a three-year Bible study course

SEARCH THE SCRIPTURES

General Editor
Alan M. Stibbs

InterVarsity Press
Downers Grove
Illinois 60515

InterVarsity Press is the book-publishing division of Inter-Varsity Christian Fellowship, a student movement active on campus at hundreds of universities, colleges and schools of nursing. For information about local and regional activities, write IVCF, 233 Langdon St., Madison, WI 53703.

Distributed in Canada through InterVarsity Press, 1875 Leslie St., Unit 10, Don Mills, Ontario M3B 2M5, Canada.

ISBN 0-87784-856-4

Printed in the United States of America

---

20 19 18 17 16 15 14 13 12 11 10 9
93 92 91 90 89 88 87 86 85 84 83

PREFACE

This course of Bible reading was first issued in 1934 in response to a widespread demand from Christian students and others for a systematic plan which could be used daily. Its aim is to guide the reader through the whole Bible in three years of regular daily study.

The General Editor of the original edition was G. T. Manley. In 1949 a new and revised course was prepared by H. W. Oldham and others. The present fresh and thorough revision has been undertaken by a large team of helpers, each of whom has worked on an allotted section. These include G. L. Carey, D. Catchpole, M. J. Cole, J. C. Connell, P. A. Crowe, A. E. Cundall, D. R. J. Evans, M. R. W. Farrer, P. K. Finnie, R. T. France, P. H. Hacking, A. R. Henderson, J. B. Job, Dr. and Mrs. A. Johnston, F. D. Kidner, G. E. Lane, Mrs. A. Metcalfe, H. Peskett, Mrs. M. Roberts, Miss E. M. Scheuermeier, J. A. Simpson, J. K. Spence, Miss M. Sugden, J. B. Taylor, Miss R. E. Wintle, D. R. Wooldridge and D. F. Wright; with A. M. Stibbs acting as General Editor.

As G. T. Manley wrote of the compilers of the earlier editions, all who have shared in preparing this revision 'know well the difficulty of sustained Bible study, and how many a hindrance Satan will put in the way. But they pray that the guidance here given may, by the grace of God, stimulate such a taste for His Word as to make the time daily spent upon it a delight as well as a source of strength'.

OVER-ALL PLAN OF THE COURSE

NEW TESTAMENT

Gospels

SUGGESTIONS ON METHOD OF STUDY

Aim of the course

The aim of this course is to help Christians young and old in their daily study of the Word of God. It differs from other schemes which have a similar aim in a number of important respects. First, the whole Bible can be covered in a period of three years. Second, the method employed is to set a number of questions on the content, meaning and application of each passage to be studied. These are designed to encourage a personal searching of the Scriptures to discover God's particular teaching and message for the reader from each portion of His Word. Third, explanatory notes are reduced to an absolute minimum on the principle that the truth which we dig out for ourselves is more likely to be remembered. There is real profit and enjoyment in wrestling with a difficult passage, as the many thousands who have already used the course can testify.

The right approach

The term 'Bible study' has been used to describe this course, but it is a phrase that needs some interpreting. We must not approach the Bible merely academically, as if it were some textbook we are required to read for an examination. We read and study our Bible because this is a means appointed by God by which we can encounter Him. It is vital that we seek the Lord, and desire to know His will as it applies to us. Otherwise, answering a question can become an end in itself and instead of a joyful meeting with our God our Bible study will become either a rather boring duty, or, at best, nothing more than an intellectually absorbing pastime.

While it is true that in our study of the Bible we must use our minds, employing all the intellectual faculties which God has given us, our primary requirement is not intellectual but spiritual. The

Bible itself declares: 'The unspiritual man does not receive the gifts of the Spirit of God, for they are folly to him, and he is not able to understand them because they are spiritually discerned' (1 Cor. 2: 14). Similarly, our Lord reveals in one of His prayers that the things of God are often hidden from those whom men reckon wise, and revealed to those He calls 'babes' (Mt. 11: 25, 26). Our approach to God's Word must be wholly without pride and self-confidence. We should begin with a humble acknowledgment of our dependence upon God, and a prayer that His Holy Spirit will open our blind eyes and give us spiritual discernment and understanding.

At the same time we must remember that God has been pleased to reveal His truth in documents written originally in ancient languages and in a particular historical environment. Consequently full discovery of all that God has to say to us through them demands diligent study involving patient and persistent enquiry and the use of all proper available aids to understanding. Bible study ought to be regarded, therefore, as demanding the serious and concentrated exercise of all one's intellectual powers. God rewards those who seek in order to find.

The time required

Those who originally planned *Search the Scriptures* had in mind people who would give at least twenty minutes a day to their personal Bible study. But experience over many years has shown that to get the maximum amount of help from the course rather longer than this may be required. Without it, prayerful meditation on the passage, which is a necessary preliminary to answering the questions, may well get curtailed. Those with little time to give would therefore be well advised to seek some slightly less demanding scheme as an aid to their Bible study.[1] But for those who can set aside, say, half an hour a day, experience has shown that this course can be of immense spiritual benefit. In addition, the question and answer method provides valuable practical training in how to study the Bible for oneself.

Arrangement

The full course can be completed in exactly three years by anyone who will keep at it and do the study each day without fail. This is the challenge it presents. But it is intended to act as a servant, not as a task master, to assist rather than to discourage. Obviously, illness

[1] For example, the introductory Bible study course, *Learning to Live* (IVP, Leicester), which provides approximately six months' study.

or a change in circumstances may necessitate a change in routine. Others may find that they benefit by a move to another Bible study method for short periods. The important thing is to keep constantly before one's mind the aim of completing a personal study of the whole Bible, even though one finds it takes longer than the recommended three years.

The order in which it is suggested that the books of the Bible should be studied has been worked out with some care. There are both deliberate sequence and planned variety. Except where other considerations have demanded some different arrangement, Old Testament books are studied in their historical order. Since, however, 1 and 2 Kings are studied as part of this historical sequence, 1 and 2 Chronicles are inserted towards the end of the course as a final review of the history of the kingdoms of Israel and Judah.

Only where the study of a book occupies more than four weeks has its study been subdivided into sections to be taken with intervals in between. Studies which occupy the first year have been chosen to help the beginner. They contain, for instance, a much larger proportion of New Testament reading than is possible in the remainder of the course.

Those who are accustomed to reading only a short passage of Scripture each day may find the length of some of the Old Testament allocations rather forbidding. But there is much to be said for the practice of reading large sections (and even whole books) at a sitting. After all, this is what we usually do when reading for study or pleasure. With the time available, the detailed study of particular verses is less important than a broad, general acquaintance with the contents and main spiritual truths of the passage.

One big advantage of a course of this kind is that it can so easily be adapted to suit individual needs. For example, if the order of study recommended is not what the reader wants, it can very easily be altered. Again, the larger books of the Bible, which in this course are divided into sections, can, if preferred, be read without interruption in their entirety. Cross references are provided from the end of one section to the beginning of the next to make this simpler. If, on the other hand, it is preferred to break the books down into even smaller sections for the sake of variety, there is nothing to prevent the course being adapted in this way. Another suggestion is that readers may wish to increase the amount of New Testament study they do in the later stages of the course by turning again to some of the books studied in Part One. This will lengthen the time taken to complete the course but some may well decide that other considerations are more important.

To make this easier, the books are listed in their biblical order on pp. vi vii and viii with the total number of studies allocated to each and the page where each section begins. But any deviation from the prescribed order ought not to be allowed to interfere with the ultimate aim of completing for oneself a study of the whole Bible.

A check-list on which each book or section can be ticked when completed appears at the beginning of each of the three Parts; and each individual study can also be ticked as it is done, in the small 'boxes' provided for the purpose.

Requirements

(a) *A Bible*

The course is based in general upon the Revised Standard Version of the Bible, and can naturally be used with this alone. There will be occasions when other translations may be helpful to the study of the passage; and there are, of course, numerous other versions of the Bible or New Testament available today. While care should be taken in their use (sometimes they are paraphrases rather than translations), they can often throw light on a passage that might otherwise be somewhat obscure.

(b) *A notebook*

This can be used both for rough notes made during the study each day and also for writing up more carefully those findings which are felt to be of more permanent value. Some have found it wise to leave the recording of these notes to a later time when the value of the daily discoveries can be seen in perspective. In the initial thrill of discovery all sorts of things may be thought to be of great and lasting worth which will not appear quite so relevant a week later. The majority, however, will probably not have time to come back to each study in this way. A good loose-leaf book can serve for both purposes.

(c) *Other aids to Bible study*

A Bible and a notebook are the only two *essential* requirements, but the following reference books can be recommended as useful aids to Bible study.

(i) *The New Bible Commentary Revised.*[1] A one-volume commentary on the whole Bible. Some explanatory notes and a certain amount of background information are provided in the course, but to have a commentary available for reference can be very valuable. If time is limited, however, such helps should be used only sparingly.

[1] IVP, Leicester; Eerdmans, Grand Rapids, Michigan. See also the Tyndale Commentaries on individual books (IVP, Leicester; Eerdmans, Grand Rapids, Michigan).

What is discovered personally from a study of the Bible will mean far more than what is read hurriedly in a commentary.

(ii) *The New Bible Dictionary*.[1] This contains a great deal of useful information concerning places, customs and the meaning of words and ideas. Again, care must be taken to see that the time set apart for personal study is not replaced by reading some of the fascinating facts recorded in the Dictionary! On the other hand, such a reference work can be a very helpful supplement to the study of the Bible.

Procedure

What follows is put forward merely as a suggestion for those starting the course. After a while, each individual will naturally wish to make his own adaptations of this procedure as seem best to him in the light of his experience.

1 Begin with prayer along the lines previously suggested.

2 Read the portion of Scripture appointed for study. It is best not to read the questions before reading the Bible passage itself. Knowing what the questions are may mean that one's interest becomes limited too soon to those particular points.

3 Read the questions and any notes on the passage. Think about the passage in the light of the questions asked. Then try to work out the answer to these: they will be found a very useful aid to concentration.

4 Write answers to the questions in the notebook. The user of the course is strongly advised to discipline himself to do this, and not just to pass over the questions with a vague idea that they have been answered. Greatest profit will be derived from actually committing to paper what has been discovered from the passage. At the same time it is possible to be too dependent on the questions. Especially in the larger Old Testament sections the questions set obviously do not exhaust the meaning of the passage. The reader may even feel that at times they miss what is to him the main point of the passage or jump to application too quickly. Fair enough! If readers find themselves wanting to formulate their own lines of inquiry instead of being tied to the questions set, one of the aims of the course is being achieved.

Some users of the course may wonder at times whether their answer to a question is in fact the one intended! This does not really matter provided that scriptural teaching is being better understood. But where other Scripture references are provided for comparison these will often indicate the kind of answer expected. But it is better to concentrate first on getting an answer from the verses

[1] IVP, Leicester; Eerdmans, Grand Rapids, Michigan.

set for study, and to leave the references to other Scriptures until that has been done. The temptation to study the cross references rather than the passage set must be avoided.

It can also be very helpful to have a weekly review of the ground covered, and of the outstanding truths which have been learnt or more fully appreciated.

Some people may find that all this gives them too much to do in the time they have allocated to Bible study. In that case an attempt could be made to adapt the course so that only one question is dealt with each day, concentrating on the one which seems likely to be the most profitable. Then move on to the next study. To do otherwise means that the course may well take six years or even longer to complete. When it is only occasionally that one finds there is not enough time to finish, it may well be possible to complete the study later in the day or at the weekend, while the reading is still comparatively fresh in the mind.

Where more than two questions are provided for the same study, the third (or fourth) question is to be regarded as an optional extra; or as an alternative to the first two; or for possible use when the same Bible passage is studied later. One of the advantages of a course of this kind is that it can be used repeatedly.

5 Use the passage as a basis for worship and praise. Pray over the lessons learnt. There will be some particular thought (or thoughts) which is God's word to you for the day. Seek to discover it, and then in prayer relate it practically to your own life. Remember that God's inspired Word has been given to us for an essentially practical purpose; to teach us, to reprove us, to correct us, to instruct us in righteousness, and to make us spiritually mature and equipped for every good work (2 Tim. 3: 16, 17).

ABBREVIATIONS

Books of the Old Testament: Gn., Ex., Lv., Nu., Dt., Jos., Jdg., Ru., 1, 2 Sa., 1, 2 Ki., 1, 2 Ch., Ezr., Ne., Est., Jb., Ps. (Pss.), Pr., Ec., Ct., Is., Je., La., Ezk., Dn., Ho., Joel, Am., Ob., Jon., Mi., Na., Hab., Zp., Hg., Zc., Mal.

Books of the New Testament: Mt., Mk., Lk., Jn., Acts, Rom., 1, 2 Cor., Gal., Eph., Phil., Col., 1, 2 Thes., 1, 2 Tim., Tit., Phm., Heb., Jas., 1, 2 Pet., 1, 2, 3 Jn., Jude, Rev.

AV	Authorized Version (1611)
ICC	*International Critical Commentary*
LXX	Septuagint Version (*i.e.*, translation of the Old Testament into Greek, *c.* 250 BC)
mg.	margin
Moffatt	*A New Translation of the Bible* by James Moffatt (1935)
NBCR	*The New Bible Commentary Revised* (1970)
NBD	*The New Bible Dictionary* (1962)
NEB	The New English Bible (1961–70)
RSV	Revised Standard Version (1946–52)
RV	Revised Version (1885)
TNTC	*Tyndale New Testament Commentaries*
TOTC	*Tyndale Old Testament Commentaries*
Way	*Letters of St. Paul and Hebrews* by Arthur S. Way (1921)
Weymouth	*The New Testament in Modern Speech* by R. F. Weymouth (1902)

PART ONE

Check-list of material contained in this part (tick when completed):

LUKE 1:1–9:56

Introduction

This Gospel is proved by its style and language to have been written by a Greek doctor, who was identical with the writer of the Acts of the Apostles, and, as the latter book shows, was a companion of Paul. Only Luke, 'the beloved physician', fits these conditions, and as he was not a man of note, there would have been no inducement to attribute the Gospel to him had he not actually been the author.

The most probable explanation of the abrupt ending to Acts is that Luke brought that book up to date, and that Paul was still in his first imprisonment at Rome when Acts was finished. This would give a date of about AD 62 for Acts, and a year or two earlier as the latest date for the Gospel.

This Gospel lays a special emphasis on the human nature of the Lord Jesus, though witnessing also with no doubtful voice to His Deity (see, *e.g.*, 10: 21, 22; 24: 26, 49). His sympathy with the suffering and bereaved, the despised and the outcast, is brought into clear view: and the universal nature of the gospel, intended for Samaritan and heathen as well as the Jew, is strongly emphasized. The free offer of salvation and the impossibility of acquiring merit come out again and again (*e.g.*, 15: 11–32; 17: 7–10; 18: 9–14; 23: 39–43).

Analysis

1: 1 – 2: 52	The birth and childhood of Jesus and John the Baptist.
3: 1 – 4: 13	The preaching of John; the baptism and temptation of the Lord.
4: 14 – 9: 50	The ministry in Galilee.
9: 51 – 19: 28	Journeyings towards Jerusalem.
19: 29 – 21: 38	Last days of public teaching.
22: 1 – 24: 53	The last supper, the arrest, trial, death and resurrection of the Lord.

☑ STUDY 1 Luke 1: 1–25

1 What was the mission assigned to John the Baptist? What was to be the nature of his greatness (verse 15)? *Cf.* verses 76, 77.

2 What was the cause of Zechariah's punishment (verse 20)? What made him hesitate to believe the angel's message? What similar temptations to unbelief do you face? Why ought Zechariah to have believed, and why ought we to believe?

3 Verses 1–4. What do these verses tell us of (a) the sources of Luke's information, (b) the importance which he attached to giving a truthful record, and (c) his purpose in writing the Gospel?

Note. Verse 3. The title 'most excellent' suggests that Theophilus was a high official, probably not a Christian, but with some knowledge of and interest in Christianity.

☑ STUDY 2 Luke 1: 26–38

1 Verses 31–33, 35. How many features of the person and mission of the promised Child can be discerned in the words of the angel? Make a list of them.

2 Contrast Mary's reception of the angel's message with that of Zechariah (see previous study, Question 2). *Cf.* verse 45. What did Mary's response involve? Are you prepared similarly to ask the Lord to fulfil His word in you?

Note. Verse 31. 'Jesus' is the Greek form of Joshua, which means 'God saves'. *Cf.* Mt. 1: 21.

☑ STUDY 3 Luke 1: 39–56

1 What does Mary's song reveal of (a) the character of God (see especially verses 49, 50), and (b) His way of working among men (verses 51–53)? How were these facts demonstrated in the manner of the Saviour's coming?

2 What features in Mary's character are revealed in this song? What may we learn from her example?

☑ STUDY 4 Luke 1: 57–80

The song of Zechariah may be divided thus: verses 68–70, thanks to God for the coming of the Messiah; verses 71–75, the purpose of the Messiah's coming; verses 76, 77, the mission of John; verses 78, 79, further picture of the Messiah's coming.

1 Trace in the song of Zechariah the successive stages in the unfolding of God's plan of salvation through the Old Testament and up to the coming of the Messiah. How does it reveal the unity of the Old and New Testaments?

2 What, according to this song, is the *purpose* of salvation? Is this your experience?

Notes

1 Verse 69. 'A horn of salvation': *i.e.*, one who is strong to save. The horn of an animal was a common symbol of strength; *cf.* Ps. 18: 2.

2 Verse 80. 'The wilderness': the desolate region around the Jordan and the Dead Sea.

STUDY 5 Luke 2: 1–20

1 What may we learn from the circumstances of our Saviour's birth, and the status of His first worshippers?

2 What do the angel's message and the rejoicing of the heavenly host teach us of the *importance* of the birth of Jesus? How is the shepherds' response to this message an example to us?

3 Verses 1–7. How do these verses illustrate that God controls all human affairs, effecting His own purpose through the free actions of men? *Cf.* with verse 4, Mi. 5: 2.

STUDY 6 Luke 2: 21–39

1 What did the appearance of Jesus mean to Simeon and to Anna? What, according to verses 30–32, was to be the scope of His work?

2 Verses 34, 35. What was to be the effect of Jesus' coming on different classes of people? What would be the cause of men's falling and rising? *Cf.* 1 Pet. 2: 6–8.

Notes

1 Verses 21–24. After the circumcision of the Child two rites had to be performed: first, His presentation to God (verses 22, 23; *cf.* Ex. 13: 2); second, the sacrifice of purification for the mother (verse 24; *cf.* Lv. 12: 2–8).

2 Verse 25. 'Looking for the consolation of Israel': *i.e.*, for the coming of the Messiah. *Cf.* verse 38 and 24: 21.

STUDY 7 Luke 2: 40–52

1 Verse 49. What was the consequence in His life of Jesus' unique relation to God? In what way does this truth apply to us, as sons of God? *Cf.* Jn. 14: 31.

2 How does the story illustrate the truths of verses 40 and 52?

☑ STUDY 8 Luke 3: 1–22

1 What, according to the preaching of John, are the cause (verses 7–9, 16, 17), nature (verses 8, 10–14), and outcome (verses 3, 15–17) of repentance?

2 What did Jesus' baptism, and the voice from heaven, mean (a) to Jesus Himself, and (b) to the others present? *Cf.* Jn. 1: 32–34.

3 Consider the fearless honesty of John. Note also its result (verses 19, 20).

Notes

1 Verse 1. The date is thus fixed probably as AD 28–29. See *NBD*, p. 223.

2 Verse 22. The voice combines references to the Old Testament Messianic figures of the Son of God (Ps. 2: 7) and the suffering Servant of the Lord (Is. 42: 1), thus setting the tone of Jesus' ministry.

☑ STUDY 9 Luke 3: 23 – 4: 13

1 Notice the time of the temptation, immediately after the revelation of 3: 22, and at the opening of Jesus' ministry. What light does this throw on the devil's challenge, 'if you are the Son of God' (4: 3, 9)?

2 Consider the special subtlety of each temptation, and the means by which Jesus in each case parried the thrust. *Cf.* Eph. 6: 17. What does this teach us for our own defence against temptation?

3 What may we learn from this passage of the nature of temptation? Note, *e.g.*, at what times temptation may come, what sort of circumstances the tempter may use (4: 2; *cf.* Mk. 14: 38), *etc.* How does the passage show that temptation is not sin?

Note. 3: 23–38. The genealogy differs from that of Matthew in that (a) it goes back beyond Abraham, and the origin of the Jewish race, to Adam, and the origin of the whole human race; (b) the list from David to Jesus is different except for two names. For the explanation of this last fact, and the significance of the genealogies, see *NBD*, pp. 458–459.

☑ STUDY 10 Luke 4: 14–30

1 Verses 16–21. Jesus speaks to the people of Nazareth, His own home town. What does His use of Is. 61: 1, 2 teach them of His mission? Why is the claim of verse 21 so startling?

2 Verses 22–30. The people were moved but not convinced (verse 22). How did Jesus interpret to them their unspoken thoughts (verse 23), and what did He go on to imply (verses 25–27)? What made them so angry?

☐ STUDY 11 4: 31–44

1 What two facts about Jesus particularly impressed the people in the synagogue? Note also the even more discerning testimony of the demons (verses 34, 41). Why did Jesus silence this?

2 This passage illustrates the busy-ness and urgency of Jesus' mission (see especially verse 43). Why then did He retire to a lonely place (verse 42)? *Cf.*, in this Gospel, 5: 16; 6: 12; 9: 18, 28; 11: 1; *etc.* What may we learn from this example?

Notes

1 On the nature of demon possession, see *NBD*, pp. 1010–1012.

2 Verse 40. The Jewish day ended at sunset. The people waited until the Sabbath was over, and then brought their sick for healing.

☐ STUDY 12 Luke 5: 1–11

1 Put yourself in the place of Simon. Trace the development of his attitude to Jesus in the successive phases of the story. In what ways is he an example to us?

2 Jesus needed fellow-workers. How and where did He find them? What marked out Simon and his colleagues as suitable? What were, for them, the conditions of being used?

☐ STUDY 13 Luke 5: 12–26

1 Compare the faith of the leper with that of the friends of the paralytic. Of what was the former uncertain? And how did the latter display their faith? What can we learn from these miracles about prayer?

2 Verses 21–24. What claims are implied in Jesus' answer to the scribes' challenge?

☐ STUDY 14 Luke 5: 27 – 6: 11

1 These verses record four encounters with the scribes and Pharisees. What were the grounds of their growing opposition to Jesus? And what were the truths and the principles which (as His answers reveal) determined the actions of Jesus?

2 5: 36–39. What happens when formal religion encounters the new life which Jesus brings? How do the incidents in today's passage illustrate the truth of these verses? *Cf.* 1 Sa. 15: 22; Heb. 10: 8, 9.

Note. 6: 1. This was allowed on other days (Dt. 23: 25), but was regarded by the scribes as work, and therefore prohibited on the Sabbath.

☐ STUDY 15 Luke 6: 12–36

1 Verses 20–26. Contrast Jesus' picture of a blessed life with the world's idea of happiness. Why is a Christian happy in such circumstances? What makes the difference?

2 Verses 27–36. A picture of unselfish love. What should be the source and pattern of our love (verses 35, 36)? Think of practical cases in your own situation to which the principles laid down in these verses apply.

3 Verses 12–19. Note the increasing pressures on Jesus (verses 17–19; *cf.* verse 11). What two special actions did He take?

☐ STUDY 16 Luke 6: 37–49

1 Verses 37–42. What sort of attitude towards the faults of others does Jesus prescribe, and why? What positive actions are here enjoined?

2 Verses 43–49. On what does effectiveness and stability in the Christian life depend? What is the remedy for a weak or inconsistent Christian life?

☐ STUDY 17 Luke 7: 1–17

1 Verses 1–10. What are the characteristics of the centurion's approach to Jesus? What can he teach us about a right attitude in prayer?

2 What do we see in these two stories of the character of Jesus (a) of His appreciation of, and love for, people, and (b) of His unique authority? *Cf.* Jn. 5: 24.

☐ STUDY 18 Luke 7: 18–35

1 Verses 18–23. What exactly was the doubt in John's mind? Do you find a clue to this perplexity in 3: 16, 17? What is the significance of Jesus' reply? *Cf.* Is. 35: 5, 6; 61: 1.

2 Verses 24–35. How had the Jews gone wrong in their reaction to John's preaching? What had they failed to see? What does Jesus' estimate of John teach us concerning the greatness of our privilege? *Cf.* 10: 23, 24.

Note. Verses 26–28. John, the last and greatest of the prophets of the 'old covenant', marks the beginning of a new and better era, 'the kingdom of God'.

☐ STUDY 19 Luke 7: 36 – 8: 3

1 Compare the Pharisee's attitude to Jesus with that of the woman. How did Jesus answer his criticisms of verse 39? How did the parable of verses 41, 42 apply to him?

2 What made the woman act as she did? *Cf.* 8: 2, 3. Have you a similar incentive? How can it be expressed?

Note. 7: 47. 'For' here indicates the evidence rather than the cause of her forgiveness.

☐ STUDY 20 Luke 8: 4–21

1 Verses 4–15. What sorts of people do the four kinds of soil represent? What experience have you of the truth of this parable in yourself and in others?

2 Verses 16–21. What do these verses teach of (a) the responsibilities and (b) the privileges of Jesus' followers?

3 Why did Jesus now adopt the method of teaching by parables (verses 9, 10)? Do verses 4 and 18 provide a clue?

☐ STUDY 21 Luke 8: 22–39

1 Verses 22–25. 'Where is your faith?' In what way was their faith defective? What did they learn from the incident?

2 Verses 26–39. Compare the man's condition before and after he met Jesus. What evidence can you find of the reality of the change? What may we learn from this about Jesus' power to save?

3 Verses 35–39. What caused the different reactions to Jesus of the cured man and his fellow-countrymen? Why did Jesus grant the request of those who wanted to be rid of Him, and refuse that of the man He had saved?

☐ STUDY 22 Luke 8: 40–56

1 Verses 43–48. Try to enter into the woman's hopes and fears. What made her touch different from that of the rest of the crowd? Have you any experience and testimony similar to hers?

2 What do these two stories teach us of the importance and nature of faith, and the need to continue in faith? *Cf.* Heb. 3: 14.

☑ STUDY 23 Luke 9: 1–17

1 Verses 1–6. A new development in the work. Picture the twelve itinerating as here described. What lessons would they themselves learn, and what would be the impact on those who saw and heard them?

2 Verses 10–17. What light do these verses throw upon the unselfish love of Jesus, and on His concern for both physical and spiritual needs? Putting yourself in the place of the disciples, what would you have learned from the incident?

☑ STUDY 24 Luke 9: 18–36

1 Verses 18–27. Trace the connection between the three sections, verses 18–20; 21, 22; 23–27. What does this teach us concerning (a) the goals which Jesus was out to reach, and (b) the demands He makes on those who would follow Him?

2 Verses 28–36. What lessons would the disciples learn from this experience about the real character and mission of Jesus? Can you find any connections with the truths they had been taught the previous week (verses 20–27)?

Notes

1 Verse 23. 'Take up his cross': like a condemned criminal on the way to execution.

2 Verse 27. See *NBCR*.

3 Verse 30. Moses and Elijah represent the Law and the Prophets. They were God-given guides whose endorsement of fresh teaching was important. *Cf.* Mal. 4: 4–6.

☑ STUDY 25 Luke 9: 37–56

1 Verses 37–43. Note the disciples' failure (verse 40). Do you find any significance in the fact that this followed a week of new revelations (verses 22–27)? What ought we to learn from this?

2 Verses 43–56. Further failures of the disciples. Why did they find it so hard to understand Jesus' teaching or to practise it? Do you find the same difficulties? How are they overcome? *Cf.* Phil. 2: 3–8.

Note. The Analysis shows a new section of the Gospel begins at verse 51. But verses 51–56 are included in this study because they also record an example of failure on the part of the disciples.

For Studies 26–47 on the second part of Luke's Gospel see p. 18.

GENESIS 1 - 26

Introduction

The title Genesis comes from the Septuagint Greek translation of the Old Testament and means 'origin' or 'beginning'. The book justifies its title in three ways.

(a) As *history* it tells the story of the creation, of the earliest civilization, of the Flood, and of the origins of the chosen people of God.

(b) As *revelation* it teaches primary truths about God and man: and with regard to the way of salvation it tells first of the coming of sin into the world through the Fall; then of the utter failure of early man to save himself, culminating in the Flood; and finally of God's choice of one family in which all families of the earth should be blessed. The fact of God's redemptive purpose, first foreshadowed in the garden of Eden (Gn. 3: 15), shines out from time to time with increasing clearness as the book proceeds.

Genesis is thus the story first of man's need of salvation, and then of the early stages in the unfolding of God's wonderful plan of redemption.

(c) As *practical teaching* it introduces us to personalities of profound and universal religious significance, such as Abel and Cain, Noah, Abraham, Jacob and Esau and Joseph, and by its unforgettable stories teaches lessons of abiding value, showing God at work in human life.

Authorship

The Pentateuch, or Five Books, of which Genesis is the first, was attributed to Moses by universal tradition of the Jews, which our Lord takes for granted, and endorses with His own authority (*e.g.*, Mk. 12: 26; Jn. 5: 46, 47). This is not the place to attempt to discuss the questions raised by modern criticism, but the following remarks may be made here.

(a) To put the composition of the Pentateuch centuries after the time of Moses means much more than a judgment on its authorship; it inevitably involves surrendering its claim to be reliable history, and, moreover, it involves the unreliability of a great part of Bible history outside the Pentateuch, as the course of modern criticism shows.

(b) There is an important external check on the claim of the Pentateuch to be historical, namely, its representation of the customs of the ancient Near East. Archaeology has shown that these were just such as they are represented in Genesis to be in the period referred to, but that in many respects they had become quite different long before the exile.

Analysis

1 – 11 Primaeval history.

12 – 50 The ancestors of the chosen people. There is some overlapping, but each patriarch is the leading figure within the section to which his name is attached below:

12: 1 – 25: 18	Abraham
25: 19 – 26: 35	Isaac
27 – 36	Jacob
37 – 50	Joseph

☐ STUDY 1 Genesis 1 and 2

1 What truths stand out regarding (a) the character of the whole creation, (b) the character of man and his relation to God?

2 'And God said' is found ten times. *Cf.* Ps. 33: 6, 9; Heb. 11: 3. What does this suggest concerning the mode of creation? What further light is provided by Jn. 1: 1–3; Col. 1: 15–17?

3 Why did God make men 'male and female'? What pattern for marriage is here divinely ordained? *Cf.* Mt. 19: 3–6.

Note. Interest should be concentrated on theological truths not to be learnt from text-books of natural science.

☐ STUDY 2 Genesis 3

1 What does Genesis 3 teach about (a) Satan's methods, (b) the first false steps which lead to sin in act, (c) the results of sin?

2 What simple positive principles of action, if acted on, would have given Adam and Eve victory over temptation?

3 What is the significance of Gn. 3: 15?

☐ STUDY 3 Genesis 4 and 5

1 Trace in chapter 4 the growth of sin, and the evidence of its power and its effects.

2 Abel died and Cain lived. But what had Abel that Cain had not? *Cf.* 1 Jn. 3: 12; Heb. 11: 4.

3 Try to picture to yourself the life of Enoch as described in Gn. 5: 21–24. What new light does Heb. 11: 5, 6 throw upon it?

☐ STUDY 4 Genesis 6

1 What do we learn here concerning (a) the fallen condition of human nature, (b) God's attitude to sin, (c) the provision of a way of salvation? *Cf.* Mt. 24: 37–39; 1 Pet. 3: 20; 2 Pet. 2: 5.

2 'Noah found grace in the eyes of the Lord.' What were his characteristics? *Cf.* Heb. 11: 7.

Notes

1 In Gn. 6: 3 the words 'a hundred and twenty years' probably refer not to the average length of human life, but to the respite for repentance which the race was to have from that time to the Flood.

2 The value of the New Testament references is specially great in this study.

☐ STUDY 5 Genesis 7: 1 – 8: 19

1 What was God's part in Noah's salvation, and what was Noah's? *Cf.* Eph. 2: 8; Phil. 2: 12, 13; 1 Pet. 1: 5.

2 In the ark Noah was not saved from being affected by the Flood at all, but he was brought safely through it. *Cf.* 'saved through water', 1 Pet. 3: 20. In what similar way does the gospel of Christ offer us salvation from God's judgment upon sin?

☐ STUDY 6 Genesis 8: 20 – 9: 29

1 What did Noah's altar and burnt offerings signify? To what would they correspond in our lives today? *Cf.* Rom. 12: 1; Heb. 13: 15, 16.

2 Reflect on Noah's position after the deluge. In what ways did God encourage him?

3 What makes human life supremely precious? What kind of penalty is here ordained for the murderer?

4 What may we learn here concerning the place and manner of covenant making? Can you think of other visible tokens and pledges which seal covenants?

Note. 9: 13. This does not imply that the rainbow was now seen for the first time, but that God now made it a token of His covenant of promise to Noah.

☐ STUDY 7 Genesis 10: 1 – 11: 9

1 What does Gn. 10 teach about the origins of the nations and about their relation to one another and to God? *Cf.* Acts 17: 26; Rom. 3: 29.

2 See 11: 1–9. What was wrong with the attitude and activity of these men? What kind of judgment does God bring on those who seek supposed success in their way rather than in His way? See Ps. 2: 1–4; Lk. 11: 23; *cf.* Gn. 3: 22–24; Is. 14: 12–15; contrast Jn. 11: 49–52, especially verse 52.

☐ STUDY 8 Genesis 11: 10 – 13: 4

1 Consider the inseparable intermingling of command and promise in God's call to Abram. How, in consequence, did Abram's faith express itself? *Cf.* Heb. 11: 8. Compare and contrast Gn. 11: 31 with 12: 5. In what ways is a similar response demanded by the gospel of Christ?

2 In what two respects did Abram's faith fall short under the tests of famine and fear? When he acted unworthily how was he rebuked? What may we learn from Gn. 13: 3, 4? *Cf.* Rev. 2: 5.

☐ STUDY 9 Genesis 13: 5 – 14: 24

1 Put yourself in Lot's place when Abram's offer was made to him. What was the motive that decided his choice, and how did it end? What did Abram lose by letting Lot choose first? *Cf.* Mt. 16: 25.

2 What fresh light do the events of chapter 14 throw on Abram' character?

☐ STUDY 10 Genesis 15

1 How are God's words in verse 1 exactly related to Abram's circumstances and condition?

2 In utterly hopeless human circumstances (see Gn. 11: 30; 15: 3) how did Abram obtain hope of having descendants? What else did

he gain by such response? What principle of the gospel of Christ does this illustrate? *Cf.* Rom. 4: 2–5, 13–25.

3 What grounds for his faith did God give to Abram? Why did God also make a covenant with Abram? Note the use of a visible token and pledge. *Cf.* Heb. 6: 13–18.

Note. Verses 9, 10, 17 describe an ancient ritual used to seal a contract. *Cf.* Je. 34: 18, 19. The smoking pot and flaming torch represent the Lord passing between the divided carcasses, and thus ratifying the covenant.

☐ STUDY 11 Genesis 16 and 17

1 Gn. 16: 1–6. In what ways did Abram act wrongly in having a son by Hagar? How was he misled? Was Sarah right to blame Abram for the wrong done to her? What ought Abram to have thought, said and done in the face of such a situation?

2 Gn. 17. Note the characteristics of covenant-making which are mentioned here. What were the blessings of which Abraham was thereby assured? What did Abraham have to do to embrace the assurance which the covenant afforded?

3 Gn. 16: 7–15; 17: 18–21. What do we learn here of God's character and purposes from His dealings with Hagar and Ishmael? What Christian truths are here prefigured?

Notes
1 16: 13. Hagar not only realized that God is One by whose all-seeing eye none are unseen or overlooked; but also that He had personally manifested Himself to her, and that she had seen God without dying. Mention of 'the angel of the Lord' (verse 7) occurs here for the first time in the Bible. In verse 13 he is described as 'the Lord who spoke to her'. This suggests an anticipation of the incarnation, an appearance in person of God the Son.
2 Chapter 17. The covenant was pledged by God in His Name. In witness of the benefits which they were to receive under it, Abraham and Sarai were both given significant new names. Abraham and every male of his house were circumcised as 'a sign of the covenant' between God and him.
3 17: 18–21. Note that Abraham's suggestion that Ishmael might be accepted by God, as the son concerning whom God's special covenant promises were made, was not accepted by God.

☐ STUDY 12 Genesis 18

1 Let us learn from Abraham's example how it is possible to receive the Lord as our guest, to enjoy fellowship with Him, to become those whom He calls His friends. *Cf.* Heb. 13: 2; Rev. 3: 20; Jas. 2: 23; Jn. 15: 13–15. What were the fruits of this fellowship in Abraham's experience? What enrichment, in consequence, did Abraham gain for himself, and was able to bring to others?

2 Verses 22–33. What are the chief characteristics of Abraham's intercession? Make a list of those which should also mark our praying. Note the effect of Abraham's intercession. *Cf.* Gn. 19: 29.

Note. Verses 23–25. Note that in praying for Lot and for Sodom Abraham appealed not to God's special covenant mercy or faithfulness, but to His universal righteous judgment.

□ STUDY 13 Genesis 19

1 What is revealed in this chapter about (a) the evil latent in the heart of man, (b) the certainty of divine judgment, (c) the priority of divine mercy, and (d) the urgency of immediate action while there is time to escape? *Cf.* Lk. 17: 23–32; 2 Pet. 2: 6; Jude 7.

2 What did Lot gain for himself and his family by his association with Sodom? In what ways should he be a warning to us?

□ STUDY 14 Genesis 20: 1 – 21: 21

1 What may we learn from Gn. 20 of the weakness of human nature, even in a believer; and of God's protecting care and saving grace? *Cf.* Ps. 94: 18; Mk. 14: 38; 1 Cor. 10: 12; 2 Tim. 2: 13.

2 Gn. 21: 1–7. 'Isaac' means 'laughter'. What is the difference between Sarah's laughter in 18: 12 and in 21: 6? How was the change brought about? See also 17: 17–19. To what two complementary truths did the name Isaac thus bear witness? *Cf.* Mt. 19: 26.

3 Gn. 21: 8–21. From what was Ishmael cast out, and why? *Cf.* Rom. 9: 6–9; Gal. 4: 28–30. Why did God nevertheless hear Ishmael's voice, and grant him His blessing and His presence?

Notes

1 20: 18. The use here of God's covenant name 'LORD' or 'Jehovah' is significant. It was He who intervened to preserve Sarah as the intended mother of the promised son. Contrast 21: 17–20, where we read that 'God', not 'the LORD', heard Ishmael's voice, *etc.*

2 21: 9. 'Playing with': the sense is probably better conveyed by the AV and RV 'mocking'. Ishmael did not laugh like Sarah; he made fun. Thus Isaac, the object of holy laughter, was made the butt of unholy mockery.

□ STUDY 15 Genesis 21: 22 – 22: 24

1 Gn. 22. In what ways was the command of verse 2 a most severe test of Abraham's faith in God? Note the significance of the comment in Heb. 11 : 17, 18. Whence did Abraham expect to get, and where did he expect to find, the answer to the questions which he could not answer? How did his faith express itself? *Cf.* Jas. 2: 20–24.

2 Gn. 21: 22–34. What was it about Abraham that made Abimelech believe that a covenant between them which would be kept was a serious possibility? Do we covet similar evidences in our lives which will make others trust us and reverence our God? *Cf.* Mt. 5: 16; 1 Pet. 2: 12.

☐ **STUDY 16 Genesis 23**

1 What features in Abraham's character does the story of this chapter bring out? With verse 4 *cf.* Heb. 11: 9, 10, 13–16. What may we learn from his example concerning the right way to face both life and death?

2 What is Sarah's character as shown in Genesis? *Cf.* Heb. 11: 11; 1 Pet. 3: 5, 6. How many wives today become what the Bible calls 'her children'?

☐ **STUDY 17 Genesis 24: 1–60**

1 What can we learn from the attitude of Abraham's servant in his relation to (a) his master, and (b) the task given to him? What were his confidence and concern? *Cf.* Col. 3: 22–24.

2 Examine the manner in which the servant made his choice, and the test he employed. Of what did he become particularly conscious? Can we learn from this about choosing a life-partner?

3 What picture do we get of Rebekah?

☐ **STUDY 18 Genesis 24: 61 – 25: 34**

1 What light do we get from this portion on the kind of man Isaac was? See 24: 63–67; 25: 28.

2 Contrast Jacob and Esau, as described in 25: 27–34, in their habits, character and spiritual outlook. What lesson is drawn in Heb. 12: 14–17 from Esau's conduct in regard to his birthright?

3 Review Abraham's life. What gives him an outstanding place in world history and makes him a conspicuous example to us all? *Cf.* Is. 41: 8; Gal. 3: 9, 29.

☐ **STUDY 19 Genesis 26**

1 Why did Isaac fail so badly after receiving striking promises from God? What was different about his reaction when the promises were repeated?

2 What can we learn from the quarrel over the wells concerning the way to behave in the face of opposition or hostility? *Cf.* 1 Pet. 2: 23.

For Studies 20–42 on the second half of Genesis see p. 24.

LUKE 9 : 57 - 19 : 28

☑ STUDY 26 Luke 9: 57 – 10: 12

1 9: 57–62. How would you describe the three different types referred to here? Why was Jesus not satisfied with their response to His summons to follow Him? Contrast Jesus' own attitude (verse 51).

2 10: 1–12. How do these verses show the urgency both in Jesus' own concern for evangelism, and in the work He gives to His disciples? What is the reason for this urgency? In what activities ought it to make us engage?

Note. 9: 59, 60. The man wants to delay until after his father's death, which may be imminent. In Jesus' reply 'the dead' are those who have no spiritual life.

☑ STUDY 27 Luke 10: 13–24

1 What do these verses show of the greatness of our privileges in Christ? In how many of them are you sharing?

2 Verses 21, 22. What caused this outburst of joy? What does this prayer teach us of (a) the Father's method of working, (b) Jesus' unique relationship to the Father?

Notes

1 Verses 13–15. Chorazin, Bethsaida, Capernaum: towns of Galilee.

2 Verses 18, 19. The language is symbolic of triumph over Satan and all evil.

☑ STUDY 28 Luke 10: 25–42

1 Consider the summary of the law in verse 27. Is it an adequate summary? How does Jesus' story guard against a misinterpretation of it? Who is *your* neighbour? And how can you prove yourself to be a neighbour?

2 Verses 38–42. Martha and Mary were concerned about different things. Which did Jesus consider the more important, and how did He solve the tension between them?

Note. Verse 42. The 'one thing' may well be a pun, implying that there is no need for an elaborate meal, and Mary, by choosing to listen to Jesus, has chosen the best dish!

☑ STUDY 29 Luke 11: 1–13

1 Verses 2–4. This abbreviated version of the Lord's Prayer gives, as it were, the 'iron rations' of prayer. Consider what aspects and themes of prayer are selected as the most essential. How does your prayer measure up to this pattern?

2 Verses 5–13. What attitude in prayer is commended in these verses? What results may such prayer expect? What reasons are we given for confidence in prayer?

Note. Verse 8. 'Importunity': what this describes is a persistence in solicitation that is literally 'shameless' or 'impudent'.

☑ STUDY 30 Luke 11: 14–36

In verses 15 and 16 are recorded two attacks on Jesus: a charge of collusion with Satan, and a demand for a sign to authenticate His mission. The first is answered in verses 17–26, the second in verses 29–32.

1 How does Jesus show the falsity of the charge that He cast out demons by demonic power? What, on the contrary, do His exorcisms prove about Him?

2 What is the sign of Jonah? *Cf.* Mt. 12: 40. Why should the generation to whom Jesus preached stand condemned at the judgment? What was their sin?

Notes

1 Verse 19. 'Your sons': Jewish exorcists. Verses 20–22 show Jesus' complete mastery over Satan in comparison with the imperfect cures of the exorcists (verses 24–26).

2 Verses 34–36. The function of the eye, as the organ by which the body makes use of the light which shines on it, is taken as an analogy for the faculty of spiritual perception, which must be in good order to receive the light of revelation. The allusion is to the spiritual blindness of 'this generation'.

STUDY 31 Luke 11: 37–52

1 Verses 37–44. How would you summarize the faults of the Pharisees? Translate them into terms of modern life. What attitude and action does Jesus recommend?

2 Verses 45–52. What three charges does Jesus level against the lawyers? Translate these, too, into modern terms. Who may still be guilty in this way? How may such sins be avoided?

Notes

1 Verse 44. Contact with a grave caused defilement (Nu. 19: 16).

2 Verse 51. For Abel, see Gn. 4: 8; for Zechariah, see 2 Ch. 24: 20–22. As Chronicles was the last book in the Hebrew Old Testament, the whole range of Old Testament history is thus indicated.

STUDY 32 Luke 11: 53 – 12: 12

1 In a context of growing opposition and publicity, what does Jesus teach of the security of His people, and of the help God gives in time of need?

2 What, then, should be the disciple's reaction to persecution, both in his outward response and in his inner attitude?

STUDY 33 Luke 12: 13–34

1 Was the rich man wrong to make provision for the future? Where did he go wrong? In what *does* a man's life consist (verse 15)?

2 What should be the central motive in the life of a Christian? If this is taken seriously, what does Jesus here promise with regard to material needs? How could this apply practically in your own situation?

STUDY 34 Luke 12: 35–59

1 Verses 35–48. What reasons do these verses give us for being alert? In what ways can we be ready for our Master's return? Against what dangers are we here warned?

2 Verses 49–59. Jesus addresses first His disciples (verses 49–53), and then the crowds (verses 54–59); what warnings does He give to each group about the effects of His coming?

Notes

1 Verse 50. The 'baptism' is His coming suffering. The agony of Gethsemane was already felt.

2 Verses 58, 59. A parable of the need to be reconciled with God before the day of judgment.

☑ STUDY 35 Luke 13: 1–17

1 Trace the connection of thought between verses 1–5 and the parable of verses 6–9. In the light of the parable, what is meant by 'repent' (verses 3, 5)? *Cf.* 3: 8a.

2 Verses 10–17. What, in Jesus' view, was wrong with the attitude of the ruler of the synagogue? Compare his reaction to Jesus' miracle with that of the woman and the crowd. What made the difference?

Note. Verse 1. The reference is to some massacre in the Temple, typical of Pilate's brutality.

☑ STUDY 36 Luke 13: 18–35

1 Verses 23–30. What is Jesus' answer to the question of verse 23? What determines whether a person is saved or not? What inadequate grounds of confidence are here exposed?

2 Verses 31–35. With what attitude and emotions does Jesus meet the opposition and unbelief of men. What may we learn from Him in this?

3 Verses 18–21. What do these similes teach about the expansion of the kingdom of God? *Cf.* Mk. 14: 9. What is the relevance of this to evangelism?

Note. Verses 32, 33. 'Today and tomorrow and the day following': an idiomatic expression for a short period.

☑ STUDY 37 Luke 14: 1–24

1 Verses 7–14. How does Jesus' teaching in these verses run counter to the ways of the world? How did His own life exemplify this teaching?

2 Verses 15–24. How is Jesus' parable related to the remark of verse 15? What is it that keeps people out of the kingdom, and who will in fact get there?

☑ STUDY 38 Luke 14: 25–35

1 Note the reason for this stern teaching (verse 25). What, according to verses 26, 27, does discipleship involve? Was this teaching for that time only, or does it apply still?

2 Verses 28–35. What is the safeguard against spiritual wrecks and ineffectiveness?

Notes

1 Verse 26. 'Hate': *i.e.*, love less than Me, especially when there are conflicting demands. *Cf.* Mt. 10: 37.

2 Verse 27. The picture is of the condemned criminal carrying his cross through the jeering crowds to execution.

STUDY 39 Luke 15: 1–32

1 Show how these three parables answer the Pharisees' objections (verse 2). What are the Son, the Spirit and the Father all eager to see happen and to bring about?

2 What does the story of the prodigal son teach about sin, repentance and the love of God?

3 Verses 25–32. What were the Pharisees meant to learn from this episode? Can you see the same tendency in yourself?

STUDY 40 Luke 16: 1–13

The point of this parable lies not in the dishonesty of the steward's plan, but in his prudent provision for the future.

1 Verses 1–9. For what did the steward's master commend him? What ought Christian disciples to learn from the wisdom of the world? How can money be used to provide 'spiritual capital' for the future? *Cf.* 1 Tim. 6: 18, 19.

2 Verses 10–13. How do these verses show that Jesus was not condoning the steward's dishonesty? How ought material possessions to be seen in perspective?

Note. Verses 9, 11, 13. 'Mammon' means 'money'. It is called 'unrighteous' because of the way it easily leads men to dishonesty. *Cf.* 1 Tim. 6: 10.

STUDY 41 Luke 16: 14–31

1 For what was the rich man punished? In what way does this parable reinforce the lesson of verse 9?

2 What does the parable teach about the reality of future punishment and the means of avoiding it? What ought men to be doing now? And why?

Note. Verses 16, 17. The ministry of John the Baptist marked the end of the Jewish prerogative. Men of every race and kind could from now on press into the kingdom. Yet the moral law remained unchanged; *e.g.*, verse 18, the sanctity of marriage.

☐ STUDY 42 Luke 17: 1–19

1 Verses 1–10. Four characteristics of a true disciple are presented in these verses. Can you sum them up in four words? Note the demand for personal application (verses 3, 10); and the need to pray for an increase (verse 5) in such qualities.

2 Verses 11–19. What was required before the men could be healed? And what did Jesus expect of them afterwards? Can we learn anything from this for our own prayers?

☐ STUDY 43 Luke 17: 20–37

1 What does Jesus here teach concerning the nature of (a) the kingdom of God, and (b) the coming of the Son of man? What is the difference, and what the connection?

2 What aspects of His return does Jesus here emphasize? How will it find the world? And how should it find His own people?

Note. Verse 37. The figurative language (*cf.* Jb. 39: 27–30) suggests that, 'Where there is spiritual decay, judgment will come.' Or it is perhaps a proverbial saying meaning simply, 'When the time is ripe, it will happen.'

☐ STUDY 44 Luke 18: 1–17

1 Verses 1–8. Why ought we to be persistent in prayer? How does the parable illustrate this? Note the elements both of comparison and of contrast.

2 Verses 9–14. What was the Pharisee's error? Was he wrong to give thanks? What does God require in prayer?

3 Verse 17. To what characteristics of children do you think Jesus was referring?

☐ STUDY 45 Luke 18: 18–34

1 Verses 18–30. What did this ruler lack? Why are possessions so dangerous?

2 Do you see any connection between the radical demand of verses 22 and 29, and Jesus' own self-sacrifice (verses 31–33)? *Cf.* 1 Pet. 2: 21.

☐ STUDY 46 Luke 18: 35 – 19: 10

1 Compare and contrast these two men in their need and their

attitude to Jesus. What may we learn from the different way in which Jesus dealt with each?

2 Who took the initiative in the salvation of Zacchaeus? What may we learn from the expression of his repentance?

☑ **STUDY 47 Luke 19: 11–28**

1 What does the parable teach (a) about the present responsibility of the followers of Jesus, and (b) about future judgment?

2 Was the third servant's excuse a valid one? On what grounds was he condemned? What is his case intended to teach?

For the remaining Studies 48–63 on Luke's Gospel see p. 30.

GENESIS 27 – 50

☐ **STUDY 20 Genesis 27: 1–45**

1 Trace the parts played by each of the actors in the story. What motive influenced each one? Why was God pleased to bless Jacob? *Cf.* Rom. 9: 10–13.

2 What was the nature of Esau's grief (verses 34, 38)? Did it have anything to do with repentance? *Cf.* Heb. 12: 17; 2 Cor. 7: 10.

☐ **STUDY 21 Genesis 27: 46 – 28: 22**

1 How does the fundamental difference between the two brothers now manifest itself increasingly? What truth concerning God's choice does Isaac now explicitly recognize?

2 What was the significance of Jacob's dream? At what point in his experience did it happen? Of what great truths was he then made aware concerning (a) God, and (b) God's purpose for his own life? What response did he make? How far have you gone in similarly making God's promises your own?

☐ STUDY 22 Genesis 29: 1–30

1 Compare Laban's trickery in his deals with Jacob with Jacob's earlier trickery in his dealings with Esau and with Isaac. Can we discern God's hand here? What practical lessons did Jacob thus learn? See 31: 42; 32: 10–12.

2 Are the determination and energy shown by Jacob here a new feature in his life? Do you, like him, have a purpose and object in life to give you a similar single-mindedness?

Note. Verse 27 seems to mean that Jacob had to fulfil the week of wedding festivities for Leah; then he received Rachel and served seven more years for her after marrying her. See 30: 25, 26; 31: 41.

☐ STUDY 23 Genesis 29: 31 – 30: 43

1 Which of Jacob's wives was the ancestress of our Lord? *Cf.* Pr. 16: 9; Heb. 7: 14. And of what did his years with Laban make him most conscious?

2 What does this passage show about polygamy? Does Jacob's possession of several wives provide an example of a warning concerning right ideals for marriage?

☐ STUDY 24 Genesis 31: 1 – 32: 2

1 Six more years have passed (31: 41). To what extent is Jacob the deceiver now a changed man? See 31: 6, 38–42. Also, what evidence is there that he has come to a deeper knowledge of God? See 31: 3–13, 42.

2 What factors combined to make Jacob sure that God's time for him to return to Canaan had come? How was the inevitable opposition of Laban overcome? What may I learn for my own encouragement from such a record?

Note. 31: 42,53. 'The Fear of Isaac': *i.e.*, the God whom Isaac reverently worshipped.

☐ **STUDY 25 Genesis 32: 3–32**

1 What is good, and what is defective in Jacob's prayer in verses 9–12? Was he relying most upon God, or upon his own resourcefulness? If the former, ought he to have been so greatly afraid (verse 7)? *Cf.* Mk. 4: 40; 5: 36.

2 What is suggested by the picture of wrestling with God? How far does God bless us only when we echo Jacob's prayer in verse 26? What are the cost and the reward of such a prayer? Did Jacob prevail by his own strength, or by faith? *Cf.* Ho. 12: 3, 4a.

☐ **STUDY 26 Genesis 33**

1 What is the importance of the title which Jacob gives to God in verse 20? How has he named Him previously? See 31: 5, 42, 53; 32: 9. *Cf.* Ps. 63: 1.

2 In the story of this chapter how far did Jacob live up to his new name Israel? Is it significant that he is still called by the old name? Recall the terms of his vow in 28: 22. How far does our behaviour match our Christian profession and express our new nature? *Cf.* Rom. 7: 20, 24, 25a.

Note. In other cases of change of name in Scripture the new replaces the old; so we read of Abraham instead of Abram, of Peter instead of Simon (but see Jn. 21: 15–17), of Paul instead of Saul. But after Peniel the old name Jacob still occurs seventy times in Genesis, and Israel only forty times.

☐ **STUDY 27 Genesis 34**

1 In this sordid story, which appears the more honourable, Shechem and his father, or the sons of Jacob? How contrary to 1 Pet. 2: 12; 4: 15! *Cf.* 1 Cor. 10: 12.

2 What evidence is there that Jacob left everything to his sons, instead of taking action himself as the head of the family? When he did finally rebuke them, about what was he chiefly concerned? What considerations ought to have moved him to think, speak or act differently?

☐ **STUDY 28 Genesis 35**

1 How did Jacob's repentance show itself, and how was it rewarded? Note what personal sorrows accompanied God's blessings to Jacob. *Cf.* Heb. 12: 6–11; Ps. 119: 67, 71.

2 What actually provoked Jacob's repentance, and what new

revelation was given to him after his repentance? What does this record thus demonstrate concerning God's character and His demands? *Cf.* Ho. 14: 4–7; 2 Tim. 2: 19.

☐ STUDY 29 Genesis 36

In chapter 10, before the writer concentrates on the line of Abraham, the names of other nations are recorded. In a similar way in this chapter, before concentration on the family of Jacob a list of Esau's descendants is given.

1 Jacob and Esau were both sinners. What, however, was the vital and decisive difference between them? Do we ever read anything similar to 35: 1–7 recorded of Esau? *Cf.* Heb. 12: 16, 17.

2 It was foretold before their birth that each of Rebekah's twin sons would beget a nation (25: 23). Was it the case with the nations, as it was with their progenitors, that the one was chosen of God and the other rejected, and, if so, why? *Cf.* Ob. 1–4, 8–10, 17, 18; Mal. 1: 2–5.

☐ STUDY 30 Genesis 37

1 What three things specially aroused the envy and hatred of Joseph's brothers against him? To what other sins did their envy lead them? *Cf.* Jas. 3: 16.

2 Can you approve of (a) Jacob's possessive love for Joseph, (b) his favouritism in his treatment of him, (c) the unrelieved gloom to which the loss of Joseph led him? What ought we to learn from such a story?

Note. Verse 3. 'A long robe with sleeves': a garment of distinction, perhaps implying freedom from manual toil. The ordinary tunic had no sleeves.

☐ STUDY 31 Genesis 38 and 39

1 Chapter 38. From what initial false step did all the events of sin and shame originate? What can we learn from this? *Cf.* Gn. 24: 3; 26: 34, 35; 27: 46 – 28: 4.

2 Chapter 39. How did Joseph exemplify the best qualities of his ancestors: the faith and faithfulness of Abraham, the meekness of Isaac, the energy and ability of Jacob, the beauty of Rachel?

3 Over what temptations did Joseph win the victory? What was the key to his success?

☐ STUDY 32 Genesis 40: 1 – 41: 13

1 What qualities in Joseph are shown in this passage? Try to find at least five.

2 How did God make Joseph's prison experiences work together for good? Why were victory over temptation, and use of opportunities to prove God and help others, so important at this stage?

☐ STUDY 33 Genesis 41: 14–57

1 What in Joseph so impressed Pharaoh and his court that he was made ruler of Egypt? Compare your own character and consistency with his, and consider where you fall short.

2 If we have found in Christ the Bread of life, and men around us are perishing, what spiritual lesson may we draw from verses 54–57?

☐ STUDY 34 Genesis 42

1 What was the motive of Joseph's apparent harshness towards his brethren? For his real feelings see verses 24, 25. Have we here an illustration of the methods which God also uses? *Cf.* Heb. 12: 6, 11; Je. 31: 18, 19.

2 What brought the brothers to the recognition of their guilt? See verse 21.

3 How mistaken was the attitude of Jacob in verse 36! What may we learn from this about our own attitude when everything seems against us? *Cf.* Ps. 43: 5; Phil. 4: 6, 7.

☐ STUDY 35 Genesis 43

1 Why did Jacob yield to Judah's appeal when he had refused the earlier appeal of Reuben in 42: 37, 38?

2 Why do you think Joseph gave to Benjamin a portion five times as large as to the others? Was it affection for Benjamin or a further test for his brothers? See 37: 4.

☐ STUDY 36 Genesis 44

1 How do the actions of Joseph's brothers in this chapter show a real change in them? Contrast their behaviour towards their father and another beloved son in 37: 18–31.

2 Observe how in this second visit to Egypt Judah takes the lead; see 43: 3, 8; 44: 14, 16, 18. What qualities are revealed in his speech in verses 18–34? How does this teach us that we should not despair of anyone? See 37: 26, 27; 38: 1; Ps. 119: 59.

☐ STUDY 37 Genesis 45

1 What were the reasons for Joseph's intensity of feeling in verses 1–15? What was his attitude to the sufferings that preceded the reconciliation? What can we learn from this of God's longing to reconcile His sinful creatures, at whatever cost?

2 What blessings did the restoration of family harmony bring with it?

☐ STUDY 38 Genesis 46: 1 – 47: 12

1 In what way would the fulfilment of the promise in 46: 3 be easier in Egypt than in the nomadic conditions of Canaan? What may we learn from this of God's providence?

2 What trait in Joseph is revealed by his management of Jacob's arrival? *Cf.* Is. 11: 2.

3 How does this passage illustrate, typically or otherwise, (a) Jn. 14: 6; (b) 2 Cor. 4: 17, 18?

☐ STUDY 39 Genesis 47: 13 – 48: 22

1 By their own confession what did Joseph do for the people of Egypt? How did he remain true to his father's God amid all the pressures of his office?

2 What different points of view produced the two retrospects of Jacob in 47: 9 and 48: 15, 16? Which is more worthy of our imitation?

3 Note Jacob's confident faith and prayer for his two grandsons. *Cf.* Heb. 11: 21; Gn. 18: 18, 19; Dt. 6: 4–7; Ps. 78: 5–7. What can we learn from this concerning the privilege and responsibility of Christian parenthood?

☐ STUDY 40 Genesis 49

1 Consider how diverse and unpromising were the human materials which God chose for the fulfilment of His purposes. *Cf.* Dt.

7: 7, 8; 9: 4, 5. One secret of how God could do this is described in verses 24, 25a. Is this a secret of victory which you have learnt for yourself? *Cf.* Phil. 4: 13; 2 Cor. 12: 9.

2 Consider especially Reuben, Judah and Joseph. In whom was the promise of verse 10 fulfilled? (See RSV for sense; *cf.* Ezk. 21: 27.) *Cf.* also 1 Ch. 5: 1, 2.

☐ **STUDY 41 Genesis 50**

1 Comparing 50: 1–13 with 28: 13–15, reflect how faithful God had been in the fulfilment of His promises even in Jacob's own lifetime. *Cf.* Ps. 146: 5, 6.

2 Why were the brothers slow to believe that Joseph had forgiven them? What was Joseph's reaction? Do we ever similarly grieve God?

3 How long a time elapsed between Jacob's coming to Egypt and Joseph's death? What took place during those years? See verses 22, 23; Ex. 1: 7. How does this make Joseph's faith (see verses 24, 25) the more conspicuous? *Cf.* Heb. 11: 22.

☐ **STUDY 42 Genesis 37 – 50: Revision**

1 Why did Joseph remain so free from bitterness in the face of undeserved suffering, and so unspoilt by sudden great responsibility? See Gn. 39: 9c; 50: 20; Acts 7: 9, 10.

2 Consider Joseph as a type of Christ. How many parallels can you find?

LUKE 19 : 29 – 24 : 53

☑ **STUDY 48 Luke 19: 29–46**

1 Verses 29–40. What was Jesus' purpose in making this public

entry into Jerusalem? *Cf.* Zc. 9: 9. What was He intending to teach about the nature of His Kingship? Contrast Rev. 19: 11.

2 Verses 41–46. What was it about Jerusalem that moved Jesus to pity and to anger? How do these verses show that love does not exclude judgment?

☐ STUDY 49 Luke 19: 47 – 20: 26

1 Observe the atmosphere of hostility and intrigue in this passage. In this situation, what was the purpose of the parable of 20: 9–18? To whom does it refer, and what does it imply about the status of Jesus?

2 20: 19–26. Why was Jesus' answer so effective? Apply both halves of verse 25 to your own situation.

3 20: 1–8. Why did Jesus answer one question by asking another? Or was He treating their enquiry seriously? If so, why did He refuse to tell them the answer to their original question?

☐ STUDY 50 Luke 20: 27 – 21: 4

1 20: 27–40. The Sadducees repudiated the doctrine of a life after death, both because of the practical difficulties it involved, and because it was not taught in the Five Books of Moses, which they regarded as the only authority. How did Jesus meet their objections on both grounds? *Cf.* Mk. 12: 24.

2 21: 1–4. What does God look for in those who make gifts for His work? *Cf.* 2 Cor. 8: 12. Contrast these verses with 20: 46, 47.

3 20: 41–44. 'Son of David' as a title for the Messiah carried the implication of a national, political deliverer. What does Jesus here teach about the true status of the Messiah, and about the character of His reign?

Note. 20: 37, 38. God's covenant with those who are His is such that death cannot break it. If He is still called the God of Abraham, then Abraham cannot be dead.

☐ STUDY 51 Luke 21: 5–24

In this chapter two themes seem to be intertwined; the coming destruction of Jerusalem and its Temple (which happened in AD 70), and the second coming of the Lord. It is not always clear which is in view, but in verses 5–24 the reference is probably to AD 70 throughout.

1 Jesus speaks of the destruction of Jerusalem as 'days of vengeance' (verse 22); what then was its cause? *Cf.* 11: 49–51; 13: 34, 35; 19: 41–44.

2 What dangers and problems will confront the disciples? How are they to be ready to meet them? *Cf.* Jn. 15: 18–21; Rev. 12: 11.

☐ STUDY 52 Luke 21: 25–38

If detailed predictions are first given about AD 70 in verses 5–24, and about our Lord's second coming in verses 25–28, it seems probable that in a concluding summary our Lord first referred again to AD 70 in verses 29–32, and then to the end of the age and the final day of the Lord in verses 33–36.

1 Contrast the attitude of Christians with that of other men in times of crisis and judgment. What makes the difference?

2 In the light of our expectation of our Lord's return, how ought we to live? What will enable us to stand firm?

☐ STUDY 53 Luke 22: 1–13

1 Verses 1–6. As events move towards the climax, what interested parties are mentioned here, and what is the attitude of each to Jesus? What ought we to learn from the part played by Judas, who was 'of the number of the twelve'?

2 Verses 7–13. Do you think it is significant that Jesus' death occurred at Passover time? *Cf.* 1 Cor. 5: 7; Ex. 12: 3–13; 1 Pet. 1: 18–20.

☐ STUDY 54 Luke 22: 14–30

1 Verses 14–23. What indication do you find in this passage of (a) the necessity and (b) the purpose of Jesus' death?

2 Verses 24–30. How does Jesus here reverse the world's standards? Consider how His own life and work exemplified His teaching.

Note. Verses 19b, 20. Luke's Gospel apparently did not originally contain the fuller account of the institution of the Lord's Supper found in Matthew, Mark and 1 Corinthians 11, from which it was later inserted here.

☐ STUDY 55 Luke 22: 31–46

1 Verses 31–34. Compare the empty confidence of Peter with Jesus' knowledge of his danger. What may we learn from this? What is the safeguard against similar failure?

2 Verses 39–46. Why did Jesus shrink from the cross? Could the physical suffering alone have caused this? What does this teach us both about Jesus Himself and about His death? Consider your share in the responsibility for that agony.

3 What sort of impression of the quality of Jesus' disciples do you get from this passage as a whole? Is this an encouragement to you?

Notes

1 Verse 32. Jesus' prayer referred not to the denial (He *knew* Peter would deny Him), but to the time after it, when Peter's role would be vital. For he would be the key to the restoration of the whole group of disciples, who were all to be the objects of Satan's attack. Note that 'you', verse 31, is plural, and 'you', verse 32, singular.

2 Verse 36. Not a command to resist, but a picturesque warning of dangerous times ahead. *Cf.* Mt. 26: 52.

☐ STUDY 56 Luke 22: 47–62

1 Verses 47–54. Compare the attitude of Jesus with that of His disciples (*cf.* also Mk. 14: 50), and His enemies. What made the difference? Do verses 41, 42, 45, 46 suggest an answer?

2 Verses 54–62. What does this passage show both of the strength and of the weakness of Peter? Trace the stages of his failure from verse 33 to verse 60. What brought him to repentance?

☐ STUDY 57 Luke 22: 63 – 23: 12

1 How would you describe the attitude to Jesus of the following people: the guards, the religious leaders, Pilate, Herod? What sort of people are their counterparts today? Have they anything to teach us?

2 Consider what Jesus had to suffer, and how He bore it. Read 1 Pet. 2: 19–23; Phil. 2: 5–8.

☐ STUDY 58 Luke 23: 13–31

1 Trace in this chapter the stages in Pilate's capitulation. What was his ruling motive? What would you have done in his place?

2 Verses 26–31. Try to picture Jesus on the way to crucifixion. What impression must His condition and His words have made on the bystanders? What occasioned this warning and implied call for repentance?

Note. Verse 31. A proverbial expression probably meaning here: 'If the Romans so treat the innocent Jesus, what will be the fate of the guilty Jerusalem?'

☑ STUDY 59 Luke 23: 32–43

1 Consider (a) the attitude to Jesus' suffering of the different people mentioned, and (b) His attitude to them.

2 Verses 39–43. What brought this criminal to repentance and faith? What may we learn (a) from his confession and request, and (b) from Jesus' response to his prayer? *Cf.* Lk. 18: 13, 14.

☑ STUDY 60 Luke 23: 44–56

1 What indication does the narrative give of the significance of Jesus' death? What was its effect on the various people present? And what gave it this effect?

2 Verses 50–56. Jesus had apparently failed. What does the action of Joseph and the women at such a time teach us?

☑ STUDY 61 Luke 24: 1–12

1 Try to put yourself in the place of the women on Easter morning. Ought they to have been perplexed? Why had they not remembered Jesus' words?

2 To the disillusioned apostles the story was wishful thinking (verse 11). What does it mean to you?

☐ STUDY 62 Luke 24: 13–35

1 Verses 25–27. Would you have merited the same rebuke? What does Jesus' use of the Old Testament here and in verses 44–47 teach us of its importance and reliability, and the way we should use it?

2 Contrast the attitude of the two disciples before and after their meeting with Jesus. Why were they so slow to recognize Him? In what ways is their experience a parable for our instruction?

☐ STUDY 63 Luke 24: 36–53

1 *Cf.* verse 11. What changed the apostles' minds? Why do *you* believe that Jesus rose from the dead?

2 What are the fundamental facts of the gospel to which witness must be borne throughout the world? Who are to bear that witness, and in what power? Are you personally involved? Or, if not, why not?

PSALMS 1 - 12

Introduction

The book of Psalms may be regarded as the inspired hymn-book of the Jewish church, containing psalms for both public and private worship. Those with the superscription (or subscription[1]) 'To the choirmaster' seem specially intended for public worship. Others were, perhaps, originally personal meditations which were taken over for use in the service of the sanctuary and in family worship at home. There are also didactic poems and historical recitals. The book stood at the head of the third section of the Hebrew Scriptures, to which it often gave its name. This section followed the books of the prophets. (*Cf.* Lk. 24: 44.)

The contents of the book were composed at various periods during the whole of Israelite history from the exodus to the Babylonian captivity. One psalm at least is the work of Moses (Ps. 90). Many are by David, one or two by Solomon, a few by certain of the Temple singers, and many again are anonymous. Some have a title and others have none. The Psalms divide into five divisions, as follows: 1–41, 42–72, 73–89, 90–106, 107–150. The end of each division except the last is marked by the word 'Amen'.

This third section of the Old Testament Scriptures, at the beginning of which the Psalms stand, may be said to strike, on the whole, a more individual note than the preceding ones. While the

[1] A reference to Hab. 3: 19 (last clause) suggests the probability that, in those of the psalms which have headings or titles, the musical part of the title, including words 'To the choirmaster', should really be attached to the end of the preceding psalm.

prophets write largely (though not, of course, entirely) from the point of view of the outward and national life, the Psalms deal largely with personal, spiritual matters. It is needless to say that they look forward, as do the prophets, to the Person and work of our Lord Jesus Christ.

☑ STUDY 1 Psalms 1 and 2

1 In Ps. 1 the righteous and the wicked are contrasted. Compare their characters (verses 1, 2), the pictures given of them and their final end (verses 3–6). In what do you delight? And with whom are you most at ease?

2 Ps. 2. What is the Lord's purpose for 'his anointed', and what is involved in its accomplishment? *Cf.* Acts 4: 24–28. What response does this demand from men, and what hope does it offer to them?

Note. Ps. 2 is the first of what are known as Messianic psalms, *i.e.*, psalms which prophesy the sufferings and glory of the coming Messiah.

☑ STUDY 2 Psalms 3 and 4

For the probable circumstances of both psalms, see 2 Sa. 15–17.

1 Ps. 3 is a morning psalm. As David wakes, what adverse conditions confront him (verses 1, 2)? *Cf.* 2 Sa. 16: 5–8. How does David react (verses 3, 4)? What are the consequences of his trust in the Lord (verses 5–8)? What may we learn from his example?

2 Ps. 4 is an evening psalm. In verses 2–5, David addresses his adversaries. What counsel does he give them? In what does he find his own strength, joy and security?

Note. 3: 5. If this psalm was written, as seems likely, on the second morning after David's flight from Jerusalem, it was a great encouragement to him that the night had passed without an attack. *Cf.* 2 Sa. 17: 1–4, 14.

☑ STUDY 3 Psalm 5

1 What does this psalm reveal about God? Write out a list of the truths which you discover here, and let them inform your responsive worship.

2 The psalm is an example of David at prayer. When, how, why and for what does he pray? Do my prayers express the same urgent concern and expectant faith?

☑ STUDY 4 Psalm 6

Another example of prayer. David seems to have suffered both from sickness and the taunts of his enemies. His sickness gave them occasion to point to him as one 'smitten of God'.

1 Verses 1–7. Explain in your own words the state of David's heart and mind as he made his prayer. What does he (a) confess to God, and (b) expect from God?

2 Note in verses 8–10 how David has come to an assurance of answered prayer and certain deliverance—an assurance which he openly confesses before God and men. Have you had any similar experience?

☐ STUDY 5 Psalms 7 and 8

1 In Ps. 7 David is experiencing persecution. On what grounds does he make his appeal to God (verses 1–11)? In what two ways does he see judgment will overtake the wicked (verses 12–16)? Learn from verse 17 how prayer should end.

2 Ps. 8. What two truths here make the psalmist worship and wonder? And, more particularly, what is here declared concerning the place of man in the mind and purpose of God? *Cf.* Heb. 2: 5–10.

☐ STUDY 6 Psalms 9 and 10

These psalms were probably originally one, as is shown by the fact of their common 'alphabetic' structure. In the LXX they are one psalm. The contents are, however, different. Ps. 9 is mainly a song of praise, celebrating victory over foreign nations; but Ps. 10 consists mainly of prayer, pleading for the overthrow of the wicked within Israel.

1 Make a detailed list of the truths we may learn about the Lord from these psalms.

2 From Ps. 9 what do we learn of the actions and longings of David, and of his experience of the Lord? Contrast this with the thoughts and actions of the wicked as described in Ps. 10. To what extent is your own action, experience and longing similar to David's?

Note. 9: 17. The meaning is that through the judgments which God is executing the life of the wicked will be cut short by death.

☐ STUDY 7 Psalms 11 and 12

1 In Ps. 11 why does David not follow the advice of those who

see the situation as hopeless (verse 3) and suggest flight? What gives him confidence to stand firm? Do you have this confidence?

2 How are the word of man and the Word of God contrasted in Ps. 12?

Note. 11:3. See RV mg. The righteous have not been able to effect any change for the better; why then remain in the midst of danger?

For Studies 8–21 on the Psalms see p. 70.

ACTS 1:1 - 12:24

Introduction

In one of the most exciting books of the Bible Luke tells how the gospel spread from Jerusalem—the capital of the Jewish world—to Rome—the centre of the Gentile world. He shows how Christianity emerged from within the framework of the Jewish nation to become a universal religion. These developments are consistently traced to the continued activity of the risen and ascended Christ and to the working of the Holy Spirit.

The theme of the book is found in the opening section (1:1–11) where Luke draws our attention to (a) the continued activity of Jesus, risen and ascended; (b) the apostles as the leaders Christ had chosen; (c) the Holy Spirit as the source of power and (d) Jesus' programme for the future. These facts dominate throughout the book.

Analysis

The book of Acts falls into two main parts: chapters 1–12, which give the story of the rise of the church in Jerusalem and its extension to Judaea, Samaria and Antioch; and chapters 13–28, which describe Paul's three missionary journeys, his arrest in Jerusalem, imprisonment in Caesarea, and journeys to Rome. A more accurate analysis, however, reveals that there are (apart from the introductory paragraph, 1: 1–11) six divisions or periods, each concluding with a brief summary of progress.

	1: 1–11	Introduction.
1.	1: 12 – 6: 7	Progress in Jerusalem.
2.	6: 8 – 9: 31	Extension to Judaea and Samaria.
3.	9: 32 – 12: 24	Reception of Gentiles into the church.
4.	12: 25 – 16: 5	A door of faith opened to the Gentiles.
5.	16: 6 – 19: 20	Extension to Macedonia, Achaia and Asia.
6.	19: 21 – 28: 31	Paul's journey to Rome.

☐ STUDY 1 Acts 1: 1–11

1 What did Jesus teach His apostles about their future work before He ascended? Does this still apply to us today?

2 What is said in these verses about (a) the authority of God the Father, (b) the agency of God the Holy Spirit, and (c) the activity of Jesus, the Son of God? The whole story of this book flows from these facts. Are they transforming your life?

☐ STUDY 2 Acts 1: 12–26

1 What two actions did the disciples take during this waiting period? Can you suggest reasons why?

2 Compare Judas (especially verses 16, 17) with Jesus' brothers (verse 14). *Cf.* Jn. 7: 5. What warning and encouragement do they give you?

☐ STUDY 3 Acts 2: 1–13

1 What three signs were given in connection with the coming of the Spirit? See verses 2–4, and 6, 8, 11. They express in symbol what our Lord had already stated in word (*cf.* 1: 8), that the coming of the Spirit would lead to power, inspired utterance and universal testimony. What purposes of God was the Spirit thus given to fulfil?

2 What was the reaction of the disciples, the crowd and the mockers to the coming of the Holy Spirit? What do you think your reaction would have been?

Notes

1 Pentecost was the Greek name for the feast called in the Old Testament 'the feast of harvest' (Ex. 23: 16), or 'the feast of weeks' (Dt. 16: 9, 10). It

marked the end of the grain harvest, and began on the fifteenth day from the day after the Passover sabbath (Lv. 23: 15, 16). The season of the year being favourable for travelling, Jerusalem was crowded with Jews from all parts (Acts 2: 9–11).

2 If possible see *Acts* (*TNTC*), pp. 55–57 for comments on 'tongues'.

☑ STUDY 4 Acts 2: 14–36

1 What three passages of the Old Testament does Peter quote in his address and what facts of the gospel does he support by them? What may we learn from this concerning the place and use of the Old Testament today?

2 What characteristics does Peter show in his preaching? Remember what he had been like eight weeks earlier. Wherein lay the change? Can this apply to your Christian service?

☑ STUDY 5 Acts 2: 37–47

1 What twofold offer is made in verse 38, and on what condition?

2 What features marked the lives of these new believers and of the early church according to verses 42–47? How many of these are true in your experience?

Note. The receiving of the Holy Spirit in 2: 4 is an extraordinary event. The receiving of the Holy Spirit in 2: 38 is the ordinary New Testament pattern. Note how baptism with water symbolizes the two gospel benefits of cleansing from sin and of new life from above by the baptism of the Spirit.

☑ STUDY 6 Acts 3: 1–26

1 The cripple's physical cure (verses 1–11) is a picture of the spiritual truths of the gospel of salvation. Note how it shows (a) man's need, (b) the necessity of faith, (c) the importance of personal witness, (d) the assurance of salvation, (e) the miracle of salvation itself. (Peter explains how it happened in verses 12–16.) Have you been the link between Christ and a person in need as Peter was that day?

2 In addressing the people of his own nation, what sins does Peter charge against them? What promises does he make to them and on what conditions? How far are his words applicable to us who are not Jews?

Notes

1 Verse 6. 'In the name of Jesus' means 'by the authority', 'with the power' of Jesus. *Cf.* verse 16; 4: 12.

2 Verses 13, 26. 'Servant': *cf.* Is. 52: 13 (also 42: 1–4; 49: 5, 6; 50: 1–10). Peter is making a fearless proclamation of the Lord's Messiahship. *Cf.* 4: 27, 30.

☐ STUDY 7 Acts 4: 1–31

1 Verses 1–22. Persecution. The leaders of organized religion now openly persecute the disciples. What caused the arrest (verse 3) and the release (verse 21) of Peter and John? What verbal and visible evidence did Peter offer in their defence? Does fear of men sometimes make us silent when we ought to speak?

2 Verses 23–31. Prayer. Going back to their fellow-Christians, the disciples pray. Trace the threefold reason (verses 24–28), request (verses 29, 30) and result (verse 31) found in their prayer. Could you pray with such boldness and willingness in a similar tough situation?

☐ STUDY 8 Acts 4: 32 – 5: 16

In this insight into the fellowship of the early church the sincere self-sacrifice of Barnabas is compared with the hypocrisy and greed of Ananias and Sapphira.

1 In 4: 32–37 what essentials of fellowship are demonstrated? See one result of them in verse 33.

2 What made the sin of Ananias and Sapphira so grave and what led to it? Why was such a divine judgment necessary? What result did it produce?

3 What example can you follow from the action of Barnabas and what danger can you avoid from the attitude of Ananias and Sapphira?

Notes

1 5: 4. This verse shows that the giving spoken of in 4: 34–37 was entirely voluntary.

2 5: 9. 'Tempt': the word means to put God to the test, to challenge or provoke Him. *Cf.* Ex. 17: 2, 7; Acts 15: 10.

☐ STUDY 9 Acts 5: 17–42

1 In spite of persecution and warnings (*cf.* 4: 17–21) the apostles continue to witness. Consider the different parts played by the angel (verse 19), the Holy Spirit (verses 20, 32), and Gamaliel (verses 34–40) in making this possible. Do you know something of the same constraint—to speak to others about Christ?

2 Consider the four different reactions of the religious opposition (verses 17, 24, 26, 33). Finally they beat the apostles. *Cf.* 1 Pet. 2: 20, 21. Are you afraid to suffer through faithful witness?

□ STUDY 10 Acts 6: 1 – 7: 8

1 How did the apostles deal with the incipient troubles mentioned in 6: 1? What three results followed for the widows, the Seven, and the Twelve? What lessons may we learn from their handling of the situation?

2 Notice three things about Stephen's life and ministry (6: 5–15): (a) the outstanding features of his life (verses 5, 8); (b) the nature of the persecution against him (verses 11–13); (c) the charges laid against him (verses 13, 14). *Cf.* Mk. 14: 57, 58 and Acts 21: 27, 28. What are the indispensable qualifications for, and the possible consequences of, faithful witness for Christ?

Notes

1 6: 1. 'Hellenists' denote Jews who had lived abroad and spoke Greek. 'Hebrews' were Jews of Palestine who spoke the Jewish language.

2 Stephen's ministry marked a vital stage in the growth of the early church. His teaching 'first drove a wedge between Judaism and Christianity' (see *Acts* (*TNTC*), p. 75).

□ STUDY 11 Acts 7: 9–43

Stephen's speech seeks to show (a) that God's presence with His people is not limited to a particular place or building (verses 2, 9, 10, 30–34, 38, 44–49); and (b) that far from overthrowing Moses, Christ is the promised prophet like Moses of whom Moses himself spoke (verse 37).

1 God intended Joseph (verses 9–16) and Moses (verses 20–43) to deliver His people from bondage. Notice (a) the places in which they lived, (b) the work they had to do, (c) the treatment they received from their brethren, and (d) the results they achieved. In what ways do they foreshadow the work of the Lord Jesus Christ?

2 The tragedy of Israel's spiritual blindness is described in verses 25 and 35–43. How did it manifest itself first in thought, will and desire (verse 39) and finally in action (verses 40–43)? What was its penalty? Does God still deal with His people like this?

□ STUDY 12 Acts 7: 44 – 8: 4

1 In his conclusion (7: 44–53) how does Stephen teach the divine origin and yet the inadequacy of both the Tabernacle or 'tent of witness' and the Temple or 'house' which Solomon built? What charges does he bring against his accusers? To what positive truths here indicated or implied ought we to pay heed?

2 Consider the likeness between Stephen and his Lord in his life,

character, and in his death. What did this likeness come from? How may we follow his example? *Cf.* 2 Cor. 3: 18.

3 What were the results for the church of Stephen's witness (a) in suffering (see 8: 1, 3), and (b) in expansion (see 8: 4, 5; 11: 19, 20)? Notice what God can do through one man fully yielded to His service.

☐ STUDY 13 Acts 8: 5–25

1 Measure the success of Philip's ministry in Samaria by the difficulties with which he had to contend. *Cf.* Jn. 4: 9. To what was his success due? *Cf.* Jn. 14: 12; Acts 1: 8. What results followed when the power of God was manifested? See verses 6, 18–21. In what ways should such a record make us give heed?

2 Simon was intellectually convinced of the truth and power of the gospel, but his heart was unchanged. How did this come to light? In what ways is it right or wrong for us to covet the power of God's Spirit?

Note. Verses 14–17. The reason, no doubt, why the Holy Spirit had not yet fallen upon the Samaritan believers was that, as this was the first extension of the church beyond the borders of the Jewish people, it was fitting that the seal of the Spirit (Eph. 1: 13) should be given through Peter and John, as representatives of the apostles. In a similar way Peter was chosen to go to Cornelius (10: 5), though Philip was probably in Caesarea at the time.

☐ STUDY 14 Acts 8: 26–40

1 Note how much of active interest and response the Ethiopian was already showing before Philip met him. What more did he need before he was able to go 'on his way rejoicing'? What similar aids may we use in order to find God and to discover more of His truth for ourselves?

2 Learn from Philip (a) the qualities needed in, and (b) the methods used by, one man when leading another person to trust Christ. Are you willing to be sent on such an errand (verses 26, 29)?

☐ STUDY 15 Acts 9: 1–19a

1 What do these verses reveal of Christ's power, majesty and glory and also of His compassion, love and grace? *Cf.* 1 Tim. 1: 12–14.

2 What task was Ananias given to do? In what way is he an example of the help we can give to a recently converted person?

☐ STUDY 16 Acts 9: 19b–31

1 How did Paul prove his sincerity from the very beginning of his Christian life? *Cf.* 1 Jn. 3: 14; Acts 26: 19, 20.

2 Comparing verse 31 with 6: 7, notice how the church had extended its boundaries. Notice, also, the two marks of healthy spiritual life that are especially mentioned in verse 31. Are these marks, together with those seen in Paul's life (Question 1), found in yours?

3 Compare the Jewish opposition and the Christian fellowship that Paul experienced at Damascus (verses 22–25) and Jerusalem (verses 26–30). May becoming a Christian today still give a person new enemies and new friends?

Note. The visit to Arabia of which Paul speaks in Gal. 1: 17 should probably be fitted in between verses 21 and 22 of the story in Acts 9.

☐ STUDY 17 Acts 9: 32–42

1 What evidences do you find in these verses that a widespread revival was going on at this time, and that Christ, dwelling in His people, still moved among men as Saviour, Teacher, Healer and Friend? What prayer ought such a record to stir us to pray?

2 How do you picture Dorcas? What ideals of Christian character and service are exemplified in her? Can you find ways to go and do likewise?

3 Peter continues to heal in the name of the Lord Jesus. (a) *Cf.* also 3: 6, 7, 16; 4: 30; 5: 12–16; 6: 8 and 8: 6, 7 for other examples. (b) Compare what Peter did with the work of his Master. With verse 34, *cf.* Mk. 2: 11 and Jn. 5: 8; and with verses 40, 41, *cf.* Mk. 5: 35–43. (c) Peter was experiencing what Christ had promised in Jn. 14: 12. Peter believed the promises of Christ and experienced the co-operating power of God the Spirit. The question is—Do we? And if not, why not?

☐ STUDY 18 Acts 9: 43 – 10: 33

1 See Notes 1 and 2. Contrast the two towns of Joppa and Caesarea, and the two men and Cornelius. The scene is now set for the Gentiles to receive the gospel. Whose intervention was necessary to bring it about? Whom ought we to thank for our reception of the gospel?

2 How did God teach new truths to both Peter and Cornelius? Notice the prejudice that had to be removed and the obedience that was shown. Are you also willing to obey God when He teaches you something new and different from your natural prejudice or preference?

Notes

1 9: 43. This verse really belongs to the Cornelius story. Joppa was a very Jewish town, loyal to ancient tradition; Caesarea was a semi-pagan city, modelled on Rome.

2 10: 1. Cornelius was a Gentile and a God-fearer, who joined with the Jewish worship, without becoming a proselyte.

3 10: 4. 'As a memorial': the word is that used in Lv. 2: 2 in connection with the remembrance offering. The angel's message assures Cornelius that though, in his uncircumcision, he had no share in the sacrifices of the Temple, yet his prayers and alms were acceptable before God.

□ STUDY 19 Acts 10: 34–48

1 What new truth had Peter learned from the vision? See verses 34, 35 and *cf.* verse 28. Notice that the work could not develop until Peter had learned this. Is our unwillingness to learn some divinely-revealed truth hindering God's work in and through us?

2 When Peter addressed Jews, what truths did he use to awaken their conscience (*cf.* 2: 36 and 3: 13–15)? What truth did he use now? Do you find any other indications in this address that it was spoken before a Gentile audience? What ought we to learn from these features concerning our presentation of the gospel to non-Christians?

3 Consider the character of Cornelius as revealed in this chapter. If he was such a devout man before, what did he gain by believing on Jesus? *Cf.* 11: 13–15.

Note. Verses 34, 35. The meaning of Peter's words is not that men can be saved by their own good works, but that men like Cornelius and his friends are not excluded from God's favourable regard on the ground of their nationality. Their devout spirit is just as pleasing in God's sight as a similar spirit and behaviour would have been in a Jew.

□ STUDY 20 Acts 11: 1–18

The circumcision party (verse 2) was a conservative group in the church at Jerusalem, who insisted on the necessity of circumcision for all. *Cf.* 15: 1, 5. Peter has to explain to them his action with Cornelius.

1 What main point does Peter emphasize when he recounts his meeting with Cornelius? Notice what Peter says about prayer; the vision and action of God; the part played by the angel and the Holy Spirit. What was the result of God's action upon (a) the Gentiles

(verses 14, 17, 18), (b) the circumcision party (verse 18), and (c) Peter (verses 16, 17)?

2 Compare 1: 5 with 11: 16, 17 and Eph. 3: 6. Peter had to learn that there was more truth in God's word than he realized at first, and that he must not keep up social, national and religious barriers when God has removed them. Do you retain any such barriers between yourself and someone else which ought to be removed?

□ STUDY 21 Acts 11: 19–30

The city of Antioch, capital of the Roman province of Syria, was one of the three largest cities of the Empire. It was famous for its commerce, art and literature, and infamous for its vice and frivolity. It was to become 'the jumping-off point' for Paul's missionary journeys.

1 What was the distinctive feature that from the beginning marked the preaching of the gospel at Antioch, and with what far-reaching results?

2 What stages marked the establishment of the church there, and what part did Barnabas play? How can we teach and encourage young Christians?

3 Verses 27–30. A young Gentile church helps the older church at Jerusalem. Note the signs of this church's vitality, influence and Christian spirit. *Cf.* 2: 44, 45; 4: 34–37. Does your Christian faith find expression in practical giving like this?

Note. Verse 26. The onlooking world, realizing that this clearly was not a synagogue of Jews, gave them a new distinctive name—'Christians'.

□ STUDY 22 Acts 12: 1–24

1 Sum up Herod's character from verses 1–4 and 18–23. How and why was his life abruptly ended? Are we living to the glory of God? *Cf.* 1 Cor. 10: 31.

2 Prayer was the church's weapon to free Peter. Note (a) its character (verse 5), (b) its obstacles (verses 6–11), (c) its results (verses 12–17). Those who had prayed did not believe that what had happened was true (verses 14, 15). Do you believe that intercessory prayer can do great things? *Cf.* 2 Cor. 1: 8–11 and Eph. 3: 20, 21.

For Studies 23–56 on the rest of Acts see p. 51.

EXODUS 1 - 20

Introduction

The name Exodus, taken from the Septuagint translation, means 'going out'. By applying the word 'redeem' to the great deliverance from Egypt (Ex. 6: 6; 15: 13), the book itself shows us in which direction to look for the spiritual meaning lying behind the historic fact. These twenty chapters are indeed full of teaching: not only the Exodus itself, but also the Red Sea, Marah, Elim, the manna, the rock, and the life-giving water, to name only the chief examples, all speak to us of spiritual truth.

In these chapters we read:

(a) Of redemption from bondage by power, and from death by the shedding of blood.

(b) Of the love of God, manifesting itself first in compassion for His suffering people, then in action for their deliverance, and in wonderful patience with their faithlessness and obstinacy.

(c) Of the holiness of God demanding consecration, separation and purity, and giving a law which must be observed.

(d) Of the amazing ingratitude of man, despite the countless benefits showered upon him, and of a ready promise (so soon broken) to do all that God commanded.

(e) But also of one man, Moses, who, like Abraham and Joseph before him, lived in the consciousness of God's presence and showed steadfast fidelity and conspicuous faith.

Analysis

1: 1 – 7: 7	Israel in bondage; the call and training of Moses.
7: 8 – 15: 21	Israel redeemed: the plagues, the Passover, and the crossing of the Red Sea.
15: 22 – 18: 27	Israel in the wilderness; needs met, despite ingratitude and unbelief.

19 and 20 — Israel at Sinai; the revelation of the majesty of God, and the giving of the ten commandments.

☐ **STUDY 1 Exodus 1 and 2**

1 What are the contrasting attitudes of the Israelites towards their circumstances, as revealed in this passage? *Cf.* Heb. 11: 23–25. What is God's attitude to the situation? See especially 2: 23–25.

2 By what varied means from birth onwards was Moses prepared for his life-work? *Cf.* Acts 7: 20–29. What does this reveal concerning God's ways of working?

☐ **STUDY 2 Exodus 3: 1 – 4: 17**

1 Consider God's revelation of Himself in the incident of the burning bush. How would you sum up God's being and character as revealed in this incident?

2 Was Moses' reluctance to accept God's call to be commended? *Cf.* 2 Cor. 3: 5; Rom. 12: 3. Why was God angry with him?

☐ **STUDY 3 Exodus 4: 18 – 6: 9**

1 Contrast 4: 29–31 with 5: 20, 21. What had happened to change the people's attitude? How did Moses react?

2 Consider God's answer to Moses' cry. What does it teach us about the faithfulness of God and the reliability of His promises?

Notes

1 4: 24. This seems to mean that Moses was struck down by a severe and dangerous illness, the result of his neglect to circumcise his son; and his life was saved by Zipporah's prompt action. He could not act as God's instrument while in disobedience to His covenant. *Cf.* Gn. 17: 10.

2 6: 3. 'Did not make myself known': *i.e.*, as One whose name is 'the LORD' or 'I AM'. *Cf.* 3: 14. Once only in Genesis did God use that name of Himself, and then without emphasis or explanation (Gn. 28: 13).

☐ **STUDY 4 Exodus 6: 10 – 7: 25**

1 God had called Moses and promised deliverance to the people. Why did He delay so long in fulfilling His promise? What did Moses learn from these difficult experiences and delays?

2 Why was Pharaoh so confident and so adamant in disobeying God's command? See particularly 7: 11–13, 22, 23. How does this kind of opposition to God show itself now? *Cf.* 2 Tim. 3: 1–9.

Note. 6: 12. 'Of uncircumcised lips': uncircumcision symbolizes unfitness for God's presence, and hence, more generally, unfitness for His service. *Cf.* 4: 10.

☐ STUDY 5 Exodus 8

1 What is mentioned in this chapter as the double purpose of the plagues? *Cf.* Is. 45: 22–25; Rom. 1: 18.

2 What new evidences are given of God's power, and how would these encourage the Israelites?

Note. Verse 26. A reference to the sacrifice in Israelite worship of bulls, cows or oxen, which in Egypt were sacred to Isis and therefore sacrosanct.

☐ STUDY 6 Exodus 9

1 How does Pharaoh's attitude show the difference between sorrow for the consequences of sin and true repentance?

2 Contrast the nature and the consequences both of faith in God's word, and of unbelief, as illustrated in this chapter.

☐ STUDY 7 Exodus 10 and 11

1 What was the outcome in Pharaoh's life of his persistent refusal to heed God's warnings? See particularly 10: 29.

2 What lesson can we learn from Moses' consistent refusal to compromise where God's command was concerned? What was the source of Moses' great courage? *Cf.* also Heb. 11: 27.

☐ STUDY 8 Exodus 12: 1–36

1 Why did the angel of death pass over the houses of the Israelites? How does this illustrate our redemption in Christ? *Cf.* 1 Pet. 1: 18, 19.

2 How were the Israelites to use the lamb's blood and its flesh? What is the New Testament counterpart of this? Why was unleavened bread used? *Cf.* 1 Cor. 5: 6–8; 2 Tim. 2: 19.

☐ STUDY 9 Exodus 12: 37 – 13: 22

1 What are the two major responses that God expects from those who are redeemed?

2 What lessons about guidance are taught in 13: 17–22?

□ STUDY 10 Exodus 14: 1 – 15: 21

1 Chapter 14. What can we learn here about God, about faith, and about the completeness of God's salvation?

2 Chapter 15. What does this song of triumph teach us about how to worship God? How ought we to follow its example?

□ STUDY 11 Exodus 15: 22 – 16: 36

1 What reason is given twice in this passage as to why God allowed His redeemed people to suffer thirst, disappointment, and hunger? *Cf.* Dt. 8: 2, 3; 1 Pet. 1: 6, 7.

2 What response is demanded from those for whom God provides? In what ways does God's provision test this response?

Note. 1 Cor. 10: 1–6 indicates that these experiences in the wilderness were spiritual as well as physical and material.

□ STUDY 12 Exodus 17

1 What is the significance of the sequence of the two events recorded in this chapter?

2 What lessons are taught here about the importance of prayer and its relationship to activity in the life and witness of the church? What further lesson was Israel meant to learn from the defeat of Amalek (verses 14–16)?

□ STUDY 13 Exodus 18

1 Consider the parts played by Jethro, Moses and God in this chapter. What can we learn about guidance from this?

2 What kind of men are to be chosen as rulers of the people of God? *Cf.* Acts 6: 1–4.

□ STUDY 14 Exodus 19 and 20

1 What revelation is given in these chapters concerning (a) the character of God, and (b) His purposes for His people?

2 What are the standards of worship and behaviour that God expects of His people? Try to summarize them briefly in your own words.

For Studies 15–29 on the second half of the book of Exodus see p. 106.

ACTS 12:25 – 28:31

☐ STUDY 23 Acts 12: 25 – 13: 12

With the return of Barnabas and Saul to Antioch (12: 25) begins the story of a great expansion of the gospel among the Gentiles.

1 What parts were played by (a) the Holy Spirit and (b) the local church in initiating the new advance? Note that the church may have been praying about possible future developments of their work when guidance came through a prophet inspired of the Holy Spirit. What does this teach you about guidance?

2 Paul and Elymas meet in a head-on clash (verses 6–12). What was (a) the cause of the clash, (b) the reason for Paul's strong condemnation of Elymas, (c) one purpose of the judgment which visibly fell upon him? Are you as prepared as Paul to rebuke and resist direct opposition to the Lord Jesus?

Notes

1 Verses 6–8. As a court magician Bar-jesus or Elymas feared his job would be in danger if the proconsul became a Christian.

2 Verse 9. 'Saul, who is called Paul': Luke changes from the apostle's Jewish name to his Roman and Gentile name to stress Paul's special ministry as the apostle to the Gentiles which was now beginning. Note also that Paul takes over as leader from Barnabas: *cf.* verse 1 with verse 13. Doubtless, because Paul was a Roman citizen, the proconsul treated him as superior to Barnabas.

☐ STUDY 24 Acts 13: 13–43

Paul's journey from Paphos to Antioch involved an ascent of 3,600 ft from the sea coast to a high plateau which was a flourishing region of Graeco-Roman civilization. This probably accounts for the return of John Mark, who was thus faced with more than he expected when he set out. Note also the presence in the synagogue at Antioch of two classes—Jews and God-fearing Gentiles (verses 16 and 26).

1 In the first part of his address (verses 16–25), how does Paul show

that the coming of Jesus was the culminating point in God's activity in the history recorded in the Old Testament?

2 When speaking of the resurrection (verses 30–39), what does Paul say about (a) the reasons for, (b) the Old Testament prophecies about, and (c) the result of, Jesus' resurrection? Of what particular blessing is it a God-given pledge? *Cf.* Rom. 4: 25.

Note. Verse 39. Paul here sets side by side two contrasting methods of justification: the one, by the works of the law, failing to achieve the end desired; the other, through faith in Jesus, bringing the person into the immediate blessing of full justification. *Cf.* Phil. 3: 6–9.

☐ STUDY 25 Acts 13: 44–52

The Jews at Antioch became jealous (verse 45) because Paul's message of forgiveness through Christ was drawing away the God-fearers, whom they hoped would eventually become fully committed to Judaism.

1 What was the result of this jealous opposition upon the work of Paul and Barnabas? *Cf.* 18: 5, 6; 28: 28. Do you ever allow opposition to silence your testimony or halt your Christian work? Of what may the refusal of some to respond be an indication?

2 Paul and Barnabas now turn to the Gentiles. What two reasons are given in verses 46, 47 (see Note 1), and what two results follow in (a) the wider proclamation of the gospel and the ingathering of believers, and (b) the experience of the converts?

Notes

1 Verse 47. *Cf.* Is. 49: 6. Supremely this refers to Jesus Christ, but Paul sees himself as continuing the mission to the Gentiles that Jesus began.

2 Verses 46 and 48. The Jews' exclusion was their own fault. The Gentiles' inclusion was due wholly to God's grace and a fulfilment of His foreordained purpose. This illustrates two sides of scriptural truth which need always to be held in balance.

☐ STUDY 26 Acts 14: 1–12

Paul continues his missionary visits to the towns and cities of Asia Minor. He always chose the strategic centres from which to work. Iconium was a prosperous commercial city on one of the main trade routes from east to west, where there would be both Jews and Gentiles. Lystra was a smaller and more country town, with a simpler and less-educated population.

1 Each verse of verses 1–7 describes a fresh development in the events at Iconium. From these identify the three main stages of the work. Are you finding that opposition (human or satanic) follows blessing in your Christian work?

2 Verses 8–12. At Lystra a cripple is healed. What are (a) the condition of the man, (b) the cause and the character of his faith, and (c) the reaction of the people?

☐ STUDY 27 Acts 14: 13–28

1 What five elemental truths about God are set forth by Paul in verses 15–17? What application does he draw from them? *Cf.* verses 11, 14, 15. To whom do you think Paul would bring this kind of message today?

2 Verses 19–25. Despite opposition Paul and Barnabas return to the cities where churches have been founded to strengthen them. In what ways did they encourage these young Christians? What may we learn from this about helping one another in our faith?

3 Paul and Barnabas report to the church that had sent them out. *Cf.* 13: 1–3 with 14: 26–28. What is their emphasis in the way they report?

☐ STUDY 28 Acts 15: 1–12

1 The point at issue between the newly-established Gentile church at Antioch and the older Jewish church at Jerusalem was: 'On what terms can Gentiles be saved?' What answer was given by (a) Paul and Barnabas (see 14: 27), and (b) the teachers from Judaism (verses 1, 5)? Write down what you think is essential for salvation.

2 Verses 7–11. Of what three facts did Peter remind the Council at Jerusalem, and what conclusions does he draw from them? Is it possible for old established churches to impose upon young churches of a different culture, or for mature Christians to impose upon new converts, patterns of behaviour or ceremonies that are not essential to Christianity?

Note. Verses 6–21. Luke records only the closing speeches of a discussion that may have lasted for some days and been marked by deep feeling.

☐ STUDY 29 Acts 15: 13–34

1 Verses 14–21. Here James, the leader of the Jerusalem church, the Lord's brother, and probably President of the Council, sums up. What judgment does he give, and for what reasons? Do you think this would satisfy both Jew and Gentile?

2 Verses 22, 23. In what ways was the decision to be made known to the Gentiles, and with what results? From the whole debate what principles can you draw out to guide you when there is a disagreement among fellow-Christians (a) on essentials of the faith and (b) about non-essentials and matters of individual conscience?

☐ STUDY 30 Acts 15: 35 – 16: 5

1 What was the contention between Paul and Barnabas? Which was right, or were both wrong? *Cf.* Jn. 21: 21, 22; 2 Tim. 4: 11. Can you disagree with another Christian without falling out with him?

2 What provision did God make for Paul when he lost the help of Barnabas and John Mark? What was the keynote of their work at this stage? *Cf.* 14: 21–23; 18: 23. In what ways can you help a young Christian to be strong in the faith?

3 12: 25 – 16: 5. List the developments which took place in this fourth period (see Analysis).

Note. 16: 3, 4. Paul firmly opposed the circumcising of Gentile believers as something necessary to salvation. This is shown by his passing on of the decision of the Jerusalem Council. But Timothy in Jewish eyes was a Jew by birth; and, in fresh evangelism, it would cause needless offence if he did not wear the sign of his Jewish nationality. *Cf.* 1 Cor. 9: 20; Gal. 5: 6; 6: 15.

☐ STUDY 31 Acts 16: 6–15

A new period begins here, recording Paul's greatest missionary effort and achievement: the evangelization of three important Roman provinces—Macedonia, Achaia and Asia.

1 Verses 6–10. By what various means was Paul guided at this time? Trace on a map how remarkable the guidance was. What indication is there from this that God does not always guide us in the way we might expect?

2 Verses 11–15. The gospel comes to Europe. What evidence is there (a) that Luke, the author of Acts, joined Paul at this time; (b) that the work began in a small way (with verse 13, *cf.* 13: 14–16; 14: 1, 2 and Zc. 4: 10a), and (c) that Lydia was truly born again of the Holy Spirit? Do you ever try to organize great work for God, rather than let God start a lasting work in a small way?

☐ STUDY 32 Acts 16: 16–40

1 Verses 16–24. What was the origin of the persecution, and in what way did it differ from all those hitherto recorded? Note the successive stages of it, as described in Luke's very vivid account. Do you find yourself tempted or persecuted in new ways in your Christian life?

2 A beating with rods (verse 22) was very severe. Yet Paul and Silas are calm and rejoicing. What caused them to triumph? *Cf.* Phil. 4: 13; 2 Tim. 1: 7, 8. Paul insists that a public declaration of their innocence is made (verse 37). What use would this be to the

advance of the gospel? Are there any ways we can use public authority to help advance the gospel?

3 What caused the jailer to believe? What was essential to his salvation? What change was immediately found in his life? *Cf.* 8: 39; 13: 52. Does your salvation give you the joy of the Lord?

Note. Verses 20, 21. Philippi, as a Roman colony, was proud of its Roman connections and privileges. Hence the charges brought against the missionaries would excite the people and magistrates.

□ STUDY 33 Acts 17: 1–15

Thessalonica was the metropolis and most populous city of Macedonia, a centre for both inland and maritime trade. Berea was a smaller town some sixty miles to the south-west.

1 What do we learn from Paul's visits and preaching at Thessalonica and Berea about (a) the places where he preached, (b) the features of his preaching, (c) his chief message, (d) those who believed, and (e) the persecution that arose? The same events are written about by Paul in 1 Thes. 1: 1 – 2: 16. Do you realize that opportunities for strategic Christian witness may last only a short time? What ought you to do?

2 Verses 11, 12. How are those who attended the Jewish synagogue in Berea described, and why are they commended? Are these features found in your life and Bible study?

□ STUDY 34 Acts 17: 16–34

Paul at Athens faces philosophers, who are eager to hear another man's views in order that they may add these to their rag-bag of ideas, and who also have no background understanding of the Old Testament. See, if possible, *Acts* (*TNTC*), pp. 136–146 for a most helpful explanation of Paul's visit.

1 Verses 16, 21. From what motives, and by what methods, did Paul proclaim the gospel? Do you know anything of a divine jealousy provoked by the fact that people do not give Christ the allegiance which is His right?

2 Verses 22–34. Study Paul's sermon and note (a) how he gained the interest of his hearers (verses 22, 23), (b) what he taught about God in relation to the universe, mankind, idols and images (verses 24–29), and (c) the response he argued which men needed to make to God (verses 30–34). Paul sought to make the Christian message relevant to the thought and background of his hearers .He had no slick phraseology. What do you learn from this about preaching today?

☐ STUDY 35 Acts 18: 1–17

The city of Corinth was the capital of the Province of Achaia, and one of the greatest cities in the Empire. It was famous for commerce and learning, but infamous for its wickedness.

1 Consider the enormous task Paul faced in an evil and pagan city as he sought to found a church there. Note (a) the value of Christian fellowship (verses 2, 3; 5; 7, 8) and (b) the command and promises of God's word to Paul (verses 9–11). *Cf.* 1 Cor. 2: 3. Is this God's answer to a depressed Christian worker? Do these things encourage you in difficult situations?

2 Compare the three distinct stages in Paul's ministry mentioned in verses 4, 7 and 12. What hindrances did Paul face and what encouragements came to him? Notice that with the hindrances came new opportunities and new encouragements. Let us pray for grace to be equally faithful.

☐ STUDY 36 Acts 18: 18–28

1 Paul ends his second missionary journey (verses 18–23) with travels of more than a thousand miles. Luke reviews many months very briefly. Note, with the help of a map, the places Paul visited and the purposes he hoped to achieve.

2 We have a thumb-nail sketch of Apollos in verses 24–28. What is said about (a) his knowledge of the Scriptures, (b) his enthusiasm, (c) the help Aquila and Priscilla gave, (d) his preaching, and (e) the value of his ministry (*cf.* 1 Cor. 3: 6)? Take each of these five points and ask yourself what *you* can learn from the life of Apollos.

Notes

1 Verse 18. 'He had a vow': it is not known why Paul made a vow. The practice was, however, common among the Jews.
2 Verse 22. 'He went up': *i.e.*, to Jerusalem.

☐ STUDY 37 Acts 19: 1–20

Ephesus was the metropolis of the large and wealthy Province of Asia, a centre of commerce and religion, famous for its image and its temple dedicated to the goddess Diana.

1 Apollos had taught only the baptism of John (18: 24, 25) at Ephesus. When Paul arrived, what did he find these disciples lacked in knowledge and assured experience? Is this experience yours? Have you realized how essential it is for you to understand fully in order to teach others accurately?

2 Verse 20 summarizes both Paul's ministry at Ephesus and Luke's

whole section from 16: 6 to 19: 20, which covers the evangelization of Macedonia, Achaia and Asia. What methods and special incident led to such a result in Ephesus (verses 8–19) and by what power were great results achieved in the three provinces? *Cf.* 16: 14; 18: 9 and 19: 11. Does this review highlight any weaknesses in your Christian life?

☐ STUDY 38 Acts 19: 21–41

Luke's vivid description of the riot at Ephesus is a close study in crowd psychology as well as a faithful account of the persecution which Paul and his companions faced.

1 Verses 21, 22. What were Paul's plans for the future? To where was his eye turned? But what two things must first be done? *Cf.* Rom. 15: 19, 23, 24. Is your Christian work planned or haphazard?

2 What was the cause of the riot and persecution? How did it spread and how was it quieted? Note especially (a) the challenge of the Christian faith to a man's business and wealth (verses 25, 27); (b) the blindness of religious people (*cf.* verses 26, 27, 35, 36); (c) the cost, fellowship and protection Paul found in missionary service (verses 28–31, 37–41). To which of these truths do I personally most need to pay attention?

☐ STUDY 39 Acts 20: 1–16

Paul revisits the churches in the province of Macedonia to encourage them.

1 With 19: 21 compare 20: 1–6 and 13–16. How was Paul's original plan modified and why? Follow Paul's route on a map and discover what advantage this opposition was to Paul. *Cf.* Gn. 50: 20.

2 Paul is seeking to encourage and strengthen the young churches. What part do personal example (verse 4), fellowship (verse 7), and instruction (verse 11) have in this? With verses 7–12, *cf.* 2: 42. Are the spirit and the marks of these Jewish and Gentile churches found in you and your church today?

☐ STUDY 40 Acts 20: 17–38

Paul's farewell address to the leaders of the church at Ephesus (verses 17–35) and his departure for Jerusalem (verses 36–38).

1 Verses 17–27. Paul reviews his ministry at Ephesus. Notice, especially, what he says about his behaviour, service, faithful preach-

ing of Christ and the overriding ambition of his life. As you measure your outward service and inward spirit against Paul's, in what respects do you feel you come short?

2 Verses 28–35. What counsel does Paul give those to whom God has given positions of leadership? How can they guard the flock against the dangers that threaten? Have you begun to experience the truth of Christ's words quoted in verse 35?

☐ STUDY 41 Acts 21: 1–16

1 Paul continues his journey to Jerusalem. Follow the route of the voyage on a map. Note, especially, the moving scene in verse 5, and the part that hospitality played (verses 4, 7, 8, 16). What insights does this give us about the influence of a Christian home on visitors and children?

2 How are we to understand these warnings of the Spirit? To Paul's friends they seemed to say 'Do not go up to Jerusalem'. But Paul himself did not so interpret them. Is the explanation that the Spirit gave clear warning of peril and suffering, and Paul's friends in their human affection interpreted this in one way, while Paul regarded it in another and deeper way? *Cf.* 20: 23, 24; Mt. 16: 21–23. What would your reaction have been in the same situation?

☐ STUDY 42 Acts 21: 17–36

1 Verses 17–26. Paul's arrival at Jerusalem. He relates to the leaders of the church at Jerusalem all that God has done among the Gentiles. (a) What problem did James consider would thus arise (verses 20–22)? (b) What practical action is recommended to Paul (verses 23–26)? (c) What principles determined Paul's action? *Cf.* 20: 24; 1 Cor. 9: 20–23; 10: 32, 33. How might these principles affect your own attitudes to others?

2 Verses 27–36. Paul's arrest at Jerusalem. Try to picture the vivid scenes. Why did it happen? Trace the parallels—at least five—between the treatment given to Paul and to Christ. Do you expect men to treat you better than they did Christ?

Note. Verse 23. 'We have four men': these men were Jewish Christians who were about to complete a Nazirite vow by offering the prescribed sacrifices (see Nu. 6: 13–21). It was considered a meritorious act to defray the expenses of poor Nazirites.

☐ STUDY 43 Acts 21: 37 – 22: 16

In the face of a murderous mob, and by permission of the captain of the guard, who at first misunderstood who he was, Paul makes his defence.

1 Paul uses, not a sermon, but personal testimony. Notice what he says about his background, religious activity, conversion and calling to serve the Lord Jesus. Have you realized how powerful a weapon you possess in your personal Christian testimony? Do you use it?

2 Paul seeks to put no unnecessary offence before the Jews: notice the language he uses, and what he says about Ananias as a Jew. Here was a man being utterly faithful to Christ, and concerned for his enemies. Can you care, in the same way, for those who badly treat you?

☐ STUDY 44 Acts 22: 17–29

1 Paul argues in verses 19, 20 that he is well qualified to take the gospel to the Jews. Why? Yet God commands him to go to the Gentiles (verse 21). What practical lessons about Christian service and God's working may we learn from this?

2 With verses 22–29 compare 16: 22, 23, 37–39. Paul mentions his Roman citizenship to prevent scourging; yet at Philippi he had acted otherwise. Compare the circumstances and consider the reasons for Paul's action. Are you prepared to forgo your personal rights for the sake of God's glory? *Cf.* 1 Cor. 9: 12.

☐ STUDY 45 Acts 22: 30 – 23: 10

1 What is Paul's testimony concerning his behaviour and his belief? *Cf.* 24: 16 and 2 Tim. 1: 3. He sought always to live to the glory of God. Are you able to testify in the same way concerning your behaviour and belief?

2 Consider Paul's tactics in the courtroom: (a) his righteous anger (verses 3–5), and (b) his division of the court (verses 6–10). Once again the enquiry was abandoned. Was Paul more concerned for his own welfare and a settlement of the whole matter, or for the truth?

Notes

1 23: 1. 'Lived': literally 'lived as a citizen'. Paul's meaning was: 'Men and brethren, I have fulfilled my duty to the Commonwealth of Israel in all good conscience, in the sight of God, until this day.'

2 23: 5. This was not a formal meeting of the Jewish Council, at which the high priest was present, but a meeting summoned by the chief captain and no doubt presided over by himself. Paul, therefore, did not know that the voice that spoke was that of the high priest.

☐ STUDY 46 Acts 23: 11–35

1 Consider how greatly Paul must have needed encouragement because of (a) the physical strain he had undergone, (b) the pain of Israel's unbelief, (c) the seeming failure of his witness, and (d) the danger of which he would be aware next day. How would the vision and the words spoken by the Lord meet all these needs? What words of the Bible have you found a help in such times? Do you memorize them?

2 God sends deliverance in many different ways. How did He send deliverance in this case? Paul must have been greatly encouraged by what his nephew did. Are you able to do any acts of kindness that will bring gladness to some person in need or loneliness or anxiety?

☐ STUDY 47 Acts 24: 1–21

1 The Jewish prosecution employed on this occasion a trained advocate, Tertullus. What four charges are brought against Paul? What evidence is produced in support?

2 How did Paul answer these charges? See verses 11–13; 14–16; 17, 18. Note especially (a) that Paul had to contend with unsupported and false accusations (verses 19–21). He was firm but calm in refuting them. Are you, when you are in the same situation? (b) Paul was able to give a reason for the hope that he had (verses 14–16). Can you? (c) Paul was really on trial because he believed in the resurrection of the dead (verse 21). Does this truth make a practical difference to your life?

☐ STUDY 48 Acts 24: 22 – 25: 12

1 24: 22–27. Paul before Felix. What four motives controlled Felix's treatment of Paul? Do self-interest and fear ever stop you from doing what is right?

2 25: 1–12. Paul before Festus. Why did Paul refuse Festus' offer for a trial in Jerusalem, and instead, as a Roman citizen, claim his

right to appeal to Caesar? Do you think Paul was taking the right course of action regardless of the consequences?

Note. 25: 11. A Roman citizen could appeal to a higher Roman magistrate against his sentence, or at any stage in his trial. Paul now appeals to Nero.

☐ STUDY 49 Acts 25: 13–27

1 What evidence is there that Festus can be commended for his fair dealings with Paul? Nevertheless, what major fault did he reveal (*cf.* Mk. 15: 15; Acts 24: 27; 25: 9)? Do you believe that God sometimes uses non-Christians, with their faults, for His own purposes? *Cf.* Is. 45: 1. Should this alter our attitude towards people in authority?

2 What promises of God are now being fulfilled in Paul's experience? *Cf.* Acts 9: 15, 16; 22: 15. What condition did Paul have to satisfy? How would God's word prevent him from feeling that the last two years awaiting trial had been a waste of time?

☐ STUDY 50 Acts 26: 1–18

1 Paul makes his defence before King Agrippa. He deals with three themes: (a) his life before he was converted (verses 4–11), (b) his conversion (verses 12–15), and (c) his commission to serve Jesus Christ (verses 16–18). Sum up in a few words each of these three periods in Paul's life. What made this change and what was the real question at issue in this trial? See verses 6–8; 13–15.

2 How does the Lord Jesus, in the commission which He gave to Paul (verses 16–18), describe (a) the lost condition of mankind, (b) the content of salvation, and (c) the method of salvation?

☐ STUDY 51 Acts 26: 19–32

1 What do you learn about obedience from Paul's example (verses 19–23)? Note especially (a) the place where he witnessed, (b) the message he gave, (c) the cost involved, and (d) the help God gave. Does your obedience cost you anything?

2 What was the motive that enabled Paul to speak so boldly and yet politely before such men as Festus and Agrippa? *Cf.* verse 29 with 1 Cor. 9: 16–22 and 2 Cor. 5: 14. Is this true in your life?

☐ STUDY 52 Acts 27: 1–20

1 Follow the voyage on a map. What were the outstanding events in the voyage, and what encouragements did Paul receive during the early part of the journey? Has God given you an unexpected blessing in a difficult time?

2 Why was Paul's advice disregarded at first, but heeded later? *Cf.* verses 9–12 and 21–25.

Note. Verse 9. 'The fast': the Day of Atonement, which came in the latter part of September, and was considered by the Jews as marking roughly the close of the safe season for sea travel.

☐ STUDY 53 Acts 27: 21–44

1 In the time of testing and danger that all on the ship went through, compare the reactions of Paul (verses 24, 25; 33–36) with the sailors (verses 30–32), and the soldiers (verses 42, 43). Why was Paul able to behave so calmly and inspire others with his example? Do you have inner resources that help you to stand in times like these?

2 Notice that the shipwreck was caused through not taking Paul's advice. See Study 52, Question 2. Is this a warning to you not to make shipwreck of your life through disobedience of some plain command of God (*e.g.*, 2 Cor. 6: 14 and Mt. 6: 33)?

☐ STUDY 54 Acts 28: 1–16

1 The disastrous journey is almost ended. What opportunities of service and witness did Paul find in Malta? Have you found opportunities of service for Christ when things, seemingly, go wrong in your life?

2 'So we came to Rome' (verse 14). *Cf.* 19: 21; 23: 11; Rom. 1: 13; 15: 22, 23. This was the goal, but what can one learn from the fact that God had other ways for it to be achieved than Paul at first realized?

☐ STUDY 55 Acts 28: 17–31

1 Paul at Rome (verses 17–22). What was Paul's chief concern on reaching Rome? It would seem he was anxious that no discredit should be laid against the Christian faith by his house-arrest. Are you anxious always to commend the Christian faith by your life?

2 Verses 23–28. What was Paul's message to the Jews at Rome? What reasons does he give for the persistence of so many in unbelief? What reaction did he expect the Gentiles would show? Is this still the same today?

3 List the main facts with which Luke summarizes Paul's ministry as a prisoner at Rome (verses 30, 31). Consider the influence Paul had during those years through people coming to him, and through letters he wrote to the churches he had visited.

☐ **STUDY 56 Revision**

1 Trace through the following key verses in the book: 1: 8; 6: 7; 9: 31; 12: 24; 16: 5; 19: 20 and 28: 31. What reasons can you list from them for the growth of the early church? What lessons do you learn about obedience to God's Word, trust in God's power, and witness to the Lord Jesus Christ?

2 In such passages as 20: 18–35; 21: 13, 14; 23: 1; 24: 16; 26: 19–23, 29 and 27: 22–25, we have an insight into the real personality and spirit of Paul. List the qualities that are outstanding. Were these natural or divine qualities? Can they be yours?

AMOS & HOSEA

Introduction

These two prophets are linked together in that both prophesied to the northern kingdom of Israel about the same time.

Amos was the earlier by a few years. His ministry took place in the latter part of the reign of Jeroboam II. He himself belonged to Judah, and was a herdsman when called of God to prophesy to northern Israel (Am. 7: 14, 15). The kingdom was at that time outwardly prosperous, but all kinds of evil were rife in the land, and the people, thinking themselves secure in Jehovah's favour, resented any reproof (Am. 5: 10). They did not realize that they were not worshipping Him in the way that He desired, and that their sins were bringing judgment near. Amos, filled with a vision of the majesty and righteousness of God, denounced the sins of the land, and the false worship that was offered. Let them not imagine that because they were the people of Jehovah, therefore they would escape punishment (Am. 3: 2).

The first three chapters of Hosea also belong to the closing years of the reign of Jeroboam II, but the remaining chapters reflect the chaotic conditions of the period that followed Jeroboam's death. Hosea was a native of the northern kingdom, and had been deeply taught in the school of sorrow. His own sad history was used by the Holy Spirit to fit him in a unique way to see into the heart of God, and to depict the sorrow which His people's ingratitude and unfaithfulness cause Him. No prophet so clearly shows us the love of God, without in any way weakening the claims of His holiness; and thus he prepares the way for the perfect revelation of God's love and holiness given in our Lord Jesus Christ. In understanding Hosea's message, however, it must be borne in mind that the Israelites had adopted many Canaanite religious practices, including that of gross sexual immorality in worship. In the light of this, the 'harlot' theme in Hosea has both a literal and a metaphorical meaning.

Analyses

Amos

1: 1, 2	Introduction.
1: 3 – 2: 16	Oracles against surrounding nations, ending with Judah and Israel.
3 – 6	'A series of addresses, three of which begin "Hear ye this word" (3: 1; 4: 1; 5: 1) and end with a threat introduced by "therefore" (3: 11; 4: 12; 5: 11, 16); and two begin with "Woe" (5: 18; 6: 1). In these the crimes and impending punishment of Israel are set forth at length' (Kirkpatrick, *The Doctrine of the Prophets*, p. 105).
7: 1–9	Three visions.
7: 10–17	Amos expelled from Bethel.
8: 1 – 9: 10	Two more visions of coming doom.
9: 11–15	The ultimate restoration.

Hosea

1 – 3	Hosea's personal history as an illustration of God's relation with Israel.
4 – 8	Israel's guilt and the corruption of the nation.
9: 1 – 11: 11	Israel's doom is necessary and inevitable.
11: 12 – 13: 16	Israel's ingratitude and unfaithfulness deserve destruction, yet Jehovah yearns over His people.
14	One day, after the punishment, Israel will repent and be restored.

☐ STUDY 1 Amos 1 and 2

1 What are the particular sins of the nations (1: 3 – 2: 3) which call for God's judgment? What may be learnt from this about the things God hates?

2 Judah and Israel are judged because they have failed to live up to God's Law—a different standard of judgment from that applied to the nations. In what ways does 2: 4–16 show the social, economic, and religious guilt of God's people? How do we fall short on the same issues?

Notes

1 1: 3. Heavy machines for threshing grain had been used as instruments of torture on the people of Gilead.

2 2: 1. Desecration of the dead was considered specially wicked.

3 2: 8. *Cf.* Ex. 22: 26. The judges demanded unjust fines, accepting payment in clothing and wine, then made use of these at their sacrificial feasts.

☐ STUDY 2 Amos 3 and 4

1 3: 3–8. These verses, by a statement of the law of cause and effect, underline the fact that the unexpected prophecy of 3: 1, 2 is indeed from God. What does this prophecy teach regarding the responsibility of the people of God?

2 3: 9–15. What is the significance of the invitation to the Philistines and Egyptians to come and see the evil done in Samaria?

3 What does chapter 4 teach on the following issues: (a) the evil of luxury, (b) religious formalism, and (c) God's attempts to bring Israel to her senses? Notice the solemn conclusion of verse 12.

Notes

1 4: 1. A reference to the wealthy women of Samaria. The cattle of Bashan were noted for their quality.

2 4: 5, 6. These verses are ironical in tone.

☐ STUDY 3 Amos 5 and 6

1 5: 1–17. God uses various methods to draw men back to Himself. Chapter 4 mentioned natural calamities; this chapter, a plea for right living. What sins are rebuked in these verses, and what is the one way of escape?

2 5: 18–27. What is necessary to make our worship acceptable to God? How did Israel fail? Is our worship in danger of falling under the same judgment?

3 Chapter 6. Why were the Israelites insensitive to the approaching judgment? What warning does this contain for us?

Notes

1 5: 25, 26. These verses are obscure, but seem to mean that the idolatrous tendency in Israel found expression in the days of the wilderness wandering, as it was doing now in Amos' day.

2 6: 2. Probably a reference to cities which have recently fallen. Israel is no more secure than they were.

3 6: 10. This reference to burning the dead indicates a time of emergency.

☐ STUDY 4 Amos 7: 1 – 8: 3

1 What is the significance of each of Amos' four visions (7: 1–9 8:1–3)? What truth is demonstrated by the difference between the first two and the last two?

2 7: 10–17. How does this section reveal the fearless courage of the prophet and the danger to which his obedience to God's call exposed him? What may we learn from this concerning the demands of God's service?

Notes

1 7: 4. 'The great deep': probably a reference to the ancient belief in underground depths which supplied water for streams, springs, *etc. Cf.* Gn. 7: 11.

2 7: 10. Bethel was the chief sanctuary of the northern kingdom.

☐ STUDY 5 Amos 8: 4 – 9: 15

1 Why is social injustice the burden of Amos' prophecy? What seven forms of judgment are spoken of in 8: 7–14? Are these in any way related to the sins of the nation?

2 9: 1–10. How does this final vision show that none can escape the hand of God?

3 What does this final chapter teach about the relationship between judgment and restoration in the purposes of God?

☐ STUDY 1 Hosea 1 and 3

Hosea's life-story is outlined in these two chapters.

1 What evidence do you find (a) that at the time of his marriage Hosea was already conscious of his prophetic calling, and did all things, including his marriage, with his eyes upon the Lord; (b) that he was not aware, when he married Gomer, that she would prove unfaithful; and (c) that on looking back later upon the whole matter, he recognized that God had brought him through this bitter experience in order that he might understand what Israel's unfaithfulness meant to God? What ought we to learn from such a record? *Cf.* Gn. 50: 20.

2 Gomer, having proved unfaithful, appears to have forsaken Hosea and sunk to the position of a slave. Hosea, loving her still, redeemed her, but placed her for a time under discipline. How does the prophet use this to illustrate God's love and Israel's future?

Notes

1 1: 4. See 2 Ki. 10: 11, 30. Jehu was right in what he did, but not in the spirit in which he did it.

2 1: 10 – 2: 1 is a prophecy of the future, in which the divine love interrupts the message of doom. This is characteristic of Hosea.

3 3: 4, 5. This is a reference to the exile.

☐ STUDY 2 Hosea 2

1 The adulterer seeks satisfaction in unlawful relationships; the harlot debases high possessions for material gain. How does Hosea show that this is what Israel has done in relation to the Lord Himself?

2 What promise is given in verses 14–23 of the final triumph of God's love? How is it to be achieved? Does this chapter in any way illustrate the conduct and the one sure hope of God's people today?

Notes

1 Verse 5. 'My lovers': a reference to the local gods of the land (or 'the Baals', verse 13), whom the Israelites in their backsliding conceived to be the givers of nourishment ('bread and water'), clothing ('wool and flax') and joy ('oil and drink'), and to whom accordingly they offered worship (verse 13).

2 Verses 14, 15. The Israelites, after leaving Egypt, wandered in the wilderness, and entered the promised land by the valley of Achor. Now they shall again be brought into the wilderness (*i.e.* the exile), but after this time of affliction, they shall return to Canaan, and will find the valley of Achor, not, as at the first, a place of trouble (Jos. 7: 24), but a door of hope. *Cf.* Is. 65: 10.

3 Verses 18–23. A beautiful picture of peace (verse 18), communion with the Lord (verses 19, 20), and abounding blessing (verses 21–23). Jezreel, which means 'God sows', is used in verse 22 as a name for Israel.

☐ STUDY 3 Hosea 4: 1 – 5: 14

1 Note down in chapter 4: 1–14 (a) the outward sins which caused the Lord to have a controversy with His people, and (b) the inward condition of which these sins were the outcome. How far might this description be applied to our society today?

2 4: 15–19. This passage may be interpreted as a warning to the southern kingdom of Judah not to ally herself with Israel. Why this warning, and what message has it for us?

3 What in chapter 5 are shown to be the real obstacles that separate the people from God, and God from the people? Who are charged with responsibility for this condition of things?

Notes

1 4: 15. 'Beth-aven': 'house of vanity', used ironically for 'Beth-el', 'house of God'.

2 4: 17. 'Ephraim': the leading tribe of the northern kingdom, therefore used as a synonym for Israel. Only in chapter 13 does it refer to the tribe.

3 5: 7. 'The new moon': *i.e.*, the next new moon. Within a month ruin will be upon them.

☐ STUDY 4 Hosea 5: 15 – 8: 14

1 The passage 5: 15 – 6: 6 is a dialogue between God and the people, in which God has expressed His purpose to withdraw His presence (5:15), the people light-heartedly profess repentance, and their confidence in God's restored favour (6: 1–3); but the true situation is far from what the people think (6: 4–6). What does God desire to find in His people?

2 The remainder of today's portion consists of descriptions of the state of the nation: the sinfulness of priests, kings, and people (6: 7 – 7: 7); their instability and folly (7: 8 – 8: 3); God's anger against both their rulers and their idols—all alike man-made (8: 4–13). What do you find here (a) about the sins that abounded; (b) about false alliances that blinded their eyes; (c) about the real cause of their perilous position?

☐ STUDY 5 Hosea 9 and 10

These chapters are prophecies of coming judgment, and show how the people's sin will bring upon them (a) exile (9: 1–8); (b) a diminished population (9: 9–17); and (c) the destruction of both the sanctuaries and the throne, and the reducing of the nation to servitude (10: 1–15).

1 9: 1–8. This passage was perhaps spoken at a religious festival, when people were making merry after the manner of the heathen

at their festivals (9: 1). How does Hosea describe the changes that exile will bring?

2 9: 9–17. God Himself speaks. He sees lust prevalent in the nation, as in the most shameful days of Israel's history. To what results would it lead?

3 What different kinds of sin are spoken of in chapter 10? What counsel does the prophet give as to the one way of escape from the coming judgment?

Notes

1 10: 1. 'Pillars': a common feature of a Canaanite shrine, imitated by the Israelites in their worship.
2 10:5, 6. *Cf.* 1 Ki. 12: 28, 29.
3 10: 10. 'Their double iniquity': perhaps meaning the sins of the throne and of worship.
4 10: 11. The position of Israel is to be changed from that of a heifer treading the threshing-floor and eating freely (Dt. 25: 4) to the heavy labour of the yoke.
5 10: 14. 'As Shalman destroyed Beth-arbel': the reference is uncertain. Shalman is probably the same as Shalmaneser, 2 Ki. 17: 3.

☐ STUDY 6 Hosea 11 and 12

In chapter 11 another aspect of God's dealings with Israel breaks into view—His persistent love. Judgment there must be (11: 5–8), but God will not make a final end of His sinning people.

1 How was God's love manifested in Israel's beginnings? See 11: 1–4; *cf.* Dt. 7: 6–8. How was this love still manifested, in spite of all His people's backsliding? See 11: 8–11.

2 In chapter 11 God has spoken of His attitude to Israel; now in 11: 12 – 12: 2 He speaks of Israel's attitude to Himself. Then the prophet reminds the people of the very different history of their ancestor Jacob (12: 3, 4). What is the attitude to Himself which God desires (12: 6; *cf.* 6: 6; 10: 12)? What, however, was Israel's response to all God's pleadings (12: 7–14)?

☐ STUDY 7 Hosea 13 and 14

1 In what four ways is the coming judgment described in chapter 13 (verses 3, 7–8, 15, 16)? And what four reasons are given for this judgment (verses 1–2, 4–6, 9, 16)? What may we learn from this about the nature of sin?

2 Chapter 14 describes the final triumph of God's love. What, according to this chapter, does repentance involve (14: 1–3, 8), and what is the divine response?

PSALMS 13 - 29

☐ STUDY 8 Psalms 13 and 14

1 In Ps. 13 what is David having to endure? And how does he avoid depression and despair?

2 What can we learn from Ps. 14 about the fundamental reasons why men say, 'There is no God'? *Cf.* 2 Cor. 4: 3, 4. How should this affect our approach to such people? How are they sometimes made aware of the living God?

☐ STUDY 9 Psalms 15 and 16

1 Go through Ps. 15 verse by verse, and use it as a test for your own life and holiness. Then turn to 1 Jn. 1: 8, 9.

2 What according to Ps. 16 are the marks of the believing man (verses 1–4)? What his privileges (verses 5–8)? And what his prospects (verses 9–11)?

Notes

1 15: 5a. *Cf.* Lv. 25: 35–38; Dt. 23: 19, 20. The laws against usury were enacted more as a protection of the poor than against the legitimate use of capital in the interests of trade. *Cf.* Mt. 25: 27.

2 16: 10. Quoted by Peter (Acts 2: 27) and by Paul (Acts 13: 35) with reference to Christ. As with Ps. 15, the psalm is fulfilled in Him, and in us through Him.

☐ STUDY 10 Psalm 17

1 In verses 1–7 on what two grounds does David base his plea? *Cf.* 1 Jn. 3: 21, 22.

2 Contrast the inward character, the aims and the actions of David and his enemies as revealed in this psalm. In what ways do you resemble David, and in what ways his enemies?

☐ STUDY 11 Psalm 18: 1–30

1 David begins by expressing his love for the Lord (verses 1–3). God was to him a rock, fortress, shield and stronghold. What are the equivalent defences and securities in which men trust today? Is God to you all that these can give, and more? *Cf.* Hab. 3: 17, 18; Heb. 13: 5, 6.

2 From David's testimony concerning God's answer to his prayer, what can we learn as to (a) God's power to help, (b) the sort of person God will help, and (c) the reasons why this help will be forthcoming?

Notes

1 Verses 9–16 are probably not intended to be taken literally, but as a poetic description in vivid imagery of the strength and majesty with which God came to David's aid.

2 Verse 29a. There is a possible allusion here to 1 Sa. 30: 8; and in verse 29b to 2 Sa. 5: 6, 7.

☐ STUDY 12 Psalm 18: 31–50

1 Make a list of all that God did for David as set forth in these verses. What corresponding help may we expect from Him in spiritual service? *Cf.* 1 Cor. 15: 10; Eph. 1: 19.

2 Verse 49 is in Rom. 15: 9 referred to Christ. Does this mean that the whole psalm can be taken as being in some way prophetic of Christ? If so, to what does it draw attention?

☐ STUDY 13 Psalm 19

1 God has revealed Himself in His creation. What do the things the psalmist mentions in verses 1–6 tell us about God? *Cf.* Mt. 5: 45; Rom. 1: 19–21.

2 Contrast this with the revelation given in 'the law of the Lord' (verses 7–11). Note how great is the advance, both in clearness and in fullness of effect. Note in particular its effect upon the psalmist (verses 12–14). Is your study of God's Word producing similar results in your experience?

Note. Verse 4. 'Their voice': the Hebrew (see mg.) says 'line', *i.e.*, their 'measuring line'. *Cf.* Je. 31: 39. The boundary or extent of their message is earth's farthest limit.

☐ STUDY 14 Psalms 20 and 21

These two psalms are closely linked together. In Ps. 20 a battle is about to take place between the king of Israel at the head of his people and his foes. Sacrifices have been offered, and the king and his people commit their cause in faith to God. In Ps. 21 the battle is won, and the people give thanks to God for their king and look forward to further victories.

1 What does Ps. 20 reveal is the attitude of the king and his people as they set out against their foes? On what is the confidence of verse 6 based? Is this sort of confidence characteristic of God's people today?

2 Ps. 21 falls into two parts, verses 1–7 and 8–12, with a concluding prayer. To whom is the first part addressed, and to whom the second? In what ways does what is said of the king find its fulfilment in Christ?

☐ STUDY 15 Psalm 22: 1–21

1 Note the things that seem to make the sufferings here described the harder to bear. How closely does this psalm picture the sufferings of Christ? *Cf.* Mt. 27: 35–46; Jn. 19: 23, 24.

2 In these sufferings upon what does the faith of this man stay itself?

☐ STUDY 16 Psalm 22: 22–31

1 Trace in these verses the happy results of the sufferings described in verses 1–21. Note (a) how far-reaching is their effect, and (b) to whom they mean most.

2 List those things that are stated will be the reaction of people to the deliverance of the sufferer, and see how far this is true of your own reaction to the resurrection of Jesus Christ.

Note. Verse 22. This is applied to Christ in Heb. 2: 12.

☐ STUDY 17 Psalms 23 and 24

1 David knows the Lord as his shepherd. In Ps. 23 note the effect this has upon his thoughts about his present and his future. Has your knowledge of the Lord had this effect for you?

2 From Ps. 24 what do we learn of the Lord? What is required, therefore, of those who worship Him?

Note. Ps. 24 was probably written for the occasion when David brought the ark of God to Jerusalem. See 2 Sa. 6.

☐ STUDY 18 Psalm 25

1 What are the main petitions made here by the psalmist? What light do these petitions throw upon his circumstances and spiritual experience? How far can you make these petitions your own?

2 In verses 6–15 what is said about God and what He does for those who fear Him? How far is this true in your own experience? What does this psalm teach about how you can experience more of the friendship, guidance and deliverance of the Lord?

☐ STUDY 19 Psalm 26

1 Describe in your own words the main trend of David's life as he describes it here. Can you make similar claims for yourself?

2 In verse 12, David seems to be assured that God will answer his prayer. On what has it been based that he can have this assurance? *Cf.* Ps. 66: 18; Jas. 4: 3.

Note. Verse 12. 'Level ground': *i.e.*, a place of safety and ease, where he can fulfil the promises of verses 6, 7.

☐ STUDY 20 Psalm 27

1 What do verses 1–6 reveal of David's attitude in life and of his chief desire? Upon what is this attitude and desire based? What equivalent desire should we have today? *Cf.* 1 Pet. 2: 4, 5; 1 Cor. 6: 19, 20.

2 In verses 7–14 what are David's seven petitions? How does he address God, and how does he encourage himself to continue in prayer?

☐ STUDY 21 Psalms 28 and 29

1 In Ps. 28 David's prayer is answered. What difference does this make to him? Are you always as thankful about God's answers to your prayers?

2 Ps. 29 is the description of a thunderstorm viewed as a manifestation of God's glory. What spiritual lessons does it teach regarding God, and regarding our duties and privileges as His people?

Note. 29: 3. 'The voice of the Lord': *i.e.*, thunder, and so throughout the psalm. *Cf.* Ps. 18: 13.

For Studies 22–35 on the Psalms see p. 119.

1 & 2 THESSALONIANS

Introduction

Almost certainly these two letters were the first books of the New Testament to be written. They were written in Corinth during Paul's second missionary journey, and not long after the church at Thessalonica had been founded, about 50 AD (Acts 17: 1–10). In them we get an insight into the life of a local Christian church within about twenty years of the death and resurrection of our Lord. The first letter was written on Timothy's return from a visit to Thessalonica, and the second a few months later. They are among the most personal of the apostle's letters in the New Testament, and present a vivid picture both of himself and of his readers, while revealing also the marvellous results of his missionary work in a great heathen city, the capital of Macedonia.

The apostle was greatly encouraged by the report, which Timothy brought, of the church's steadfastness under persecution and of its continued progress. But there were some matters that gave him concern, in particular the wrong views that were held about the second coming of Christ. This is then the chief theme of the two letters. It is shown to be a comfort in bereavement, a motive for endurance, an inspiration to hope, a safeguard in temptation, a help to purity, a challenge to watchfulness, a ground of rejoicing, and a separating and sanctifying power. The apostle's great aim is summed up in 1 Thes. 3: 13.

Analyses

1 Thessalonians

1: 1–10	The founding of the church.
2: 1–20	Service for Christ.
3: 1 – 4: 12	Sanctification and daily behaviour.
4: 13 – 5: 28	The second coming and Christian conduct.

2 Thessalonians

1: 1–12 The second coming and persecution.
2: 1–12 Further teaching about the second coming.
2: 13 - 3: 18 Final exhortations.

☐ STUDY 1 1 Thessalonians 1

1 What explanation does this chapter give of the way in which these Thessalonians became Christians? Am I taking a similar share in the reception and spread of the gospel of Christ?

2 Pick out the outstanding features of the Christian life and character of these converts. Making every allowance for the difference in circumstances, is our Christian life of this kind?

3 What marks of a work of the Holy Spirit are mentioned here? Can we share in a similar experience?

Note. Verse 3. Their faith issued in active obedience, their love toiled on for others' good, their hope of Christ's return endured, as they lived in communion with Him who had become their God and Father. *Cf.* Heb. 11: 27b.

☐ STUDY 2 1 Thessalonians 2

1 Verses 1–12, 17–20. List all the characteristics of a faithful Christian worker which these verses mention. Which do I particularly need to covet?

2 Verses 13–16. Consider the place of the Word of God in the work of the gospel. What differing responses does it evoke from those who hear it? Is this still true today?

Note. Verses 14–16, 18. He who seeks either to receive or to spread the gospel will meet the opposition of Satan and his agents. *Cf.* Mk. 4: 15; 1 Thes. 3: 5.

☐ STUDY 3 1 Thessalonians 3

1 In what ways did Paul show his love and concern for the Thessalonian Christians? When, like Paul, we pray for our fellow-Christians, what does his example suggest that we ought to pray for them?

2 What is here taught concerning suffering for Christ? *Cf.* Jn. 16: 33; 2 Tim. 3: 12. To what dangers does such an experience expose us (*cf.* 1 Pet. 5: 8, 9), and how are they to be successfully faced?

3 Verses 11–13. How are love and sanctification linked in these verses? Does this teach us anything important about what is involved in becoming holy?

☐ STUDY 4 1 Thessalonians 4

1 Verses 1–12. What aims and aspects of Christian living are emphasized in these verses? Why should we so live? And what makes such a standard of living possible for us?

2 Verses 13–18. In what ways do these words on the Lord's return bring comfort? State in your own words what Paul says will happen. On what grounds can we be sure of our share in such a wonderful hope?

Notes

1 Verse 8. 'Who gives his Holy Spirit to you': the indwelling Holy Spirit is the seal of God's ownership, the evidence that we are His. *Cf.* Eph. 1: 13; Rom. 8: 9b. It is by the power of the Spirit that we overcome the flesh. *Cf.* Gal. 5: 16.
2 Verses 11, 12. *Cf.* 2 Thes. 3: 10–12; Eph. 4: 28.
3 Verses 1–12. Notice the repeated emphasis in the verses, not only on upright behaviour, but on the need to advance and progress in the things of God.

☐ STUDY 5 1 Thessalonians 5

1 Verses 1–11. How will the 'day of the Lord' break upon the world, and what will it mean (a) for men in general, and (b) for Christians? *Cf.* Mt. 24: 32–44; Lk. 21: 25–28.

2 What practical effects should the prospect of the Lord's return have on our attitude and behaviour? Make your own list of the injunctions of this chapter and examine your own life in the light of them.

Notes

1 Verse 2. 'The day of the Lord': an Old Testament phrase, signifying God's future intervention in history in salvation and judgment (Is. 2: 12; 13: 6; Zp. 1: 14; 3: 11, 16), and applied in the New Testament to the second coming of Christ (Lk. 17: 24; 1 Cor. 1: 8, *etc.*).
2 Verses 6, 7, 10. The word 'sleep' is used in this passage in three meanings; in verse 6 in the sense of spiritual insensibility, in verse 7 in the meaning of natural sleep, and in verse 10 in the sense of physical death, as in 4: 14, 15 (*cf.* 4: 16 'the dead in Christ').

☐ STUDY 6 2 Thessalonians 1

1 Verses 5–12. When men suffer for Christ what two prospects of things which are to be fulfilled by Christ at His return should be a comfort to them? What two complementary things will Christ then do?

2 Notice the subjects of Paul's thanksgiving and prayer for his fellow-Christians at Thessalonica. Is this how you pray for others? Compare your aims in the Christian life with those here implied to be desirable.

Notes

1 Verse 5. 'This evidence of the righteous judgment of God': it affords proof—since God is righteous—that His day of judgment and just recompense will certainly come.

2 Verses 7–10. *Cf.* Is. 66: 15, 16; Mt. 13: 40–43; Lk. 3: 17.

☐ STUDY 7 2 Thessalonians 2: 1–12

1 What advice and warnings does Paul give here to encourage a healthy attitude towards the Lord's return?

2 Examine the methods, motives, power and end of Satan and his human agents. What does this teach us about the subtlety and nature of sin? Who are to be deceived thereby, and for what reasons?

Note. Verse 3. 'The man of lawlessness': in the New Testament this seems to refer to both a principle and a person. *Cf.* 1 Jn. 2: 18. In the last days he will appear in his final form as the incarnation of evil, the Antichrist, but he has had and will have precursors up till that time.

☐ STUDY 8 2 Thessalonians 2: 13 – 3: 17

1 2: 13–15. We are shown here that God has taken the initiative in our salvation. What steps has He taken? What is His purpose for us? And what part is our responsibility?

2 Consider Paul's four prayers for his readers and also the prayer which he asks them to pray for himself. What can we learn about Paul's circumstances and about his ambitions, both for himself and for the Thessalonians? Do we share similar ambitions when we pray?

3 3: 6–13. What is the place and importance of daily work and other mundane tasks in the life of the Christian? Is there a tendency to underestimate the importance of these nowadays?

Note. 3: 2–4. From the unbelief of men Paul turns to the faithfulness of the Lord. This is how turning to the Lord to pray can afford fresh confidence and hope.

JOSHUA

Introduction

The book of Joshua tells us nothing about its authorship, but in Jos. 15:63 we have a clear indication that it was written before David's capture of Jerusalem.

The book tells the story of the crossing of Jordan, the conquest of the promised land and its division among the tribes, ending with the death of Joshua after he had obtained from the whole people a solemn promise (soon to be broken) that they would be faithful to God.

The apparent discrepancy between the seemingly universal conquest of Palestine (in 9–11) and the stubborn and often unsuccessful fighting referred to in the latter part of the book and in the early part of Judges, is explained by the fact that in 9–11 the united army of Israel was meeting and crushing organized resistance. But, after the division of the land, the Israelite army broke up into its component tribes, each of which attempted to possess its own lot, meeting with a stubborn resistance from those who had fled from the united army or had not come in its way. Other factors may have been the spiritual declension of the people and the ruling geographical factor of Palestine, the division into the hill country and the coastal plain. The latter remained unconquered until David's time.

The book is an account of the Israelites' fight to claim their promised inheritance. The lessons they learnt concerning the conditions of possession can teach us much about the conditions of our obtaining the blessings promised to us in Christ (*cf.* Heb. 4:1, 2, 8–11; 11:30).

Analysis

1 Introductory.

2–5 Preparations for the conquest: Rahab and the spies; Jordan crossed; the people circumcised.

6–8	The first victories; Jericho and Ai taken; the fall of the latter delayed by Achan's sin.
9	Gibeon makes peace by a trick.
10, 11	The crushing of organized resistance first in the south, then in the north.
12	The list of the conquered kings.
13–19	The division of the land: the tribes attempt to take possession of their lots.
20, 21	The cities of refuge and the Levitical cities.
22	The altar of witness beyond Jordan.
23, 24	Closing scenes in the life of Joshua; the people's promise.

☐ STUDY 1 Joshua 1

1 Verses 1–9. *Cf.* Dt. 31: 7, 8. List the promises God made to Joshua. What conditions of success was he given? What picture of Joshua is given in this chapter?

2 What principles, warnings or encouragement to be found here can I apply to my own life?

Note. Verses 12–18. These Israelites wished to settle east of Jordan, but had promised to help in the conquest of Canaan. See Nu. 32.

☐ STUDY 2 Joshua 2

1 How does the story in this chapter justify the statement in Heb. 11: 31? Compare Rahab's words with the actual position of the Israelites at the time, and note especially verse 11.

2 Observe how Rahab's faith kindled the faith of the spies. What stimulus does this give us in the life of faith? What parallel is suggested to you by the house protected by the scarlet thread? With verse 19, *cf.* Ex. 12: 22.

☐ STUDY 3 Joshua 3 and 4

1 Work out the order of events, as the people entered the promised land. Note the parts played by God and by the people. What principles of progress in the Christian life are here illustrated?

2 Compare and contrast the position and attitude of the people here with that of their fathers in Nu. 14: 1–10. Which group reflects your own attitude?

☐ STUDY 4 Joshua 5 and 6

1 Before the conquest of Jericho come the events described in chapter 5. Note their order. What is their significance (a) for the Jews; (b) for Joshua; (c) for us?

2 6: 1, 2; *cf.* Heb. 11: 30. What may we learn here concerning the conditions and demands of conquering enemy strongholds by faith? Have you a faith that perseveres? *Cf.* Heb. 3: 14; 6: 11, 12; 10: 35, 36.

3 Follow the rest of Rahab's life in 6: 22–25 and Mt. 1: 5, 6. Salmon may have been one of the spies. What truths does Rahab illustrate concerning God's ways of dealing with men?

☐ STUDY 5 Joshua 7

1 What sins are described here? What were their results? *Cf.* also Is. 59: 1, 2.

2 What steps were necessary to rectify the situation? Why was the punishment so drastic? How ought this chapter, Is. 53: 5 and 1 Pet. 2: 24 to affect our view of sin?

☐ STUDY 6 Joshua 8

1 Using a map, follow the plan of campaign. Note the contrasts and similarities to the conquest of Jericho. What principles of victory emerge from chapters 6 and 8 for the people of God?

2 The background to verses 30–35 is to be found in Dt. 11: 26–29; 27: 1 – 28: 68. What were the purposes of this dedication service?

☐ STUDY 7 Joshua 9

1 See Dt. 7: 1–6 as the background to this chapter. What factors led to the disobedience of Joshua and his leaders?

2 Having realized their error, how did the Jewish leaders deal with the situation? What principles can we draw from this for ourselves?

3 Trace the subsequent history of the Gibeonites, seen in Jos. 10: 2; 11: 19; 2 Sa. 21: 1–9; 2 Ch. 1: 1–13.

☐ STUDY 8 Joshua 10

1 Use a map briefly to clarify in your mind the events described

here. In what ways is this chapter an interesting sequel to chapter 9? What lessons had Joshua and Israel learnt?

2 These things 'were written down for our instruction' (1 Cor. 10: 11). What examples can we follow? See verses 6ff.; 16–22; 24, 25; 26–40; 42; and *cf.* Ps. 15: 4 and Col. 3: 5.

Notes

1 Verses 12, 13. See *NBCR*, p. 243. By the action of God's sovereign providence conditions were granted, which we cannot fully explain, which enabled the Israelites to gain a complete victory.

2 Verse 40. 'The Negeb' was the arid southern land.

☐ STUDY 9 Joshua 11 and 12

1 Again the aid of a map is needed to follow this summary of a war which lasted several years. Which area is covered here? To what causes was Joshua's final victory due?

2 Note the verses which point out the finality and harshness of the treatment which Joshua carried out. Why was this necessary? What spiritual lesson can we learn from this? *Cf.* Mt. 18: 8, 9; Col. 3: 5.

3 Meditate on the statement at the end of chapter 11 in the light of the continued conflict in chapters 13ff. See esp. 13: 1. In what ways does this history provide encouragement and challenge to us today? *Cf.* the order and progress of Rom. 6–8.

Notes

1 11: 20. See Dt. 9: 4, 5; Gn. 15: 16; and *cf.* Ex. 9: 12. The Canaanites, like Pharaoh, were in the end provoked to go further on their already self-chosen evil way. This brought their judgment to a head.

2 In 11: 21 we read that Joshua cut off the Anakim from Hebron, Debir and other places; in chapters 14 and 15 it is Caleb and Othniel who take Hebron and Debir; while in 10: 36–39 we have read that at a still earlier time Joshua took Hebron and Debir, and 'destroyed all the souls that were therein'. The explanation is that those whom Joshua is said to have killed on the earlier occasion were those whom he captured in the cities when he took them the first time; a considerable part of the population must have fled before he attacked the cities, and must have returned and reoccupied them while he was away in the north. 11: 21 describes in summary form operations which covered a long time, and attributes to Joshua as Commander-in-Chief what was done by Caleb and others under his orders.

☐ STUDY 10 Joshua 13: 1 – 15: 12

1 13: 1–7. Consider how exactly the Lord amplifies the statement at the end of 13: 1. Are there in your life blessings promised to us in Christ which are not yet possessed, and remaining enemies to be subdued? Ask Him to reveal them to you with similar precision.

2 Note the inheritance given to the different tribes and individuals; notice particularly the contrast between Levi and Caleb, and the reasons given for each. With 14: 6–13, *cf.* Nu. 13: 17 – 14: 10.

Note. 14: 7, 10. These verses, combined with Dt. 2: 14, show that the preliminary conquest of the land took seven years.

☐ STUDY 11 Joshua 15: 13 – 17: 18

1 Is your environment as unpromising as the arid, giant-ridden Negeb seemed to Achsah? If so, compare her attitude with Lk. 11: 13 and Phil. 4: 19, and be thankful!

2 Whose inheritance is described in today's section? What attitudes were shown by the tribes and by Joshua? Why were the people of Joseph not praised as Caleb had been (14: 13), when they made a particular claim to territory?

3 Using a concordance, study the character of Ephraim. Do you agree with Ellicott's statement that 'They were constantly asserting their right to the supremacy in Israel, without exhibiting any qualification for it'?

Note. 15: 63, together with 2 Sa. 5: 6, 7, shows that this book was written before David's time.

☐ STUDY 12 Joshua 18 and 19

1 With 18: 3, *cf.* Heb. 4: 1. What attitude is Joshua's pointed question designed to correct? See Heb. 6: 11, 12.

2 What evidence do you find in these chapters that God's promised blessings in Christ, though ours already by God's gift, are claimed and experienced only through the fight of faith, resolute action, and steady progress? *Cf.* 2 Pet. 1: 4–11; 1 Tim. 4: 13–16.

☐ STUDY 13 Joshua 20 and 21

1 Check the facts. Using a map, find the cities of refuge. In whose area were they, and in what type(s) of territory? Why were they established? And who became responsible for them? Why were the Levites given property? What type of property was it? Who provided it and on what plan?

☐ STUDY 14 Joshua 22

1 What was Joshua able to commend in the conduct of these tribes? What charge did he give them? With verse 5, *cf.* 1: 8.

2 What roused the remaining tribes to anger? Was their anger justified? (For the background to the reference in verse 17, see Nu. 25: 1–9.) What warning can we take from this incident?

☐ STUDY 15 Joshua 23

1 Verses 1–13. To whom was Joshua speaking on this occasion? On what conditions does the fulfilment in verse 5 depend?

2 How is the faithfulness of God shown in this chapter? *Cf.* the similar statements in 21: 43–45 and 1 Sa. 7: 12. Can you endorse these?

☐ STUDY 16 Joshua 24

1 Note the place chosen by Joshua for this occasion. *Cf.* Gn. 12: 6, 7; 33: 18, 19; Jos. 8: 32–35; Acts 7: 16. In what other ways did he seek to make this as impressive and memorable an event as possible? Consider verses 2–13; 14, 15; 19, 20; 22, 23; 25–28.

2 What evidence is there in this chapter, despite all that God had done, of the superficiality and instability of the Israelites' religious life? *Cf.* Ho. 6: 4.

☐ STUDY 17 Revision

1 By looking through the book of Joshua as a whole, clarify the outline of events in your mind.

2 What encouragements and warnings have you gained? What does the book teach of (a) the character of God, and (b) His purposes for His people?

GALATIANS

Introduction

The particular situation with which the Epistle deals must be kept in mind if its great argument is to be understood. Paul had preached the gospel of salvation by faith in Jesus Christ to the Galatians, who were of Gentile race. They had welcomed him with enthusiasm, and many had believed (4: 14, 15). But they had later been visited by Jewish-minded Christian teachers who had told them that it was not enough simply to believe on Jesus Christ: they must also be circumcised and keep the law of Moses. These teachers had further cast doubts upon Paul's apostleship, and had sought to undermine his authority. We can understand with what mingled sorrow, indignation and deep concern Paul refutes the teaching of the legalists, and defends both his own position and the truth of the gospel which he had proclaimed.

The question at issue assumes a different form today, but is none the less vital. Is acceptance with God to be obtained by any effort of ours, or is it, as the gospel declares, the free gift of God's grace through the redemptive work of Christ, to be obtained by faith alone? The enduring value of this Epistle lies in the answer given by Paul, under the inspiration of the Spirit, to this question.

Analysis

1: 1–10	Introduction.
1: 11 – 2: 21	Paul declares that the gospel which he preached is not of human origin, but came to him by the revelation of Christ.
3: 1 – 5: 1	Acceptance with God is not obtained by doing what the law commands, but by faith in Jesus Christ.
	3: 1–9. The facts of their own experience confirmed by the case of Abraham.

	3: 10–14. The hopeless position of those under the law, from which the death of Christ alone delivers. 3: 15–18. The original covenant of promise is not superseded by the law. 3: 19–24. The true function of the law. 3: 25 – 4: 7. The blessedness of those who have believed in Christ. 4: 8–20. Appeal not to backslide. 4: 21 – 5: 1. The spiritual freedom of the believer illustrated from 'the law' itself.
5: 2 – 6: 10	The life of the Christian: (a) faith, hope, love; (b) walking in the Spirit.
6: 11–19	Conclusion.

☐ STUDY 1 Galatians 1

1 What does Paul say in verses 1–10 (a) about God; (b) about Christ; (c) about himself; (d) about the gospel? Note these things carefully, for they lay the foundation on which the Epistle rests.

2 Verses 11–24. How does Paul show that the gospel is a revelation of God? What does his personal testimony demonstrate? What significance has this for the Christian?

Note. Verse 10 is parenthetical. Paul appears to have been charged by his opponents with being a man-pleaser. So, after writing verses 8 and 9, he interjects a pertinent question. What he means is: 'Words such as I have just written do not look like man-pleasing, do they?'

☐ STUDY 2 Galatians 2

1 Verses 1–10. Why does Paul consider his Jerusalem visit significant? What issues were at stake, and what facts were confirmed?

2 Verses 11–21. What were Paul's motives for his opposition to Peter? How does he justify the stand which he took? Try to express in your own words the truths declared in verses 16 and 20.

3 What may we learn from this chapter concerning the principles which should govern Christian fellowship, church unity and ministerial co-operation?

☐ STUDY 3 Galatians 3: 1–18

These verses are a fourfold argument in proof of 2: 16: (a) verses 1–5, an argument from experience, (b) verses 6–9, an argument from Scripture teaching about Abraham, (c) verses 10–14, an argument from the meaning of Christ's death, and (d) verses 15–18, an argument from the fact that the covenant of promise was long prior to the giving of the law.

1 Unravel the arguments used by Paul in these verses to demonstrate that justification and enjoyment of the gift of the Spirit are by faith in Christ, and not by 'works of the law' (*i.e.*, our own law-keeping).

2 Verses 10–18. Distinguish between law and promise and between works and faith as bases in God's dealing with men. What two benefits has Christ made available for us by His redeeming work?

Notes

1 Verses 2, 5. 'By hearing with faith': this is an abbreviated expression for hearing the word of the gospel and receiving it with responsive or obedient faith. *Cf.* Rom. 10: 8–17.

2 Verse 7. 'The sons of Abraham': in the sense of spiritual likeness. *Cf.* Jn. 8: 39.

3 Verses 8, 9. Paul interprets the promise of Gn. 12: 3b to mean that just as Abraham received the blessing of justification by faith (Gn. 15: 6), so a time would come when men of all nations would 'in Abraham', *i.e.*, through his seed, which is Christ (verses 14, 16), receive the same blessing in the same way.

☐ STUDY 4 Galatians 3: 19 – 4: 7

1 3: 19–24. Paul seems to have made light of the law. How does he state its purpose in this passage?

2 In what way does 3: 25 – 4: 7 demonstrate the amazing privileges and position of a Christian? Make a list of them in your own words.

Note. 3: 19, 20. 'Added because of transgressions': *i.e.*, the law gave to sin the form of transgression and so made men conscious of guilt before God when they sinned. *Cf.* Rom. 3: 19, 20; 5: 20; 7: 7, 13.

'It was ordained by angels through an intermediary': Paul introduces these words to show that the promise is superior to the Law even in the very manner of its promulgation. In the case of Abraham God Himself spoke the promises directly, whereas the giving of the law was through intermediaries on both sides—God being represented by angels (*cf.* Dt. 33: 2, LXX; Acts 7: 53; Heb. 2: 2), and the people by Moses.

☐ STUDY 5 Galatians 4: 8 – 5: 1

1 According to this passage, what does Christian freedom imply?

2 In what ways is Paul's reaction to the Galatians' condition indicative and illustrative of pastoral concern? Do we know any similar concern for the spiritual well-being of others?

3 Verses 21–31. Paul uses Gn. 16 as an allegory. In this picture,

what is the position of those 'under law', and what, in contrast, that of believers? What is the point of Paul's quotation of (a) Is. 54: 1, and (b) Gn. 21: 10–12?

Note. 4: 17, 18. A reference to the new teachers, who were eager to win the favour of the Galatian believers in order to cut them off from Paul and his gospel so that they would have no-one to turn to but themselves. If these teachers had really come to do good, Paul would have raised no objection (verse 18).

☐ STUDY 6 Galatians 5: 2–24

Spiritual freedom may be lost in two ways: (a) by false teaching, in this case the teaching of the necessity of circumcision (verses 2–12); and (b) by living to please self (verses 13–15). The secret of victory is to give the Holy Spirit full sway within us by obeying His promptings. He will subdue the flesh, and bring forth in us the fruit of Christ-like living (verses 16–25).

1 Verses 2–12. To be circumcised meant taking the way of the law. What four results would follow if the Galatians did so? What is the way of the gospel?

2 Verses 13–15. How should the Christian use his freedom?

3 Verses 16–24. Seek to grasp the antithesis between 'flesh' and 'spirit'. What should be the attitude of the Christian towards each? Note that the right attitude demands expression in positive action.

Notes

1 Verses 5, 6. 'The hope of righteousness': *i.e.*, the hope of future glory that springs from justification through believing on Jesus Christ. *Cf.* Rom. 5: 1, 2; 1 Pet. 1: 3. Notice also the collocation here of faith, hope and love.

2 Verse 18. The Christian is free from the law as a rule to be obeyed in order to obtain life (*cf.* 3: 12), yet, when 'led by the Spirit' he does all that the law demands (see verses 24, 25; *cf.* Rom. 8: 4).

3 Verse 24. *Cf.* 2: 20; Rom. 6: 6.

☐ STUDY 7 Galatians 5: 25 – 6: 18

1 5: 25 – 6: 10. What is the effect of 'walking by the Spirit' in the realm of social relationships? Make a list of what you find, and test your own relation to fellow-Christians by it.

2 What, according to 6: 11–16, is the core of Christianity? What must be given up in order to embrace it?

3 Gather together from the Epistle as a whole the teaching given about (a) the cross of Christ, and (b) the Holy Spirit.

Note. 6: 2. 'The law of Christ': *cf.* Jn. 13: 34; 1 Jn. 4: 21.

PROVERBS

Introduction

Proverbs 1: 7 provides the key to the book and to the whole of the Wisdom Literature (Job, Proverbs, Ecclesiastes). It all starts from the creed of one God—Jehovah, or the Lord—and wisdom is to know and do His will. The term 'proverb' has the double meaning of a short parable and a pithy saying.

The proverbs are all intensely practical, covering the human race and the whole of its activity, aiming at giving 'knowledge and discretion', or the building up of the 'perfect man', by fixing truth in the memory. As expressing eternal spiritual principles many of them can receive their full meaning only when applied to the believer in Christ.

Analysis

1 – 9	The appeal of wisdom.
10: 1 – 22: 16	Short proverbs of Solomon.
22: 17 – 24: 22	'Words of the Wise'.
25 – 29	Proverbs of Solomon collected by Hezekiah.
30, 31	Words of Agur and Lemuel, and an acrostic on the excellent wife.

□ STUDY 1 Proverbs 1

1 From the purpose of the book, as expressed in verses 1–6, what personal profit may we expect to gain from studying it? How, according to verse 7, can we (a) begin right, or (b) show our folly? (See Note under Study 17.)

2 List some of the attractions in the enticing talk of verses 11–14. What positive attitudes will forearm me against them?

3 What is the essence of the outlook deplored in verses 20–32? And of the promise given in 33?

☐ STUDY 2 Proverbs 2 and 3

1 What directions are given in these chapters for the attaining of wisdom? Make a list of them as a guide to your own life.

2 What benefits does wisdom bring us, and from what evils does it preserve us? How far have I proved this in my own experience?

3 'My son': what application does the writer of the Epistle to the Hebrews give to these words? *Cf.* Heb. 12: 5–10.

☐ STUDY 3 Proverbs 4 and 5

1 What are the main lessons that the speaker seeks in these chapters to impress upon us? What heed have I given, and am I giving, to these most urgent counsels?

2 4: 23–27 provide an admirable guide to successful living. Heart, lips, eyes, feet: what directions are given concerning each? Note how much is implied for the Christian by verse 18.

3 What are the results, at various levels, of neglecting this way of wisdom? See 4: 19; 5: 9–14; 5: 21–23.

☐ STUDY 4 Proverbs 6 and 7

1 Verses 1–5 give warning against foolish financial commitments and pledges. What other warnings are given in these chapters?

2 In what forms do the sins here spoken of manifest themselves at the present day?

3 Test your life in the light of 6: 16–19.

☐ STUDY 5 Proverbs 8

1 Contrast the description of wisdom with that of the woman in 7: 5–27. How do they differ in speech, in conduct, in what they offer, and in the goal to which they lead their followers?

2 What is said of wisdom in verses 22–31 concerning (a) its existence from the beginning; (b) its part in creation; (c) its communion with God; (d) its interest in man? Consider how in all these respects there is here a foreshadowing of Christ. *Cf., e.g.,* (a) Jn. 17: 5; (b) Jn. 1: 1–3; Col. 1: 15–17; (c) Mt. 11: 27; (d) Heb. 2: 17, 18.

3 What similar but greater gifts than those which wisdom offers in 8: 32–36 are offered in Christ? *Cf., e.g.,* Mt. 11: 29; Lk. 11: 28; Jn. 14: 21; 17: 2, 3; 3: 36.

☐ **STUDY 6 Proverbs 9**

1 Set 9: 1–6 and 9: 13–18 side by side. In what respects are wisdom and folly (9: 13, RV mg.) alike, and wherein do they differ?

2 In my reactions to criticism and advice, do I show any of the symptoms of the scoffer or of the wise man, as shown in verses 7–9?

☐ **STUDY 7 Proverbs 10: 1 – 11: 13**

1 In 10: 2–6 there are four conditions of well-being in circumstances, mind and character. What are they?

2 In the light of Jas. 3: 10, what uses of the faculty of speech are here (a) commended, and (b) to be avoided?

3 What will the possession of integrity secure for a man (11: 1–13)?

☐ **STUDY 8 Proverbs 11: 14 – 12: 28**

1 What two kinds of sin or sinners are said in this passage to be an abomination to the Lord?

2 What other sins are here condemned? In what verses are they traced to their origin in the *heart*? *Cf.* 4: 23; Mt. 12: 34, 35; 15: 18, 19.

3 Apply to yourself the five principles for the using of money expressed in 11: 24–28.

☐ **STUDY 9 Proverbs 13: 1 – 14: 21**

1 'Consider the outcome of their life' (Heb. 13: 7). What is said in today's portion concerning the outcome of their life in the case of the righteous and of the wicked respectively?

2 Gather out what is taught about 'fools' and 'folly'. If we are wise, what should be the manner of our life (a) in relation to the Word, (b) in relation to our neighbours, and (c) in conduct and speech?

☐ **STUDY 10 Proverbs 14: 22 – 15: 23**

1 What is said in this passage about the beneficent effects of right words?

2 What is said about 'the Lord'? How may we discern the fear of the Lord in our own hearts?

3 Can I claim to have the four things making for satisfaction which are enumerated in 15: 13–17?

☐ **STUDY 11 Proverbs 15: 24 – 16: 33**

1 How does 15: 24–33 illustrate what has been called 'the sanity of religion'?

2 Gather out what is said in today's portion about the Lord, and about man's proper attitude to Him.

3 Consider in 16: 27–30 the multiplied evil wrought by evil men. *Cf.* Jas. 3: 6–10.

☐ **STUDY 12 Proverbs 17 and 18**

1 Make a list of the sins condemned in chapter 17. What choices concerning our conduct ought we to make, if we wish to avoid them?

2 What reasons are given in chapter 18 why we should 'watch the door of our lips'?

3 Consider the two fortresses in 18: 10, 11; and *cf.* Jn. 10: 27, 28; Lk. 12: 15–21.

Note. 18: 10. 'The name of the Lord' denotes the character of God Himself, as revealed to us in the Scriptures. *Cf., e.g.,* Ex. 34: 5ff. For us it is summed up in 'Jesus'.

☐ **STUDY 13 Proverbs 19: 1 – 20: 13**

1 Make a list of the varied conditions and circumstances in respect of which counsel is given in this passage. Which of them apply more particularly to yourself? Note particularly the warning and the challenge of 20: 6. *Cf.* Mt. 7: 21.

2 What is said about the Lord? Note carefully how the fact of His presence forms the foundation on which the writer's counsels are based.

☐ **STUDY 14 Proverbs 20: 14 – 22: 16**

1 Gather out from this passage those principles for wise living that most impress you.

2 Make a list from 20: 17–25 of different kinds of action which ought to be avoided; and notice why.

3 20: 24 speaks of God's sovereignty, and 20: 27 of man's responsibility. What other verses in this passage touch on these two complementary truths?

Notes

1 20: 27. 'The spirit of man': here a synonym for the conscience.
2 22: 16. 'He who . . . gives to the rich': *i.e.*, solely with his own advantage in view—'to increase his own wealth'.

☐ STUDY 15 Proverbs 22: 17 – 23: 35

1 According to 22: 17–21 what steps are involved in a full reception of God's word? What blessings are promised as the outcome?

2 What are the marks of a wise 'son' (23: 15)? What will he avoid and what will he practise?

3 What, according to 23: 29–35, are the effects of too much indulgence in wine?

☐ STUDY 16 Proverbs 24

1 What missionary call is heard in verses 11, 12? Am I saying concerning those who are going down to death, 'Behold, we did not know this'?

2 What other sayings here challenge my standards of neighbourly love?

3 What did the wise man learn from the field of the sluggard? Find and ponder the positive teachings of this chapter on thoroughness and forethought.

☐ STUDY 17 Proverbs 25: 1 – 26: 12

1 How does our Lord in one of His parables adapt the teaching of 25: 6, 7?

2 Observe in 25: 8–28 how many illustrations are given of the power and influence of words both to do good and to do harm. Am I sufficiently careful in this matter?

3 In what ways does the passage 26: 1–12 enforce the familiar injunction, 'Don't be a fool'? Among whom did Christ find 'fools'? *Cf.* Mt. 7: 26; 23: 17; 25: 2; Lk. 11: 40; 12: 20; 24: 25.

Note. The 'fool' is one who is wilfully unresponsive to the teaching of divine wisdom, and, going his own self-chosen way, hurts himself and others.

☐ STUDY 18 Proverbs 26: 13 – 27: 27

1 What various kinds of wrong speech are exposed in 26: 18–27: 2?

2 'Be wise, my son' (27: 11). What directions for wise living do you find in 27: 5–22, especially in regard to friendship?

3 What, according to 27: 23–27, is the reward of diligence? *Cf.* also 27: 18; 28: 19; Rom. 12: 11.

Note. 27: 25, 26 should more probably read, 'When the hay is removed and the after-growth appears, and the grass of the mountains is gathered, then thy lambs will supply thee with clothing, and thy goats furnish the price of a field' (*ICC*).

☐ STUDY 19 Proverbs 28 and 29

1 Gather out in these chapters the verses which present a contrast between the righteous and the wicked. How do these differ in character and conduct? Consider also their influence for good or evil on society, especially if they hold positions of authority.

2 What is said about the importance of keeping the law, and about a right attitude to the poor? There are four references to the first, and at least five to the second.

3 Put a mark against verses in these two chapters that you feel to be specially incisive and memorable.

☐ STUDY 20 Proverbs 30

The last two chapters of Proverbs are appendices. Chapter 30 gives the words of Agur, of whom nothing further is known. Agur first looks Godward, and is humbled by the mystery of the divine being and power. Later he looks out upon the world of men and animals and notes a number of striking facts, which he records.

1 Notice the definiteness, urgency, content and motive of Agur's prayer. Compare with it the prayer which our Lord taught His disciples to pray.

2 Are the classes of men mentioned in verses 11–14 still present? State in four words the sins of which they were guilty.

3 What four lessons may the four creatures mentioned in verses 24–28 teach us?

☐ STUDY 21 Proverbs 31

1 What three virtues did King Lemuel's mother urge upon him

(verses 1–9)? Are they any less necessary for all who will occupy positions of responsibility?

2 Make a list of the qualities of the ideal housewife as depicted in verses 10–31.

Notes

1 Read verses 6, 7 in the light of verses 4, 5, *i.e.*, as 'a cutting reminder that an administrator has better things to do than anaesthetize himself' (*Proverbs* (*TOTC*), p. 182).

2 Verse 10. 'Good': the Hebrew word includes both moral worth and practical efficiency. *Cf.* 12: 4. Ruth was such an one. See Ru. 3: 11.

3 Verse 18b. This does not mean that she worked all night, but that her house was well ordered and ready against emergencies. *Cf.* 13: 9.

ROMANS

Introduction

The Letter to the Romans was written by Paul from Corinth during three months which he spent in the province of Achaia, as described in Acts 20: 2, 3. Its purpose is to present to the church in Rome (which he had not founded, but which he hoped soon to visit) a reasoned statement of the gospel which he preached, together with a discussion of the great problem of Jewish unbelief and of the relation of both Jews and Gentiles to Jesus Christ and His salvation. From 15: 23, 24 it would seem that the apostle to the Gentiles felt that he had done everything possible to carry out his task in the east. The time had now come to put into operation his plans for extending his work westwards. In such a task it would no doubt be an advantage to have the prayerful support and practical fellowship of the church in the metropolis. Rome was a strategic centre and the church there would seem to have been as cosmopolitan as the city. A clear statement of the gospel which he would be preaching would be the best means of clearing up any misunderstandings which might arise through Jewish–Gentile tensions or through other causes, and of gaining for Paul the fellowship and co-operation he desired.

At the outset Paul declares that the gospel is the power of God for salvation to everyone that believes. The great themes of the Christian gospel are dealt with in turn: human guilt; redemption by grace; righteousness which comes from God; justification by faith; the new life in Christ; the work of the Holy Spirit in the believer; the certainty of the final triumph of the Christian; the divine sovereignty; and the inclusion of 'the nations' in God's purposes of mercy. These are followed by a section on the practical outworking of the gospel in all spheres of life. Little wonder that this Epistle, with its comprehensive treatment of the gospel and the compelling logic of its argument, is regarded by many as the most remarkable book in a volume of remarkable books.

Analysis

1: 1–15	Opening greetings and introduction.
1: 16, 17	The theme of the letter stated.
A. 1: 18 – 11: 36	*The gospel as revealed to Paul.*
1: 18 – 3: 20	THE UNIVERSAL SINFULNESS OF MEN.
	1: 18 – 2: 16. The exposure of the Gentiles.
	2: 17 – 3: 18. The exposure of the Jews.
	3: 19, 20. The guilt of all men.
3: 21 – 5: 21	THE WAY OF RIGHTEOUSNESS.
	3: 21–31. Righteousness as God's gift.
	4: 1–25. Righteousness reckoned to Abraham.
	5: 1–21. Righteousness offered to all men through Christ.
6: 1 – 8: 39	THE WAY OF HOLINESS.
	6: 1–23. Life under grace.
	7: 1–25. The law and the flesh.
	8: 1–39. Victorious life in the Spirit.
9: 1 – 11: 36	THE JEWS AND THE GENTILES.
	9: 1–29. God's sovereignty in election.
	9: 30 – 10: 21. Man's responsibility.
	11: 1–36. God's sovereign purposes.
B. 12: 1 – 15: 13	*Christian living.*
12: 1–21	Christian relationships.
13: 1–7	The Christian and the state.
13: 8–14	Christian duty.
14: 1 – 15: 13	Balancing liberty and charity in the Christian community.
15: 14 – 16: 27	Concluding greetings and exhortations.

☐ STUDY 1 Romans 1: 1–17

1 What does the apostle say in these verses about himself? See verses 1, 5, and each verse from 9 to 16. With verse 14, *cf.* 1 Cor. 4: 1; 9: 16, 17.

2 What does Paul say about the gospel, its origin, content, purpose, power and propagation? Have you any eagerness or sense of obligation to preach it?

Note. Verse 17. The phrase 'the righteousness of God', here and in 3: 21, means a righteousness provided for man by God in Christ. It should be distinguished from 'the justice of God' (3: 5) or 'God's righteousness' (3: 25). which means God's character as righteous.

☐ STUDY 2 Romans 1: 18–32

1 How does Paul show the sin of man to be (a) deliberate, and (b) inexcusable? How did it begin, and what spiritual, mental, moral and physical effects does it have?

2 How is God's wrath said to manifest itself? Notice the three stages in verses 24, 26 and 28. *Cf.* Ps. 81: 12; Acts 7: 42. In what ways do you see God's wrath at work in the world of today? *Cf.* Rom. 12: 19; 13: 4.

☐ STUDY 3 Romans 2: 1–16

1 What four things are said about God's judgment in verses 2, 6 11 and 16? What else do you learn about it in this passage?

2 By what general test will God judge men? See verses 7–10. How will this bring condemnation on (a) the self-righteous person, (b) the Gentile, and (c) the Jew? Why does God delay the day of wrath?

Notes

1 Verses 7 and 10 in no way contradict the truth that salvation cannot be earned by works. Paul is not dealing at this point with the method of salvation, but with the nature of the test in the day of judgment. The test is righteousness (*cf.* 1 Jn. 3: 7, 10). If a man is not righteous in heart and life, he will be condemned. Later Paul will show that the only way to become righteous in God's sight is through faith in Christ.

2 Verses 12–15. The meaning is that men will be judged by the light they have had. If they have been under the law of Moses they will be judged by that; if not, they will be judged by the standards they possess by nature through reason and conscience.

☐ STUDY 4 Romans 2: 17–29

1 In verses 17–20 Paul enumerates a number of privileges upon

which the Jews of his day were inclined to congratulate themselves. If you make a list of them you should find ten in all. Racial and religious pride are by no means confined to the Jews only, however. Substitute 'Christian' for 'Jew' and 'the Word' for 'the law', and show how the argument could be applied to professing Christians today.

2 Verses 25–29. The Jews rested upon circumcision as the seal of God's covenant with them. What else does Paul show here to be required without which the outward sign ceases to have value? *Cf.* 1 Sa. 16: 7. How would you frame the argument in relation to Christian ordinances?

☐ STUDY 5 Romans 3: 1–20

1 In verses 1–8 the apostle answers four objections which he found that men raised against the gospel. (The objections are stated in verses 1, 3, 5 and 7, 8a; the answers are given in verses 2, 4, 6 and 8b.) These will repay careful study; in particular note how Paul describes the Old Testament Scriptures, to what two attributes of God he holds fast, and what kind of conduct he strenuously repudiates.

2 In verses 10–18 Paul gives the general verdict of Scripture upon man in his fallen condition. What does Scripture say (a) about the general trend of human life (verses 10–12, *cf.* Is. 53: 6a); (b) about man's speech (verses 13, 14); and (c) about his conduct and inner attitude to God (verses 15–18)? How does this witness confirm the verdict of experience already given in 1: 18–32 and 2: 17–29 and lead to the conclusion of 3: 19, 20?

3 Do you assent to the truth that it is impossible for any man, by his own efforts, to escape condemnation at the bar of God's judgment?

Notes

1 Verse 20. 'Works of the law': a phrase which occurs also in verse 28. It denotes conduct achieved by a man's own efforts in obedience to a divinely-given statute. *Cf.* Gal. 3: 10–12.

2 Verse 20. 'Justified' means 'declared' or 'pronounced righteous'.

☐ STUDY 6 Romans 3: 21–31

1 The answer to the question how guilty man can be saved is found in the revelation of a righteousness of God, *i.e.*, a righteousness provided by God (see Study 1, Note). It will help greatly to

clarify what is said about this righteousness in this all-important paragraph (verses 21–26) if the various points are written down and appreciated one by one. There are twelve to fifteen of them.

2 What two inferences follow? See verses 27, 28 and verses 29, 30. *Cf.* 1 Cor. 1: 29–31; Gal. 3: 28. What is Paul's answer to an objector who might say that the gospel of salvation by faith, which Paul preached, made the law of no account?

☐ STUDY 7 Romans 4: 1–15

Paul has made three statements which were directly opposite to the Jewish interpretation of Scripture. The first was in 3: 20, that by the works of the law shall no flesh be justified; the second in 3: 30, that God would justify the Gentiles through faith without circumcision; and the third in 3: 19 and 28, that salvation is given independently of the law. Paul proceeds, therefore, in chapter 4 to show that Scripture supports these propositions. He bases his argument mainly on Gn. 15.

1 Abraham, and David also, were men pre-eminently in the favour of God (*cf., e.g.*, Is. 41: 8; Acts 13: 22). On what basis, then, according to Scripture, was righteousness reckoned to them? See verses 1–8.

2 At what *time* in Abraham's life was his faith reckoned to him as righteousness? How does this vitally affect the question at issue regarding the admission of Gentiles? See verses 9–12.

☐ STUDY 8 Romans 4: 16–25

1 Consider the correspondences between Abraham's faith and ours, for example, (a) the promise to Abraham (Gn. 15: 5, 6) and the corresponding promise to us (verses 20–24); (b) the inability of Abraham in himself (verses 18, 19) and our corresponding inability (see 3: 20); (c) the God in whom Abraham believed (verse 17) and the God in whom we believe (verse 24); (d) the result to Abraham (verse 18) and to us (5: 1, 2).

2 Verse 25. In what sense are our sins the reason for Christ's death, and our justification the purpose of His resurrection? *Cf.* Is. 53: 4–6, 8b, 11; 1 Pet. 2: 24; 1 Cor. 15: 17.

☐ STUDY 9 Romans 5: 1–11

1 Verses 1, 2, 9–11. What blessings does justification bring with it? List the things which are now ours to enjoy. Note how much is covered by these statements. What ought such awareness to make us do?

2 Someone, however, may say: 'But what of the sufferings attending the Christian life? Do they not detract from its blessedness?' What is Paul's answer to this? See verses 3–5. What is the value of suffering, and how may we be sure that our hopes are not mere wishful thinking?

3 Verses 5–8. By what evidence may we be doubly sure that God loves us? Notice the importance of having at least two witnesses. *Cf.* Dt. 19: 15; 2 Cor. 13: 1. In what ways are the witnesses mentioned here different and complementary?

☐ STUDY 10 Romans 5: 12–21

1 What are the consequences for men (a) of Adam's fall into sin, and (b) of Christ's 'obedience' or 'act of righteousness'? In what respects are the latter both similar to, and different from, the former? What ought we to recognize about the character of the benefit which becomes ours in Christ?

2 What four 'reigns' are spoken of in this passage? Two of them are the sad experience of all men. How do the other two operate? What benefits do they bring? How can we enter into their enjoyment?

☐ STUDY 11 Romans 6: 1–14

1 What is now the position of those who are spiritually united with Christ (a) in relation to sin, and (b) in relation to God? How had this change been effected?

2 This being our position in Christ, how are we so to enjoy and express it as to live a life of victory over sin? See verses 11–14; and note the key-words, 'consider', 'let not', 'yield'.

Notes

1 The question in verse 1 arises out of what Paul has said in chapter 5, especially verse 20.

2 Verses 3–10 are an exposition of verse 2.

3 Verse 6. 'The sinful body' means 'the body in which sin ruled', whose members were employed in sin's service (see verses 13 and 19).

4 Verse 7. A statement of the general principle that death ends all obligations and relationships (*cf.* 7: 1, 2) is here applied to our former relationship to sin.

☐ STUDY 12 Romans 6: 15 – 7: 6

Two questions may arise out of Paul's argument so far; the first, 'Shall we then continue to sin?' and the second, 'How is it possible to be not under law?' The first is answered in 6: 15–23, and the second in 7: 1–6.

1 In 6: 15–23, what two masters are contrasted? What kinds of service do they respectively demand, and with what result? In view of all these things, what is the only possible answer to the question whether we should continue in sin?

2 To answer the second question ('How is it possible to be not under law?') Paul finds in the marriage tie an illustration of a person being subject to law and subsequently set free from it (verses 1–3), and applies it to the case of the Christian (verse 4). In the case of the Christian, by whose death is his old position under law brought to an end? Who is the new husband? And what are the fruits of this new union, as contrasted with those of the old? See verses 5 and 6.

Note. 7: 4. When Christ's body was broken in death, He passed to a life free from all subjection to legal ordinances, and we, having died with Him, are also set free. Sharing in His resurrection life, we are able to live no longer in legal bondage but in the glad obedience of love.

☐ STUDY 13 Romans 7: 7–25

Man's true life under the law frustrated and spoiled by sin.

1 Verses 7–13. To speak about passions being aroused by the law might suggest that the law itself is sinful. What evidence does Paul give in these verses to show that the law is holy and good, and yet (a) reveals sin; (b) provokes sin; (c) results in death? What does it thus bring to light concerning the character of sin?

2 Verses 14–25. Which is the stronger force in a man's life, the law or sin? What, then, is the inevitable result of life under the law, even at its best?

Note. In verses 14–25 the apostle expands what he means by 'the old written code' (7: 6). The law of God commands from without, but sin as a power *within* compels obedience to its own dictates. Two things are needed: (a) deliverance from the condemnation which the law of God pronounces, and (b) a power within greater than that of sin to enable us to do God's will. Both are provided in Christ, as Paul shows in chapter 8, expounding the meaning of his words 'the new life of the Spirit' (7: 6).

☐ STUDY 14 Romans 8: 1–17

1 Verses 1–4. What is the happy condition of those who are 'in (union with) Christ Jesus'? How has their deliverance been brought about, and what is God's purpose in effecting it?

2 Verses 5–17. Life according to the flesh, and life according to the Spirit, are here contrasted. What is it that effects the change from one to the other? How do we know that life in the Spirit carries

with it also ultimate victory over death? If this life is ours what is our present duty and why? And what are our present privileges?

Notes

1 Verse 1. 'Condemnation' probably means 'the punishment following sentence', *i.e.*, penal servitude.

2 Verse 2. The Spirit, sin, and death are regarded as powers exercising authority, and the Spirit proves the stronger. *Cf.* Gal. 5: 16, 17.

3 Verse 3. 'In the death of His own Son, who has come in our nature to make atonement for sin, God has pronounced the doom of sin, and brought its claims and authority over men to an end' (Denney).

4 Verses 5–8, 12, 13. 'Flesh' here denotes our corrupt human nature.

☐ STUDY 15 Romans 8: 18–39

1 What threefold ground of confidence does Paul give in verses 18–27 that the present time of suffering will issue in glory? See verses 18–22, 23–25 and 26, 27, noting the words 'groan', or 'sighs'. *Cf.* Ex. 2: 23–25; Rom. 5: 3–5.

2 In verses 28–39 how many distinct reasons does Paul give for the Christian to rejoice, though everything in this world should seem against him?

Note. Verse 28. *Cf.* NEB: 'in everything, as we know, he (the Spirit, verse 27) co-operates for good with those who love God.' *Cf.* 1 Cor. 2: 9.

☐ STUDY 16 Romans 9: 1–13

In chapters 9–11 Paul deals with the great problem of the rejection of their Messiah by the bulk of the Jewish nation, and God's consequent rejection of them. Two questions arise: (a) 'Has God broken His promises?' and (b) 'If not, how are they to be fulfilled?' Paul answers the first question in chapters 9 and 10, and the second in chapter 11.

1 Chapter 8 is full of triumphant joy. How, then, can Paul speak of having great sorrow and unceasing pain in his heart? See especially 9: 3. What made him sorrowful? How much of this Christian joy and how much of this Christian sorrow do we ourselves know?

2 Verses 9–13. The question with which Paul is here dealing is: 'If God reject those Jews who reject Jesus as Messiah, has not His word come to nought? For were not the promises (verse 4) made to the Jews?' How does Paul answer this question? And what two principles of God's election does he find in the Old Testament stories of the births of (a) Isaac and (b) Jacob and Esau?

☐ STUDY 17 Romans 9: 14–29

1 How does Paul show that in His election of men God retains

absolute liberty of action (a) without compromising His own righteousness, and (b) without giving man any just ground for complaint? See verses 14–22. At the same time, observe how Paul lays emphasis upon God's mercy. See verses 15, 16, 23–26.

2 What is the purpose of God's election, and how do the scriptures which Paul quotes illuminate that purpose? How does this truth concern me?

☐ STUDY 18 Romans 9: 30 – 10: 21

1 What are the two ways of seeking acceptance with God which are here contrasted? How are they shown to be mutually exclusive? See 9: 30 – 10: 9. What was the cause of Israel's failure?

2 Righteousness by faith (10: 8–15). What does the apostle say regarding (a) its simplicity; (b) its universal application; and (c) the necessity of proclaiming it?

3 What light does 10: 14–21 throw upon man's responsibility (a) in proclaiming the gospel; (b) in hearing it?

☐ STUDY 19 Romans 11: 1–10

1 What three reasons are given in this passage to show that God has not cast Israel wholly away?

2 How have the remnant who have been saved come into that blessedness, and how have the others failed to obtain salvation? What has been God's part in the result, and what man's?

☐ STUDY 20 Romans 11: 11–24

1 If a man trips and stumbles, he may either rise again or fall and perish. What reasons does Paul give here for his confidence that Israel's rejection is not final?

2 Against what spirit does he warn Gentile believers? What lessons ought we to learn for ourselves from God's dealings with Israel?

3 How does this passage encourage the vigorous prosecution of Christian mission to the Jews?

Note. Verse 16. *Cf.* Nu. 15: 17–21. As the offering of the first-fruits was regarded as consecrating the whole harvest, so in the choice of the patriarchs the whole nation became set apart for God. *Cf.* verse 28.

☐ STUDY 21 Romans 11: 25–36

1 What is God's ultimate purpose for Israel, and how do the scriptures cited confirm that purpose?

2 Consider the plan of God as revealed in chapters 9–11. By what successive steps has God acted, and will He still act, to bring about the result stated in verse 32? Does the argument of these chapters lead you as naturally as it led Paul to the doxology of verses 33–36?

☐ STUDY 22 Romans 12

In the second part of his letter Paul now shows what quality of life should characterize those who believe in the gospel as set out in chapters 1–11. The close connection between belief and conduct is emphasized by the significant word 'therefore' in 12: 1. See Analysis.

1 What should be the believer's attitude (a) to God, and (b) to the world? What results should such a right attitude produce?

2 It has been suggested that the teaching of verses 3–8 might be summed up in the word 'humility', and that of verses 9–21 in the word 'love'. How far is this true? At what points do I particularly come short of these standards?

Notes

1 Verse 2. 'Transformed': the same Greek word is used three other times in the New Testament, in Mt. 17: 2 and Mk. 9: 2 ('transfigured'); and in 2 Cor. 3: 18 ('changed').

2 Verse 20. 'Burning coals': a figurative emblem of severe pain, here the pain of shame and contrition.

☐ STUDY 23 Romans 13

1 What three main reasons does Paul give in verses 1–7 why it is right to submit to the civil power? How will this submission express itself in practice?

2 What single guiding principle should control the Christian's life in society? See verses 8–10.

3 Verses 11–14. Paul gave in 12: 1 one powerful motive for living the life set forth in these chapters, namely, 'the mercies of God'. What further motive does he present here? What will wearing the armour of light mean for you, both negatively and positively?

Note. Verse 2. 'The state can rightly command obedience only within the limits of the purposes for which it has been divinely instituted—in particular the state not only may but must be resisted when it demands the allegiance due to God alone' (*Romans* (*TNTC*), p. 237).

☐ STUDY 24 Romans 14

1 'A Christian man is a most free lord of all, subject to none' (Luther). What do verses 1–12 teach about Christian liberty?

2 'A Christian man is a most dutiful servant of all, subject to all' (Luther). For what reasons should Christian liberty be qualified? What are the most important things to be preserved at all costs in the Christian community?

3 If in doubt ourselves about the lawfulness of a thing, can we do it because we see other true Christian people doing it? If not, why not?

Notes

1 Verse 1. *Cf.* NEB: 'Accept him without attempting to settle doubtful points.'

2 Verse 5. There is no need to suppose that Paul was thinking of the weekly sabbath here, but rather of Jewish holy days.

3 Verse 6. There is an important principle here, akin to that of verse 23b. It is that if we can thank God in what we do, receiving it as His gift, it is right to do it; otherwise not.

☐ STUDY 25 Romans 15: 1–13

1 The counsel given in verses 1, 2 is by no means easy to follow. What three sources of help and encouragement are suggested in verses 3–5?

2 What does following Christ's example involve (verses 7–12)? Why does Paul lay such emphasis upon the inclusion of the Gentiles?

3 What should characterize the life of the Christian church? See verses 2, 5–7, 13.

☐ STUDY 26 Romans 15: 14–33

The Epistle from 1: 16 onwards has been more like a treatise than a letter. Paul now resumes the epistolary form, and there are many links between this closing section and 1: 1–15.

1 How does Paul in verses 15–21 describe his work—in relation to its nature, scope, power and results? How far is the description applicable to our own work in connection with the gospel?

2 What matters lay nearest to Paul's heart at this time, as shown in verses 20–25? Also, what may we learn about the importance which he attached to intercessory prayer? Have we a kindred spirit and outlook?

Notes

1 Verse 16. The figure here is that of the sacrifices of the Old Testament ritual. Paul's work was to bring the Gentiles to God as an offering, sanctified by the Holy Spirit.

2 The contributions of the Gentile churches to the poor of the church in Jerusalem were the result of much labour on Paul's part, and he looked for important results in the drawing together of Jewish and Gentile believers. *Cf.* 2 Cor. 8 and 9, especially 9: 12–15.

☐ STUDY 27 Romans 16: 1–16

1 What may we learn about Phoebe from her name and the place where she lived (see Note 1), from the description of her as 'sister' and 'deaconess of the church', and from the service which she rendered? What did Paul ask for her from the Christians at Rome, and on what grounds?

2 Looking down the list of names, note the references to (a) diligent service; (b) sufferings borne for Christ; and (c) Christian character. *Cf.* 2 Cor. 5: 9, 10.

3 How often do you find the phrase 'in the Lord' or 'in Christ Jesus' or 'in Christ'? Notice also the different connections in which it is used. What significance do you attach to the phrase?

Notes

1 Verse 1. The name Phoebe, being that of a goddess, suggests that Phoebe had a heathen background. But now she is a sister in the Lord, one of the household of faith. Cenchreae, the eastern port of Corinth, was not an easy place in which to live as a Christian.

2 Verse 7. 'My kinsmen': this probably means 'fellow countrymen', 'fellow prisoners'; they may at the time have been imprisoned with Paul because of the gospel.

3 Verse 13. Rufus, possibly the same as in Mk. 15: 21.

☐ STUDY 28 Romans 16: 17–27

1 (a) How may perverters of the gospel be recognized? *Cf.* 1 Tim. 6: 3; Mt. 7: 15–20. (b) How may we be safeguarded from them? *Cf.* 2 Jn. 10; 2 Tim. 2: 14–16; 1 Thes. 5: 22. (c) What encouragement have we in the conflict?

2 How is God described? How does the present age differ from all that went before? What is the one all-important end to be achieved? *Cf.* 1: 5. What is the method to be adopted?

Note. Verses 25, 26. The mystery spoken of is fully expounded in the Epistle to the Ephesians. *Cf., e.g.*, Eph. 3: 3–6.

EXODUS 21 - 40

Introduction

Although the twentieth chapter of the book of Exodus divides it into two distinct parts, we must remember that the book is really one. The narrative of the opening chapters leads up to the law-giving of the later ones, and is bound to it with an intimate connection. When our section opens, Israel is encamped at the foot of Sinai. Behind them are the great experiences of God's judgments upon Egypt, the Passover, the passage of the Red Sea and the wilderness journey. 'Not a hoof' was 'left behind' (Ex. 10: 26). God had delivered Israel from bondage and separated them from Egypt that He might call them to Himself and make known His will to them. In just the same way God has called us from the bondage of sin and the world, redeemed us with the precious blood of Christ, baptized us with His Holy Spirit, and separated us unto Himself. Israel met with God on Sinai. We have met with Him too, not only among the thunders of the law, but also in the face of Jesus Christ. Holiness is His intention for us, as it was for them.

This shows how relevant these chapters of the Bible are. There are many pictures not only of holiness and holy living which we can apply to our own lives, but also pictures of the great principles and doctrines of atonement, and above all of the suffering of our Saviour in redeeming us from sin.

The immediate context

The voice of God had proclaimed the ten commandments from Sinai (Ex. 20: 1–16). On account of the people's fear they fled from the mountain (20: 18, 19) and asked that Moses should tell them God's commands. Moses therefore went up into the mountain (20: 21, 22), and the words of chapter 21 are the words of God spoken to Moses alone on the mountain, with the command that he is to pass them on to the people.

Analysis

21: 1 – 23: 13	Civil and criminal laws.
23: 14–33	Various religious laws and promises.
24	Making of the covenant.
25 – 31	Directions for making the Tabernacle and for its worship.
32 – 34	The people's sin and its forgiveness.
35 – 40	Making of the Tabernacle.

☐ STUDY 15 Exodus 21: 1–32

The laws in this portion concern relations between people, particularly those between slaves and masters. While slavery is tolerated, its severity is mitigated in various ways.

1 What are the principles underlying the laws about persons? In particular, what kind of relationship between slave and master is contemplated in verses 2–6? *Cf.* also Dt. 15: 12–18; Je. 34: 12–17.

2 For what kinds of transgression was the death penalty inflicted? See also 22: 18–20; 31: 15. Why is this? *Cf.* Mk. 9: 43–48.

☐ STUDY 16 Exodus 21: 33 – 23: 19

The laws in 21: 33 – 22: 15 relate mainly to questions of property, and the remainder of the portion contains miscellaneous precepts.

1 What instances of careless neglect, leading to injury or loss for others, are given in 21: 33 – 22: 15? And what does God demand of the offender in such cases? Can you think of modern parallels to the careless neglect described here?

2 Gather out from 22: 16 – 23: 19 illustrations of the truth of the claims God makes here concerning Himself. For these claims see 22: 27; 23: 7. Against what sin does He say that His wrath will wax hot?

Note. Some of these laws are similar to those found in the famous code of Hammurabi, but the provisions are much more merciful. (*Cf. NBD*, pp. 501, 502.) Notice in 22: 31 the reference to being 'consecrated' to God. *Cf.* Lv. 11: 44, 45.

☐ STUDY 17 Exodus 23: 20 – 24: 18

1 23: 20–33. Consider the promises God makes to the people and the demands He makes of them. Can you think of parallel spiritual promises made to Christians and demands made of them in the Christian life?

2 24: 1–18. Why was this a day of significance and importance in the history of Israel? To what did the people commit themselves? Why is this covenant called (in 2 Cor. 3: 7, 9) a 'dispensation of condemnation' and of 'death'? What was God's answer to the situation thus created? *Cf.* Lv. 17: 11; Heb. 9: 22.

□ STUDY 18 Exodus 25

1 What was the twofold purpose of the Tabernacle? See verses 8, 22 in particular.

2 Notice the three articles of furniture described in this chapter, but observe specially the ark and what is said of it in verses 20, 22. What is the significance of the fact that only above the mercy seat could God and man meet and commune together? *Cf.* 1 Jn. 2: 1, 2.

Note. Verses 17–22. The 'mercy seat' or propitiatory covering was a slab of pure gold, with cherubim at either end. This acted as a lid on the ark, covering the tables of testimony inside. On it the high priest sprinkled blood to make atonement. *Cf.* Lv. 16: 15, 16.

□ STUDY 19 Exodus 26 and 27

1 Chapter 26. What four layers of curtains covered the Tabernacle? What appearance would it have from without, and what from within? *Cf.* the contrast between Christ seen from without (Is. 53: 2), and seen from within (Phil. 3: 8).

Note. It will prove helpful to draw a ground plan of the Tabernacle so far as it has been described in these two chapters, with the court, the holy place, and the most holy place, and the altar, table of shewbread, candlestick and ark in their proper positions.

□ STUDY 20 Exodus 28

1 For the order in which the priest's garments were put on, see Lv. 8: 7–9. Each has some significance: the coat of pure linen (verse 39) indicating the high priest as a righteous man; the blue robe (verses 31–35) as a heavenly man; the ephod with the names of the tribes (verses 3–29) as a representative man; the mitre with its golden plate (verses 36–38) as a holy man. Reflect how in all these ways the high priest of Israel in his priestly garments was a type of Christ.

2 What may we learn from this chapter concerning the way in which to draw nigh to God on behalf of others? How must we be clad, and what ought we to be concerned to do?

Notes

1 The ephod was a shoulder garment, covering breast and back.

2 The breastplate was probably a bag or pouch fastened to the front of the ephod, and called 'the breastplate of judgment' because it contained the Urim and Thummim, which were used to ascertain the divine will. *Cf.* Nu. 27: 21; Ezr. 2: 63. Their exact form and use is not now known.

3 Aaron bore the names of the tribes upon his shoulders (the place of strength) and upon his heart (the place of affection).

☐ STUDY 21 Exodus 29

1 In this instruction concerning the consecration of the priests, distinguish the various parts of the ceremony: the cleansing, the robing, the anointing, and the sacrifices. How does our High Priest stand out in marked contrast to Aaron? *Cf.* Heb. 7: 26–28.

2 Verses 38–46. What was the significance of the daily burnt offering morning and evening? What are the counterparts to these activities which are possible for us to share in?

☐ STUDY 22 Exodus 30 and 31

1 Chapter 30. The altar of incense and the bronze laver speak of the need for prayer and for daily cleansing. *Cf.* Ps. 141: 2; Jn. 13: 10; 1 Jn. 1: 8, 9. What lessons can we learn from this chapter on these important subjects?

2 Chapter 31. What was God's part and what man's in the designing and making of the Tabernacle? See verses 1–11 and *cf.* 25: 2, 9.

☐ STUDY 23 Exodus 32

1 How does Aaron illustrate the dangers of compromise when essentials are at stake? What did compromise lead to? Why was God's anger kindled against the people?

2 What features of Moses' character stand out in this chapter? What may we learn from his example?

☐ STUDY 24 Exodus 33

There follows a period of suspense, during which the people mourned, and Moses set up a tent outside the camp. Here God came in the pillar of cloud to speak with him.

1 What was God's attitude at this time (a) towards the people, and

(b) towards Moses? What were Moses' three petitions? What answers did God give?

2 How do the prayers and answers of this chapter show (a) the growth of Moses' desire and faith, and (b) the richness of God's grace?

Notes

1 Verses 1–3. The cause of mourning seems to be that God threatens to revoke the promise of 25: 8; 29: 45, 46 and to return to the earlier method of guidance by His angels (*cf.* 14: 19; 18: 20–23).

2 Verse 7. This tent of meeting cannot be the Tabernacle (although it was sometimes called by that name: 29: 42–44; 35: 21), because it was not yet built. It was apparently an ordinary tent pitched outside the camp during the period of suspense.

☐ STUDY 25 Exodus 34

1 Show how fully God answered Moses' request, fulfilling the promise of 33: 19. Against what things was Moses, as representative of the people, sternly warned?

2 As a result of his communion with God the skin of Moses' face shone. What, in the case of Christians, issues from the contemplation of the glory of Christ? *Cf.* 2 Cor. 3: 18; Lk. 11: 36.

☐ STUDY 26 Exodus 35: 1 – 36: 7

1 What illustration do we find in this passage of the way in which the service of God in His church calls for the contribution of all His people, whatever may be their talents, rank or age? *Cf.* 1 Cor. 15: 58.

2 What examples for ourselves may be found in the spirit in which the people wrought or brought gifts, and in the value and abundance of their giving? *Cf.* 2 Cor. 8: 1–7.

☐ STUDY 27 Exodus 36: 8 – 37: 9

1 36: 8–38. Try to picture the holy place, as seen from within. What would the sides, the roof, the ends, and the floor consist of? Of what were these a symbol?

2 37: 1–9. In what way do the ark and the mercy seat speak of Christ?

Note. The pronoun 'he' in 36: 10, 11, *etc.*, does not represent any particular individual. It might be better rendered 'they', as in Moffatt's translation. But the ark (37: 1) was Bezaleel's own work.

☐ STUDY 28 Exodus 37: 10 – 38: 31

1 The Tabernacle signified both God's approach to man and also man's way of drawing near to God. In view of this, what is the significance of the table of shewbread, the candlestick or lamp-stand, and the altar of incense? *Cf.* Jn. 6: 57; 8: 12; Heb. 4: 16.

2 Whence came the brass for the laver? Consider the part played by women in the making of the sanctuary. Whence came the silver sockets of the sanctuary? *Cf.* also 30: 11–16. Is the fact that the Tabernacle was founded on atonement money significant?

☐ STUDY 29 Exodus 39 and 40

1 Try to picture the Tabernacle and its furniture as here described. What New Testament truths does it foreshadow? *Cf., e.g.,* Heb. 9: 8–12.

2 What phrase occurs repeatedly in this passage concerning the making of the Tabernacle? What does this teach us about our own service for God? *Cf.* Jn. 15: 14.

Note. 40: 26. 'The golden altar': *i.e.,* the altar of incense, called 'golden' to distinguish it from the brazen altar of burnt offering in the outer court (40: 29).

I CORINTHIANS

Introduction

This Epistle was written by Paul from Ephesus (16: 8, 9, 19) during his third missionary journey (Acts 19: 1–10) about AD 56 or 57. It is well to have in view, in reading the Epistle, the great Greek city of Corinth, with its pride of intellect, its idolatries and immoralities, and its busy commerce and thronging life. The purpose of the Epistle was partly to answer questions sent to Paul by the Corinthians (7: 1; 8: 1; 12: 1), partly to deal with distressing news which had come to him from Corinth about factions and other abuses in the church (1: 11; 5: 1; 6: 1; 11: 18, 20). Paul had already written at least one letter to the Corinthians (5: 9).

It will be seen from the Analysis that the Epistle is very largely concerned with questions of practical morality, and as such it has a deep interest for our own as for every age. But these questions are not dealt with on a basis of psychological analysis, but on the ground of the relation of the person to God. For example, the factious spirit is wrong because a saving relation with God is not obtained by intellectual brilliance but by humble faith, and because the ministers of God's gospel are simply His servants, responsible to Him. Again, immorality is a defiling of the temple of the Holy Spirit, a misuse of the blood-bought property of the Redeemer. The ruling principles which Paul lays down in the problem of meats offered to idols are first, that our liberty must not hurt the brother for whom Christ died, and second, that we cannot partake of the table of the Lord and the table of demons. Thus in morals, as in doctrine, the great truth prevails that Christianity is Christ. Also, these principles which inform and guide Paul's attitude here are of abiding value. They can and ought equally to inform and guide our own action, when we are confronted by problems which, however different in outward form, are the same in their fundamental spiritual issues.

The Epistle contains two of the grandest passages in the New Testament, the beautiful description of Christian love in chapter 13, and the defence and explanation of the doctrine of the resurrection in chapter 15.

Analysis

1: 1–9	Introduction.
1: 10 – 4: 21	Factions in the church.
	1: 10 – 2: 16. The spirit of factions rests on intellectual pride, which is contrary to the essence of the gospel. There is a heavenly wisdom, but the natural man cannot understand it.
	3: 1 – 4: 8. Ministers of the gospel are not leaders of parties, but servants of God: to Him they are responsible and their work must pass His tests.
	4: 9–21. The apostolic example of humility and patience: but there is also apostolic authority.
5 and 6	Moral disorders in the church.
	5. A great offender judged, and disciplinary rules laid down.

	6. Litigation between Christians in heathen courts forbidden; the spiritual basis of purity of life.
7	Marriage and celibacy; answers to questions asked.
8: 1 – 11: 1	Meat offered to idols; principles and considerations which should determine the Christian's attitude.
	8. Liberty must be restrained by love.
	9. Paul's example. Application in his life of the same governing principles.
	10: 1 – 11: 1. Above all, no compromise with idolatry.
11: 2–34	Abuses in the church assemblies.
	11: 2–16. Rules for the conduct of women in the church.
	11: 17–34. The profanation of the Lord's Supper rebuked.
12 – 14	Spiritual gifts.
	12. No gift ought to be magnified above another, though there is a sense in which there are greater and lesser gifts.
	13. Love is greater than all spiritual gifts.
	14. Prophecy is more to be desired than speaking with tongues; the first consideration must be the edification of Christ's church.
15	The resurrection; both of Christ Himself and of all His people.
16	The collection for the saints. Conclusion.

☐ STUDY 1 1 Corinthians 1: 1–17

1 Paul is setting out to deal with various divisive factors in the life of the church at Corinth. What is significant, therefore, about his approach in verses 1–9? What may we learn from these verses about our privileges and prospects as Christians?

2 What were the main causes of the dissensions in the church at Corinth? See verses 10–17; *cf.* 3: 3, 4, 21. How may similar dissensions arise in church life today? According to this passage why are they fundamentally wrong and what is the remedy for them?

Note. Verse 12. Apollos was a Jew from Alexandria, a centre of philosophy. He was a man of learning and eloquence, and very able in argument. See Acts 18: 24–28. It seems probable that some at Corinth preferred him to Paul for these reasons.

☐ STUDY 2 1 Corinthians 1: 18 – 2: 16

1 List Paul's reasons for preaching the word of the cross in the way he did. See verses 1: 17 – 2: 5.

2 See 2:6–3:2. What does Paul teach here about (a) 'human wisdom', and (b) 'a secret and hidden wisdom of God'? How is the latter to be possessed, and by whom alone is it understood?

3 Looking back over the passage, pick out the work of the Father, the Son, the Holy Spirit and the human preacher respectively in man's salvation. Is the Lord Jesus Christ to you all that Paul speaks of in 1:30, 31?

Notes

1 2:6. There would appear to be three groups of people in Paul's mind: (a) 'the mature' (*cf.* 'spiritual men', 3:1); (b) 'men of the flesh' (or 'babes in Christ', 3:1); (c) 'the unspiritual' (or 'natural') man of 2:14.

2 2:12, 13. The wisdom of God can be understood by the preacher, interpreted and imparted to others, and received by the hearers, only through the aid of the Holy Spirit. *Cf.* 2:4, 5.

☐ STUDY 3 1 Corinthians 3 and 4

1 3:1–4:2. Discover and summarize all that this section has to teach concerning the place and tasks of Christian workers. What is, or should be, their relationship to (a) God, (b) each other, and (c) those among whom they work?

2 4:1–21. What lessons are to be learnt from the earthly lot of the apostles? Why are men's judgments concerning the worth of Christian ministers' work of such little value? How and when will the real worth of a man's work for God be made plain? Can the value of what he does affect his own salvation? Or what will it affect? See 3:13–15.

Notes

1 3:12, 13. The different materials here mentioned can be taken to represent the teachings of those who were ministering in the church; the gold, silver and precious stones being the doctrines of the Spirit, and the wood, hay and stubble the wisdom of the world.

2 4:6. 'To live according to scripture': literally, 'not beyond what is written'. This was probably a familiar catchword of the day. AV supplies verb 'to think', which gives a more pointed sense in context than RSV 'to live'.

☐ STUDY 4 1 Corinthians 5 and 6

1 Notice in chapter 5 the distinction in the attitudes enjoined towards sinning Christians and sinning non-Christians. What special actions are here demanded of the local church, and why are such actions necessary?

2 6:12–20. These verses stress the permanent significance of the

Christian's body. List the points here mentioned. What does it mean to glorify God in your body? What kind of actions are (a) appropriate, and (b) undesirable or even unthinkable?

3 6: 1–11. What reasons does Paul give here for viewing the public washing by Christians of their dirty linen as a denial of the church's mission in the world?

Notes

1 5: 2. 'Arrogant': or 'puffed up'. Used often by Paul in this letter (4: 18, 19; 5: 2; 8: 1; 13: 5).
2 5: 5. Paul implies that physical affliction may follow excommunication.
3 5: 6–8. Paul enforces his point by referring to the Passover practice of searching out and destroying all the old leaven before (not after) the Passover Lamb is eaten. See Ex. 12: 14, 15, 19.

☐ STUDY 5 1 Corinthians 7

In this chapter Paul is answering specific questions about marriage. These questions had been sent to him by the church at Corinth. His instructions are strict in view of the moral laxity of pagan Corinth and the 'distress', *etc.* referred to in verses 26–35. He shows that marriage and the single life are equally permissible and that each person must find out in which state God intends him to live (see verse 7).

1 Why did Paul remain single (verses 7, 8)? See verses 25–35. Are his reasons relevant for us today?

2 In verses 17–24 Paul is dealing with the wider question of the Christian's position in the society of his day. What rule is laid down for the Christian three times in these verses? How does this apply to us?

3 Gather out Paul's practical teaching about married life (2–5, 10–16) and compare his more theological treatment in Eph. 5: 22–33.

Notes

1 Verse 14. There seems to have been a fear in some minds that continued union with an unbeliever after conversion to Christ might be defiling to the Christian partner. Paul says the opposite can happen.
2 Verses 17–24. Being 'called' in this section refers not to a person's place and function in human society, but to God's call through Christ to sinners.
3 Verses 26, 28, 29, 31–35. The trying and transitory character of this present world, the added anxieties of married life, and desire to give undivided devotion to the Lord may provide reasons for abstaining from unnecessary change or involvement.
4 Verses 36–38. A difficult section. Paul was probably advising a young man about his fiancée. But he could have been advising a father or guardian about a girl under his care (see RV).

☐ STUDY 6 1 Corinthians 8 and 9

The church in Corinth had asked about the eating of food which had been offered before an idol. Picture yourself as a Christian in Corinth, invited to a social banquet in a temple, or seated as a guest in the house of a non-Christian friend, and offered food which had been presented in sacrifice to an idol.

1 8: 1–13. Using the knowledge of truth as their sole guide (such truth as is stated in verses 4–6), what decision did the Corinthians come to about eating food offered to idols? Did Paul agree? List the reasons why he also says that in certain circumstances he would abstain from such eating.

2 9: 1–27. What basic principles which should govern Christian action does Paul here illustrate from his own conduct? In particular what rights does he show Christian workers to have, and what are his reasons for not using them?

Notes

1 8: 12. 'Wounding . . . when it is weak': note the contrast. What requires tender handling is brutally treated. *Cf.* 9: 22. 'The weak': *i.e.*, those whose grasp of Christian truth is feeble, and who are timid in exercising their liberty in Christ. *Cf.* Rom. 14: 1–3.

2 8: 13. This declaration is conditional and personal, not absolute and general. The significance of this should not be overlooked. *Cf.* 10: 27–30.

☐ STUDY 7 1 Corinthians 10: 1 – 11: 1

1 10: 1–13. The people of Israel, who came out of Egypt, enjoyed similar privileges to those of Christians. What lessons then can we learn from their failures? Why is the inevitability of temptation no occasion for despair?

2 Paul distinguishes between eating in an idol temple (verses 14–22), and eating meats bought in the market, which had been offered before an idol (verses 23–30). Why does he condemn the former, but permit the latter, except in the circumstances of verses 28, 29? What principles does he lay down, in conclusion, to guide Christians in all such matters?

☐ STUDY 8 1 Corinthians 11: 2–34

This chapter deals with two irregularities in public worship. The first concerns the proper way for women to dress when they take part in public worship. The second concerns unchristian behaviour at the social meal, which was the occasion of the observance of the Lord's Supper.

1 What were the arguments that Paul brought forward to insist that in Corinth women should be veiled in public worship? How far are these arguments of permanent validity? May their application

vary where prevailing social customs differ from those of Paul's day?

2 What (according to verses 23–26) is the central significance of the Lord's Supper? What were the causes of some receiving it unworthily? See verses 17–22 and 27–32. How can we make our reception more worthy?

Notes

1 Verse 10. 'Because of the angels': Christian worship was probably regarded as conducted in their presence and open to their view.

2 Verse 10. The veil was both a symbol of authority, reminding the woman that her husband was her head, and also a sign of her modesty and chastity, for no respectable woman was seen without one in Corinth at that time.

☐ STUDY 9 1 Corinthians 12

1 List the different kinds of gift and of service which Paul mentions in this chapter. On what principle are they given, and for what purpose? What responsibility does the possession of such a gift put upon the person who has it?

2 Consider how the character of the human body illustrates both the unity and the diversity of the church. What other lessons does the apostle draw from this illustration?

Note. Verses 1–3. The necessary and decisive test of the presence of the Spirit of God in those exercising spiritual gifts is loyalty to Jesus as Lord. *Cf.* 1 Jn. 4: 1–3.

☐ STUDY 10 1 Corinthians 13

The apostle has urged the believers at Corinth to be zealous to possess the more excellent of the gifts (12: 31), but before going on to explain what he means by this (chapter 14), he pauses to point out that spiritual gifts are of profit only when exercised in love.

1 Verses 1–3. Why is love so all-important? In what ways does Paul show further in verses 8–13 that love is greater than all other gifts? How may it find expression in my life? *Cf.* 1 Jn. 4: 7, 12; Gal. 5: 22, 23.

2 In verses 4–7 there are fifteen ways of describing love. Write them in a column and then try to put opposite each a single word summarizing it, and, if possible, an incident in Jesus' life illustrating it. Then ask yourself: Is this found in me?

☐ STUDY 11 1 Corinthians 14

1 Try to form a mental picture of the church's worship in Corinth.

In what ways did it differ from the church's worship today? Did it include any features, no longer familiar, which it would be good to see restored?

2 What two principles should govern the conduct of public worship and of church gatherings? How did Paul apply these principles in his directions about public worship in Corinth?

3 Many in the church at Corinth seem to have coveted speaking with tongues. What assessment does Paul make of this gift? What was Paul's counsel to those eager for manifestations of the Spirit? Which gift do you earnestly desire?

Note. Verse 3. Prophecy might include foretelling of the future (Acts 11: 28), but was more normally a forthtelling of God's will for present 'upbuilding and encouragement and consolation'. In contrast to an unintelligible 'tongue', it was readily understandable and practically relevant to the hearers.

☐ STUDY 12 1 Corinthians 15: 1–34

One group at Corinth did not believe in life after death at all, another did not believe in the resurrection of the body. In this classic passage Paul deals with both groups.

1 What strikes you about the content and the proclamation of the gospel as summarized in verses 1–4? What benefit does it offer to men, and how is this benefit to be enjoyed? *Cf.* 1 Tim. 1: 15.

2 What is the significance of the evidence which Paul marshals in verses 5–11 for the resurrection of Christ? What for Christians are the five far-reaching consequences of denying the doctrine of the resurrection of the dead? See verses 12–19. Does death set any limit to your hope in Christ?

3 What are to be the full and final consequences of the resurrection of Christ? Of what ultimate consummation is it the promise and pledge? Why are Christians able triumphantly to face death for Christ's sake?

Notes

1 Verse 28. No change in the eternal relations between the Persons of the Trinity is meant here. It is the Son's willing subjection in love. *Cf.* 11: 3.

2 Verse 29. The exact meaning of this reference is uncertain. What is obviously implied is that the practice mentioned is pointless if there is no life beyond death.

☐ STUDY 13 1 Corinthians 15: 35–58

1 What does the analogy of the seed suggest about the relation between our present natural body and our future spiritual body?

In what ways will the latter be different from the former? What does verse 38b also imply?

2 What will take place when Christ comes again? *Cf.* 1 Thes. 4: 13–18. In view of this, what should be the character of our present life and service?

Notes

1 Verse 36. Resurrection in Paul's view is not a strange thing, but is embedded in the heart of God's creative plan, both in nature and in grace.
2 Verse 49. 'The image of the man of heaven' signifies the likeness of Christ in His glorified body. It is this likeness that we are to share. *Cf.* Rom. 8: 29; Phil. 3: 20, 21; 1 Jn. 3: 2.
3 Verse 51. 'We' means 'we Christians'. Some will be alive when Christ comes.

☐ STUDY 14 1 Corinthians 16

1 Verse 1: 'The contribution for the saints'. Paul was concerned about a fund which he had initiated among the Gentile churches to aid the poor of the church in Jerusalem. What may we learn from his practical directions about the collection and sending of this money?

2 What may we learn from this chapter about the plans, movement and ministry of Christian workers? How may we help such more effectively to do 'the work of the Lord'?

3 How were the five commands of verses 13, 14 particularly relevant for the church at Corinth as we know it from this letter? Let me also examine my own life in order to discover in what ways I, too, need to heed these commands.

PSALMS 30–41

☐ STUDY 22 Psalm 30

1 From what danger had God delivered David? What indications

are there that the danger had been very great? What was David's state of mind (a) before the danger, (b) during its presence, and (c) after he was delivered from it?

2 In regard to his experience, to what conclusions does David come about (a) the salutary effects of the affliction, and (b) the purpose for which he had been delivered? What can he now do that he could not do in the same way before? *Cf.* 2 Cor. 1: 8–11.

☐ STUDY 23 Psalm 31

1 What would you pick out as the most bitter ingredients in David's cup of sorrow (verses 9–18)? What would you do if you were in a similar situation? What did David do?

2 In the rest of the psalm what witness does David bear to God both in his prayer and praise? What message does he bring to fellow-believers everywhere?

Note. Verse 5a. *Cf.* Lk. 23: 46 as evidence that this psalm was in our Lord's mind upon the cross.

☐ STUDY 24 Psalm 32

1 According to this psalm what are the indispensable conditions for enjoying the forgiveness of God? *Cf.* Pr. 28: 13.

2 What great blessings does the forgiven soul receive, filling the heart with joy? What conditions of their continued enjoyment are laid down? Are you fulfilling these conditions?

☐ STUDY 25 Psalm 33

This psalm begins where Ps. 32 left off. The Hebrew word translated 'rejoice' in verse 1 is the same as that translated 'shout for joy' in Ps. 32: 11.

1 The call to praise (verses 1–3) is followed by reasons for praise (verses 4-19). What are these, and do they help you to join in praising God?

2 What reasons are given as to why the nation whose God is the Lord is blessed above other nations? What is the psalmist's response to this (verses 20–22)?

Note. Verse 3. 'A new song': the song of the redeemed. *Cf.* Ps. 40: 3. 'Play skilfully': *verb. sap.* for all who aspire to lead the praises of God's people.

☐ STUDY 26 Psalm 34

This is a psalm that shines with new light when we know the probable circumstances of the time when it was composed. See the psalm heading and 1 Sa. 21: 10 – 22: 2. Perhaps it was sung in the cave of Adullam for the instruction of David's followers.

1 Who are those who may expect the Lord's blessings? Note the various ways in which they are described. Are we ourselves entitled to claim blessings on the same ground?

2 Make a numbered list (avoiding repetition) of the blessings God gives to His people, as stated in this psalm.

☐ STUDY 27 Psalm 35

1 The psalm falls into three divisions, each ending with a promise to give God thanks. Discover these sections, and give to each an appropriate heading, summarizing its contents.

2 David gives a vivid picture of the vigour, subtlety and malice of his persecutors, and reacts against them with equal vigour. What is the main cry of his heart, and on what grounds does he plead? In what respects is he an example to us?

Notes

1 Verses 4–6. Concerning this and similar prayers in the Psalms, see *NBD*, p. 1058.

2 Verses 11 and 12. Malicious insinuations were made against David, which had never even entered his mind. *Cf.* 1 Sa. 24: 9, 17.

☐ STUDY 28 Psalm 36

1 Note the contrast in this psalm in the attitude, action and end of the wicked and of those who know the Lord. What should this teach us (a) to avoid, and (b) to do?

2 Which of God's attributes are here extolled and what blessings flow from them? Are you living in the enjoyment of these blessings? Do you pray, as the psalmist did, for their continuance?

☐ STUDY 29 Psalm 37: 1–20

1 What things are we told not to do in these verses, and what reasons are we given for this?

2 What positive counsels are contained in verses 1–11? Note also the promises attached. How far are you personally obeying these injunctions?

☐ STUDY 30 Psalm 37: 21–40

1 Verses 21–31. This section of the psalm expands in fuller measure what was said of the reward of the righteous in verses 4, 6, 9, 11. What do verses 21–31 say about the righteous? How do you measure up to this description?

2 Upon what does the salvation (past, present and future) of the righteous depend? See verses 22, 23, 24, 28, 33, 39, 40.

☐ STUDY 31 Psalm 38

1 If this psalm was written when David's great sin first came to light and struck dismay and horror into the hearts of his friends, can we wonder that its tone is so subdued? How great the contrast with Ps. 35! What light does the psalm throw upon the effects of discovered sin in the life of a believer?

2 The three divisons of this psalm are marked by the fact that they all begin with an address to God. Do you discern a progress in faith from one section to the next?

Notes

1 Verse 5. 'My wounds': *i.e.*, my stripes, a poetic description of God's scourging.

2 Verse 11. 'My plague': his friends regard him with horror as if he were a leper.

☐ STUDY 32 Psalm 39

1 Why was the psalmist at first silent, and why did he break silence and speak? When he gave utterance to his thoughts, to whom did he speak? What can we learn from this? *Cf.* Ps. 62: 8; Jas. 3: 5, 6.

2 It seems that God had many lessons to teach David, and that after his fall his eyes were opened to some of them in a new way. Discover from this psalm what some of these lessons were, and ask yourself, 'Have I learnt them?'

☐ STUDY 33 Psalm 40: 1–10

This psalm consists of two parts, which differ widely in their content. The first part is full of joyous thanksgiving for recent deliverance; the second pleads for help in the midst of distress and danger.

1 What five things does David say in verses 1–3 that God did for him? And what effects did his deliverance have upon those who witnessed it? Have you a corresponding experience of God's deliverance, and has it had a similar effect? *Cf.* Acts 9: 34, 35, 41, 42.

2 To what reflections, resolve and actions did his deliverance give rise in David's own heart and life? See verses 4–10.

Note. Verses 6–8 are quoted in Heb. 10: 5–7, but from the LXX version, which has a different reading in the second line of verse 6. The general meaning is not, however, essentially different. 'As the ear is the instrument for receiving the divine command, so the body is the instrument for fulfilling it' (*Cambridge Bible*).

☐ STUDY 34 Psalm 40: 11–17

1 What are the reasons for the psalmist requiring God's help?

2 On what grounds does he ask for God's help, and what does he see as the result of an answer to his prayer? What lessons can we learn for our own prayer life?

☐ STUDY 35 Psalm 41

1 David from his sick-bed thinks of the words, thoughts and attitudes of other people, some of whom visited him. Note the different ways they added to the sufferings of David. In contrast to this, think of ways by which you can consider the poor, weak and those who are sick.

2 Amid the 'fighting without and fear within' (2 Cor. 7: 5), how did the psalmist's faith finally gain the victory?

Note. Verse 1. 'Considers': the Hebrew word implies wise as well as kindly consideration. LXX: 'He that understands'.

For Studies 36–42 continuing the study of the Psalms see p. 232 in Part 2.

---

2 CORINTHIANS

Introduction

This letter was written from Macedonia (2: 13; 7: 5; 8: 1; 9: 2–4) after Paul had left Ephesus (Acts 20: 1, 2). Paul had met Titus on his return from a mission to Corinth, and the report which Titus gave greatly relieved Paul's anxieties, especially in regard to the church's favourable reception of, and action upon, a severe letter which Paul had written to them (2: 3, 4; 7: 5–16). But there were still other matters which gave Paul much concern. There was a minority in the church opposed to him, and their influence had been strengthened by the arrival of Jewish Christians who claimed apostolic rank, and sought to undermine Paul's authority by making false insinuations against him.

The whole letter vibrates with strong feeling—glowing with love, weighed down with sorrow, burning with indignation. It is the most personal of Paul's letters to the churches, for he had been deeply wounded by the doubts cast upon his personal integrity, his love for those whom he had won for Christ, and upon the validity of his apostolic commission. He knew well also that in their attacks upon him his enemies were really striking at his gospel (11: 1–5). Hence the vehemence of his defence.

The letter falls into three main sections, chapters 1–7, 8–9, 10–13. The chief theme of the first is the nature of Paul's Christian ministry —its divine glory and power (2: 12 – 4: 6); its human weakness and final reward (4: 7 – 5: 10); its motive, message and methods (5: 11 – 6: 10). The theme of chapters 8 and 9 is the collection which Paul is organizing. He indicates the motives for and blessedness of Christian giving. In the closing chapters Paul feels himself reluctantly compelled to declare what manner of man he is, that his readers may know how far from the truth the slanders of his enemies are. These chapters give an insight into the apostle's character such as we find nowhere else. They also contain promises for the weak, and a much-needed warning against the cunning disguises of Satan.

Analysis

1: 1–11 — Salutation: thanksgiving for the comfort that attended his recent troubles.

1: 12 – 2: 11 — Paul vindicates himself from the charge of fickleness and states why he did not come to Corinth; he urges them to forgive the offender.

2: 12 – 6: 10 — The nature of the Christian ministry.

- 2: 12 – 4: 6 — The triumph and glory of the gospel.
- 4: 7–15 — Heavenly treasure in earthen vessels.
- 4: 16 – 5: 10 — Encouragement and reward found in things unseen and eternal.
- 5: 11 – 6: 10 — The ministry of reconciliation: its inspiration, its message and its demands.

6: 11 – 7: 4	An appeal to the Corinthians for their affection. Let them withdraw from evil associations and pursue holiness.
7: 5–16	Paul's joy at the good news brought by Titus.
8 and 9	Concerning the collection for the poor Christians of Judaea. Indication of the governing principles of Christian giving.
10: 1 – 12: 18	Paul's vindication of himself against his adversaries at Corinth.
	10 — The apostle's authority and sphere of service.
	11: 1 – 12: 18 — Paul's self-glorification—a folly forced upon him in order to expose false apostles.
12: 19 – 13: 14	Final warnings and exhortations.

☐ STUDY 1 2 Corinthians 1: 1–11

1 After a formal greeting and introduction Paul opens his letter on a note of praise. What particular aspects of God's character does Paul give praise for? Why do you think these should be particularly singled out in this letter? Can we learn from Paul's experiences any new lessons about the Christian in his personal relationships with God?

2 What reasons does Paul give in this passage for wanting the Corinthians to be fully aware of the extent of his sufferings? What spiritual gain would they get from his suffering (verse 6)? What part are they to play, and with what result (verse 11)? How faithful are we in our support of those whose Christian lives entail more than a usual amount of suffering?

3 Compare the formal greeting of this letter with similar ones in other Epistles (*e.g.*, Gal. 1: 1). On what ground does Paul rest his claim to apostleship? How does he describe the church in Corinth in spite of its defects? What blessings does he ask for its members? How far are these blessings real to you?

Note. Verses 8–10. 'To be ignorant': in the sense of 'to underrate'. The Corinthians knew of the affliction, but not of its gravity. 'I absolutely despaired of life. Yes, and when I asked, What shall be the end? the whispered answer of my heart was, Death. This taught me to rely no more on my own strength, but upon God alone, for He can raise up men actually dead' (Way).

☐ STUDY 2 2 Corinthians 1: 12–22

1 To what does Paul's conscience bear witness regarding his

relations (a) with the world, and (b) with fellow-believers? Can you say the same?

2 Paul makes the remarkable claim that his reliability is to be compared with the eternal faithfulness of God. What does he tell us here about God's faithfulness? What three special functions of the Holy Spirit are referred to in verses 21, 22?

Notes

1 Verse 12. 'Not by earthly wisdom': *cf.* 1 Cor. 2: 6; Jas. 3: 13–18.
2 Verse 13. 'It is simply untrue that I send any private communications. The only letters which I write are those which you read out to the congregation—ay, and which you do recognize as the expression of my mind, and will never cease, I hope, to recognize as such' (Way).
3 Verse 20. 'He, who has God's Son, Jesus Christ, has all God has promised' (Denney). When we believe this and utter with thankful hearts an appropriating Amen, we glorify God.

☐ STUDY 3 2 Corinthians 1: 23 – 2: 17

There had been a gross case of immorality in the church at Corinth (1 Cor. 5: 1) and Paul had written strongly about it. This was the reason for his altering his plans. He did not wish to come with a rod (1: 23; 2: 1), and had postponed his visit in the hope that his letter would achieve its purpose. This had been the case, and Paul now counselled that the offender be forgiven (2: 5–11).

1 What may we learn from the spirit in which Paul administered discipline? What can we learn from his attitude to the situation in Corinth (1: 24; 2: 4), and from the instructions he gave to the Corinthian Christians, regarding discipline and forgiveness? In what ways can a scandal in church life give Satan an advantage?

2 Does the Word of God promise that faithful preaching of the gospel will win all who hear it? How does Paul describe his own experience in this regard? *Cf.* 4: 4.

Notes

1 2: 5. 'As for him who was the cause of all this grief, it is not I whom he has grieved, but all of you—in some measure, that is, for I do not wish to be too severe' (Way).
2 Verse 14. 'Leads us in triumph': in an ancient Roman triumphal procession the captives used to carry censers of incense that diffused their scent far and wide on either side. Paul likens himself to a captive in Christ's train, diffusing the fragrance of the knowledge of Him.

☐ STUDY 4 2 Corinthians 3: 1 – 4: 6

The intruders at Corinth (see Introduction) made much, we may gather, of letters of recommendation which they carried (*cf.* Acts 18: 27), and may have said, or implied, that Paul did not possess such, though he was very ready to commend himself (3: 1).

1 In 3: 6–11 the old and new covenants are contrasted (see Note below). List the ways in which the new covenant is shown to be superior to the old.

2 In this passage Paul describes his own confidence in the work he is doing. What grounds for confidence does he find (a) in the effects of preaching, and (b) in the nature of his gospel? See 3: 1–5; 4: 1–6.

Note. 3: 6. 'The written code kills, but the Spirit gives life': Paul has condensed into these few words the teaching about the law and the gospel which is expounded fully in Rom. 7 and 8.

☐ STUDY 5 2 Corinthians 4: 7 – 5: 10

1 Why has God placed the 'treasure' of 4: 6 in a weak vessel—the earthen vessel of man's frail human nature? How does this arrangement work out in actual experience? See 4: 7–12. How do present afflictions appear to the eye of faith, and what prospect is seen at the end? See 4: 13–18.

2 In 5: 1–4 Paul defines one aspect of the future prospect more closely. What awaits him after death? Or, if Christ should come first, as would be Paul's desire (verse 4), what awaits him at His coming? How is Paul sure that this prospect is no mirage, and what effect has it upon his present aim? See verses 5–10.

Notes
1 4: 10–12. *Cf.* 1: 8–10; 6: 9.
2 5: 3, 4. 'Not be found naked': a reference to the unclothing that takes place at death, when the spirit leaves its earthly body. Paul's desire was, as verse 4 shows, that he might live to see the second coming, and so escape death. *Cf.* 1 Cor. 15: 53.
3 5: 10. The issues of the judgment here spoken of are not eternal life or death; but praise or blame, glory or disgrace. *Cf.* 1 Jn. 2: 28.

☐ STUDY 6 2 Corinthians 5: 11 – 6: 10

1 What great motive dominated Paul's life, and to what conclusion did it lead him? See verses 14–17. How far are we like Paul in this matter?

2 5: 18 – 6: 2. What does Paul say God (a) has done in Christ and (b) now purposes to do through us? What ought we to tell men, and to beseech them to do, in order to fulfil our God-given task?

3 Examine the list of twenty-eight particulars in which Paul describes the kind of life and experience into which the acceptance of Christ and of Christ's commission led him. To what extent do you find that this describes your life as a Christian?

Notes

1 5: 12. An allusion to the intruders who were undermining Paul's influence in Corinth (see Introduction). Paul's purpose in these verses (11–13) is to assure his readers that however he may appear to them, whether mad or sane, in heart he is true to God and to them.

2 Verse 21. 'The sin is laid by God upon the sinless One . . . His death is the execution of the divine sentence upon it . . . and there is henceforth no condemnation to them that are in Christ' (Denney).

☐ STUDY 7 2 Corinthians 6: 11 – 7: 16

1 In what ways does Paul show in 6: 14–16 that Christians must be a separated people? What arguments does he use in 6: 16 – 7: 1 to lead us to separate ourselves completely from all that defiles, and to endeavour whole-heartedly to make our holiness perfect? Are you willing to test your friendships and your inmost purposes by this passage? *Cf.* Ps. 139: 23, 24.

2 In what ways does Paul convey the strength of his feelings about the Corinthian Christians and their behaviour? What two kinds of sorrow for sin are here distinguished (a) in their nature, and (b) in their result? By what signs did the Corinthians show that they were genuinely penitent?

Notes

1 6: 11–13. Paul's loving heart overflows towards the Corinthians, and he yearns for a corresponding large-hearted affection from them towards him. Verse 12 means that any sense of constraint they might feel towards Paul arose not from any lack of love in him, but from the narrowness of their own affections.

2 6: 14 – 7: 1. This is a parenthesis, introduced to make clear that when Paul bids his readers to be broadened in their affections, he does not mean increased tolerance of *evil*. 'Belial' is here a name for Satan.

3 7: 10. 'Godly grief': *i.e.*, sorrow towards God, regarding the sin as an offence against Him. *Cf.* Ps. 51: 4. 'Worldly grief', on the other hand, is such sorrow as the man of the world feels, concerned only with the painful consequences of the sin, and not leading to repentance.

☐ STUDY 8 2 Corinthians 8: 1–15

Chapters 8 and 9 form the second section of the letter (see Introduction), which relates to the fund which Paul was collecting from the Gentile churches for the poor in the church in Jerusalem. It lay very near to his heart, and had great importance in his eyes, as a demonstration of the oneness of all believers as members of one body in Christ.

1 In what condition were the churches of Macedonia at this time in regard to their circumstances? Yet what was their spiritual attitude, and in what four ways did it show itself? To what does Paul ascribe it?

2 What is the chief point in the appeal which Paul makes in verses 7–15? Gather out the other points which he makes, and consider them in their application to our own giving.

Notes

1 Verse 5. 'Gave themselves': *i.e.*, for any personal service the Lord might require of them.

2 Verse 15. The story of the manna indicates God's purpose that in material things His people should have neither surplus nor want. They should, therefore, mutually help one another. *Cf.* Ex. 16: 18.

☐ STUDY 9 2 Corinthians 8: 16 – 9: 15

Today's portion falls into two parts. First, in 8: 16–24, Paul explains why he is sending Titus and two others to Corinth, and gives them his warm commendation. Second, in chapter 9, he shows the blessings of cheerful and generous giving.

1 What may we learn from Paul's example of the duty of giving praise where praise is due? What picture do you have of the personalities of the Christian workers he describes?

2 What lessons do we learn here about handling money? What kinds of giving does God value? What reward does He give?

Note. 9: 15. 'His inexpressible gift': *i.e.*, the gift of Christ, so great as to be beyond description, the spring and pattern of our giving.

☐ STUDY 10 2 Corinthians 10

In his third section of the letter (see Introduction) Paul has specially in view the disaffected minority, who were being led astray by visiting preachers, who were enemies of Paul and of the gospel. His desire is to destroy the influence of these men, so that his visit, when it comes, may not be one of strife and conflict. In this chapter he twice refers to a charge, which his enemies made against him (10: 1b, 10), that while he might be able to write vigorous letters from a distance, he was weak and ineffective when present in person. Paul answers that he has powerful weapons at his command, and that the church in Corinth falls within the sphere of his God-given authority.

1 Consider Paul's description of his ministry as a warfare (verses 3–6). What is the aim he has in view? What fortresses have to be captured, and how is victory achieved? Have you known in your own experience (a) of lawless elements in your own thought-life brought into captivity to the obedience of Christ, and (b) of winning such victories for Christ in the thought-life of others?

2 What does Paul claim for himself in verses 7–16, and what hope for future service does he express? *Cf.* Rom. 12: 3; 15: 18–24. What is the only form of commendation in which he is interested?

Note. Verse 16. 'Done in another's field': an allusion to those who came to a church already founded by someone else, to make mischief there.

☐ STUDY 11 2 Corinthians 11: 1–21a

1 Why was Paul so concerned for the Corinthian Christians? See verses 1–4, and *cf.* Gal. 1: 6–10. On what two grounds was he amazed that they should so readily tolerate these false teachers? See verse 4 and verses 19, 20. But see also verses 13–15. What warning for our own day can be drawn from what Paul says about the false teachers, their methods, and their message? Is 'another Jesus' preached today?

2 In what ways does Paul distinguish his own way of life while at Corinth from that of the 'false apostles'? Have you learnt anything new about Paul's character from this passage?

Notes

1 Verse 5. An ironical reference to the intruders at Corinth who exalted themselves so highly.

2 Verses 7–12. Paul refused to take money from the church in Corinth, and says that he will continue to refuse, one reason being that his enemies who, it is implied, did receive support from the church, would have liked to see Paul doing the same.

3 Verse 16. Paul feels ashamed to be engaged in self-praise; but in the circumstances he can do no other. *Cf.* 12: 11. He will do even this for the church's sake. It is to be noted, however, that he speaks less of what he has done than of what he has suffered. *Cf.* verse 30.

☐ STUDY 12 2 Corinthians 11: 21b – 12: 10

1 Follow Paul through the experiences which he describes. In particular let your imagination dwell clause by clause on the list of sufferings in verses 23–29. Why do you think Paul felt it necessary to 'boast' of his experiences?

2 Why did Paul believe he had been given the 'thorn in the flesh'? What did Paul do about this 'thorn' and with what result? Notice the force of the present tense in the Lord's reply. What lessons did Paul learn that changed his whole attitude to trial? Have we begun to understand these things? *Cf.* Rom. 5: 3–5; 1 Pet. 4: 14.

Notes

1 12: 5. Paul contrasts himself, as a passive recipient of divine revelations, with himself in other capacities.

2 12: 7. The 'thorn in the flesh' seems to have been severe bodily suffering of some kind, but its exact nature is not disclosed.

3 12: 9. 'He said': better, as in RV, 'He hath said'—a word of abiding application.

☐ STUDY 13 2 Corinthians 12: 11–21

1 Paul again summarizes his past ministry in Corinth and his attitude towards the Christians there. What accusations is he meeting in this passage and how does he answer them? What impresses you

most as showing the measure of his Christ-likeness? In answering this question bear in mind how deeply he has been wronged by the ingratitude and suspicion of the church.

2 In verses 20, 21 what anxieties does Paul have over the church in Corinth? What can we learn from this about our responsibility for younger Christians?

Notes

1 Verse 13. 'Forgive me this wrong!': spoken in irony.

2 Verse 14. 'I seek not what is yours but you': *cf.* 4: 5, 15; 5: 13; 13: 9.

☐ **STUDY 14 2 Corinthians 13**

1 What effect has Paul's love for the Corinthians on his attitude to their sin? In answering consider the evidence of both verses 1–6 and verses 7–10. See also 12: 20, 21.

2 Consider how closely related the exhortations and promises of verse 11 are to the teaching of the whole letter.

3 Consider how the prayer of verse 14 sums up our Christian heritage, and gives the complete solution to our threefold need—our sin, sorrow and weakness.

Notes

1 Verse 1. When Paul comes he will hold a judicial inquiry. *Cf.* Mt. 18: 16; 1 Tim. 5: 19.

2 Verses 2–4. Christ 'crucified in weakness' is not the whole gospel. He also lives by the power of God, and that power will be manifested also in His servant Paul.

3 Verses 7–10. Paul would rather that the Corinthians should act rightly, and so make it needless for him to rebuke them, than that he should gain prestige by the demonstration of his apostolic authority.

MICAH

Introduction

Micah was a contemporary of Isaiah, but whereas Isaiah was a prophet of the court and of the city, Micah came from Moresheth-gath (1: 1, 14), a country town near the western border of Judah. Notice, *e.g.*, how often he used the image of a flock and its shepherd (2: 12; 3: 2, 3; 4: 6, 8; 5: 4, 8; 7: 14). His prophetic ministry began only a few years after that of Hosea, and there are many traces in his book of the influence upon him both of Hosea and of Isaiah. See, *e.g.*, Mi. 1: 7 and Ho. 2: 13; 8: 6; 9: 1; and again Mi. 7: 1 and Is. 24: 13, *etc.* Mi. 4: 1–3 and Is. 2: 2–4 are almost verbally the same. Yet Micah was no plagiarist. He had his own message, and exercised a profound influence, as is seen from the reference to him in Je. 26: 16–19. As Jonah's prophetic word moved the king of Nineveh to repent, so Micah's similar prophecy moved King Hezekiah; and so deep was the impression Micah made that these things were remembered about him a century later, and were instrumental in saving the life of the prophet Jeremiah.

Micah's word still lives, because the Spirit of God is in it, and he has important lessons to teach us for our own day.

Analysis

1 and 2 Judgment must come, but in the end there will be blessing.

1: 1–16. A vision of Jehovah come in judgment; Samaria falls and country towns in the lowland of Judah will be overwhelmed.

2: 1–11. The sins of the wealthy and powerful which brought the judgment.

2: 12, 13. A prophecy of restoration.

3 – 5 Further prophecies of coming judgment, and further blessing.

3: 1 – 4: 7. The sins of rulers, prophets and priests will bring destruction upon Jerusalem; yet in the latter days it will be restored and the rule of Jehovah established.

4: 8–13. Zion must suffer exile, but later will be victorious.

5: 1–15. Temporary humiliation will lead to future triumph.

6 and 7 Jehovah in controversy with His people states His real demands; then denounces Judah's sin and gives warning of the consequences. The prophet, speaking in the name of a penitent people, laments the terrible conditions of social family life, but waits for God in confidence and hope, and is assured of the final fulfilment of all God's promises.

☐ STUDY 1 Micah 1 and 2

1 Judgment falls on Samaria and (almost) on Jerusalem. The Lord God is witness for the prosecution (1: 2); the result is ruin in Samaria (1: 6, 7), consternation in Judah (1: 10–16) and grief in the prophet (1: 8, 9). What was the basic reason for the catastrophe (1: 5, 13)?

2 What classes of the community and what sins are rebuked in chapter 2? What is the penalty?

3 Promise (2: 12, 13) follows banishment (2: 10). How are God's gracious acts described? Do we, too, know the Shepherd's love (Jn. 10: 14, 15) and the King's might (2 Cor. 2: 14)? *Cf.* also Is. 40: 11; 2 Sa. 5: 20.

Notes

1 1: 5. The prophet sees the capital cities of the kingdoms of both Israel and Judah as the main sources of the corruption of the whole country, although they were the centres of worship.

2 1: 10–12. There is some word-play on the names of the towns mentioned and what they will endure. 'Grovel in the dust as Dust-town' (Beth-le-aphrah), *etc.* (see Moffatt).

3 1: 13. 'The beginning of sin': Lachish was the border town at which chariots and horses purchased in Egypt would be received in Judah. See 5: 10 and *cf.* Is. 31: 1; 36: 9.

4 1: 14, 15. The calamities coming on Judah will include separation from loved ones, deception, conquest and ignominious flight.

5 Chapter 2. Micah preaches in verses 1-5; he is interrupted by the rich in verse 6 and retorts, verse 7. God speaks in verses 8–10 and 12, 13; the prophet soliloquizes in verse 11.

6 2: 4, 5. The avaricious landowners will lament because they themselves have been dispossessed; their portion in the Lord's inheritance (verse 5) will be no more.

7 2: 6. Micah's preaching is not well received and he is told, 'Do not drivel . . .!' Verse 11 and 3: 11 describe the sort of preachers the rich wanted—and got!

☐ STUDY 2 Micah 3: 1 – 4: 7

1 The nation's rulers, prophets and priests come under scathing denunciation. Why? And with what result (see 'then', 3: 4, 'therefore', 3: 6 and 12)? The priests remembered God's promises (3: 11; *cf.* Ps. 132: 13, 14) but not His stipulations (*cf.* Ps. 132: 12). May our confidence be similarly false?

2 Notice especially the contrast between the true prophet (3: 8; *cf.* 2: 7) and the false (3: 5, 11; *cf.* 2: 6, 11). How may we recognize 'the Spirit of the Lord'?

3 4: 1–7. A new kingdom of peace (4: 3, 4) and wholeness (4: 6, 7) is to be established. What will characterize the King, and what His subjects?

Notes

1 3: 1. 'Know' here means 'care for'; the verb is used in this pregnant sense in, *e.g.*, 6: 5; Ps. 144: 3 (AV); Pr. 12: 10; Ho. 8: 4.

2 3: 2, 3. God's ideal (Am. 5: 15) had been turned on its head. The judiciary, like ravenous wild beasts, was preying on the people.

3 3: 7. 'Cover their lips': a sign of shame (Lv. 13: 45) or mourning (Ezk. 24: 17).

4 3: 10. Jerusalem was being adorned with fine buildings at the cost of the lives of the people.

5 Chapter 4. Zion will be the pre-eminent place of God's revelation (verse 2) and His rule (verses 3, 7).

6 4: 5. A parenthesis: at present men do not all give their allegiance to the Lord; this is yet to come, 'in that day' (4: 6).

☐ STUDY 3 Micah 4: 8 – 5: 15

Two prophecies with a 'Now . . . But . . .' pattern. See Analysis.

1 4: 8 – 5: 1. Zion will be besieged and her inhabitants exiled. But what will follow? On a personal level, what is man's true perspective to be? *Cf.* 4: 12 and 1 Cor. 2: 9, 10.

2 5: 2–6. From this early Messianic prophecy what do we learn of the Messiah's origins and activity? How did Jesus fulfil the longings of prophet and people?

3 5: 10–15. The life of the restored remnant of Israel will be one of God-given (verse 7) victory (verses 8, 9), but purification will be involved (verses 10–14). Disobedience is disastrous (verse 15). See 1 Pet. 2: 9–12, 16; 4: 7 and consider how the same principle still applies.

Notes

1 4: 10. 'Go to Babylon': a remarkable instance of prophetic prevision, because at the time the great enemy was Assyria, not Babylon. But see Is. 39: 6, 7.

2 4: 11. The nations gather to ogle, and worse. But one day the roles will be reversed; *cf.* 7: 10b, 17.

3 4: 13. Devoting spoil to the Lord was an old custom; *cf.* Jos. 6: 24.

4 5: 3. Israel shall be surrendered up until the Messiah is born; then, the Messiah's family will be reunited.

5 5: 5. 'Seven . . . eight': an indefinite number according to Hebrew idiom; whatever the need for leaders is, it will be met.

6 5: 6. Read (with mg.) '*he*' (*i.e.*, the Messiah) 'shall deliver us . . .'

7 5: 14. 'Cities': probably, better, 'sacrificial stones'. Verses 10–14 (like 6: 7b) hint at the sort of unfaithfulness which characterized the reign of Ahaz; *cf.* 2 Ki. 16: 3.

☐ STUDY 4 Micah 6: 1 – 7: 6

1 6: 1–8. What was the substance of the Lord's case against His

people? Do not forgetfulness and misunderstanding still characterize them? Apply Col. 2: 20 and 3: 1–4, for example. Does God find in us what He has shown to us (verse 8; 'require of' literally means 'seek in')?

2 6: 9 – 7: 6. Sin brings desolation (6: 13, 16) and social breakdown (7: 2–6). Do we (a) recognize and (b) grieve over this sad and modern tale? Do our lives shine like lights in this situation? *Cf.* 7: 8 and Phil. 2: 15.

Notes

1 6: 5. Balaam blessed Balak's enemies three times when he was expected to curse them (Nu. 22–24). 'From Shittim to Gilgal' refers to the crossing of the Jordan. 'Know' here means 'care for'; *cf.* 3: 1.

2 6: 9–16. The text is somewhat confused; but it is clear that a wicked Israel is receiving a stern warning.

3 6: 16. 'The statutes of Omri': *cf.* 1 Ki. 16: 25, 26. 'That I may make you . . . ': a final, not a causal, clause.

☐ STUDY 5 Micah 7: 7–20

1 7: 7–20. The penitent city speaks in verses 7–10, and the prophet responds to them (11–13), and to God on their behalf (14–20). In what respects does the sinful city take the right course in chapter 7? On what promises does she rest her case (verses 7–9), and what promise does she receive (verses 11, 12, 15)?

2 The end of the disobedient nations is appalling (7: 10, 13, 16, 17; *cf.* 5: 9, 15). Strict justice is the principle of God's judgment (*cf.* Rev. 16: 5–7). How was Micah's vision of a forgiving God (7: 18–20) glorious yet restricted? How does the New Testament have a broader insight into this same forgiving God? *Cf.* Jn. 3: 16; 2 Pet. 3: 9.

Note. 7: 11. 'In that day': *cf.* 4: 1, 6; 5: 10. For the promise of the verse, *cf.* Zc. 2: 1–5 and Is. 26: 15 (also 'In that day . . .', Is. 26: 1).

1 TIMOTHY

Introduction

Timothy was Paul's dearly loved companion and helper whom he first found at Lystra (Acts 16: 1–3) and ever afterwards regarded as a son (1 Tim. 1: 2, 18; 2 Tim. 1: 2; 2: 1). He was with Paul on his missionary journeys and during his imprisonment in Rome (Col. 1: 1), and was sent by Paul from time to time on important missions (1 Thes. 3: 1–6; 1 Cor. 4: 17; 16: 10, 11; Phil. 2: 19). At this time he had been left at Ephesus to check tendencies to false teaching (1 Tim. 1: 3, 4) and to superintend the affairs of the church as the apostle's representative (1 Tim. 3: 14, 15). The letter belongs to the last period of Paul's life, between his first and second imprisonments in Rome.

Paul's main purpose in writing was to guide and encourage Timothy in his work. The letter is full of practical advice concerning church affairs and the preservation of purity of life and doctrine. It exhorts the worker for God to be uncompromising in his loyalty and devotion to his duty.

Analysis

1: 1, 2 Personal address and greeting.

1: 3–20 The apostle and his gospel.

- 1: 3–11 The gospel in contrast to false teaching.
- 1: 12–17 The gospel in Paul's experience.
- 1: 18–20 The gospel as committed to Timothy.

2: 1–15 Guidance concerning praying and teaching in the congregation.

3: 1–16 Qualifications for church ministry.

4: 1–5 Warning concerning false teaching.

4: 6–16 Exhortations to Timothy concerning his teaching and personal behaviour.

5:1–6:2 Instructions concerning special groups within the church—widows, presbyters, slaves.
6:3–21 Concluding advice. Renewed warnings against false teaching and covetousness.

☐ STUDY 1 1 Timothy 1

Timothy is reminded of the purpose for which he was left at Ephesus. Verses 12–17 are a digression in which Paul breaks out into thanksgiving for God's grace towards him.

1 What is the nature of the false teaching which Paul attacks? From verses 3, 11, 12, 18 and Gal. 1: 8, 9, 12 consider why Paul would not allow any deviation from the gospel.

2 The spurious doctrine evidently exaggerated the law as a means of righteousness. How does Paul indicate in verses 8–15 the limitations of the law and the superiority of the gospel?

3 Compare your own experience of the gospel with that described in verses 12–17. What outstanding features does Paul emphasize?

Notes

1 Verse 4. 'Myths and endless genealogies': rabbinical fables (*cf.* Tit. 1: 14), and attempts to find hidden meaning in the names of the genealogies of the Old Testament.

2 Verse 20. 'Hymenaeus and Alexander': *cf.* 2 Tim. 2: 17; 4: 14. Nothing else is known of these men. 'Whom I have delivered to Satan': a form of apostolic discipline with a view to spiritual benefit. *Cf.* 1 Cor. 5: 5; 2 Cor. 12: 7.

☐ STUDY 2 1 Timothy 2

1 Verses 1–7. What theological truths form the basis for confidence in prayer?

2 For whom, and for what, should we pray (verses 1–4)? What kind of people ought we to be in personal behaviour if we wish to be effective in prayer and pleasing to God when we meet to pray? With verses 8–10, *cf.* Ps. 66: 18; Is. 59: 1–3; Mk. 11: 25.

3 Verses 9–15. Paul is not deprecating the role of women in the service of Christ (*cf.* Rom. 16: 1ff.; Phil. 4: 2, 3), but he does here forbid women 'to teach or to have authority over men' in the local church. Is it conceivable that today change may be permitted in women's part, or is Paul appealing here to the permanent consequences of the difference made by the Creator between male and female? What is the significance of verses 13 and 14? (See *NBCR*.)

Notes

1 Verse 8. 'Lifting holy hands': it was customary to stand when praying, and to spread out one's hands before God. *Cf.* 1 Ki. 8: 22.

2 Verse 15. 'Saved through bearing children': a difficult expression. It must be understood here in its context, with reference to the place and function of women. Bearing children is a function to which women are unquestionably called. In it they will experience God's saving grace provided they continue in faith, *etc.*

STUDY 3 1 Timothy 3: 1–13

1 Verses 1–7. What are the qualities required in those who exercise leadership in the church? Note what Paul says about their (a) personal character, (b) Christian experience, (c) general reputation, and (d) abilities. Why does Paul put such stress upon the personal life of a Christian leader?

2 What qualities are necessary for deacons (verses 8–10, 12, 13) and deaconesses (verse 11)? Compare your answer with the answer to Question 1. Note how largely the element of self-discipline enters into these qualifications. In the light of this passage, how do I measure up to the standard God requires?

Notes

1 Verse 1. 'Bishop': the bishop here must not be identified with a present-day bishop. The Greek word means 'one who exercises oversight'. There were a number of such men in each congregation (see Phil. 1: 1); and they were also called 'elders' or 'presbyters'. See Tit. 1: 5, 7; Acts 20: 17, 28, AV and RV.

2 Verse 2. 'Married only once': *cf.* 3: 12; 5: 9. Opinion is divided as to whether this means married only once, or having only one wife, *i.e.*, not a polygamist. The latter is more probable in the light of 1 Cor. 7: 8, 9; Rom. 7: 1–3.

3 Verse 6. 'The condemnation of the devil': this probably means to fall into the condemnation incurred by the devil for his sin of pride.

STUDY 4 1 Timothy 3: 14 – 4: 5

1 What truths about the Christian church are signified by the descriptive phrases of 3: 15? Consider each in turn. *Cf.* Eph. 2: 19–22; 2 Cor. 6: 16–18. (See Note below.) What demands ought these truths to make upon us?

2 Note whence the false teaching described in 4: 1–5 would arise; and by what kind of men it would be propagated. What, according to Paul's teaching here, is the true Christian position with regard to (a) marriage and (b) foods that may be eaten? *Cf.* Heb. 13: 4; Rom. 14: 2, 3, 6b.

3 3: 16 may quote part of an early Christian hymn. What do these statements declare concerning the Person and work of Jesus Christ? What are the sphere and the extent of His Lordship?

Note. 3: 15. 'The pillar and bulwark of the truth': *i.e.*, displaying and upholding in the world the revelation of the gospel; and so providing a public and enduring witness for God. *Cf.* Rev. 2: 5.

☐ STUDY 5 1 Timothy 4: 6–16

1 Make a list of all the things which Timothy is here told to do and to avoid in order to become 'a good minister of Christ Jesus'.

2 Distinguish in this passage (and in the list made in answer to Question 1) between actions which concerned (a) Timothy's personal life, and (b) his public ministry. What may we here learn concerning the connection of these two?

☐ STUDY 6 1 Timothy 5: 1 – 6: 2

1 Note Paul's concern for others, and his detached interest in the special conditions and needs of particular groups. What may we here learn concerning the way to treat people?

2 How ought the elderly, *e.g.*, widows, normally to be cared for? Why does Paul advise against the giving of church support to younger widows?

3 5: 19–22. Of what dangers and responsibilities is Timothy here made aware? What, in principle, can I learn from these instructions for my own guidance?

Notes

1 5: 3, 17. 'Honour': probably implies financial support.

2 5: 22. 'The laying on of hands' refers to the setting apart of individuals for specific service, *e.g.*, as elders.

☐ STUDY 7 1 Timothy 6: 3–21

1 Verses 3–5, 20, 21. What characteristics of false teachers are here mentioned? What is lacking, and what out of place, in their attitude and practice? From these statements make a list of things to be avoided, if you wish to be an acceptable teacher of the things of God. Set over against them the positive aims desirable in a true man of God (verses 11–14).

2 Verses 6–10, 17–19. What are the perils of covetousness and wealth? What is the proper attitude to, and use of, material possessions? On what should our desires and hopes be fixed?

TITUS

Introduction

Titus was a Gentile convert (Gal. 2: 3), led to faith by the apostle himself (Tit. 1: 4). He accompanied Paul on some of his journeys and was sent by him on important missions to churches, as, for example, to Corinth (2 Cor. 8: 16–18, 23; 12: 17, 18) and to Dalmatia (2 Tim. 4: 10). This letter reveals that Paul left him in Crete to establish the churches of that island (1: 5).

This letter is very similar to 1 Timothy and was probably written about the same time, in the interval between Paul's two imprisonments. It is therefore earlier than 2 Timothy. It emphasizes the importance of order and discipline in the churches. The gospel had evidently made rapid headway in Crete, but church government was as yet undeveloped (1: 5). False teaching also had to be countered, and the apostle has some strong words to say on this subject. But, above all else, the letter stresses the Christian's calling and obligation to live a holy life. It contains also two great doctrinal passages (2: 11–14; 3: 4–7), which stand out like mountain ranges in the landscape.

Analysis

1: 1–4	Opening greeting.
1: 5–16	The need to appoint elders in the churches as a safeguard against the spread of doctrinal error.
2: 1–10	Instructions concerning the conduct of various classes in the Christian community: the aged, the young, Titus himself, slaves.
2: 11–15	The doctrinal basis for the appeal to holy living.
3: 1–7	Exhortation to submission and gentleness, leading up to a further doctrinal statement.
3: 8–11	The Christian's obligation to maintain good works, and to avoid profitless discussion.
3: 12–15	Personal closing messages.

☐ STUDY 1 Titus 1

1 Verses 1–4. What does Paul tell us here concerning the origin and the aims of his ministry? What was the basis of his assurance?

2 Verses 10–14. What was wrong with those whom Paul here criticizes? Make a list of their faults and failings. How, by contrast, are sincerity and genuineness revealed?

3 Verses 6–9. Make a list of the qualifications desirable in a Christian minister which are here mentioned. Compare them with those stated in 1 Tim. 3: 1–13.

☐ STUDY 2 Titus 2

1 Verses 1–10. How may Christians 'adorn the doctrine of God our Saviour'? Examine carefully the characteristics demanded from the different classes mentioned; and summarize them briefly in your own words. Which characteristics ought you particularly to covet and cultivate?

2 Verses 11–14. What reasons are here given why a Christian should live differently? (a) What should he give up? (b) How should he now live? How far is this true of you?

☐ STUDY 3 Titus 3

1 Verses 1–7. How ought we as Christians to behave in relation to (a) civil authorities, and (b) our fellow-men? What double awareness about ourselves should inspire such conduct?

2 Verses 4–7. What are we here told about (a) the source and method of salvation, and (b) our present state and future hope? Do you realize as you ought how 'richly' (verse 6) you are endowed?

3 Verses 8–15. By what actions and by what abstinence should genuine faith in God express itself? What is necessary on our part to ensure that this happens?

2 TIMOTHY

Introduction

This letter is of peculiar interest because it is Paul's last, written during his final imprisonment in Rome when he was aware that his death could be not for long delayed. It reveals that his last days were spent without material comfort. There was no immediate earthly reward to crown his long years of labour. For one reason or another his friends had left him (1: 15; 4: 10, 12, 16). Amid the dreary limitations of his imprisonment he asks for his old cloak to be brought to keep him warm and his books for him to read (4: 13). He urges Timothy to come quickly that he may see him before his death (1: 4; 4: 9, 21).

In such difficult circumstances he exhorts his son in the faith to be faithful to the truth. He is more concerned for Timothy and for the future of the gospel than for himself. Steadfast and confident to the end, he has still the same message to give to all who are called to the service of Christ. What the Lord requires in His workers is faithfulness, even unto death; to watch, to endure, to work and fully to discharge the obligation of their office; to finish their course; and live in anticipation of the crowning day that is coming. For all such is laid up in store 'eternal glory'.

Analysis

1: 1–5	Opening greeting and thanksgivings.
1: 6 – 2: 13	Exhortation to steadfastness, single-hearted purpose and courage in the service of Christ.
2: 14–26	Rules of conduct for the servant of the Lord.
3	A dark outlook. Paul's own example. Value of the Scriptures.
4: 1–8	Final charge, made more urgent by the prospect of Paul's death.
4: 9–18	Personal details of Paul's circumstances and experiences as a prisoner.
4: 19–22	Closing greetings and benediction.

☐ STUDY 1 2 Timothy 1

1 Picture Paul's circumstances. See also 4: 9–13. What positive Christian truths sustained and encouraged Paul as he lay in prison?

2 Note how Paul reminds Timothy of the demands and cost of Christian service. Express in your own words the chief points of Paul's counsel and exhortation to him. To which of these do you particularly need to give heed?

3 What do verses 3–7 reveal concerning the value of a God-fearing and Christian home and upbringing? *Cf.* 3: 14, 15.

Note. Verses 16–18. 'Onesiphorus appears here as one separated from his household, either by absence from home, or quite possibly by death (*cf.* 4: 19). This does not mean, however, that Paul is praying for his present well-being as one dead, a practice completely unsupported elsewhere in Scripture. The prayer concerns not the intermediate state at all, but conduct in this life, and reward on the future day of judgment' (*NBCR*, p. 1178).

☐ STUDY 2 2 Timothy 2

1 What do verses 1–13 teach about the Christian life concerning (a) what it demands from those who embrace it, (b) the source of its strength, and (c) its final end? Seek personally to face the challenge of the illustrations which Paul uses.

2 Verses 14–26. What should be the Christian's dominant aim and purpose? What should be his attitude to (a) evil things, and (b) enemies of the truth? Note (a) what Timothy is here repeatedly told particularly to avoid; and (b) by what methods he is to seek to win back to the truth those who are misled.

☐ STUDY 3 2 Timothy 3

1 Verses 1–13. Of what are the evil traits here listed a characteristic expression? What by contrast ought true Christians to be like? How may we counter such evil tendencies (a) in ourselves, and (b) in the community to which we belong?

2 Verses 14–17. What great things can the right use of the Bible do for us? Note its contributions at each stage from (a) early childhood and its dependence on others, through (b) adolescence and its discipline, to (c) mature manhood and its active service. What must we do fully to enjoy these benefits?

☐ STUDY 4 2 Timothy 4

1 What ministry is Paul here urging Timothy to fulfil? Make a list of the main points in Paul's charge to him. How does this chapter also indicate the possibilities of failure, and its causes? What challenge ought I to find here concerning my own Christian service?

2 Consider Paul as he faces death. Note (a) his consciousness about the past; (b) his confession about, and his confidence in, the present; (c) his hope for the future. How far can and do I share his experience and his outlook? Note Paul's words in 1 Cor. 11: 1.

PART TWO

Check-list of material contained in this part (tick when completed):

LEVITICUS

Introduction

The third book of the Pentateuch was referred to by the Jews in various ways—the 'priest's law', 'priest's book', 'law of the offerings' —for Leviticus consists mainly of ritual law. The author is not named in the book. All we know is that it was given by divine revelation at Sinai in the time of Moses.

Leviticus is a book of great significance from many points of view. It provides us with a background to all the other books of the Bible. It helps us to understand references to sacrificial offerings and ceremonies of purification, or institutions such as the sabbatical year or the year of jubilee. Orthodox Jews have to this day found their binding regulations, their food laws, for instance, in this book. But it also shows us the way in which the God of Israel combats sin in Israel: first by means of His institutions of sacrifice and purification (social sin by means of the sabbatical year and year of jubilee, sexual sins by means of the laws of chastity) and second, by means of His promises and warnings. All this is of interest to Christians as showing the principles of atonement and purification applied in a particular context. In doing so it is natural that there should be many illustrations of the work of the Lord Jesus Christ. His atoning death on the cross is the reality of which the rituals of Leviticus are but pictures and symbols.

Analysis

1 – 7	The offerings.
8 – 10	Consecration of the priests.
11 – 15	Laws of cleansing.
16	Day of Atonement.
17 – 22	Various laws as to ceremonial and social purity.
23 – 25	Laws of sabbaths, jubilee, *etc.*
26	Blessings and curses and their conditions.
27	Laws of redemption.

☐ STUDY 1 Leviticus 1

God is now dwelling in the midst of His people, and gives them directions concerning their worship of Him and their communion with Him. Notice how throughout this book God is the speaker, through Moses.

1 What are the two outstanding features of the burnt offering mentioned here? See, *e.g.*, verses 3, 9, 10, 13.

2 What significance would the burnt offering have for the person making the offering? See, *e.g.*, verses 4, 9, 13, 17.

☐ STUDY 2 Leviticus 2 and 3

1 The cereal offering represents a blameless life. The purity of its ingredients is emphasized (see 2: 1, 11). The worshipper who is not blameless draws near to God with acceptance in the power of an offering possessing the perfection which he lacks. Consider how this offering is fulfilled in Christ. *Cf.* Heb. 7: 26; 1 Jn. 2: 6.

2 The peace offering speaks of communion, based on the blood of atonement (3: 1, 2), and expressed in a whole burnt offering pleasing to the Lord (3: 5). Do you know the heart-satisfaction of such a relation to God?

☐ STUDY 3 Leviticus 4: 1 – 6: 7

1 What is it that distinguishes the sin and guilt offerings from the burnt, meal, and peace offerings? See 4: 2, 13, 22, *etc.* Of what divine provision for our need are we here assured? *Cf.* Lv. 17: 11.

2 Notice particularly what was done with the body and with the blood of the sacrifice in the sin offering (4: 6, 7, 11, 12). How do these solemn ordinances indicate God's hatred of sin, and suggest some of the fearful results that may arise out of sin?

Note. The sin and guilt offerings have much in common, but the sin offering had reference rather to the person of the offender in his guilt towards God, whereas the guilt offering was an atonement for the offence especially in its relation to man. Hence the sin offering differed for different classes of persons (4: 3, 13, 22, 27); and in the guilt offering the guilty party, in addition to his offering, had also to make amends for the wrong done (5: 16; 6: 4, 5).

☐ STUDY 4 Leviticus 6: 8 – 7: 38

Distinction must be made between public and private offerings. In addition to the private burnt offerings of the people, there was a daily, public burnt offering morning and evening. *Cf.* Ex. 29: 38–42. It is this daily sacrifice that is referred to in 6: 9, 12, with directions that the fire must not be allowed to go out on the altar.

1 Neither the sacrifice nor the fire was to fail. What lessons can we learn from that? *Cf.* Heb. 6: 11, 12.

2 7: 11–21. In the peace offering the people offered to God the spontaneous gifts of their love. What were the three kinds of peace offerings which individuals might bring? What about us? *Cf.* Heb. 13: 15, 16.

Note. A 'wave offering' (7: 30) means an offering or part of an offering presented to the Lord by waving it towards Him, before receiving it back from Him. In a 'heave offering' (7: 32) the word 'heave' does not mean to throw, but to lift or take off, and indicates the part of the offering taken off for the priests.

☐ STUDY 5 Leviticus 8

Cf. Ex. 29: 44. The directions for the ceremony were given in Ex. 28 and 29; this chapter gives the account of it.

1 What is the order in which the dedication of priests and Tabernacle took place? Do you see any significance in this order?

2 In the sacrifice of the ram of ordination (*i.e.*, of dedication to special service), what special use was made of the blood? What symbolic significance does this have? *Cf.* Rom. 6: 13.

☐ STUDY 6 Leviticus 9 and 10

The Tabernacle and priests have been sanctified and dedicated; all was now ready for the normal work of the priesthood to begin.

1 What was Aaron's first offering at the start of his ministry? Though pardoned, anointed and consecrated, he still needed mercy through atoning blood. But when all was duly offered, how did God show His acceptance of His people's worship? With 9: 22a, *cf.* Nu. 6: 22–27.

2 What did Nadab and Abihu do? What happened? Why did God act like this?

Notes

1 10: 1. 'Unholy fire': this may mean fire not taken from the altar, but the central thought is that it was fire which God had not authorized.

2 10: 8–11. It has long been thought that Nadab and Abihu may have been indulging in wine; hence this prohibition.

3 The significance of 10: 16–20 seems to be that Aaron realized that Nadab and Abihu had taken part in the offering of the sin offering and that this rendered it unacceptable and unclean. This is a touching story of Aaron's full acceptance of God's verdict on his own sons.

☐ STUDY 7 Leviticus 11

1 What would the distinction between clean and unclean teach Israel about God and His worship? See verses 44, 45. Consider the

great changes in their habits that the coming of God to dwell among them brought about. *Cf.* 1 Pet. 1: 14–16; Eph. 4: 22–24.

2 How did our Lord show that such distinctions are not now binding? What constitutes defilement in God's sight? *Cf.* Mk. 7: 14–23.

☐ STUDY 8 Leviticus 12: 1 – 13: 46

1 Did the mere fact of being born a Jew give a child a place in the covenant? See 12: 3, Note 1 below, and Dt. 10: 15, 16; 30: 6. How do the principles illustrated here apply today?

2 From chapter 13 trace some of the parallels that exist between the plague of leprosy and the plague of sin.

Notes

1 12: 3. Circumcision had a twofold significance, namely, identification with God's covenant people, and purification from unfitness for such a role.
2 12: 8. *Cf.* Lk. 2: 22–24.

☐ STUDY 9 Leviticus 13: 47 – 14: 32

1 If leprosy is an illustration of sin, what is the general teaching of 13: 47–59 regarding sin-contaminated habits and practices?

2 What is the significance of the fact that the leper had to be healed before he was cleansed from the defilement of his leprosy? *Cf.* Jn. 3: 3; Gal. 6: 15.

☐ STUDY 10 Leviticus 14: 33 – 15: 33

1 How does this portion show that sin, wherever found and in whatever form, is defiling in God's sight, and prevents acceptance before Him?

2 Chapter 15 is usually taken to represent the defilement of secret sin. Notice (a) how it pollutes the whole life and all around it, and (b) that this kind of defilement requires atonement just as much as other forms of sin. *Cf.* Pss. 19: 12; 51: 6–9.

☐ STUDY 11 Leviticus 16

1 Sketch out the order of the ceremonies of the Day of Atonement.

2 What do you learn from this chapter about (a) the conditions of approach into God's presence; (b) the complete removal of sin's guilt through substitution; (c) the necessity on man's part of submission in penitence and faith to God's way of salvation?

Note. Verses 8, 10, 26. 'Azazel' means 'destruction'. This goat, upon which the lot fell for destruction, is referred to in the AV as the 'scapegoat', a term with which we are more familiar.

☐ STUDY 12 Leviticus 17

There are two main instructions in this portion: first, that all domestic animals which are to be killed shall be brought to the Tabernacle (verses 3–9); and second, that no blood must be eaten (verses 10–16). The former of these instructions points to a time when animals were not killed except in connection with worship of some kind.

1 What would this first instruction (verses 3–9) teach Israel about God? Where is it suggested in these verses that this instruction is directed against idolatrous worship?

2 Why was the eating of blood so strictly forbidden? See verse 11 in particular. What is the significance of this for us?

☐ STUDY 13 Leviticus 18

In chapters 18–20 we pass from the worship of the people to their behaviour. Chapter 18 prohibits unlawful marriage, unchastity, and Molech worship; but the last is dealt with more fully in 20: 2–5.

1 What reasons are given for Israel's obedience to these laws and how important is this obedience? See verses 1–5 and 24–30.

2 What light is thrown by this chapter upon God's command for the extermination of the Canaanites?

☐ STUDY 14 Leviticus 19 and 20

1 What particular attribute of God receives emphasis in these chapters as a ground of obedience to His commands? *Cf.* 1 Pet. 1: 14–17.

2 Which one of the ten commandments do these laws elaborate? What significant summary of the law of God is to be found here?

Note. Molech was the national god of Ammon. Great cruelty seems to have been associated with worship of him. Children were offered in sacrifice and burned with fire. Hence God's implacable opposition to all such worship.

☐ STUDY 15 Leviticus 21 and 22

1 What words and expressions occur frequently, giving the reason why these instructions are imposed? List some ways in which we ought to be showing similar concern.

2 What can we learn here about the serious effects on our Christian lives of things which are apparently small, but spiritually unclean?

☐ STUDY 16 Leviticus 23

1 List the feasts and note the general character of each. What did they have in common? And what were their differences?

2 What are the New Testament parallels to the three main feasts and what is the significance of each? (a) The Passover. *Cf.* 1 Cor. 5:7, 8. (b) The Feast of Weeks, or Pentecost. *Cf.* Acts 2:1–4. (c) The Feast of Tabernacles, the final ingathering of the harvest. *Cf.* Rev. 7:9, 10.

Notes

1 Verse 11. The sheaf of the first-fruits of the barley harvest waved on the morrow after the sabbath points to Christ's resurrection. *Cf.* 1 Cor. 15:23.
2 Verse 16. 'Fifty days': hence the name 'Pentecost', *i.e.*, the 'fiftieth' (day).
3 Verse 17. 'Two loaves of bread to be waved': the first-fruits of the wheat harvest, representing the church of Christ in its first beginnings (Jn. 12:24).

☐ STUDY 17 Leviticus 24

1 Consider the significance of the words 'pure' and 'continually' which recur in verses 1–9. Apply these words to your own worship and Christian service.

2 What attributes of God's character are set side by side in this chapter? *Cf.* Heb. 10:19–31. What constraint should such awareness put upon us?

☐ STUDY 18 Leviticus 25

1 How was the year of jubilee reckoned, and what was its genera purpose? Are there any corresponding spiritual blessings in Christ? And how may we enjoy them? *Cf.* Gal. 2:4; 5:1, 13.

2 What light is shed in this chapter on the principles governing our relationship to God and to one another in Christ? See especially verses 17, 23, 35, 36, 38, 42, 43, 55.

☐ STUDY 19 Leviticus 26

1 What spiritual blessings are promised to obedient Christians, corresponding to these promised here to an obedient Israel?

2 What are the reasons for punishment and the conditions for restoration given here? How do these apply in the Christian life?

☐ STUDY 20 Leviticus 27

Instruction as to what is to be done where an offering has been made to the Lord and the giver wants to redeem it; also a regulation about tithes.

1 What can be redeemed and what cannot be redeemed? What does this teach us about the seriousness of vows made to God? Is there any exception to the statement in verse 29? *Cf.* Ps. 49: 7–9, 15; Mk. 10: 45.

2 What does this chapter show of the Lord's character? What does He require in His people?

THE LETTER TO THE HEBREWS

Introduction

The Epistle is an exhortation and warning to Jewish believers to continue in the faith of Christ and not to fall back into Judaism. Christ is set forth as the fulfilment of Old Testament type and prophecy, and the faith and endurance of the Old Testament saints are held up as examples to believers. Needless to say, the teaching of the Epistle has a scope and value far beyond what was of immediate concern to Jewish believers of the first century. It shows the new covenant, of which Jesus, the Son of God, is Mediator, to be not only far superior to the first covenant, but the final and perfect religion, both as regards revelation (1: 1 – 2: 18) and redemption (3: 1 – 10: 18). The Epistle also contains practical teaching concerning life under the new covenant. It constitutes a divine call to all who have professed themselves Christians to see that their faith is a reality, and to continue in it, and a very definite challenge to those who have not yet put their faith in Christ. It sets forth Christ very fully in His capacity as our High Priest, shows His divine nature, and yet points out the reality of His humility and suffering as man in a way no other book does in the whole Bible, the Gospels not excepted.

Analysis

1: 1 – 2: 18	Christ the perfect Revealer, better than angels (a) as the Son of God (1: 5–14); and (b) as the Son of man (2: 15–18).
3: 1 – 10: 18	Christ the perfect Redeemer, better than Moses (3: 1–6) and better than Aaron (a) in His Person and character (4: 14 – 5: 10); (b) in the 'order' of His priesthood (7: 1–25); and (c) in His ministry (8: 1 – 9: 12) and in His offering (9: 13 – 10: 18).
10: 19 – 12: 29	Practical teaching.
13: 1–25	Final counsels and greetings.

Within this outline are contained five passages of solemn warning:

2: 1–4	Against the danger of drifting.
3: 7 – 4: 13	Against the danger of missing God's promised rest.
5: 11 – 6: 20	Against the danger of losing salvation.
10: 26–39	Against the danger of drawing back.
12: 25–29	Against the danger of refusing to hear God's final word.

☐ STUDY 1 Hebrews 1

1 Verses 1–4. List the statements made about Christ in verses 2 and 3. What do these statements tell us about His Person and work? In what ways is He greater than prophets and angels?

2 How do the scriptures quoted in verses 5–14 confirm the statement of verse 4? Define for yourself the ways in which what God says of Christ is different from what He says of angels.

Notes

1 The emphasis laid upon Christ's superiority to angels, which to us seems obvious, is explained by the fact that, to the Jews, one of the chief glories of the Old Testament revelation was that it was given through angels. See 2: 2.

2 Verse 7. Angels are created beings; they are God's servants; and their form and appearance suffer change and transformation at God's pleasure. Contrast the royal dominion and unchanging being of the Son (verses 8–12).

☐ STUDY 2 Hebrews 2

1 Verses 1–4. Why ought we to 'pay the closer attention to what we have heard' (verse 1)? Sort out the reasons here stated. Against what practical dangers is this warning directed?

2 What, according to the Scriptures (*e.g.*, Ps. 8), is man's divinely-intended destiny? How do we here see God's purpose for man being brought to its fulfilment? What path did the Son of God have to tread to make it possible for sinful men to share in this fulfilment? What, in consequence, can He now do for us?

☐ STUDY 3 Hebrews 3: 1–6

1 Verses 1, 6. Christians are here described as those who confess Christ and respond to His call. If these activities are to be fully meaningful, we must 'consider Jesus' as our 'apostle and high priest'. What, then, can Christ do for us, and what does He demand from us as (a) our Apostle, and (b) our High Priest?

2 Verses 2–5. Find three ways in these verses in which Christ is said to excel Moses.

Notes

1 Verse 1. As 'Apostle' Jesus was sent from God to men to reveal; as 'High Priest' He offered Himself for men to God to redeem and to reconcile. *Cf.* 1: 1, 2a, 3b; 2: 3, 17; 4: 14; 5: 1; 8: 1.

2 Verses 2–6. 'God's house': this refers to God's people or household, not to the Tabernacle or Temple. Now it is we Christians who are God's house. Our heavenly calling makes us 'holy brethren' in God's family (verse 1).

☐ STUDY 4 Hebrews 3: 7 – 4: 13

1 3: 7 – 4: 2. What is the danger against which we are here warned? Why were the Israelites overtaken by it in the wilderness? How may we avoid similar disaster?

2 4: 1–13. In what ways does God use His Word in His dealings with us? What promise of His still stands open for our enjoyment? What are the conditions of obtaining its fulfilment in our experience? Can any avoid having dealings with Him?

Note. 3: 12, 13; 4: 1. In each of these verses an exhortation is addressed in the plural to the many, exhorting them all to take care lest any single one of their number fall away.

☐ STUDY 5 Hebrews 4: 14 – 5: 10

1 4: 14–16. What truths concerning our Christian High Priest are we here exhorted to confess, and what consequent privileges open to our enjoyment are we here exhorted fully to possess?

2 5: 1–10. What qualifications for high priesthood are set forth in verses 1–4? How are these possessed by Christ at a higher level and in a fuller way than could ever be true of a Levitical priest? What benefit can He consequently make ours, and on what condition?

Notes

1 The order of treatment in 5: 1–4 is reversed in 5: 5–10. The three points dealt with are (a) function, (b) understanding sympathy, (c) appointment to office.

2 5: 3. Every Jewish high priest was 'bound to offer sacrifice for his own sins'. Contrast 4: 15. Jesus was sinless.

3 5: 7–9. These verses give an amazing insight into our Lord's true humanity and earthly humility.

☐ STUDY 6 Hebrews 5: 11 – 6: 8

1 5: 11–14. What is the writer's complaint about his readers? What does he imply are the conditions of spiritual growth? By these standards, considering how long I have been a Christian, by this time what ought I to be?

2 6: 1–8. What teaching constitutes the foundation of the gospel? See Acts 2: 38; 20: 21; 26: 18. What reason is given here for not laying this foundation again? What were the only possibilities now open to such people?

Notes
1 5: 11. As the writer is about to begin his exposition of the Melchizedek priesthood of Christ, he is arrested by a sense of the difficulty of expounding it to those who have become spiritually so dull of hearing.
2 5: 14. Note the practical evidence of maturity. *Cf.* Is. 7: 16.
3 6: 4–8. To understand these verses compare the writer's earlier reference to the Israelites in the wilderness. It was impossible for Moses to take them back into Egypt, and to bring them out through the Passover and the Red Sea a second time. Either they must go on with God and enter in, or come under God's judgment, and be finally shut out. See 3: 10–12.

☐ STUDY 7 Hebrews 6: 9–20

1 Verses 9–12. What gives the writer confidence concerning his readers' final salvation? In what ways does he desire to see improvement in their Christian living? Examine yourself to see in which of these characteristics you are strong or weak.

2 Verses 13–20. If we have made Christ our refuge, what three unshakable grounds of assurance have we that our confidence and hope will not disappoint us? In what ways is Jesus Himself like an anchor? What benefits does He guarantee?

Notes
1 Verses 10–12. Note the mention of love, hope and faith. *Cf.* 1 Thes. 1: 3; 5: 8.
2 Verse 12. 'Sluggish': in 5: 11 the same Greek adjective is translated 'dull'. Other renderings are 'lazy' or 'slothful'.
3 Verses 11, 12. 'Until the end'; '. . . and patience'. This is an emphasis typical of this letter. *Cf.* 3: 14; 6: 15; 10: 35, 36.

☐ STUDY 8 Hebrews 7: 1–14

1 Verses 1–10. On what grounds is Melchizedek said to be greater than Abraham and consequently superior to the Levitical priesthood? By what the scriptural record both does and does not tell us about him, in what ways is Melchizedek made to resemble the Son of God?

2 Verses 11–14. Why could not Jesus possibly be a priest after the order of Aaron? What does the promise in the Old Testament of a new order of priesthood (see Ps. 110: 4) imply concerning the existing Levitical priesthood? If the priesthood is changed, what must inevitably be changed as well?

Notes
1 Verse 1. 'This Melchizedek, king . . . priest': among the Israelites these two offices were never held by the same person.
2 Verse 2. 'First . . . righteousness, and then . . . peace': *cf.* Is. 32: 17.
3 Verse 12. The priesthood was so fundamental to the old covenant between God and His people, that any change in the order of priesthood must of necessity involve a change in the whole constitution; *i.e.*, it implies nothing less than an accompanying new, and indeed better, covenant. See 7: 22.

□ STUDY 9 Hebrews 7: 15–28

1 Verses 15–25. What are the distinctive differences between the Levitical and the Melchizedek orders of priesthood—in qualification for office, in continuance in office and in efficacy? In relation to Christ's office what is added by God's oath?

2 Verses 23–28. How do these verses show that in Jesus we have a perfect High Priest, and that He perfectly meets the sinner's need? In what ways is He unique both in Person and work?

Note. Verse 25. 'For all time': the Greek phrase means 'to the uttermost' both of time and of degree: 'completely' (RV mg.).

□ STUDY 10 Hebrews 8

1 Verses 1–6. Jews were used to seeing Levitical priests fulfil their ministry in an earthly sanctuary. As Christians they needed to appreciate that Christ's ministry is different and 'much more excellent' (verse 6). In what ways is this true? What is the significance of His being already seated at the right hand of God's throne (verse 1)? *Cf.* 10: 10–14; 4: 14–16; Eph. 4: 8.

2 Verses 7–13. Why did the first covenant fail? Was there anything wrong with it? In contrast to it, in what ways does the new covenant meet our need, give us 'better promises' (verse 6), and make success certain?

Note. Verses 10–12. Experimental progress into the enjoyment of the blessings of the new covenant is best appreciated from the bottom to the top as (a) forgiveness of sins, (b) personal knowledge of the Lord, (c) covenant relation to Him, (d) the indwelling Spirit turning the external restraint of the law into an internal constraint to do God's will.

☐ STUDY 11 Hebrews 9: 1–15

1 Verses 1–10. In what respects did the earthly sanctuary and its ceremonies come short, and for what reasons?

2 Verses 11–15. In what ways is the ministry which Christ fulfilled superior to, and more effective than, the Levitical ceremonies? List its far-reaching consequences.

Notes
1 Verse 9. 'Perfect the conscience': *i.e.*, free it from guilt and defilement, or 'purify' it (verse 14).
2 Verse 12. The Greek does not say that Christ took blood into God's presence, like the Levitical high priest took blood into the inner shrine (verse 6). Rather He entered 'through' (see RSV mg.) His own blood, *i.e.*, on the ground of His death or shed blood. For by this the veil had been rent which shut men out. *Cf.* Mk. 15: 37, 38; Heb. 10: 19–22.

☐ STUDY 12 Hebrews 9: 15–28

1 Verses 15–23. What are the reasons why Christ's death was necessary? Of what benefits can we be sure because it has occurred?

2 Verses 24–28. What differences are here indicated between what the Jewish high priest did and what Christ has done? What are the consequences of Christ's one sacrifice of Himself? How can it affect what happens to us when this life is over?

Note. Verses 15–22. According to ancient practice covenants were sealed in blood, by the symbolic introduction of the death of the parties making it. Also, once a transgression of a covenant obligation had been committed, death became necessary for a second reason, to pay the penalty of such failure. So 'without the shedding of blood there is no forgiveness of sins' (see *NBCR*, pp. 1206f.).

☐ STUDY 13 Hebrews 10: 1–18

1 Write down as many contrasts as you can find between the sacrifices of the Tabernacle and the sacrifice offered by Christ. Why did the latter succeed where the former failed?

2 What consequences of Christ's sacrifice (a) are enjoyed by Him, and (b) can be enjoyed by us?

3 To what truths does the Holy Spirit bear witness in the Old Testament passages which are here quoted?

Notes
1 Verses 5–9. The truth emphasized here is that a moral act of personal obedience has superseded ritual ceremonies, which in themselves had no inherent worth. They were only 'a shadow of the good things to come' (verse 1).

2 Verses 1, 10, 14. 'Perfected' and 'sanctified': the meaning is that by Christ's one sacrifice we are brought for ever into a perfect, unalterable relationship of acceptance with God and consecration to His service. No further offering for sin is necessary (verse 18).

☐ STUDY 14 Hebrews 10: 19–39

Having finished his doctrinal exposition, the writer proceeds to give practical counsel for the life we are to live under the new covenant.

1 Verses 19–25. How are we here exhorted to give expression to our faith, hope and love? Seek in your own life to discern ways in which these exhortations demand your obedience.

2 Verses 26–39. For those who have God-given light concerning the way of salvation, what is the only alternative to going on with God? Why are its consequences so serious? On what grounds does the writer here expect, and appeal for, the best from his readers?

Notes

1 Verse 22. As the high priest and his sons at their consecration for service in the earthly sanctuary were washed with water and sprinkled with the blood of sacrifice (Ex. 29: 4, 21), so we in 'heart' and 'body' (that is, inwardly and outwardly, in our whole being) have been 'sanctified' by Christ's sacrifice.

2 Verses 26, 29. The writer has in mind deliberate and persistent apostasy—self-chosen denial and defiance of both the Son of God and the Spirit of grace. The closing words of verse 26 mean that no second atoning sacrifice is provided for those who reject the sacrifice of Christ and His sanctifying blood.

☐ STUDY 15 Hebrews 11: 1–22

1 Faith deals with things unseen and things future, and, in particular, with the living God and His faithful doing (verses 1, 6). It is sure of the present reality of the one, and of the coming fulfilment of the other. Notice in detail how these characteristics of faith were exhibited in the lives of the individuals here mentioned. What does this teach me I need to covet if my life is to please God?

2 Verses 7–16. To what should faith in God take heed, and what does its full expression involve? Where is the crowning fulfilment of its hopes to be enjoyed? How should such awareness affect my present outlook, action, and attitude to life?

3 Verses 17–19. What apparent contradiction was involved (as Abraham at first saw it) between God's promise and God's command concerning Isaac? How did Abraham's faith in God triumph over this test, and what new hope did Abraham have in God?

☐ STUDY 16 Hebrews 11: 23–40

1 Verses 23–28. Note how Moses' faith gave him the twofold awareness and assurance emphasized in verse 1. What choices did

such faith lead him to make (a) concerning the world in which he had grown up, and (b) concerning the cost of siding with the Israelites? How ought similar faith to affect my attitude towards the interests to which I choose to devote my life?

2 Verses 28–31. What different steps and stages of faith and its expression are illustrated by these four instances? What kind of faith did the capture of Jericho demand? *Cf.* 3: 14; 6: 11, 12; 10: 35, 36. Is my faith at all weak in this last quality?

3 Verses 32–40. These verses give a summary of the achievements and the sufferings of the men and women of faith. Note that the victories are of all kinds; and that the most outstanding witness is given by the 'martyrs' who suffered and died rather than deny their faith. In what ways am I more privileged than they? Would I be ready to follow their example, or does their faith put mine to shame?

☐ STUDY 17 Hebrews 12: 1–17

1 Verses 1–4. What quality does the Christian race particularly demand? What conditions must be fulfilled if it is to be run successfully? How may I gain the help I need to finish my course?

2 Verses 5–11. For what purpose does God in His providence order some of the earthly experiences to His children? What goal has He in view for us? Upon what kind of response from us does our full enjoyment of benefit depend?

3 Verses 12–17. What dangers beset those who are spiritually slack and careless? How may a whole group be affected by one renegade? What practical steps to avoid these dangers are here (either explicitly or implicitly) given?

☐ STUDY 18 Hebrews 12: 18–29

1 Verses 18–24. List the ways in which our Christian privileges under the new covenant excel the experiences of the Israelites at Sinai. Of what ought we by faith deliberately to be conscious when we draw nigh to God through Christ and His shed blood?

2 Verses 25–29. What is here said to be impending and inescapable? How do we know this? *Cf.* Mk. 13: 31; 2 Pet. 3: 9–14. How, in consequence, ought we to live our present earthly lives?

Notes

1 Verse 23. 'The assembly of the firstborn': *i.e.*, the church (Greek, *ecclesia*) of the privileged who have a heavenly inheritance and whose names are written in heaven. *Cf.* Lk. 10: 20; Rev. 21: 27.

2 Verse 23. 'The spirits of just men made perfect': *i.e.*, either Old Testament saints, or all the faithful departed.

☐ STUDY 19 Hebrews 13: 1–8

1 List in detail the various aspects of Christian duty which are here enjoined or implied. Examine your own life and circumstances in order to discover ways in which your practical obedience is demanded.

2 Verses 5, 6, 8. What makes the Christian adequate to face every possible circumstance? Why is there for him nothing to fear, and no-one who can really harm him? For his encouragement what use may he make of the Old Testament Scriptures?

3 Verse 7. In what ways should Christian leaders, whose life on earth has ended, be remembered?

Note. Verse 1. 'Continue': *cf*. 6: 10; 10: 32–34.

☐ STUDY 20 Hebrews 13: 9–25

1 What decisive choice and action are here demanded of the first readers of this Epistle between their old Jewish associations and their new Christian allegiance? What comparable choices do those who wish to follow Christ still have to make today?

2 Verses 15, 16, 20, 21. What may we count on God to do for us, and why? What is the purpose in view? What sacrifices may we now offer in God's service? How far is this purpose finding fulfilment in my life?

☐ STUDY 21 Revision

1 Review the doctrinal teaching of this Epistle. See the Introduction and Analysis. List the ways in which what is ours under the new covenant is better than the things which the Israelites enjoyed under the old covenant. What do we have to do to gain full possession of these benefits? Why is rejection of them so serious?

2 Consider the positive exhortations to be found in the following passages: 2: 1; 4: 1, 11, 14, 16; 6: 1; 10: 22–24; 12: 1, 28; 13: 17, 22. Which of these exhortations do I particularly need to heed, and to act upon?

NUMBERS

Introduction

In the book of Numbers the narrative of Israel's journey from Egypt, interrupted at the foot of Sinai (Ex. 19) for the giving of the law, is resumed. The history, however, is throughout the book alternated with further laws and enactments. The book is a story of failure. The people are brought to the edge of the promised land, but owing to unbelief and disobedience are prevented from entering it. Then follows the long forty years of wandering in the wilderness, passed over almost in silence, except for one or two incidents. Finally, the people come again to Kadesh-barnea, the whole generation that came out of Egypt as adults being dead, with three exceptions. Their first conquests are recounted, and their destiny foretold in the mysterious prophecies of Balaam.

Analysis

1 – 4	Numbering and order of the tribes. Work of the Levites.
5, 6	Various civil and religious laws.
7 – 9	Dedication of the Tabernacle. Observance of the Passover.
10 – 12	Journeyings and complaints.
13, 14	The spies are sent into the land. The people refuse to go forward.
15	Religious laws.
16, 17	The rebellion of Korah.
18, 19	Laws concerning the Levites and concerning purification.
20, 21	Approach to the land and conquest of the Amorite kings.
22 – 25	Prophecy of Balaam, and sin at Baal-Peor.
26	Numbering of the tribes.
27 – 30	Various civil and religious laws.
31	Conquest of the Midianites.
32	Inheritance of the two and a half tribes.
33, 34	Statistics.
35, 36	Various civil and religious laws.

☐ STUDY 1 Numbers 1 and 2. Numbering and order of the tribes

1 Israel's immediate future was to be characterized by war and worship. How is this shown in chapter 1? Can the two be separated in the daily life of the Christian? *Cf.* 2 Cor. 10: 3–6; Eph. 6: 10–13.

2 What point is there in the detailed ordering of the tribes as given in chapter 2? What are the central and governing interests? *Cf.* 1 Cor. 12: 7, 11, 12; 14: 40.

☐ STUDY 2 Numbers 3 and 4. Work of the Levites

For background details concerning the tribe of Levi, see Ex. 6: 16–25; 32: 25–29; Lv. 10.

1 How was the work assigned to the Levites divided between the three 'families' of the tribe? How, if at all, might the command 'each to his task' (4: 49) apply to Christians? Do these two chapters throw any light on the possible implications of such a command? See especially 3: 5–10, 25, 31, 36, 45; 4: 46–49.

2 Whom did the Levites represent? Why did the first-born belong to God? What does 'redemption' mean in this context? Is there a New Testament counterpart which involves us?

3 How does 4: 1–20 bring out the 'frighteningly' sacred character of the Tabernacle? *Cf.* 1: 51b, 53; 2 Sa. 6: 6–11; Rev. 4: 8. What truths does this illustrate and enforce?

☐ STUDY 3 Numbers 5: 1 – 6: 21. Civil and religious laws

Many of the civil and religious laws of Israel and the rites connected with them are hard for us to understand. They may seem strangely abhorrent, sometimes inhumane or quasi-magical in character. It is important to bear in mind (a) the authority of the priest in every sphere of Israel's life, including that of cleanliness and hygiene, which were as much a part of 'religious' ceremony as the worship in the Tabernacle; (b) the background of religious rites common to the whole of the ancient Near East and used by Israel, though transformed both by her faith in the one true God, and in order to make them usable in His worship; and (c) the need that this new, God-chosen nation should be constantly reminded of the holiness and moral demands of her God.

1 What sort of people were to be 'put out' of the camp, and why? *Cf.* Lv. 13: 46; 15: 31. What interests of humanitarian justice are satisfied in the commands of 5: 11–31? These seem like purely magical rites, but note verses 16, 18, 21 and 30.

2 How did the Nazirite's separation to God find expression? What was the point of it all, since it was apparently *not* an act of service

which could be offered to God as acceptable in and of itself apart from the regular offerings of the Tabernacle? See 6: 14–16; and *cf.* Lv. 1–7 for details. How far is there a similar challenge to consecration confronting the believer in Christ? *Cf.* Heb. 9: 10–14; Rom. 12: 1, 2.

Note. 6: 2. A 'Nazirite' was a man who desired for a period to set himself apart for God in an unusual way. The Hebrew root, *nazir*, expresses the idea of separation or consecration.

☐ STUDY 4 Numbers 6: 22 – 7: 89. Dedication of the Tabernacle

1 What did it mean for Aaron and his sons to 'put' God's name 'upon the people of Israel'? How did the blessing effect this? See Dt. 28: 9, 10; Dn. 9: 18, 19; and *cf.* 1 Cor. 6: 11; 2 Cor. 13: 14.

2 Notice how often the words 'offering' or 'dedication offering' are used in chapter 7. The solemnity is emphasized by repetition. In what way is 7: 89 a fitting climax to this 'build-up'? What did it all mean to Israel? Do *we* 'offer' to God in this atmosphere of reverence? What similar climax may we expect when we thus approach God? *Cf.* Heb. 3: 7; 4: 16.

Note. 6: 26. 'Peace' (Heb. *shalom*) does not mean simply 'cessation of hostility'. It indicates 'completeness', 'perfection' or 'well-being'.

☐ STUDY 5 Numbers 8: 1 – 9: 14. Observance of the Passover

1 Chapter 8 is a re-assertion of the 'separatedness' of the Levites. How was this made clear to Israel? What is a wave offering? *Cf.* Lv. 10: 15; 23: 20; a probable meaning is 'contribution'. What was the relationship of the Levites to God, priests and people respectively?

2 9: 1–14. How is the importance of the Passover shown here? *Cf.* Ex. 12: 24–27. What are we to learn from this?

3 What do we see here of Moses' way of exercising leadership? How did he deal with practical problems when individuals brought them to him?

☐ STUDY 6 Numbers 9: 15 – 10: 36. The journeying begins again

1 Israel were made very sure of God's guidance. Without the actual symbols of cloud and fire can we claim the same assurance? *Cf.* Acts 16: 6–10; Rom. 8: 14. Why the repetition of the words 'at the command of the Lord'?

2 Notice the correspondences *and* the differences between 10: 14–28 and 2: 3–31. What is there in chapter 10 to show that, although God led and protected the children of Israel, He did not expect them to be utterly passive and to do nothing for themselves?

3 What was the significance of the trumpets (10: 1–10)? *Cf.* Lv. 23: 24; Nu. 29: 1. It has been said, 'When God remembers, He acts'. *Cf.* Gn. 8: 1; 19: 29; 30: 22.

Note. 10: 35, 36. These were the words uttered publicly by Moses at the beginning and end of each day's journey. Note their expression of dependence upon God's protection and desire for His abiding Presence.

☐ STUDY 7 Numbers 11 and 12. Complaints

1 What different attitudes are shown here by the people, the rabble, Joshua, Miriam and Aaron, and Moses? How does Moses stand out as 'different'?

2 How did God 'deal' with the various complaints made?

Note. 12: 3. 'Meek': not concerned for his own interests or prestige, and so able to pay no attention to the unfair attacks upon himself.

☐ STUDY 8 Numbers 13: 1 – 14: 10a. The spies are sent into the land

1 To what places in Canaan did the spies go? Look up Hebron and the Valley of Eshcol on a map. What were they commissioned to discover, and what report did they give?

2 What lay behind the opposing views expressed in 13: 30 and 31? Were Caleb and Joshua being unrealistically optimistic and refusing to face facts? What was the outcome of the people's fear and unbelief? Notice how *few* believed, and the frequent occurrence of the word 'all' in 14: 1–10. *Cf.* Heb. 4: 1, 2.

Note. 13: 32. 'A land that devours its inhabitants': this probably refers to the constant wars between its people, and their ferocity in internecine strife.

☐ STUDY 9 Numbers 14: 10b–45

1 What can we learn from Moses' prayer, especially concerning governing motives and grounds of appeal to God?

2 Although forgiven, the people suffered the consequences of their sin. How? In what way do they show themselves throughout this story (Nu. 13 and 14) to be typical of us?

☐ STUDY 10 Numbers 15. Religious laws

1 What do verses 1–21 teach us about making offerings which are pleasing to God?

2 Why was there no way of atonement for the person who sinned 'with a high hand'? What does this mean? *Cf.* Mk. 3: 28, 29; Heb. 10: 26–31, 39; Ps. 19: 13.

3 Notice by whom the deliberate law-breaker had to be dealt with and in what way. *Cf.* Mt. 18: 15–17; 1 Cor. 5; Heb. 12: 15. Why is such church discipline so little practised?

Note. Verse 38. 'Tassels': these were made of twisted thread and attached by a blue ribbon to the robe, to remind the wearer of the commandments of the Lord, and of his obligation to keep them.

☐ STUDY 11 Numbers 16: 1–35

1 There is evidence here of a double revolt: one by Korah (a Levite) 'and all his company' against Moses and Aaron; and one by Dathan and Abiram (Reubenites) against Moses. What was the ground of complaint in each case? See 16: 3 and 16: 13, 14. To what extent was it justified? *Cf.* Heb. 5: 4; 2 Cor. 10: 18.

2 What lay behind the revolts which made them serious enough to warrant so drastic a punishment and warning to the people? See especially verses 11, 19, 28, 30.

Note. Verse 1. That such men should lead an open revolt against the authority of Moses and Aaron meant that it was a very serious outbreak of discontent.

☐ STUDY 12 Numbers 16: 36 – 18: 7

1 How is the exclusive Aaronite priesthood strengthened and confirmed? What does the service of the priesthood involve? Notice especially 16: 48, and compare the work of Christ as great High Priest. *Cf.* Heb. 5: 1, 9, 10; 7: 25–28; 9: 11, 12, 26.

2 How could our service be transformed by thinking of it as a gift (18: 7)? *Cf.* 1 Tim. 1: 12–14; 2 Tim. 1: 6.

☐ STUDY 13 Numbers 18: 8 – 19: 22

1 What does 18: 8–32 teach us about offerings which are holy and belong by right to God?

2 What are the special features of the sacrifice described in 19: 1–10? Note the use to which the ashes were put (19: 9, 12, 17–19). What are the 'dead works' from which we need to be purified?

Notes

1 18: 19. 'A covenant of salt': *i.e.*, an indissoluble covenant. *Cf.* 2 Ch. 13: 5.
2 19: 9, 12, 17–19. The cleansing virtue of the sacrifice already made was thus symbolically stored up and applied, as need arose, to the unclean. *Cf.* Heb. 9: 13, 14; 1 Jn. 1: 7–9.

☐ STUDY 14 Numbers 20

1 Notice Moses' and Aaron's reaction to the people's discontent (verse 6). What did God desire to achieve through this incident? See verses 6, 8, 12. How did Moses and Aaron fail, and in what terms is their failure described? See verses 10, 12, 24; *cf.* 27: 14; Dt. 32: 51.

2 God's anger with Moses and Aaron may at first seem to us out of proportion to the extent of their failure. What ought we to learn from this? What ought we also to learn from the fact that even 'meek' (12: 3) Moses 'spoke words that were rash' (Ps. 106: 33)?

☐ STUDY 15 Numbers 21. Conquest of the Amorite kings

1 Israel's reaction to adversity gets a little monotonous (verse 5), and it is easy to say, 'Why cannot they learn to trust God?' But are not we often as unbelieving? Notice how Jesus uses this story (verses 6–9) as a 'type' in Jn. 3: 14, 15. What parallels are there in the condition of the afflicted and in the means of salvation in each case? Why a serpent on the pole? *Cf.* 2 Cor. 5: 21.

2 It is worth tracing Israel's journey on a map from 20: 1 onwards. Notice how circuitous it was. What evidence is there, as *against* 20: 2, 3 and 21: 4, 5, that Israel *was* learning trust and obedience through discipline? What discipline? *Cf.* Dt. 8: 2.

☐ STUDY 16 Numbers 22. The story of Balaam

This is a difficult story. Before tackling it, it will probably be helpful to read 2 Pet. 2: 15, 16; Jude 11; Nu. 31: 16 and Rev. 2: 14, which give a clue as to Balaam's true character and motives.

1 Balaam's influence and relationship to God are interesting. Think about them. Consider also Moab's fear in the face of Israel's advance. What does this show concerning the ways in which God works?

2 What was the 'chink' in Balaam's armour? Why did his 'guidance' seem all confused after that? Contrast verse 12 with verses 20, 22, 32, 35. What ought we to learn from his failure? Do you think Rom. 14: 22b, 23 and 1 Tim. 6: 9, 10 give us a similar warning?

□ STUDY 17 Numbers 23 and 24 (first study)

1 Two studies are to be given to these chapters. On this occasion concentrate attention on Balaam's oracles. Make a list of the statements in them which indicate God's special purpose for, and care of, the people of Israel.

2 Seek to appreciate the full significance of each one of these statements. What were the grounds of Balaam's assurance of Israel's victory and success? What similar grounds have we for thankfulness and wonder? *Cf.*, *e.g.*, 1 Pet. 2: 9, 10.

Note. 23: 10. 'The righteous': the word is plural, and refers here to the Israelites.

□ STUDY 18 Numbers 23 and 24 (second study)

1 What can we learn from Balaam about the demands of being a spokesman for God, and a steward or minister of His Word? Note carefully the answers which Balaam gives to Balak's suggestions. *Cf.* 1 Cor. 9: 16, 17.

2 23: 19. What is here said to make God's words different in character from those of men? When God gives us His word, of what else can we be sure? *Cf.* 1 Thes. 5: 24.

□ STUDY 19 Numbers 25 and 26

1 Chapter 25. Why was God's anger so fierce against the sins of His people? *Cf.* 1 Cor. 10: 6–12. In this situation what two complementary concerns stirred Phinehas to action? Who likewise was moved to action on our account by similar concerns?

2 Chapter 26. Compare the numbering in chapter 1. This is a new generation. See verses 64, 65. Notice which tribes had increased and which decreased. What explains the survival of Caleb and Joshua?

Note. 25: 1–5. Nu. 31: 16 and Rev. 2: 14 reveal that these developments were due to Balaam's activities. The Israelites were seduced into idolatry and immorality.

□ STUDY 20 Numbers 27 and 36. Laws of inheritance

1 What was the principle lying behind the request of the daughters of Zelophehad, and to what did the request lead? What was the importance of all this?

2 What was Moses' overriding concern before his death? How was Joshua's commission different from that of Moses? Was it inferior?

☐ STUDY 21 Numbers 28 and 29. Review of Israel's sacrifices

1 Distinguish between the daily sacrifice throughout the year offered every morning and evening (28: 3–8) and the additional sacrifices: (a) on the sabbath (28: 9, 10); (b) at the new moon each month (28: 11–15); (c) throughout the feast of unleavened bread and at the Passover itself (28: 17–25, see Note below); (d) at the Feast of Weeks (28: 26–31); (e) at the blowing of trumpets (29: 1–6); (f) on the Day of Atonement (29: 7–11); (g) at the Feast of Tabernacles (29: 12–38).

2 It was easy for these sacrifices to become mere ritual—so much so that later prophets strongly condemned their misuse. Am. 5: 21–24 and Is. 1: 11–18 give a clue as to the purpose of these offerings and to God's real requirements in and through them. *Cf.* also Heb. 10: 1–18.

Note. 28: 24. The meaning is that the sacrifices prescribed above in verses 19-22 are to be offered daily throughout the feast.

☐ STUDY 22 Numbers 30

1 How does this chapter show our responsibility in speech? *Cf.* Mt. 5: 33–37; 12: 36.

2 Do you think the woman's relationship to father and husband should be viewed as merely local Israelite custom, or is there an implied principle which holds in the twentieth century too?

☐ STUDY 23 Numbers 31. Conquest of the Midianites

1 This is another difficult passage unless you bear in mind (a) that it records only the bare outline of an event far greater in scope; (b) that it is recorded from a particular standpoint (the Midianite account was probably quite different from this one); and (c) that its message concerns a God of love who *must* purge of evil everything that is His. What are the forms of purging found in this account? In what directions ought a Christian to act with comparable severity? *Cf.* Col. 3: 5–11.

2 What does the chapter teach about sharing and giving? On what grounds were portions given to the priests and Levites?

☐ STUDY 24 Numbers 32. Inheritance of the two and a half tribes

1 What was wrong with the request of Reuben and Gad? What was the result which Moses feared might arise from it, and on what

conditions only could it be granted? Why is this event particularly significant for Israel as it arrives in the promised land, and begins to form itself into a tribal confederacy? How will its future life as a 'nation' differ from all that it has been up to now?

2 What great principle with regard to sin and its consequences is expressed in verse 23? Can you think of instances in Scripture which illustrate its working? *Cf.* Gal. 6: 7, 8.

Note. Verses 1-5. The tribes of Reuben and Gad understandably thought tha the land of Jazer and Gilead would suit their large herds of cattle. But their self-willed choice brought their descendants into constant trouble in later times. The territory lacked natural frontiers and was somewhat isolated and exposed to attack. Often in later centuries the other tribes had to come to their rescue. *Cf.* 1 Sa. 11; 1 Ki. 22: 3.

☐ STUDY 25 Numbers 33 – 35

1 What details stand out in this statistical account which make one aware of the particular interests and concerns of Moses (see 33: 2) the 'statistician'? What does he want his readers to take note of and remember?

2 The theme of entry into a promised inheritance appears several times in the New Testament. *Cf.* especially Acts 20: 32; Rom. 8: 17; Gal. 3: 29; Heb. 6: 11, 12. Heb. 11 makes it clear that our *real* inheritance, both Israel's and Christians', is a heavenly one. What does Israel's entry into its earthly inheritance teach us about preparing for and claiming our true inheritance? To what warnings ought we to pay heed?

3 What can we learn from chapter 35 concerning God's standards of judgment as regards manslaughter and murder?

Note. For consideration of Numbers 36, see Study 20 above.

MARK 1-9

Introduction

It is generally held that this Gospel was written by John Mark, the nephew of Barnabas, and is the earliest of the four Gospels. According to tradition it is based upon the teaching of the apostle Peter, whose interpreter Mark became (*cf.* 1 Pet. 5: 13), and was written in Rome for the church there. It begins with a short preliminary statement of John the Baptist's ministry, and of the baptism and temptation of Jesus, and then passes on to His public ministry in Galilee. In common with the other Gospels, it devotes a comparatively large space to Jesus' sufferings, death and resurrection.

The story centres in the confession of Peter, 'Thou art the Christ' (8: 27–29). Up to that time it tells of our Lord's activity in preaching and healing; but after the confession of Peter, Jesus makes known to the Twelve that He must suffer and die, and be raised the third day, and His face is turned towards the cross. The disciples failed to understand; and the work of Jesus in this latter half of the Gospel consists largely in teaching His disciples, and seeking to wean them from the false ideas of the kingdom which possessed their minds.

The closing verses of the Gospel (16: 9–20) do not appear to be the original ending. Some ancient manuscripts end at 16: 8, and others have a different paragraph at the close. But these verses contain the great missionary commission and have an established claim to be regarded as a part of Scripture.

Analysis

1: 1–13	The preparation.
1: 14–45	Opening of Jesus' ministry in Galilee.
2: 1 – 3: 6	Beginnings of opposition.
3: 7 – 4: 34	Important developments.
4: 35 – 6: 6	Jesus' mighty works.
6: 7–56	Crisis and culmination of the Galilaean ministry.

7: 1 – 8: 26	Conflict with the Pharisees and departure from Galilee.
8: 27 – 9: 50	The great confession. Jesus turns His disciples' eyes to the cross.
10: 1–52	Moving towards Jerusalem.
11: 1 – 12: 44	Entry into, and last days of ministry in Jerusalem.
13: 1–37	Jesus speaks of the future.
14: 1 – 15: 15	Betrayal, arrest and trial.
15: 16 – 16: 20	Death, resurrection and ascension.

☐ STUDY 1 Mark 1: 1–15

1 Why 'the gospel' (verse 1)? How is this record different from a biography? What blessings of the gospel of Christ were anticipated in the Baptist's preaching? *Cf.* Acts 2: 38. When Jesus Himself preached 'the gospel of God' what aspects of its accomplishment and enjoyment did He stress?

2 Observe how the Father, Son and Holy Spirit are all active in the events recorded—and Satan also. What does this imply concerning the issues involved in the coming story and in our own earthly lives?

Note. Note Mark's significant use of the description 'gospel'. It is of such 'good tidings' that Isaiah had explicitly written. *Cf.* Is. 40: 9-11; 52: 7–10; 61: 1–4.

☐ STUDY 2 Mark 1: 16–34

1 In what different ways does Jesus here exercise His authority? What kind of questions did such actions make people ask? On what did they repeatedly focus attention?

2 How were these Galilaean fishermen to become personal soul-winners? What were the conditions and the cost of the realization of such a surprising suggestion? Is there any reason why a similar change could not happen in my life?

Notes

1 Verse 22. The scribes quoted the great authorities. Jesus spoke as if He Himself were the supreme authority. *Cf.* 'But I say to you' (Mt. 5: 21, 22, 33, 34).

2 Verses 25–27. Jesus did not invoke God's Name like Jewish exorcists. He spoke as if the decisive authority was His own; and it 'worked'. The unclean spirits obeyed *Him.*

☐ STUDY 3 Mark 1: 35 – 2: 12

1 After the astonishing events of the preceding day Jesus had to consider what He should do next. How did He arrive at a decision,

and to what decision did He come? In what way did the healed leper's disobedience hinder Jesus' work? What bearing has this upon (a) our prayer life, and (b) the church's missionary duty? *Cf.* Jn. 20: 21; Mk. 16: 15.

2 What evidences do you find in this story in chapter 2 of our Lord's powers of discernment? What did Jesus 'see'? And when He confirmed a verbal claim, which men questioned, by a miraculous work, which none could deny, to what truths was He bearing decisive witness?

Note. 2: 4. The house would have a flat roof, which could be reached by an outside stairway (*cf.* 13: 15).

☐ STUDY 4 Mark 2: 13 – 3: 6

1 Note how, when questions were asked about His behaviour, Jesus made Himself and the work which He had come to do the sufficient justification for His action. *Cf.* 2: 6–12. What claims was He thus making for Himself?

2 Why did not Jesus' disciples stand condemned for 'doing what is not lawful on the sabbath'? Who did stand condemned for their wrong use of the sabbath in the subsequent controversy concerning the healing of the man with a withered hand? Since Jesus used the sabbath as His day, and for men's good, how ought we to use the Lord's day?

Notes

1 2: 19. The 'bridegroom' is, according to Old Testament usage, virtually a description of God in His covenant relation to His chosen people Israel. *Cf.* Ho. 2: 16–20.

2 2: 25, 26. Note the repeated phrase 'those who were *with him*'. In such company their action could not be condemned.

3 2: 23, 24 and 3: 2. The scribes taught that to pluck ears of corn was a form of *reaping* which the law did not allow on the sabbath (Ex. 34: 21); also that it was unlawful to do the work of healing on the sabbath, *unless life was in danger.*

☐ STUDY 5 Mark 3: 7–19a

1 At this stage in His ministry, what obvious dangers and what positive desires made Jesus withdraw and go up into the hills? Whom did He take with Him, and why? What were the overriding aims and the underlying strategy of His method?

2 The Twelve are first described as 'disciples' (*i.e.*, 'learners') and later as 'apostles' (see 3: 14, mg.; *i.e.*, 'men sent on a mission'). What kind of response did each calling demand? Can we become one without becoming the other? How far have you got in this sequence?

☐ STUDY 6 Mark 3: 19b–35

1 Note the official source and the evil character of the opposition which Jesus now had to meet. His reply to their accusation falls into three parts: (a) He disproves their assertion; (b) He sets forth the true explanation of His power over evil spirits; (c) He gives a solemn warning. State His argument in your own words.

2 Jesus here distinguishes His spiritual kinsmen from His human relatives. Why did the latter misunderstand Him? How do the former reveal their kinship with Him?

Notes

1 Verses 19b–21 are connected with verses 31–35. The words 'his friends' in verse 21 mean literally 'they from His home', and might be translated 'His family'.

2 Verses 29, 30. The scribes' sin was unforgivable because it was a defiant rejection of God-given light. They were knowingly calling good evil and holy unclean.

☐ STUDY 7 Revision: Mark 1–3

1 What strikes you most about Jesus in Mark's picture of Him at the beginning of His ministry? Of what truths was Jesus most concerned to make people aware? In other words, what is the essence of 'the gospel of God' which He preached?

2 What different kinds of reaction and result did the activity of Jesus provoke? To which class of people was Jesus prepared to give most? What must I be prepared to do to belong to this class? What may I then expect Him to give me?

☐ STUDY 8 Mark 4: 1–20

1 What does this parable teach concerning (a) the reasons why even the teaching of Jesus failed to produce fruit in the lives of many of the hearers; (b) the method by which the kingdom comes in this present age; (c) the criteria by which true success is measured in gospel preaching?

2 'He who has ears to hear, let him hear.' Is the Word of God finding entrance into my heart (verse 15)? Is it taking deep root (verses 16, 17)? Am I allowing some other crop to mature in my heart (verses 18, 19)? What measure of fruit is being produced in my life (verse 20)? *Cf.* Heb. 3: 7, 8.

Notes

1 A new method in Jesus' teaching begins here. The first parable is itself an indication of the purpose of teaching by parables. See verse 13. Such a method brings hearers under judgment, and finds out the truly responsive.

The real cause of blindness to the truth is unwillingness to repent and to be forgiven. Those who, as disciples, are responsive are given fuller understanding. See verse 34.

2 Verse 11. 'The secret' or 'mystery' (AV and RV): this is not something which cannot be understood. Rather it is something specially disclosed by divine revelation to those who are ready to understand it. 'The secret of the kingdom of God' is the content of the gospel of Christ. *Cf.* Eph. 3: 4; 6: 19.

☐ STUDY 9 Mark 4: 21–34

1 Verses 21–25. What is the responsibility of the hearer (a) for what he does with his knowledge, and (b) for his personal response to what he hears? What therefore are (a) the divinely intended consequences of spiritual privilege, and (b) the conditions of spiritual progress? *Cf.* Mk. 3: 14.

2 Verses 26–29. What is suggested in this parable concerning the character and purpose of (a) the first coming, and (b) the second coming into the world of the Lord Jesus? *Cf.* Ps. 126: 6. What truth do both of the parables here illustrate concerning the seed of God's word when it is sown in human hearts?

Note. Verses 26, 30. 'Kingdom': this word (particularly its Old Testament antecedent) signifies primarily 'sovereignty', *i.e.*, the sway exercised by a king, and only secondarily 'realm', *i.e.*, the sphere or territory over which he rules. 'The kingdom of God is as if . . .' (verse 26) virtually means 'the way God exercises His sway and works out His purposes among men is like this'.

☐ STUDY 10 Mark 4: 35 – 5: 20

1 4: 35–41. What were the disciples surprised at in Jesus, and what was He surprised at in them? What was He both testing and teaching by leading them into such an experience? Why did this miracle mean more to them than anything which they had yet seen Jesus do?

2 5: 1–20. Contrast men's way of treating the demoniac with what Jesus did for him. In which way is the power of evil active in my life being dealt with?

3 Why did the people 'beg Jesus to depart' (5: 17) and why did Jesus leave the healed demoniac behind? What may be the best form of witness in a home or neighbourhood that seems not to want Christ?

Notes

1 4: 40. It is significant that Jesus did not rebuke men used to sailing on the Sea of Galilee for their failure to bring Him safely through the storm.

2 5: 1–20. This happened in Decapolis, on the south-east side of the lake, in Gentile territory. The use of the title 'Most High God' (verse 7) and the local keeping of swine (verse 11) confirm this.

☐ STUDY 11 Mark 5: 21 – 6: 6a

1 These three incidents all emphasize the same necessity for any who would enjoy the experience of Christ's saving power. What is it? Why is it sometimes lacking? What must it resist?

2 Why were the disciples puzzled by the question of Jesus (5: 30, 31)? Why did Jesus wait for a trembling woman to speak in public before a crowd? What had she to give which no-one else there possessed? Do you possess it, and are you giving it—particularly before people who think that contact with Christ makes no difference?

Note. 5: 30, 31. 'Who?': this word is in the singular, *i.e.*, 'What one person?'

☐ STUDY 12 Mark 6: 6b–30

1 What can we learn (a) from our Lord's method of preparing His disciples for the work which He intended them later more fully to do, and (b) from such details as 'two by two', 'to take nothing for their journey' (*cf.* Mt. 10: 10), 'enter a house' and 'stay there', 'if . . . they refuse to hear you', 'they . . . preached that men should repent'?

2 How would you sum up Herod's character? What were the causes of this failure?

Note. 6: 7, 30. Another new beginning—the first mission of the Twelve; and so, when they return to report, they are temporarily called 'apostles' or 'missioners'.

☐ STUDY 13 Mark 6: 30–56

1 What lessons did the disciples need to learn before Christ could use them in feeding the crowd? Are there similar lessons we need to learn before we can be of use to Him?

2 Verses 45–53. It seems from the situation described here that the disciples got into difficulty as a result of obedience to Christ's command. What light does this throw upon the life of discipleship with its trials and deliverances? Why does it say in verse 48 'He meant to pass by them'? *Cf.* Lk. 24: 28, 29.

Note. Verse 48. 'The fourth watch': *i.e.*, the last watch, beginning about 3 a.m.

☐ STUDY 14 Mark 7: 1–23

1 No-one would dispute the earnestness of the Pharisees in observing genuine historical traditions, aimed at the honouring of God.

Why then should Christ use such strong language in condemning them (verse 6), and how does He show up their inconsistency?

2 Notice in verses 21–23 that Christ makes no distinction between sins of thought and sins of deed; they all alike defile a man. *Cf.* Mt. 5:28. Are we seeking deliverance from the uncleanness of an evil heart? Or, like the Pharisees, are we content with a fair appearance outwardly?

3 Verses 17, 18a. Why do you think the disciples were so slow to understand some of Christ's simplest teaching? Are we perhaps also at fault here? If so, what ought we to do about it? *Cf.* Jn. 14:26.

Notes

1 Verse 3. 'The tradition of the elders': *i.e.*, rules and regulations drawn up by past generations of scribes to guide people how to act. The Pharisees were those who made it their aim to walk strictly according to this 'tradition'. They regarded themselves, and were regarded by others, as 'the righteous'.

2 Verse 6. 'The Lord here both quotes Scripture and adds to it, thereby interpreting it' and establishing His own authority (see *Mark* (*TNTC*), p. 118).

☐ STUDY 15 Mark 7:24–37

1 Why did Jesus at first seem to refuse the woman's request (*cf.* Mt. 15:24), and why did He use such harsh words? What can we learn from her response, and from the Lord's answer to her further plea?

2 Assuming that the deaf and dumb man knew little or nothing about Jesus due to his limitations, what would the strange actions of Jesus mean to him? How would they help him to respond in faith?

3 Is there anything we can learn here about personal witness from the example of those who brought their deaf and dumb friend to Jesus?

Note. Verse 27. The term 'dogs' is an expression of contempt and disgust. In many parts of the East the dog is still basically a scavenger and by its very nature unclean and a potential carrier of disease (see *NBD* article: 'Dog').

☐ STUDY 16 Mark 8:1–26

1 What characteristic features in the Lord Jesus stand out in the miracle of 8:1–9? What special claim had this particular crowd on the Lord's provision? *Cf.* Mt. 6:33. Of what was His provision a sign?

2 Why did Christ warn the disciples to beware of the leaven of the Pharisees and of Herod (verse 15)? Why did He question them about

the miracles that had recently taken place? How do thought and reflection of this kind help us to grow spiritually?

3 Verses 22–26. What may we learn from this incident about the way and the cost of leading someone in need to experience the saving power of Christ?

Note. Verse 15. The word 'leaven' used here symbolically refers to the unseen pervasive influence of sin.

☐ STUDY 17 Mark 8: 27–38

1 Verses 27–29. What did the disciples need to understand first of all, before Jesus could begin to explain to them about His death? Why was this so important, and why were most people so slow to understand it? *Cf.* Lk. 10: 21, 22.

2 Why was Peter unable to accept Christ's teaching about His death? What is the meaning of Christ's rebuke? In this matter of a right attitude to Christ's death, on whose side are you?

3 Verses 34–38. What two alternative courses are presented to us in these verses? Why is it so important to make the right choice? What does this involve, and what does Jesus say will be the final result of a wrong choice?

Notes
1 Verse 33. 'Get behind me, Satan!' Jesus was faced with a similar temptation in the wilderness to avoid the cross. *Cf.* Mt. 4: 8–10.
2 Verse 34. For the meaning of the word 'deny', see Lk. 12: 9; 22: 34. Here it means to disown self, to refuse to recognize the claims of self as against those of Christ.

☐ STUDY 18 Mark 9: 1–29

1 Verses 1–8. What would be the significance for the three disciples of the appearance of Moses and Elijah and also of the voice out of the cloud? *Cf.* Jn. 1: 45; Lk. 24: 27. How would this new experience be likely to help and encourage them?

2 Verses 11–13. What question did the scene on the mountain raise in the minds of the disciples, and how did Jesus reply? Consider how closely John the Baptist resembled Elijah.

3 Why was Jesus so disappointed at what He found on His return to the rest of the disciples? What does this incident teach us about the chief causes of failure in our Christian witness and service (see verses 23 and 29)?

Note. Verse 24. 'I believe; help my unbelief!' This implies, 'Help me just as I am, a doubter who wants to believe.'

☐ **STUDY 19 Mark 9: 30–50**

1 Verses 33–37. How does Jesus explain the way to become spiritually great? What especially ought we to learn from the example of a little child? *Cf.* Mt. 18: 4.

2 Verses 38–41. What three reasons does Jesus give here why the disciples should not have acted as they did? Why did they fail to gain similar understanding about His teaching concerning what was going to happen to Him (verses 30–32)?

3 Verses 43–48. What spiritual truth is Jesus seeking to convey here? In what sense are we to cut off a foot, or pluck out an eye? Why may it be necessary to apply such drastic measures?

Notes

1 Verses 44, 46, 48. 'Gehenna' (Greek) is a reference to the Valley of Hinnom outside Jerusalem, where the refuse of the city was cast and burnt. It had become a synonym for 'hell', *i.e.*, the place of final ruin and destruction.
2 Verse 49. 'Salted with fire': subjected to a fiery process of discipline to purge out corruption. *Cf.* 1 Pet. 4: 17; Heb. 12: 11.

For Studies 20–35 on Mark's Gospel see p. 189.

DEUTERONOMY

Introduction

The book of Deuteronomy finds the people again on the threshold of the land after the forty years of wandering. Moses, who is about to lay down his great task, addresses them before his death. The book consists chiefly of his addresses. Naturally, there is much matter repeated from earlier portions of the Pentateuch and, just as naturally, it is generally in a rather different form. Laws that were promulgated in the wilderness are adapted for use in the land. New matter, such as that relating to the central sanctuary and the setting up of the kingdom, is introduced. Finally, Moses, after solemn warnings to the people, appoints his successor, and ascends Mount Nebo to be laid to rest by God.

Analysis

1–3 Moses reviews the events of the past 38 years, proving to them God's faithfulness to His people in spite of their disobedience and unbelief.

4–11 Moses appeals to the people to render obedience to God as the only guarantee of a happy life in the promised land.

12–26 Moses outlines in detail the code of laws which God is giving them to observe in the land. These fall into three main categories: religious (12: 1 – 16: 17); civil (16: 18 – 18: 22); social (19–26).

27–30 Moses resumes his appeal for obedience to these laws, emphasizing this by foretelling the blessings or cursings that would come upon the people according to their manner of life. All this is set out in the form of a covenant (29, 30).

31–34 The end of Moses' life and ministry, including his instructions to Joshua (31); his great hymn to God (32); his blessing on the tribes (33); and the account of his death and burial (34).

☐ STUDY 1 Deuteronomy 1

1 The burden of this chapter is the people's sin in refusing to go forward to the promised land. How is the sin described (see verses 26, 27, 32) and what made the guilt of it greater (see Note on verses 9–18; also verses 31–33)?

2 What solemn lesson is taught in verses 40–45? *Cf.* Is. 59: 1, 2; Je. 11: 14; Heb. 12: 17.

3 What does this chapter teach us about the importance of knowing history, especially Bible history? *Cf.* Pss. 78: 1–8; 44: 1–8; 1 Cor. 10: 6–13; Rom. 15: 4.

Note. Verses 9–18. These verses seem to be introduced to show that the people were both numerous and well organized when they reached Kadesh, and therefore fully ready to enter the land if their eyes had been upon the Lord.

☐ STUDY 2 Deuteronomy 2

1 What do we learn from this chapter of the sovereignty of God over the nations? *Cf.* 32: 8; Acts 17: 26.

2 Why were Edom, Moab and Ammon spared on this occasion, whereas the Amorites were exterminated? Note verses 4, 5, 9, 19; and *cf.* Am. 1: 11 – 2: 3.

3 What do verses 24 and 31 teach about the relationship between divine grace and human faith? *Cf.* Eph. 2: 8.

Notes

1 Verse 1. 'Many days': nearly thirty-eight years; *cf.* verse 14.

2 Verses 4–8. This is not the same incident as that of Nu. 20: 14–21, but a later instruction when Israel had reached the eastern border of Edom.

3 Verses 10–12 and 20–23 are parenthetical notes on ancient history.

4 Verse 30. A judicial hardening, *i.e.*, to punish one already opposed to God.

5 Verse 34. 'Utterly destroyed': 'devoted to destruction', *i.e.*, under God's curse.

☐ STUDY 3 Deuteronomy 3

1 How did the conquest of Sihon and of Og disprove the faithless fears of forty years before? *Cf.* 1: 28 with 2: 36 and 3: 4–6. What use did later generations make of the memory of these victories? *Cf.* Jos. 2: 10; Pss. 135: 10, 11; 136: 18–20.

2 What do verses 21, 22 teach us about the duty of mutual encouragement? *Cf.* how Paul sought to share his assurance (2 Tim. 1: 12) with others (Phil. 1: 6).

3 Try to imagine the intensity of Moses' desire in verses 24, 25. What insight are we given into prayer and its answer by this incident? *Cf.* Nu. 20: 12; Ps. 106: 32, 33.

4 Verse 26: 'Let it suffice you.' Moses must be content with his own place in God's work. He was the law-giver, and Joshua (Hebrew form of 'Jesus') was the conqueror. How does Jn. 1: 17 throw light on this?

Notes

1 Verse 11. 'Bedstead': or possibly 'sarcophagus'. It was eleven feet long and six broad.

2 Verses 13–15. This double division of the tribe of Manasseh greatly weakened it, thus fulfilling Gn. 48: 14ff., in which Ephraim, although the younger of the two sons of Joseph, is given priority over Manasseh.

3 Verse 29. 'Beth-peor': 'house of Peor', the Moabite god through which the people sinned (Nu. 25).

☐ STUDY 4 Deuteronomy 4: 1–40

This is the second part of Moses' first discourse, and consists of an exhortation based upon God's gracious dealings, as described in chapters 1 to 3.

1 What is said about God in this portion, and about His relation to Israel?

2 What is said about the word of God, spoken by Moses? With verse 2 *cf.* 12: 32; Pr. 30: 6; Mt. 5: 17, 18; Rev. 22: 18, 19.

3 Against what sin in particular are the people warned, and by what arguments is the warning reinforced?

☐ STUDY 5 Deuteronomy 4: 41 – 5: 33

With chapter 5 begins Moses' second discourse, extending to chapter 26 Chapter 4: 44–49 is the introductory superscription.

1 What is the significance of the pronouns 'you' and 'your' which occur throughout the ten commandments? *Cf.* Lv. 19: 3; Ps. 62: 12; Je. 17: 10 ('every man').

2 The ways in which the people reacted to the hearing of the commandments (5: 23–27) indicate abiding principles concerning the ways in which all men should react to God's law. What kind of effect do the reactions here suggest that God's law should produce? *Cf.* Heb. 12: 21; Rom. 7: 9; Gal. 3: 24.

3 What was it in the temper of the people that drew from God the words of commendation in 5: 28, and the expression of His desire that it might so continue always (verse 29)?

Note. **5: 3.** 'Our fathers': *i.e.*, 'our forefathers', *viz.* the patriarchs. *Cf.* 4: 37; 7: 8.

☐ STUDY 6 Deuteronomy 6

In chapters 6–10 Moses outlines some *general* implications of the ten commandments before proceeding to apply them in detail to *particular* situations.

1 What was God's purpose in giving the law, and what was the primary duty of the Israelite? What was he to do, and what was he to beware of and not to do?

2 Verses 10–15 concern forgetfulness of God in a time of prosperity. What ways of guarding against this danger can be found either explicit or implicit in this passage?

3 What insight is given in this chapter into the necessity and method of family religion?

Notes

1 Verse 6. 'Be upon': literally 'imprinted on'.
2 Verse 13. Alluded to by Christ in answer to Satan (Mt. 4: 10).

☐ STUDY 7 Deuteronomy 7

1 In what *four* ways were the Israelites to deal with the idolatrous inhabitants of Canaan (verses 1–5)? What points regarding the Christian's duty of separation from sin and the world do they illustrate? *Cf.* Eph. 5: 11; 2 Cor. 6: 14–18; 1 Jn. 5: 21.

2 In verses 6–11 what *three* reasons does God give the people for this drastic attitude? What New Testament principles correspond to this? *Cf.* 1 Pet. 1: 15, 16; 2: 9–12.

3 In verses 12–16 what *three* blessings does God promise will attend the faithful pursuit of this policy? What blessings are promised in the New Testament to the Christian who practises spiritual separation? *Cf.* 2 Cor. 6: 17, 18; 1 Jn. 2: 15–17.

4 In verses 18–26 how does God answer their question of verse 17? What does this teach about the power given to the Christian to 'be separate'? *Cf.* 2 Cor. 2: 14–16; Jn. 16: 33; Rom. 5: 10; 1 Jn. 5: 4.

Notes

1 Verse 2. 'Utterly destroy': the Hebrew word means 'to separate to a deity' and hence 'to put to death' or 'destroy' as here, and in verses 25, 26.

2 Verse 20. 'Hornets' are powerful insects, whose attack in large numbers is dangerous and may prove fatal. Some take the word, however, here and in Ex. 23: 28 and Jos. 24: 12, in a figurative sense, as meaning some plague or terror that spreads dismay.

☐ STUDY 8 Deuteronomy 8

1 What threefold purpose did God have in leading Israel through the experiences of the wilderness? How did our Lord apply verse 3b to His own case in Mt. 4: 4? With verse 5 *cf.* also Heb. 12: 7, 10, 11.

2 In days of prosperity what subtle danger would beset them, and how were they to guard against it? Compare the advice which Barnabas gave to the church in Antioch (Acts 11: 23b).

☐ STUDY 9 Deuteronomy 9: 1 – 10: 11

1 After they conquered the promised land, what further danger would follow on the heels of victory? How does Moses in this passage seek to safeguard them against it? *Cf.* Lk. 18: 9–14.

2 What does the example of Moses teach as to the responsibility and power of intercessory prayer? Note the costly nature of his prayer and the uncompromising dealing with sin that accompanied it. On what grounds did Moses base his plea for the people, and what was the outcome? *Cf.* Jas. 5: 16.

3 The incident as a whole demonstrates that God's dealings with His people are entirely of grace. It thus illustrates aspects of the saving grace of God revealed in the New Testament. Try to discover how the following points are illustrated in this chapter: (a) the combination of grace and justice (Rom. 3: 24–26); (b) the triumph of grace over sin (Eph. 2: 5; Rom. 5: 20, 21); (c) the provision of a mediator (Heb. 8: 6; 9: 15); (d) the establishment of a covenant (1 Cor. 11: 25).

Note. 9: 22. 'Taberah': 'burning'; see Nu. 11: 1–3. 'Massah': 'proving'; see Ex. 17: 7; *cf.* Dt. 6: 16. 'Kibroth-hattaavah': 'graves of lust'; see Nu. 11: 34.

☐ STUDY 10 Deuteronomy 10: 12 – 11: 32

Moses here uses two main arguments to persuade the people to obedience: (a) In 10: 12 – 11: 12 he shows that certain attributes and methods of God demand a corresponding response from His people. (b) In 11: 13–32 he uses the rewards of obedience and the punishments of disobedience as incentives. This raises the following questions:

1 What specifically are the attributes and ways of God particularized in 10: 12 – 11: 12 and what are their corresponding demands?

2 What rewards and punishments for obedience and disobedience are specified in 11: 13–32?

Notes

1 10: 12. 'What . . . but . . .?' does not mean these demands are slight, but that they are reasonable and to be expected in the light of God's character and His calling of Israel to be His people. *Cf.* Mi. 6: 8.

2 11: 30. 'Moreh': where the Lord appeared to Abraham; see Gn. 12: 6, 7.

☐ STUDY 11 Deuteronomy 12 and 13

See Analysis. The first part of this code of laws sets forth regulations governing the practice of religion, and is thus a detailed application of the first four commandments.

1 How does chapter 12 relate to the first commandment and chapter 13 to the second?

2 How do the regulations of chapter 13 demonstrate the priority of God's will over alleged 'results', respect of persons, ties of blood and great numbers? *Cf.* Mk. 13: 22; Gal. 1: 8; 2: 11; Lk. 14: 26; Acts 4: 19, 20.

Note. The provision of one sanctuary to which all sacrifices must be brought was a safeguard against idolatrous worship at ancient shrines of the Canaanites. *Cf.* 2 Ki. 17: 10–12.

☐ STUDY 12 Deuteronomy 14 and 15

These two chapters contain laws concerning (a) funeral practices (14: 1, 2); (b) clean and unclean foods (14: 3–21); (c) tithing (14: 22–29); (d) the seventh year or year of release (15: 1–18); (e) firstling males of the herd or flock (15: 19–23).

1 The principle underlying the laws of chapter 14 is that Christians are to behave differently from the world. What do we learn here concerning the Christian's attitude (a) to death and bereavement (verses 1, 2; *cf.* 1 Thes. 4: 13); (b) to food and bodily indulgence (verses 3–21; *cf.* 1 Cor. 6: 12, 13; 10: 23, 31); (c) to money and possessions (verses 22–28; *cf.* 1 Cor. 16: 2)?

2 What do the laws of chapter 15 teach concerning (a) redemption through Christ; (b) the Christian's duty of putting the need of his

brother before his own rights (*cf.* Mt. 5: 38–42); (c) equality in the church of God (*cf.* Acts 2: 44; 4: 34; 2 Cor. 8: 14)?

Notes

1 14: 1b. A reference to heathen mourning practices, signifying excessive grief.

2 15: 1. 'Grant a release': *i.e.*, let the debtor off.

☐ STUDY 13 Deuteronomy 16 and 17

At 16: 18 the section on the civil law commences. Here we have (a) the appointment and duties of judges (16: 18–20); (b) justice in matters of religion (16: 21 – 17: 7); (c) the final court of appeal (17: 8–13); (d) the appointment and duties of the king (17: 14-20).

1 In connection with the Feast of Weeks and the Feast of Tabernacles, what two requirements are made of the worshipper, and why? With regard to free-will offerings, on what principle is the amount of the gift to be determined? *Cf.* 1 Cor. 16: 2; 2 Cor. 8: 12; 1 Pet. 1: 8.

2 What does 17: 2–7 teach us about the need for church discipline? *Cf.* Mt. 18: 15–18; 1 Cor. 5; 1 Tim. 1: 19, 20; Tit. 3: 9–11.

3 What was to be the character of Israel's king if one were appointed, and what was to be the source of his wisdom? *Cf.* 2 Tim. 3: 15–17.

Notes

1 16: 21. The Asherah appears to have been a pole, planted by an altar, as a symbol of the god worshipped there.

2 17: 8–13. If a case is too difficult for the local judge to handle (see 16: 18–20), it is to be brought to the central sanctuary.

3 17: 16, 17. Notice the word 'multiply' three times. Horses (power), wives, and wealth were coveted by kings of the time. *Cf.* 1 Ki. 10: 26–28; 11: 3, 4.

☐ STUDY 14 Deuteronomy 18 and 19

In chapter 18 the offices of priest and prophet are included in the civil law since, Israel being a theocracy, these men were part of the government. Chapter 19 begins the section of laws governing social life, which are the detailed application of the last six commandments.

1 What were the special ministries of priests and prophets? Observe in chapter 18 how both alike were God's provision for His people's needs. Of what kind of person in heathen religion did the prophets in Israel take the place? How may we still distinguish between true and false prophets? *Cf.* Is. 8: 19, 20; 2 Pet. 1: 19; 2: 12.

2 In whom was the prophecy of 18: 18, 19 finally fulfilled? See Acts 3: 22, 23; 7: 37. Do we listen to Him as we should? *Cf.* Mk. 9: 7.

3 In what way do the regulations concerning cities of refuge both protect against injustice and at the same time enforce just penalty? See further Nu. 35.

4 How do the regulations of chapter 19 seek to apply the spirit as well as the letter of the sixth (verses 1–4), eighth (verse 14) and ninth (verses 15–21) commandments respectively?

Note. 19: 14. This law is intended to guard the inheritance of the poor against the greed of wealthy neighbours. *Cf.* 27: 17; Pr. 23: 10, 11.

☐ STUDY 15 Deuteronomy 20 and 21

These laws relate indirectly to the sixth commandment and God's requirement of perfect justice in all walks of life.

1 What general principles may be deduced from chapter 20 regarding (a) the conduct of military warfare, and (b) spiritual warfare in the army of Christ? *Cf.* Lk. 14: 25–33.

2 What illustration do these chapters give both of the compassion and of the severity of God?

3 What application do the writers of the New Testament make of 21: 22, 23? *Cf.* Jn. 19: 31; Gal. 3: 13; 1 Pet. 2: 24.

☐ STUDY 16 Deuteronomy 22 and 23

These laws are connected mainly with the sixth and seventh commandments.

1 22: 1–21. In what ways do these laws safeguard life, property and reputation, and thus put into operation the sixth commandment and the law of love to one's neighbour?

2 22: 13–30. How do these laws uphold the principle of chastity implicit in the seventh commandment? How do the laws and customs of our contemporary society compare?

3 23: 1–25. What steps were to be taken to maintain the purity of the congregation and thus of the worship of God? How is this applied in the New Testament to the church on earth and to heaven itself? *Cf.* 1 Cor. 5; Rev. 21: 27, and see Study 13.

Notes

1 22: 5. The distinction of the sexes, even in outward appearance, ought to be strictly maintained.

2 22: 9–11. Applied spiritually, these laws forbid the association of things morally incompatible; *cf.* 2 Cor. 6: 14–16.

3 22: 14, 17. 'The tokens of virginity': *i.e.*, the sheet, which became stained with blood on the first coitus.

4 23: 15, 16. The reference appears to be a slave fleeing from a foreign country, and taking refuge in a city of Israel.

☐ STUDY 17 Deuteronomy 24 and 25

1 Chapter 24. The principle behind all these regulations is that of the eighth commandment: equity and honesty in all walks of life. Make a list of the ways in which this is to be practised according to this chapter. Examine your own life by these standards in order to discover points on which you are prone to fail.

2 What application does Paul make of 25: 4? See 1 Cor. 9: 9; 1 Tim. 5: 17, 18.

3 Taking Amalek as a type of 'the flesh', that is, of our fallen carnal nature, compare what is said here with Ex. 17: 14–16; Gal. 5: 17, 24. When and where is such an enemy most likely to attack, and how ought such an enemy to be regarded by us?

☐ STUDY 18 Deuteronomy 26

This chapter concludes both the social regulations and also the whole section of the specific laws to be observed by the people in the promised land.

1 Verses 1–11: *the law of first-fruits,* to be given to God, in acknowledgment of His mercies. In what way did the law require each Israelite to reflect upon and give thanks for national mercies, and for what mercies was he specially to give thanks? Have not we far greater cause to do this? *Cf.* Ps. 103: 1–5; Col. 1: 12–14.

2 Verses 12–16: *the law of tithes,* to be given to their ministers, and to others unable to provide for themselves. Note how richly God promises to give to those who thus give to Him and to others. *Cf.* 14: 28, 29; Pr. 3: 9, 10; Mal. 3: 8–12; Lk. 6: 38.

3 Verses 16–19 are the closing exhortation of the discourse begun in chapter 5. What covenant obligations did God and Israel respectively undertake? What may we learn from these verses concerning God's purposes for us as His covenant people?

☐ STUDY 19 Deuteronomy 27: 1 – 28: 14

See Analysis.

1 What ways does God use, through His servants, Moses, the elders and the priests, to impress upon His people how absolutely He requires obedience to all the laws of chapters 5–26?

2 What abiding principles emerge from chapter 27 concerning (a) the authority of ministers to pronounce judgment on sinners in God's name (*cf.* 1 Tim. 5: 20; Tit. 1: 13; 2: 15), and (b) the failure of the law to bring life? *E.g.*, although Israel literally obeyed verses

2–8 (see Jos. 8: 30–35), they soon broke the other laws. *Cf.* Rom. 8: 2–4; Gal. 3: 10–12.

3 Contrast the nature of the blessings of 28: 1–14 with the New Testament phrase 'every spiritual blessing in the heavenly places' (Eph. 1: 3). What difference between the old and new covenants is here indicated? To what extent do the promises of Dt. 28: 1–14 still apply to us?

Note. 27: 15–26. Note that the offences mentioned here are mainly such as might escape the detection and punishment of courts of law.

☐ STUDY 20 Deuteronomy 28: 15–68

Verses 15–19 are in direct contrast to verses 1–6. Thereafter the curses are described in five paragraphs, which are somewhat similar in content: (1) verses 20–26; (2) verses 27–37; (3) verses 38–44; (4) verses 45–57; (5) verses 58–68.

1 Examine these five paragraphs, noting their similarities. What are the evils contained in these curses?

2 This chapter shows God's people brought under a judgment worse than any that has befallen a heathen nation. It was fulfilled to some degree in the Assyrian and Babylonian captivities, but mainly in the Fall of Jerusalem in AD 70, and the subsequent history of the Jews. How does this emphasize the teaching that it is better not to begin to seek God rather than subsequently to turn away? *Cf.* Mt. 12: 43–45; Heb. 2: 1–4; 10: 26–31; 2 Pet. 2: 20–22.

Note. Verse 46. 'A sign and a wonder': a sign of divine judgment, and a wonder causing astonishment.

☐ STUDY 21 Deuteronomy 29 and 30

1 Picture the moving scene described in 29: 1, 2, 10, 11, and consider what strong reasons the people had for being loyal to the Lord. Why, then, did Moses fear that they would not prove steadfast? See 29: 4, 18, 19; *cf.* Acts 20: 29, 30.

2 For what purpose is revelation given, according to 29: 29? *Cf.* Jas. 1: 22. What is God's character as revealed in chapter 30? And what is His people's responsibility?

3 Compare 30: 11–14 with Rom. 10: 6–9 and note ways in which the Old Testament law and the New Testament gospel are identical.

Note. 29: 19. 'The sweeping away of moist and dry alike': a proverbial expression meaning 'to destroy *all*'. It expresses here that the outcome of the idolater's attitude and action is utter destruction.

☐ STUDY 22 Deuteronomy 31

1 What made it possible for Israel, and what makes it possible for us, to 'be strong and of good courage' and not to 'fear or be in dread' even when great human leaders pass away? See verses 1–8 and *cf.* Heb. 13: 7, 8.

2 In how many different ways did the Lord, through Moses, seek to safeguard Israel against the backsliding which He knew, nevertheless, would take place? What alone can keep us steadfast? *Cf.* 1 Pet. 1: 5; Gal. 5: 16. *Cf.* also Dt. 32: 46, 47.

3 How does this chapter emphasize the need for something beside the law of God to promote obedience? *Cf.* Rom. 8: 3, 4; 2 Cor. 3: 5, 6.

☐ STUDY 23 Deuteronomy 32: 1–47

The analysis of this magnificent poem is as follows:
(a) The writer's purpose and hope, verses 1–3 (see Note 1 below).
(b) God's perfections, and Israel's perversity, verses 4–6.
(c) God's goodness to Israel, verses 7–14.
(d) Israel's backsliding, verses 15–18.
(e) Divine judgment upon Israel, verses 19–29.
(f) The victory of heathen nations over Israel is of God's permitting, verses 30–35.
(g) But He will finally avenge His people and show them His mercy, verses 36–43.

1 What is said of God in His essential attributes? And what, in contrast, of the nature of Israel?

2 What did God do for Israel (at least seven things are mentioned in verses 7–14), and how did Israel requite His loving-kindness?

3 What is God's purpose in His judgments, and what will be the final outcome?

Notes

1 Verse 2. 'May my teaching drop as the rain': an expression of the writer's hope that his words may act upon the hearts of men as the rain and dew upon the soil.

2 Verse 4. 'The Rock' (see also verses 15, 18, 30, 31, 37): a figure expressing the thought of a refuge and place of defence.

3 Verse 8. 'According to the number . . .': *i.e.*, He reserved for Israel an inheritance adequate to their numbers.

4 Verse 15. 'Jeshurun': a poetical name for Israel, signifying 'the upright one'. *Cf.* Dt. 33: 5, 26; Is. 44: 2.

5 Verse 29. 'Discern their latter end'; *i.e.*, discern whither their perversity must lead.

6 Verse 34. God is not unmindful of the sins of Israel's enemies.

☐ STUDY 24 Deuteronomy 32: 48 – 34: 12

Chapter 33, like Gn. 49, requires for its full understanding much research.

1 Chapter 33. Whence and why did these blessings come to the Israelites? Define for yourself the character or significance of each of the blessings here promised, and compare with them our blessings in Christ.

2 32: 48–52; 34: 1–12. Ponder (a) the character and work of Moses, and (b) the time and manner of his death. What may we learn from this record?

MARK 10 – 16

☐ STUDY 20 Mark 10: 1–16

1 Verses 1–12. What is Christ's teaching about divorce, and on what grounds does He base it?

2 Verses 13–16. No doubt the disciples were trying to be thoughtful here by guarding their Lord from unnecessary intrusion; why then was Christ so indignant? In what ways am I also in danger of obscuring Christ from those who are seeking Him?

3 Verse 15. What does it mean to 'receive the kingdom of God like a child', and why is this so essential? *Cf.* Mt. 18: 2–4.

☐ STUDY 21 Mark 10: 17–31

1 What basic wrong assumption was made by this man about salvation and eternal life? *Cf.* Eph. 2: 9. Why did Jesus stress to him the demands of the Law? What was the real hindrance that held him back?

2 Why did Jesus say it would be hard for those with riches to enter the kingdom? *Cf.* Lk. 14: 33. Are there any things in my life that are holding up spiritual progress?

3 What promises does Jesus make to those who are willing to renounce earthly wealth to follow Him without reservation? What is the meaning of the warning in verse 31? *Cf.* 1 Cor. 13: 3.

Note. Verse 25. 'There does not seem to be good early evidence for the view that the *eye of a needle* is a postern-gate in the city wall'. The phrase is better understood as a vivid description of sheer impossibility. (See *Mark* (*TNTC*), p. 165.)

☐ STUDY 22 Mark 10: 32–52

1 Verses 32–34, 45. What new aspects of His sufferings does Jesus introduce here? *Cf.* 9: 31. Why does He continue to stress this subject? Why were His disciples amazed and afraid, and what ought we to be?

2 What motives do you think were behind the request of James and John, and what was the meaning of Christ's reply to them? Do our own aims in life also reveal the same spiritual shallowness? What is the governing principle of true Christian greatness?

3 What were the progressive steps which led Bartimaeus to the recovery of his sight? What can we learn from this incident that will both guide and encourage us when trying to help those who are spiritually blind to find their way to Christ?

Note. Verse 38. The terms 'baptism' and 'cup' are sometimes used symbolically in Scripture to denote suffering which has to be endured. In this passage they are forceful reminders of the cost of following Christ. *Cf.* Lk. 12: 50; Mk. 14: 36.

☐ STUDY 23 Mark 11: 1–19

1 What truths concerning our Lord's Person are specially evident in the incidents here described? Jesus had previously refrained from publicly declaring His Messiahship. See 3: 11, 12; 8: 30; 9: 9. Why then did He declare it now?

2 Verses 1–6. When the two disciples were sent out by the Lord on this special errand, in what ways were they put to the test, and how would they benefit from the experience? Do we display the same faith and boldness in our service for Christ?

3 In what way does the fig tree described here typify Israel as a nation? What was Jesus seeking to teach His disciples from this acted parable? Before passing judgment, ought we not first to search our own hearts? *Cf.* Rom. 11: 20, 21.

Note. Verse 13. 'It was not the season for figs': it is fair to presume that the Lord was looking for the small early ripe figs that ripen with the leaves before the main crop.

☐ STUDY 24 Mark 11: 20–33

1 Verses 20–25. What does Jesus say here are the essential conditions of effective prayer? What more does prayer involve apart from just asking for pleasant things we desire? *Cf.* Mk. 14: 35, 36.

2 Why did Jesus refuse to answer the question put to Him by the Jewish leaders? What was the point of His question to them? Was He trying to be evasive? What was the root of the trouble, and how is this a warning to us? *Cf.* Heb. 3: 12.

Note. Verse 25. 'Unless we forgive our fellow men freely, it shows that we have no consciousness of the grace that we ourselves have received (Mt. 18: 32, 33), and thus that we are expecting to be heard on our own merits' (see *Mark* (*TNTC*), p. 181).

☐ STUDY 25 Mark 12: 1–27

1 Verses 1–12. How does this parable clarify Christ's unique position in relation both to God and to the prophets? What does it teach us (a) about the character of the motives which lay behind His final rejection, and (b) about His own expectation of vindication and victory?

2 Verses 13–17. How does this incident reveal both the wisdom of Christ and the insincerity of His questioners? What important truth was Jesus trying to convey to them, and of what relevance is this to us? *Cf.* Rom. 13: 1, 2, 6, 7.

3 Verses 18–27. The Sadducees were obviously attempting to make spiritual truth look ridiculous by interpreting it with the grossest of literalness. How does Christ show them their mistake? On what grounds does He base the certainty of the resurrection?

Note. Verses 1–12. Since the Lord was obviously using Isaiah 5: 1–7 as an Old Testament back-cloth for this parable, His hearers would know that He was referring to Israel, and that this was yet another parable of judgment. See *Mark* (*TNTC*), pp. 183–184.)

☐ STUDY 26 Mark 12: 28–44

1 Verses 28–34. Jesus pronounced this scribe to be 'not far from the kingdom of God'. What would he have needed to do to enter in?

2 Verses 41–44. Jesus did not deny that the rich gave much, but merely stated that the widow had given more. What does this teach us about the way God measures our giving? How do we match up to this standard? *Cf.* 2 Cor. 8: 12; 9: 7.

3 The scribes undoubtedly had an intellectual mastery of Scripture and professed to accept its authority without question. Why then

did Christ condemn them and in what way is this a warning to us? *Cf.* Lk. 12: 47, 48.

☐ STUDY 27 Mark 13: 1–23

1 Verses 1–13. Notice how Christ translates the abstract enquiry of His disciples into the personal and moral realm. What spiritua dangers does He warn them about? How can we prepare ourselves to meet similar dangers?

2 Verses 14–23. What is here foretold? How are Christ's followers to act when it happens? To whom are they to look for deliverance? Of what are they to beware? What may we learn from such a passage concerning God's sovereignty and man's responsibility?

Notes

1 Verse 14. 'The desolating sacrilege': this is the sign of the impending destruction of the Temple for which the disciples had asked (verses 1–4). It refers to the desecration of the holy place by Roman invaders. *Cf.* Dn. 11: 31.
2 Verse 15. 'Him who is on the housetop': the flat roofs of houses in Palestine were used for places of rest and social intercourse. *Cf.* Acts 10: 9.

☐ STUDY 28 Mark 13: 24–37

1 Among the many puzzling details of this passage concerning the coming of the Son of man, what are the facts about which we can be certain? What particular error do we need to avoid?

2 If we are expecting Christ to return, what difference should this make to the way we live our lives, and why? *Cf.* 2 Pet. 3: 10a, 11b, 14.

Notes

1 Verses 24, 25. The phraseology may, as in the Old Testament, symbolize national and international upheavals. *Cf.* Is. 13: 10; 34: 4; Ezk. 32: 7, *etc.*
2 Verses 33–37. 'Watch': *i.e.*, be wakeful and alert.

☐ STUDY 29 Mark 14: 1–25

1 Verses 1–9. What some said about the value of the ointment and the need of the poor was perfectly true. Why then did Jesus commend Mary for her extravagance? What does this incident teach us about right priorities in Christian service?

2 Verses 10–21. What do these verses suggest was the motive which lay behind Judas' act of betrayal? Is our own attitude one of condemnation, or are we prepared to share the solemn heart-searching of verse 19?

3 Verses 22–25. Consider the use here of the words 'bread', 'blood', 'my', 'gave', 'take', 'drank', 'covenant'. What light do they throw on the nature and method of salvation? *Cf.* 1 Pet. 1: 18, 19.

Notes

1 Verses 8, 9. Note Jesus' remarkable prediction of the future world-wide preaching of 'the gospel'; *cf.* 13: 10. There was in the woman's action a recognition both of the unique Person and of the impending work of Jesus; and these are both essential gospel truths.

2 Verse 22. The expression 'This is my body' corresponds to the Passover formula, 'This is the bread of affliction which our fathers ate in the land of affliction'. It indicates a symbolical commemoration, not an actual 'transubstantiation'.

☐ STUDY 30 Mark 14: 26–52

1 Verses 26–31. Peter evidently found it much easier to apply the Lord's words to the other disciples than to himself. What wrong attitude does this reveal? Do we ever refuse to accept what the Lord is plainly trying to teach us?

2 Verses 32–50. What caused our Lord's distress? What is meant here by 'the hour' and 'this cup'? Why was Jesus ready, in a way His disciples were not, for what had to be faced? What exactly was His petition? Was it answered. and if so, how? *Cf.* Heb. 5: 7, 8; Ps. 119: 50, 92.

☐ STUDY 31 Mark 14: 53–72

The object of the Jewish council was to find legal grounds for putting Jesus to death. It had been previously decided that He must die (14: 1), but some ground must be sought, which would justify their action in condemning Him, and enable them to secure Pilate's confirmation of the verdict. *Cf.* Lk. 23: 1, 2.

1 Verses 53–65. Note that the one definite charge, on which the decision to have Jesus put to death was taken, was His claim to be the Christ. *Cf.* 15: 26. How did Jesus declare that His claim would be vindicated? *Cf.* Acts 2: 32–36. What is your attitude to His claim?

2 Observe the experiences through which Peter passed on this eventful night. What were the contributing factors which finally led up to his denial of Christ? See 14: 29, 37, 50, 54. What can we learn from all this that will help us to be prepared for temptation?

☐ STUDY 32 Mark 15: 1–21

The main concern of the Jewish leaders now was to get their verdict carried into effect. For this they required the Roman governor's decision, for the Romans reserved to themselves the right of capital punishment.

1 What mistakes did Pilate make, and what were the reasons underlying them? Are there any of these that we are in danger of repeating? If so, what positive action can we take to avoid them?

2 Notice the amazing silence of Jesus (verses 4, 5; *cf.* 14: 60, 61a). Try, also, to picture the mocking of the soldiers, remembering that Jesus had just been scourged, a punishment of brutal severity. Why did Jesus submit without protest to such treatment, and why did God allow it to happen to Him? *Cf.* Phil. 2: 8; 1 Pet. 2: 22–24.

□ STUDY 33 Mark 15: 22–41

1 With what words did the passers-by and the chief priests and scribes mock and revile Jesus? What have you seen, which they failed to see, which makes you believe that, nevertheless, He is the Christ?

2 What is the answer to the question in verse 34? What is the significance of the rending of the veil, and what consequent benefit can we now enjoy? *Cf.* Is. 59: 2; Gal. 3: 13; Heb. 9: 8; 10: 18–22.

□ STUDY 34 Mark 15: 42 – 16: 8

1 What deliberate acts of Joseph are mentioned here? Considering who he was and the situation at the time, what qualities of character are shown by his behaviour? Which of these qualities is most lacking in my life?

2 Although the women who went to anoint the body of Christ were told that He had risen and they could see the empty tomb, and although they were given the privilege and the command to tell others, yet 'they said nothing to any one' (16: 8). Why was this? What did they still need to give them calmness, conviction and boldness in testimony? Are you at all like them?

□ STUDY 35 Mark 16: 9–20

1 What three appearances of the risen Christ are recorded in these verses? What were the reasons for the rebuke of verse 14? Is our spiritual perception and growth hindered by the same two besetting sins? *Cf.* Heb. 3: 12, 13.

2 If we truly believe what is recorded in verse 19, what challenge and encouragement are there for us in verses 15 and 20? And what does verse 16 reveal concerning the issue with which the gospel confronts men, when it is preached? *Cf.* Rom. 10: 11–15.

Note. Verses 9–20. 'This section is the so-called "Longer Ending" of Mark, omitted in some MSS. . . . Therefore it seems reasonable to see this as an early attempt, known at least as early as Irenaeus, to "round off" a Gospel whose original ending had become in some way maimed or lost' (see *Mark* (*TNTC*), pp. 257–258).

JUDGES

Introduction

The author of the book of Judges is not known. The most likely date for the completion of the book is during the reign of David or the early part of Solomon's reign (observe the favourable attitude to the monarchy implied in 19: 1; 21: 25).

The book opens with an introductory section, in two parts. The first (1: 1 – 2: 5) gives extracts from a history of the conquest, stressing the failure of many of the tribes to possess their 'lots'. It also tells how they were rebuked by the angel of the Lord. The second (2: 6 – 3: 7) shows the falling away after Joshua's death and provides a summary of the salient features of the period. The main portion of the book (3: 8 – 16: 31) gives the history of the judges, of whom twelve are mentioned, namely, Othniel, Ehud, Shamgar, Deborah, Gideon, Tola, Jair, Jephthah, Ibzan, Elon, Abdon and Samson. It will be noted that the usurper Abimelech is not included. Six of the twelve judges (Othniel, Ehud, Deborah, Gideon, Jephthah and Samson) receive extended mention, whilst the other six are little more than named (for which reason they are sometimes referred to as 'the minor judges'). The final section of the book (17: 1 – 21: 25) narrates two instances of the moral and religious declension which characterized the period of the judges. The apostasy, lawlessness and immorality which they reveal are a vivid witness to a situation when 'every man did what was right in his own eyes' (17: 6; 21: 25).

The book bears testimony to the faithfulness of God, showing both His righteousness and His enduring mercy. It contains some memorable examples of faith, and reveals also the hideous blackness of human sin. There is also much instructive teaching in it on the workings of God's providence, especially in regard to the instruments which He can use in the working out of His purposes.

Analysis

I. The incomplete conquest (1: 1 – 2: 5).

(a)	1: 1–21	The conquest of southern Canaan.
(b)	1: 22–26	The capture of Bethel.
(c)	1: 27–36	A catalogue of unoccupied territory.
(d)	2: 1–5	The effect of the broken covenant.

II. Israel in the period of the judges (2: 6 – 16: 31).

(a)	2: 6 – 3: 6	General introduction.
(b)	3: 7–11	Othniel and Cushan-rishathaim of Aram.
(c)	3: 12–30	Ehud and Eglon of Moab.
(d)	3: 31	Shamgar and the Philistines.
(e)	4: 1 – 5: 31	Deborah and Barak deliver Israel from Jabin and Sisera of Canaan.
(f)	6: 1 – 8: 35	Gideon and the Midianites.
(g)	9: 1–57	The usurper Abimelech.
(h)	10: 1–5	Tola and Jair.
(i)	10: 6 – 12: 7	Jephthah and the Ammonites.
(j)	12: 8–15	Ibzan, Elon and Abdon.
(k)	13: 1 – 16: 31	Samson and the Philistines.

III. Appendices

(a)	17: 1 – 18: 31	Micah's household and the Danite migration.
(b)	19: 1 – 21: 25	The outrage at Gibeah and the punishment of the Benjamites.

☐ STUDY 1 Judges 1: 1 – 2: 5

The many parallels between this chapter and the book of Joshua show that it is a valuable supplementary account of the conquest. It deals with events *after* the main victories had been gained, when the tribes had dispersed to attempt the occupation of their allocated territory. The opening words of the book, 'After the death of Joshua', do not necessarily relate to the events of the first chapter, but are a general title to the complete book of Judges.

1 Judah began well. Why did they fail to complete their task? Ought their advance to have been checked by 'chariots of iron'? *Cf.* Dt. 20: 1; Jos. 17: 16–18; Jdg. 4: 13–15; Mt. 9: 29; Heb. 11: 33.

2 Notice the general movement from south to north in chapter 1. Can you document a corresponding deterioration in the situation as the chapter progresses?

3 What charge did the angel of the Lord bring against Israel? What were the consequences of their failure? What may we learn from this concerning the folly of compromise? *Cf.* Heb. 12: 14–17; Rom. 6: 16.

□ STUDY 2 Judges 2: 6 – 3: 6

1 Backsliding, judgment, deliverance, renewed backsliding—trace this unvarying cycle in the history of the period, as summed up in this section. What sort of spiritual life corresponds to this in the life of the individual? *Cf.* Col. 3: 5, 6; Rev. 3: 1–3.

2 What may we learn from 2: 7, 10 and 3: 6 concerning the importance of (a) Christian example, (b) Christian teaching of the young, and (c) Christian marriage? *Cf.* Mt. 5: 13; Dt. 6: 6, 7; Eph. 6: 4; 1 Cor. 7: 39 (last clause); 2 Cor. 6: 14.

□ STUDY 3 Judges 3: 7–31

1 Observe what the Lord did *against* Israel (verses 8 and 12), and what He did *for* Israel (verses 9 and 15). What caused Him to do the first, and what caused Him to do the second? What insight does this give into the principles of God's dealings with His people? *Cf.* Pss. 34: 12–18; 103: 8–14; 2 Ch. 7: 13, 14.

2 Compare and contrast Othniel and Ehud, both in their achievements and their methods. What quality was present in both men which enabled God to use them? *Cf.* 2 Ch. 16: 9.

□ STUDY 4 Judges 4

1 Why do you think Barak was unwilling to undertake the campaign without Deborah? Does this reveal a defect in his faith? What insight does this give into God's willingness to bear with our human frailty? *Cf.* Ex. 4: 13–16; Je. 1: 6–8; 2 Cor. 3: 5, 6.

2 Who was the real architect of Israel's victory? *Cf.* Ex. 14: 13; 2 Sa. 8: 6, 14; 2 Ch. 20: 15–17. What practical application has this for us today?

□ STUDY 5 Judges 5

The story falls into four parts: (a) verses 1–5, an introductory hymn of praise; (b) verses 6–8, the situation before the deliverance; (c) verses 9–18, the rallying of the tribes and the rebuke of the irresolute; (d) verses 19–31, the victory, and the death of Sisera.

1 Observe to what dire straits backsliding had reduced the tribes (verses 6–8; *cf.* 3: 31; 1 Sa. 13: 19, 22; 2 Ki. 10: 32, 33; 13: 3, 7). What parallel spiritual consequences are found in the life of the backsliding Christian?

2 What qualities are praised in the story, and what kind of conduct is condemned? Is there a present-day application in our service for God? *Cf.* Lk. 8: 14; 9: 62; Acts 15: 26.

Note. Deborah clearly approved of Jael's act, but did God approve? It was an act of treachery which abused all the accepted conventions of the age. It may be compared with Jacob's deceit of his aged father (Gn. 27), yet in both incidents there was an element which could be approved—Jacob's earnest desire for the blessing, and Jael's zeal for her people against their oppressor. In the case of Jacob we know that he suffered severely for his treachery, although he received the blessing.

☐ STUDY 6 Judges 6

The Midianite oppression took the form of an annual invasion (for seven years, 6: 1) of hordes of semi-nomads from Trans-Jordan. This is the first indication of the use of the camel in warfare (6: 5) which gave the Midianites an immense tactical superiority. The effect upon Israel is described in verses 2, 4 and 6.

1 When the people cried unto the Lord, what was His first answer? See verses 7–10, and *cf.* 2: 1, 2; Ps. 81: 8–11; Ho. 11: 1–4, 7.

2 Gideon was called to deliver Israel from the Midianites. But first he must make a stand for God in his own house (verses 25–32). Has this a bearing upon your Christian service? *Cf.* 2 Tim. 2: 19, 21; Mk. 5: 18, 19; Acts 1: 8.

3 By what three visible signs did God strengthen Gideon's faith? Consider what these signs would teach Gideon.

☐ STUDY 7 Judges 7: 1–23

1 What other principles, in addition to that expressly stated in 7: 2, appear in the choice of few out of many to be the instrument of God's victory? In answering, observe the character defects of those rejected in the two tests. *Cf.* 1 Cor. 9: 26, 27; 10: 12.

2 Consider the transformation in Gideon's attitude from spiritless acquiescence in bondage (6: 13, 15) to a complete assurance of victory (7: 15). Do you know such confident assurance in your battle against the forces of evil? *Cf.* Rom. 8: 37; 2 Cor. 2: 14; 1 Jn. 5: 4, 5.

☐ STUDY 8 Judges 7: 24 – 8: 35

1 Note (a) Gideon's dealings with the complaints of Ephraim and with the lack of co-operation of the elders of Succoth and Penuel; (b) the vigour of his pursuit and capture of Zebah and Zalmunna, and the respect which these princes showed him. What various aspects of character are here revealed?

2 What temptation did Gideon overcome? Contrast, however, the frequent references to God's guidance in the earlier part of the

narrative with the entire absence of this in 8: 24–27. Why did Gideon, who had given such able leadership in the national crisis, fail to give adequate leadership in a time of peace? Is it true that we tend to rely upon God only when we are 'up against it'?

Note. The ephod of the high priest (Ex. 28) was a shoulder garment covering the breast and back, ornamented with gems and gold, and having in front the breastplate containing the Urim and Thummim, which were manipulated to discover God's will. Gideon's ephod (8: 24–27) may have been an elaborate reproduction, or it may have been some kind of free-standing image. In any case it was used to ascertain God's answer in a particular situation, but the people came to regard it as a kind of idol.

□ STUDY 9 Judges 9: 1 – 10: 5

1 Consider in this story (a) the sin of Gideon in associating with a Shechemite woman and having a son by her (see 8: 31; *cf.* Dt. 7: 3); (b) the sin of the men of Shechem (9: 4, 5, 16–18); (c) the sin of Abimelech (9: 1–5). Compare verses 56 and 57 and consider how in each case the words of Nu. 32: 23b were fulfilled.

2 Shechem was a Canaanite city which, most probably, had been assimilated into Israel. What does this chapter teach us about the dangers of such a compromise?

Note. Verses 7–15. The first part of the parable contains a reference to 8: 22, 23. Verse 15 presents the incongruous picture of great trees seeking shelter under a lowly bramble, and being destroyed in a forest fire which originated in the very thorn bush whose shade they had sought. The point of the parable is not that the Shechemites had chosen a king, but that they had selected the wrong person to rule over them.

□ STUDY 10 Judges 10: 6 – 11: 28

1 Why did God, at first, refuse to deliver Israel from the Ammonites? What caused the change in His subsequent attitude? *Cf.* Je. 18: 5–11.

2 What indications are there in this section that Jephthah, in spite of his unfortunate background, possessed nobility, piety and faith?

3 Summarize Jephthah's answer to the Ammonites. To what extent do you find his arguments valid?

□ STUDY 11 Judges 11: 29 – 12: 15

1 Read the story of Jephthah's vow in the light of Ec. 5: 2–6; Dt. 23: 21–23. What does this story teach about (a) the sacredness of a promise to God, and (b) the necessity of first considering what such a promise may involve?

2 Compare Jephthah's treatment of the Ephraimites with that of Gideon in a similar situation (8: 1–3). What light does this incident throw upon (a) the Ephraimites, (b) Jephthah?

Note. Whilst all earlier commentators and historians accepted that Jephthah offered up his daughter in sacrifice, well-meaning scholars from the Middle Ages onwards have tried to reduce the maiden's fate to one of perpetual virginity. But the anguish of Jephthah (verse 35), the two-month reprieve (verses 37, 38) and the institution of an annual four-day feast would be inappropriate in such a situation. The plain statement of verse 39 must be allowed to stand.

☐ STUDY 12 Judges 13

1 How did Samson's Nazirite calling differ from that of the ordinary Nazirite vow? See Nu. 6: 1–5, 13–18.

2 Observe Manoah's concern (verses 8, 12) for guidance on the subject of the upbringing of the promised child. What lessons may present-day parents learn from this? *Cf.* Pr. 22: 6; 2 Tim. 1: 5; Heb. 12: 5–11.

3 What evidences of faith do you find in Manoah and his wife? And how did the wife's faith show itself to be greater than that of her husband?

☐ STUDY 13 Judges 14 and 15

1 Note the contradictory elements in Samson's character. He was a judge in Israel, yet his life-story centres around his dubious relationships with Philistine women. His unshorn locks denoted a Nazirite consecrated to God, yet his chief aim was to please himself. How many more such contrasts can you discover? How important is it that we should be consistent in our Christian profession? *Cf.* 2 Cor. 6: 14; 1 Thes. 5: 22.

2 What does the incident of 15: 18, 19 teach regarding God's ability to supply every need of His servants? *Cf.* 1 Ki. 17: 4, 9; Phil. 4: 19.

Note. The apathetic acceptance of the Philistine yoke by the men of Judah was the most dangerous feature of this period. Samson's one-man activity was used of God to bring the danger of complete Philistine domination out into the open.

☐ STUDY 14 Judges 16

1 What may we learn from this chapter concerning (a) the folly and fruit of sin; (b) the exultation of the ungodly at the downfall of God's servants; (c) God's enduring mercy to the penitent?

2 Contrast the sad end to Samson's life with its bright dawn in the sincere desire of his parents to rear him aright (13: 8, 12). Can you suggest reasons why Samson fulfilled so little of his potential? Under what conditions is it possible for the Christian to exhibit similar powerlessness?

☐ STUDY 15 Judges 17 and 18

The story of these chapters belongs to the later period of the judges, when Philistine pressure caused the complete displacement of the tribe of Dan and forced it to migrate northwards. There is therefore a general connection with the time of Samson. The tribal league was not functioning, and Micah had no court of appeal for the wrong done to him by the Danites. The narrative shows the decline of true religion and the lawless condition of the times.

1 How would you describe the religion of Micah and of the Danites? Wherein did they fall short of true religion?

2 A Levite was supposed to be a man who stood in a special relationship to God. What impression have you formed of this particular Levite? In what respects did he fail to walk worthily of his profession? *Cf.* Is. 61: 8a; Je. 23: 11; 1 Jn. 2: 4–6.

Notes

1 17: 7. 'Of the family of Judah': the words refer to the place Bethlehem, not to the Levite, who was only a 'sojourner' in Judah. There was another Bethehem in the land of Zebulun. *Cf.* Jos. 19: 15.

2 18: 30. 'The son of Gershom': the expression need only imply a descendant, not an actual father-son relationship.

☐ STUDY 16 Judges 19

Judges 19–21 belong to the period shortly after Joshua's death. Phinehas, th grandson of Aaron, was still alive (20: 28); there is no hint of foreign oppression; the league of tribes was still functioning.

1 What does this chapter teach us of the obligations of hospitality? Are there any indications of pitfalls to be avoided? *Cf.* Heb. 13: 1, 2.

2 There are many illustrations of evil in this chapter. Make a list of the chief sins shown here, and observe how the wickedness of the men of Gibeah brought destruction upon almost their whole tribe.

☐ STUDY 17 Judges 20

1 Gibeah was a Benjamite city, and the men of Benjamin refused to deliver up their fellow-tribesmen to justice. What is the relationship between loyalty to those with whom we are connected (family, friends, business associates, *etc.*) and our loyalty to God and His commandments?

2 Note the profound effect upon the tribes of the sin of the men

of Gibeah. See 19: 30; 20: 1, 8, 11. It stabbed the people awake to the degree to which moral declension had progressed among them. Can you discover other factors which show that *some* good came out of this sordid chapter of events?

3 How would you account for the fact that the eleven tribes were twice defeated by the Benjamites, even though they had asked counsel of the Lord? What do you gather from 20: 23 about their attitude? Was it a sign of weakness, or strength?

☐ STUDY 18 Judges 21

1 The tribes recognized after their victory that in the heat of the moment they had gone too far in making the vow of 21: 1. The sense of the unity of the tribes caused great distress at the thought that one tribe was in danger of extinction, in spite of the fact that they had suffered severely at the hands of Benjamin. How did they solve their dilemma? Did they keep, or break, their second vow (21: 5)? Would you condone the action they took in verses 10–12 and 19–23? What does the whole story suggest with regard to the taking of vows?

2 To what does the writer attribute this weak and unhappy condition of things in Israel? Do you consider this an adequate explanation of the moral and spiritual condition of Israel? If not, what would you add?

---

1 PETER

Introduction

This letter is attested by very early external evidence as a genuine writing of the apostle Peter. When Peter wrote it he was 'in Babylon' (5: 13). It seems best to regard this as a reference to Rome. A probable date for the writing of the letter is AD 63.

The letter is addressed to 'the exiles of the dispersion' in Asia

Minor. But though Peter was the apostle of the circumcision, and the term 'dispersion' was ordinarily applied to the Jews scattered among the nations, the letter itself contains clear evidence that its readers at least included converted Gentiles (1: 14; 2: 9, 10; 4: 3, 4), who were addressed as the spiritual Israel dispersed among the heathen.

The letter had a double purpose: to comfort and encourage the Christians in a time of persecution actual or threatened; and to exhort them, all the more on account of this danger, to holiness of living and to hope of glory. The problem of suffering, especially the suffering of God's people, was the main subject of the book of Job, and we have met with contributions to its solution in Isaiah and in the Gospel of John. In this letter, as in Job, it is of primary importance, and here we find a noble and satisfying answer to Job's despairing questionings. Compare, for example, Jb. 10 with 1 Pet. 1: 6–9. Peter has a key to the problem which Job had not. He knew that a sinless One had suffered and died, bearing our sins in His body on the tree; so that undeserved suffering has the halo of His glory round it, and to bear it aright is to follow in the steps of the Redeemer. Also, His resurrection and heavenly enthronement (1: 21; 3: 22) are proof that suffering in the will of God leads to certain eternal reward.

Analysis

1: 1, 2	Introduction.
1: 3–12	The glorious destiny and present joy of the believer, despite suffering in this world.
1: 13–21	Therefore he must be holy, remembering at what cost he was redeemed.
1: 22 – 2: 3	The privilege of belonging to God's elect people.
2: 4–10	The expression, source and food of his new God-given life.
2: 11–17	The Christian citizen.
2: 18–25	The Christian slave; when ill-treated let him remember the example of Christ our Redeemer.
3: 1–7	The Christian wife and husband.
3: 8–12	The Christian community; how to live together.
3: 13 – 4: 7	Further advice and warning for the Christian in a hostile world, enforced by the example of Christ.
4: 8–19	Have fellowship in mutual love, use God's gifts for His glory, endure persecution patiently.
5: 1–4	The pastoral office: elders exhorted.
5: 5–11	Be humble, watchful, steadfast.
5: 12–14	Closing salutations.

☐ STUDY 1 1 Peter 1: 1–12

1 What do Christians mean by 'salvation'? How is it provided? What benefits does it offer? What kind of understanding and response are essential to its full enjoyment?

2 How can Christians 'rejoice with unutterable and exalted joy' while they 'may have to suffer various trials' (verses 6, 8)? What causes of joy does Peter enumerate in verses 3–9?

3 What light is thrown in verses 10–12 upon (a) the work of the prophets, (b) the ministry of the Spirit, and (c) the task of preachers of the gospel? What is their common interest and concern? Is it yours?

Note. Verse 2. 'Sprinkling with his blood': this signifies, for all who come under it, the ratification of the new covenant, and personal participation in its blessings and demands. *Cf.* Ex. 24: 7, 8; Heb. 9: 19–22; 12: 24; 13: 20, 21.

☐ STUDY 2 1 Peter 1: 13 – 2: 3

1 What has God provided to make possible (a) our redemption, (b) our new birth, and (c) our growth to full salvation? What response is necessary on our part to enjoy the benefits divinely intended for us?

2 In what ways ought our new God-given life as Christians to be expressed? What changes or new standards should characterize our daily living?

Notes

1 1: 17. 'With fear': *i.e.*, 'with reverence and awe'. *Cf.* Heb. 12: 28.

2 1: 17. 'Your exile': *i.e.*, your temporary sojourning in a place to which you no longer belong. *Cf.* 2: 11.

3 1: 19. 'Blood' here signifies blood shed, or life laid down, in sacrificial death.

4 2: 2. 'Spiritual milk': in Greek the adjective is *logikos*. 'Logical' milk suggests food for the mind rather than the stomach. Mention in 1: 23 of the divine 'logos' or 'word' suggests a further reference here to the same divine agent, the 'milk of the word' (AV).

☐ STUDY 3 1 Peter 2: 4–17

1 Verses 4–10. Under what figures does Peter here speak of the Christian church? What determines whether men find a place in it or not? Each figure suggests special blessings and responsibilities. Seek to identify these, and to face up to the practical challenge o each.

2 Verses 11–17. What instructions concerning worthy Christian conduct are given here? In what ways are a right attitude and

corresponding right action important (a) for our own spiritual well-being, and (b) for effective witness for God in the world? How can God use our 'good conduct'? *Cf.* Mt. 5: 16.

Notes

1 Verses 4–8. Peter justifies his comparison of Christ to a stone from three Old Testament passages: Ps. 118: 22; Is. 8: 14; 28: 16. To the believer Christ is the corner-stone on which the whole building depends; to the unbeliever He is a cause of stumbling.

2 Verse 16. 'A pretext for evil': *i.e.*, 'an excuse for base conduct' (Weymouth). *Cf.* Gal. 5: 13.

☐ STUDY 4 1 Peter 2: 18–25

1 In what ways does Christ's suffering provide an example for us to follow? What does Peter here suggest that 'servants' or 'slaves' should learn from it? Do I need to appreciate that this is also part of my Christian calling?

2 Why was the sinless Jesus willing without protest to submit to the full penalty due to the worst of sinners? What purpose was His sacrifice intended to serve? What response and what results ought to follow in my life?

Note. Verse 24. 'Bore our sins': to 'bear sin' means to 'endure its penalty'. 'On the tree': the wording suggests 'up on to the tree', *i.e.*, to the extreme limit of shameful crucifixion and, in Jewish eyes, of coming openly under the curse of heaven. *Cf.* Dt. 21: 23; Gal. 3: 13.

☐ STUDY 5 1 Peter 3: 1–12

1 Verses 1–7. What qualities in wife and husband make for a happy and harmonious wedded life? In addition, what special results can sometimes follow if the individuals concerned behave as a Christian wife or husband should?

2 Verses 8–12. What characteristics are mentioned here which should mark Christians in their relations (a) with one another, and (b) with non-Christians who work or speak evil against them? What is the way to blessing according to (a) Ps. 34: 12–16 (here quoted), and (b) our Christian calling? *Cf.* Mt. 5: 11, 12, 44, 45. Apply these standards to your own life in self-examination and prayerful concern.

☐ STUDY 6 1 Peter 3: 13 – 4: 6

1 3: 13–17. In what spirit should the Christian (a) face suffering 'for righteousness' sake', and (b) explain his faith and hope to a hostile questioner?

2 3: 18 – 4: 3. What were the nature, purpose and issue of Christ's sufferings? How, in consequence, ought we to face, and to spend, the rest of our earthly lives?

Notes

1 3: 14. Such suffering should be regarded not as one's unhappy lot, but as an added privilege. *Cf.* 4: 13, 14. It means one is the object of special divine favour. *Cf.* Lk. 1: 48. If God so wills it (3: 17), such suffering must be for some good reason and purpose. See 3: 18; 4: 1.

2 3: 18b–20. After His death on the cross Christ was at once able, as One alive in the spirit, to go and proclaim His triumph to the rebellious and imprisoned evil spirits who had involved men in sin and judgment.

3 3: 20. In the ark Noah and his family were 'saved through water', *i.e.*, brought safely through the judgment of God which fell upon a sinful world.

4 4: 6. This is best understood as meaning that this is why the gospel was preached during their earthly lives to those believers who are now dead.

☐ STUDY 7 1 Peter 4: 7–19

1 Verses 7–11. In what practical activities ought all Christians to engage? Make a brief list of them from this passage. In what way do they all start? At what end should they all aim? What is my gift (verse 10), and am I properly exercising it in ministry?

2 Verses 12–19. What kinds of suffering should the Christian (a) avoid, and (b) rejoice in? How should the latter kind of suffering be faced, and what good may be expected to issue from enduring it?

Note. Verse 14b: *i.e.*, because God will specially manifest His presence to you and with you. *Cf.* Ex. 40: 34.

☐ STUDY 8 1 Peter 5

1 Verses 1–4. How is oversight or the shepherd-care of God's flock to be exercised? What characteristics should a good pastor (a) avoid, and (b) exhibit? Note (a) how Peter speaks of himself, and (b) who is the chief Shepherd.

2 Verses 5–14. What according to these verses is 'the true grace of God', and how are we to 'stand fast in it' (verse 12)? In other words, what purpose is God working out for our good, and what must we do to co-operate with Him, and to enjoy the full enrichment of all His grace?

RUTH

Introduction

The general tone shows the setting of the story to be that of the time of the Judges. The book was read at the time of the Feast of Pentecost. The outstanding lesson of the book is the way in which the hand of God is seen guiding the faithful in the details of everyday life, as also in the events through which the way was prepared for the birth of the Son of David (see Mt. 1: 5).

Analysis

1: 1–22	Ruth's faithfulness to Naomi.
2: 1 – 4: 12	Ruth's contact with Boaz.
4: 13–22	Ruth's marriage.

☐ STUDY 1 Ruth 1 and 2

1 Put yourself in Ruth's place, and consider the cost of her decision to follow Naomi into the land of Israel. Orpah, too, had been a good daughter (1: 8), but what differences were there between her attitude and Ruth's? What lessons may Ruth teach us about our following Christ? *Cf.* Lk. 9: 23, 57–62; 14: 25–33.

2 Notice how an apparently chance happening (2: 3, 20) was overruled by God for blessing. Can you recall similar experiences? Also, in chapter 2 what qualities are outstanding (a) in Boaz, and (b) in Ruth?

Note. For the background to chapter 2 see Lv. 23: 22.

☐ STUDY 2 Ruth 3 and 4

1 How does the whole story show the Lord's loving-kindness to those who trust Him? *Cf.* La. 3: 22–26, 31–33; Na. 1: 7; Rom. 8: 28.

2 What example are we given in chapter 4 on matters affecting the rights of others?

Note. 3: 12. 'Near kinsman': the Hebrew word (*goel*, meaning 'next of kin') has a technical meaning in Hebrew law. The next of kin had certain duties and privileges, among them being that of redeeming the land or person of a kinsman who had been compelled to sell his land or himself through poverty (*cf.* Lv. 25: 25, 47–49). To draw a portion of a kinsman's mantle over oneself (3: 9) was the legal way of claiming protection and redemption. A kinsman-redeemer must be able and willing to redeem and pay the redemption price in full. *Cf.* 4: 4–6; Gal. 3: 13, 14.

---

1 SAMUEL

Introduction

The two books of Samuel formed a single work known as 'Samuel' in the Hebrew Canon. The Septuagint translators made the division. They grouped 1 and 2 Samuel with the two books of Kings to form the four 'Books of the Kingdoms'. The story is that of the development of the nation from the state described at the end of Judges to the established monarchy under David and the events of David's reign.

The chief religious theme is that Israel are the people of God, who alone is their true Ruler. First, they are rebuked for their decadence and sin by Samuel, who accedes to their demands for a king. But he warns them fully of the consequences. Saul, the sort of king the people wanted, is anointed at God's command and his history proves the danger to the nation of a self-willed leader. Finally, David is appointed and leads the people with the one aim of pursuing the will of God, until in his turn he falls into sin. The incidental events are all evidences of the inherent sinfulness of the natural man and proof of the enabling power of God granted to those who go forward in faith, as Samuel and David did. The underlying history is a continuation of that of the Pentateuch and Judges, with the theme 'a people for my name'.

Analysis

1 – 6 Eli's high-priesthood and its failure.
7 – 15 Samuel as judge; the first king rejected.
16 – 31 David during the reign of Saul.

☐ STUDY 1 1 Samuel 1

1 Verses 1–16. List the phrases describing Hannah's distress. Do you find her retaliating against her rival? How did she dispel her grief? *Cf.* Pss. 62: 8; 142: 1–3; 1 Pet. 2: 23.

2 Account for the change of verse 18b. How can a similar experience be mine? *Cf.* Mk. 11: 24; Jn. 4: 50; 1 Jn. 5: 15.

3 With verses 26–28 compare Ps. 116: 12–14; Ec. 5: 4, 5. Do you find all the encouragement you ought in the faithfulness and unforgetfulness of the Lord?

☐ STUDY 2 1 Samuel 2: 1–11

This Old Testament 'Magnificat' (*cf.* Lk. 1: 46–55) possesses an astonishing range of ideas concerning the character of God, His dealings with all sorts of men even to the ends of the earth, and the coming of His anointed king.

1 Compare the exaltation of verse 1 with the dejection of 1: 6–10. What or who should be the object of our joy? *Cf.* Pss. 9: 1, 2; 5: 11, 12; 1 Pet. 1: 8.

2 What does Hannah say about (a) God's character, and (b) the way in which time and again He reverses the lot of men? What will be the final end as described in verses 9, 10? What warning and what encouragement do you take from these truths? *Cf.* Ps. 2: 11, 12.

Note. Verse 6. 'Sheol' was the Hebrew name for the place where the dead go.

☐ STUDY 3 1 Samuel 2: 12–36. (Read also 3: 11–14)

1 What aspects of the sins of Eli's sons were specially grievous in God's sight? See 2: 12, 17, 25, 29; 3: 13. What serious warning ought we to take from 2: 25, 30 and 3: 14?

2 How did Eli fail? *Cf.* Pr. 29: 17; Mt. 10: 37. Over against 2: 31 and 3: 14 set 2: 35. What may we learn from all this concerning the ways of God? *Cf.* 16: 1.

Notes

1 Verses 12–17. The misappropriation of Eli's sons ('the men' of verse 17) was twofold. They took what they wanted rather than what was offered them; and they insisted on receiving their raw portion, before the Lord's portion—the fat (Lv. 3: 3–5)—was burned upon the altar.

2 Verses 18, 28. The 'ephod' was an item of priestly dress or equipment.
3 Verse 25. The tense shows that Eli's sons habitually did not listen to their father. Notice that it was the Lord's will to slay them for disobedience, but not the Lord's will that they should be disobedient.
4 Verse 30. 'Go in and out before me': a phrase describing the enjoyment of God's favour. *Cf.* verse 35.

☐ STUDY 4 1 Samuel 3: 1 – 4: 1a

1 Notice the expressions used about Samuel in 2: 18, 21; 3: 1, 7, 19. What new thing came into Samuel's life in the experience described in 3: 1–14? Why did Samuel have to tell the vision (3: 15–18)? *Cf.* 1 Cor. 9: 16.

2 What was lacking in Israel at this time, and what did God do to meet the need? Do you know places that need similar divine provision? *Cf.* Jn. 1: 6, 7; Lk. 3: 2, 3; Rom. 10: 14, 15.

Notes

1 3: 1. In those days there was no prophet regularly active to give the people messages from God; contrast 3: 20 – 4: 1a.
2 3: 10. 'The Lord . . . stood forth': this vivid language is paralleled in Jb. 4: 15, 16.

☐ STUDY 5 1 Samuel 4: 1b–22

1 Try to picture what a crushing blow these events were for Israel. What is the right answer to the question 'Why?' in verse 3?

2 The ark was the visible symbol of the Lord's 'glory' or manifested presence (see verses 21, 22). Why, then, did the Israelites' use of it prove unavailing? In what ways may Christians today make a similar mistake?

☐ STUDY 6 1 Samuel 5: 1 – 7: 2

1 Read the story of 5: 1–5 in the light of Je. 10: 1–16. Contrast the idols with the Lord of hosts. How ought such evidence to influence our fears and our faith?

2 Because the ark of the Lord was associated with His law (*cf.* Dt. 31: 9), it was also associated with judgment—as in this passage. Why did such a dire punishment fall on the men of Beth-shemesh, and with what result? *Cf.* Ex. 19: 21; Heb. 12: 28, 29; and see Note 2 below.

Notes

1 5: 6, 12; 6: 4, 5. The association of tumours and mice suggests an outbreak of bubonic plague.
2 6: 19. The ark, according to God's command, was to be kept closely covered, when not in the Holy of Holies. *Cf.* Nu. 4: 5, 6, 15, 20.

STUDY 7 1 Samuel 7: 3 – 8: 22

1 How does the story of chapter 7 reveal the conditions of victory even on the field of former defeats? Have you had some such experience?

2 Wanting a king was not necessarily wrong (*cf.* Dt. 17: 14, 15), especially in view of the situation described in 8: 1–3. Why then did God, while granting their request, at the same time rebuke the people for making it? Why was the desire to be 'like all the nations' (8: 5, 10) wrong? Contrast Samuel's actions with the attitude of the people.

Notes

1 7: 6. The pouring out of water symbolized separation from sin.
2 8: 7. The 'you' and 'me' in the last clauses are emphatic. The people were rejecting God (*cf.* 10: 19), as later Saul did (15: 23).
3 8: 10–18. The behaviour described is typical of oriental despots.

STUDY 8 1 Samuel 9: 1 – 10: 16

This passage describes Saul's private anointing to be king. 10: 20–24 describes his public identification by lot as the man of God's choice. 11: 14, 15 describes his public enthronement.

1 9: 1–14. What encouragement may we take from the fact that the free movements of young men and girls, of asses and God's prophet, are here overruled to bring about God's purposes?

2 What three confirmatory signs were given to Saul? How would they give him assurance that Samuel's words in 10: 1 were indeed true? How does this section also show that when God calls, He equips?

Notes

1 10: 3, 4. It was remarkable that the men should give Saul part of the offering which they probably intended to sacrifice at the sanctuary.
2 10: 8. *Cf.* 13: 8–14. The event of 11: 14, 15 is an interlude and not the visit to Gilgal referred to in 10: 8.

STUDY 9 1 Samuel 10: 17 – 11: 15

1 How does the story of Saul's public election demonstrate God's forbearance? See especially 10: 19. *Cf.* Pss. 103: 14, 15; 78: 37–39; Rom. 2: 4.

2 To what does Scripture attribute Saul's vigorous action and his success? *Cf.* Acts 1: 8. Do these verses come to you as a challenge, or a rebuke?

3 Consider what noble qualities Saul displays. See 9: 21; 10: 9, 16b, 22, 27c. Does your life give evidence of a similar work of God?

Note. 11:9. The men of Jabesh never forgot Saul's rescue of them from the Ammonites. See 31:11–13.

☐ STUDY 10 1 Samuel 12

1 What was the point of Samuel's historical recital? Unlike the Israelites, do we (a) remind ourselves constantly of the great things God has done for us, and (b) allow this reminder to have a full effect upon our behaviour?

2 What were the outstanding features in Samuel's character as seen in this chapter?

3 Summarize the counsels and warnings of verses 20–25. Note especially what Samuel says about prayer. Yet, if the people will not turn from their wicked ways, will prayer avail? See verse 25; *cf.* Je. 15:1; Ps. 99:6, 8.

☐ STUDY 11 1 Samuel 13

1 Consider the Israelites' great danger. See verses 5, 6, 19–22. In such a situation what ought they to have known to be the one indispensable and sure secret of survival and victory? See 12:14, 15.

2 What was wrong with Saul's professed desire to entreat the favour of the Lord, and with the action he took to further it? What warning do you take from the irreparable consequences following on one specific sinful act? Why does God expose men to such searching tests? See Dt. 8:2.

Notes

1 Verse 1. Some numbers are lacking here. Thirty would in each case suitably fill the gap.

2 Verse 2. Many years must have elapsed. In 9:2 Saul is described as a 'young man'. Here his son Jonathan is old enough to command a fighting force.

☐ STUDY 12 1 Samuel 14

1 How was it that Jonathan was so courageous? *Cf.* verse 6 with 2 Ch. 14:11; 1 Sa. 2:9, 10.

2 What indications do you find of Saul's impatience, and how did it lead him to hasty and wrong decisions? Yet what evidence is there that with all his self-will Saul was anxious not to offend the Lord? How do you account for this?

Notes

1 Verse 6. 'The Lord will work for us': the Old Testament is full of the God who *acts* in different ways. *Cf.* 1 Ki. 8:32; Je. 14:7; Ps. 22:30, 31.

2 Verse 24. Saul's purpose was probably religious, *viz.*, by fasting to obtain God's favour.

☐ STUDY 13 1 Samuel 15

1 Trace the course of Saul's disobedience—his excuses (verses 20, 21, 24) and his self-interest (verse 30). Trace also the course of Samuel's warning (verse 1), denunciation (verses 14, 18, 19), and declaration of divine judgment (verses 22, 23, 26, 28, 29). What may we here learn concerning God's ways and the demands of His service?

2 From verse 11, and from Samuel's reply to Saul in verses 22, 23, what do we learn concerning the divine reaction against ritual without obedience, against outward religious observance which masks an inner disobedience? Have God's requirements or His attitude changed?

Notes

1 Verse 15. The whole point about the sacred ban was that *everything* must be destroyed; not one thing must be spared or looted. *Cf.* Jos. 7: 1.

2 Verse 35. 'Samuel did not see Saul again.' 'See' here means 'visit' or 'go to see'. So 19: 24 involves no contradiction with this passage.

☐ STUDY 14 1 Samuel 16

1 How is true obedience illustrated in Samuel's behaviour? What can you learn from his example?

2 What great truth was brought home to Samuel at Bethlehem? Consider how this truth is emphasized in Jesus' teaching. See Mt. 6: 1; 7: 15, *etc. Cf.* Rom. 2: 28, 29.

3 Here men twice sent to fetch David; why? When he comes into sight, what do we learn about him? Make a list of his characteristics. What was the chief evidence that God had chosen him and rejected Saul? *Cf.* 2 Cor. 1: 22.

Note. Verses 21, 22. David became an 'armour-bearer'—possibly a military title. The phrase 'remain in my service' does not imply continued physical presence. If it did, 17: 55, 56 would be unintelligible.

☐ STUDY 15 1 Samuel 17: 1–54

1 What was it that made David view the situation differently, and gave him courage, when all the men of Israel were much afraid? *Cf.* Ps. 42: 5, 11; Is. 51: 12, 13.

2 How did David's past experiences of the Lord's deliverance give him confidence to face the present challenge? What practical lessons does this teach about (a) the value of remembering, and (b) the importance of proving God's presence and power in ordinary daily living?

3 What do you think of Saul's reasoning (verse 33), and of his provision for David (verses 38, 39)? Did he understand what he was saying, in his words to David: 'The Lord be with you!'? What was lacking? See verse 47.

Notes

1 Verses 4ff. The giant was over nine feet tall, and carried 125 lb. of armour.
2 Verse 18. 'Some token': *i.e.*, that they are well, *etc.*

☐ STUDY 16 1 Samuel 17: 55 – 19: 24

1 How were fear and jealousy like a cancer in Saul's spirit? How did they show themselves? How do you explain God's action in this matter? By what means were Saul's attempts to destroy David foiled?

2 How did Jonathan and Michal show their love for David? Do we ever risk anything for our friends? See 1 Jn. 3: 16, 18.

Notes

1 18: 5. 'Was successful': a pregnant Hebrew word is used meaning 'deal wisely' with the implied consequence of success. *Cf.* Is. 52: 13a.
2 18: 10. *Cf.* 1 Ki. 22: 22.
3 19: 13. 'An image': Hebrew 'teraphim', *i.e.*, household gods; *cf.* Gn. 31: 19. This deceived Saul's messengers into thinking that David was ill in bed.
4 19: 23, 24. 'Naked': *i.e.*, with his outer garment laid aside; *cf.* Is. 20: 2; Mi. 1: 8. Saul lay in a trance for a day and a night. The origin of the proverb about Saul is recorded in 10: 12. His behaviour here evidently caused men to recollect it.

☐ STUDY 17 1 Samuel 20: 1 – 21: 9

1 What was David's purpose in seeking Jonathan? What request did Jonathan in turn make of David? What components of true friendship does the relationship of these two men illustrate?

2 What characteristic of true 'loyal love' (20: 14) does this passage reveal? Compare it with (a) 1 Cor. 13: 4–7, and (b) your own life.

3 When human need and ceremonial obligations conflict as in 21: 6, what guidance do we find here as to the right course to take? *Cf.* Mt. 12: 3–8.

Notes

1 20: 6. Such were the standards of morality that even the best of the people seemed to have no scruples in using lies and deception to save life. See 19: 17; 20: 28, 29; 21: 2. But note how deceit brought down Saul's wrath upon Jonathan (20: 30), just as it brought disaster upon Ahimelech and his associates (22: 18, 19).
2 20: 14. *Cf.* 2 Sa. 9: 3.

3 20: 23, 42. The idea of God being between two covenant partners to watch and to judge is illustrated by Gn. 31: 49, 53.
4 20: 26. Saul thought that ceremonial uncleanness accounted for David's absence from the feast. See Lv. 7: 19, 20.
5 21: 7. 'Detained before the Lord': perhaps because of a vow.

☐ STUDY 18 1 Samuel 21: 10 – 22: 23

1 Do you gather from 21: 10–15 and 22: 3–5 that David's flights out of the holy land were done without God's guidance? What seems to have determined David's actions? Contrast 22: 23. Are you free from the fear of men? *Cf.* Pr. 29: 25.

2 Consider the character of the motley crew of which David now became the leader. Why did they turn to him? How can God today transform any group under Christian leadership? *Cf.* 1 Cor. 6: 9–11; note especially the phrase, 'such were some of you'.

3 Read the story of 22: 7–19 in the light of Pr. 6: 34; 14: 30; 27: 4. How can the Christian be zealous without being jealous? *Cf.* 1 Ki. 19: 10, 14; Jn. 2: 17.

☐ STUDY 19 1 Samuel 23 and 24

1 In what ways did God's protecting hand cover David, and what special encouragements did he receive? *Cf.* Ps. 37: 23, 24.

2 What held David back from killing Saul when it was in his power to do it, and when his followers were urging him on? What virtues shine out in his self-restraint, and what lessons do you learn from this? *Cf.* Rom. 12: 19, 20.

3 Were Saul's words and weeping accompanied by a real change of heart? *Cf.* Ho. 6: 4; Is. 29: 13. What does real repentance involve?

Notes
1 24: 13, 14. David uses the proverb to demonstrate his innocence. The wicked action one would expect from a wicked man has not been forthcoming in his case. 'A dead dog . . . a flea': something harmless, elusive, unimportant.
2 24: 20, 21. Saul apparently knew God's purpose, though he strove to avert some of its consequences.

☐ STUDY 20 1 Samuel 25 and 26

1 Nabal was rich and satisfied; but what did he lack? What, in contrast, were the outstanding features of Abigail's character? Can you think of situations where you could act as she did?

2 Chapter 26. What basic convictions motivated David's actions? How does his faith in God's purpose for him stand out? In particular, what principle emerges from 25: 39 and 26: 10, 23?

Note. 26: 19, 20. To be driven out of the promised land (*cf.* 27: 1) is to be driven out not from the dominion of the Lord (see many psalms), but certainly from His special covenanted presence to lands where other gods are worshipped.

☐ STUDY 21 1 Samuel 27 and 28

1 Contrast David's words in 27: 1 with 17: 37. Into what action did depression drive him, and what price had he to pay for it? Are you ever overcome by circumstances in this way? *Cf.* 2 Ch. 19: 2; Jas. 4: 4.

2 Looking back over the story of Saul, how did he come to his final sorry state? What warning ought we to take from his confession in 28: 15? *Cf.* 1 Tim. 1: 19.

Note. 28: 7. Consulting a medium was expressly forbidden in the law of God. See Lv. 19: 31. Saul, too, was resorting to something he himself had disowned. See 28: 9.

☐ STUDY 22 1 Samuel 29 and 30

1 Chapter 29. Into what great difficulty had David brought himself, and how was he delivered? Do I ever give the world cause to say, 'What is that Christian doing here?' *Cf.* 2 Cor. 6: 14.

2 Chapter 30. Strength in defeat and generosity in victory. How does this chapter illustrate these characteristics? Have you learnt David's secret of inner strength? *Cf.* 23: 16; Ps. 18: 2.

☐ STUDY 23 1 Samuel 31 and Revision

1 Compare the defeat of chapter 31 with that of chapter 4. What were the reasons for these defeats? *Cf.* 1 Ch. 10: 13, 14. What challenge does this bring to your own life?

2 How did David's experiences, as recorded in chapters 16–31, all serve to prepare him for his future work as king?

EPHESIANS

Introduction

This Epistle, together with Philippians, Colossians and Philemon' form a group known as the 'Prison' Epistles, because all four were' as is generally believed, written from Rome when Paul was a prisoner there, as described in Acts 28: 16, 30, 31. The words 'at Ephesus' (1: 1) are omitted in a number of important manuscripts, and this has led many to suppose that the Epistle was not intended for Ephesus alone, but for all the churches of the Lycus valley, of which the church at Ephesus was the chief.

It was God's purpose from before the foundation of the world to form a people for Himself. But mankind fell into sin and death, and only when Christ came was it revealed that God's purpose was to find accomplishment through the creation of a new humanity in Christ, made up of both Jew and Gentile, reconciled to God and to one another through the blood of the cross, and indwelt by the Holy Spirit. This 'new man' consists of the whole redeemed community of which Christ is the Head, and stands in contrast to the 'old man' whose head is Adam, and which is under the dominion of the world, the devil and the flesh, and is subject to divine condemnation.

This new humanity in Christ is the theme of the Epistle. The doctrine of individual salvation by faith, as expounded in Romans and Galatians, is here less prominent, and the apostle dwells rather upon the corporate aspects of salvation under the image of the church as the body of Christ, together with the vision of a final oneness of all things in Him.

Analysis

Theme: 'The New Humanity in Christ.'

1 – 3 God's purpose concerning His people.

4: 1 – 6: 9	Conduct befitting Christians 4: 1 – 5: 21. In relation to fellow-believers and to the world. 5: 22 – 6: 9. In family life.
6: 10–18	Conflict with the powers of evil.
6: 19–24	Final personal request, and benediction.

☐ STUDY 1 Ephesians 1: 1–14

These verses deal with God's purpose to form a people for Himself and to sum up all things in Christ. Note the reiteration of 'in Christ' or 'in him'.

1 In verses 3–6 we are shown this people as conceived in the mind of God. What do we here learn concerning God's choice of us, His gifts to us, and His purpose for us? Do such thoughts immediately move us, as they moved Paul, to say 'Blessed be . . . God'? See Note 2 below.

2 In verses 7–14 we are shown this same people in process of redemption from sin. What parts are played in this work by (a) God the Father, (b) God the Son, and (c) God the Holy Spirit? Of what benefits are we here assured? What response is necessary on our part for their enjoyment?

Notes

1 Verse 3. 'In the heavenly places': a phrase emphasizing that the believer's blessings are spiritual, in contrast to the earthly and material blessings promised to Israel under the first covenant. *Cf.* Dt. 28: 8. The phrase occurs five times in this Epistle. See 1: 20; 2: 6; 3: 10; 6: 12. It refers to what today we might term 'the spirit realm', or 'the heavenly sphere'.

2 Verses 6, 12, 14. Note the recurring reference to 'the praise of his glory'. 'The design of redemption is to exhibit the grace of God in such a conspicuous manner as to fill all hearts with wonder and all lips with praise' (Charles Hodge).

3 Verse 13. 'Sealed': a mark of God's ownership.

4 Verse 14. 'Guarantee' or 'earnest' (AV, RV): a first instalment given as a pledge that all promised will be paid in full.

☐ STUDY 2 Ephesians 1: 15–23

1 What may we learn from this example concerning the way to pray for our fellow-Christians? When we do so, what ought to be our chief interest and concern? What are the three great spiritual truths which the apostle here prays that his readers may grasp?

2 Consider Christ's present position as set forth in verses 20–23 in relation to (a) God, (b) other powers and authorities, (c) the universe, and (d) the church. In the light of these verses has our conception of Christ been big enough?

Notes

1 Verse 18. 'His glorious inheritance in the saints': be careful to note that this is a reference not to our inheritance in Him but to His inheritance in us. *Cf.* Ex. 19: 5, 6; Tit. 2: 14.

2 Verses 22, 23. 'The church, . . . his body, the fulness of him': as God of old dwelt in the Temple and filled it with His glory, or as the fullness of the Godhead dwells in Jesus (Col. 1: 19; 2: 9, 10), so Christ now dwells in His church in His fullness. He fills it with His presence.

☐ STUDY 3 Ephesians 2

1 Verses 1–10. Work out the contrast between man's condition by nature and his position in Christ. What are we here said to be saved (a) from, and (b) for, or to enjoy? How has this amazing change been effected, and how does its enjoyment become ours?

2 Verses 11–22. Before Christ came, Jew and Gentile remained separate—kept apart in the Temple courts by a 'dividing wall' (verse 14). How did God deal with this situation through Christ's coming? What is now the position of believers, whether Jews or Gentiles, in relation to (a) God, and (b) one another? What three metaphors are used in verses 19–22 to show the complete equality of privilege which Gentile believers enjoy in Christ with those of Jewish birth?

Note. Verses 2, 3. 'Sons of disobedience', 'children of wrath': these phrases follow in their form Hebrew idioms. They describe those who are deliberately giving themselves to active rebellion against the will of God, and consequently are exposed to His active displeasure.

☐ STUDY 4 Ephesians 3

The apostle shows that the union of Jews and Gentiles in one body in Christ was in God's purpose from the beginning, though only now fully revealed to men.

1 Verses 1–13. What were Paul's personal calling and commission in relation to (a) the gospel, and (b) the Gentiles? Why was he chosen, and how was he qualified, for such service? Do you share his conviction that to suffer in such a cause is something to glory in rather than to be depressed about?

2 Verses 14–21. Trace the progressive stages in Paul's prayer for his readers. What blessings would its full answer bring into our lives? What guarantees that such an answer is more than possible? What ought we also to learn concerning the way to pray for our fellow-Christians?

3 What are the things included in the eternal purpose of God in Christ, in which Paul and all members of Christ's church are called to share? How may we more fully enter into our calling?

Notes

1 Verse 1. *Cf.* 6: 19, 20. Paul knew that his imprisonment was in the will of God, and in the interests of the truth and the spread of the gospel.

2 Verses 2 and 9. 'Stewardship', 'plan': Greek *oikonomia*. The word refers originally to household management. In verse 9 (*cf.* 1: 10), the reference is to God's administration, to His working out of His purpose in Christ. In verse 2, it is used of Paul's part in this—*i.e.*, of the special commission assigned to Paul. *Cf.* 1 Cor. 9: 16, 17.

3 Verses 3, 4, 9. 'The mystery': *i.e.*, divine truth hidden from natural discovery by men, but now specially revealed by the Spirit—particularly here the full content of God's plan for men's salvation.

☐ STUDY 5 Ephesians 4: 1 – 5: 2

1 Express in your own words the difference between the unity described in 4: 3–7, as already existing among Christians, and that mentioned in 4: 13–16, which Christians are to seek. How is the first to be preserved and how is the second to be attained?

2 From 4: 25 – 5: 2 list the things which must be put away, and those which ought to take their place. Notice also in each case the reason given by the apostle why we must live thus.

3 In what ways does Paul's fourfold description of the life of the Gentile world (4: 17–19) apply to the life of the non-Christian today? In contrast, what three principles are to govern the behaviour of Christians (4: 20–24)?

Notes

1 Verse 7. 'Grace': used here, as also in 3: 2, 8, of God's gifts to His people in Christ in appointing them to His special work. *Cf.* Mk. 13: 34; Mt. 25: 14, 15.

2 Verse 12 should be read with the first comma omitted, 'for the equipment of the saints for the work of ministry'.

3 Verses 22–24. The tenses in the Greek show that the 'putting off' of the old man and 'putting on' of the new are definite acts, whereas the 'being renewed' is a process. The living of this new Christian life is made possible for us through the continual renewing of the Spirit, enabling our minds to lay hold of the truth in Christ.

4 Verses 26, 27. While there may be anger which is not sin, anger is dangerous. It may lead to some action which gives the devil scope to strike a blow at the body of Christ.

☐ STUDY 6 Ephesians 5: 3 – 6: 9

1 5: 3–20. What are the positive motives and guiding principles of worthy Christian action, which the apostle here emphasizes? Add further items to your list (from Study 5) of actions, words and thoughts which ought (a) to be abandoned, and (b) to be expressed. Test your own life in this light. Why is constant watchfulness so necessary? What help does God give to make such living possible?

2 5: 21 – 6: 9. The opening verse states a governing principle. Consider how it is here applied to the common personal relations of everyday life—particularly those of wives, children and servants. What are the distinctive complementary responsibilities of husbands, parents and masters? Particularly notice in each case how the person concerned is in his (or her) action to relate himself (or herself) to Christ.

3 5: 23–32. Study in detail what we are here told concerning the relation between Christ and His church. What is the goal in view? How is it reached and realized?

Notes

1 5: 14. Paul is here possibly quoting from a Christian hymn, addressed to those who have not yet believed in Christ. *Cf.* Is. 60: 1.

2 5: 26. 'The washing of water with the word': here some simply compare Jn. 15: 3; 17: 17, but the majority recognize a reference to baptism. 'The word' may then refer to (a) the gospel preached, *cf.* Lk. 24: 27; (b) the formula used in Christian baptism, *cf.* Mt. 28: 19; or (c) the answering confession of the person being baptized, *cf.* 1 Pet. 3: 21, AV; Rom. 10: 9.

3 5: 32. 'A great mystery': the word 'great' here does not indicate that this truth is something 'very mysterious', but that this 'mystery' or 'divinely-revealed truth' is one 'of great importance'.

☐ STUDY 7 Ephesians 6: 10–24

The same apostle and Epistle that show us how heavenly, complete and free is redemption in Christ, now indicate how certain, fierce and protracted is the conflict to be faced by those who belong to Christ.

1 Why is conflict inevitable for all who belong to Christ? What is its character? What dangers which beset us are here particularly in mind? *Cf.* 2 Cor. 10: 3–5; 11: 3. By what achievement is victory here repeatedly described? How alone may it be achieved?

2 Some interpreters take 'truth' to mean inward sincerity and 'righteousness' to mean integrity and fidelity. Others think 'truth' here means the truth of the gospel, as in 4: 21, and take 'righteousness' to mean 'the righteousness of God' given to us in Christ (see Rom. 3: 22). Can you find a decisive answer? How alone can we make our standing sure before God, men and the devil? *Cf.* Rom. 5: 1, 2; 8: 33, 34; Pss. 15; 24: 3–6; 51: 6.

3 Verses 18–20. Consider what is here implied about Christian praying—concerning its place, its character, its demands, its scope, and its particular interests and requests. Measure your praying by these standards.

Notes

1 Verse 10. 'Be strong': literally 'be strengthened'. 'A person cannot strengthen himself; he must be empowered' (*Ephesians* (*TNTC*), p. 170). Our strength is to be continually maintained (present tense) by the outworked vigour of God's inherent power.

2 Verses 11, 13. 'The whole armour of God': the complete outfit is thought of as one whole. What is most emphasized is its divine source.
3 Verse 12. The word for 'contending', literally 'to wrestle' (see AV, RV), implies personal hand-to-hand conflict.
4 Verse 15. For such fighting one needs to have a sure foothold.
5 Verse 16. 'Flaming darts': devil-inspired thoughts or desires, evil in their nature, and tending to inflame the passions.

JOB

Introduction

Outside the book itself, Job, the chief character, is mentioned only in Ezk. 14: 14, 20 and Jas. 5: 11. We know very little about him therefore, and the date and the placing of the story are matters of surmise. All absence of clear links with the patriarchal or post-conquest Israel point to an early date, and it is reasonable to take the descriptions of scenery and climate as referring to a country on the western edge of the desert. The book is written in Hebrew by a Hebrew.

We are given a portrait of a good man suddenly overtaken by extraordinary disasters. The main action of the book lies in a series of speeches between Job, his three friends, the young man Elihu, and, in the end, God Himself. In these speeches interest is sustained throughout by the presentation of opposing ideas about Job's misfortunes. Sharp divergences of temperament and belief reveal themselves. The friends insist that suffering comes only when a man has sinned. So let Job repent and his restoration will follow immediately. But Job knows that he has not sinned, at least not so greatly as to deserve so devastating a punishment. The principal agony lies, not in his diseased body, but in his bewildered mind. His cry to God to explain Himself is maintained with growing impatience. Job's real trial is theological. For he, like his friends, had once believed that men suffer here for their sins.

At last his desire is granted. God speaks to him, but very differently from his expectation. The sole divine answer consists of a vision of God's great power. Job, seeing his small concerns against this vast back-cloth, is humbled and silenced. Then God commends him, and he is restored.

The book is usually considered to be an enquiry into the reasons for innocent suffering, with Elihu seeing furthest into its meaning and purpose. Suffering is a merciful deterrent, aimed at reforming. Yet, from the standpoint of the Prologue, it is disinterested goodness which is under discussion. Satan asks, 'Does Job fear God for nought?' implying that he fears God because he has been weighed down with wealth and possessions. Job then, by divine permission, becomes a test case, to see whether he does fear God for the inducements to do so which he gets from it. Stripped of family, wealth, health, reputation and friends, he emerges at last from the experiment unscathed and believing God when all comforting proofs of His presence had been withdrawn.

Perhaps this book also teaches in a limited way how God justifies a man who has faith. He does it, not by explaining to him why life is as it is, still less by vindicating his alleged sinlessness. He does it by a personal showing of Himself to the man who cries for Him to hear, and clings to the hope of a revelation. And in that marvellous vision of power with which the book ends, totally unexpected, yet coherent and convincing as it is, Job, like Thomas before the risen Christ, is delivered from his doubt, and bows in worship. God, in showing Himself to a faithful man, in the very act justifies him. Revelation in response to faith is justification. Job was 'right', but not for the reasons he supposed.

The study of the subordinate themes in the book is well worth the time. Job's preoccupation with death, for example, and his hopes of an after-life; his certainty that somewhere a mediator will be found; his irony, his reactions to his suffering, and his character; the characters, too, of his friends, so full of truths, so far from the truth. To these, and other matters, attention is drawn in the Notes and the Questions.

Analysis

1, 2	Of the happy and exemplary life of Job. Why and how he suffered.
3	Job complains, and wishes that he had never been born.
4 – 14	The first cycle of speeches.
15 – 21	The second cycle of speeches.
22 – 31	The third cycle of speeches.

32 – 37	The speeches of Elihu.
38: 1 – 42: 6	The speeches of the Lord and Job's replies. Job regrets having questioned God's goodness.
42: 7 – 17	After Job has prayed for his friends, he is commended by God and given twice as much as before.

☐ STUDY 1 Job 1 – 3

1 1: 1 – 2: 6. What is said here about Job's (a) character, (b) position in life, and (c) sufferings?

2 2: 7 – 3: 26. In 2: 10 Job expresses his faith in God. In 3: 11 he wants to die; and in 3: 23 blames God for his troubles. How are we to account for this change?

Notes

1 2: 13. The seven-day silence of Job's friends is a rite of mourning for a man they consider as good as dead, struck down because of his sins.

2 Compare 3: 1-26 with Je. 20: 14-18.

The First Cycle of Speeches (4 – 14)

The three friends, seeing Job's suffering, assume his guilt, and with mounting zeal urge him to repent. At first Job is only grieved and hurt by this lack of understanding, but soon becomes irritated and angry. He wants God to explain Himself, and is acutely miserable.

☐ STUDY 2 Job 4 and 5. Eliphaz' first speech

1 4: 1–11. According to Eliphaz, what was Job forgetting?

2 4: 12 – 5: 7. What did Eliphaz learn from his vision?

3 5: 8–27. What is his view of Job, of God, and of divine chastening?

Notes

1 5: 2. 'Vexation': an impatient, querulous or presumptuous attitude.

2 5: 6, 7. Troubles in life come as sparks come, from somebody's actions. There must be a human cause. *Cf.* 4: 8.

3 5: 27. An appeal to scholarly research to buttress his orthodoxy.

☐ STUDY 3 Job 6 and 7. Job's reply to Eliphaz

Job is hurt by Eliphaz' attitude. He had hoped for help, not criticism (6: 14). He flings questions at God.

1 6: 1–30. What does Job's condition make him long for (a) from God, and (b) from men? What may we learn from his double disappointment?

2 7: 1–10. By what metaphors does Job describe his present life? 7: 11–21. What is the substance of his complaints against God?

Notes
1 6: 5, 6. Even animals cry out in misery: and human beings exclaim at distasteful food. Why shouldn't Job complain?
2 6: 20. Thirsty caravans perish in the desert pursuing a mirage. Job is similarly cheated by his friends.
3 6: 30. 'Cannot my taste . . .' means 'Am I quite without good reason for my complaints?'

☐ STUDY 4 Job 8: 1 – 9: 24. Bildad's first speech and Job's reply

1 To what authority does Bildad appeal for what he says? How trustworthy do you think that authority is? What are Bildad's views (a) about God, and (b) about wicked men?

2 What difficulties does Job find in his way as he tries to make God explain Himself?

Notes
1 8: 4. A cruel remark. Job's children died because they sinned, according to Bildad.
2 8: 11. Reeds wither without water. So wicked men fade away.
3 9: 2. The meaning is, 'How can a man establish his righteousness before God?'
4 9: 13b. Rahab is probably another name for the dragon. See RSV mg. note to 9: 8b.

☐ STUDY 5 Job 9: 25 – 10: 22. Job's reply to Bildad (continued)

1 9: 33. The 'umpire' is mentioned for the first time in the book. Keep a list of the occurrences, noticing what new features each fresh mention brings. Suggest ways in which Jesus Christ has made Job's great wish a reality for us.

2 What is Job's main desire in chapter 10? Do you think God is angered by such plain speaking? *Cf.* Pss. 55: 1–8, 22; 62: 8.

Notes
1 9: 35. 'Deep in my heart I have no guilty fears.'
2 10: 12. An extraordinary verse to find in a long complaint. Either it means 'Even in deep misery I am aware of an overriding loving purpose'; or 'Even my past happiness was designed as a prelude to my present misery.'

☐ STUDY 6 Job 11 and 12. Zophar's first speech and Job's reply

1 Observe (a) the sharp rebuke in 11: 6; (b) the steps to repentance in 11: 13, 14; (c) the picture of blessing in 11: 15–19. Why do you think Zophar failed to help Job?

2 Eliphaz spoke of visions, and research, Bildad of the wisdom of the ancients. To what authority does Zophar appeal to support his conviction that sin and suffering are inevitably linked?

3 Zophar and Job each speak of divine wisdom. Compare the various examples of it which they cite.

Note. 12: 5–12. Perhaps Job is ironically quoting Zophar's views back at him. Job's point is that these platitudes are irrelevant to his situation. He does not deny them.

☐ STUDY 7 Job 13 and 14. Job speaks again

For convenience the first cycle has been considered as ending at 14. It could equally finish at 12, with 13 and 14 beginning the fresh round of opposing speeches.

1 What is Job's chief accusation against his friends? What two demands does he now make to God?

2 In the long dirge on man's uncertainties in chapter 14 there is one small but significant gleam of hope. What is it? Compare and contrast the Christian's view of this hope with Job's. (Note, however, that in chapter 18 Job relapses into a deeper pessimism still.)

The Second Cycle of Speeches (15 – 21)

Unable to persuade Job that he is wrong, his friends now use blunter accusation and scarcely-veiled threats. They dwell on the fate of the wicked. Job, by this time very upset, sinks into repeated moanings about his troubles. Then, quite suddenly, at the deepest point of misery he revives a little (16: 19; 19: 25), and in 21 attacks this antique idea of his friends that 'It's always the bad who get the pain', and accuses them of preaching a dogma denied by life. Their observations are inaccurate.

☐ STUDY 8 Job 15 – 17. Eliphaz' second speech and Job's reply

1 Read chapter 15 and compare its tone and approach with Eliphaz' first speech in chapters 4 and 5. Note the emphasis on human depravity. How should Eliphaz have dealt with a younger man who would not agree with him? Why was he so sure he was right? To whose shortcomings was he blind?

2 16 and 17. Even in the depths, Job finds some particles of hope. What form do these take?

Notes

1 15: 4. Eliphaz accuses Job of being an enemy of true religion and godliness because he denies the traditional orthodoxy.

2 15: 11b. A reference to the earlier speeches of Job's friends.

3 15: 18, 19. Eliphaz claims that his doctrine is ancient and pure, untainted by foreign heresies.

4 16: 2. Ronald Knox renders this: 'Old tales and cold comfort; you are all alike.'

5 16: 19, 21. A further reference to the mediator.
6 17: 16b. Taken as a statement, not a question, this indicates a sudden further advance in Job's hopes.

□ STUDY 9 Job 18 and 19. Bildad's second speech and Job's reply

1 In 18 trace the sequence of events which happen to the wicked and the ungodly.

2 In 19 Job says he feels imprisoned and alone. List the metaphors under which he pictures his solitary confinement. How does he picture his release? To what grand assurance does his faith triumphantly rise?

Notes
1 18: 2. 'How long before you make a capture of mere words?' *i.e.*, before you stop mouthing empty ideas. 'Consider': *i.e.*, say something worth saying, and our answer will be weighty.
2 18: 4. The world's natural laws will not be altered to suit Job.
3 19: 25–27. Even if Job had no hope of vindication in this life he believed that God must vindicate him and that, after death, he would see God and find God on his side. *Cf.* Rom. 8: 33–39.
4 19: 28b. 'The real cause of the trouble is himself' possibly expresses the sense intended.
5 19: 29. 'Trouble will come to them if they go on rejecting his cries for pity' is what Job here means.

□ STUDY 10 Job 20 and 21. Zophar's second speech and Job's reply

1 Place Zophar's views of the state of the wicked in this world alongside Job's. *Cf.* 20: 6–28 with 21: 6–26. At what points do they (a) agree, and (b) disagree?

2 In this second cycle Job's friends, gaining no victory, utter threats. Is defeated conservatism bound to take refuge in acid predictions of gloom? Had Job something to teach them if only they were willing to learn?

Notes
1 20: 5. *Cf.* Pss. 37 and 73 on the sudden end of bad men.
2 20: 7. 'Dead men are dead.' Job's hopes about another life receive short measure from Zophar.
3 20: 17. 'The rivers': *i.e.*, of paradise.
4 21: 34. Job means that they have not troubled to check their thesis against life itself. So they are dealing in lies.

Concluding note to the section chapters 15–21. Job's friends have nothing new to say: but Job has. He is stumbling towards the truth that death itself will provide a way out of his impasse, when a shadowy but friendly Redeemer will acquit him.

The Third Cycle of Speeches (22 – 31)

Only Eliphaz speaks at length to Job in this third cycle. Zophar says nothing (see, however, the Note on 27: 7–22). The friends' case against Job is already leaking badly. Eliphaz sinks it by shouting false charges at Job, which Job later (31) refutes. Job ends by repeating his innocence, and his perplexity.

☐ STUDY 11 Job 22 – 24. Eliphaz' third speech and Job's reply

1 Chapter 22. Of what does Eliphaz accuse Job (verses 6–9)? List God's blessings on the humble (verses 21–30). Why does Eliphaz' list of blessings (verse 3) make so little impression on Job?

2 Chapter 23. Job earnestly desires to find God (verse 3). How is he now thinking of God? See verses 5, 6, 10, 13, 16. Is it as a Friend or a Foe?

3 Chapter 24. What anomalies does Job see in society around him? Compare what 'you' say (verses 18–20) with what Job says. Does this chapter teach us anything about how to make observations on life?

Note. 22: 2–4. Eliphaz' argument is that God's treatment of man is not with a view to any gain or advantage to Himself but for man's sake. Since we cannot suppose that He punishes them for their piety (verse 4), it must be because of their sin.

☐ STUDY 12 Job 25 – 27. Bildad's third speech and Job's reply

1 How do Bildad and Job speak of (a) God's holiness, and (b) His omnipotence?

2 The knowledge of God's power does not help Job now. To what does he cling (27: 1–6)? Was he right in this?

3 Does 27: 7–22 add any fresh ideas about the wicked?

Note. 27: 7–22. Some part of the otherwise lost third speech of Zophar is possibly here. The thought echoes 20: 12ff.

☐ STUDY 13 Job 28 and 29. The search for wisdom: Job's final speech

1 Chapter 28. What is here expressed concerning (a) human skill, and (b) human inability? What are (a) the source, and (b) the essence of true wisdom? *Cf.* 1: 1; 2: 3; Ps. 34: 11–14.

2 Chapter 29. What may we learn from Job's description of his manner of life before tragedy overwhelmed him? What most stands

out in his memory? What then gave enrichment and direction to his daily living?

Notes

1 Chapter 28 reads like an independent insertion—a poem in praise of wisdom. The 'wisdom' meant is not simply mental ability, but understanding of the right way to act in the face of life's mystery. Supremely, as known only to God, it means the master plan behind the created order. The New Testament declares that this wisdom is found and expressed in Christ. *Cf.* 1 Cor. 1: 30; Col. 2: 23.

2 Job's speech in chapters 29–31 is best understood as a concluding monologue, summing up the whole situation.

☐ STUDY 14 Job 30 and 31. Job's final speech (continued)

1 Chapter 30. Contrast Job's present condition with his previous prosperity surveyed in chapter 29. In what different ways is Job now beset by misery and distress? What is his chief reason for perplexity and complaint?

2 Chapter 31. Of what sins, secret and public, does Job here declare himself innocent? Make a list and use it for self-examination. In contrast to the judgment of his friends, what is Job here seeking to prove about his present condition?

The Speeches of Elihu (32 – 37)

☐ STUDY 15 Job 32 and 33. The introduction and first speech of Elihu

Elihu is a young man who has overheard the friends and Job speaking. Both sides anger him, and he wants to put things right. His main beliefs are these: God is incapable of making a mistake; pain is a divine deterrent aimed at keeping men from sin.

1 What made Elihu angry? On what grounds does he claim a right to speak? What do you think of the way he begins his speech?

2 Job had said that God treated him unjustly (33: 8–11), and that He made matters worse by refusing to talk to him (33: 13). What replies does Elihu give to Job about this? See verses 12, 14–33. In what ways does he say God speaks? And for what purpose?

☐ STUDY 16 Job 34 and 35. Elihu's second speech

1 According to Elihu Job says (a) that God is wronging him (34: 5, 6), and (b) that there is no profit to be gained from delighting in God and doing His will (34: 9; 35: 3). How does Elihu answer these contentions? What precious truths about God does he declare?

2 'In the setting of the book of Job it is not a question whether Elihu is right or not—obviously he is right, at least in large measure—but whether he contributes anything to the solution of Job's "Why?" Obviously he does not' (H. L. Ellison). Do you agree with this judgment? Why did a man who knew so much fail to be helpful? Of what danger should this make us aware?

Notes

1 34: 13–15. The thought here seems to be that God as Creator has no motive for injustice; and that the existence and preservation of the universe is an evidence of God's interest in His creatures.

2 34: 23–30. There is no need for God to act as men do by process of trial and judgment. God knows all and acts at once.

3 35: 10. God is the only source of all true comfort. *Cf.* Ps. 42: 8; 2 Cor. 1: 3, 4.

☐ STUDY 17 Job 36 and 37. Elihu's last speech

1 What does Elihu here assert concerning (a) the character of God's rule, and (b) the evidences of His greatness? To what conclusion about his troubles does he seek to lead Job?

2 Of what is Elihu profoundly aware concerning (a) the character and the ways of God, and (b) his own attempts to describe them? *Cf.* Rom. 11: 33–36.

Note. 37: 20. Elihu expresses dread at the thought of contending with God.

The Speeches of the Lord and Job's Replies (38: 1 – 42: 6)

☐ STUDY 18 Job 38: 1 – 40: 5. The first speech of the Lord and Job's reply

1 Consider the examples of God's handiwork here depicted. What relation had this to Job's condition and perplexity? What response ought this to produce in us? *Cf.* Pss. 97: 1–6, 12; 104: 1, 24.

2 Job had pleaded for an interview with God in which his innocence could be established. See 13: 3; 23: 3, 4; 31: 37. God proves his littleness. Why do you think Job is answered like this? What does Job confess in his reply?

Notes

1 38: 2. This means: 'You are obscuring the truth by speaking without thinking.'

2 38: 4ff. The reader should take good note of the bold, magnificent images employed here. The world is like a building erected by one man (verse 4). The sea's birth was like a child's issuing from the womb (verse 8). Dawn shakes the earth like an open-air sleeper rising and shaking out of his blanket the

creatures which came in for warmth (verses 12, 13). 'God is now speaking to deeper need, to the hidden fear, hardly realized by Job and certainly unconfessed, that there might be somewhere where the writ of God did not run, where God was not all-sovereign' (H. L. Ellison).

3 40: 2. This means: 'Can you prove yourself right only by proving me wrong?'

[ ] STUDY 19 Job 40: 6 - 42: 6. The Lord's second speech and Job's reply

1 God brings before Job two powerful wild creatures—the hippopotamus (40: 15-24) and the crocodile (41: 1-34). What does God intend that Job should learn from these animals? What questions does He ask Job?

2 Job has been given no explanation of his sufferings. What brought him to the deep humbling and self-abasement described in 42: 1-6?

Note. 'The point in these descriptions is the prodigality of Created Might' (H. R. Minn).

[ ] STUDY 20 Job 42: 7-17. The Epilogue

1 Job's friends would certainly have agreed with all that God said to Job. Yet God is angry with them. 'You have not', He says, 'spoken of me what is right' (verse 7). Why was this so? Was it their haste in condemning Job, their doctrinal prejudice, their lack of sympathy, or what was it?

2 Job had quarrelled with God, doubted His justice, insisted on his own innocence, wanted to end his life. Yet God said he had spoken 'what is right'. Why?

[ ] STUDY 21 Revision: Job 1-42

Re-read your notes on the main teaching of the book of Job. What have you learnt about (a) the origin and purpose of suffering, or so-called 'evil' (42: 11); (b) the way to bear it; and (c) the way to help others to bear it?

PSALMS 42 - 51

☐ STUDY 36 Psalms 42 and 43

These two psalms were probably originally one. Notice the thrice-repeated refrain (42: 5, 11; 43: 5).

1 What phrase does the psalmist repeat four times in these two psalms to describe his spiritual condition? What were the chief causes of his sorrow, and what his chief desire?

2 What can we learn from the psalmist's example as to how to deal with depression in our lives?

☐ STUDY 37 Psalm 44

A national appeal to God in a time of great suffering.

1 What does the psalmist say about (a) God's dealings in the past on behalf of His people, and (b) His relationship with them? See verses 1–8. In spite of past happenings, what seems to be the situation at the present time? See verses 9–22.

2 What can we learn from this psalm as to what we should do when it seems as if God has deserted us? *Cf.* Is. 50: 10; Lk. 18: 1.

☐ STUDY 38 Psalm 45

A marriage song of a king. If the king be a type of Christ (see Heb. 1: 8, 9), the bride may symbolize the church.

1 What features in Christ's character are here portrayed?

2 How can we apply to ourselves the counsel given to the bride concerning the winning of the king's favour?

☐ STUDY 39 Psalms 46 – 48

These psalms are a trilogy of praise in memory of a great deliverance, most probably that of Jerusalem from the king of Assyria. They should be read in the light of 2 Ki. 18 and 19.

1 Gather out what is said about God in these psalms: His power, His character, His relation to the world, and His relation to His own people.

2 What is the leading thought of each of the three psalms? What should be the response of God's people to such a manifestation of His power and love?

Notes

1 46: 5. 'Right early': better, 'When the morning dawns', *i.e.*, the morning of deliverance. See RV mg. and *cf.* Mk. 6: 48, 51.

2 47: 2 and 48: 2. 'The great King': *i.e.*, the true great king in contrast to the Assyrian monarch, who bore this title. *Cf.* Is. 36: 4.

3 47: 9. 'Shields': meaning 'rulers'. *Cf.* Ps. 89: 18. The verse is prophetic of Christ's final victory. *Cf.* 1 Cor. 15: 24, 25; Rev. 15: 3, 4.

☐ STUDY 40 Psalm 49

An inspired meditation, addressed to all men, on the vanity of riches. It anticipates our Lord's teaching in Lk. 12: 13–21.

1 How do men in general regard wealth? See verses 6, 13, 18. But what are the facts? What can wealth *not* do (verses 7–9)? And what is the end of the rich man (verses 10–14, 17–20)?

2 Why is it better to trust in God than in riches? See verses 14, 15. And what is the psalmist's counsel to himself and to us? See verses 5 and 16.

Note. Verses 7 and 9 should be read together, verse 8 being parenthetical. With verse 7 *cf.* Ex. 21: 30. There were cases where, in human relationships, life could be redeemed with money; but it is not so when God summons the soul.

☐ STUDY 41 Psalm 50

A picture of God's judgment of His people. There are four sections: (a) Introduction (verses 1–6); (b) God speaks to His people (verses 7–15); (c) God speaks to the wicked (verses 16–21); (d) Epilogue (verses 22, 23).

1 What can you discover of God's character in His capacity as Judge in verses 1–6? What further truth about Him is emphasized in verses 7–13?

2 What does God require of His people if they are to please Him, and what benefits does He promise to them? See verses 14, 15, 23. In what ways do the wicked displease God, and what is their end compared to those who fulfil His requirements?

☐ STUDY 42 Psalm 51

Note the occasion of the psalm, as given in the title.

1 What may we learn about confession and the grounds of for-

giveness from verses 1–5? Note (a) the terms which David uses to describe himself and his wrongdoing, and (b) where his hope lies.

2 David realizes that his whole nature is sinful, and that God requires sincerity and integrity in the innermost part of his being (verse 6; *cf.* 1 Sa. 16: 7). What, therefore, (in verses 7–12) does he ask for in addition to forgiveness? Also what does he promise shall be the outcome of God's answer to his prayer? See verses 13–17.

Note. Verse 4. This does not mean that David had not also done wrong against man (note in verse 14 his confession of 'bloodguiltiness'), but that he now saw his wrongdoing in this one outstanding aspect of it, as being sin against God. *Cf.* Gn. 39: 9; 2 Sa. 12: 13.

For Studies 43–56 on the Psalms see p. 239.

---

2 SAMUEL

For Introduction, see p. 208.

Analysis

1 – 8 David consolidates his position and takes Jerusalem.
9 – 12 David the king, to the time of his great sin.
13 – 20 The punishment of sin: Absalom's rebellion.
21 – 24 An appendix containing other historical incidents and summaries, and David's last words.

☐ **STUDY 1 2 Samuel 1**

1 The Amalekite thought he was bringing David good news (*cf.* 2 Sa. 4: 10), but he had mistaken his man. Why did David have him killed?

2 What light does this episode, and the lament for Saul and Jonathan (verses 19–27), throw on David's character? Bearing in mind the faults of the king to whom David was so loyal, are there any lessons here for me?

☐ STUDY 2 2 Samuel 2 and 3

1 Compare David's actions as a public figure (2: 4–7; 3: 20, 21, 28–39) with the trouble he was building up in his family life (3: 2–5, 13, 14). Am I in any respect guilty of double standards in my own life?

2 Make a character study of the figures of Abner and Joab from these chapters. Note the relationship of Joab and his brothers to David (Zeruiah was the daughter of David's mother by her first marriage), and David's words in 3: 39.

☐ STUDY 3 2 Samuel 4: 1 – 5: 16

1 In what respects was the crime of Rechab and Baanah worse than that of the Amalekite?

2 David waited for seven years for the decision at the beginning of chapter 5. Why did the Israelites now choose him as king? *Cf.* Dt. 17: 15.

3 How did David succeed in taking the stronghold of Zion, and why?

☐ STUDY 4 2 Samuel 5: 17 – 6: 23

1 Why was it David won these two battles with the Philistines?

2 Why did Uzzah die? *Cf.* 1 Sa. 6: 19; Nu. 4: 15; 1 Ch. 15: 15. What was God teaching through this incident?

3 What was the real reason for Michal's contempt for David, and what her pretended reason? Why was it David behaved as he did on this occasion? Can I learn anything from his exuberance 'before the Lord'?

☐ STUDY 5 2 Samuel 7

1 David is eager to build a house for God—God's reply is to make a 'house' for David. List what He has already done, and what He promises for the future.

2 It has been said that what a man is on his knees before God, that he really is. What does David's prayer reveal (a) about himself, (b) about his relation to God?

☐ STUDY 6 2 Samuel 8 and 9

1 Use a map to follow the path of David's victories. What reasons does the writer emphasize for David's success?

2 How does David's treatment of the spoils of war differ from the way in which he dealt with the gods of the Philistines captured in battle (1 Ch. 14: 8–12)? Is there a reason for this? *Cf.* Dt. 7: 5.

3 Do you see any parallel between David's treatment of Mephibosheth and God's acceptance of us?

☐ STUDY 7 2 Samuel 10 and 11

1 Why is Hanun's treatment of David's envoys inexcusable?

2 Joab shows up in a better light here. What does this add to what we already know of his character?

3 At what stage in his career did David fall? Where should he have been at the time? How did the temptation grow? Was he able to keep his sin secret? Do your answers to these questions, and your reading of the passage, suggest any general lessons about sin?

☐ STUDY 8 2 Samuel 12: 1 – 13: 37

1 How did God open David's eyes to his sin through Nathan's words? Are you prepared for Him similarly to open your eyes?

2 What may we learn from chapter 12 about (a) repentance, (b) forgiveness, and (c) discipline? *Cf.* Ps. 32: 3–5; Heb. 12: 6, 11.

3 13: 1–37. What lessons emerge from a comparison of Amnon's sin with David's? What was wrong with the way in which Amnon was treated by (a) David, and (b) Absalom?

☐ STUDY 9 2 Samuel 13: 38 – 14: 33

1 What is laudable in the actions here recorded of (a) Joab and (b) David, and what gives rise to misgivings?

2 How does David's predicament illustrate the situation confronting God with the human race? How is the gospel 'solution' at once more far-reaching and more satisfactory than the expedient adopted by David?

3 Study Absalom's character, and list his faults.

Note. 14: 7. Those who demanded the murderer's death had justification according to the law (see Dt. 19: 11–13). The woman based her plea on her own great need.

☐ **STUDY 10 2 Samuel 15: 1 – 16: 14**

1 How was it that Absalom 'stole the hearts of the men of Israel'? What do you make of David's reactions here?

2 Contrast the behaviour of Absalom with that of Ittai and Hushai.

3 Consider how the rebellion shows certain men in their true colours (16: 1–14). Again note David's reactions.

☐ **STUDY 11 2 Samuel 16: 15 – 17: 29**

1 What are the reasons for Ahitophel's first piece of advice to Absalom? What do you think would have been David's first thought (*cf.* 12: 11, 12)? Is this the key to David's rather defeatist attitude?

2 17: 1–14. Was Ahitophel's counsel good? If so, why was it that Hushai's advice won the day?

3 How was David rewarded for his previous generosity? Notice who Shobi was (see 2 Sa. 10: 2).

☐ **STUDY 12 2 Samuel 18: 1 – 19: 8**

1 What is good and what is bad about David's concern for Absalom?

2 Consider Joab's conduct throughout this passage, separating the good and bad points.

☐ **STUDY 13 2 Samuel 19: 9–39**

1 Why did David not make an immediate re-entry into the capital? How does his attitude contrast with that of Saul and other leaders in the same mould? See 1 Sa. 8: 10–18.

2 What qualities in David stand out in his treatment of (a) Shimei, (b) Mephibosheth, and (c) Barzillai? What can be learnt from the attitude of each of these men to David?

Note. Verse 11. The fact that Absalom's rebellion centred in Hebron (15: 7–12) shows how deeply the tribe of Judah was implicated in it.

☐ **STUDY 14 2 Samuel 19: 40 – 20: 26**

1 Analyse the quarrel between Israel and Judah: (a) its cause; (b) the arguments used; (c) the spirit in which it was conducted; (d) its tragic outcome.

2 How was the threatened disaster averted? What part was played respectively by David, by Joab, and by the wise woman in the town of Abel?

3 What considerations aggravate Joab's sin in murdering Amasa? *Cf.* 2 Sa. 17: 25; 19: 13.

☐ STUDY 15 2 Samuel 21

1 Why was Saul's attempt to exterminate the Gibeonites wrong? How was David careful not to make the same mistake? Do we stand by our word? *Cf.* Ps. 15: 4c.

2 There was a law that those who were hanged were to be buried the same day. What was the reason for this law? *Cf.* Dt. 21: 23. How does it explain the exception that is made here?

3 What significance is there in the fact that giants troubled David right to the end of his life?

Note. Verse 19. *Cf.* 1 Ch. 20: 5 which seems to have preserved more accurately the original text.

☐ STUDY 16 2 Samuel 22

See Psalm 18 for questions already set on this psalm.

1 Are there any passages in this psalm which we could not echo as Christians?

2 Does the psalm bring to mind any particular incidents recorded in 2 Samuel?

☐ STUDY 17 2 Samuel 23

1 Compare verses 3 and 4 with verse 5. What apparent conflict is there between the two reasons given by David for his happiness and prosperity? Is this conflict real? *Cf.* Phil. 2: 12, 13.

2 What light is cast on verses 6 and 7 by David's advice to Solomon in 1 Ki. 2: 5, 6? *Cf.* 1 Ki. 2: 31–33.

3 Consider what David's followers were willing to do for their king; and at what stage in his career (verse 13). What lessons are there here for a Christian?

☐ STUDY 18 2 Samuel 24

1 (a) Compare the length of time taken by Joab to count, and by the angel to slay the Israelites. (b) Compare the atonement required by God for David's adultery (2 Sa. 12: 15, 18) with that exacted

here. What sin on David's part is being dealt with? What two lessons are taught about it? *Cf.* Pr. 16: 5.

2 Where was Araunah's threshing-floor? See Note on verse 16. What outstanding event had happened there previously? See Gn. 22: 2. What was the site eventually used for?

3 Is there a lesson for us in David's declaration of verse 24?

Note. Verse 16. We learn from 2 Ch. 3: 1 that Araunah's threshing-floor was on Mount Moriah, which became the site of the Temple.

PSALMS 52 - 72

☐ STUDY 43 Psalms 52–54

Of these three psalms the second (Ps. 53) is a duplicate (with slight variations) of Ps. 14. For the occasion of Pss. 52 and 54 see their titles and *cf.* 1 Sa. 22: 9; 23: 19.

1 52: 1–7; 53: 1–5. How is the godless man described? In what does he put his trust, and what is his end? In what does the godly man put his trust, and what is the result for him? See 52: 8, 9; 53: 6.

2 What may we learn from Ps. 54 of (a) the severity of faith's trial; (b) the ground of faith's confidence; (c) faith's assurance of triumph?

☐ STUDY 44 Psalm 55

1 Of the two ways of meeting trouble mentioned in verses 6, 7 and 22 respectively, which is the better? What other verses show that the psalmist is turning to God for help, rather than seeking to escape from the scene of his distress?

2 What was the bitterest element in the psalmist's grief? See verses 12–14, 21 and *cf.* 2 Sa. 15: 31; Jn. 13: 21. Observe, however, the difference between David's cry in verse 15, and our Lord's word concerning Judas (Mk. 14: 21).

Notes

1 Verses 9–11. Violence, strife, iniquity, mischief, wickedness, oppression, fraud, seem to be personified as walking on the walls and in the streets of the city.

2 Verse 22. 'Your burden': the Hebrew word translated 'burden' means literally 'what he has given you'. See RSV mg. The thought seems to be, 'Take back to God, and cast upon Him the burden He has laid upon you, and He will sustain you under it. For He has given it to you to bring you to Himself.' *Cf.* Ps. 107: 23–30.

☐ STUDY 45 Psalms 56 and 57

These two psalms are closely connected and, according to their titles, should be read against the background of 1 Sa. 21: 10 – 22: 1.

1 In these two psalms how does David (a) describe the trials by which he is surrounded, and (b) express his confidence in God?

2 What does David confess that God has done, and can do, for him, and in what ways does he say that he will show his gratitude? How far can you make some of the words of these psalms your own?

Note. Ps. 56: 8. *Cf.* Mt. 10: 30.

☐ STUDY 46 Psalms 58 and 59

1 Ps. 58. When earthly rulers pervert justice and 'deal out violence', what can the righteous do? What will prove to them that 'there is a God who judges on earth'? Notice the vivid imagery in verses 6–9.

2 Ps. 59. Make a list of the different ways in which David here addresses God. How are the truths of the previous psalm here applied more personally to the psalmist's own circumstances? Can you make some similar personal application?

☐ STUDY 47 Psalm 60

For the occasion of this psalm see the title and 2 Sa. 8: 13, 14. The circumstances are not wholly clear. It would seem that while David was engaged in a campaign against Syria (Aram), the Edomites invaded Judah from the south, creating a situation of grave danger. The psalm was written when David first heard the news.

1 Note the content of David's prayer. What does he do first (verses 1–5), second (verses 6–8), third (verses 9–12)?

2 What may we learn from David's example concerning the way (a) to meet bad tidings, and (b) to find help in God?

Notes

1 Verse 6. Shechem west of the Jordan, Succoth east of it, thus representing the whole land.

2 Verse 8. 'Upon Edom': better, 'to Edom', as in RV mg. Moab and Edom were to have a menial place in God's household, as compared with Israel.

☐ STUDY 48 Psalms 61 and 62

Pss. 61–63 form another trilogy, like 46–48. They were all most probably written shortly after David's flight from Absalom (see 63 title) and should be read against the background of the story of 2 Sa. 15–17.

1 Ps. 61. Consider David's circumstances—a fugitive, his throne occupied by another, his life sought. What were his heart's chief desires, as expressed in his prayers (verses 1–4)? Observe also his confident hope, and his whole-hearted devotion (verses 5–8). Is he not in this a 'type' of our Lord?

2 Ps. 62. How did David's situation appear in the eyes of his enemies (verse 3), and how to the eye of faith (verses 6, 7)? Out of the fullness of his own joyous confidence in God, what message was David able to give his followers (verses 8–12)? Have you also found that faith leads to testimony?

Note. 62: 11, 12. 'Once . . . twice': a Hebrew idiom for 'repeatedly', here signifying that the truth David sets forth in these verses had sunk deep into his heart.

☐ STUDY 49 Psalm 63

The title of the psalm assigns it to the time when David was crossing the wilderness of Judah, *i.e.*, from Jerusalem to Jordan, in his flight from Absalom, as described in 2 Sa. 16. The psalm begins in a mournful way, but suddenly, at verse 2, the note changes, and the psalm becomes one of joyous praise. The most satisfactory explanation of the change, and of David's words '*So* I have looked upon thee in the sanctuary', is that there, in the wilderness, David was given a vision of Jehovah as vivid and glorious as ever he had seen Him in the sanctuary, and it transformed for him the whole outlook.

1 Consider how full of sorrow David's heart must have been at leaving Jerusalem, and especially the sanctuary of God. See verse 1, and *cf.* 2 Sa. 15: 24–30. Though he seemed outwardly to have lost everything, in what was he still able to rejoice?

2 In what assurance about the future was David able to rest? Have you any similar confidence?

☐ STUDY 50 Psalms 64 and 65

Ps. 64, like 58 and 59, has for its theme the certainty of God's judgment upon the wicked. Ps. 65, on the other hand, is a psalm of praise to God, as the God of the whole earth, the only Saviour from sin, and the Giver of fruitful harvests.

1 Ps. 64. How are the psalmist's enemies described (verses 1–6)? What are the purpose and result of God's judgment? What truths should we take to heart, and act on when in similar circumstances?

2 Ps. 65. In verse 1, the psalmist says that praise is due to God. In the remaining verses, what can you find which moves you to praise God for all He is, and has done? Are the experiences mentioned in verses 3 and 4 known to you?

☐ STUDY 51 Psalms 66 and 67

Ps. 66 is a summons to the nations to join in praise to God for a great deliverance which He has wrought for His people, such as the deliverance of Jerusalem from Sennacherib. If this was the occasion, the speaker in verses 13–20 may well be King Hezekiah himself, speaking as the representative of the nation. Ps. 67 may belong to the same time. See Is. 37.

1 Ps. 66. Note in detail what God is here said to do with and for His people. What response ought this to move me to make? What is the condition of sharing in such an experience?

2 Ps. 67. Do we share the longing of the psalmist that all nations might know God and His salvation? By what means did he think it would be achieved? *Cf.* Mt. 5: 14–16; 1 Pet. 2: 9, 10.

☐ STUDY 52 Psalm 68: 1–18

This psalm describes the onward march of God through history to His final triumph. The threefold reference to the sanctuary in verses 17, 24, 35 suggests that, like Ps. 24, it was written to celebrate the bringing of the ark to Jerusalem. See 2 Sa. 6: 15, 17, 18.

1 What effect does the appearing of God have on (a) His enemies (verses 1, 2), (b) the righteous (verses 3, 4), and (c) those in need (verses 5, 6)?

2 In the historical retrospect of verses 7–18, what aspects of God's character are revealed?

Notes

1 Verse 7. *Cf.* Jdg. 5: 4, 5.

2 Verses 13b, 14. The meaning is uncertain. Verse 13b may mention an item of spoil: see verse 12 and *cf.* Jdg. 5: 30. Or it may describe a symbol—like the golden wings of the cherubim (see Ex. 25: 20–22)—of a theophany. Verse 14 may be a picture of the kings and their armies fleeing as snow-flakes driven before a storm.

3 Verses 17, 18. God enters Zion with His heavenly hosts. *Cf.* Eph. 4: 8; Ps. 24: 7–10.

☐ STUDY 53 Psalm 68: 19–35

1 Verses 19–27. How is the blessedness of God's people described? In your own experience do you know God as He is here set forth? What may we also learn from these verses concerning the character and place of public worship?

2 Verses 28–35. What God has done (verses 7–18) and is doing (verses 19–27) is but the prelude to greater triumphs. What vision does the psalmist see of a world-wide homage paid to God, and how is this confirmed by other scriptures?

Note. Verse 30. 'The beasts that dwell among the reeds' represent Egypt; and the 'bulls' followed by their 'calves', other kings and their peoples.

☐ STUDY 54 Psalm 69

This psalm is notable, first because the New Testament quotes from it several times, and second, because amidst prayers of humble supplication, the psalmist suddenly breaks into cries of passionate imprecation (verses 22–28).

1 What is the cause of the psalmist's troubles? What is the chief concern of his prayer, and what does he expect will happen in the end?

2 What features in the psalmist's sufferings most closely prefigure those of our Lord, helping us to understand how deeply He tasted of human woe? *Cf.* Heb. 4: 15. Verses 20, 21 take us specially to Gethsemane and the cross; but at the point of deepest suffering, where the psalmist breaks out in imprecatory prayer, what did our Lord pray? See Lk. 23: 34.

3 In what respects do verses 22–28 foreshadow the judgment that has fallen upon the Jewish people? *Cf.* verses 22, 23 with Mt. 13: 14; Rom. 11: 9, 10; and verse 25 with Mt. 23: 38.

☐ STUDY 55 Psalms 70 and 71

These psalms are both reminiscent of other psalms. Ps. 70 is taken bodily from Ps. 40. Ps. 71: 1–3 is taken from Ps. 31: 1–3; and the rest of Ps. 71 is largely made up of fragments also found in other psalms.

1 What does the psalmist expect God to be to him, and to do for him, and what will such things make him do? Do you make similar confessions to God when you pray?

2 Observe the triple movement in Ps. 71: (a) faith, praying, rises to hope and praise (verses 1–8); (b) faith, under a renewed sense of urgent need, falls back into prayer, and again rises to hope and praise (verse 9–16); (c) faith, for the third time driven to prayer, rises quickly to assurance, praise and witness, and there abides (verses 20, 22–24). What does this teach us concerning continuance in prayer?

☐ STUDY 56 Psalm 72

This is a prophetic psalm, in which Christ is typified by Solomon, whose name means 'peace'.

1 What are the two outstanding personal characteristics of Christ as King, as seen in this psalm? See verses 1, 2 and 12–14; and *cf.* Ps. 116: 5. What does the psalm say will be (a) the results of His rule (verses 3–7, 12–14, 16, 17), and (b) the extent of His rule (verses 8–11)?

2 Does not this psalm give a perfect picture of that happy earth which men are vainly trying to bring into being by their own wisdom and work? But, according to Scripture, who alone can bring it to pass, and to whom therefore should men look for its accomplishment? See verses 1, 17–19; and *cf.* Acts 4: 12; Eph. 1: 3.

Notes

1 Verse 8. The 'River' is the Euphrates.

2 Verses 18, 19. This doxology is not part of the original psalm, but is added as the close of Book 2.

For Studies 57–70 on the Psalms see p. 379.

---

1 KINGS

Introduction

1 and 2 Kings form a single unit, the present somewhat arbitrary division having originated in the Vulgate. They give an account and complete history of the kings and the kingdoms ('of the kingdoms' is the probable literal rendering of the titles). The account bears marks of being the work of a single author using as his sources various documents (see 1 Ki. 11: 41; 14: 19, 29; 15: 7, *etc.*) including prophetic memoirs. It is important to remember that the whole is written from the religious and prophetic point of view, not from that of the secular historian. As *The New Bible Commentary* remarks: 'This is the explanation why certain of the kings who were most important for their contemporaries, *e.g.*, Omri (1 Ki. xvi. 23–28), Azariah or Uzziah (2 Ki. xv. 1–7), Jeroboam II (2 Ki. xiv. 23–29), are passed over in virtual silence. It is spiritual, not political lessons,

that we are to learn. That is why the two periods of crisis, the reigns of Ahab for the north and of Hezekiah for the south, are given at special length.'

Expressed concisely, the theme of the book is that of Israel as the redeemed people of Jehovah, bearing His Name, and the kings as His representatives. Thus a wicked king is a paradox, as well as historically evil, and a good king by righteous acts is setting forth the rule of God. The sin of the people inevitably leads to the captivities, and throughout, political incidents are shown to be the effect of the fidelity or idolatry of the people. One proof of this is that prophetic activity is prominent in the reigns of wicked kings.

Analysis

1 – 11 The last days of the united kingdom.

- 1: 1 – 2: 11 David's last days and charge to Solomon.
- 2: 12 – 4: 34 Solomon, his character and wisdom.
- 5 – 8 The Temple.
- 9 – 11 Solomon's magnificence and failure.

12 – 16 The division, and the divided kingdoms to the accession of Ahab.

17 – 22 Elijah.

☐ STUDY 1 1 Kings 1

1 Get hold of the story. Who supported Adonijah, and who supported Solomon, and by what means was Adonijah's attempt to seize the throne frustrated? What may we learn about the character of each of these men?

2 This is the last mention of Nathan in Scripture. In his actions here and also in 2 Sa. 7 and 12 how does he exemplify by his faithful and disinterested conduct our duty as servants of God?

Notes

1 Verse 5. Adonijah, as David's eldest surviving son (see 2 Sa. 3: 4), had a claim to recognition (see 1 Ki. 2: 15). At the same time this might be overruled by the king (verses 20 and 27).

2 Verses 52, 53. Solomon spares Adonijah on certain conditions, but commands him to withdraw from public affairs.

☐ STUDY 2 1 Kings 2

1 Enumerate the points David made in his final advice to his son Solomon.

2 How and why were Adonijah, Joab, and Shimei put to death? Solomon's own reaction was to let bygones be bygones, but David counselled against this, and Solomon acted accordingly. What do

you think was David's motive in giving the counsel he did? What lessons may we learn from Adonijah's life-story?

☐ STUDY 3 1 Kings 3 and 4

1 Solomon's request was pleasing to God (3: 10), but was it the highest gift he could have asked? *Cf.* Ex. 33: 13; Phil. 3: 8, 10. What do you put first in prayer? What do we learn of God's dealings with man from the way in which He answered Solomon's request?

2 What good things are said about Solomon in these two chapters, and what benefits did his rule bring to his people? What, according to the writer, was the deepest ground of his prosperity?

Note. 4: 4b. This was true only at the very beginning of Solomon's reign See 2: 35.

☐ STUDY 4 1 Kings 5

1 To what great task did Solomon first set his hand, and what motives moved him to undertake it? Are we as ready to speak to a non-Christian friend of the goodness of God and of our desire to serve Him, as Solomon was to speak to Hiram?

2 What may we learn from the fact that even in the arrangements which Solomon made with Hiram for materials and skilled labour, he acted according to the wisdom given him by God? *Cf.* Eph. 5: 15–17; Jas. 1: 5; 3: 17.

☐ STUDY 5 1 Kings 6: 1 – 7: 12

1 Try to form a mental picture of 'the house of the Lord'. What was its length, its breadth, its height? What the size of the porch, and what of the most holy place, here called 'the inner sanctuary' (RSV) or 'the oracle' (AV)? Notice, too, the side rooms, arranged in three storeys round the sides and back of the house. These would take away from the narrow appearance of the building, and provide space for storage, *etc.* It may help you to draw a sketch, keeping to scale (a cubit was about eighteen inches). Draw in also the five buildings in the outer court (7: 1–12).

2 Of what material were the walls made, with what were they lined on the inner side, and how adorned? Observe also the care expended upon the design and workmanship of the two sets of doors. What may we learn from these things? *Cf.* 1 Ch. 22: 5, 14–16; 1 Cor. 3: 12–15.

Note. 7: 2. 'The House of the Forest of Lebanon': so called because of the number of pillars made from the cedars of Lebanon. It was a Hall of Assembly.

☐ STUDY 6 1 Kings 7: 13 – 8: 11

Today's portion describes (a) the making of the brass (or bronze) furnishings and implements for the Temple court, 7: 13–47; (b) the golden furniture and utensils for the house itself, 7: 48–50. Many of the details are difficult to grasp, but it is possible to distinguish the two great pillars, with their ornamental capitals, the great basin resting upon twelve oxen, and the ten carriages with wheels, richly ornamental, and carrying lavers; and also within the house the golden altar of incense, the table of shew bread, and ten candlesticks or lampstands. There was also a brass altar in the Temple court, which is mentioned later (see 8: 64).

1 What may we learn concerning our own service for Christ from the spirit and aim that animated Solomon (*cf.* 2 Cor. 9: 7; Rom. 12: 11), and from the fact that he pursued the task through seven years until it was finished (*cf.* Acts 14: 26; 20: 24; 2 Tim. 4: 7; Lk. 14: 28, 29)?

2 Finally, when all was prepared, the ark was brought in to the place reserved for it under the wings of the cherubim in the most holy place. Is the Lord Christ thus enthroned in you, His temple? *Cf.* Eph. 3: 16, 17. In what ways is His indwelling manifested in your life?

☐ STUDY 7 1 Kings 8: 12–66

1 Verses 14–21. What promise is here spoken of as having been fulfilled? Are there experiences in your life of which you can say 'God . . . with his hand has fulfilled what he promised with his mouth'? Observe how, in verses 22–53, thanksgiving for the fulfilment of the promise stimulated further prayer. What seven particular petitions did Solomon make, and on what grounds did he base his prayer?

2 Verses 54–62. In this 'blessing' how did Solomon sum up Israel's story? What two petitions did he offer, and to what ends, and what charge did he give the people? Consider how applicable his words are to ourselves.

Notes

1 Verse 12. 'Thick darkness': there was no light in the most holy place, to symbolize the inscrutable mystery of the divine nature. The ark symbolized His presence in the midst of His people.

2 Verse 16. 'My name': a phrase used frequently in this chapter as signifying God in the fullness of His self-revelation.

3 Verse 51. 'Iron furnace': *i.e.*, one in which iron is smelted.

4 Verse 65. 'Seven days' or 'seven days and seven days': *i.e.*, seven for the dedication of the altar, and seven for the feast, as explained in 2 Ch. 7: 8, 9.

☐ STUDY 8 1 Kings 9: 1 – 10: 13

1 Comparing 9: 3 carefully with 8: 29, in what two respects did God exceed Solomon's request? Observe also the close relation between God's promise and His commands, and between His fulfilment of His promise and man's obedience. *Cf.* Jn. 14: 14, 15, 21; 15: 7; 1 Jn. 3: 22. What do we see in today's passage of the fulfilment to Solomon of God's promise in 3: 12, 13?

2 In what ways is the Queen of Sheba an example to us? Consider the purpose of her visit, the difficulties of it, and her reward.

Notes

1 9: 14. A talent of gold, it is reckoned, would be the equivalent of £6,150, but would in those days have a far higher purchasing power.

2 9: 25. *Cf.* 2 Ch. 8: 13, 14.

☐ STUDY 9 1 Kings 10: 14 – 11: 43

1 Solomon was outwardly at the height of his power, wealth and fame (see 10: 14–29). But what was going on within his heart in respect (a) of his affections, and (b) of his relation to God (see 11: 1–8)? Read Pr. 4: 23–27. What was God's chief charge against him?

2 How does the account of the events of 11: 14–40 bring out God's overruling hand? *Cf.* Dn. 4: 34, 35; Ps. 135: 5, 6. What effect should this truth have upon a believing heart? *Cf.* Acts 4: 23–30.

☐ STUDY 10 1 Kings 12: 1–32

1 Study the characters of the two kings, Rehoboam and Jeroboam. To what factors would you attribute the division of the kingdom?

2 What four actions of Jeroboam are spoken of in verses 25–32, and what was their purpose? Clever as they were politically and according to human judgment, wherein lay their fatal error? See verse 30; 13: 33, 34; 2 Ki. 17: 21.

☐ STUDY 11 1 Kings 12: 33 – 13: 34

1 What was the root fault in Jeroboam's character, and how did God in His mercy seek to show him the folly of the course he was pursuing? See 12: 33 – 13: 10.

2 What punishment fell upon 'the man of God . . . out of Judah' and why? *Cf.* 20: 36, and contrast our Lord's firmness in Mt. 16: 22, 23.

☐ STUDY 12 1 Kings 14

1 Jeroboam and Ahijah had both been called of God, the one to be king (11: 31), and the other as prophet. What was the difference between them in their carrying out of their office, and how does this show what qualities are required in a servant of God?

2 What two pictures of Rehoboam's reign are given in verses 21–31? What light do they throw upon the state of the kingdom of Judah, and upon Rehoboam's character?

Notes

1 The name Abijah, given by Jeroboam to his son, shows that Jeroboam still worshipped Jehovah, for Abijah means 'my father is Jah'.

2 Verse 17. 'Tirzah' was the residence of the kings of the northern kingdom. *Cf.* 15: 21; 16: 15.

3 Verses 23, 24. All that is mentioned in these verses was associated with idolatry. *Cf.* Je. 2: 20.

☐ STUDY 13 1 Kings 15: 1 – 16: 7

1 In this portion two kings of Judah are mentioned and two of Israel. Who were they? What facts do we learn about each of them?

2 What is the one standard by which these men are judged in Scripture? In relation to this standard, which of them were disapproved, and why? And which of them was approved, and why? What does this teach us concerning eternal values?

Notes

1 15: 10. 'His mother's name': strictly his grandmother (see verses 2 and 8). Maachah apparently continued to be officially 'queen mother' (see verse 13).

2 15: 17. 'Ramah' was only five miles from Jerusalem to the north.

3 16: 7. 'Because he destroyed it': *cf.* 15: 27, 29.

☐ STUDY 14 1 Kings 16: 8–34

1 In the northern kingdom the dynasties of Jeroboam and Baasha were utterly destroyed, as later was that of Omri (see 21: 22). How does the story of this kingdom show that the people departed farther and farther from God until the climax was reached with Omri (verse 25) and Ahab (verse 30)? What may this teach us as to the self-propagating power of sin? Yet in Judah the royal line of David continued. Why this difference? Consider what is said in 11: 36 and 15: 4.

2 What was the special sin of Ahab, by which he provoked the Lord to anger? How did he go beyond what previous kings of Israel had done, and what led him to do it?

Notes

1 Verse 24. Omri was an able and powerful ruler, whose name is mentioned in the ancient Assyrian records and in the Moabite stone of Mesha. His selection of Samaria as the capital was an important event in Israel's history.

2 Verses 31, 32. The calves set up by Jeroboam (see 12: 28) were supposed to represent the God of Israel. Ahab's sin was greater in that he worshipped Baal, the god of Tyre, and built in Samaria a 'house of Baal'.

☐ STUDY 15 1 Kings 17 and 18

1 How was the prophet trained in faith and obedience for the supreme struggle on Mount Carmel? What did the experiences at the brook Cherith and in Zarephath teach him? What was the supreme issue at stake between him and King Ahab?

2 What was the secret of Elijah's strength and victory? See 18: 41–45; Jas. 5: 17, 18, and *cf.* 17: 1 with Heb. 11: 27b.

Note. 18: 45, 46. 'To Jezreel': about seventeen or eighteen miles. This extraordinary feat of endurance indicates that the prophet was keyed up to a high degree of nervous tension.

☐ STUDY 16 1 Kings 19

Prophets among the people of Israel were held in high regard. Elijah therefore supposed that after so great a moral victory as that won on Mount Carmel, king and nation would return to Jehovah. But Jezebel had no such awe in her heart, and Elijah found himself faced by her wrathful fury. It was a rude shock to all his hopes.

1 What difference do you notice between the account of Elijah's flight at this time and that of his previous flights to Cherith and Zarephath? What causes for his deep depression and sense of failure can you think of? Read the story of verses 4–18 in the light of Ps. 103: 13, 14. How did God comfort, teach and restore Elijah?

2 When God's call came to Elisha, how did he respond? Are you thus ready to do God's will, in whatever sphere of service He may appoint? *Cf.* Mk. 1: 15–20. What do we learn from this passage about the way God plans for His work to be begun by one of His servants and carried on by another? *Cf.* 1 Cor. 3: 6.

Notes

1 Verse 8. 'To Horeb the mount of God': the site of God's covenant with Israel (see Dt. 4: 9–20). This was probably the object of Elijah's journey from the first.

2 Verse 19. 'Twelve yoke of oxen' indicates a wealthy farm.

☐ STUDY 17 1 Kings 20

The reappearance of true prophets of Jehovah in this chapter is striking. It seems to indicate that Elijah's ministry had effected a change in the whole attitude of public opinion, and even in Ahab himself.

1 What was the difference between Ben-hadad's two demands which made Ahab reject the second, though he had yielded to the first? What threat did Ben-hadad make, and what was Ahab's answer?

2 How many times in this chapter is the intervention of a prophet recorded? What may we ourselves learn from the messages these men were sent of God to deliver?

☐ STUDY 18 1 Kings 21

1 Consider the parts played by Ahab, Jezebel, and the elders of Jezreel respectively in the murder of Naboth. What was the special guilt of each? What was it that distinguished Elijah from all these? What do we learn from his example of the qualities God wants in us if He is to do His work?

2 Sum up what you have learnt of Ahab's character from chapters 20 and 21.

Notes

1 Verses 2 and 3. Ahab's offer was fair in itself, but when he failed to gain his desire he was displeased. Yet Naboth, according to the law, had the right to refuse. See Nu. 36: 7.

2 Verse 15. We learn from 2 Ki. 9: 26 that Naboth's sons were also put to death, that there might be no surviving heir.

☐ STUDY 19 1 Kings 22

1 Compare the attitude of the two kings in regard to asking counsel of the Lord. Did they not both err: Ahab because he would not have done it at all but for Jehoshaphat, and Jehoshaphat because he did it *after* the decision was made? Do we sometimes find ourselves committing both these errors?

2 What may we learn from Ahab's foolish hatred of Micaiah? What was the reason for it, and to what end did it lead? *Cf.* Jn. 8: 40. Are we ever guilty of asking advice only from people who will tell us what we want to hear?

Notes

1 Verse 3. 'Ramoth-gilead': possibly one of the towns mentioned in 20: 34.

2 Verse 6. These prophets were probably prophets of the calf-worship which Jeroboam had established (12: 28, 29). In name they may have been prophets of Jehovah, God of Israel, but they were not true prophets as Micaiah was.

3 Verse 31. An ungrateful return or Ahab's clemency; see 20: 31–34. It underlines the truth of the unknown prophet's prediction in 20: 42.

JOHN 1 - 12

Introduction

The author of this Gospel claims to have been an eye-witness of the scenes that he records (1: 14; 19: 35; *cf.* 1 Jn. 1: 1–3), and in 21: 24 his identity with 'the disciple whom Jesus loved' is asserted. Among the many reasons for identifying this disciple with John the son of Zebedee, one of the most striking is the Evangelist's habit of referring to the Baptist as 'John' only, and never mentioning the son of Zebedee by name.

The other three Gospels are chiefly concerned with our Lord's ministry in Galilee; a bare hint is all that they give us that He so much as visited Jerusalem between His baptism and the final Passover (Mt. 23: 37; Lk. 13: 34; and Lk. 4: 44). John, on the other hand, has little to say about our Lord's work in Galilee (2: 1–12; 4: 43–54; 6); for the most part the scene of his narrative is Judaea, and especially Jerusalem, where almost from the first the Lord was rejected (1: 11; 4: 43, 44; 5; *etc.*).

It is important to observe that in the record of Jesus' ministry up to His death, seven miracles are recorded in this Gospel. These are (1) the turning of water into wine (2: 1–11); (2) the healing of the nobleman's son (4: 46–54); (3) the healing of the impotent man (5: 2–9); (4) the feeding of the five thousand (6: 4–13); (5) the walking on the water (6: 16–21); (6) the healing of the man born blind (9: 1–7); (7) the raising of Lazarus from the dead (11: 1–44). John calls these miracles 'signs', by which he means that they have a meaning beyond themselves, and point to the identity of Jesus as the Christ, and to His corresponding works in the spiritual realm, such as the raising of the spiritually dead, the opening of the eyes of the spiritually blind, *etc.*

The purpose of the Gospel, and particularly of the signs recorded in it, is clearly stated, 'that you may believe that Jesus is the Christ, the Son of God, and that believing you may have life in his name' (20: 31). It shows the divine Word coming to His own people, revealing the Father to them both by teaching and by 'signs', and yet rejected and persecuted to the death. To the world this Gospel reveals the tremendous claims of the Lord Jesus and the awfulness of rejecting Him. To the disciple it reveals the implications of accepting Him, showing the interdependence of love and obedience, of life and feeding upon the Lord, of fruit-bearing and abiding in Him.

The section 7: 53 – 8: 11 is omitted by all the oldest Greek manuscripts now existing, with one exception, and its style and vocabulary are more like those of Luke (in whose Gospel four manuscripts insert it) than those of John. But though this section was probably not written by John, it bears every evidence of truth, and we may thankfully accept it as part of the inspired Word of God.

Analysis

1: 1–18	The Preface or Prologue. The eternal, divine Word became flesh and dwelt among us.	
1: 19 – 12: 50	Jesus reveals Himself to the world.	
	1: 19–51	By the testimony of the Baptist and the first disciples.
	2 – 4	By signs and teaching among Jews, Samaritans and Galilaeans.
	5	The healing of the paralytic in Jerusalem begins the conflict between Jesus and the Jews.
	6	Jesus is revealed as the sustainer of life.
	7: 1–52	Jesus at the Feast of Tabernacles; the people divided; vain attempt to arrest Him.
	7: 53 – 8: 11	The woman taken in adultery.
	8: 12–59	Jesus is the light of the world, and the I AM.
	9	Blindness cured, and blindness intensified.
	10	Jesus is the Good Shepherd, and He is One with the Father.
	11	Jesus is the resurrection and the life.
	12	Jesus is about to be glorified through death. Summary of the effects of His ministry.
13 – 17	Jesus reveals Himself to His disciples in the farewell discourse and the High-Priestly prayer.	
18 – 21	Jesus is glorified in His arrest, His trial, His passion and His resurrection.	

☐ STUDY 1 John 1: 1–18

1 Why is Jesus here called 'the Word'? What is His relation to God; to the world; to men? See the whole passage.

2 Who does not, and who does become a child of God? By what means is one brought into this new status?

3 Note all the allusions to 'light' and associated ideas (*e.g.*, 'glory') in this passage. How much of the purpose of Jesus' coming does this explain?

Note. Verse 16. 'Grace upon grace': *i.e.*, one grace succeeding another.

☐ STUDY 2 John 1: 19–34

1 What do we learn here about (a) the character, (b) the work, of John the Baptist? See also verses 6–8 and 3: 28–30.

2 Verses 26–34. What testimony does John the Baptist here bear to Jesus? How much of this did John learn about Him through his experience at Christ's baptism? Do these truths mean something to you?

Note. Verse 29. 'He saw Jesus coming': probably after the forty days in the wilderness, when He was tempted by Satan. That Jesus' baptism had already taken place is shown by verse 32. *Cf.* Lk. 3: 21, 22.

☐ STUDY 3 John 1: 35–51

1 Describe what it was that brought each of these five men to Jesus. How far did they understand who Jesus was? What account of Him can *you* give to others?

2 Verses 48, 49. Why did Jesus' answer elicit the response of Nathanael? See 2: 25. What do verses 47–50 reveal of Nathanael's character?

Notes

1 Verse 42. Cephas = Peter = Rock.
2 Verses 47, 51. An allusion to the story of Jacob in Gn. 32: 24–29 and 28: 12, 13.
3 Verse 51. This word, as shown by the plural 'you', was spoken not about Nathanael only, but about all the disciples. Jesus would be revealed to them as the true and final Mediator between God and man.

☐ STUDY 4 John 2: 1–22

1 Verses 1–11 present the first of the seven 'signs' (see Introduction), which reveal the identity of Jesus and stimulate faith (verse 11). What particular aspect of Jesus' glory does this miracle display?

What change in our life does turning the water into wine represent? *Cf.* 2 Cor. 5: 17. What can we learn from Mary's response to Jesus?

2 The idea of the 'Temple' unites verses 13–17 with 18–22. How does Jesus appear in each incident? By what authority does He drive out the traders? *Cf.* Mal. 3: 1–3. What crisis does this incident foreshadow in the mind of Jesus? What did He foresee concerning the cost and character of His mission?

Notes

1 Verse 4. The English, even in RSV, makes Jesus' words seem disrespectful, but in the Greek the form of address is perfectly courteous. Jesus makes it clear that He depends upon no human instructions, even from His mother, but only upon that which God appoints. He is awaiting His Father's instructions.

2 Verses 14–16. See *TNTC* (p. 61) for discussion whether there were two cleansings of the Temple, one at the beginning of Jesus' ministry, as here, and one at the end, as recorded in the Synoptics.

☐ STUDY 5 John 2: 23 – 3: 21

1 Why was Jesus not satisfied with the faith spoken of in 2: 23? *Cf.* 4: 48; 6: 26, 30; Mt. 13: 14. Is my faith the kind that pleases God?

2 What was right and what was lacking in Nicodemus' assessment of Jesus? How did Jesus' answer correct him? What is involved in being 'born of the Spirit', and why is it needed? *Cf.* Mt. 18: 3; Jn. 1: 12, 13; 2 Cor. 5: 17; Rom. 8: 8, 9.

3 Why was the lifting up of the Son of man necessary? (Note 'must' in verse 14.) On what ground are men judged and condemned? Where do you stand in relation to these truths?

Notes

1 Verse 5. 'Born of water' probably refers to John's baptism.

2 Verse 8. As with the wind, so with the movement of the Spirit, the effect is real and recognizable, although the process is hidden.

3 Verses 12, 13. The gospel speaks of heavenly things, of which Christ is the sole revealer. *Cf.* 3: 31, 32; Mt. 11: 27.

☐ STUDY 6 John 3: 22–36

1 How might one have expected John to have replied to the statement of verse 26? Consider the quality of character and the principles brought out in his answer. How far do you share his attitude to Christ? How does it apply to your situation?

2 What is said about Jesus in verses 31, 32, 34, 35, which set Him apart from and above all others?

3 'Receives his testimony', 'believes in the Son', 'does not obey the Son' (verses 33, 36). What kinds of response to Jesus Christ do these phrases describe? To what consequences do they lead?

Notes

1 Verse 32. 'No one': *i.e.*, generally speaking; it is qualified in verse 33.

2 Verse 33. 'Sets his seal': he both confirms his acceptance of the truth of God's word and in his consequent experience proves the truth of it. *Cf.* 7: 17.

☐ STUDY 7 John 4: 1–26

1 What did our Lord mean by 'living water' (verse 10)? Why, when He had wakened in the woman a desire for it, did He not at once grant her request? What was necessary before He could do so?

2 Trace the successive steps by which Jesus brought the woman to feel her need of salvation, and pointed her to Himself. What can we learn from this to help us as we seek to lead others to Him?

3 In verses 19, 20 was the woman evading the demand for a personal response? How does Jesus' answer meet the need of those today who evade the claims of God by professing to follow a correct form of worship? Where must all look for salvation?

Note. Verse 20. 'This mountain': *i.e.*, Mount Gerizim, where the Samaritans had built a temple. The temple had been destroyed, but the Samaritans regarded the place as holy.

☐ STUDY 8 John 4: 27–54

1 How do the previous verses explain and verses 35–38 develop the truth which Jesus expressed in verse 34? What gives you most satisfaction in life?

2 Two groups of Samaritans and the Capernaum official all believed in Jesus, but through different means. What was the particular truth about Him which brought each of them to faith? To what did 'the second sign' (verse 54) point? What aspect of the Lord's character or power led you to Him?

3 Verse 48 seems to be a test of the man's sincerity. How would you explain Jesus' words here?

Note. Verses 35–38. In the natural world there were yet four months until harvest, but in the spiritual sphere in this instance reaping was possible at once. Someone else had done the sowing.

☐ STUDY 9 John 5: 1–29

1 Verses 2–9, the third 'sign'. What features of Jesus' power does it reveal? What did He do for the man, and demand from the man, apart from making him walk? See verses 6 and 14.

2 Verses 17–29. In what terms is Jesus' relationship with God described? What functions concerning judgment has God given to Jesus, and why? How do these truths concern us?

3 Verses 16–18. What connection has Jesus' statement in verse 17 with His healing on the sabbath? How does this agree with Gn. 2: 2, 3, and how does it answer the Jews' criticism of His action?

Note. Verse 25. What is meant here is spiritual resurrection from the death of sin. Contrast verses 28, 29.

☐ STUDY 10 John 5: 30–47

1 To what four different testimonies to Himself does Jesus appeal? Which does He Himself regard as of least importance, and why? Contrast 8: 14.

2 Verses 39, 40. Is it still possible to study the Bible without finding life? If so, what is lacking? What reasons does Jesus give for the Jews' failure? *Cf.* 2 Cor. 3: 14–16.

Note. Verse 31. 'Not true': in the sense of not being accepted as true. *Cf.* Dt. 19: 15; Mt. 18: 16; Jn. 8: 13, 14.

☐ STUDY 11 John 6: 1–21

1 Taking this fourth 'sign' in the context of verses 1–13, note what it reveals concerning (a) why the people were attracted to Jesus; (b) His own attitude to the people; (c) His testing of His disciples' faith; (d) His use of their co-operation; (e) the source of the answer to men's need. What over-all lesson was this miracle intended to convey?

2 Verse 15. Why did not Jesus wish to be made king by these people? What may we learn from His withdrawing from the place of success to be by Himself? *Cf.* Lk. 5: 15, 16.

Notes

1 Verse 7. A denarius may be valued as a day's wage for a labourer; *cf.* Mt. 20: 2.

2 Verse 14. 'The prophet who is to come': *cf.* Dt. 18: 15; Mt. 11: 3; He is here identified by the people with the Messiah, as verse 15 shows.

☐ STUDY 12 John 6: 22–40

The miracle of verses 4–13 is the basis of the dialogue between Jesus and the Jews in verses 25–59.

1 The people saw the outward form of the miracle, but failed to discern what it signified spiritually (verse 26). Why? From what

motives did they seek Jesus? Are you more concerned about spiritual development than material prosperity (verse 27)?

2 'Labour' in verse 27 is literally 'work for'. How did the people relate this word (a) to the work they were expected to do (verse 28), (b) to the work of Moses compared with Jesus (verses 30, 31)? What work did Jesus (a) require from them (verse 29) and (b) offer from Himself (verse 32–40)? What, therefore, is the answer to the question in verse 28?

3 How do verses 35–40 present God's answer to man's hunger?

Note. Verses 22–25 explain the astonishment of the crowd at finding Jesus next day on the Capernaum side of the lake. They had noticed that He had not gone with the disciples.

☐ STUDY 13 John 6: 41–71

Today's portion falls into four parts: (a) verses 41–51, Jesus' reply to murmurings of the Jews; (b) verses 52–59, Jesus' answers to the wranglings of the Jews; (c) verses 60–65, Jesus' reply to murmurings of His disciples; (d) verses 66–71, Jesus asks the Twelve, 'Will you also go away?'

1 Comparing verses 36, 37 with 43–45, why do you think some people will not accept Jesus' words? By what steps do others come to experience salvation?

2 The closing verses 60–71 make clear that what Jesus offers to men is not fleshly or material gain (*cf.* verse 27), but spiritual life through union with Himself. What three reasons does Peter give why he and his fellow disciples remained faithful when many others went back?

3 How did Jesus give His flesh for the life of the world? What is meant by eating His flesh and drinking His blood?

Notes

1 Verse 62. The return of the Son of man to heaven (*cf.* 3: 13) will be a greater wonder than the words just spoken. It will confirm the divine character of Jesus and of His words.

2 The approaching Passover Feast was clearly in our Lord's thought as He spoke, and there may be anticipating allusions to the Lord's Supper; but Jesus is speaking in this discourse, not of the sacrament itself, but of the truths of which the sacrament is only one expression. Note the manner of true participation (verses 35, 63, 68, 69).

☐ STUDY 14 John 7: 1–24

Chapters 7: 1 – 10: 21 give an account of Jesus' visit to Jerusalem at the Feast of Tabernacles six months before His death. The story vividly portrays the various attitudes towards Jesus among different groups. These groups fall into two main classes: one, 'the Jews', who included the chief priests,

Pharisees, rulers and 'the people of Jerusalem', and the other, 'the people', that is, the general multitude from all parts, who were attending the feast. The first of these two classes was, in the main, hostile to Jesus.

1 How do the words of Jesus' brothers in verses 3-8 show that they did not understand Him? What did Jesus mean by 'my time'? The world's attitude to Jesus prevented Him from showing Himself to them, as other men might (verses 4, 7). Can *you* expect any different reception from the world (*cf.* 15: 18-21)? Has verse 13 any reproach for you?

2 Verses 17, 18. What two tests does our Lord suggest by which a man can discover whether Jesus' teaching was true and of divine origin? What will it cost you to apply these tests?

Notes

1 Verses 8, 10. Jesus did not break His word. He meant that He was not going up to the feast just then, and at their direction.

2 Verses 21-24. The law of Moses commanded circumcision on the eighth day after birth (Gn. 17: 12; Lv. 12: 3), and it was the practice of the Jews to perform the rite on that day, *even if it fell upon the sabbath*. Jesus argued that to make a man's whole body well on the sabbath had even more justification than to circumcise him.

☐ STUDY 15 John 7: 25-52

1 What illustrations are found in these verses (a) of the deep impression made by the Lord Jesus upon many; and yet (b) how their incipient faith was checked by ignorance (verses 27-29), or prejudice (verses 35, 36), or pride (verses 48-52)? Is one of these hindering me?

2 The chief priests and the Pharisees by no means saw eye to eye in most matters, but they were united against Jesus. What action did they take at this time, and what prevented its success? It is often said, 'No thinking person now believes that . . . '. What example of this attitude can you find in this passage?

3 In what way is the promise of verses 37, 38 an advance on that of 4: 13, 14? What difference does the Holy Spirit make to your life? *Cf.* Acts 1: 8.

Note. Verse 39. The Spirit was already present and active in the world, but the particular promise of Joel 2: 28 was not fulfilled until the ascended and enthroned Christ gave the Holy Spirit on the Day of Pentecost. See Acts 2: 16-18, 33.

☐ STUDY 16 John 7: 53 - 8: 29

1 For the passage 7: 53 - 8: 11, see Introduction. It has perhaps been introduced here as an illustration of 8: 15. What two different types of sinner can you see in the Pharisees and in the woman? Why

did Jesus treat her so gently? Would His words to her bring conviction of her sin?

2 In verses 13–29 what does Jesus say about His origin, His ultimate destination, His relation to the world, His relation to God?

3 What was lacking in the Pharisees which prevented them from recognizing the truth of Jesus' words? How can I see the light of truth? How does light lead to life? See verses 12, 24.

Notes

1 8: 12. An allusion to the pillar of fire which guided the Israelites on their journey through the wilderness (see Nu. 9: 15–23), and which was commemorated during the Feast of Tabernacles by brilliant lighting of the Temple.

2 Verses 13, 14. There is no contradiction with 5: 31. There Jesus says that if He had been the sole witness in His own cause, His witness would not have been true. But in both passages He goes on to point out that He is not alone in His witness. See verses 17, 18.

□ STUDY 17 John 8: 30–59

1 The form of expression in Greek in verse 31 shows that 'the Jews' here did not commit themselves to Jesus as much as the 'many' in verse 30. What steps leading to full freedom are seen in verses 31–36? What is this freedom? In what sense did the Jews claim to be free? Are you truly free?

2 This section is concerned with the real meaning of parentage. For what reasons did Jesus argue that these Jews were not truly the children of Abraham or of God, but of the devil? What evidence did Jesus give that He is God's Son? Why were they not able to see this?

Notes

1 Verse 51. 'He will never see death': *i.e.*, know the experience of that death which is God's judgment on sin; *cf.* Gn. 2: 17; Jn. 5: 24; 11: 26.

2 Verse 56. 'My day': Abraham in faith saw ahead to the day of Christ's incarnation, and anticipated His saving work.

3 Verse 58. 'I am': the divine name, as in Ex. 3: 14.

□ STUDY 18 John 9

1 This is the sixth of the seven 'signs'. To which aspect of Jesus' work does it point? See verses 5, 39. In how many ways is the opening of this man's eyes to be compared with the giving of spiritual sight? Does your personal experience of Jesus' power give you the same assurance in answering His critics as this man had?

2 Explain verses 39–41. Detail the ways in which the words and actions of the Pharisees in verses 13–34 illustrate this passage.

Note. Verse 14. The 'work' for which the Pharisees condemned Jesus as breaking the sabbath was making clay, as well as healing. The latter was allowed, but only in an emergency.

☐ STUDY 19 John 10: 1–21

Compare Je. 23: 1–4. By their attitude to the blind man of chapter 9 the Pharisees, who claimed to be the spiritual guides of Israel as the people of God, had shown themselves to be 'thieves and robbers' (verses 1, 8), like the false prophets of the Old Testament.

1 Verses 1–10. Why does Jesus call Himself 'the door of the sheep'? What are the privileges and blessings of those who enter in? How do the sheep recognize the true shepherd? What does he do to them? Do you know his voice?

2 What are the marks of the good shepherd? Can you find in verses 11–18 (a) proof that our Lord's death was not a mere martyrdom, (b) the purpose of His life and death, and (c) an incentive to missionary work? *Cf.* Rev. 7: 9, 10, 15–17.

Notes

1 Verse 3. 'Hear': *i.e.*, listen attentively to, and so obey.

2 Jesus is both 'door' and 'shepherd'. Others also are under-shepherds (Acts 20: 28, 29; 1 Pet. 5: 2–4) who must themselves first enter through the 'door'.

☐ STUDY 20 John 10: 22–42

1 Why would a plain answer to the Jews' question of verse 24 have been useless? What indications of the nature of Jesus' Person were already being given? See verses 25, 32, 37, 38. Why were the Jews incapable of seeing this? Do your works corroborate your words?

2 In the statements of verses 27, 28 how is the sheep's relation to the shepherd described, and how the shepherd's relation to the sheep? On what grounds given in verses 28, 29 can you be sure that you will never perish?

3 In what terms does Jesus describe His relationship with God, and what evidence does He give in support of His claim? How far are the words of the Jews at the end of verse 33 correct? What ought they to have done?

Notes

1 Verse 30. The word 'one' is neuter in the Greek: 'a unity', not 'one person'.

2 Verses 34–36. See Ps. 82: 6. Even the judges of Israel, acting as God's representatives, were called 'gods'. The Jews should have seen that Jesus was far superior to them. This comparison with the men of the Old Testament is sufficient argument to refute the charge of blasphemy. Jesus does not imply that He is merely a man like them.

□ STUDY 21 John 11: 1–27

The seventh 'sign'.

1 Compare verse 4 with 9: 3. Explain the apparent contradiction both in verse 4 and also in verses 5, 6. See verses 14, 15. Can you see why God sometimes seems to delay answering your prayer?

2 What direction and assurance do verses 9, 10 give for the conduct of your life? *Cf.* 9: 4, 5.

3 In verses 21, 22, 24 Martha makes three correct but limited statements. In respect to each of them Jesus' answer in verses 25, 26 reveals that He has within Himself infinitely greater powers than she knew. What are they?

Note. Verse 26. 'Shall never die': for the believer death is no longer death. It introduces him into a new state of life. See Note on Jn. 8: 51.

□ STUDY 22 John 11: 28–44

1 What is the special significance of this seventh 'sign'? How is it related to the events which Jesus was shortly to experience as the climax of His work? In what way was the glory of God revealed?

2 Why did Jesus pray aloud before calling Lazarus from the tomb? What does this teach about the means by which His miracles were accomplished? *Cf.* Jn. 5: 19, 20; 14: 10.

Note. Verses 33–38. The word 'weep' in verse 33 is the wailing of mourners; that in verse 35 implies silent tears of sympathy. The rendering of RSV in verse 33, 'he was deeply moved in spirit', does not give the full force of the Greek, for which Prof. Tasker suggests, 'He was enraged in spirit and troubled Himself' (*TNTC*, p. 140). His anger was roused against the evil powers of death, which caused such distress to mankind, and which He was about to conquer, here by a mighty display of divine power, and finally on the cross by His own death and resurrection.

□ STUDY 23 John 11: 45 – 12: 19

1 Observe the varied effects of the miracle. See especially 11: 45, 46, 47–53, 54; 12: 10, 11, 17–19; and *cf.* Lk. 16: 31. How is it that the same act quickens faith in some, and hatred in others? *Cf.* 11: 47, 48; 12: 11, 19; Mt. 27: 18.

2 12: 1–8. What insights does Mary's action reveal? How far does your love for the Lord lead you to understand Him, and to serve Him without counting the cost?

3 In 11: 47–53 and 12: 12–16 there are two examples of God overruling men's words and actions to fulfil His own purposes. What is the real purpose of God to which each points?

Note. 11: 48. The Jewish leaders feared that Jesus might lead a revolt for which the Romans would exact severe punishment.

☐ STUDY 24 John 12: 20–36

The Greeks who inquired for Jesus were a token of the world of people beyond Israel who would be saved through Jesus' atoning death and resurrection (*cf.* 10: 16; 12: 32). Their coming therefore introduces the consummation of Jesus' work; see verse 23.

1 Give examples of the ways in which you can love your life, or hate it. To whom does Jesus primarily refer in verse 24? In view of this, what is involved in following Him (verse 26)?

2 In what sense did the coming 'hour' (verse 23) bring about the glorifying of the Son of man and of the Father (verse 28)? How did His being lifted up involve the judgment of this world (verses 31–34)?

3 Verses 35, 36 give Jesus' last appeal to the nation. What is meant by walking and believing in the light? Are you doing this?

☐ STUDY 25 John 12: 37–50

This passage presents the problem of unbelief in face of manifest evidence of God's power and presence.

1 Both quotations from Isaiah in verses 38–40 speak of Christ, the latter because Christ's glory is included in the vision of God's glory in Isaiah 6. Who has and who has not 'believed our report'? Why has God blinded their eyes, *etc.*? Does this apply today to (a) Jews, and (b) non-Jews? Why do *you* believe?

2 The *seriousness* of rejecting Jesus is the subject of verses 44–50, in which John summarizes the teaching of Jesus on this matter. Why is it so serious to reject Jesus? See especially verses 45, 46, 50, and compare Pr. 1: 20–33. Why will Jesus' word be the judge (verse 48)?

Notes

1 Verse 42. 'Put out of the synagogue': *cf.* 9: 22. This was a very severe punishment, involving separation from public worship and from social intercourse.

2 Verse 45. 'Sees': here is the concept of careful observation leading to spiritual insight.

For Studies 26–42 on the second half of John's Gospel see p. 270.

2 KINGS

For Introduction, see p. 244.

Analysis

1: 1 – 2: 11	Elijah (continued).
2: 12 – 13: 25	Elisha.
14 – 17	The course of events leading to the captivity of Israel.
18 – 20	Hezekiah (and Isaiah).
21	Manasseh's evil reign.
22, 23	Josiah's reformation.
24, 25	The captivity of Judah.

☐ STUDY 20 2 Kings 1 and 2

These two chapters contain the last two stories about Elijah.

1 Contrast the end of King Ahaziah with Elijah's end. What was the fundamental difference between these two men? *Cf.* 1 Jn. 2: 15–17; 5: 4.

2 In what three ways was Elisha tested (see 2: 1–15), and what qualities in him does his conduct reveal? Have we the same resolute spirit? See Note 1 below. Elisha's miracles are parables of spiritual truths. What do you learn from this first miracle (2: 19–22)?

Notes

1 2: 9. Elisha wanted to be fully equipped for the high service to which he was called.

2 2: 23–25. 'Small boys': better 'young lads', as in RV mg. These were youths of Bethel, whose attitude reflected the spirit of the place. Coming out to meet Elisha in a large band, they mocked the prophet, who was bald in mourning for his master (*cf.* Jb. 1: 20), and said 'Go up', *i.e.*, 'Ascend to heaven as you say your master did'. It was a grievous insult, and Elisha, righteously angry, invoked the judgment of God upon them. Shaken by the whole episode, he did not enter Bethel but made his way to Carmel.

□ STUDY 21 2 Kings 3: 1 – 4: 7

1 What was the cause of the attack upon Moab, and how was Elisha brought into the situation? A map should be used to identify the route taken by the attacking armies, and the place where the miracle was wrought. How does the story show what one man of faith can do to save a multitude?

2 How does the story of 4: 1–7 illustrate the working of faith? Was it easy for the woman to do what Elisha bade her do? Has this any lesson for you in your own life?

Notes

1 3: 1. *Cf.* 1: 17. The apparent discrepancy may be explained by the fact that father and son frequently reigned together during the latter part of the father's life.

2 3: 11. 'Who poured water . . .': *i.e.*, he was Elijah's attendant.

3 3: 20. Travellers report that in that region there is water under the sand.

□ STUDY 22 2 Kings 4: 8–44

1 Verses 8–37. In what ways is the woman of Shunem an example to us? What do you learn about the reasons why God allows His servants to undergo acute suffering? What lessons are to be drawn from Gehazi's failure?

2 What features in Elisha's character are brought out by the incidents in this passage?

Note. Verse 42. The present was for Elisha; and if there was still scarcity of food (verse 38), the gift would be the more precious. But Elisha shared it with all who were with him.

□ STUDY 23 2 Kings 5: 1 – 6: 7

1 Chapter 5. There are four important figures in this chapter: the captive maid, Naaman, Elisha and Gehazi. What lessons may we learn from each?

2 6: 1–7. Think about this incident in relation to Elisha's position as a spiritual leader. Are there lessons here for the Christian church?

Notes

1 5: 17. The idea in Naaman's mind was that Jehovah, the God of Israel, could not be rightly worshipped except on Israelitish soil. His faith was still very imperfect, as verse 18 also shows.

2 5: 22. 'A talent of silver': *i.e.*, 'four hundred pounds' (Moffatt), a very large sum to be asked for two young men of the sons of the prophets.

□ STUDY 24 2 Kings 6: 8 – 7: 20

1 6: 8–23. Why was the young man afraid, and why was the prophet not afraid? Have we learned the secret of the conquest of fear? *Cf.* Heb. 11: 27.

2 Observe the severity of the siege, and the greatness of the faith that enabled Elisha to speak as he did in 7: 1. How does the judgment that fell upon the unbelieving officer illustrate the punishment that will follow all wilful unbelief? *Cf.* Mk. 16: 16b; Jn. 3: 36.

3 What lessons do you learn from the part played by the four lepers in this story?

Notes

1 6: 25. 'Ten pounds in silver was paid for the head of an ass and twelve shillings for a pint of doves' dung' (Moffatt).
2 6: 30, 31. Elisha appears to have been sustaining the hopes of the king and people by the promise of divine deliverance. The king's faith now gave way, and he burned with anger against the prophet.
3 7: 1. 'A shekel': 'half-a-crown' (Moffatt).

☐ STUDY 25 2 Kings 8 and 9

Today's portion contains (a) two incidents connected with Elisha's ministry; (b) a brief summary of the reigns of two kings of Judah; (c) the story of the revolution under Jehu, through which the house of Ahab was destroyed.

1 8: 1–15. How does the first of these two incidents illustrate God's watchful care over His own? *Cf.* Ps. 33: 18–22; Rom. 8: 28. In the second incident why did Elisha weep? *Cf.* Je. 8: 16 – 9: 1; Lk. 19: 41–44.

2 Ponder the vivid story of the revolution, as given in chapter 9, noticing especially how it began, and the references to the word of God and its fulfilment. *Cf.* Heb. 10: 31; 12: 29; 2 Ki. 10: 30.

3 Consider throughout the history of the kings of Israel and Judah the results of marriage alliances with those who are the enemies of God.

Notes

1 8: 10. The sickness in itself was not fatal, but Elisha was given a vision of other things that would happen, which filled him with horror. Moffatt translates verse 11 thus: 'The man of God's face became rigid with horror, absolute horror.'
2 Verse 13. Hazael was elated at the prospect of doing such deeds.
3 Verse 16. It is important to distinguish between Jehoram, son of Jehoshaphat, king of Judah, and Jehoram (or Joram), son of Ahab, king of Israel. Their reigns were in great measure contemporaneous.
4 Verse 26. Athaliah was the daughter of Ahab and Jezebel, and therefore the granddaughter of Omri. See 1 Ki. 16: 29–31. She married Jehoram, king of Judah (verse 18).

☐ STUDY 26 2 Kings 10

1 Trace the course of Jehu's rise to power. Looking back to chapter 9, where was he first anointed, and acclaimed as king? Whither did he then go, striking down in swift succession Jehoram, Ahaziah and

Jezebel? Whom did he further slay, as recorded in 10: 1–14, and by what means?

2 From this account of his reign, what do you learn about Jehu's aim, his character, and his attitude to God?

Note. Verses 9, 10. Jehu quietens the people of Samaria, by reminding them that all that was happening was but the fulfilment of God's word through Elijah. See 1 Ki. 21: 21, 23, 24.

☐ STUDY 27 2 Kings 11 and 12

In today's portion we pass from the history of the northern kingdom to the re-establishment in Judah of the worship of Jehovah.

1 What was Athaliah's purpose, and by what two persons, under God, was it brought to nought? What new light does 2 Ch. 22: 11 throw upon the story? Compare with the faith and courage of Jehosheba and Jehoiada that of Moses' parents (*cf.* Heb. 11: 23).

2 What signs of healthy moral and spiritual life do you find in these chapters, and in what respect shortcoming? What part did Joash play in this? See further 2 Ch. 24: 17–24.

☐ STUDY 28 2 Kings 13 and 14

This is another composite portion, containing first a brief account of two kings of Israel, Jehoahaz, and Jehoash or Joash (to be distinguished from the king of Judah of the same name); then two incidents connected with Elisha; and finally an account of the reigns of Amaziah, king of Judah, and Jeroboam II of Israel.

1 What evidence is there that in the reign of Jehoahaz Israel was greatly impoverished? Also what reason is assigned for this state of things?

2 In what ways did all four kings, whose reigns are described in chapter 14, fall short of what God required of them?

Notes

1 13: 5. A reference to Jeroboam II; see 14: 27.
2 14: 13. 'Four hundred cubits': about 200 yards.
3 14: 23. Jeroboam II had a long and successful reign, during which the northern kingdom of Israel was greatly extended. See verse 25.
4 14: 25. 'The entrance of Hamath' may refer to the pass between Hermon and Lebanon in the north; 'the sea of Arabah' is the Dead Sea. There is no other reference in Scripture to this particular prophecy of Jonah.

☐ STUDY 29 2 Kings 15 and 16

These two chapters cover a period of about eighty years. It is helpful to make a list in parallel columns of the kings of Judah and Israel respectively, mentioned in today's portion, with the length of their reigns.

1 Taking first the kings of Judah, how does Ahaz stand out in sharp contrast to his father Jotham, and his grandfather Azariah (Uzziah)? What two particular acts of folly, one political, the other religious, are recorded of him? *Cf.* Ps. 146: 3–5; Is. 7: 1–9.

2 How long did the dynasty of Jehu continue in Israel? See 10: 30 and Ho. 1: 4. What happened after the dynasty came to an end? What great loss did the northern kingdom suffer in the reign of Pekah? Do you find any good thing recorded of any of the kings of the northern kingdom in these two chapters? *Cf.* Ho. 7: 7; 8: 4; 13: 11.

□ STUDY 30 2 Kings 17

This chapter tells of the end of the northern kingdom of Israel, with the causes of its downfall, and what followed after it.

1 Can you trace a progressive deterioration in Israel's moral and spiritual condition in verses 9–18? Compare the phrase 'did secretly . . .' in verse 9 with 'sold themselves . . .' in verse 17. What are the modern counterparts of the sins which Israel committed? *Cf.* Col. 3: 5; Heb. 12: 25.

2 Consider what great events had taken place in Israel's history in the territory of the northern kingdom, which had brought glory to God, and deliverance to the people. To what condition was it now reduced? *Cf.* 2 Tim. 3: 5; Is. 29: 13.

Notes

1 Verse 2. In what way Hoshea sinned less grievously than preceding kings is not explained.

2 Verses 33, 34. The word 'fear' is used here in two senses; in verse 33 of outward worship, and in verse 34 of heart reverence.

□ STUDY 31 2 Kings 18: 1 – 19: 7

1 What four points about Hezekiah's attitude and conduct with reference to God are mentioned in 18: 3, 5 and 6? Are these things true of us? How did Hezekiah's faith manifest itself in action, and what evidence had he of God's favour and blessing? See verses 4, 7 and 8.

2 In what ways did the Assyrian speaker, Rabshakeh, threaten the people of Israel? What were the reactions to this attack of (a) the people, and (b) Isaiah? *Cf.* Ex. 14: 13; 1 Sa. 17: 44, 45; Dn. 3: 15–18. Are you able to encourage others by your faith, or are you among those that fear and need encouragement?

Notes

1 18: 22. Hezekiah's reforming zeal was no doubt unpopular with many. Rabshakeh knew this, and sought to turn it to advantage for his own ends.

2 19: 3b. A figure of speech denoting a crisis of extreme gravity.

☐ STUDY 32 2 Kings 19: 8–37

1 Comparing Hezekiah's action and words in verses 14–19 with those of the earlier crisis in verses 3, 4, what evidence do you find that Hezekiah's faith had grown stronger?

2 How did Sennacherib appear to merely human judgment? How did he appear as seen by Isaiah with the eyes of faith? Are we learning to look at the world situation today in relation to God? *Cf.* Jn. 14: 1. What does the whole story teach as to the difference which faith in God makes in individual and national life?

Note. Verse 29. The meaning is that only in the third year from the time at which the words were spoken would there be normal sowing and reaping. The fulfilment of the prophet's pronouncement would attest his divinely given authority.

☐ STUDY 33 2 Kings 20 and 21

The events described in chapter 20 happened in the earlier part of Hezekiah's reign before the invasion of Sennacherib (see verses 6 and 13, and also 18: 15, 16), and are introduced here as a kind of appendix to the story of Hezekiah.

1 Put yourself in Hezekiah's place, and try to picture the effect on him of Isaiah's announcement. What did he do (*cf.* Ps. 102: 24), and what did God then do? How would these experiences help to prepare Hezekiah for the greater tests of faith that he was to meet when Sennacherib attacked him? In spite of his faithfulness to God, in what way did Hezekiah fail in the incident recorded in 20: 12–19? *Cf.* Pr. 29: 5. How did Isaiah view the incident, and what word of judgment was given him to speak? For its fulfilment over a century later see chapter 25.

2 Summarize in your own words Manasseh's flagrant idolatry. What judgments did God declare through His prophets? Do you think it can have been easy for the prophets to speak thus? *Cf.* Mi. 3: 8.

Notes

1 20: 12. Merodach-baladan (see Is. 39: 1) was a northern chieftain, who had seized Babylon and was looking round for every possible means of strengthening his position. His reign did not last long, and it would have been folly for Hezekiah to enter into alliance with him.

2 21: 13. The first half of the verse means that Jerusalem will receive the same measure of judgment as Samaria and the house of Ahab. The metaphor in the second half of the verse is a very strong and vivid one.

☐ STUDY 34 2 Kings 22 and 23

1 Make out a list of all that Josiah did, both positively to promote true religion, and negatively to destroy the false. Are our lives marked by a similar eagerness to depart from iniquity and to live

in covenant with God? *Cf.* 2 Cor. 6: 14 – 7: 1. What was the mainspring of Josiah's reforming zeal? *Cf.* Ps. 119: 161b; Is. 66: 2; see also 2 Ki. 23: 25; and contrast the behaviour of Jehoiakim in Je. 36: 23–25.

2 Examine the part played by Huldah the prophetess, and compare with the influence of other women mentioned in previous chapters.

☐ **STUDY 35 2 Kings 24 and 25**

1 Looking back to 23: 31, what four kings reigned between Josiah's death and the fall of Jerusalem? What was the length of their reigns, and what was their record, as described in these chapters?

2 In what ways was Nebuchadnezzar's treatment of Jerusalem after his second capture of it much more severe than when he captured it the first time? What reasons are given in chapter 24 for the captivity? *Cf.* 23: 26, 27; Je. 15: 1–4; Dt. 4: 26, 27. What does this teach us about the end of persistent sinning? Yet what star of hope is seen shining in the closing verses of the book? *Cf.* 2 Sa. 7: 14, 15.

Note. 25: 22. 'Gedaliah the son of Ahikam': see 22: 12; Je. 26: 24. The story of his assassination is told more fully in Je. 40: 1 – 41: 10.

JOHN 13–21

☐ **STUDY 26 John 13: 1–20**

1 Verse 13. 'Teacher and Lord.' What degrees of Lordship are revealed in verses 1 and 3? Did Jesus perform the task of a servant in spite of, or because of, His relation to the Father? *Cf.* Phil. 2: 5–8.

2 What important lesson did Jesus teach in response to Peter's interruptions? See verses 8 and 10. *Cf.* Tit. 3: 5; 1 Jn. 1: 7.

3 What further application did Jesus make of His action as an example to His followers? *Cf.* Lk. 22: 22–27. Are you giving sufficient heed to this matter? See verse 17.

Notes

1 Verse 10. 'Bathed': the disciples had been cleansed; all except Judas (verse 11). *Cf.* 15: 3.

2 Verse 20. 'Anyone whom I send': *i.e.*, the apostles and all subsequent witnesses to Christ. So also verse 16.

☐ STUDY 27 John 13: 21–32

1 Trace the action of Satan upon the heart of Judas as shown in this Gospel. See 6: 70; 12: 4–6; 13: 2, 27. If the giving of the morsel to him in verse 26 was Jesus' last appeal of love, what state of heart does verse 27a indicate? What connection has verse 30 with 12: 35, 36?

2 Compare verses 31, 32 with 12: 23, 28. Verses 31 and 32a point to the action of the Son and 32b to that of the Father. To what impending events did these words point? How can the Father be glorified in you?

☐ STUDY 28 John 13: 33 – 14: 14

1 Trace the connection between 13: 33–37 and 14: 1–6. Where was Jesus going? Why could they not follow until later? To what event does 'I will come again' refer?

2 In what respect were the questions of both Thomas and Philip short-sighted? How is Jesus the way, the truth and the life, especially in relation to the Father?

3 What prospect does Jesus set before His disciples as a consequence of His return to the Father? See verses 12–14. Do you know anything of this in your experience? Why are the works of the believer called 'greater works'?

☐ STUDY 29 John 14: 15–24

1 Three times in this passage Jesus speaks of loving Him (verses 15, 21, 23). How does our love for the Lord Jesus show itself? Is this true of you? Since love is personal, can you see to what personal relationship this love leads?

2 In what sense does Jesus 'come' to us (verse 18)? How is this related to the coming of 'another Advocate' (see Note 1)? Give examples of ways in which Jesus proved to be the first 'Advocate'.

3 Why cannot the world 'see' the Spirit or Jesus (verses 17, 19)? *Cf.* 1: 11; 3: 19; 5: 37; 7: 34; 8: 19, 47; 12: 37–40. What explanation did Jesus give here in answer to Judas? How can the eyes of men be opened to see Him?

Notes

1 Verse 16. 'Counsellor': literally, one called to one's side to plead on one's behalf. 'Advocate' is a better translation. *Cf.* 1 Jn. 2: 1.

2 Verse 18. 'Desolate': better, 'bereaved'.

3 Verse 22. *Cf.* 7: 4. The disciples also naturally expected that the Messiah would display His power to the world.

☐ STUDY 30 John 14: 25 – 15: 8

1 The disciples were distressed at the thought of Jesus going away and leaving them alone in a hostile world; *cf.* 16: 6. What promises does Jesus give in verses 25–29 to answer their fears? Why does His going to the Father bring greater benefit than if He had remained as He was? What also does verse 31 teach about Christ's reason for facing the cross?

2 What does the parable of the vine teach about (a) the purpose for which the branches exist, (b) the vinedresser's dealing with the branches, and (c) the dependence of the branches upon the vine? With verses 3 and 7 compare 14: 15, 21, 23; see also 8: 31, 32. What kind of fruit do you bear? *Cf.* Gal. 5: 22, 23.

Notes

1 14: 28. 'The Father is greater than I': *cf.* 10: 29, 30. He is not greater in being more *divine*, but in the eternal Father-Son and God-man relationships. (See *NBCR*, p. 959.)

2 14: 30. 'The ruler of this world': *cf.* 12: 31; 16: 11; 2 Cor. 4: 4; Eph. 2: 2; 1 Jn. 5: 19. The RSV 'has no power over me' gives the true sense of these words. There is nothing in Jesus over which the devil can claim possession, and therefore domination.

☐ STUDY 31 John 15: 9–25

1 People think of the Christian life as a joyless observance of rules. What answer to this idea is contained in these verses? Is it your experience?

2 If we are disciples of Jesus, why must we expect hatred from the world? Why did many hate and persecute Jesus?

3 Love not only feels, but acts. By what actions is (a) the love of the Father shown to the Son, (b) the love of the Son to His disciples, and (c) the love of the disciples to one another? *Cf.* 3: 35; 5: 20; 1 Jn. 3: 16–18.

☐ STUDY 32 John 15: 26 – 16: 15

1 What evidence do you find in 16: 1–7 that the disciples were cast down by Jesus' words? Why did He say that He had not spoken of these things before, and why did He speak of them now? Notice,

however, that He did not lighten in any way the dark picture He had drawn, but rather shaded it more deeply (16: 2).

2 What new force, does Jesus say, will be brought to bear upon the world, and through whom (see 15: 26, 27)? What threefold result will follow (16: 8–11)? How would this make Jesus' departure an advantage instead of a loss?

3 What results ought this situation to have upon the disciples (a) in their dependence on the Holy Spirit, and (b) in the place of the Holy Spirit and the Person of Jesus Christ in their thinking? Is this true of us? See 16: 14, 15.

Notes

1 16: 2: 'Put you out of the synagogues': see Note on 12: 42.

2 16: 5. The questions of Thomas (14: 5) and Peter (13: 36, 37) concerned their own following of Jesus. No-one was now asking about the glory to which Christ was going in His return to the Father.

3 16: 8–11. The Holy Spirit will convince men of their false standards of sin, righteousness and judgment (*cf.* Is. 55: 8, 9). He will show them that the essence of sin is unbelief in Christ; that true righteousness is not that of the Pharisees (works of the Law) but the righteousness seen in Christ, and declared in the gospel; and that judgment awaits all who follow the ruler of this world. At Pentecost the heavens were convinced by the Spirit's witness through the apostles, exactly as Jesus says here.

4 16: 13. 'Declare to you the things that are to come': *i.e.*, interpret the significance of Christ's impending crucifixion and resurrection, as well as other divine actions.

□ STUDY 33 John 16: 16–33

1 'A little while'. In the light of verses 16–22 do you consider that this refers to the time between the death of Jesus and His resurrection; between His ascension and Pentecost; or both?

2 Note the RSV in verse 23, 'You will ask me no questions.' With the Spirit to enlighten (*cf.* verses 12–15) and the Father to supply our needs, what do we learn in verses 23–28 about the place of prayer? On what do we rely when we pray in the name of Jesus Christ? *Cf.* 14: 13, 14; 15: 16.

3 In verse 33 Jesus sums up the situation. In what two opposing spheres would the disciples live? What would be their experience in the one and in the other? What can be the ground of your courage and confidence?

□ STUDY 34 John 17 (first study)

Jesus' prayer falls into three divisions: (a) verses 1–5, for Himself; (b) verses 6–19, for the immediate circle of disciples; (c) verses 20–26, for the great company who should afterwards believe.

1 The hour of Jesus' supreme sacrifice has come (verse 1; *cf.* 2: 4; 7: 6, 30; 8: 20; 13: 1). How is this related to the glorifying of the Son and the Father (verses 1–4)? Already the glory of God has been seen in Jesus (1: 14); how is it seen also in His disciples (verse 22)? When will they see the full glory of the Son (verses 5, 24)?

2 In verses 6–14 note how many things Jesus has already done for His disciples.

3 What does our Lord pray that the Father will do for those whom He has given Him? Is this prayer being answered in you? Are you 'consecrated in truth' (verse 19)?

Notes

1 Verse 2. 'Power': better, 'authority', as in RV. The whole of humanity lies within the sphere of Christ's commission. *Cf.* Ps. 2: 8; Mt. 28: 18, 19.

2 Verse 5. A prayer that the glory of which for a time He had 'emptied himself' (Phil. 2: 6, 7) might be restored to Him.

3 Verses 17, 19. Note the repetition of the word 'to consecrate'. Jesus consecrated Himself to the holy Father in fulfilment of His perfect will, particularly in offering Himself as the sacrifice for sin. *Cf.* Heb. 10: 5–10. This shows what true consecration involves.

☐ STUDY 35 John 17 (second study)

1 What is our relationship to the world? How should we ourselves pray regarding people in the world?

2 Verses 20–23. Is the Lord praying for the uniting of all branches of the Christian church as in the ecumenical movement? What is the object of His prayer? What will its fuller realization mean?

3 Observe the significance of the 'word' or 'words' of the Father and the Son in this passage.

☐ STUDY 36 John 18: 1–27

Jesus' arrest and trial before Caiaphas.

1 In verses 4–11 and 19–23 what qualities of our Lord's character appear in relation to (a) those who came to arrest Him, (b) His disciples, and (c) His accusers?

2 How did Peter's own actions contribute to his fall? Of what was he afraid? Does fear ever prevent you from declaring your association with Jesus Christ?

Note. Verses 5, 6, 8. 'I am he': the thrice-repeated use of this phrase point to its special significance. It is virtually a reiteration of the divine name, 'I AM'. *Cf.* Ex. 3: 14; Jn. 8: 58. Note the effect of Christ's statement on the hearers.

☐ STUDY 37 John 18: 28 – 19: 16

The trial before Pilate.

1 Trace through this passage the attempts made by Pilate to spare Jesus from death, and the steps taken by the Jews to counter his efforts. The full charge brought against Jesus is given in Lk. 23: 2. (Note the Jews' use of both religious and political threats to overcome Pilate's resistance; see 19: 7, 12.) What features of the character of Pilate and of the Jews are revealed here? Could we be guilty of similar injustice?

2 'The King of the Jews.' Note how this title forms the central interest from 18: 33 to 19: 22. What is the real nature of Jesus' Kingship? How does it differ from the world's? How is Jesus' royal dignity shown here? How does the use of the title reveal the sin of the Jews, and the glory of Jesus' sacrifice?

Notes

1 18: 28. 'Praetorium': the headquarters of the Roman governor.

2 18: 31b. The Romans did not allow the Jews to inflict capital punishment. Hence Pilate's words in 19: 6 imply that there was no ground in Roman law for Jesus' death. However he spoke a deeper truth than he realized.

☐ STUDY 38 John 19: 17–37

1 The story of the crucifixion is told in seven incidents, namely verses 17–18, 19–22, 23–24, 25–27, 28–29, 30, 31–37. How does each incident manifest some fresh aspect of the glory of the suffering Saviour?

2 Which scriptures are quoted in this portion as having found fulfilment in this hour? To which aspects of Jesus' sufferings and of His saving work do they point?

☐ STUDY 39 John 19: 38 – 20: 10

1 What made both Joseph of Arimathea and Nicodemus now come out into the open? With 19: 38 *cf.* Lk. 23: 50, 51; and trace Nicodemus' growing faith, 3: 1–15; 7: 45–52. Both were members of the Sanhedrin, the Council of the Jews which had condemned Jesus.

2 20: 1–10. How do these verses show that the disciples were not expecting the resurrection of the Lord? What does the description of Peter and John's visit to the tomb reveal about each of their respective temperaments? What was it that John believed?

Notes

1 19: 39. 'About a hundred pounds' weight': an exceptionally lavish amount.

2 20: 5, 7. The position of the clothes showed that they had not been unwound from Jesus' body. He had gone out, just as later He came in, where the doors were shut, without the doors being opened (20: 19, 26).

☐ STUDY 40 John 20: 11–31

1 Why was Mary so concerned that the body had gone from the tomb? What did Jesus convey to her when He said 'Mary'? Why did He say, 'Do not hold me'? Is it possible for us to miss the best in the Lord while holding on to the good?

2 Does verse 19 show that the disciples were still doubting? What convinced them that Jesus was truly raised from the dead? Why was Thomas moved to make the complete avowal of faith, to which none of the others had yet attained? Was it only that he saw Jesus? How can one who has not seen Him be led to faith in the risen Lord (verses 29–31)?

3 In verses 21–23 the risen Christ commissions His apostles. By what authority, with what power, and for what purpose does He send them?

Note. Verse 17. Note the distinction, 'my Father and your Father'. Jesus never said of Himself and His disciples, 'Our Father', as though their relation to God was the same as His. He is the only begotten Son; we are sons of God 'in Him'.

☐ STUDY 41 John 21: 1–14

1 Compare this passage with Lk. 5: 1–11, noting the similarities and the differences. Why did the disciples take up their old work again? What did they learn from this experience?

2 What did the Lord reveal here (a) about Himself, (b) about the work which the disciples were to do? How does this revelation of the risen Lord affect your own life and work?

Note. Verse 14. 'The third time': first time, 20: 19–23; second time, 20: 24–29; third time, now in Galilee. See Mk. 16: 7. Probably the third recorded by this Gospel is meant here.

☐ STUDY 42 John 21: 15–25

1 What is the significance of (a) Jesus' use of the name Simon in addressing Peter (*cf.* 1: 42); (b) the phrase 'more than these' (verse 15; *cf.* Mk. 10: 28–30; 14: 29); (c) Jesus asking Peter three times, 'Do you love me?' (*cf.* 13: 38)?

2 Though Peter had failed, Jesus re-commissioned him. What does this teach about (a) the Lord's nature, (b) Peter's spiritual condition?

Can you expect always to be restored after a fall? What does the Lord require from you?

3 What may we learn from verses 18–23 about (a) the different ways in which the Lord directs the life of each one of His people; (b) what our own main concern is to be?

Notes

1 Verses 18, 19. According to tradition Peter died as a martyr in Rome.

2 Verse 23. A statement introduced to correct a current misunderstanding of what the Lord had said about John.

ISAIAH 1 - 39

Introduction

Isaiah, the 'evangelical prophet', began his ministry at the end of Uzziah's reign, and continued through the reigns of Jotham, Ahaz and Hezekiah. A Jewish tradition, to which allusion is perhaps made in Heb. 11 : 37, states that he was slain in the reign of Manasseh by being sawn asunder. He was a man of outstanding faith in God, and came to exercise a large influence upon his fellow-countrymen. He had to contend with many difficulties, for the moral and spiritual condition of the people was corrupt. The rich oppressed the poor, and revelled in wanton luxury; justice was shamelessly bought and sold. When in distress, men turned to idols; and when in danger, they sought alliances with heathen powers. Isaiah urged a quiet trust in Jehovah, as the only sure path of safety; and when, in the supreme crisis of the Assyrian invasion, his counsel was followed, it was triumphantly vindicated in the destruction of the Assyrian army.

Isaiah spoke much of impending judgment; but he foresaw also the coming of the Messiah, and the establishment of His kingdom. His interest was not confined to his own nation of Judah only. He prophesied also concerning the northern kingdom of Israel (whose overthrow he witnessed), and the heathen nations surrounding Palestine.

The last twenty-seven chapters (40–66) contain a very remarkable group of prophecies, spoken primarily for the comfort and warning of those who lived in the period of the Jewish captivity in Babylon after the destruction of Jerusalem by Nebuchadnezzar about 150 years after Isaiah's time. It is not possible here to discuss the modern contention that chapters 40–66 are not the work of Isaiah, but of one or more prophets who lived in the period of exile, or later. The problem is dealt with in the Introduction to Isaiah in *The New Bible Commentary Revised*, where the arguments adduced in favour of and against the unity of the book are carefully set down and analysed. Suffice it to say here that these studies are based upon the view, not lightly held, and supported by ancient Jewish tradition, and by the writers of the New Testament, that Isaiah was the author of the whole book. He had already foreseen in the vision of 13: 1 – 14: 23 (to which his name is attached; see 13: 1) and in other visions (*e.g.*, 21: 1–10; 35; 39: 6) the rise of Babylon to power and glory, and then her downfall, and the release of her Jewish captives. But in these later prophecies the glad message of redemption is revealed to him in far greater fullness. He takes his stand in prophetic vision in that later age, and declares the messages which God puts into his heart and upon his lips.

The chapters fall into three main sections (see Analysis), each ending with a statement of the doom of the wicked (48: 22; 57: 20, 21; 66: 24). Embedded in these chapters are four prophecies, usually known as the 'Servant' passages (see Analysis), in which the prophet describes God's ideal Servant, and, in so doing, draws a perfect picture of the Lord Jesus Christ. This is an illustration of a notable feature of the prophecies of these chapters, that they look far beyond the period of the return under Cyrus to the coming of Jesus Christ, and the final events of this present age. While spoken primarily to and of Israel, they have a message to all who belong to Christ. The triumphant faith in God, the revelation of God's character, and of the principles of His working, the insight into the human heart in its sin and weakness, the 'exceeding great and precious promises', with which these chapters abound, these and other features make this part of Scripture a veritable mine of wealth to the Christian reader.

Analysis

1	Introductory. God's controversy with His people.
2 – 4	Prophecies of judgment, lying between two Messianic oracles.
5	The Song of the Vineyard. A series of woes. Vision of an invading army.
6	Isaiah's call.

7: 1 – 10: 4	Events connected with the alliance of Ephraim (*i.e.*, northern Israel) and Syria against Judah, and prophecies arising out of them, some Messianic.
10: 5–34	Assyrian invasion of Judah, and its results (a) for Assyria, (b) for Judah.
11 – 12	Messianic prophecies.
13 – 23	Prophecies against the nations, except 22: 1–14 (Jerusalem) and 22: 15–25 (Shebna and Eliakim).
24 – 27	Prophecies of the Day of the Lord, in its twofold aspect of world judgment, and deliverance for Israel.
28 – 33	Prophecies connected with a proposed alliance with Egypt. Some speak of judgment, others of deliverance, and of Messiah's coming.
34 – 35	Vengeance upon Edom, contrasted with the salvation of the redeemed of the Lord, as they return from exile.
36 – 39	Historical.
40 – 48	The glad tidings of Israel's redemption from captivity through the agency of Cyrus. The supremacy of Jehovah over the nations and their gods. 42: 1–7 The first of the 'Servant' passages.
49 – 57	Messages of encouragement and comfort, with rebuke of those who practise evil. 49: 1–9, 50: 4–9, 52: 13 – 53: 12 — The second, third and fourth of the 'Servant' passages.
58 – 66	Rebuke of sin. Visions of Zion's glory. Prayer for God's intervention, and God's answer, that the people will be sifted. The true Israel will inherit 'the new heavens and the new earth', and those who refuse to turn to God will be destroyed.

☐ STUDY 1 Isaiah 1

1 What were the sins that had brought God's judgment on the nation of Israel? See verses 2, 4, 13b, 15. Why should God condemn their formal religious observances (verses 10–17)? See also Ps. 40: 6–9; Am. 5: 21–24; Mi. 6: 6–8.

2 What is the double purpose of God's judgment revealed in verses 24–31? Can you link it with verses 19 and 20?

Notes

1 Verses 5, 6. Sinful Israel is pictured as a body suffering all over from sword wounds, scourge bruises, and abscesses.

2 Verse 10. In God's sight His people are as depraved as Sodom and Gomorrah. *Cf.* 3: 9; Mt. 11: 23, 24.

3 Verse 22. Silver and wine are probably metaphors for the leaders of the nation.

☐ STUDY 2 Isaiah 2–4

The prophet's lofty vision of future possibility in 2: 2–5 gives way to a picture of coming judgment in 2: 6–22, made inevitable by man's failure. From a description of the anarchy (3: 1–8) which will result from the prevalent sins of the ruling class, both men and women (3: 9 – 4: 1), he turns to a more confident expectation of the glory which will follow the judgment (4: 2–6).

1 Try to build a comprehensive picture of the hope for the future given in 2: 2–5 and 4: 2–6. What is said about the word of the Lord, the peace of the world, the holiness of God's people, and their blessedness under His protecting care?

2 Can you detect from these chapters what Isaiah regarded as the greatest sin, and why it is so abominable?

Notes

1 **2: 2–4.** A prophecy almost identical with Mi. 4: 1–3, and probably borrowed by Micah from Isaiah.

2 **2: 6.** The striking of hands may refer not only to friendship but to trade bargaining. Commercial greed is further condemned in verse 7a.

3 **3: 12.** A reference to the childishness and effeminacy of King Ahaz.

☐ STUDY 3 Isaiah 5

1 Compare Isaiah's song of the vineyard with Christ's parables of the wicked husbandmen (Mk. 12: 1–9) and the barren fig tree (Lk. 13: 6–9). Note the differences, and then work out the one great lesson taught in all three passages. How can it be applied to our lives today? *Cf.* Jn. 15: 8.

2 Make a list of the six 'Woes' in verses 8–24, finding twentieth-century words to describe each sin denounced.

Note. Verse 14. 'Sheol' (Greek 'Hades') is the place where all the dead go. It is depicted as a dim and shadowy underworld.

☐ STUDY 4 Isaiah 6

1 What did Isaiah's vision of God in His glory teach him (a) about the character of God, and (b) about himself and his needs? What may this teach us concerning God's provision of cleansing for sinners who deserve judgment?

2 How was Isaiah prepared for his task of carrying God's message to his own people? Consider the message itself; what does it reveal of the inevitable outcome of rebellion against God? *Cf.* Acts 28: 23–28.

Note. Verses 9, 10. In seeking to understand these verses (with which *cf.* Mk. 4: 10–12, where Jesus quotes them), remember these two facts:

(a) Although the Word is preached in order to bring salvation to those who will hear, it inevitably brings condemnation to those who will not. *Cf.* Jn. 3: 16–21.

(b) The Old Testament, with its unshakable faith in God's sovereignty, often refuses to distinguish between intention and inevitable result, between God's permissive and directive will. Thus, to say 'Preach to them and they will not respond' could equally well be expressed, 'Preach to them in order that they may not respond.'

☐ STUDY 5 Isaiah 7: 1 – 8: 15

Isaiah now turns his attention from the internal condition of Judah to the realm of international politics. The historical background of chapters 7: 1 – 10: 4 is the so-called Syro-Ephraimitic confederacy, when King Rezin of Syria and King Pekah of Israel conspired against Judah (735 BC). Ahaz of Judah, overcome with panic (7: 2), rejected the counsel of Isaiah that he should trust in God (7: 3, 4), and appealed to King Tiglath-Pileser of Assyria, an act which Isaiah predicted would have disastrous consequences in the end, even though at first apparently successful (7: 17 – 8: 4).

1 What did Ahaz lose, both personally and politically, through his refusal to trust in the Lord?

2 How is the historical 'sign' to be given to Ahaz a foreshadowing of the future coming of the Messiah? *Cf.* Mt. 1: 21–23. In daily experience do you know Christ as 'Immanuel'—'God with us'?

3 How could the Lord be both a sanctuary and a stumbling-block (8: 13–15), and how may He be to us the former and not the latter? *Cf.* 1 Pet. 2: 7, 8.

Notes

1 The two names, Shear-jashub ('A remnant shall return') and Maher-shalal-hash-baz ('Speed, spoil, haste, prey'), sum up Isaiah's double message of doom and hope.

2 7: 3. Ahaz was probably making preparation for the siege when Isaiah met him.

3 7: 14–16. The primary meaning seems to be that before a certain child (as yet unborn) emerges from infancy, his diet will have to be limited to curds and honey, since the devastated land will yield no better food (7: 21, 22). But the child's remarkable name, and the mention of the 'young woman' or 'virgin' (mg.; *cf.* Mt. 1) who is to be his mother, provide a prophetic reference to the Messiah.

4 8: 6. 'The waters of Shiloah': *i.e.*, the water supplies of Jerusalem, dependent on subterranean springs and reservoirs under the Temple area, here used symbolically of God's providence. The phrase 'this people' must refer either to Israel or a pro-Syrian party in Judah, unless, as some think, the verb Isaiah used was not the word 'rejoice' (AV, RV), but a word of similar letters meaning 'faint before' ('melt in fear before', RSV).

☐ STUDY 6 Isaiah 8: 16 – 10: 4

The prophet will withdraw his disciples, and the elect remnant will thus take shape (8: 16–18). The dark days (8: 19–22) will end in the coming of a great light, the advent of the Messiah (9: 1–7). The remainder of chapter 9 is a prophecy of judgment upon the northern kingdom of Israel. Let Judah then beware (10: 1–4)!

1 When disaster comes, and God seems to have hidden His face, what is man tempted to do (8: 19)? *Cf.* Lv. 19: 31; 1 Sa. 28: 6, 7. What must the child of God do in such a case? What test does Isaiah propose for spiritist teachings?

2 Contrast the condition of things under God's anger (8: 21, 22; 9: 8 – 10: 4) with Isaiah's picture of Messiah's reign (9: 1–7). What do the names given to the coming King in 9: 6 reveal of His nature?

Note. 9: 1. The anguish of the northern kingdom 'in the former time' no doubt refers to Tiglath-Pileser's invasion mentioned in 2 Ki. 15: 29. 'The latter time', though future to the prophet, is described with the past tense of prophetic certainty. For the fulfilment, in part, of the prophecy, see Mt. 4: 15, 16.

□ STUDY 7 Isaiah 10: 5–34

A prophecy of the Assyrian invasion of Judah.

1 Contrast the invasion as seen in the mind of the Assyrian king (verses 7–10, 13, 14), and as seen in the purpose of God (verses 5, 6, 12, 16–19). How does this passage help us to understand how the holy God can use evil men or nations to carry out His purposes?

2 In the stress of the trial it might have seemed that God had cast off His people. But was it so (verses 20–23)? *Cf.* Rom. 9: 27–29. What was the purpose of God's chastening?

3 How does today's portion make more clear the two predictions implied in the names of the prophet's two sons? See Study 5, Note 1.

Notes

1 Verse 17. 'The light of Israel' and 'his Holy One' are names for God.

2 Verse 20. 'Him that smote them': *i.e.*, the king of Assyria. The 'remnant' will have learned the lesson Ahaz had failed to learn.

3 Verses 28–32. A vivid picture of the approach of the enemy, checked only at the very walls of Jerusalem.

□ STUDY 8 Isaiah 11 and 12

The Assyrian cedar would be irrevocably felled, but out of the stump of the pollarded Judaean tree will come forth a shoot—the Messiah, in whom Isaiah's hope for the future is centred. His glorious reign (11) is considered (a) in relation to human society (2–5); (b) in relation to the brute creation (6–9); and (c) in relation to world history (10–16). There follows (12: 1–6) a song of thanksgiving to God for His forgiveness, together with a vision of a united Israel (*cf.* 11: 13) enjoying the blessings of salvation, and engaging in missionary activity among the nations.

1 What are to be the characteristics of the coming Messiah (11: 1–5)? Compare this picture of His reign with 9: 1–7, and notice any new truths brought out.

2 Chapter 12 is the song of those who have discovered that God's anger is turned away from them. What results of salvation are mentioned here, and are you experiencing them all?

☐ STUDY 9 Isaiah 13: 1 – 14: 23

Here we leave the Book of Immanuel, and enter what has been called the 'jungle of prophecy' (chapters 13–25). See Analysis. It contains the 'burdens of the Lord', oracles concerning foreign nations, many parts of which are now obscure. The first oracle concerns Babylon, and is directed first against the city (13: 1 – 14: 2), and second, against the king (14: 3–23). Its predictions have been literally fulfilled.

1 For what sins was Babylon condemned by God (14: 5, 6, 12–14)? How did God administer judgment?

2 In what respects may Babylon be regarded as a picture of the world in opposition to God (as Jerusalem or Zion is a picture of God's people), and the king of Babylon a picture of Satan, the prince of this world? *Cf.* Gn. 11: 1–9; 2 Thes. 2: 4; Rev. 18: 2, 3.

Notes

1 13: 2–6. 'The day of the Lord' is the day of His manifestation and here denotes the day of His vengeance upon Babylon.

2 13: 12. The population will be so reduced, that men will be scarcer than gold.

3 14: 9–17. The departed spirits in Sheol assemble, surprised and scornful, to greet the arrival of the king whose pomp is now stripped from him.

☐ STUDY 10 Isaiah 14: 24 – 16: 14

A series of denunciatory oracles directed against Assyria (14: 24–27), Philistia (14: 28–32), and Moab (15; 16).

1 14: 24–27. What two attributes of God are emphasized in these verses? How do they encourage us to trust in His Word?

2 In the prophecy against Moab consider (a) the severity of the judgment, (b) the sympathy of the prophet with Moab in her sufferings, and (c) the reason why her doom is inevitable. Are you moved by the thought of the judgment which awaits those who reject Christ?

Notes

1 14: 29. 'The rod which smote you is broken': a reference probably to the death of Tiglath-Pileser of Assyria who died just before Ahaz. However, it was no use rejoicing at this, for the power of Assyria would be revived in a form more deadly than ever.

2 14: 30–32. The meaning is that while even the poorest in Judah shall be secure (verses 30a and 32), Philistia shall be destroyed.

3 15. The proper names are Moabite towns, known and unknown. On the signs of grief and mourning in verses 2 and 3, *cf.* 22: 12; Mi. 1: 16.

4 16: 1–5. The Moabites are advised to send tribute in the form of lambs (*cf.* 2 Ki. 3: 4) to the king of Judah. Verses 3–5 is the Moabites' plea for refuge.

☐ STUDY 11 Isaiah 17–19

Oracles concerning Damascus (*i.e.*, Syria) and Ephraim, Ethiopia, and Egypt, with a short oracle (17: 12–14) prophesying the overthrow of the Assyrian hosts.

1 How is Ephraim's sin described in 17: 10, together with its inevitable issue? *Cf.* Dt. 8: 19, 20.

2 Gather out from these chapters what is said of the results of God's judgment in causing men to turn to Him. What encouragements for missionary work, especially in certain countries, may be derived from these chapters?

3 Contrast in chapter 18 man's scheming and planning with God's attitude of quiet watchfulness, knowing what He will do (verses 4–6). *Cf.* Ps. 2: 1–5.

Note. 18: 1, 2. A description of Ethiopia, whose ambassadors have come to consult with Judah about plans to resist Assyria. The 'whirring wings' is probably an allusion to the swarms of insects which infest the land. Isaiah gives the ambassadors a message to take back (verses 2b–7), that God is watching, and will shortly deal with the Assyrian menace.

☐ STUDY 12 Isaiah 20: 1 – 22: 14

The story of an acted prophecy on the futility of reliance upon Egypt (20) is followed by four oracles concerning Babylon (21: 1–10), Edom (21: 11, 12), Arabia (21: 13–17), and Jerusalem (22: 1–14).

1 In what ways did Isaiah's responsibility to convey God's message prove demanding and costly? Are you prepared to sacrifice your pride in your service for God (chapter 20)? Do you spare time to wait on God (21: 8, 12)?

2 In what two respects does Isaiah in 22: 1–14 find fault with the people of Jerusalem? Do you find the same spirit prevalent today?

3 In what ways does this passage teach us that God is behind the events of history, knowing all beforehand, and carrying out His purposes?

Note. 22: 1–3. The prophet bewails the conduct of the people, thronging the house-tops, shouting and rejoicing when calamity was near. 'Without the bow' (which had been cast aside) they were captured.

☐ STUDY 13 Isaiah 22: 15 – 23: 18

1 Why did God depose Shebna and put Eliakim in his place? If God can say of you 'my servant', how are you filling your position? *Cf.* Mt. 24: 45–51.

2 Isaiah foresees a day when Tyre's riches will be no longer hoarded for her own selfish enjoyment, but will be lavished upon Jehovah and His people. If then he is not condemning wealth in itself as evil, what is he attacking in the earlier part of the chapter? What should be the Christian's attitude towards wealth and material prosperity? *Cf.* 1 Tim. 6: 6–10, 17–19.

☐ STUDY 14 Isaiah 24 and 25

Chapter 24 begins the long apocalyptic vision of the Day of the Lord which continues until chapter 27. It seems impossible to give it any certain historical background, and it was probably intended to be an ideal description of the last great judgment which will engulf the whole world. The horizon is very black except for the bright gleam of light which appears in verse 23, and which leads on to the burst of praise in chapter 25, just as chapter 12 follows chapter 11. First in his own name (25), and then in the name of the redeemed community (26), the prophet gives thanks for their certain deliverance from the final judgment and for their everlasting bliss and security.

1 In chapter 24 contrast the emotions of unbelievers when faced with the calamity of God's judgment with the reactions of believers. Can you still praise God in the midst of seeming disaster? *Cf.* Hab. 3: 16–19.

2 What does chapter 25 teach us about God's 'faithful and sure' plans for this world and for His people?

3 Compare this Old Testament picture of God's ultimate purpose for His people with the New Testament one in Rev. 7: 15–17; 21: 1–4.

Note. 25: 2. In this verse, as in 24: 10, 12 and 26: 5, 6, 'the city' refers to no special town, but to any stronghold of opposition to God, in contrast to God's 'strong city' (26: 1). The former will be 'made a heap', but the latter fortified with impregnable bulwarks.

☐ STUDY 15 Isaiah 26 and 27

1 Think over the attitudes of heart described in 26: 3, 4, 8, 9, 13 and 19, and ask yourself if you share this trust and faith in God. What should be the response of God's people to His mercy and judgment?

2 How does chapter 27 express the principle underlying God's chastisement of His people, and also His ultimate purpose?

Notes

1 26: 19. The prophet's answer to the people's plaint is the promise of resurrection. His words here and in 25: 8 are among the clearest utterances of the Old Testament upon that subject.

2 27: 1. The three monsters represent three world powers, probably Assyria, Babylon and Egypt.

☐ STUDY 16 Isaiah 28

This is the first of four chapters of warning to Judah. Their main theme is the folly of seeking help from Egypt. Warnings of terrible judgment (observe the recurrence of the word 'woe', see 28: 1; 29: 1, 15; 30: 1; 31: 1) intermingle with assurances of God's intervention in mercy. The divisions of chapter 28 are as follows: verses 1–4, judgment upon Samaria; verses 5, 6, after the judgment; verses 7–13, the drunken rulers of Judah rebuked; verses 14–23, the coming storm of God's judgment will sweep away all man-made policies; verses 23–29, if the farmer acts with wisdom, how much more God?

1 How many consequences of intemperance can you discern in verses 1–4, 7 and 8? What was God's message to His intemperate people, and why would they not listen (verses 9–15)?

2 What do verses 16–29 teach us about the inevitable triumph of God's will in human affairs, and the futility of unbelief and rebellion? How does the parable in verses 23–29 encourage us to see that God has foreseen and arranged all?

3 What foreshadowing of Christ is there in the final fulfilment of God's plans? *Cf.* verse 16; 1 Pet. 2: 6, 7; Acts 4: 11; Mt. 21: 42.

Note. Verses 15, 18. Isaiah calls the proposed alliance with Egypt 'a covenant with death'. 'The overflowing scourge' is Assyria.

☐ STUDY 17 Isaiah 29: 1 – 30: 17

1 29: 9–16. What were the reasons for the people's spiritual blindness and lack of spiritual discernment, and in what ways did they show this? What causes the spiritual transformation of verses 17–22? See verses 18, 24.

2 On what various grounds does Isaiah urge upon his hearers that they should rely upon God rather than upon Egypt? Trace out in 30: 8–17 the respective issues of the two ways.

3 Observe the contrast between the extreme distress of Jerusalem in 29: 2–4, and her complete triumph in 29: 5–8. How may this encourage us in times of severe trial?

Note. 29: 1–8. 'Ariel' is a name for Jerusalem. It may mean 'lion of God' or, as is more probable here, 'hearth of God' (RV mg.). Jerusalem will become an altar hearth soaked with the blood of many victims.

☐ STUDY 18 Isaiah 30: 18 – 32: 20

1 What blessings does God promise to His people after their trials? *Cf.* 30: 18–29; 32: 1–8, 15–20. How has the promise of a Teacher been fulfilled to us in Christ? Look up Jn. 14: 26; 16: 13, in this connection. Are we sensitive to the promptings of the Holy Spirit (30: 21)?

2 Many trusted in Egypt because she seemed strong (31: 1). How does Isaiah here show the folly of this, as compared with trusting the Lord?

Notes

1 30: 25, 26. A poetic description of the blessings of the new age, to be interpreted symbolically as showing the abundance of God's provision. For the phrase 'when the towers fall', *cf.* 2: 11–17.

2 30: 27–33. Notice the wealth of imaginative metaphor—the storm, the flood, the bridle. The meaning of verse 32 is not fully clear. Moffatt renders 'He clubs them down to peals of merry music'. 'Topheth' (verse 33, mg.) was the name given to the valley of Hinnom outside Jerusalem, where the foul rites of human sacrifice were practised in honour of the god Molech. Its original meaning seems to have been 'fire place', and Isaiah declares that God has prepared such a place for a great holocaust in honour of the king (of Assyria). There is a play upon words in the Hebrew, for the word for 'king' is *melek* (= Molech).

☐ STUDY 19 Isaiah 33–35

The opening verses of chapter 33 reflect the excitement and panic which preceded Sennacherib's approach (verses 7–9) and the prophet's triumphant faith that the proud Assyrian would suffer defeat (verses 1–6, 10–12). The remainder of the chapter shows the profound effects of this deliverance, and paints a glowing picture of the coming kingdom. Chapters 34 and 35 present a striking contrast between the fearful doom of God's enemies, symbolized by Edom (34), and the glorious future which awaits God's redeemed people (35).

1 In the picture of the Messiah's kingdom, given in 33: 14–24, (a) what are the characteristics of His people, (b) what will the Lord be to them, and (c) what blessings will they enjoy?

2 Applied spiritually, what blessings are spoken of in chapter 35 which are available to believers now? In particular, can you discover in verses 8–10 four or five characteristics of the 'highway', *i.e.*, the Christian life?

Notes

1 33: 18, 19. The things that terrified them before, such as Assyrian officials counting the tribute, will all belong to the past.

2 34: 6, 7. God's judgment of Edom pictured as a sacrifice in Bozrah, an Edomite city.

3 34: 16. 'The book of the Lord': this probably refers to a collection of Isaiah's previous prophecies. None of them shall fail. The Spirit of God will accomplish in history what the mouth of God's servant has declared in prophecy. *Cf.* 55: 11; Je. 1: 9, 10.

☐ STUDY 20 Isaiah 36 and 37

We have now reached 701 BC, the year of Sennacherib's siege of Jerusalem, so long predicted. Chapters 36–39 repeat, with a few omissions and additions, the history recorded in 2 Ki. 18: 13 – 20: 11. The course of events seems to have been as follows: (1) After receiving the tribute demanded (2 Ki. 18: 14–16),

Sennacherib sent three envoys with an army to demand further the surrender of Jerusalem (36: 1 – 37: 7). (2) This was refused and the Assyrian troops withdrew, but Sennacherib sent a letter to Hezekiah renewing his demands (37: 8–35). This also was rejected, and the chapter concludes with a brief account of how God fulfilled His word (37: 36–38).

1 36: 4–10, 13–20. How did the Rabshakeh try to shake the confidence of the defenders of Jerusalem in the power of God to save them? What fact did he ignore which invalidated the basic assumption of his argument? *Cf.* 37: 18–20, 23–29.

2 Both Hezekiah and Isaiah recognized in Sennacherib's challenge a blasphemous insult to the living God (37: 6, 7, 17, 23). How did this give them confidence? *Cf.* 1 Sa. 17: 26, 36, 45–47.

Notes

1 36: 1. The chronological note is wrong, for 701 BC was Hezekiah's twenty-sixth year. Possibly the note belongs properly to 38: 1, and has become misplaced. See Note under Study 21 below.

2 36: 2, 3. Rabshakeh was the title of the Assyrian chief-captain, second to the Tartan or commander-in-chief. As there were three envoys (2 Ki. 18: 17), so three Jewish high officials were sent to meet them.

3 36: 7. Whether in ignorance or in subtlety, the Rabshakeh spoke of Hezekiah's religious reformation (2 Ki. 18: 4), as if it had been an act of disrespect towards God. Possibly to a heathen mind it appeared in that light.

☐ STUDY 21 Isaiah 38 and 39

The events of these chapters preceded Sennacherib's invasion. Hezekiah reigned twenty-nine years (2 Ki. 18: 2). He probably fell ill in the fourteenth year of his reign. See Note on 36: 1 in Study 20 above.

1 How does chapter 38 show forth (a) the power of prayer (*cf.* Jas. 5: 16b), (b) a loving purpose behind suffering (*cf.* Ps. 119: 71, 75), (c) the completeness of God's forgiveness (*cf.* Ps. 103: 12; Mi. 7: 19), (d) the duty of praise (*cf.* Ps. 13: 6)?

2 Wherein lay Hezekiah's sin in displaying his royal treasures and military might to the envoys of Merodach-baladan? *Cf.* 2 Ch. 32: 25, 31. How does the incident reveal what was in his heart?

Notes

1 38: 7, 8. The sign was a miraculous alteration of the shadow on the sun-dial, and not necessarily of the sun in the sky. It may have been caused by eclipse or reflection, and appears to have been a local phenomenon only (*cf.* 2 Ch. 32: 31).

2 38: 11 and 18. The thought that death cut them off from God made it a cause of dread to Old Testament believers. Contrast 1 Cor. 15: 20, 55, 56.

3 39: 1. Merodach-baladan made himself king of Babylon in defiance of Assyria in 721 BC, but was taken captive by the Assyrian king Sargon in 709. Before his downfall he sought to secure himself against Assyria by foreign alliances, one of which was with Judah in 714. Hezekiah's sickness and remarkable recovery gave him occasion to make a first approach. *Cf.* 2 Ch. 32: 31.

For Studies 22–42 on Isaiah see p. 294.

THE EPISTLES OF JOHN

Introduction

1 John and the Epistle to the Hebrews are the only two New Testament letters written anonymously; and in 2 and 3 John, the author merely introduces himself as 'the elder'. It is clear, however, that the three Johannine Epistles are by the same person, and there is a very strong case for saying that it is the same person as the author of John's Gospel. The evidence of the letters themselves, and the witness of early Christians, suggest that the writer is the apostle John. He writes as an eye-witness who has personally known the Lord (1: 1–4; 4: 14). He writes as a teacher with great, indeed, with apostolic authority (2: 8, 17; 3: 6; 4: 1; 5: 20, 21). He writes as a pastor, with a deep concern both to defend and confirm the faith of the church (2: 1, 26; 4: 1–6; 2 Jn. 9; 3 Jn. 4).

In the first Epistle, John sets forth three marks of a true knowledge of God and of fellowship with God. These marks are, first, righteousness of life, second, brotherly love, and third, faith in Jesus as God incarnate. Such characteristics distinguish true Christians from false teachers who, for all their lofty profession and Christian language, neither believe nor obey the truth.

In 2 and 3 John, the writer deals with the problem of giving hospitality to visiting Christians. False teachers were abusing the generosity of Christian people, and some advice was needed to help Christians in dealing with the situation.

Analysis of 1 John

1: 1–4 Introduction. The apostolic witness—its authority, content and aim.

1: 5 – 2: 27 *God is light;* and the test of true fellowship with Him is threefold:

- 1: 5 – 2: 6 (i) Confession of and cleansing from sin, and obedience to Christ.

	2: 7–11	(ii) Brotherly love.
	2: 12–14	Digression on the church.
	2: 15–17	Digression on the world.
	2: 18–27	(iii) Confession that Jesus Christ is come in the flesh.
2: 28 – 4: 6	*God is love;* and the test of true sonship to Him is, as before, the threefold evidence of:	
	2: 28 – 3: 10	(i) Practical righteousness.
	3: 11–18	(ii) Brotherly love.
	3: 19–24	Digression on assurance.
	4: 1–6	(iii) Confession that Jesus Christ is come in the flesh.
4: 7 – 5: 12	*God is love;* and the test of our dwelling in Him, and His dwelling in us is, as before:	
	4: 7–21	(i) Mutual love.
	5: 1–3	(ii) The keeping of God's commandments.
	5: 4–12	(iii) Belief that Jesus is the Son of God.
5: 13–21	Conclusion. Five Christian certainties.	

Analysis of 2 John

1–3	Opening salutation.
4–11	Message.
12, 13	Conclusion.

Analysis of 3 John

1–8	The message to Gaius.
9, 10	Diotrephes condemned.
11, 12	Demetrius approved.
13, 14	Conclusion.

☐ STUDY 1 1 John 1: 1 – 2: 2

1 To what unique experience in his life is the writer referring in verses 1–4? How does he describe it? *Cf.* Jn. 1: 14. To what inestimable privilege did it lead him, and why does he want to make it known? *Cf.* 1 Thes. 3: 8, 9.

2 The nature of God determines the conditions of fellowship with Him. See verses 6–10. How has He made fellowship with Himself possible for sinful man? What is His provision to enable fellowship to be maintained, and to meet failure if it should occur? If men deny in one way or another their need of this provision, what may we conclude concerning them? See verses 6, 8, 10.

Note. 1: 5. 'Light': used in Scripture in various meanings, as signifying truth, goodness, joy, safety, life; just as 'darkness', on the contrary, denotes falsehood, evil, sorrow, peril, death. Here, 'light' signifies perfect truth and goodness, without any vestige of evil.

☐ STUDY 2 1 John 2: 3–27

1 Verses 3–11. If a man claims to know God, to abide in Christ and to be in the light, what must be his attitude to (a) Christ's word and commandment; (b) the example of Christ's life on earth; (c) fellow-Christians?

2 Verses 18–29. Amid false teachers and defection, what three safeguards for continuance in the faith does John give? See especially verses 24–27. If a professing Christian falls away from the truth, what is proved thereby which, before the falling away, may not have been at all obvious?

3 Verses 15–17. With what two arguments does John support the commandment of verse 15? How may this commandment be reconciled with Jn. 3: 16?

Notes

1 Verse 7. *Cf.* Jn. 13: 34, 35; 15: 12.

2 Verse 8. John calls the old commandment new, both because Jesus Christ, by His teaching and living, has invested the old idea with a richer and deeper meaning, and because experimental Christianity is always new in kind or character.

3 Verse 15. 'The world': here it denotes human society as an ordered whole, considered both apart from, and in opposition to, God.

☐ STUDY 3 1 John 2: 28 – 3: 10

We enter today upon the second section of the Epistle (see Analysis).

1 2: 28 – 3: 3. The apostle, having begun in verse 29 to show that the test of sonship is righteousness of life, is carried away by the marvel of the new birth into a rapturous outburst of wonder and joy. Whence comes our sonship? How does the world regard it? What will be its future glory? How should this affect us now? *Cf.* Col. 3: 4, 5.

2 3: 4–9. These verses resume and expand the truth of 2: 29. What five reasons are given to show that sinning is utterly incompatible with being a child of God?

Notes

1 2: 28. This verse gives clear proof that John, no less than Paul and Peter, believed in the Lord's second coming. See also 3: 2; 4: 17.

2 2: 29. 'Born of him': the first reference to sonship in this letter.
3 3: 6, 9. These verses do not mean that a Christian is incapable of sinning, nor that one sin is proof of an unregenerate nature, but that it is impossible for a true child of God to persist in habitual sin.

☐ STUDY 4 1 John 3: 11 – 4: 6

1 3: 11–18. By what various arguments does John show, in verses 11–15, that mutual love is the essential mark of the children of God and that hatred is inadmissible? After what manner should we love? See verses 16–18 and *cf.* Jn. 15: 12; Eph. 5: 1, 2.

2 3: 19–24. A digression on the subject of assurance before God. The apostle first considers the case of a Christian whose heart condemns him. How is such a person to be reassured? See verses 19, 20. *Cf.* Heb. 6: 9, 10. Next the apostle considers the case of a Christian whose heart does not condemn him, because he is practising all the characteristics of a truly Christian life—obedience, love and faith. What blessings does this man enjoy? See verses 21–24.

3 What two tests are given here by which to know whether a prophet is, or is not, speaking by the Spirit of God? See especially 4: 2 and 6; see also Note 2 below.

Notes
1 3: 14. *Cf.* Jn. 5: 24. This gives the practical test whether a professed faith in Christ is genuine. *Cf.* Gal. 5: 6b; Jas. 2: 15–17.
2 4: 6. 'We are of God': the pronoun 'we' in the first half of this verse refers primarily, as in 1: 1–3, to John as representing the apostles, while not excluding those who, following after them, base their teaching upon the apostolic foundation.

☐ STUDY 5 1 John 4: 7 – 5: 3

We now begin the third section of the Epistle (see Analysis).

1 4: 7–10. What arguments are used in verses 7 and 8 to show that true Christians must love one another? In verses 9 and 10 the apostle speaks of the manifestation of God's love in Christ. How does he describe the gift? What does he say of its purpose? By what means was this purpose achieved, and for whom did God do this?

2 4: 11–18. The apostle goes over the same ground as before, but at a higher level. How does he here describe the Christian's relationship to God? How does he show that no higher or closer relationship can be conceived? Out of the depths of that relationship, the believer bears his testimony through the Spirit (verses 13–16; *cf.* Jn. 15: 26, 27).

3 4: 19 – 5: 3. In view of Mt. 22: 36, 37 why does not the apostle say in verse 11, 'Beloved, if God so loved us, we ought also to love God'? Why does John say, 'We ought also to love *one another*'? What other test of our love for God is also mentioned?

Notes

1 4: 17, 18. 'Because as he is . . .': *cf.* Jn. 3: 35 with 16: 27. Those who are loved of the Father need not look forward with dread. If we are still afraid, the remedy is to concentrate more upon the love of God shown in the cross and the resurrection.

2 5: 1. Faith in Jesus as the Christ implies receiving Him as such, and to receive Him is to be born of God (Jn. 1: 12, 13).

☐ STUDY 6 1 John 5: 4–21

1 The apostle has already given a warning against the subtle attraction of the world (see 2: 15–17). Now he reveals how the world may be conquered. Who does he say will overcome the world, and by what means? See verses 4–6; see also Note 1 below.

2 A faith that can effect such great results must be well attested. What fivefold witness is given in verses 7–11, and what marvellous fact does the witness attest?

3 Verses 13–20. There are here five great certainties concerning which John says 'We know'. What are they? Are you building your life upon this foundation?

Notes

1 Verse 6. This verse probably refers to our Lord's baptism and death, and not to Jn. 19: 34. He came not only to call us to repentance by the witness of His baptism, but also to wash away our sins with His blood. The two sacraments of the Christian church are the standing memorials of these things.

2 Verses 9 and 10. God has spoken to man in Jesus with the utmost clarity and finality. He that believes has an inward witness: he that believes not makes God a liar.

3 Verse 16. 'A mortal sin': *i.e.*, the deliberate, purposeful choice of darkness in preference to light.

4 Verse 21. 'Idols': anyone professing to worship God, but who denies that Jesus is the Son of God, is worshipping a false God. 'Be on your guard against all such idols' is John's final word.

☐ STUDY 7 2 and 3 John

1 Compare the tests of a true Christian found in 2 John with those given in 1 John.

2 Consider the three men mentioned in 3 John, all professing Christians. What does the apostle praise in Gaius? What faults does he find in Diotrephes? What threefold witness does he give in praise of Demetrius?

3 What dangers arise from listening to false teachers? What is John's answer to the claims of 'advanced thought'? See Note 3.

Notes

1 2 Jn. 2. *Cf.* NEB, 'whom I love in truth . . . for the sake of the truth'.
2 2 Jn. 4. 'Following the truth . . .': *i.e.*, living true Christian lives in obedience to the command which we have received from the Father.
3 2 Jn. 9. 'Goes ahead': *i.e.*, claims a knowledge superior to God's revelation.
4 3 Jn. 5. *Cf.* Heb. 13:2.

ISAIAH 40 - 66

☐ STUDY 22 Isaiah 40

The prophecies of chapters 40–48 have as their main theme the proclamation that God is about to restore the exiled Jews in Babylon to their own land. See Introduction. They refer to a time when the words spoken to Hezekiah (39:5–7) have been fulfilled. The first eleven verses are a prologue in which the prophet hears heavenly voices declaring to Jerusalem the glad message of redemption.

1 In verses 1–11 what four great facts are proclaimed by God to give comfort to His people? How does this prophecy of the future coming and glory of the Lord find fulfilment in the New Testament? *Cf.* Mt. 3:3; 1 Pet. 1:23–25; Jn. 10:11.

2 In verses 12–26 how is God shown to be beyond the petty mind of man to comprehend or to explain? How may we, as His creatures, draw on His infinite strength and power? See verses 29–31.

☐ STUDY 23 Isaiah 41

In this magnificent chapter the supremacy of the God of Israel is further demonstrated. First the nations (verses 1, 2) and then their gods (verses 21-29) are summoned before Him, and challenged as to what counsel they can give, and what control they can exercise in regard to the world-shaking onward march of Cyrus. They know nothing and can do nothing. It is the holy One of Israel who alone can predict the future, for He has planned all, and brought it to pass. Let Israel lift up his head, for he is God's elect and for him He has great purposes in view (verses 8–20).

1 The nations in their fear make new idols (verses 5–7). How are these idols shown to be worthless (verses 23, 24, 28, 29)? The reference in verses 2 and 25 is to Cyrus; what is God's relation to this mighty conqueror, and to the events of history in general (verses 2–4, 25–27)?

2 Tabulate the promises made to Israel in verses 8–20. How far and in what sense are they true for us today? *Cf.* 2 Cor. 1: 20. In what measure have we tried and proved God's promises?

Notes

1 Verses 2, 3. Here the first actor is God, and the second Cyrus.
2 Verses 21–24. The idols are now summoned before God. Note how they are challenged.

☐ STUDY 24 Isaiah 42: 1 – 43: 13

In chapter 41 Isaiah has shown that God has great purposes for Israel, His servant. That purpose is now declared. It is a purpose of blessing to all nations (42: 1–4 and 5–9; *cf.* Gn. 12: 3b). In order to accomplish it, God will redeem His people from their present plight (42: 13–16), confounding those that trust in idols (42: 17), and calling forth from far and near a paeon of praise to His Name (42: 10–12). Israel's present condition, under God's chastisement for her sins, is indeed pitiable (42: 18–25), but God will ransom His people, letting other nations suffer subjection in their stead (43: 1–7), and Israel shall then bear witness before the assembled nations to Jehovah's sovereign might and glory (43: 8–13).

1 42: 1–4. The prophet, in this picture of God's ideal Servant, perfectly portrays the Lord Jesus. *Cf.* Mt. 12: 18–21. What is said concerning (a) His relation to God; (b) His equipment for His task; (c) the purpose and scope of His mission; (d) the qualities that characterize Him; (e) the method of His ministry; (f) His endurance; (g) the final fulfilment of His work?

2 What does God promise to do for His people Israel in their distress (42: 16, 17; 43: 1–7)? What witness will Israel, when redeemed, bear to God and His saving power (43: 10–13)? Have we a similar testimony to the world around us concerning the reality of God's work of redemption?

Notes

1 42: 19. 'Blind': *i.e.*, to destiny and mission.
2 43: 3, 4. The meaning seems to be that God will give to Cyrus other people to serve him in payment for setting the Jews free.

☐ STUDY 25 Isaiah 43: 14 – 44: 23

In making reference to Babylon's impending downfall (43: 14, 15) God answers an unspoken objection that such a thing is incredible. 'Do you not remember what I did at the Red Sea?' He asks (43: 16, 17). 'Yet what I am about to do now is greater still' (43: 18–21). He answers, too, a deeper cause of their unbelief, namely, a guilty conscience (43: 21–24). 'I know it all,' He says, 'but I will pardon all' (43: 25). 'My purpose toward you is one of blessing' (44: 1–5).

1 What was the new thing that God was about to do, greater even than His deliverance of Israel at the Red Sea? *Cf.* chapter 35. What application has it to ourselves?

2 How does 43: 22–28 show that Israel was not justified by works, but only by free grace? *Cf.* Rom. 3: 23, 24. What further gift had God in store for His redeemed people, and what blessings will it bring (44: 3–5)? *Cf.* Jn. 7: 37–39.

3 What is the effect of idolatry on the mind of the worshipper? See 44: 18–20. Have you realized the greatness of our privilege in knowing the true God? See 44: 6–8.

Notes

1 43: 22–24. During the exile, God had not burdened them with demands for sacrifice and offering. But they had burdened Him with their sins.

2 43: 27, 28. 'Your first father': a reference probably to Jacob; *cf.* 48: 1. 'Your mediators' may refer to priests and prophets; *cf.* Je. 2: 8.

☐ STUDY 26 Isaiah 44: 24 – 45: 25

Allusion has already been made to Cyrus, but not by name (41: 2, 25). Now he is directly and personally addressed, as one whom God has chosen as an instrument of His purpose of good towards Israel, and the purpose for which he has been raised up is declared (44: 24 – 45: 8). Those who object to this view of God's relation to Cyrus are rebuked (45: 9–13), and there follows a remarkable prophecy of universal acknowledgment of the God of Israel as the one God, in whom alone is salvation (45: 14–25).

1 What is said in 44: 24 – 45: 8 concerning (a) God's power in creation and in human history; (b) Cyrus, and what God will do for him and through him? What assurance should such a passage afford us?

2 What is the twofold answer given in 45: 9–13 to those who question God's purposes and ways? *Cf.* Rom. 9: 20. Are you ever guilty of feeling resentment against God?

3 In 45: 14–25 what are the reasons given for the turning of men of all nations from their idols to the worship of the one true God? How does this anticipate the universal scope of Christ's redemption? *Cf.* Rom. 1: 16.

Notes

1 44: 28. 'Shepherd': used frequently with the meaning of 'ruler'.
2 45: 13. 'Not for price or reward': this seems to contradict 43: 3, 4, but that passage speaks of the reward God gave, this of Cyrus' motive.
3 45: 14–17. Spoken to Israel. Verses 14b, 15 are the confession of the nations mentioned in verse 14.

☐ STUDY 27 Isaiah 46 and 47

These two chapters concern Babylon, the first showing the impotence of Babylon's gods and the folly of worshipping them (46: 1–7), and rebuking those Jews who would not receive God's revelation of His purposes (46: 8–13); and the second depicting Babylon as a proud queen humbled to the position of a menial slave, with none to help her.

1 Observe the difference in 46: 1–4 between the gods of Babylon that have to be borne by beasts, and carried away by their worshippers, and the God of Israel who bears His people throughout their history. Is your religion one that is a burden to you, or do you know One who will bear you even to old age?

2 What sins brought about Babylon's downfall, and God's judgment upon her? What did she assume was her security against future disaster (47: 8–13)?

3 What is the attitude of the Word of God to all forms of fortune-telling, crystal-gazing, and the like? What may we learn from chapter 47 about what will happen in the hour of judgment if we have been trusting in any other than in God?

Notes

1 46: 1, 2. The inhabitants of Babylon laid their chief idols (Bel and Nebo) on beasts, and carried them away in their flight.
2 47: 6. 'I profaned my heritage': *i.e.*, allowed the holy land to be defiled by foreign conquerors.

☐ STUDY 28 Isaiah 48

There seems to have been a party among the exiles which received God's message concerning Cyrus with disfavour. God has already rebuked them more than once (45: 9–13; 46: 12, 13); and now in verses 1–11 of this chapter He answers an objection they seem to have raised that the teaching was novel, and not in accord with God's usual procedure. He tells them that in spite of their rebellious attitude, He will carry out His plans.

1 What does God condemn in the nominal religiosity of the Jews? Why did this cause God to announce His intentions beforehand (verses 3–5), and yet to keep some of His purposes hidden (verses 7, 8)? Do we grieve God by failing to acknowledge Him, and to give Him glory?

2 Verses 17–22. What conditions does God lay down before we can experience the fullness of His grace and peace in our lives?

Notes

1 Verses 3–6a. 'The former things': a reference to prophecies long foretold and now fulfilled; see also verse 5a. In verse 6b God acknowledges that He has now used a different method, keeping back the revelation of His intended action until just before it happened, but in this also He had a purpose (verse 7).

2 Verse 10. 'But not like silver': a phrase that seems to express the divine sorrow that the refining process had not given a better result, such as happens when silver is refined. *Cf.* Je. 6: 29, 30.

3 Verse 14. 'All of you' refers to Israel; 'who among them' to the nations; and 'the Lord loves him' to Cyrus.

☐ STUDY 29 Isaiah 49: 1 – 50: 3

In chapters 40–48 the prophet has been concerned to show the supremacy of the God of Israel over the nations and their gods, and that God's purpose is to be accomplished through Cyrus. These two themes now disappear, and attention is turned to Israel's glorious future. Much of the section 49–55 consists of words of encouragement, spoken to overcome the doubts, hesitations and difficulties which the message of the preceding chapters had aroused in many minds. It contains also three of the 'Servant' passages in which the mission, the sufferings, and the atoning death of the Lord's Servant are set forth. (See Analysis.)

1 Verses 1–6. The 'Servant' speaks to the nations. What does he say concerning (a) his call; (b) his equipment; (c) his initial non-success, and his attitude in face of this; (d) the new task which God gave him to do? Although the passage applies to the Lord Jesus Christ, Paul uses part of it of himself and Barnabas. See Acts 13: 47. How is this? Have we then a share in the Servant's task? *Cf.* Jn. 20: 21.

2 How does the Lord answer Zion's doubts, first that the Lord has forsaken her (49: 14); second, that her children are taken from her and lost to her (49: 21); third, that Babylon was too strong to give up its prey (49: 24); and fourth, that her covenant relation with Jehovah is broken (50: 1)?

3 Try to put yourself in the position of Israel in exile, as described in 49: 7a (*cf.* 41: 14, 'worm'); and then contemplate the faith that could see and declare the transformation announced in 49: 7b–13. On what is the prophet's faith founded? With verse 7 *cf.* Ps. 22: 6 and 27–29a.

Notes

1 49: 12. See mg. Some scholars connect 'Sinim' with China, but it seems unlikely that Jewish exiles would have travelled so far East by this period. The RSV 'Syene' refers to the more southerly country mentioned in Ezk. 29: 10; 30: 6.

2 50: 1, 2. 'What writ of divorce did I ever hand to your mother?' (Moffatt). The meaning is that the breach between God and Zion and her children is not irreparable.

☐ STUDY 30 Isaiah 50: 4 – 51: 16

1 What qualities are revealed in this picture of God's Servant? Meditate on the fulfilment of these in Christ. *Cf.* Jn. 12: 49; Mt. 26: 67. Consider from His example and experience what you may count upon God to do for you, and on what conditions.

2 What comfort and encouragement for your own faith do you find in 51: 1–6? What divine reassurances are given to those who are frightened by the hostility of men (verses 7, 8, 12–16)?

☐ STUDY 31 Isaiah 51: 17 – 52: 12

1 Consider the seeming hopelessness of Zion's condition in 51: 17–20, 23. How and why does God promise to act on her behalf (51: 22; 52: 3–6)? What must she herself do (52: 1, 2)? What message has this for a backsliding Christian? *Cf.* 1 Jn. 1: 9.

2 Let your imagination picture the joy of Zion described in 52: 7–12. What application does the apostle Paul make of this passage in Rom. 10: 14, 15 and 2 Cor. 6: 17?

Notes

1 51: 23. An allusion to the practice of making captives lie face downward on the ground, and using their backs as a road to walk on.

2 52: 8. 'Eye to eye': *i.e.*, face to face. This is how they will see the Lord when He returns to Zion.

☐ STUDY 32 Isaiah 52: 13 – 53: 12

This is the fourth of the 'Servant' passages, which portray with such marvellous accuracy the mission, character, and redemptive work of the Lord Jesus Christ. (See Introduction and Analysis.) Today's portion falls into three parts: (1) an introductory summary, announcing the Servant's exaltation after extreme suffering, and the effect of this upon surrounding nations and kings (52: 13–15); (2) the story of His life and suffering unto death, told by His now penitent fellow-countrymen (53: 1–9); and (3) the glorious issue, both for Himself and others, of His sufferings and redemptive work (53: 10–12).

1 How is God's Servant the Lord Jesus Christ depicted in 52: 13–15? Notice the depth of His suffering, His exaltation, and the effect of this upon the nations. *Cf.* 49: 7; Jn. 19: 1–5; Eph. 1: 20, 21.

2 Work out in detail the many close parallels between 53: 1–9 and the actual life of the Lord Jesus, as, for example, (a) the form of His

manifestation to the world; (b) the reception accorded Him; (c) His sufferings and the meaning of them; (d) His behaviour when arrested; (e) the manner of His death and of His burial.

3 Who are the 'offspring' spoken of in 53: 10, and what benefits are shown in this whole passage to have been procured for them by the Servant's substitutionary death? *Cf.* Heb. 2: 10. Do you belong to this number?

Notes

1 53: 1. The nations had not heard (52: 15); but Israel, hearing, had not believed.

2 53: 8. 'Considered': or possibly 'complained', in the sense of making an appeal against the sentence. All were indifferent and even scornful. *Cf.* Mt. 27: 39–44.

3 53: 11. 'By his knowledge' may mean 'by means of His knowledge' or 'by the knowledge of Him' (on the part of others). *Cf.* Jn. 17: 3.

☐ STUDY 33 Isaiah 54

1 In verses 4–10 consider all the reasons given why God's reconciled people should not fear. In what ways will God be like a 'husband' to His people (verse 4–7)? How does God reveal in His treatment of His people that He is faithful to His covenants (verses 9, 10)?

2 'This is the heritage', says the prophet, 'of the servants of the Lord' (verse 17). What is this inheritance? List the blessings here promised. What guarantees that we can enjoy them?

3 William Carey applied verses 2 and 3 to the missionary enterprise, and summoned the church to reach out to the unevangelized nations. What does this chapter mean for you? In what direction does it summon you to 'lengthen your cords and strengthen your stakes'? Have you grasped how great your God is, how far-reaching His purposes of blessing?

☐ STUDY 34 Isaiah 55

1 Is the appeal in this chapter any less applicable or less urgent in our day than it was to the Jews living in Babylon? Are you then proclaiming it to those around you? Try to state its argument in present-day language.

2 In verses 8–13 what do we learn about (a) man's inability to comprehend God; (b) God's word of promise; (c) the future for God's people? How ought we to act in response to such truths?

□ STUDY 35 Isaiah 56 and 57

The good tidings of Jehovah's purpose to bring back the exiles and to restore Jerusalem produced many repercussions among different classes of hearers. In the opening verses of today's portion the prophet replies to the questionings of two special groups: (1) non-Jews, who had joined themselves to Israel (56: 3a, 6–8), and (2) eunuchs, who feared God (56: 3b–5). Might they also participate in the promised deliverance? The Lord's answer is that if they fulfilled the conditions of the covenant, they would be welcome to a full share in its blessings. In 56: 9 – 57: 14 the prophet rebukes two other groups: the leaders of the community in Jerusalem (56: 9–12), and those who were openly practising idolatry (57: 1–14). There follows a striking description of the kind of persons with whom God will dwell, and of His purposes of grace towards His people (57: 15–21).

1 What were the spiritual conditions on which the Lord would recognize a man, whether a Jew or not, as being one of His own people? See 56: 1–8. How does this anticipate the New Testament offer of the gospel to all, and how does it fall short of it? With verse 7 *cf.* Mt. 21: 13; and with verse 8 *cf.* Jn. 10: 16.

2 What do these two chapters, and more particularly 57: 15–21, teach us about God?

3 Consider the sad picture in 56: 9 – 57: 14 of a community whose leaders were unworthy, and whose members were forsaking the Lord for idols. What warnings for ourselves may be found in it?

Notes

1 56: 3b–5. In the new community physical and racial disabilities would no longer be a ground of exclusion. *Cf.* Dt. 23: 1, 3–8.

2 56: 10. 'Watchmen': *i.e.*, the leaders of the community, also called 'shepherds' (verse 11). They loved ease, gain, and drunken carnivals.

3 57: 3. A reference to their idolatrous practices; so also in verses 7, 8.

4 57: 11. 'You went on fearlessly, in faithlessness, giving no thought to me, in your indifference. Is it not so? I said no word, I hid my face from you, and on you went, fearing me not' (Moffatt).

□ STUDY 36 Isaiah 58

1 Has fasting itself any value in God's sight? What does He look for in His people, and why is such conduct called 'fasting'? In verses 8–12, what promises of spiritual blessing does God give to those who are right in spirit towards Himself and their fellowmen?

2 Examine your own attitude to Sunday in the light of verses 13, 14.

Notes

1 Verse 4. 'You fast only to quarrel and to fight . . .' Fasting, if not done in the right spirit, is apt to make men irritable and contentious, quick to use their fist.

2 Verse 9. 'The pointing of the finger': probably a gesture of haughty contempt.
3 Verse 13. 'If you turn back your foot from the sabbath': *i.e.*, regard it as holy ground, not to be profaned by common business. *Cf.* 56: 2; Ne. 13: 15–21.

☐ STUDY 37 Isaiah 59

This chapter in its opening verses is an exposure of the sins that separate from God (verses 1–8). In verses 9–15a the people describe their sorrowful state, and make confession. But they feel that if action on God's part is to be for ever restrained by their sinfulness the position seems hopeless indeed (see Note 2 on 'justice' below). Then in the closing verses of the chapter comes the triumphant divine answer (verses 15b–21). God is not baffled, and when there is no human help He Himself comes to the rescue, in judgment upon evil-doers on the one hand, and in redemption for the penitent on the other.

1 Verses 1–15. What various sins are mentioned here, and what are the consequences in the personal, social and spiritual life of the people? With verses 1, 2 *cf.* 1: 15–17; Mi. 3: 4.

2 What is the motive of God's intervention, as described in verses 15b–21? What is its twofold purpose, and what its world-wide issue? When does St. Paul look for this to be fulfilled to Israel (Rom. 11: 25–27)? Yet, for us who believe on Jesus Christ, is it not in part fulfilled to us now, and not least verse 21? *Cf.* Jn. 14: 16, 26.

Notes
1 Verses 5, 6. The plan and plots of evil-doers working fresh evil, and giving no useful result.
2 Verse 9. The word 'justice' is used in these verses in two senses, (a) as right done by man (verse 8, 15b), and (b) as divine judgment, exercised on behalf of Israel against her oppressors (verses 9, 11, 14). The people's lament was that the latter was withheld, because the former was lacking.

☐ STUDY 38 Isaiah 60

An inspired vision of Zion, when God shall have fulfilled towards her all His purpose, and clothed her with His glory.

1 Try to build up the picture of the glorified Zion as given in this vision. Gather out the references to God, and observe carefully the place He occupies in Zion. Has He this central place in your life, and in your Christian fellowship?

2 Consider how many of the features of beauty and glory in the Zion of this chapter are to be found, in their spiritual counterpart, in a life dwelling in the fullness of the Holy Spirit. See especially verses 2, 5, 7 (last clause), 13 (last clause), 16b, and 17–21; and *cf.* 2 Cor. 3: 18; 4: 6; 6: 16; Eph. 3: 14–21.

Notes

1 Verses 8, 9. The ships coming from the west, with their white sails, looking like a flock of doves.

2 Verse 13. 'The place of my sanctuary': *i.e.*, the Temple, called also 'the place of my feet'.

3 Verse 21. 'That I might be glorified': compare 'he has glorified you' (verse 9) and 'I will glorify my glorious house' (verse 7; so also verse 13). Where God is glorified, all else is glorified in Him. *Cf.* 2 Thes. 1: 12.

☐ STUDY 39 Isaiah 61: 1 – 63: 6

1 How would you summarize the teaching of chapters 61 and 62 regarding the Lord's purpose of good for Zion? What do we learn, for example, about (a) the relation to God into which God's people will be brought (61: 6, 8, 9; 62: 4, 12), and (b) the response of God's people to His promised salvation (61: 10)? Is your experience of this kind?

2 In chapter 61 the coming salvation is proclaimed, in 62 it is prayed for (verses 1, 6, 7). If the gospel is to prevail on earth, are not both the proclamation of it and prayer concerning it still necessary? *Cf.* Rom. 10: 14, 15; 2 Thes. 3: 1. What characteristic of prevailing prayer is emphasized here?

3 In Lk. 4: 17–21 our Lord says that the opening words of chapter 61 were spiritually fulfilled in His own ministry. Why did He cut His reading in the synagogue short in the middle of 61: 2? Meditate on the scope of our Lord's ministry as revealed in these verses.

Notes

1 62: 2. 'A new name': the symbol both of a new character, and of a new relation to God. *Cf.* Rev. 2: 17; 3: 12.

2 63: 4. The day of redemption is also a day of judgment. *Cf.* 61: 2; Jn. 3: 17–19.

☐ STUDY 40 Isaiah 63: 7 – 64: 12

1 63: 7–14. How does the suppliant begin his prayer? What has Israel learnt of God's mercy and love in her past? What lesson is there here for us when in our need we pray to God? *Cf.* Eph. 1: 16; Phil. 1: 3; 4: 6; Col. 1: 3.

2 What five pleas are found in 63: 15–19? In 64: 4, 5, the suppliant begins to advance another plea. What is it, and why is he unable to continue it (verses 6, 7)? Do you know how to plead with God? What pleas may we rightly make?

Notes

1 63: 10, 11, 14. The references to the Holy Spirit in this prayer are strikingly clear and full.

2 63: 17a. The prolonging of the suffering was tending to increase the ungodliness.

□ STUDY 41 Isaiah 65

1 Verses 1–7. What picture of God is unfolded in verses 1 and 2? *Cf.* Mt. 7: 2. Why has He been unable to answer the prophet's prayer for Israel's salvation? *Cf.* 59: 1–3. How does God purpose to deal with them (verses 8–12)?

2 What is to be the lot of God's chosen people in Jerusalem in the new age that is to dawn (verses 17–25)? What in contrast is going to be the life and end of those who forsake God (verses 11–15)?

Notes

1 Verses 3–7. A condemnation of various idolatrous practices.

2 Verse 8. 'When a bunch of grapes holds some good wine, men say, "Destroy it not, it holds a blessing" ' (Moffatt). So God will save the good in Israel.

3 Verse 11. 'Fortune' and 'Destiny': the Hebrew words are Gad and Meni, the names of two gods.

□ STUDY 42 Isaiah 66

The distinction is maintained between those who are disobedient to God, and those who fear Him. The final destiny of the two classes is made clear. God will thus be fully and finally glorified. *Cf.* 2 Thes. 1: 7–12.

1 When God looks down upon men's worship, what is it He values? See verses 1–4; *cf.* Ps. 51: 17; Jn. 4: 23, 24.

2 What is the end of those who, having heard God's voice, will not give heed? See especially verses 4, 5, 6, 17, 24. What, on the other hand, is promised to Zion and her children? See verses 7–14, 20–22. While these promises are made primarily to Jerusalem and are yet to be fulfilled, they also declare the spiritual good things which God has provided for us in His Son, and which we may claim for ourselves in Him. *Cf.* Rom. 8: 16, 17, 32; 1 Cor. 3: 22; 2 Cor. 1: 20.

3 How does the prophet's vision of God's purpose for the nations fall short of the glory of the full revelation of this 'mystery' in the New Testament?

PART THREE

Check-list of material contained in this part (tick when completed):

MATTHEW 1 - 7

Introduction

It is customary to see in Matthew's Gospel the fact that Jesus is presented especially as the Messiah, the promised Son of David. This is true; but it also declares that He is the Saviour from sin (1:21) and the Son of God (1:23; 3:17; 16:16, 17); and although the writer was obviously a Jew to the core, and wrote primarily for Jewish Christians, yet he recognizes that Jesus is the Saviour, not of the Jews only, but of all nations (2:1, 11; 28:19, 20). Nevertheless, this is the most Jewish of the Gospels. It is significant that our Lord's genealogy is traced back, not to Adam, as in Luke's account, but to Abraham, the father of the Jewish race.

The story of the birth of Christ shows distinct signs of being derived from Joseph's side, as the story given by Luke would seem to come from Mary's.

The Gospel is characterized by the large place it gives to the teaching of our Lord, and in particular to His teaching in parables and about 'things to come'.

Analysis

1:4 – 4:11	Early days of the Messiah.	
	1 and 2	Genealogy, birth and childhood incidents.
	3:1–12	The heralds proclaim His coming ministry.
	3:13 – 4:11	His baptism and temptation.
4:12 – 16:12	The ministry in Galilee.	
	4:12–25	Preaching, and call of disciples.
	5 – 7	The Sermon on the Mount—the kingdom expounded.

	8 – 16: 12	Teaching, preaching and healing, mainly in Galilee. Commissioning and sending forth of the Twelve. Increasing opposition.
16: 13 – 18: 35	Peter's confession. Prediction of the cross. The transfiguration. Teaching of the Twelve.	
19: 1 – 21: 16	Journey to Jerusalem and entry into the city.	
21: 17 – 25: 46	Last days in Jerusalem.	
	21: 17 – 23: 39	Final words. Reciprocal rejection.
	24: 1 – 25: 46	Teaching the Twelve about 'things to come'.
26: 1 – 27: 66	The finished work.	
	26: 1–56	Last supper and betrayal.
	26: 57 – 27: 66	Trial, crucifixion and burial.
28: 1–20	The new beginning. The resurrection and the great commission.	

☐ STUDY 1 Matthew 1

1 Consider the names in the genealogy and note how sinful some of them were. How does this chapter indicate that the coming of Jesus was in God's plan from the beginning? In what ways does it demonstrate that in Jesus Old Testament prophecy is fulfilled? What truths are here indicated concerning His Person and work?

2 What do verses 18–25 teach us about the virgin birth? What is the importance of this truth for the Christian?

3 Examine the character of Joseph as revealed in these verses (*cf.* 2: 13–23). What may we learn from his courageous obedience?

Notes

1 Verse 17. This arrangement into three periods of fourteen generations each is not exact, some generations being omitted. Possibly this artificial arrangement is for easy memorizing.

2 Verse 19. According to Jewish law, Mary, being betrothed to Joseph, was already legally regarded as his wife.

☐ STUDY 2 Matthew 2

1 Consider the significance of the coming of the wise men from the East in the light of such passages as Is. 49: 6; Lk. 2: 32; Jn. 10: 16.

2 Note the different reactions to the birth of Jesus from the wise men, the chief priests and scribes, and Herod. How does this prove the truth of Jn. 9: 39; 18: 37?

3 Notice the accuracy of fulfilment of prophecy in our Lord's infancy (verses 15; 17, 18; 23). What does this teach us about the nature and authority of prophecy?

Notes

1 Verse 1. 'Wise men': the word 'Magi' (see RV mg.) refers to learned astrologers or those who practised magical arts. There is nothing but tradition to make them kings.

2 Verse 23. There is no Old Testament quotation about the Messiah as a Nazarene. Matthew may be making a play on the Hebrew word *netser* meaning 'branch' from Is. 11: 1 and Je. 23: 5. Or the phrase may refer to the contempt associated with Christ's home background. *Cf.* Jn. 1: 46; Is. 53: 2, 3.

☐ STUDY 3 Matthew 3

1 John the Baptist saw himself as preparing the way for Christ (verse 3). In what ways did he do this through (a) his preaching, and (b) his administration of baptism?

2 What do verses 13–15 tell us about the importance of His baptism to Jesus? How do you link this moment with the cross? *Cf.* Ps. 40: 7–8; Lk. 12: 50; 2 Cor. 5: 21. Can you see the Trinity clearly at work in these verses?

☐ STUDY 4 Matthew 4

1 Consider the temptations of Jesus as a testing of the kind of ministry He was going to exercise. What was the special point of appeal in each temptation? Can you link these three typical temptations with the threefold division of 1 Jn. 2: 16?

2 In what way do verses 1–11 help us to understand the meaning of temptation and the way in which Satan may be defeated?

3 What was Christ's first message? Try to define repentance. *Cf.* Acts 2: 38; 20: 21; Lk. 15: 18; Mt. 3: 8. What further demand did He make on those who became disciples, and why? Has your response to Christ been of this kind?

Note. The incidents recorded in Jn. 1: 29 – 4: 3 must have happened between verses 11 and 12 of this chapter.

☐ STUDY 5 Matthew 5: 1–16

1 Describe the qualities of the happy life as detailed in verses 1–12. What makes them such? To what rewards do they lead, and why?

2 Verses 13–16. What is the significance of the two metaphors with which our Lord describes the relation to the world of those who belong to the kingdom? And in what ways does He warn them that they may fail to exercise their proper function?

Note. Verse 3. 'Poor in spirit': *i.e.*, aware of their spiritual poverty and of their need of divine help. *Cf.* Is. 57: 15; Lk. 18: 13.

☐ STUDY 6 Matthew 5: 17–48

1 Our Lord demonstrates His respect for the law in verses 17–20. What does verse 20 mean? Does it leave us any hope? *Cf.* Rom. 3: 20–22; 8: 3, 4. In what way does our Lord make the law more demanding?

2 What is the relevance in our modern world of Christ's teaching in verses 33–48 on the subject of oaths and taking vengeance? Consider the application of the question in verse 47, 'What more are you doing than others?' to the whole subject of Christian love.

3 Comparing verses 31, 32 with 19: 3–9, what is our Lord's teaching on the sanctity of marriage and the possibility of divorce?

Notes

1 Verse 18. 'Not an iota, not a dot': a reference to the smallest letter or significant part of a letter in the Hebrew language.

2 Verse 48. 'Perfect' has more the meaning of 'mature' or full-grown than any concept of sinless perfection. *Cf.* Lk. 6: 36.

☐ STUDY 7 Matthew 6: 1–18

1 What was wrong with the religion of the scribes and Pharisees, here called 'hypocrites', and what kind of religion does our Lord commend in contrast? *Cf.* Je. 17: 10. How do you 'practise your piety' (verse 1)?

2 In the Lord's prayer, what may we learn (a) from the order of the petitions, and (b) from the kind of subjects which are particularly mentioned? What must be our relation (a) to God, and (b) to our fellow-men, if we are to make it our prayer?

Note. Verses 2, 5, 16. The word 'hypocrite' means an actor, *i.e.*, one who plays a part.

☐ STUDY 8 Matthew 6: 19–32

1 Verses 19–24 are a word to the rich. What should be a Christian's attitude to material possessions? In what way do these verses portray the character and danger of worldliness?

2 Verses 25–34 are a word to the not-so-rich. Note the recurrence of the phrase 'Do not be anxious', and list the reasons given why anxiety is wrong.

Note. Verse 23. An eye which is 'not sound' (RSV) or 'evil' (AV, RV) signifies a covetous or niggardly disposition. *Cf.* Dt. 15: 9; Pr. 28: 22; Mt. 20: 15 (mg.).

☐ STUDY 9 Matthew 7: 1–12

1 Compare verses 1–5 with verses 6, 16; and see Jn. 7: 24. If judging is not always wrong, what is our Lord here condemning?

2 What is the teaching of verses 7–12 on the practice of prayer? What place is there for persistency, and what place for trusting? Is there any conflict between these two ideas?

Note. Verse 6. This indicates that, while Christians must not be guilty of condemning anyone, they must learn to discriminate in their witness. *Cf.* Pr. 9: 8.

☐ STUDY 10 Matthew 7: 13–29

1 In verses 13–23 what threefold responsibility does our Lord lay upon those who would enter His kingdom (a) as to a right choice at the beginning (verses 13–14); (b) as to a right discrimination between false and true (verses 15–20); and (c) as to the condition of being acknowledged by Him at the last (verses 21–23)?

2 To what categories of men do verses 24–27 refer? In what way do the two houses differ? How is it possible to be building—yet building foolishly?

3 Verses 15–20. In what way may we tell the false prophet? *Cf.* Dt. 13: 1–5; 1 Jn. 4: 1–6. Can you think of any modern guise in which he appears?

For Studies 11–28 on the second section of Matthew's Gospel see p. 325.

JONAH

Introduction

Jonah is mentioned in 2 Ki. 14: 25 as having predicted the victories of Jeroboam II by which the borders of the kingdom of Israel were greatly enlarged. If Jonah prophesied at the beginning of Jeroboam's reign, he would precede Amos by about twenty years only. At that time Assyria was already a great power, and had begun to reach out westwards: in fact, Jeroboam's victories were partly due to Assyrian raids upon Damascus and neighbouring states, which weakened these kingdoms. It would seem that Jonah was afraid of Assyria, whose cruelties were well known, and whose power was dreaded.

To this man came the commission to go to Nineveh and cry against it. One might have thought that such a commission would not be unwelcome, but to Jonah it was so hateful that he resolved rather to resign his prophetic office than obey it. The book is the story of what happened. It is one of the most remarkable books in the Bible, and rich in spiritual teaching.

Analysis

1 Jonah's disobedience and its result.
2 His prayer of desolation and thanksgiving.
3 A recommissioned Jonah preaches in Nineveh with astonishing effect.
4 Jonah's anger, and God's reproof.

☐ STUDY 1 Jonah 1 and 2

The key to Jonah's flight is found in 4: 2. He feared the tenderness of God. If he went to Nineveh as commanded, Nineveh might repent, and be spared (*cf.* Je. 18: 8) to become later the destroyer of Israel. If he did not go, God's judgment would fall upon Nineveh, and Israel would be saved.

1 'But Jonah' (verse 3); 'But the Lord' (verse 4). *Cf.* Acts 11: 8, 9 (where the context also concerns Gentiles). Of what truth had Jonah lost sight? *Cf.* 1 Tim. 2: 4. How did the Lord retain control of the situation? With 1: 7b *cf.* Pr. 16: 33, and notice 'appointed' in 1: 17.

2 Jonah (like Adam and Eve, Gn. 3: 8–10) tried to escape from the presence of the Lord (1: 3, 10; *cf.* 2: 4). Why was this impossible? In the light of this passage, look up Ps. 139: 23, 24 and apply it to yourself.

3 Jonah's prayer, remarkable for its lack of direct petition, speaks of distress and passes into thanksgiving. What was the fundamental cause of his distress? What caused the transition?

Notes

1 1: 3. 'Flee . . . from the presence of the Lord': this amounted to renouncing his vocation, for the prophet stood in the presence of the Lord (*cf.* 1 Ki. 17: 1).

2 1: 17. 'Three days and three nights': *cf.* Mt. 12: 40. According to Jewish reckoning this may mean one full day with the night before and the night after.

3 2: 7. To the Hebrews, 'remembering' could be much more than a bare mental process; it could mean recreating to the imagination the historic deeds of the Lord; the use of the word repays detailed study. With this passage *cf.* Pss. 77: 11, 12; 105: 4–6; 143: 5.

4 2: 9. The vow was probably some sort of sacrificial thank-offering. Vowing is a biblical practice; but the Old Testament counsels against hasty (Pr. 20: 25) and empty (Ec. 5: 5) vows.

☐ STUDY 2 Jonah 3 and 4

1 God is unchangeably consistent in His attitude to men. What moral action is necessary to avoid judgment and find mercy? *Cf.* Joel 2: 12–14; Acts 10: 34, 35. How did Jesus commend the Ninevites' action? *Cf.* Mt. 12: 41.

2 Jonah the patriot almost hides Jonah the prophet. How do 4: 2b, 4, 10 and 11 rebuke his attitude? Contrast the attitude of Jonah with that of Jesus the Jew. *Cf.* Mt. 23: 37, 38; Mk. 10: 45.

3 What aspects of the character of God stand out in this short book?

Notes

1 3: 3. 'An exceedingly great city': the administrative district of Nineveh, which could be referred to here (as distinct from the city alone), was thirty to sixty miles across.

2 4: 2. 'Repentest of evil': the Hebrew root means 'to breathe heavily'. A change of mind is not so much meant; the thought is almost that the Lord takes a deep breath of relief that He does not have to act in judgment as the consistency of His character would otherwise demand.

3 4: 6. 'A plant': a fast-growing, trailing or climbing plant with broad leaves.
4 4: 9-11. 'Jonah (for selfish reasons) pities the insignificant plant for which he was not responsible. Should not God much more (and unselfishly) have pity on the poor ignorant inhabitants with their cattle in the evil city of Nineveh?'

JOEL

Introduction

Nothing is known of this prophet beyond what is stated in the first verse of his book, and the evident fact that he prophesied to Judah. It is generally agreed that he was either one of the earliest of the prophets, or one of the latest. The date is not important for the study of his message.

The occasion of his prophecy was an unprecedented plague of locusts, apparently accompanied by drought (1: 18–20). He summoned the people to national repentance and self-humbling, and on their doing this, he was authorized to declare the speedy departure of the locusts and the restoration of the land.

But the prophet was given also a more distant vision. The plague of locusts was a symbol of the approaching day of the Lord, and Joel foresees the outpouring of the Spirit, and the gathering of the nations to answer for their misdeeds towards Israel. The Lord will triumph, and Israel be blessed.

Analysis

1: 1 – 2: 17	The plague of locusts and a national summons to repentance.
2: 18–27	The locusts will be destroyed, and the land will recover its fertility.
2: 28–32	The outpouring of the Holy Spirit.
3: 1–21	The day of the Lord; the judgment of the nations, and blessings upon Judah and Jerusalem.

☐ **STUDY 1 Joel 1: 1 – 2: 17**

Two addresses on the plague of locusts, both describing in different ways its severity, and summoning the people to repent.

1 What teaching is given in this passage on the need for corporate repentance for national sin? What essentials of true repentance are given in 2: 12, 13?

2 Gather together the teaching on 'the day of the Lord' in this passage. What is its significance?

☐ **STUDY 2 Joel 2: 18 – 3: 21**

1 What is God's reaction to His people's repentance? What principle does this teach?

2 How has the prophecy of 2: 28, 29 been fulfilled far more wonderfully than Joel foresaw?

3 Chapter 3 is a vision of mercy upon Israel, and judgment on her enemies. In what ways had the nations angered God by their treatment of Israel, and what judgment would fall on them? What according to 3: 17 and 21 is the supreme blessedness of God's people?

ZEPHANIAH

Introduction

Zephaniah prophesied in the reign of Josiah, and probably in the early years of that reign, before Josiah began his religious reforms. For when Zephaniah delivered his message, idolatrous customs, which Josiah abolished, were still openly practised (*cf.*, *e.g.*, 1: 4, 5 with 2 Ki. 23: 4, 5). Zephaniah was therefore a contemporary of Jeremiah and possibly began his ministry somewhat earlier. If the

Hezekiah from whom his descent is traced (1 : 1) was, as many think probable, the king of that name, then Zephaniah was related to the royal house.

The theme of his prophecy is the day of the Lord, which was about to break. It is pictured as a day of terrible judgment, under the imagery of war and invasion, in which Judah and Jerusalem would be thoroughly purged of those who practised wickedness. But the judgment would embrace all nations; it was to be a day of universal judgment.

When the judgment was completed there would be a remnant of Israel, a lowly but upright people who, trusting in the Lord, would rejoice in His favour. Zephaniah foresaw also that other nations would 'call on the name of the Lord and serve him with one accord' (3 : 9). His message is marked by breadth of view and profound insight, and charged with an ardent vehemence of moral passion.

Zephaniah's words received a striking fulfilment in the fall of Nineveh, and a quarter of a century later in the fall of Jerusalem. But the fulfilment is not yet complete. The final day of God's judgment has yet to come.

Analysis

1 : 1–18	The approaching day of the Lord, with special reference to Judah and Jerusalem.
2 : 1 – 3 : 7	A summons to repentance; prophecies of judgment against other nations; and the failure of Jerusalem to amend her ways.
3 : 8–20	The remnant that will survive the judgment; their character and their felicity.

☐ STUDY 1 Zephaniah 1

The effects of God's universal judgment (verses 2, 3) upon Judah and Jerusalem are described in detail (verses 4–13). The chapter ends with a terrifying picture of the day of the Lord (verses 14–18).

1 On whom particularly will God's judgment fall according to this chapter, and why? Can you think of any modern counterparts to the sinful actions described?

2 Having considered the reasons for judgment, now ponder the accompaniments of the day of the Lord in verses 14–18. What may we learn from these about God's view of sin? *Cf.* Pr. 11 : 4; Ezk. 7 : 19.

Notes

1 Verse 4. To 'cut off . . . the name of' mean to 'obliterate the memory of'.

2 Verse 5. 'Milcom': a foreign deity of this or a similar name was worshipped in several of the countries surrounding Judah.

3 Verse 12. 'Thickening upon their lees': *cf.* Je. 48: 11. This picture, taken from the wine-trade, refers to the sedimentation of wine. The idle, stagnant, muddy-minded men in Jerusalem, who thought they could settle down in their godless indifference, will be punished.

☐ STUDY 2 Zephaniah 2: 1 – 3: 7

1 What phrases are used to describe the nations over whom judgment is impending? See 2: 1, 10, 15. What was especially sinful about Nineveh's attitude (2: 15; *cf.* Is. 47: 6–11), and has it a modern counterpart? What qualities does God look for in those who desire his help (2: 3)?

2 'Hidden on the day of the wrath of the Lord' (2: 3). Is there such a hiding-place? *Cf.* Je. 23: 24; Am. 9: 3; Rev. 6: 15–17; Rom. 5: 9; 1 Thes. 1: 10.

3 The indictment against Jerusalem is the most grievous of all (3: 1–7). *Cf.* Lk. 12: 47, 48. List the evils found in her, and consider especially how they were sins against the Lord.

Notes

1 2: 1. 'Come together . . .': *i.e.*, in solemn assembly to seek the Lord.

2 2: 13–15. No man alive at the time had known anything but the greatness and glory of Assyria. So these words would have had an astonishing impact.

3 3: 5–7. The Lord's faithfulness in judgment on their enemies is matched by the shamelessness of His people. They were heedless of the lessons He was seeking to teach them.

☐ STUDY 3 Zephaniah 3: 8–20

1 Throughout this passage the Lord is seen acting. What is He pictured as doing? How many of these actions were, or can now be, fulfilled in Christ? Are there some which still await fulfilment, and, if so, why?

2 Consider the character of the remanant that the Lord leaves (verses 12, 13). Compare 2: 3; and contrast 2: 1; 3: 1, 2. Does 3: 17 suggest a reason for this change of character? How is it brought about? *Cf.* 2 Cor. 5: 17; Eph. 4: 24.

Note. Verses 9, 12. To 'seek refuge in the name of the Lord' is an expressive figure for trust in the Lord's revealed character. Truly to call Him Lord means to acknowledge Him as such, and to give Him the service that is His due. *Cf.* 1 Pet. 3: 6a.

NAHUM

Introduction

In the prophet Nahum God found a man who, with flaming conviction, proclaimed the astonishing message that great Nineveh, still at the height of her power and glory, must fall and disappear. Nahum concentrates on this seemingly incredible event to the exclusion of all else. With great poetic skill and vivid realism he portrays the attack upon the city and her final end. We can almost see the battle, the capture, the looting, and hear the noise of her fall and the silence of her desolation. Nahum's purpose in writing, however, is not to gloat over the downfall of the great enemy of his people. It is to magnify the God of Israel, to declaim that He is, on the one hand, faithful to His promises and strong to save those who put their trust in Him, and, on the other hand, the Holy One, who is the Adversary and Judge of the wicked. It is because the Assyrian Empire was built with ruthless cruelty upon the principle that might is right that God, as the moral Governor of the world, rises up to smite it to the dust.

Nahum prophesied between the overthrow of Thebes in Egypt, about 663 BC (to which he makes reference in 3: 8), and the fall of Nineveh in 612. There is no certain clue as to a more exact date, but the most likely period for his ministry seems to be in the early years of King Josiah. If so, he preceded Jeremiah by only a few years.

Analysis

1: 1	Title.
1: 2–15	The Lord, who is good to those who trust in Him, is terrible to His enemies, and will utterly destroy Assyria.
2	The attack upon the city, its capture and overthrow.
3	Nineveh's guilt and punishment. Her end is final, and all that hear of it shall clap their hands.

☐ STUDY 1 Nahum 1

1 What do we learn in this chapter about God (a) in relation to His own people, and (b) in relation to His enemies? *Cf.* Lk. 18: 7, 8; 2 Thes. 1: 8; Nu. 14: 17, 18; Ps. 46: 1.

2 Nineveh's boastful spirit is seen in Is. 36: 18–20; 37: 23–25; Zp. 2: 15. But how does Nahum regard her in relation to God's power? See verses 3b–6, 9–12a, 14; and *cf.* Ps. 37: 35, 36.

3 Consider how verse 7 is illustrated in the story of 2 Ki. 18 and 19, which happened less than a century before Nahum's time. Have you your own illustration to give out of your own experience?

Notes

1 Verse 1. 'An oracle concerning Nineveh', or 'The burden of Nineveh': see Note on Je. 23: 33–40. Where 'Elkosh' was is not known with certainty; it may be in Judah.

2 Verse 2. 'A jealous God': behind this description lies the figure of the marriage relation used in Scripture of Israel's relation to God. 'Just as jealousy in husband or wife is the energetic assertion of an exclusive right, so God asserts and vindicates His claim on those who belong to Him alone.' Or, in terms of kingship, it is His 'passionate determination' that His sovereignty be recognized among all men, 'to the benefit of the humble and loyal among his subjects and the confusion of the presumptuous'. *Cf.* Ex. 34: 14; 1 Cor. 10: 20–22.

3 Verse 7. 'Knows': *i.e.*, takes care of.

4 Verses 8–10. The translation here is often difficult: see mg. The RSV too readily follows alternative readings. In verse 8 read with mg. 'her place', *i.e.*, probably the sanctuary of Nineveh or its goddess Ishtar. Verse 10 has been rendered (*cf.* mg.): 'Though tangled as thorns, and drenched as their drink, they shall yet be consumed as stubble fully dry' (Eaton), *i.e.*, however tricky an enemy (for men) to deal with, God's flame will run through them like dry stubble.

5 Verse 11. Possibly a reference to Sennacherib. *Cf.* Is. 10: 7–11.

6 Verses 12, 13 and 15 are addressed to Judah, and verses 11 and 14 to Nineveh.

7 Verse 12b. RV mg. reads: 'So will I afflict thee, that I shall afflict thee no more' (*i.e.*, 'I shall not need to'). *Cf.* verse 9. Then the verse is addressed to Nineveh.

8 Verse 14. 'Vile' here does not mean depraved, but rather abject, reduced to the meanest condition.

9 Verse 15. The 'good tidings' is the news of Nineveh's downfall.

☐ STUDY 2 Nahum 2 and 3

These two chapters are two separate odes describing the fall of Nineveh. In chapter 2 the prophet depicts the approach of the enemy (verse 1a) and ironically summons the people to defend their city (verse 1b). Then follows a description of the attackers within and without the walls (verses 3–5). The river gates are forced, the palace is in panic, the queen captured, the people flee (verses 6–8), and looting follows (verse 9). The chapter ends with a picture of Nineveh overthrown, lying desolate in her ruins. Chapter 3 declares the city's guilt and her punishment (verses 1–7), and bids her take warning from the fate of Thebes (verses 8–10). Nineveh's strength fails (verses 11–15a). Though her people are without number, and her merchants are as numerous as locusts, yet, like locusts, they will fly away (verses 15b–17). Her rulers perish, her people are scattered. All who hear of her fall will rejoice (verses 18, 19).

1 Read each chapter aloud, if possible in Moffatt's translation. What were Nineveh's sins that brought upon her so terrible a retribution? See also 1: 11. What does this show of God's attitude even to non-Christian societies? Does He care whether they are righteous or corrupt? If God cares, should we?

2 How does Nahum show the converse of Rom. 8: 31; *i.e.*, if God be against us, who can be for us? *Cf.* Ps. 34: 16; Je. 37: 9, 10. Have you ever experienced this in your own life, with all circumstances going against you, that in fact God was against you?

Notes

1 2: 5. 'Officers': or '*elite* troops'. The same word is rendered 'nobles' in 3: 18. A 'mantlet' is a missile-proof screen under the shelter of which the attackers advance.

2 2: 7. 'Mistress': the word may refer to the queen (*cf.* verse 6), or to the Assyrian goddess Ishtar or her image.

3 2: 8. Nineveh is compared to a breached reservoir.

4 2: 11. 'Cave': 'pasture' (RSV mg., AV), or 'feeding place' (RV).

5 2: 13. 'Messengers': envoys; *cf.* 2 Ki. 19: 9, 23.

6 3: 4–6. The use of this figure to symbolize Nineveh was doubtless suggested by the sacred prostitution prominent in the cult of Ishtar.

7 3: 8. 'Sea': *i.e.*, the mighty waters of the Nile.

8 3: 9. 'Put': an African people, perhaps from Somalia or Libya.

HABAKKUK

Introduction

We know nothing about Habakkuk himself except that he was a prophet, and the only clear historical reference in the book is to the Chaldeans in 1:6, on the basis of which a date just after the Battle of Carchemish (605 BC) is suggested, when this 'bitter and hasty' nation was marching westwards to subjugate Jehoiakim, king of Judah. Habakkuk was thus a contemporary of Jeremiah, but the two men were very different. Jeremiah's problem was how God could destroy His people. Habakkuk's problem was how God could use so evil a nation as the Chaldeans as His instrument (*cf.* Isaiah and the Assyrians). The problem is set forth in chapter 1, and God's answer is given in chapters 2 and 3 in words of extraordinary depth and grandeur.

Analysis

1:1–4	How long will lawlessness go unpunished?
1:5–11	Incredibly, God points to the Chaldeans in reply.
1:12–17	How can God allow the inhumanity and the idolatry of this wicked nation?
2:1–5	The expectant prophet receives God's answer: Pride comes before a fall, but the truthfulness of the righteous will be his salvation.
2:6–20	A series of woes directed against the Chaldeans.
3:1–19	A psalm consisting of a prayer, a revelation of God coming in judgment and salvation, and a confession of faith.

☐ STUDY 1 Habakkuk 1:1 – 2:5

1 What is the prophet's first complaint, and what is to Habakkuk God's strange answer? See 1:2–4, 5–11.

2 What further problem does this raise in the prophet's mind, and what answer is he given? See 1: 12–17 and 2: 2–5.

3 What course of action does 2: 1 suggest that the Christian should adopt when perplexed at God's dealings? *Cf.* Ps. 73: 16, 17; Mi. 7: 7. Are you faithful in this way?

Notes

1 1: 7b. The Chaldeans' so-called 'justice and dignity' are arbitrary and self-determined.

2 2: 2. God's answer is to be written down plainly so that it may be read at a glance.

3 2: 4, 5. God's answer is in two parts. (a) The arrogant Chaldean, whose soul is not upright, shall fail and pass away. *Cf.* Is. 2: 12–17. (b) The righteous man will endure. He will live by his faith, a faith inspired by God's faithfulness, which keeps him steadfast. The profound truth here expressed is seen in its full significance in the gospel of Christ. *Cf.* Rom. 1: 16, 17.

☐ STUDY 2 Habakkuk 2: 6–20

1 Sum up in one or two words each of the evils against which the five 'woes' of these verses are pronounced. Are these evils found in the world today? What may those who commit them expect?

2 In contrast to verses 18, 19, ponder the promise of verse 14 and the command of verse 20. How were these a warning to the plunderer, and a comfort to the plundered? What response should they inspire in us? *Cf.* Ps. 73: 16–26.

☐ STUDY 3 Habakkuk 3: 1–15

Habakkuk prays that God will show Himself once again as long ago (verses 1, 2), and then describes a vision of God coming to deliver His people. Past, present and future are intermingled. God's self-revelation in the past at Sinai, at the Red Sea and at the entrance into Canaan are pictured under the image of a thunderstorm rolling up from the south and breaking upon Palestine. The same 'Holy One' is at work also in the present, and the tumults of the nations are the tokens that He has come in judgment to work salvation for His people.

1 Habakkuk considered God's working in the past with longing and fear (verses 1, 2). Do we know such longing? *Cf.* Pss. 85: 6; 143: 5, 6; Is. 64: 1–3. Why was he afraid? *Cf.* Heb. 12: 21, 28, 29.

2 The poetry describes political upheavals. *Cf.* Is. 29: 5–8. Yet the poetry also is full of God's acts. How does this vision teach us to regard the world-happenings of our own day? What is God's purpose through them? *Cf.* Ps. 74: 12; Lk. 21: 25–28.

Notes
1 Verse 3. 'Teman', 'Mount Paran': *i.e.*, the region of Sinai.
2 Verse 4. Allusions to lightning and thick clouds.
3 Verse 8. The answer is found in verses 13–15.

☐ STUDY 4 Habakkuk 3: 16–19

1 What two effects did the vision have upon Habakkuk? With verse 16, *cf.* Dn. 10: 8; Rev. 1: 17. With verses 17, 18, *cf.* Ps. 73: 25, 26; Phil. 4: 11–13. Are we as sensitive as Habakkuk was to the glory and the faithfulness of the God with whom, by grace, we have to do?

2 What three things did God—trusted and rejoiced in—do for the prophet? *Cf.* Ps. 18: 32, 39; Zc. 4: 6; Is. 40: 31. Which of these do you particularly need God to do for you?

Notes
1 Verse 16. 'Rottenness enters': a Hebrew idiom expressing complete loss of strength. *Cf.* Pr. 12: 4; 14: 30. With the last part of this verse, *cf.* 2 Thes. 1: 6–8.
2 Verse 19. To 'tread upon my high places': a picture of triumph and security. *Cf.* Dt. 33: 29c.

OBADIAH

Introduction

Obadiah's message is almost entirely a denunciation of Edom for unbrotherly conduct to Israel, and a prophecy of the destruction of that proud kingdom and people. But the prophet associates Edom's fall with the day of the Lord, and foresees Israel's recovery of their promised possessions, and the universal triumph of God's reign and kingdom.

The Edomites, as the descendants of Esau, and the Israelites, as the descendants of Jacob, were enemies from the time that Israel took possession of Canaan (see Nu. 20: 14–21), and there are many references in the historical and prophetic books to Edom, which show the antipathy between Edom and Israel, and the difference in their destinies. See, *e.g.*, 2 Sa. 8: 14; 2 Ki. 14: 7; Je. 49: 7–22; Ezk. 25: 12–17; Am. 1: 11, 12; Mal. 1: 1–5.

Analysis

1–9 The doom of Edom, despite his confidence in his impregnable strongholds.
10–14 The sin for which Edom is to be punished.
15–21 The day of the Lord is at hand when Edom shall be punished and Israel shall triumph.

☐ **STUDY Obadiah**

1 By act and attitude Edom had sinned against God and against His people. Trace the details of the sin; then look up 1 Cor. 10: 11, 12 and apply Obadiah's warnings to your own life.

2 The prophet claims divine inspiration (verses 1, 4, 8, 18). What do we learn of the Lord's character from this book? What wonderful truth had yet to be revealed which goes beyond verse 15? *Cf.* Rom. 8: 3, 4.

3 The prophet's words speak of searing (verse 18) and possession (verses 17, 19, 20). How do the words 'holy' (verse 17) and 'the kingdom shall be the Lord's' (verse 21) change the complexion of the situation? The Christian's expectation is the same: 'Thy kingdom come.' How and why does its spirit differ? *Cf.* Mk. 1: 14, 15; Mt. 12: 28; Acts 8: 12; Jn. 18: 36; Rev. 12: 10, 11; Mt. 5: 3; Rom. 14: 17.

Notes

1 Verse 1. The section 'We have heard . . . let us rise against her for battle!' is in parenthesis, suggesting the means by which Edom will be brought low.

2 Verse 3. RSV mg. draws attention to a possible pun here; *Sela* means 'rock', but it was also the name of the capital city of Edom, later called Petra.

3 Verses 5, 6. Thieves or grape-stealers leave something behind; but when God plunders, the pillage is complete.

4 Verse 7. The principle here is enunciated in verse 15b; this principle of strict justice is the basis of God's moral law. *Cf.* Gal. 6: 7.

5 Verses 10–14. *Cf.* Ps. 137: 7; La. 2: 15, 16.

6 Verse 16. The 'cup' of God's wrath was a vivid prophetic picture of divine punishment and consequent disaster. *Cf.* Je. 25: 27, 28; Is. 51: 17; Rev. 14: 10.

MATTHEW 8 - 18

☐ STUDY 11 Matthew 8: 1–22

1 Consider how different the people were who received healing, and how different our Lord's methods with them were. What does this teach us concerning (a) His power, and (b) our work for Him?

2 What was so remarkable in the centurion's faith as to elicit Christ's great commendation? Contrast Jn. 4: 48. Note how the statement of verses 11, 12 anticipates the revolutionary developments recorded in the Acts. See Acts 13: 45–48.

3 Verses 18–22. Why did our Lord leave the crowds, and why did He check two would-be disciples? *Cf.* Lk. 14: 25–27.

Note. In chapters 8 and 9 Matthew records nine miracles of our Lord, in three groups of three. Matthew has this habit of grouping in subject-matter rather than in strict chronological order.

☐ STUDY 12 Matthew 8: 23 – 9: 8

1 In 9: 6 and 8 the word 'authority' is used to characterize Christ's ministry. In what three realms is this seen in this passage?

2 9: 1–8 reveals Christ's power to deal with the deepest trouble of man. What is this? How do these verses illustrate the means whereby a man may find this healing? What follows from it as a visible proof of it?

3 Demon-possession was clearly treated seriously by our Lord. What may we understand by the demons' witness to Christ in 8: 29 (*cf.* Mk. 1: 24; 3: 11, 12; Acts 16: 16–18)? In what way does the incident of 8: 28–34 have any parallel in the ministry of the Spirit today?

□ STUDY 13 Matthew 9: 9–34

1 In what ways do verses 9–17 disclose the revolutionary character of the ministry of Jesus? What do they teach us of the character of God (verse 13), and of the way a Christian ought to live amongst sinners?

2 Considering the miracles as signs, define the lessons we may learn from the incidents of verses 18–34 about the ability of our Lord to deal with the spiritual problems of weakness, deadness, blindness, dumbness. Have you such a problem which ought to be dealt with?

□ STUDY 14 Matthew 9: 35 – 10: 23

1 Some of the instructions given to the twelve here are clearly temporary and would not apply to every situation. But what principles of Christian service can you find, which are always applicable?

2 Verses 16–23 offer the prospect of both persecution in, and power for, service. In this situation, what is to be the attitude of disciples?

Note. 10: 23 has probably no reference to the second advent, but rather to Christ's coming in triumph after the resurrection, or to His coming in judgment in the fall of Jerusalem.

□ STUDY 15 Matthew 10: 24–42

1 With all the realism of the warning in verses 24, 25, Christ encourages His disciples not to fear. Consider the reasons given in verses 26–33 to encourage confidence.

2 In what way do verses 34–42 demand of the Christian both militancy and tenderness? How do you equate the statement of verse 34 with the thought of Christ as Prince of Peace?

□ STUDY 16 Matthew 11: 1–24

1 What may we learn of the character of John the Baptist from his problems and doubts concerning Jesus, and from our Lord's commendation of him (verses 1–19)?

2 Verses 20–24. We may discern here some important principles behind God's judgment of mankind. What are they, and what relevance do they have in our situation?

Notes

1 There is a unity in chapters 11 and 12. Apparently disconnected incidents are linked together around the theme of the reality and nature of the Messiahship of Jesus.

2 Verse 12 may suggest either the dynamic of John's ministry or the cost of becoming a member of the kingdom.
3 Verse 19 may read 'deeds' or 'children' (mg.). In either case the verse means that God's ways are justified by their results.

☐ STUDY 17 Matthew 11: 25 – 12: 21

1 In 11: 25–30, there is an amazing combination of Christ's claims to unique authority and to humility. Can both be true? What do these verses teach concerning (a) His Person, and (b) the attitude He asks from us?

2 Summarize the main principles of sabbath observance outlined in 12: 1–14. In what way may we be guilty of the sin of the Pharisees? How are we to avoid a secularization of the Lord's day?

3 12: 15–21. These verses indicate the significance of the Suffering Servant passages in Isaiah for an understanding of Jesus and His ministry. *Cf.* 8: 17; Lk. 2: 29–32; 22: 37; Jn. 12: 37, 38. What are the outstanding features of this ministry?

☐ STUDY 18 Matthew 12: 22–50

1 Verses 22–32. What do you understand by the 'unforgivable sin' interpreted in the light of its context here? Consider the solemnity of these warnings; and note the connection with them of verses 43–45.

2 What is taught in verses 33–37 about the dangers of evil or foolish speaking? In what way may a Christian deal with failure at this level?

3 Why does Christ refuse to give a *special* sign to the Pharisees (verses 38, 39)? What is the significance of His references to the Old Testament in verses 40–42? What may we learn from verses 41, 42 and 50 concerning our right response to Christ?

☐ STUDY 19 Matthew 13: 1–23

1 The parable of the sower (or 'the soils') may be regarded as a parable to explain why our Lord taught in parables. How did this method serve to reveal truth to some and to hide it from others? What was the simple and searching condition of gaining benefit?

2 In the parable of the sower what were the reasons why the same seed produced such different results? What conditions are signified by the different kinds of soil? What is indispensable to fruitfulness?

☐ STUDY 20 Matthew 13: 24–52

1 What is the teaching of the parable of the wheat and the tares (verses 24–30)?

2 Verses 31–33 record two parables on the theme of growth. What is the main message of these verses? May these verses include warning against possible dangers?

3 Verses 44–50 illustrate different ways by which individuals may enter the kingdom. What are these? Why is there a mixture of good and bad? What is the condition of true enjoyment?

☐ STUDY 21 Matthew 13: 53 – 14: 12

1 What may we learn from the closing verses of chapter 13 about the nature of prejudice? Of what may it deprive us, and why?

2 In the story of 14: 1–12, identify the distinctive characteristics of both Herod and John the Baptist; what is the difference between John's faithfulness and Herod's keeping of his promise?

☐ STUDY 22 Matthew 14: 13–36

1 Consider the miracles of these verses as parables in action. What particularly do you learn from the response and failure of the disciples? For what qualities do we need to pray if we are to be found faithful?

2 From the same stories consider the light cast upon the Person of Christ. What characteristics are unmistakably revealed?

☐ STUDY 23 Matthew 15: 1–20

1 For what reasons does Christ condemn the religious outlook of the Pharisees? How may we be in danger of similar failure?

2 These verses emphasize the importance of man's heart. *Cf.* 5: 8, 28; 12: 34; 18: 35. What is meant here by the word 'heart'? *Cf.* Is. 10: 7, AV and RV. How then can a man's actions be put right?

3 What are the three groups of people to whom Christ speaks in these verses? Do you notice any difference in His manner of teaching them? Has this any implication for Christian teaching today?

□ STUDY 24 Matthew 15: 21–39

1 Verses 21–28. Why did our Lord treat the Canaanite woman in this way? Do you see the purpose behind it? *Cf.* Lk. 11: 8; 18: 1; 1 Pet. 1: 7. Contrast Mt. 8: 23, 26; 15: 28, 30, 31.

2 In all the miracles in this passage Christ seems to be dealing with Gentiles. Note the phrase 'the God of Israel' in verse 31. This seems to be contrary to the principle of verse 24. What was our Lord thus beginning to reveal concerning the full purpose of His mission? *Cf.* Mt. 24: 14; 28: 19; Rom. 1: 16 (the last nine words).

Note. Verse 37. The word for 'basket' here is *sphuris*, the large Gentile basket, contrasted with the Jewish *kophinos* in 14: 20. The same accuracy of distinction is found in 16: 9, 10.

□ STUDY 25 Matthew 16: 1–20

1 Christ condemns, in verses 1–4, the Jews' inability to read 'the signs of the times'. What does He mean by this? How were the disciples similarly guilty? See verses 5–12. What response should such signs produce?

2 Verses 13–20. This incident at Caesarea Philippi is clearly the 'hinge-point' of the Gospel narrative. From now on Christ withdraws from the crowds, and concentrates on teaching the disciples. Why is the question about His Person so crucial? *Cf.* 1 Jn. 4: 2, 3; 5: 1a, 5.

3 Note the three things which our Lord says to Peter in verses 17–19. With verse 17, *cf.* 1 Cor. 12: 3; with verse 18, *cf.* 1 Cor. 3: 11; 1 Pet. 2: 4–6; and with verse 19, *cf.* 18: 18; Jn. 20: 23.

Note. Verses 18, 19. There is a play on words in Greek in verse 18 (see mg.). '*Petros*' means 'stone'; '*petra*' means 'rock'. Note that Christ did not say, 'On *thee* I will build my church.' Peter had just made the classic confession of faith in Christ. Equally in verses 22, 23 he can be seen as an agent of Satan. The power of the keys, *i.e.*, of 'loosing' and 'binding', is one of great authority; but it is that of a steward rather than a door-keeper. The keys are the keys of knowledge (*cf.* Lk. 11: 52) which Christ entrusts to those who preach the gospel, and thus 'open the kingdom of heaven to all believers'.

□ STUDY 26 Matthew 16: 21 – 17: 13

1 16: 21 indicates Christ's clear awareness of the cross ahead. The word 'must' expresses a sense of inward necessity. What does this reveal about the character of Christ's death?

2 What are the terms of discipleship (verse 24)? What incentive does Christ put forward in verses 25–28 to encourage His disciple to pay the cost? What did Peter particularly need to learn (verse 22, 23)?

3 In the story of the transfiguration (17: 1–13), can you see its purpose (a) for Christ Himself, and (b) for His disciples?

Note. 16: 28. The reference here to 'the Son of man coming in his kingdom' would seem to be not to His second advent but to His post-resurrection triumph and exaltation to the throne.

☐ STUDY 27 Matthew 17: 14–27

1 Verses 14–20. What were the reasons for the powerlessness of the disciples? What does Christ tell them is the one indispensable secret of success?

2 Verses 24–27. What practical lesson is enshrined in the story o the Temple tax? What does it teach about the Christian's responsibility towards his fellow-men? *Cf.* 1 Cor. 10: 31–33; Rom. 13: 6, 7.

☐ STUDY 28 Matthew 18: 1–35

1 Verses 1–14. Consider Christ's teaching on children (see also 19: 13–15). What are the qualities of the childlike spirit suggested in verses 3, 4? How should the Christian act towards children or those young in faith?

2 What do verses 15–20 teach us about the way of reconciliation? What do we also learn here concerning the nature and the ministry of the local church, and concerning the practical value of acting together with others?

3 How does the parable in verses 23–35 answer Peter's question in verse 21? What other lessons does it teach?

For Studies 29–48 concluding Matthew's Gospel see p. 341.

JEREMIAH 1 - 25

Introduction

Anathoth, the home of Jeremiah, was a small town some three miles north-east of Jerusalem. Jeremiah's father was a priest, possibly a descendant of Abiathar (*cf.* 1 Ki. 2: 26), and the family owned some property in Anathoth (32: 8). Jeremiah's fellow-townsmen were among those who turned against him and sought to slay him (11: 21).

Born probably towards the end of the reign of Manasseh, Jeremiah lived through the reigns of Josiah (thirty-one years), Jehoahaz (three months), Jehoiakim (eleven years), Jehoiachin (three months), and Zedekiah (eleven years). His prophetic ministry lasted for forty years, from his call in 626 BC, the thirteenth year of Josiah, to the fall of Jerusalem in 587 BC (1: 2, 3). Of the five kings Josiah alone was loyal to the Lord. Jehoiakim was hostile to Jeremiah, and Zedekiah, though personally friendly, was weak and unstable. Under these two kings Jeremiah endured much physical suffering at the hands of his enemies. His life, however, was preserved, and after the fall of Jerusalem he was permitted to stay with the remnant in the land, and was carried with them into Egypt (43: 4–7).

In the earlier years of his ministry, though his outward lot was easier, Jeremiah suffered great mental conflict, revealed in a series of soliloquies in which he struggles to accept the burden of his prophetic calling and message. He saw more and more clearly that the nation was thoroughly corrupt, and that judgment was at hand. The false prophets, who cried 'Peace, Peace', were misleading the people (14: 13, 14). The inevitability of disaster filled Jeremiah's heart with dismay and sorrow. It seemed as if God were annulling His covenant and casting off His people, and if that were to happen, what hope was left? God, however, revealed to Jeremiah that He still had a purpose of good beyond the judgment, and that He could and would make a new covenant of a different kind, in which He would give His people a new heart and put His fear in their inmost being: and the hope of this glorious future sustained him as he watched the dying agonies of his nation, and suffered with them. As a result of all this, 'Jeremiah's personality is the most sharply etched of any of the Old Testament prophets' (*NBD*, p. 608), and part of the distinctiveness of the book lies just here.

Jeremiah was appointed a prophet not only to Judah, but to the nations (1: 5, 10), and he kept an ever-watchful eye on the movements of neighbouring peoples. In Josiah's reign the power of Assyria was waning, and both Egypt and Babylon sought to take advantage of this for their own ends. Three events especially affected the kingdom of Judah, and had a profound influence upon Jeremiah's life and outlook. The first was the capture of Nineveh and of the Assyrian Empire by Babylon (612–609 BC), the second, the battle of Megiddo, when King Josiah was slain (608 BC), and the third, the battle of Carchemish, when Pharaoh-Necho of Egypt and Nebuchadrezzar of Babylon met face to face in a trial of strength and the Babylonian armies won (605 BC). From that time Jeremiah was assured that Babylon was to reign supreme for many years, and that Judah would be wise to yield submission. In fearlessly proclaiming this he seemed in the eyes of many a traitor to his own nation, and aroused great opposition and enmity against himself; but his devotion to God and to his fellow-countrymen stands out clearly on every page, though from time to time he breaks out into passionate cries for vengeance upon his persecutors.

The prophecies are not all in chronological order. In some, mention is made of the king in whose reign they were uttered, but in others the date must be judged from the contents. The following may be taken as a rough guide:

The reign of Josiah: 1–6.
The reign of Jehoiakim: 7–20, 22, 25, 26, 30, 31, 35, 36, 45.
The reign of Zedekiah: 21, 23, 24, 27–29, 32–34, 37–39.

Analysis

1 Call of Jeremiah.
2–6 The sin of Israel. Call to repentance. The enemy from the north.
7–10 In the Temple gate. Prophecies of judgment. Jeremiah's sorrow.
11, 12 The broken covenant. Jeremiah's complaint and God's answer.
13 The linen waistcloth and other prophecies.
14, 15 The drought. Jeremiah's pleadings and God's reply.

16, 17	Jeremiah told not to marry as a sign of coming judgment; and other prophecies.
18–20	At the potter's house; and the breaking of the flask. Incident of Pashhur; Jeremiah's complaint.
21	Answer to Zedekiah at the beginning of the siege.
22	The doom of the royal house of David.
23	The faithless shepherds, and false prophets.
24	The two baskets of figs.
25	The seventy years' captivity.
26	In the court of the Temple. Jeremiah's life preserved.
27, 28	'Serve the king of Babylon and live.' Incident of Hananiah.
29	Jeremiah's letter to the exiles in Babylon.
30–33	The book of consolation. Prophecies of hope.
34	Zedekiah's captivity foretold.
35	The fidelity of the Rechabites.
36	Jehoiakim burns the scroll of Jeremiah's prophecies.
37, 38	Jeremiah's imprisonment and rescue.
39	Fall of Jerusalem.
40–43	Jeremiah left in the land; his final prophecies before being taken to Egypt.
44	Prophecy to Jews in Egypt.
45	Message to Baruch.
46–51	Prophecies against surrounding nations.
52	Historical appendix.

☐ STUDY 1 Jeremiah 1

1 Verses 4–10 and 17–19. What did God require from Jeremiah, and what did He promise him? How can this apply to us?

2 What is the divine interpretation of the two visions which Jeremiah saw?

3 What aspects of God's character and activity are brought before us in this chapter? *Cf.* Eph. 1:4.

Notes

1 Verse 5. 'Knew': in the sense of 'regarded', almost equivalent to 'chose'. 'I consecrated you': set you apart for Myself. For 'prophet', see verse 9.

2 Verse 11. 'A rod': probably meaning a straight shoot just beginning to blossom. The word for almond tree is from the same root as the word 'watching over' in verse 12 (see mg.). Moffatt translates 'wake-tree'. The almond was so called because it was the first to awake after the sleep of winter.

3 Verse 13. The boiling pot is ready to pour out its fiery contents southwards.

4 Verse 15. 'His throne': *i.e.*, of judgment.

☐ STUDY 2 Jeremiah 2: 1 – 3: 5

A review of Israel's backslidings from the beginning.

1 According to this section, what are the components of backsliding? Compare Israel's beginnings with her later condition. Is any of this story true of you? *Cf.* Gal. 5: 7.

2 2: 12, 13. 'Living' water means fresh water from an ever-flowing spring. *Cf.* 6: 7; Jn. 4: 13, 14. What do the 'fountain of living waters' and the 'broken cisterns' stand for in spiritual experience? Do you take as serious a view of backsliding as God does?

3 What evil results does Jeremiah say have already followed from the nation's forgetfulness of God?

Notes

1 2: 10. 'Kedar' was a tribe east of Jordan. The verse means 'search from east to west . . .'

2 2: 16. 'Memphis' and 'Tahpanhes': cities of Egypt.

3 2: 25. 'Do not run thy foot bare, and thy throat dry in the eager pursuit of strange gods' (Driver).

4 3: 4. An allusion probably to the feigned penitence of many at the time of Josiah's reform. *Cf.* 3: 10; 2 Ch. 34: 33.

☐ STUDY 3 Jeremiah 3: 6 – 4: 31

1 3: 6–20. What is the offence of Judah? And what aggravated it in the eyes of God? What forms does this sin take today? *Cf.* Jas. 4: 4; 1 Jn. 5: 20, 21. What does God offer, and on what conditions?

2 Trace the process of restoration as outlined in 3: 21 – 4: 4. What is meant by such phrases as 'Break up your fallow ground' and 'Circumcise yourselves to the Lord'? *Cf.* 9: 26; Dt. 10: 16; Rom. 2: 28, 29.

3 4: 5–31. A vivid picture of the approach of an invader from the north. What place does he have in the purposes of God?

Notes

1 3: 8. An allusion to the conquest of northern Israel in 721 BC by the Assyrians.

2 3: 10. See Note on 3: 4.

3 3: 14. 'Master': in the sense of 'husband'. *Cf.* verses 19, 20 for similar mixing of metaphors from the family.

☐ STUDY 4 Jeremiah 5 and 6

Further indictments of Judah (5: 1–5—all classes are alike corrupt), warnings of coming judgment, and depictions of the invasion and its effects.

1 Make a list of the main sins charged against the people. Are we in danger of any of these sins? Note especially Judah's response to God's word and messengers.

2 Was judgment inevitable? Was God not willing to pardon? What are we taught here about the 'kindness and severity of God' (Rom. 11: 22)? *Cf.* Rom. 4: 4, 5.

Notes

1 6: 1. Tekoa and Beth-Haccheram were a few miles south of Jerusalem. The 'signal' (*i.e.*, a beacon; *cf.* Jdg. 20: 38) would alert the south, or perhaps guide the refugees from Jerusalem.

2 6: 3. 'Shepherds with their flocks' here means kings and their armies.

3 6: 16. 'By the roads': *i.e.*, Judah must return to the cross-roads to regain the right path. *Cf.* 18: 15.

4 6: 27–30. Jeremiah's work is described as that of a tester of silver. But no pure silver results from the process of refining. *Cf.* 9: 7.

□ STUDY 5 Jeremiah 7: 1 – 8: 3

It is thought by many that this is the address given by Jeremiah in the fourth year of Jehoiakim, as described in 26: 1–9.

1 How does this passage show the uselessness of outward worship when separated from the daily practice of godliness? What was lacking in the people of Jerusalem? Are your worship and your life all of a piece? *Cf.* Mt. 5: 23, 24.

2 In what ways may we in our day act in a spirit similar to that rebuked in 7: 10? What is involved in a Christian's being 'delivered' or 'saved'? *Cf.* Col. 1: 13; Tit. 2: 14; Mt. 7: 21–23.

3 How does this section illustrate our Lord's warning in Lk. 8: 18?

Notes

1 7: 4, 8. Confidence in the Temple itself as a protection was a delusion. *Cf.* 1 Sa. 4: 3–11.

2 7: 10b. 'Thinking you are now quite safe—safe to go on with all these abominable practices' (Moffatt).

3 7: 12. Shiloh was probably destroyed around the time of the disaster recorded in 1 Sa. 4.

4 7: 18. 'The queen of heaven': probably Ashtoreth, a goddess widely worshipped in the Semitic world.

5 7: 22, 23. Such a categorical statement ('not this . . . but that . . .') is a Hebrew idiom to express where the real emphasis falls. The essence of the covenant made at the exodus was, on Israel's side, obedience (11: 6, 7). God did not commission sacrifice for its own sake—or for *His* own sake—but to be the expression and embodiment of heart-devotion and ethical obedience. *Cf.* 6: 19, 20; 11: 15; 1 Sa. 15: 22; Is. 1: 10–17. Where these were absent, mere external ritual was worse than nothing. Hence in 7: 21 the people are bidden to eat the meat of the burnt offerings, which were wholly offered to God, as well as their proper portions of the other sacrifices. Emptied of all spiritual significance, it was now merely meat, and might as well be eaten.

But in the worship of a purified people, sacrifices would again have their rightful place. See 17: 24–26; 33: 18.
6 7: 32. 'The valley of the son of Hinnom': a valley on the south side of Jerusalem, where the city refuse was cast. The day will come, says the prophet, when the slain will be so many that they will have to be buried even in this unclean spot.

☐ STUDY 6 Jeremiah 8: 4 – 9: 22

Further exposure of the moral and spiritual plight of the people, and descriptions of the coming judgment. Jeremiah's heart is almost broken.

1 What specific charges does God level against His people in these chapters? Are there any traces of these faults in your own life?

2 Consider the evidence this passage gives of the effects of sin upon a nation's morale and prosperity. See, *e.g.*, 8: 14, 15, 20; 9: 5, 6.

3 Compare 8: 11 with Jeremiah's anguish. What modern counterparts to the former must we beware of? Are we ready to sorrow for others like Jeremiah, and to keep on pleading with them as he did? See 25: 3.

Notes
1 8: 4–7. The sin of Judah runs counter to the pattern of nature. *Cf.* Is. 1: 3.
2 8: 20. Probably a proverbial saying expressing the thought that it is too late.

☐ STUDY 7 Jeremiah 9: 23 – 10: 25

1 9: 23, 24. What is better than wisdom, power and wealth? *Cf.* also 1 Cor. 1: 26–31; Phil. 3: 8–11. What do you set most store by in the normal course of life?

2 Set down, on the one hand, the characteristics here mentioned of the idols of the heathen, and on the other, the character of the living God.

3 What are the implications of 10: 23, 24? Have you learnt to live by them? See 30: 11 and *cf.* Pr. 3: 5–7, 11, 12.

Notes
1 9: 25, 26. All these nations practised circumcision, and Judah, despite the fact that her circumcision was ordained to mark a unique relationship with God, takes her place here between Egypt and Edom because her spiritually uncircumcised state (*cf.* 4: 4; Rom. 2: 28, 29) has rendered her physical circumcision no more meaningful than theirs.
2 10: 11. See mg. Probably originally a reader's marginal comment, in response to the denunciation of idols.
3 10: 17. 'Bundle': a few hastily gathered possessions for immediate flight.
4 10: 21. 'Shepherds': see 2: 8 and mg.; 3: 15.

☐ STUDY 8 Jeremiah 11 and 12

These chapters fall into three sections: 11: 1–17, Judah's stubborn idolatry and breaking of the covenant; 11: 18 – 12: 6, a complaint of the prophet because of plots against his life, and God's answer to his questionings; and 12: 7–17, which seems to refer to the attacks of surrounding peoples (see 2 Ki. 24: 1, 2), and closes with a remarkable promise to these nations on condition of their turning from idols to worship the Lord.

1 What were the constituent elements of 'this covenant' (11: 2)? What was God's part and what the people's? *Cf.* 2 Cor. 6: 14 – 7: 1.

2 What did Jeremiah do with his perplexities, and what answer did he receive? Can we come with his confidence? Note 12: 5 and 6 in particular. What does this answer of God imply? *Cf.* Heb. 12: 3, 4.

3 Jeremiah is often described as a Christ-like figure. As you read the book chapter by chapter, note the similarities. With 11: 21 and 12: 6, *cf.* Mk. 3: 21; Lk. 4: 24, 29; 21: 16.

Notes

1 11: 15. See Note on 7: 22, 23.

2 12: 13. 'They': *i.e.*, the people of Judah.

☐ STUDY 9 Jeremiah 13

1 What is the purpose of the incident of the waistcloth? Which is a truer description of you, verse 10 or verse 11?

2 Consider the images used to describe the coming judgment, and their usefulness for preaching today. See Notes below; and *cf.* Pss. 1: 4; 60: 3; Is. 8: 22; 51: 17; Mi. 3: 6, 7; Jn. 12: 35; 2 Thes. 2: 11, 12.

3 Verse 23. What answer does the New Testament give to this question? See Rom. 5: 6; 2 Cor. 5: 17.

Notes

1 Verses 13, 14. 'Drunkenness' is used in a figurative sense to describe mental fear and bewilderment, when men in their panic turn against each other.

2 Verse 16. 'Give glory to the Lord': a Hebrew expression for confession of sin, recognizing God's holiness, and turning from sin to obedience. *Cf.* Jos. 7: 19; Mal. 2: 2; Jn. 9: 24.

3 Verse 18: *i.e.*, Jehoiachin and his mother Nehushta (2 Ki. 24: 8, 9). Queen mothers regularly wielded great influence at court.

4 Verse 19. 'The Negeb' is the area of Palestine south of Beersheba.

5 Verse 21. Another translation reads 'he', *i.e.*, God, instead of 'they' (Driver). *Cf.* Dt. 28: 13, 44; La. 1: 5.

☐ STUDY 10 Jeremiah 14 and 15

These two chapters consist of a kind of colloquy between Jeremiah and God. The prophet is driven to prayer by a time of drought (14: 1–6).

1 What pleas of the people does the prophet present before God in 14: 7–9, and what does God's answer (14: 10–12) tell us of the people's confession? *Cf.* 3: 10; 15: 6, 7; Is. 59: 1, 2. What further pleas does Jeremiah urge in his second and third prayers (14: 13 and 19–22)? What are God's answers in each case?

2 The prophet, ceasing to pray for the people, breaks into a lament (15: 10) and prays for himself (15: 15–18). Observe carefully God's answer, especially in verses 19–21. How well did Jeremiah know himself? What new element is added in verse 19? Have you ever had a comparable answer to prayer? *Cf.* 2 Tim. 2: 19–21.

Notes

1 14: 2; 15: 7. 'Gates': *i.e.*, cities.
2 14: 7, 21. 'For thy name's sake': God's Name is 'His nature as revealed in the covenant, which is the ultimate ground of prayer' (Cunliffe-Jones). *Cf.* Ex. 33: 19; 34: 5–7.
3 15: 1. *Cf.* Ps. 99: 6–8. Moses (*e.g.*, Ex. 32: 11–14, 30–32) and Samuel (*e.g.*, 1 Sa. 7: 8, 9) were outstanding in intercession for their people.
4 15: 4. See 2 Ki. 21: 1–5, 16.
5 15: 11. The Hebrew is very difficult, and RSV, AV, and RV all differ considerably from each other.
6 15: 12. A reference to the Chaldeans. There is no hope of breaking their power.
7 15: 19. The tone is severe. Jeremiah must return to a more undivided allegiance. For 'stand before', *cf.* verse 1 and Note 3 above, and 18: 20.

☐ STUDY 11 Jeremiah 16: 1 – 17: 18

1 Consider how hard it must have been for a man of Jeremiah's affectionate and sympathetic nature to obey the commands of 16: 2, 5 and 8. Why did God lay this burden upon him? What other trials that Jeremiah had to bear are referred to in 17: 14–18?

2 How does the passage illustrate Jeremiah's oft-repeated statement concerning God's dealings with His people: 'I will not make a full end of you'? See 4: 27; 5: 10, 18; 30: 11; 46: 28. *Cf.* Ps. 94: 14; Rom. 11: 1–5.

3 Contrast, clause by clause, 17: 5 and 6 with 17: 7 and 8. How do verses 9–13 reinforce the certainty of curse or blessing? Examine yourself in the light of this contrast. *Cf.* Ps. 146.

Notes

1 16: 6, 7. Mourning customs. *Cf.* Am. 8: 10; 2 Sa. 12: 17; Pr. 31: 6b.
2 17: 1, 2. 'The tablet of their heart': *i.e.*, their inmost being. 'The horns of

their altars': an allusion to their polluted idolatrous sacrifices (*cf.* Lv. 4: 7, 30; and with verse 2, *cf.* 2: 20). 'Asherim': probably wooden images of the Canaanite goddess, Asherah.
3 17: 15. *Cf.* 2 Pet. 3: 3, 4.

☐ STUDY 12 Jeremiah 17: 19 – 18: 23

1 The issue between God and His people turned on the question of obedience. How was it brought in 17: 19–27 to a single test? In your Christian obedience are there test issues of this kind, which, although possibly not themselves the most important subject, are the heart of the question of obedience at the time?

2 To Jeremiah the condition of the people made the destruction of the kingdom inevitable; yet the destruction seemed to involve the failure of God's purposes. How does the illustration of the potter throw light upon this problem (18: 1–12)? What other lessons about God does it teach? *Cf.* Rom. 9: 20, 21.

3 How does 18: 13–23 reveal the costliness for Jeremiah of being a more faithful spokesman of the Lord? *Cf.* Mt. 10: 24, 25, 28–33.

Notes
1 17: 26. 'The Shephelah': *i.e.*, the lowlands of Palestine between the coastal plain and the higher central hills.
2 18: 14. The Hebrew is uncertain, but the meaning is clear. The snows of Lebanon remain, and its streams do not run dry; but God's people have failed.
3 18: 18. 'The law shall not perish . . .': the people refused to believe that the present order of things would be destroyed.

☐ STUDY 13 Jeremiah 19 and 20

1 Reflect on Jeremiah's courage, and what it must have cost him to deliver the message of 19: 1–13. What was his immediate reward? See 19: 14 – 20: 6.

2 The strain and tension caused the prophet to break out into a more bitter lament than he had yet uttered (20: 7–18). In the midst of it his faith triumphed in the assurance of God's protection, and he was able even to sing His praise (20: 11–13). Then once more waves of sorrow swept over him. In the light of this passage, try to enter into the loneliness, hardship and suffering of Jeremiah's life. Note especially verse 9. Do we know anything of this almost irresistible constraint to speak God's word, even when we are daunted by the costliness of speaking? *Cf.* Acts 5: 27–29.

Notes
1 19: 5, 6, 11b. See 7: 31–33 and Note on 7: 32.
2 19: 13. 'Defiled': *i.e.*, by dead bodies.
3 20: 16. 'The cities': *i.e.*, Sodom and Gomorrah; see Gn. 19: 24, 25.

☐ STUDY 14 Jeremiah 21 and 22

These chapters refer in turn to the last five kings of Judah: Josiah (22: 15, 16), Jehoahaz or Shallum (22: 10–12), Jehoiakim (22: 13–19), Jehoiachin or Coniah (22: 24–30), and Zedekiah (21).

1 Zedekiah's hope was that God would work a miracle, as He had done in the days of Hezekiah, a little over a century before (21: 2; 2 Ch. 32: 20–22). What was Jeremiah's answer, and what light does this throw on 'unanswered prayer'? *Cf.* 7: 16; 11: 14; 14: 11, 12; Is. 59: 1, 2.

2 Chapter 22. Why did Jeremiah condemn injustice and outrage? Consider the contemporary application of this word from the Lord. Are we guilty of conforming to any current social iniquities or sharp practices?

3 22: 21. (The northern kingdom behaved in the same way—see 3: 25.) Reflect upon this verse as depicting the pattern of Judah's history.

Notes

1 22: 6. Gilead and Lebanon typify prosperity.
2 22: 20. 'Abarim': a mountain range to the south-east of Palestine.
3 22: 22. 'Shepherds': see 2: 8 and mg.

☐ STUDY 15 Jeremiah 23

1 Verses 1–8. To meet the situation created by the failure of Judah's rulers, what does God say He will do? *Cf.* Ezk. 34: 1–16. How much of what is promised here has been fulfilled? *Cf.* Jn. 10: 1–18; Lk. 1: 32, 68–70; 1 Cor. 1: 30.

2 What does Jeremiah say concerning (a) the religious life, worship and ministry of the prophets of his day; (b) their moral character and conduct; and (c) their influence? What qualifications are essential in those who are called to speak in the name of the Lord?

Notes

1 Verse 1. 'Shepherds': see 2: 8 and mg.
2 Verse 5. 'Branch': better, 'shoot' or 'sprout', *i.e.*, a growth of new life. *Cf.* 33: 15; Is. 11: 1.
3 Verses 7, 8. 'The new and more wonderful Exodus' (C. R. North).
4 Verse 9 describes the effect of God's words upon Jeremiah himself.
5 Verses 33–40. The Hebrew word translated 'burden' could also mean, figuratively, a solemn utterance, an oracle, normally of ominous import (*cf.* Is. 13: 1; 15: 1; 17: 1). The people had evidently been speaking mockingly of the prophet's utterances as 'burdens'. Jeremiah uses it to rebuke its users (verses 33, 39), and forbids its employment in such an irreverent context.

☐ STUDY 16 Jeremiah 24 and 25

Chapter 24 dates from the reign of Zedekiah. Chapter 25 declares to Judah and the surrounding nations that they shall all be brought under the power of Babylon with great slaughter.

1 Who are the good figs and who the bad, and what will happen to them respectively? *Cf.* Ezk. 11: 14–20.

2 25: 1–11. The fulfilment of the vision of the boiling pot (1: 13–15). Much of what is said in these verses is found in preceding chapters. See, *e.g.*, 7: 6, 7, 13; 16: 9; 18: 11, 16. What, however, do you find here that is new?

3 'The supreme factor in history for the Hebrew is the activity of the eternal God.' Illustrate this statement from today's portion. Note especially 25: 29. *Cf.* Am. 3: 2; 1 Pet. 4: 17, 18. What is the correlative of special privilege?

Notes

1 25: 12–14. These verses break the sequence of thought, and were possibly introduced at a later date; so also the words 'as at this day' in verse 18 (they are not in the LXX) and the last clause of verse 26.

2 25: 23. Dedan, Tema and Buz were tribes of northern Arabia. Unlike the Jews (Lv. 19: 27), they shaved the hair from the sides of their forehead. *Cf.* 9: 26.

For Studies 17–35 on Jeremiah see p. 348.

MATTHEW 19 - 28

☐ STUDY 29 Matthew 19: 1–22

1 In Christ's answers to the Pharisees and the disciples on the subject of marriage (19: 1–12), what does He teach about the place and character of marriage, and what does He say about the celibate life?

2 Verses 16–22. What do you find commendable in the young man in this incident? What were the factors which nevertheless made him turn away from Christ?

☐ STUDY 30 Matthew 19: 23 – 20: 28

1 Consider the teaching of Jesus on riches and possessions. With verses 23–26, *cf.* Lk. 6: 24; 8: 14; 12: 13–21. Compare Paul's teaching in 1 Tim. 6: 7, 10, 17. But note that Christ gladly received help from the rich (*cf.* Lk. 8: 2, 3).

2 Is there a place for the concept of reward in Christian service? What do verses 27–30 teach about this?

3 Verses 1–16. What is the main teaching of the parable of the labourers in the vineyard? What does it have to say about the legalistic spirit in Christian service?

4 Verses 17–19 are the third prediction by Christ of His own passion. *Cf.* 16: 21; 17: 22, 23. What new details are added here? What do verses 22 and 25–28 reveal of the mind of Christ with regard to what was ahead?

5 In what ways do verses 20–28 prove the disciples to be out of sympathy with Christ at this moment? What do both Christ's teaching and His example demand of us?

☐ STUDY 31 Matthew 20: 29 – 21: 22

1 What claims concerning the Person and work of Jesus are here (a) publicly made by Jesus Himself, and (b) openly acknowledged by others? What particularly provoked either rebuke and indignation, or prayer and acclamation? Can you keep silent?

2 What was Christ condemning in His cleansing of the Temple (21: 12, 13), and in His cursing of the fig tree (21: 18, 19)? If He similarly came into our church or examined our lives, what would He see and say?

☐ STUDY 32 Matthew 21: 23–46

1 Verses 23–27. People often ask for more understanding or for more proof before they respond to Christ. How did Christ Himself answer such a demand? What are the conditions of receiving more light? *Cf.* Jn. 7: 17. In what way does the brief parable of verses 28–32 underline the same teaching?

2 Verses 33–44. What is taught by this parable concerning the character of God, the Person of Christ, the responsibility of men, and the reality of judgment? Do you find anything significant in the reaction of the Pharisees in verses 45, 46?

Note. Verse 44 (see mg.) is omitted in many manuscripts. But it teaches that there will be brokenness either in repentance or in final judgment.

□ STUDY 33 Matthew 22: 1–14

1 In this parable what are we taught about the pattern of Christ's ministry, and what challenge do you find to evangelistic outreach?

2 In verses 11–13 what do you understand to be the significance of the wedding garment? *Cf.* Zc. 3: 1–5. Consider the balance in these verses of the free invitation of the gospel and the demand for holiness, 'without which no one will see the Lord' (Heb. 12: 14).

□ STUDY 34 Matthew 22: 15–46

1 Comparing the teaching of Jesus in verses 15–22 with Paul's teaching in Rom. 13: 1–7, outline the duty of the Christian to the state.

2 Verses 23–33. On what does Christ base His teaching about the fact of resurrection? What features of the life of the world to come emerge from this teaching?

3 Verses 41–46. Christ's counter-question here makes some clear claims. What are these? Ps. 110: 1 is cited in verse 44. Consider the use made of this elsewhere in the New Testament. *Cf.* Acts 2: 33–36; Heb. 1: 13; 10: 11–13. Of what truths and hopes are we thereby assured?

□ STUDY 35 Matthew 23: 1–22

1 Verses 1–12 are an indictment of the Pharisees because of their concern for personal prestige and outward show. Do you see how this may happen within the Christian church? In what ways may this temptation come?

2 Note the repetition of the word 'hypocrite' or 'play-actor'. How is this seen in the attitude of the Pharisees to others (verses 13–15), and in their vows and promises (verses 16–22)? What do we need to do to avoid becoming like them?

Notes

1 Verse 5. The phylactery was a small box of leather containing portions of the law and strapped to forehead and to left arm. The fringes of the garments were four in number, attached to the dress as a symbol of the law.

2 Verse 15. 'A child of hell': Greek *Gehenna*, meaning 'worthy of suffering punishment in the after-life'.

☐ STUDY 36 Matthew 23: 23–39

1 The Lord accuses Pharisees in verses 23–26 of a serious lack of proportion in their practice of religion. Can you find modern examples of this dangerous tendency?

2 The chapter comes to a climax with our Lord's teaching on the inevitability of judgment (verses 29–39). Yet consider the love of Christ for Jerusalem which is clearly shown. What was it that made judgment inevitable?

☐ STUDY 37 Matthew 24: 1–31

1 What is the pattern of future history as predicted by Christ in verses 1–14? Make a list of the prominent features and see how they apply to our present age.

2 According to the teaching of these verses how should a Christian react in days of political upheaval and world-wide distress? On what can he count?

Notes

1 The teaching of this chapter is in answer to the two questions of verse 3. The disciples seemed to think of these events as contemporaneous. Christ sees the fall of Jerusalem as a foreshadowing of the day of His return. It is impossible to be dogmatic about the division of the chapter, since references to the two events are so interwoven, but the following is suggested. Verses 4–14: general principles. Verses 15–28: the siege and destruction of Jerusalem. Verses 29–31: the day of Christ's coming. Verses 32–51: preparation for both events.

2 Verse 15 refers back to Dn. 11: 31 and in this context seems to point to the setting up of the Roman ensign within the sacred precincts of the Temple.

3 Verse 27. 'Coming' is in Greek *parousia*, meaning the official visit of a king. *Cf.* verses 3, 37, 39.

☐ STUDY 38 Matthew 24: 32 – 25: 13

1 What truths concerning our Lord's return are unmistakably certain, and what matters are left uncertain? What, in consequence, ought the Christian's attitude to be?

2 The parable of the ten virgins (25: 1–13) teaches a final division. What is the basis of that division? How can we join the company of the wise? *Cf.* Mt. 7: 21–27.

☐ STUDY 39 Matthew 25: 14–46

1 Verses 14–30. Compare this parable with that in Lk. 19: 11–27. What is the message underlying both parables? Can you distinguish the particular emphasis of each parable?

2 Verses 31–46. What claims does Christ here make concerning Himself? How is men's final destiny determined?

3 What does this passage teach about the gravity of the sin of omission? What does the absence of good works prove?

Notes

1 Verse 34. This is the only place in the Gospels where Christ speaks of the Son of man as King. No doubt there was too great a danger of the popular misunderstanding of that title for its frequent use to be possible.

2 Verse 46. 'Eternal': this speaks primarily not of endless duration but of that which in quality is characteristic of the age to come.

☐ STUDY 40 Matthew 26: 1–16

1 Note the difference between the prophecy of Christ in verses 1, 2, and the plans of the Jewish religious leaders in verses 3–5. Whose word, in fact, prevailed, and why? *Cf.* Acts 2: 23; Ps. 33: 10, 11.

2 In verses 6–16 consider the contrast between the action of Mary, anointing Christ, and Judas selling Him. How does this demonstrate the truth of Lk. 2: 35b? What were the motives behind these different actions?

☐ STUDY 41 Matthew 26: 17–29

1 What does the phrase in verse 18, 'My time is at hand', teach us of Christ's understanding and control of the situation even at this moment? Notice the repetition of this reference to 'the hour' (verse 45). *Cf.* Jn. 12: 23, 27; 13: 1. Note also in verse 24 the combined recognition of God's foreordained purpose and man's personal responsibility.

2 In the institution of the Lord's Supper, Matthew notes the idea of a covenant in verse 28. In what way does this link with Ex. 24: 6–8 and with Je. 31: 31–34? What ought drinking from such a cup to mean to us?

☐ STUDY 42 Matthew 26: 30–56

1 How do these verses indicate the strength to do God's will that Christ found through His knowledge of Scripture? Consider how frequently during these last hours our Lord quoted the Old Testament. What ought we to learn from this concerning the way to face the demands of Christ's service?

2 Wherein lay the particular agony to Jesus of the experience in the garden? Why did He shrink so much from the cross? Consider this section in the light of Heb. 5: 7–9; 10: 4–10; 1 Pet. 2: 24.

3 What does our Lord pinpoint as the reason for the disciples' failure in the garden? Consider in how many ways they did fail that night, and how relevant this is to our situation. *Cf.* what Peter wrote in 1 Pet. 5: 8, 9.

☐ STUDY 43 Matthew 26: 57–75

1 The trials of Jesus and Peter were running concurrently, but with such different results. What was Peter's failure, and what was the reason for it? Do you see any difference between this and the failure of Judas?

2 Verses 59–68. In what ways was the trial of Jesus unworthy of the name of justice? In contrast note the majesty of Jesus at this point. What would you consider the salient characteristics of His witness here?

Note. Verse 64. 'You have said so' is more than the equivalent of 'Yes'. It indicates that Christ's Kingship was real, but different from the concept in Caiaphas' mind.

☐ STUDY 44 Matthew 27: 1–14

1 What lessons concerning the inevitable judgment upon sin are to be found in the account of the death of Judas? Can you see any sense in which we may be tempted to act like Judas in our situation, or is he unique?

2 Consider the silence of Jesus in these last hours of His life. *Cf.* Lk. 23: 9. In the light of this, read 1 Pet. 2: 21–23 and note the lessons for our own life and witness.

☐ STUDY 45 Matthew 27: 15–31

1 In these verses the Jewish people made a fateful choice. Note especially verses 20 and 25. It was the choice of what kind of saviour they wanted (see Note below). What was the result of this choice in the life of the nation?

2 In how many ways did Pilate seek to avoid a decision about Christ? *Cf.* Lk. 23: 7. Read again the question in verse 22. Is this not a question which I, too, must ask and answer?

Note. Verses 16, 17. There is good textual evidence in favour of reading 'Jesus Barabbas'. This makes the question of verse 17 even more telling. This was a choice between a false claimant and the true Saviour.

☐ STUDY 46 Matthew 27: 32–50

1 What were the real sufferings of Christ? In what way are physical, mental and spiritual sufferings here indicated?

2 What, if any, truth is there in the taunt of verses 41–43? Why did God not intervene? What is the meaning behind Christ's own sense of desertion in verse 46? Can you hold this truth with that contained in 2 Cor. 5: 19, 'God was in Christ reconciling the world to himself'? See also 2 Cor. 5: 21.

☐ STUDY 47 Matthew 27: 51–66

1 What is the significance of the torn curtain of the Temple (verse 51)? *Cf.* Heb. 9: 8; 10: 19–23. How are the manifestations recorded in verses 52, 53 linked with these truths?

2 What made Joseph of Arimathea (and Nicodemus, Jn. 19: 39) come out into the open at this late stage? Is it not at first sight strange that they should now publicly associate themselves with Christ? What, in the purposes of God, did such a burial demonstrate and make possible?

Note. Verse 62. 'Next day, that is, after the day of Preparation': it looks as if, in their concern to safeguard the tomb, the Jewish leaders even broke their own sacred sabbath laws.

☐ **STUDY 48 Matthew 28: 1–20**

1 Note the foremost place taken by women disciples in the story of the resurrection appearances. Why should this be (*cf.* Jn. 14: 21)? Contrast the effect of the news of the resurrection on the disciples with the response of Christ's enemies recorded in verses 11–15. How does this prove the truth of Lk. 16: 30, 31?

2 Verses 18–20. Note the fourfold repetition of the word 'all' in Christ's final commission. What is the threefold task given to the Christian church? Are we obeying, as we ought to do, in the light of (a) Christ's authority, and (b) the promise of His presence?

JEREMIAH 26 - 52

☐ **STUDY 17 Jeremiah 26**

Jehoiakim was a very different king from Josiah. At the beginning of his reign, therefore, God sent Jeremiah to warn the people against being led astray into further disobedience to Him.

1 What reason does God give for sending His servant on this dangerous mission? See verse 3 and *cf.* 2 Ch. 36: 15; 2 Pet. 3: 9; Lk. 13: 34, 35.

2 Note the points of resemblance between Jeremiah and Jesus (see Study 8, Question 3; and Mt. 16: 14); *e.g.*, *cf.* Mt. 24: 1, 2; 26: 61; 27: 4, 24, 25. Consider also the experiences of Jeremiah and Uriah in the light of what Jesus foretold for His disciples. *Cf.* Jn. 15: 18–20; 16: 33; 1 Pet. 4: 12, 13.

Notes

1 Verses 4–6. It seems probable that this brief summary of Jeremiah's words is given more fully in chapter 7.

2 Verse 18. 'Micah of Moresheth': see Mi. 1: 1, 14.

3 Verse 24. 'Ahikam the son of Shaphan': one of those sent by King Josiah to consult the prophetess Huldah (2 Ki. 22: 12, 13), and the father of Gedaliah, who was made governor after the fall of Jerusalem (40: 5, 6).

☐ STUDY 18 Jeremiah 27 and 28

Five kings of surrounding nations seek Zedekiah's co-operation in an attempt to throw off the yoke of Babylon. Jeremiah opposes the plan.

1 What means did Jeremiah use to impress upon the five kings the futility of resistance to Babylon? Notice the claim which God made for Himself in His message to these heathen rulers (27: 4–7).

2 What did Jeremiah condemn in the propaganda of the prophets?

3 In chapter 28 we have a leading prophet of the time attacking Jeremiah, and we can consider the two men at close range. In what respects did they resemble each other, and in what respects did they differ? Ponder Jeremiah's now unwavering courage in predicting passive acceptance of Babylonian control in the face of prominent *religious* opposition. What ought we to learn from this?

Note. 27: 16–22. Only a part of the vessels of the Temple had at this time been carried off to Babylon.

☐ STUDY 19 Jeremiah 29

Those who had been carried into exile in the first captivity under Jehoiachin (2 Ki. 24: 14–16) were being made restless by prophets who prophesied falsely that they would soon be set free. Jeremiah therefore wrote a letter to them declaring that the exile would last seventy years.

1 What, as revealed to Jeremiah, were the Lord's thoughts (a) towards the exiles in Babylon, and (b) towards Zedekiah and those who remained in Jerusalem? With verse 17, *cf.* chapter 24.

2 Verses 10–14. What is God's doing and what man's in the promised restoration? Note the divine initiative and sovereignty throughout this chapter, and indeed throughout the book. Note also how its benefits are to be enjoyed.

3 What three prophets are mentioned by name by Jeremiah? What accusations did he bring against them, and what judgment did he pronounce upon them?

Notes

1 Verse 24. 'Shemaiah': that he, too, was a prophet is seen from verse 31.

2 Verse 25. 'Zephaniah': probably the same as the Zephaniah who in 52: 24 is called 'the second priest', *i.e.*, second to the high priest. *Cf.* 21: 1.

☐ STUDY 20 Jeremiah 30: 1 – 31: 26

See Analysis. This passage forms part of a group of prophecies. It was a time of darkness and despair, and Jeremiah himself apparently derived much comfort from the message (31: 26).

1 This passage falls into sections which are all variants of the one theme, that after judgment will come restoration. See 30: 1–3, 4–11, 12–22, 23, 24; 31: 1–9, 10–14, 15–20, 21–22, 23–25. What are the blessings promised?

2 To what extent have these blessings been fulfilled? Observe that they are spoken of northern Israel as well as of Judah (30: 4; 31: 1). *Cf.* Rom. 11: 25–27.

3 Meditate on the greatness of the blessings here promised as fully realized only in Christ. *Cf.* Jn. 7: 37, 38; 15: 9–11; 16: 27.

Notes

1 30: 14. 'All your lovers': *i.e.*, the nations with whom Israel had sought alliance. *Cf.* verse 17b.

2 31: 2. 'The wilderness': here denoting the place of exile.

3 31: 15. 'Rachel is weeping for her children': a graphic picture of the sorrows of the exile. Rachel, the mother of Joseph and Benjamin, is depicted weeping in her grave, which was near Ramah, as the exiles pass by. *Cf.* 40: 1; also Mt. 2: 17, 18.

☐ STUDY 21 Jeremiah 31: 27–40

1 Verses 31–34. If Israel has broken the covenant between herself and the Lord, how can there be any future blessing for her? What is God's answer to this question? Note the four occurrences of 'says the Lord', and the repeated use of 'I'. *Cf.* Jn. 15: 5c.

2 What four features of the new covenant are set forth in 31: 33, 34? With verse 33, *cf.* Ex. 31: 18; 2 Cor. 3: 6; and with verse 34 contrast Ex. 20: 19. See Heb. 8: 3–13 and 10: 14–22 for the fulfilment in Christ.

3 Verses 35–40. How do these verses show the certainty and completeness of the restoration? See Note on verses 39, 40. *Cf.* 33: 20–22.

Notes

1 Verse 28. *Cf.* 1: 10–12.

2 Verses 29, 30. It appears likely that among the exiles, the proverb of verse 29 was being quoted as if they, the innocent, were suffering for their parents' sins. Part of the new order will be the certain accountability of every individual to God personally.

3 Verse 32. The writer to the Hebrews, in quoting this passage, follows the LXX. See Heb. 8: 9.

4 Verse 34. The word 'know' is used here not of intellectual knowledge, but of personal intimacy.

5 Verses 39, 40. The localities Gareb and Goah are not now known. The 'valley of the dead bodies' is the valley of Hinnom. The meaning is that in the new city all shall be holy.

□ STUDY 22 Jeremiah 32 and 33

1 What was Jeremiah's response to God's command to purchase land (a) immediately (32: 9–12), and (b) subsequently (32: 16–25)? What has this to teach us when faced by perplexities of Christian obedience? What was God's answer to Jeremiah's prayer? What was the significance of his being commanded to buy land at such a time?

2 What blessings are promised in chapter 33? Which of them are for us also under the new covenant? *E.g.*, with 33: 3, *cf.* Eph. 1: 17–19a; 1 Cor. 2: 9, 10.

Note. 33: 1. 'The court of the guard': Jeremiah's friends would be able to visit him, but he would not go outside the court.

□ STUDY 23 Jeremiah 34

Two incidents that occurred during the siege of Jerusalem at the end of Zedekiah's reign.

1 Nebuchadrezzar doubtless thought that he, with his numerous and powerful forces (verse 1), was master of the situation. But who is revealed here as the controlling power, deciding the fate of cities and kings? *Cf.* Is. 40: 15, 17, 21–24; Lk. 3: 1, 2.

2 Why was the failure to go through with the freeing of the slaves so severely condemned? *Cf.* Ec. 5: 4, 5; Mt. 7: 21; 21: 28–31a; Lk. 9: 62. With verse 17, *cf.* 22: 16. Do I owe some promised obedience which has not yet been performed?

Notes

1 Verses 2–5. *Cf.* 32: 3–5; 52: 11.

2 Verse 14. *Cf.* Dt. 15: 12–15.

3 Verse 17. 'Liberty to the sword': *i.e.*, freedom to be destroyed by conquest.

4 Verses 18, 19. The ceremony of the covenant of repentance (verse 15) included the participants' passing between the parts of a calf which had been cut in two (*cf.* Gn. 15: 7–18). By such ritual they asked to be put to death in a similar violent manner, if they failed to keep their promise. See verse 20.

□ STUDY 24 Jeremiah 35

The Rechabites were a small class or sect who regarded Jonadab (*cf.* 2 Ki. 10: 15) as their father or founder, and had received a charge from him to abstain from wine, from settled dwellings and from agriculture, *i.e.*, the marks of a settled civilization. They normally lived a nomad life, but, in fear of the advance of the armies of the north, they had taken refuge in Jerusalem.

1 What test did Jeremiah, at God's command, apply to the Rechabites? And what message did God then give him to take to the people of Jerusalem?

2 Verses 13–17. Consider the frequency of this complaint: see 7: 13, 25, 26; 25: 3, 4, 7; 26: 4, 5; 29: 19; 44: 4. Are you careful to heed God's word to you, *e.g.*, through teachers and preachers?

3 What traits of the Rechabites should be the distinguishing features of Christians today? *Cf.* Mt. 24: 12, 13; Heb. 10: 36, 38, 39.

☐ STUDY 25 Jeremiah 36

1 The events of this chapter cannot have been very long after those of chapter 26 (compare the dating in verse 1 with 26: 1). God in His compassion bids Jeremiah make one more appeal. In what respects does it differ from that of chapter 26 (a) in its content, (b) in the manner of its delivery, and (c) in its outcome?

2 Why do you think the princes felt they must tell the king (verse 16)? Was it to get Jeremiah silenced (*cf.* Am. 7: 10–13), or in the hope that the king might hearken to God's word, as Josiah had done (2 Ki. 22: 10, 11)? With verse 24, *cf.* Is. 66: 2. Do you have the impression that this was a fateful moment for the nation, and that very much depended on the king's action? Are there comparable decisions in your life?

3 Compare verses 19 and 26. How do I describe a successful action or activity of my own?

Notes

1 Verse 5. 'I am debarred': perhaps because of the fear of his causing a disturbance (*cf.* the impact of his Temple sermon in chapter 26), or perhaps because of some ceremonial defilement.

2 Verse 8. This verse sums up in brief the story of the following verses. Note from verses 1 and 9 the time taken to complete the scroll. The incident of chapter 45 falls between verses 8 and 9.

☐ STUDY 26 Jeremiah 37 and 38

Although Egypt had been decisively defeated by the armies of Babylon at Carchemish twenty years before (46: 2), now a new king had arisen in Egypt who sought to oppose Nebuchadrezzar's southward advance. He sent an army, while Nebuchadrezzar was besieging Jerusalem, whose approach forced the Chaldeans to raise the siege. This excited great hopes, but Jeremiah was not deceived. The Chaldeans, he said, would come back and burn the city with fire.

1 How do these two arrests of Jeremiah illustrate 1: 18, 19? His arrest seems to have contributed to his safety (37: 21). Should we expect to find God's goodness in our hardest experiences? *Cf.* Ps. 23: 4; Acts 27: 21–25.

2 Which do you think were harder to bear—the physical sufferings or the reproaches hurled at him? Why did he not keep silent and so escape censure? See 20: 7–11; Acts 4: 18–20; 5: 29.

3 What can we learn from the character of Zedekiah as revealed in these chapters? *Cf.* Pr. 29: 25a; Jas. 1: 8.

Note. 37: 12. 'To take over some property among his own people' (Moffatt).

☐ STUDY 27 Jeremiah 39–41

The fall of Jerusalem and the events immediately following.

1 What message did Jeremiah give to Ebed-melech, and why? *Cf.* Mt. 10: 40–42. Is your faith equally practical? *Cf.* Jas. 2: 21–24.

2 Note carefully 40: 2, 3. Could the matter be better summed up than in these words of a heathen officer? *Cf.* Pr. 29: 1; Is. 30: 9–14.

3 Most Christians are too ready to believe evil of others. Gedaliah was the opposite. What can we learn from this example? Note that as a public leader he had responsibility for others (40: 10; 41: 10) as well as for himself.

Notes

1 39: 3. 'Rabsaris' means chief of the princes; and 'Rabmag', chief of the magi.

2 39: 4. 'Between the two walls': *i.e.*, of the city, probably 'the wall along the west side of the east hill, and along the east side of the west hill' (Driver).

3 39: 5. 'Riblah': in the far north, fifty miles south of Hamath.

4 41: 1. Ishmael was probably jealous that Gedaliah had been appointed governor, and sought to get the remnant of the Jews under his control (41: 10).

☐ STUDY 28 Jeremiah 42 and 43

1 It is clear that the remnant of the people left in the land were obsessed by fear—fear of the Chaldeans (42: 11) and fear of famine (42: 16). From both these evils Egypt appeared to offer a secure place of refuge (42: 14). But what did God say they ought to do? And what did He say would happen to them if they went to Egypt?

2 Why did the people, in spite of their promise to obey God, take a wrong course? What did they lack spiritually that they failed so badly? Read carefully 42: 20, 21 (see Note 1 below), and *cf.* Mt.

15: 7, 8; Heb. 3: 18, 19. What does this teach us about our attitude in seeking to know the will of God? Note 42: 6. Are we guilty of making up *our* minds in advance? *Cf.* 43: 2.

3 Over against the people and their failure contrast the character of Jeremiah. God had made the same promise to him that He now made to these Hebrews (see 1: 18, 19); but how different was the response in Jeremiah's case? What are the outstanding features that you observe in Jeremiah in these chapters?

Notes

1 42: 21. Jeremiah anticipates the reply they were about to make in their fixed resolve to seek refuge in Egypt. Perhaps during the interval (verse 7) preparations for flight had been in hand.

2 43: 7. 'Tahpanhes' was on the eastern branch of the Nile not far from the Mediterranean.

3 43: 10–13. Nebuchadrezzar did invade Egypt before two decades were out.

☐ STUDY 29 Jeremiah 44 and 45

This is the last recorded scene of Jeremiah's life. The now aged prophet, exiled in Egypt, visits some place where his fellow-countrymen are gathered and delivers a last message from their God, a message which they resolutely reject, thus drawing upon themselves their own destruction. Chapter 45 is a much earlier fragment, belonging to the fourth year of Jehoiakim (see Note on 36: 8).

1 How would you sum up Jeremiah's message in 44: 2–14? What was the spiritual condition of the people as revealed in their reply (*cf.* 17: 9; Is. 44: 20)? And what was God's final word to them through His servant? *Cf.* 1 Jn. 5: 21.

2 44: 17, 18, 21–23. Here are two divergent interpretations of Judah's recent past. Outwardly, at least, there seems much to support the idolaters' standpoint. Since Josiah's reformation Judah had experienced nothing but trouble and calamity. Could outward events *alone* adjudicate between these two interpretations? Is there always an immediate correspondence between godliness and prosperity? *Cf.* Ps. 73.

3 Chapter 45. Baruch was the son of a princely house. His brother Seraiah held an important office under the king (see 51: 59), and he himself probably had ambitions (45: 5). His work for Jeremiah would reveal to him the doom of the city and the kingdom. What were his natural reactions? What was God's message to him, and what may we learn from it for ourselves? Was Baruch's distress greater than the Lord's in having so to deal with His people (verse 4)? *Cf.* Mk. 10: 42–45; Mt. 10: 24, 25a.

Notes
1 44: 1. The three cities represent Jewish settlements in northern Egypt, and Pathros was the name given to Upper (*i.e.*, southern) Egypt.
2 44: 17. 'The queen of heaven': see Note on 7: 18 (p. 335).

☐ STUDY 30 Jeremiah 46 and 47

46: 1 introduces chapters 46–51 (see Analysis). Chapter 46 falls into three sections: verses 2–12 (description of Egypt's bid for power and defeat by the Chaldeans at Carchemish); verses 13–26 (prophecy of Nebuchadrezzar's invasion of Egypt); and verses 27, 28 (a message of comfort for Israel: see these verses in their original setting at 30: 10, 11). Chapter 47 prophesies the Chaldean conquest of Philistia.

1 Read each section aloud, perhaps in Moffatt's translation, to catch the rhythm and force of these utterances. What is the relation of the God of Israel to the clash of these mighty powers? *Cf.* 46: 10, 15, 25–26; 47: 4, 6, 7. Note that God's chosen people is not directly involved. *Cf.* Am. 9: 7; Is. 40: 15, 17, 23; 41: 2. What does this tell of God's control of the history of *all* the nations of the world, even if that control is hidden from our sight? *Cf.* Ps. 22: 28.

2 How is Egypt described (a) before the battle, (b) after it, and (c) during the invasion? Compare all this with her boast in 46: 8, and read again 9: 23–26.

Notes
1 46: 9. 'Put' and 'Lud' were African tribes of uncertain location.
2 46: 15. 'Apis': *i.e.*, the sacred bull of Egypt, the supposed incarnation of Osiris.
3 46: 16. 'And they said': the reference must be to foreign settlers or traders in Egypt, or to foreign mercenaries (verse 21).
4 46: 18. 'Like Tabor . . . like Carmel': *i.e.*, 'towering above' the nations.
5 46: 22. The fleeing Egyptians are likened to a snake gliding away before the woodcutters, *i.e.*, the invading armies from the north.
6 46: 25. Thebes was the famous capital of Upper Egypt, and Amon its local god.
7 47: 1. 'Before Pharaoh smote Gaza': it is uncertain when Necho smote Gaza. The LXX omits the phrase.
8 47: 4. 'Caphtor' is the name used of Crete, the original home of the Philistines, and also of the neighbouring coastal regions which came under its control.
9 47: 5. 'Baldness' and 'gash yourselves' are tokens of mourning. *Cf.* 16: 6 (and see Note, p. 338); 48: 37. The 'Anakim' were among the pre-Israelite inhabitants of Palestine.

☐ STUDY 31 Jeremiah 48

Within Jeremiah's lifetime, Moab was in league with the Chaldeans against Judah during Jehoiakim's reign (2 Ki. 24: 2; *cf.* Je. 12); and later, in Zedekiah's reign, discussed with other nations a possible revolt against Babylon (27: 1–11).

1 The chapter may be divided into five sections: verses 1–10, verses 11–20, verses 21–27, verses 28–39, verses 40–47. What heading would you give to each of these sections to sum up its contents?

2 What reason for the judgment is given in verse 11? What warning should we take for ourselves? *Cf.* Dt. 8: 11–18; Is. 47: 8–11; Am. 6: 1–7; Zp. 1: 12. What other reasons for the judgment are set forth in this chapter?

Notes

1 All the numerous place-names refer to Moabite territory. Some have not been identified, including 'Madmen' (verse 2; the LXX reads 'Yet you, *i.e.*, Moab, shall be brought to silence').

2 Verses 7, 13. 'Chemosh': the god of Moab. 'Bethel, their confidence': see Am. 5: 5; 7: 10–13 for false worship at Bethel. Bethel means 'house of God', and there may be present also an allusion to false trust in the Temple; see Je. 7: 1–15.

3 Verses 11, 12. An illustration from the treatment of the juice of grapes. It is left in a vessel until a sediment called 'lees' has formed at the bottom; then the liquid is poured into another vessel, and so repeatedly, until the liquid is clear. Moab had experienced no such purifying process, and so retained its original unrefined character.

4 Verse 26. 'Make him drunk': *i.e.*, stagger with shock and despairing grief. *Cf.* 13: 13 (and see Note, p. 337); 25: 16.

☐ STUDY 32 Jeremiah 49: 1–33

This chapter contains prophecies on four neighbouring nations, namely Ammon (verses 1–6), Edom (verses 7–22), Damascus (verses 23–27), and Kedar and the kingdoms of Hazor (verses 28–33). Ammon was concerned along with Moab in the two incidents mentioned in the introduction to chapter 48. Antagonism between Israel and Edom was long standing, and Edom had recently taken advantage of the fall of Jerusalem in 587 BC to occupy cities in southern Judah (Ob. 10–14). Edom had also considered revolt against Babylon (27: 3). Kedar was a nomadic Arabian tribe, and Hazor is probably used collectively of the region occupied by semi-nomadic Arabs (*cf.* 25: 23, 24).

1 What was Ammon's sin against Israel? *Cf.* Am. 1: 13; Ex. 20: 17; Lk. 12: 15. In what was her trust placed? *Cf.* 48: 7; Pr. 10: 28; Mk. 10: 23, 24. What was to be her punishment?

2 Notice the vivid metaphors describing the severity of Edom's fate, as, *e.g.*, in verses 9, 10, 19, 20. Note, too, its comprehensiveness, from Teman and Bozrah in the north, to Dedan, south of Edom in Arabia. Why is the judgment against Edom (Esau's descendants) so severe? *Cf.* verse 16; Mal 1: 2–4; Heb. 12: 16, 17.

3 The sins that brought judgment upon Damascus and Kedar are not specified. Read again 25: 15–38, and note the reasons given there for judgment upon nations mentioned in this chapter.

Notes

1 Verses 1, 3. 'Milcom' was the national deity of the Ammonites. The Ammonites took advantage of the deportation of the Gadites by the Assyrians in 733–732 BC (2 Ki. 15: 29).

2 Verse 3. The word 'daughters' here refers to towns and villages which looked to Rabbah as their head. In verse 4 'daughter' refers to the whole people.

3 Verse 8. 'Dwell in the depths': *i.e.*, hidden away from observation. *Cf.* verse 30.

4 Verse 17. 'Hiss': *i.e.*, draw in the breath with astonishment, gasp.

5 Verses 19, 20. The picture of a lion coming up out of the jungle on the fringe of Jordan and doing what it pleases with the flock, no shepherd being able to challenge him.

□ STUDY 33 Jeremiah 49: 34 – 50: 46

Elam was a country north of the Persian Gulf and east of Babylon. This prophecy, delivered soon after the first deportation from Judah in 597, no doubt warns the exiles against expecting relief from this direction. Jeremiah looked ahead, beyond the judgment of which Babylon was to be the instrument, to the time when Babylon herself would be judged. Chapter 50 may be divided as follows: Babylon's fall (verses 1–3); a message of comfort to Israel (verses 4–7); renewed declaration of Babylon's doom (verses 8–13); summons to the attackers to begin their work (verses 14–16); Israel's return to her land and to her God (verses 17–20); the attackers bidden to press on (verses 21–28, 29–34, 35–40); description of the attackers (verses 41–46).

1 Why are God's people to be restored?

2 Consider the solemn truth that, while God may use a nation as His instrument, this does not absolve that nation from responsibility before God. Why would Babylon receive no mercy? See especially verses 7, 11–15, 24–25, 27–29, 31; Is. 14: 5, 6, 17; 47: 6, 7; 51: 22, 23; La. 1: 7.

Notes

1 50: 2. 'Bel' and 'Merodach' are names of the supreme god of Babylon.

2 50: 7. *Cf.* 40: 3.

3 50: 16. A reference to foreigners in Babylon. *Cf.* 46: 16 and Note.

4 50: 21. 'Merathaim' (perhaps a name for southern Babylonia) and 'Pekod' (a people of eastern Babylonia) are probably used here because they are very close to the Hebrew words for 'double rebellion' (or 'bitterness') and 'punishment' (or 'visitation') respectively.

5 50: 36a. *Cf.* Is. 44: 25.

□ STUDY 34 Jeremiah 51: 1–58

This chapter may be divided as follows: Babylon's doom and Israel's vindication (verses 1–10); summons to the attackers to press home their assault (verses 11–14); the Lord in contrast to idols (verses 15–19); the Lord's fierce anger against Babylon (verses 20–26); capture of the city (verses 27–33); Israel's wrongs avenged: let her hasten her escape (verses 34–57); summing up God's judgment upon Babylon (verse 58).

1 In the time of her prosperity the idols of Babylon seemed powerful and mighty; but now in the hour of her fall how do they appear? See verses 15–19, and *cf.* 1, 2; Ps. 146: 5–10.

2 What, according to chapters 50 and 51, were the sins of Babylon which called down upon her such terrible vengeance? How far are these sins prevalent in the world today?

Notes

1 Verse 1. Note mg. The Hebrew means literally 'the heart of those who rise up against me'.

2 Verse 3a. The Hebrew is difficult. Either it means that the defenders of Babylon need not trouble to fight, for it will be of no avail (*cf.* verse 30; 31: 4; 32: 5b); or the text is to be amended, *e.g.*, by omission of the negatives.

3 Verse 20. A reference to Cyrus, the conqueror of Babylon.

4 Verse 27. 'Ararat, Minni and Ashkenaz' were three peoples north of Babylonia earlier conquered by the Medes.

5 Verse 36. 'Her sea': perhaps a reference to the great lake Nebuchadrezzar constructed for the defence of the city, or perhaps to the Euphrates.

6 Verse 55a. 'Her mighty voice': *i.e.*, the noise of the great city. Verse 55b refers to the roar of the attackers.

7 Verse 58c. 'So ends the toil of nations, ends in smoke, and pagans waste their pains' (Moffatt).

☐ STUDY 35 Jeremiah 51: 59 – 52: 34

1 51: 59–64. Note the date of this incident. At the time, Babylon was rising to the height of her power and glory, and Jeremiah was convinced that she would enjoy complete supremacy over the nations. See chapter 28 which belongs to the same year. How, then, does this commission which Jeremiah gives to Seriah illustrate the truth of Heb. 11: 1, that 'faith is . . . the conviction of things not seen'?

2 Chapter 52 is very similar to 2 Ki. 24: 18 – 25: 30. It tells once more the story of the fall of Jerusalem, the destruction of the Temple and the captivity of the people, perhaps to emphasize how complete was the fulfilment of Jeremiah's words. For example, compare verse 3 with 7: 15; verse 6 with 14: 15–18; verses 8–11 with 34: 3; verse 13 with 7: 14; 9: 11; 19: 13; 32: 28, 29; verse 15 with 16: 9–13; 21: 9; verses 18, 19 with 27: 19–22. See 1: 12. Do you believe this, and live by it?

Note. 52: 24. 'The three keepers of the threshold': denoting three high officials of the Temple who had charge of the three gates.

LAMENTATIONS

Introduction

The book of Lamentations consists of five songs or elegies, the theme of which is the sorrows of Judah and Jerusalem in the siege and destruction of the city. The cause of these calamities is traced to the sin of the people bringing God's judgment upon them, and the songs contain confessions of sin, statements of faith and hope, and prayer for the restoration of God's favour.

Tradition from the time of the LXX has assigned the authorship of the songs to the prophet Jeremiah. In the Hebrew Bible, however, the book is anonymous, and is placed not among 'The Prophets', but in the section known as 'The Writings'. The book certainly has close affinities with Jeremiah. Chapters 1–4 seem to be the work of an eye-witness of Jerusalem's fall; and if not by Jeremiah himself, may well be the work of one or more of his associates, such as Baruch. Chapter 5 probably dates from a slightly later period.

The songs are written in acrostic form. In chapters 1, 2 and 4 each verse begins with a fresh letter of the Hebrew alphabet from beginning to end. In the poem of chapter 3 there are twenty-two groups of three verses each, and each verse of each group begins with the same letter of the alphabet in order. In chapter 5 the acrostic form is not followed. This acrostic arrangement is partly an aid to memorization, but also seems intended to give a sense of completeness in confession of sin and grief.

Analysis

1 The deep sorrows of Jerusalem with contrite confession of sin.
2 It is God who has acted according to His word. Seek Him in prayer.
3 Speaking on behalf of the nation, the writer pours out his grief before God, and, staying himself upon the Lord, pleads earnestly for help.

4 The miseries of the siege. The guilt of prophets and priests. The capture of the city.
5 A prayer describing the nation's suffering, confessing sin, and pleading for salvation.

☐ STUDY 1 Lamentations 1

Verses 1–11 depict the covenant people in the guise of a widow. The second half of the chapter is a lament by the desolate widow herself.

1 What ingredients make up Jerusalem's cup of sorrow, *e.g.*, loneliness, bereavement, reversal of fortune, *etc.*? Make a list of them. How and why had Jerusalem come to such a pass? See especially verses 5, 8, 9, 12, 14, 17, 18, 20; and *cf.* Heb. 10: 29–31; Lv. 26: 27–33.

2 Do you find any note of resentment in this complaint? 'The sense of tragedy is heightened by the recognition that it was avoidable.' What is commendable in the attitude of this chapter? Note verse 18, and *cf.* Ps. 51: 3, 4; Dn. 9: 6–8; Rom. 3: 4–6.

Notes

1 Verse 2. 'Lovers . . . friend's: *i.e.*, neighbouring peoples with whom she had sought alliance. *Cf.* Je. 30: 14.
2 Verse 6. 'Her princes . . .': *cf.* Je. 39: 4, 5.

☐ STUDY 2 Lamentations 2

Verses 1–9 deal particularly with the devastation of buildings in Judah and Jerusalem, and the rest of the chapter with the sufferings of various classes of the inhabitants.

1 Try to imagine the desolation here portrayed and the intensity of the people's sorrow. *Cf.* 1: 12. What is said of God's 'right hand' in verses 3, 4? Contrast with this such passages as Ex. 15: 6, 12; Pss. 63: 8; 139: 10.

2 What evidence in this chapter suggests that already the disaster of the judgment is having one of its intended effects? *Cf.* 2 Ch. 7: 13, 14. Are we, as God's children, as sensitive as we ought to be to His disciplinary dealings?

Notes

1 Verse 2. 'Habitations': *i.e.*, country dwellings, as opposed to 'strongholds'.
2 Verse 4. 'Tent' here denotes the city.
3 Verse 6a refers to the Temple. 'He has broken down his tabernacle like a garden hut' (Gottwald).
4 Verse 22a. Instead of summoning worshippers to a festival, God has called together 'terrors on every side', so that none of His people escaped. *Cf.* Is. 28: 21.

☐ STUDY 3 Lamentations 3

1 In verses 1–20 the poet, speaking in the name of the community, pours out his heart 'like water before the presence of the Lord' (2: 19). Notice the change from the minor to the major key at verse 21. What causes it? Do the psalmists' experiences in Pss. 42: 1–5 and 73: 16, 17a provide a clue?

2 Consider how remarkable is the appearance here, in verses 22–42, of such a noble expression of assurance concerning God's mercies. What aspects of God's character are most emphasized in these verses, and what should be our attitude of mind and spirit in time of affliction or chastisement? *Cf.* Joel 2: 12–14. Why is it both foolish and wrong for a man to complain and murmur in time of chastisement (verses 37–39)? *Cf.* Je. 5: 19–24; Pr. 19: 3.

3 In verses 43–54 the poet, in the name of the people, again pours out his heart before the Lord and, having done so, is strengthened to pray again, and receives comfort. What is his prayer (verses 55–66)? What factors in the poet's situation might lead us not to judge this prayer for requital too harshly?

Notes

1 Verse 20. An alternative reading is, 'Thou wilt surely remember and bow down to me' (Gottwald).
2 Verse 38. The word 'evil' is used here in the sense of misfortune or calamity. *Cf.* Am. 3: 6; Is. 45: 7.
3 Verse 63. *Cf.* Jb. 30: 9.

☐ STUDY 4 Lamentations 4

1 Make a list of the statements in this chapter which emphasize the extraordinary severity of the divine judgment. Notice how all the classes of the community are affected. What is the particular cause here assigned for so great a calamity? *Cf.* Je. 23: 9–14.

2 With verse 17, *cf.* Je. 2: 36, 37; 37: 7, 8; and with verse 20, *cf.* Ps. 146: 3, 4; Je. 17: 5, 6.

Notes

1 Verse 6a. Note the variants in mg.
2 Verse 20. A reference to King Zedekiah; *cf.* Je. 39: 4–7.

☐ STUDY 5 Lamentations 5

1 How would you infer from this chapter that it was written some time after Jerusalem had fallen? How would you sum up the conditions in the land? How does this chapter illustrate what is said in

Heb. 12: 11? Contrast the present disposition of the people with what they formerly said (Je. 5: 11, 12; 18: 18). What did they still lack?

2 With verse 16, *cf.* Je. 13: 18, and with verse 21, Je. 31: 18. Consider how much God's word spoken before through Jeremiah meant to the people at such a time. *Cf.* Jn. 13: 19; 14: 29; 16: 4.

Note. Verse 9. A reference to the danger of attack from desert robbers when the people ventured out to reap the harvest.

PHILIPPIANS

Introduction

Paul had a special love for the Christians in the church at Philippi (see 1: 8; 4: 1). From the beginning they had entered into his labours and sufferings with financial support and prayerful personal interest (1: 5, 19; 4: 15, 16). Shortly before this letter was written they had greatly encouraged him by sending a gift to Rome, where he was a prisoner (4: 10, 14, 18). His letter is marked to an unusual degree by personal affection for his readers, and consists largely of an account of his personal experience of Christ, with special reference to his circumstances as a prisoner.

The church in Philippi seems to have been singularly free from both serious error in doctrine and moral lapses. At the same time there were threatening dangers. A measure of friction had arisen between certain members, and in the earlier part of the letter Paul urges the importance of being of one mind in the Lord. He also warns them against other dangers, and urges them to stand fast in the Lord. It is in this connection that the main doctrinal passages of the letter occur, namely in 2: 5–11 and 3: 1–21.

The letter is dominated by a spirit of joy and peace, and is an outstanding witness to the power of Christ to lift the person weighed down with the sorrow and suffering of earth to rejoicing and gladness in the Lord.

Analysis

1: 1, 2	Greeting.
1: 3–7	Thanksgiving.
1: 8–11	Prayer.
1: 12–26	Paul's present circumstances and outlook.
1: 27 – 2: 18	Encouragement to the Philippians to lead godly lives.
2: 19–30	Future plans.
3: 1–21	Warning against threatening dangers. The faith and aim of a Christian illustrated by Paul's own life.
4: 1–9	Further marks of a Christian.
4: 10–20	An appreciation of the Philippians' gift.
4: 21–23	Greetings and benediction.

☐ STUDY 1 Philippians 1: 1–11

1 Verses 3–7. Why is the joy with which Paul remembers the Philippians remarkable? *Cf.* Acts 16: 22; 1 Thes. 2: 2. How had they made up for the treatment given to Paul at the start? What made him sure that they were now permanently on the right road?

2 Verses 8–11. What twofold preparations for the return of Christ does Paul pray that the Philippians will make? Is it really they who are to make it? *Cf.* 2: 12, 13. How will this preparation be reflected in their character and behaviour? Express Paul's petitions for them in your own words, and then use them in your own praying.

3 Make a list of the places in the Epistle where Paul stresses that he is writing to *all* the Philippian Christians. (See especially verses 1, 3, 7, 8.) Does any part of the letter suggest a reason for this?

Notes

1 Verse 1. 'Saints': a name for the people of Christ as 'holy' or set apart for God's possession and service.

2 Verse 5. See 4: 15, 16.

3 Verse 6. 'The day of Jesus Christ': *i.e.*, the coming day of His manifestation in glory, in the light of which the truth about men's lives will be revealed. *Cf.* 2: 16; 1 Cor. 1: 7, 8; 3: 13; 2 Thes. 1: 9, 10.

☐ STUDY 2 Philippians 1: 12–26

1 The things that had happened to Paul must have seemed calamitous to those who loved him. Why did he himself view the situation

differently? What lesson about suffering may a Christian draw from Paul's attitude?

2 What was Paul's attitude as a Christian (a) to life, and (b) to death? What were his reasons for choosing one rather than the other? What were his overriding concerns? Have you faced every possibility that lies before you in the same way?

3 What temptation in Christian service is it clear from this passage that Paul steadfastly resisted? How had others succumbed? What kind of slant might their preaching have had in relation to Paul? In what shape does the same temptation come to us? What should be our chief reason for joy? *Cf.* Jn. 3:25–30.

□ STUDY 3 Philippians 1: 27 – 2: 18

1 Make a list of the things (a) to be coveted, and (b) to be avoided in one's life as a member of a company of Christians. Then pray, and by God's grace determine, that these things shall be (a) realized and (b) avoided in your own Christian fellowship. Note especially the direct connection between these things and witness to those who are not Christians.

2 What two qualities of personal character and conduct are here shown to be supremely exemplified in the incarnation and the redemptive work of the Son of God? What ground have we for hoping to be able to have and to express the same qualities? How ought we to act in consequence?

3 Why does disunity amongst Christians discredit the gospel? What does Paul here teach about (a) the motive for unity, and (b) the power by which it may be achieved?

Note. 2:6–11. It is generally thought that these verses are here quoted by Paul from an early Christian credal hymn. It is worth committing this section to memory and exploring it in depth.

□ STUDY 4 Philippians 2: 19–30

1 What is said here or can be inferred about the character and career of Epaphroditus? Note carefully how the two workers here mentioned personally exemplified the virtues considered under the previous study, *i.e.*, they had the mind of Christ. Compare verses 20, 21 with 4, 5; and verses 29, 30 with 5–8. Examine your own life in relation to these standards.

2 What phrase occurs three times in this passage and several other times in the letter? What clue does 4: 2 give as to one reason for this repeated emphasis? Are our hopes for the future and our relationships under the same sway as Paul's?

□ STUDY 5 Philippians 3: 1–11

Paul now turns to another subject—possibly, as some think, resuming his writing after a break. His subject now is the essential character of the Christian life from its beginning in justification by faith to its glorious consummation at the coming of the Lord; and he illustrates the theme from his own life.

1 What three characteristics of the true people of God are given in verse 3? How far are they true of me?

2 Examine carefully the reasons for 'confidence in the flesh' which Paul enumerates in verses 4–6. Are there not many church-goers today who are relying for salvation on just such grounds as these? What, in contrast to all this, is the position of the true Christian? What choice does Paul show needs to be made in order to become one?

3 Faith in Christ as the sole ground for acceptance with God led, in Paul's case, to intense desire to know Christ; nothing else seemed to him of any value (verses 8, 9). Along what two lines in particular did he want a deeper knowledge (verse 10), and to what end (verse 11)?

Notes
1 Verse 2. Note the emphatic 'Look out', repeated three times. A word meaning 'incision' or 'mutilation' is here used instead of 'circumcision', because the circumcision on which they insisted was harmful rather than helpful to spiritual well-being. *Cf.* Gal. 5: 2–4; 6: 12–15.
2 Verses 3, 4. 'Confidence in the flesh': *i.e.*, reliance upon outward privilege and personal merit. 'We are the true circumcision': *i.e.*, the true people of God. *Cf.* Rom. 2: 17, 23, 28, 29.

□ STUDY 6 Philippians 3: 12–21

1 Verses 12–17. Once a person knows he is 'saved' or 'justified', what attitude should he adopt to life? Even after he has 'grown up' as a Christian and become 'mature', what concern should still dominate his thoughts? What is he never justified in doing? How in consequence ought I to be acting?

2 Verses 18–21. What kind of outlook, interest and expectation should a Christian have, and why? By contrast, what kind of appetite and interest dominates some? What difference should the cross of Christ make to my daily life? *Cf.* Gal. 5: 24; 6: 14.

Notes

1 Verses 12, 15. 'Perfect' or 'mature': the Greek word means 'having reached its end'. It was used of persons who were full-grown or mature.
2 Verse 20. The thought here is that Christians here on earth are a colony of heavenly citizens, just as the Philippians were proud to think of themselves as a colony of Roman citizens. *Cf.* Acts 16: 12, 21.

☐ STUDY 7 Philippians 4

1 Note in detail how the believer's relationship to the Lord should make a difference (a) to his own condition, (b) to his attitude to circumstances, and (c) to his relationship to people. Note the importance of the mind and its right use; and note what God can do for our minds. *Cf.* Is. 26: 3. Examine your own life to discover ways in which you may trust Christ to make you 'different'.

2 What teaching is implicit in this passage about (a) the bond effected by Christian giving; (b) the need for regularity in it; (c) the way God looks at it; and (d) the way in which He repays it? *Cf.* Lk. 6: 38.

Notes

1 Verse 5. 'The Lord is at hand': this may mean either that the Lord is close by, at their side (*cf.* Ps. 119: 151), or that His coming is imminent.
2 Verse 18. 'A fragrant offering' (RSV), or 'an odour of a sweet smell' (AV, RV): a phrase used in the Old Testament of acceptable offerings. *Cf.* Gn. 8: 21; Lv. 1: 9, 13; Eph. 5: 2.

EZEKIEL 1 - 32

Introduction

Ezekiel was one of the many taken captive by Nebuchadrezzar in the first captivity, commonly referred to as the captivity of King Jehoiachin (*e.g.*, 1: 2), because this king himself was among those carried away. This occurred in 597 BC, eleven years before the actual destruction of Jerusalem.

Ezekiel was a priest as well as a prophet. He began prophesying in 592 BC and continued till at least 570 BC. See 1: 2 and 29: 17. His ministry was divided into two distinct periods by the destruction of Jerusalem (586 BC). Before this event it was his painful task to disillusion his fellow-exiles, to proclaim that all hopes of the early deliverance of the city and speedy return of the exiles were vain. Jerusalem must fall. After this event the character of his ministry completely changed. He sought to rebuke despair and to afford comfort and hope by promises of future deliverance and restoration.

To witness with the object first of overthrowing men's natural hopes, and then of overcoming men's inevitable despair, is a work that can be undertaken and carried through only under the constraint and by the inspiration of a divine commission. Such a commission was Ezekiel's compelling urge. He was a man whose whole life was dominated by his sense of vocation and responsibility as a prophet—as God's messenger to his fellows. Similar necessity is laid upon us to be God's witnesses, and the essential truth of Ezekiel's message should be the unchanging truth of our own. Because God is righteous, sin must be punished; old things must pass away. But because God is gracious, and has provided a salvation for sinners, there is a gospel of hope for the hopeless; in Christ all things can become new.

Analysis

1: 1 – 3: 21	Ezekiel's call and commission.	
3: 22 – 24: 27	Prophecies concerning the destruction of the city and nation (uttered before the fall of Jerusalem).	
	3: 22 – 7: 27	Symbolic representations foretelling Jerusalem's overthrow, and their interpretation.
	8 – 11	Symbolic departure of the Lord from the Temple because of idolatry.
	12 – 23	Specific proofs of the necessity of judgment.
	24	Final symbol of the scattering of the people and their purification through exile.
25 – 32	Predictions against seven heathen nations—Ammon, Moab, Edom, Philistia, Tyre, Sidon, Egypt.	
33 – 39	Prophecies concerning the restoration of the nation (uttered after the fall of Jerusalem).	
	33, 34	The moral conditions of entering the new kingdom.
	35: 1 – 36: 15	The land to be rescued from its enemies.
	36: 16 – 37: 28	The nation to be restored, purified, revitalized, and re-united.
	38, 39	The Lord's final victory.
40 – 48	A vision symbolizing the ideal state of Israel as the Lord's people.	

☐ STUDY 1 Ezekiel 1

The vision of this chapter was of supreme importance in Ezekiel's life. Not only was it the occasion of his call to be a prophet, but it was also the medium through which a new conception of God was revealed to him which was to mould his prophetic ministry.

1 As the vision of God's chariot-throne is outlined, follow the prophet's description of it, part by part: first the living creatures (verses 5–14), then the wheels (verses 15–21), with the throne on top, and finally the One who sat there. How is God described, and what is this meant to teach about the nature of God?

2 What do you find symbolized by the other features of the vision: the living creatures, the wheels, the throne, *etc.*?

Notes

1 Verse 1. 'In the thirtieth year . . .': probably of Ezekiel's age, *i.e.*, the year when he would have begun to function as a priest had he remained in Jerusalem.

2 Verse 3. 'The hand of the Lord was upon him there': a phrase used elsewhere in the book to signify a prophetic trance or ecstasy. See 3: 22; 8: 1; 33: 22; 37: 1.
3 Verse 5. 'Four living creatures': heavenly beings, yet representing the highest forms of life on earth (among birds, domestic animals, wild animals and the whole creation respectively), and indicating perhaps that all created things are under God's control.
4 Verses 19–21. Observe that there was no mechanical framework to the chariot. All was spiritual, and responsive to the Spirit.

[ ] STUDY 2 Ezekiel 2: 1 – 3: 21

1 To whom was Ezekiel sent, and how are they described? What was to be the theme of his message to them? See 2: 3–7; 3: 4–11.

2 What two meanings are symbolized by the eating of the scroll, one having reference to the prophet himself (2: 8), and the other to his ministry (3: 4)? Consider the application of these things to all who would be God's messengers.

3 What consolations are there in these verses for one called to witness for the Lord among those who are obstinately opposed to the gospel? Why is such opposition no excuse for ceasing to witness (2: 5b)? What are the four possible cases which are cited in 3: 17–21? What relevance do these have for the work of Christian ministers today?

Notes
1 2: 1, 3. 'Son of man': a phrase occurring over ninety times in Ezekiel. It is used to draw attention to the prophet's insignificance and mere humanity.
2 2: 6. 'Briers and thorns . . . scorpions': symbols of the trials he would suffer.

[ ] STUDY 3 Ezekiel 3: 22 – 5: 17

Jerusalem, under King Zedekiah, had recovered a measure of strength after its capture by Nebuchadrezzar in 597 BC, and false prophets were prophesying a period of divine favour (see Je. 28: 1–4). These reports reached the exiles in Babylon, and the burden of Ezekiel's message at this time was that, on the contrary, Jerusalem was about to experience God's judgments.

The closing verses of chapter 3 are best regarded as an introduction to the prophecies of chapters 4–24, which all relate to the approaching judgment on Jerusalem. During this time the prophet was commanded to live in seclusion, as if bound and dumb, except when God gave him some message to deliver (3: 25–27).

1 In chapters 4: 1 – 5: 4 the prophet is directed to show by four symbolic actions the impending siege of Jerusalem, with its privations and sufferings, and also the plight of those who would be carried into exile after the city's fall. What were these actions?

Which of them refer to the siege, and which to the sufferings of those who would be carried into captivity? With 4: 13, *cf.* Ho. 9: 3, 4; and note the explanation of 5: 1–4 in 5: 12.

2 What is said in 5: 5–17 of (a) the reasons, (b) the nature, and (c) the purposes of the terrible judgment that was about to fall upon Jerusalem? Some Christians are less Christian in their lives than many who reject or ignore Christ. In the light of these verses what may we infer to be God's attitude to this sad fact?

Notes

1 4: 10, 11. Food restricted to eight ounces, and water to two pints or less. *Cf.* 4: 16.

2 4: 15. Animal dung was, and still is, a recognized form of fuel in the East.

☐ STUDY 4 Ezekiel 6 and 7

1 Chapter 6. Against what sin is the Lord's anger particularly directed? In what forms is it found today?

2 What refrain frequently recurs in these two chapters? What does it teach us about the purpose behind Ezekiel's prophesying?

3 Contrast the phrase 'I will punish you according to your ways' (7: 9) with Ps. 103: 10; and see Pr. 1: 24, 29–31; 2 Cor. 6: 1, 2. What warning for the careless and indifferent does this contrast suggest?

4 What can be learnt from 7: 14–27 about the right and wrong uses of money? In what ways can it become a stumbling-block to the follower of Christ?

Notes

1 6: 3. 'Your high places': the word originally meant a height or eminence, but as these were used as the sites of temples and shrines, the word came to mean 'sanctuaries', as here. *Cf.* Dt. 12: 2, 3.

2 7: 20. 'They prided themselves upon the beauty of their silver and their gold, and made out of them . . . idols' (Moffatt). *Cf.* Ho. 2: 8.

☐ STUDY 5 Ezekiel 8

Chapters 8–11 describe what Ezekiel was shown in a prophetic trance fourteen months after his first vision. *Cf.* 8: 1 and 1: 1, 2.

1 The prophet is carried 'in visions of God' (verse 3) to Jerusalem, and is there shown four forms of idolatry, practised in or at the gate of the Temple. If you were asked what these practices were, how would you describe them? Observe also what classes of the community are seen engaging in them.

2 The idol-worshipping elders said, 'The Lord has forsaken the land' (verse 12). In what sense were their words true (*cf.* verse 6), and in what sense false? How does this chapter show that all that was happening was under the eyes and under the judgment of God?

Notes

1 Verse 3. 'Image of jealousy': *i.e.*, which provoked God's jealous anger. *Cf.* Dt. 32: 21.

2 Verse 14. 'Women weeping for Tammuz': *i.e.*, taking part in the heathen festival of mourning the death of the vegetation god, Tammuz, later known in Greek mythology as Adonis.

3 Verse 16. 'Between the porch and the altar': these men must therefore have been priests. *Cf.* Joel 2: 17.

□ STUDY 6 Ezekiel 9 and 10

Following the prophecy of judgment, which Ezekiel recorded in chapters 6 and 7, and the vision of chapter 8, which illustrated in detail why such a judgment was justified, the prophet here gives a picture of God acting in judgment in the destruction of both the people (chapter 9) and the city (chapter 10) according to His word in 8: 18.

1 Chapter 9. What was God's answer to the prophet's cry of distress? *Cf.* Je. 14: 19; 15: 1. Who alone were spared, and why? How were they distinguished from others? Compare the distinguishing marks which similarly brought men salvation, described in Ex. 12: 13; Rev. 7: 1–3; 14: 1.

2 Chapter 10. To what use were the burning coals put, and what did they symbolize? How does this differ from their function in Isaiah's vision (Is. 6: 6, 7)?

Notes

1 'The cherubim' of chapter 10 are the same as the 'living creatures' which featured in the vision of chapter 1.

2 10: 14. We would expect to find the word 'ox' instead of 'cherub', and this should probably be understood.

□ STUDY 7 Ezekiel 11

1 The political leaders in Jerusalem thought they were safe within the fortification of Jerusalem, as flesh in a pot is safe from the fire (verse 3). What does God say concerning them? For the fulfilment of the prophecy, see 2 Ki. 25: 18–21.

2 The people of Jerusalem thought that they were the favoured of the Lord, and would be given possession of the land, while those in exile would be cut off (verse 15). But what was God's purpose concerning those in exile (verses 16–20)?

3 Trace the steps by which the glory of God withdrew from His Temple. See 8: 3, 4; 9: 3; 10: 4; 10: 19; 11: 1, 23. What hint is given in chapter 11 as to the possibility of the return of the glory and under what conditions? *Cf.* 43: 1–4, 9.

Notes

1 Verse 1. 'Jaazaniah the son of Azzur': a different man from the Jaazaniah of 8: 11.

2 Verse 23b. 'The mountain': *i.e.*, the Mount of Olives.

☐ STUDY 8 Ezekiel 12 and 13

1 12: 1–20 declares by two vivid symbolic actions on the part of the prophet the doom that was in store both for the people of Jerusalem (verses 3, 4, 18, 19) and for the king (verses 5, 6, 10–16). Having grasped the significance of the prophecy, turn to 2 Ki. 25: 1–7 to see how exactly it was fulfilled.

2 Note the two scoffing remarks in 12: 22 and 27. What do these signify? How are they paralleled in modern attitudes to the second coming of Christ? *Cf.* 2 Pet. 3: 8–10.

3 Chapter 13. Condemnation of false prophets. By what two vivid images are they described (see verses 4 and 10, 11), and what is the effect of their prophesying (verses 6, 10a, 22)? What phrase differentiating them from true prophets occurs twice in the chapter?

Note. 13: 18–21. The magic armbands and veils were devices used by soothsayers and clairvoyants to deceive gullible victims. A useful section on the interpretation of this passage is to be found in *NBD* (article 'Magic and Sorcery', p. 767). The handfuls of barley and pieces of bread were probably used in forms of divination, forecasting life or death to inquirers.

☐ STUDY 9 Ezekiel 14 and 15

1 14: 1–11. (a) If men whose hearts are inwardly alienated from God come professing to seek guidance from Him, will God answer them? What must they first do? If they do not so do, what will be their end? (b) If a prophet should fail to follow this rule, and attempt to give guidance, how will God deal with him?

2 People might ask, 'Will not the presence of righteous men among a sinful nation save it from destruction?' *Cf., e.g.*, Gn. 18: 23–26. How does God in reply show that in the present instance the righteous will be saved out of the destruction, but will not be able to save others? *Cf.* 9: 4–6; Je. 15: 1. If any should escape, what purpose will this accomplish (see 14: 22, 23)?

Notes

1 Noah, Daniel and Job are probably all three patriarchal characters. It is not likely that Ezekiel would be thinking of his contemporary in exile, Daniel the prophet. We know of a Daniel from the Ras Shamra tablets of 1400 BC, and this is a more likely identification.

2 15: 2. For another example of Israel as God's vine, see Is. 5: 1–7.

☐ STUDY 10 Ezekiel 16

In this vivid allegory the prophet seeks to break down the pride of Jerusalem. She appears as the bride of the Lord God, who loved her from infancy, and did everything for her, but whose love she had requited with persistent and shameful idolatry. The chapter falls into four sections: (i) Jerusalem as a child and as a bride (verses 1–14); (ii) her sin (verses 15–34); (iii) her judgment (verses 35–52); (iv) her restoration (verses 53–63).

1 What was God's complaint against Jerusalem? With verses 22 and 32, *cf.* Dt. 32: 15–18. Notice also that God regards her sin as greater than that of Samaria and of Sodom. See verses 46–52 and *cf.* Mt. 11: 23, 24.

2 How may the teaching of this chapter be applied to one who has been truly converted, but has backslidden? What can we learn here for our warning of the peril and folly of the sin of unfaithfulness? *Cf.* Je. 2: 13, 19; Jas. 4: 4–10.

☐ STUDY 11 Ezekiel 17

In 588 BC Zedekiah rebelled against Nebuchadrezzar who, nine years previously, had installed him as puppet-king of Judah, at the time when Jehoiachin had been taken captive to Babylon. His rebellion encouraged false hopes among the exiles of a speedy end to their captivity, but Ezekiel silenced these with this parable about the eagle, the cedar and the vine. The first eagle (verse 3) was Nebuchadrezzar, removing the Davidic King Jehoiachin (the cedar twig, verse 4). Those who remained in Jerusalem under Zedekiah (the vine, verse 6) flourished for a time, but then turned towards the king of Egypt (the second eagle, verse 7), whose influence caused them to wither away.

1 What sin is the prophet specifically rebuking here? With verses 13–16, *cf.* 2 Ch. 36: 13; and with verses 7 and 15, *cf.* Je. 37: 5–8.

2 How do verses 22–24 show that neither the ambitious designs nor the perfidies of men can frustrate the purposes of God? Notice the emphatic and repeated 'I'. *Cf.* Pr. 19: 21; Is. 46: 8–13.

☐ STUDY 12 Ezekiel 18 and 19

The teaching of national retribution in chapter 16 and other passages seems to have raised doubts as to the justice of God's dealings with individuals (18: 2, 29). This is the subject of chapter 18. Chapter 19 is a lament.

1 Two fundamental principles are stated in 18: 4 in answer to the people's complaint in 18: 2. How would you express these in your own words? What verses in the New Testament can you think of which emphasize the same ideas?

2 In the remainder of chapter 18 two questions are answered: (a) Is each man responsible to God for his own acts, and for these alone (see verses 5–20)? (b) If a man turn from his past way of life, will that past affect God's judgment upon him (see verses 21–29)? How does this teaching reveal not only God's justice, but also His mercy? Why does it lead on immediately to the call to repentance of verses 30–32?

3 Chapter 19 is a lament over three of the kings of Judah. Try to identify these by comparing verses 3 and 4 with 2 Ki. 23: 31–34; verses 5–9 with 2 Ki. 24: 8–15; and verses 10–14 with 2 Ki. 25: 4–11. What did they all have in common?

Notes

1 18: 6, 11, 15. 'Eat upon the mountains': *i.e.*, join in idolatrous forms of worship. *Cf.* 6: 1–4.

2 19: 14. The fire which brought destruction sprang from the ruler himself, *i.e.*, Zedekiah. See 17: 19–21.

☐ STUDY 13 Ezekiel 20: 1–44

This section is a review of Israel's history (verses 5–31), with a prophecy of what God will yet do (verses 32–44). The review of history covers (a) the time in Egypt (verses 5–9); (b) in the wilderness (verses 10–17 and 18–26); and (c) in the land of Canaan (verses 27–31). With verses 1–3, *cf.* 14: 1, 2.

1 Analyse the repeated poetical pattern found in verses 5–9, 10–14, 15–17, 18–22. What restrained God from pouring out His wrath? What does this reveal of God's character? How does it show what is the one and only guarantee of our salvation? *Cf.* 1 Sa. 12: 22.

2 To what two conclusions does God say He will ultimately bring His people Israel (verses 42–44)? Has a like conviction been wrought in us?

Notes

1 Verse 25 is a Hebrew way of saying, 'I gave them good statutes but they had a bad effect; I thereby condemned those who were disobedient and I defiled those who performed human sacrifices.' *Cf.* Rom. 5: 20.

2 Verse 37. 'Pass under the rod': the eastern shepherd makes his sheep pass one by one under his staff, held horizontally, to count and examine them.

☐ STUDY 14 Ezekiel 20: 45 – 21: 32

The prophet is bidden to prophesy (a) against the south (of Palestine) (20:

45–49), and (b) against Jerusalem and the land of Israel (21: 1–17). The sword of the Lord is drawn from its sheath (21: 1–7), sharpened and polished (21: 8–13), and smites repeatedly in its deadly work (21: 14–17). In 21: 18–27, the explanation is given. The king of Babylon is seen, standing at the parting of the ways, seeking guidance by divination—Ammon or Jerusalem? The decision falls for Jerusalem, the city is taken, and the king (Zedekiah) slain. The closing verses of the chapter (verses 28–32) are a short prophecy of utter doom upon Ammon as well.

1 Who kindles the fire? Whose sword is drawn? Yet it was by a heathen king that the judgment was effected. What does this teach us concerning God's methods of accomplishing His purposes of judgment in the world? *Cf.* Je. 25: 9 ('my servant'); Is. 25: 1–4.

2 When human leaders and confidences all fail and are overthrown, where can we still look for the establishment of a reign of peace? See 21: 25–27; *cf.* Ps. 2: 6–9; Lk. 21: 25–28.

Notes

1 21: 21 refers to three well-known forms of divination practised by the Babylonians: drawing marked arrows from a quiver (or throwing them in the air to see how they fall); consulting the teraphim, the ancestral household gods, in some form of necromancy; and studying the marks on the entrails of sacrificial victims.

2 21: 27. 'Whose right it is': *i.e.*, the Davidic Messiah who is entitled to the kingship. *Cf.* Gn. 49: 10.

□ STUDY 15 Ezekiel 22

This chapter falls into three divisions: (a) a description of the sins committed within the city (verses 1–16); (b) the certainty of judgment (verses 17–22); and (c) an indictment of all classes of the community (verses 23–31).

1 Group the sins enumerated in verses 1–12 under the following two heads: (a) religious, and (b) social. Notice how, with the loss of a true conception of God, there follows the loss of filial piety, moral purity, and civic justice. How far are the sins mentioned here prevalent among us today?

2 What four classes are mentioned in verses 24–29, and what charges are made against them? What is the saddest feature of the situation, as stated in verse 30? *Cf.* verse 19 ('all become dross') and Je. 5: 1–5.

Notes

1 Verse 4. 'Your day': *i.e.*, the day of your judgment.

2 Verse 13. Striking the hands was an expression of horror. *Cf.* 21: 14, 17.

3 Verse 30 'Build up the wall': *i.e.*, act as a bastion against the inroads of wickedness.

☐ STUDY 16 Ezekiel 23

This chapter resembles chapter 16. Samaria and Jerusalem are condemned for their unfaithfulness in seeking alliances with foreign nations and their gods. Their conduct is represented in unusually realistic figures to make it appear how loathsome and repulsive it has been.

1 What is the main content of each of the four divisions of this chapter, namely verses 1–10, 11–21, 22–35, and 36–49?

2 Trace how Jerusalem walked in the way of Samaria and even exceeded her in wickedness, and therefore must drain to the dregs the same cup of judgment. What were the origins of her idolatrous tendencies, both on the historical and on the religious level (verses 8, 19, 27, 35)? What warning does this contain for God's people today?

☐ STUDY 17 Ezekiel 24

A last picture of Jerusalem before its destruction—a rusted pot set on a fire, with flesh being boiled in it. The flesh is taken out and scattered, symbolizing the dispersion of the people of the city; and the pot is then left on the fire, a symbol of the city lying waste and burned.

1 Verses 1–14. Compare what the chief men of Jerusalem said in 11: 3 (see Study 7, Question 1) with what God says here concerning the city and its people. What may we learn from this? *Cf.* 1 Thes. 5: 3; 2 Pet. 3: 4.

2 Verses 15–27. How is Ezekiel's wife described in verse 16? Yet God makes this painful experience also a means of ministry. What was it designed to demonstrate? See verses 24 and 27. Can you think of other instances where the sufferings of a servant of God have been made to serve God's design, no matter at what cost to the sufferer? *Cf.* Col. 1: 24.

Notes

1 Verse 23. The people would be too stunned by the evil tidings to take any action.

2 Verse 27. *Cf.* 3: 26, 27.

Introductory Note to Chapters 25–32

These chapters are a series of prophetic utterances against seven foreign nations. They are intended to show that the calamities which were falling on Judah were not arbitrary, nor an evidence of God's weakness, but that, on the contrary, He is supreme over all peoples and all His acts are governed by fixed moral principles which reveal His holy nature. By their position in the book they separate the prophecies that belong to the period of Ezekiel's ministry prior to the fall of Jerusalem from those that followed later. (See Introduction.)

☐ STUDY 18 Ezekiel 25 and 26

Chapter 25 contains four prophecies directed against Ammon, Moab, Edom and the Philistines respectively. Chapter 26 is a prophecy of the approaching destruction of Tyre through the armies of Nebuchadrezzar, together with a vivid description of the far-reaching effects of her overthrow.

1 In chapter 25, find four ways in which unbelievers and enemies of the truth act towards the people of God when the latter are brought low by calamity. How will such adversaries be dealt with, and why? *Cf.* Pss. 94: 1–5, 21–23; 46: 8–10; Is. 26: 9b.

2 What, according to 26: 2, was the ground of God's judgment upon Tyre? As we try to imagine the scenes described in 26: 7–14, and measure the fame and worldly greatness of Tyre by the dismay caused by her fall (15–18), what lessons may we learn? *Cf.* Je. 9: 23, 24; Lk. 12: 15–21.

Notes

1 25: 10. 'The people of the East' are the tribes of the desert. Moab and Ammon were before long overrun by the Nabataeans.

2 26: 2. Jerusalem had been as an open gate, by which commerce had been diverted from Tyre.

3 26: 6. 'Her daughters': *i.e.*, towns on the mainland dependent upon Tyre.

☐ STUDY 19 Ezekiel 27 and 28

Further prophecies concerning Tyre. In chapter 27 the city is pictured as a stately ship. Verses 5–11 give a description of the ship; verses 12–25 of her cargo; and verses 26–36 of her shipwreck and total loss, with the widespread mourning that ensued. In chapter 28 the prince of Tyre is regarded as personifying the genius or spirit of the city, and as incarnating in his person the principle of evil which animated it. The terms used concerning him (especially in verses 11–19) are such that the figure of the human ruler seems to merge into Satan himself, the originator of the sins of which Tyre was guilty.

1 Contrast men's judgment of Tyre (27: 4, 33) and Tyre's view of herself (27: 3) with God's judgment of her (28: 2–8). What was the pre-eminent sin of Tyre? *Cf.* Dn. 4: 29–32.

2 In what sense did Tyre become 'a terror' (AV 27: 35, 36)? See also 26: 21; 28: 19. To what kind of fear should such a catastrophe give rise in our own hearts? *Cf.* Dt. 17: 12, 13; Rom. 11: 20; 1 Tim. 5: 20.

3 28: 20-26 is a short prophecy against Sidon, which was closely linked with Tyre. What is said in verses 20–26 to be the twofold purpose of God's judgments (a) in relation to Himself, and (b) in relation to His people?

Notes

1 27: 36. Hissing expressed astonishment, rather like whistling today.
2 28: 3. 'Daniel': see Study 9, Note 1.

☐ STUDY 20 Ezekiel 29 and 30

The prophet's gaze is now directed towards Egypt, pictured in 29: 1–16 as a great dragon or crocodile, whose destruction is at hand. The remainder of today's portion consists of three further prophecies of similar import, namely 29: 17–20; 30: 1–19; and 30: 20–26.

1 Compare the explanation of the allegory in 29: 8–12 with the allegory itself in 29: 3–7. What are the two sins in particular which caused God's judgment to fall on Egypt? With 29: 7, *cf.* verse 16 and Is. 30: 5.

2 29: 17–21. This is a prophecy dated sixteen years after that of verses 1–16, *i.e.*, in 571 BC. It appears to indicate that Nebuchadrezzar had not gained the spoils of war at Tyre as he expected, and is now promised a recompense from the conquest of Egypt. What light does this passage throw on the way in which God treats heathen nations?

3 'Her proud might shall come down' (30: 6; *cf.* 30: 18). Why cannot anyone ultimately prosper who trusts, as Pharaoh did, in his own resources and achievements? *Cf.* Jb. 9: 4; Lk. 1: 51.

Notes

1 29: 14, 15. Egypt is not to be finally destroyed, like Tyre (26: 21; 27: 36; 28: 19), but reduced in status.
2 29: 18. A reference to the chafing of helmets and the carrying of packs.

☐ STUDY 21 Ezekiel 31 and 32

These chapters contain three more prophecies concerning Egypt. In chapter 31, Egypt is likened to a mighty cedar, whose fall causes the other trees to mourn. In 32: 1–6 the figure of the dragon or crocodile is resumed (*cf.* 29: 3–5), and in 32: 7, 8 Egypt is likened to a bright star. The imagery is very vivid, depicting the utter destruction of Pharaoh and his hosts. In 32: 17–32 the prophet in a vision follows Pharaoh and his armies into Sheol, and sees them there among others also slain by the sword who bear the shame of their lack of proper burial.

1 How does chapter 31 further enforce the lesson of chapter 30? What is the reason given for the tree's destruction, and what effect is this intended to have on other nations?

2 Observe how often in these chapters the personal pronoun 'I' occurs. Do we realize enough that God is the chief actor in the developments of history? Over what realms, in addition to that of Israel, is His dominion here asserted?

Note. 32: 17–32. This is not to be regarded as a literal description of the state of men after death, but as an imaginative picture intended to show that all who use violence and lawless might, causing terror on the earth (*cf.* verses 23ff.), shall alike meet with retribution. Pharaoh's only consolation will be in the multitude of his companions (verse 31).

For Studies 22–35 on Ezekiel see p. 385.

PSALMS 73 – 89

☐ STUDY 57 Psalm 73

Pss. 73–83 are all entitled 'of Asaph' (*cf.* 2 Ch. 35: 15; Ezr. 2: 41; 3: 10). These psalms are marked by certain characteristic features, among which may be mentioned the representation of God as Judge and also as the Shepherd of His people. They are, in the main, national psalms, and look back to the past history of Israel to draw from it encouragement and warning.

1 The problem of the prosperity of the ungodly oppressed the psalmist sorely. See verses 2, 13, 16. Real life seemed to mock the assertion of verse 1. What was the root of the psalmist's distress? See verses 3, 22; *cf.* Pr. 23: 17; Ps. 37: 1. What is the 'more excellent way'? *Cf.* 1 Cor. 13: 4; 1 Pet. 2: 1.

2 How did the psalmist discover the grossness of his error? What did he come to see with regard to the wicked (verses 17–20), and what did he find that he possessed in God (verses 23–26)? Can you honestly and enthusiastically make the confession of verse 25?

3 What may we learn from the psalmist's example (a) in verses 15–17 (for 'the sanctuary', *cf.* Pss. 63: 2, 3; 68: 35), and (b) in verse 28? Do you delight in being near to God, and in speaking not of doubts (verse 15), but of God's mighty works?

Notes

1 Verse 15. The psalmist realizes that to parade his doubt (verses 13, 14), or to speak like the wicked (verse 9), would be to betray the family of God.

2 Verse 20. The sense is, 'The wicked are like a dream when one awakes; and when you, O Lord, awake, you will despise their shadow.'

☐ STUDY 58 Psalm 74

The psalm starts in anguish, because of the ruined sanctuary. At verse 12 it changes completely into a resounding hymn of praise to God, Creator and Redeemer. But both sections contain earnest pleas for God to act on behalf of His name and of His own.

1 Consider (a) the psalmist's survey and summary of Israel's shattering defeat (verses 1–11); and (b) how he then reminds himself that God is Creator, Redeemer and King (verses 12–17). As a Christian, can you face disaster and discomfort with such an assurance about God? *Cf.* Rom. 8: 18, 28.

2 Note the boldness and the persistence of the psalmist's requests. See verses 2, 3, 10, 11, 18–23. What is the basis of his confidence? Have you learnt thus to plead in prayer both for church and nation? Note the reasons the psalmist gives why God should answer.

Note. Verses 4, 9. 'Our signs': *i.e.*, the outward signs of the worship of God had been replaced by heathen 'signs' set up by their enemies.

☐ STUDY 59 Psalms 75 and 76

Ps. 76 celebrates the deliverance of Jerusalem from the Assyrians in the reign of Hezekiah. Though we cannot say that Ps. 75 belongs to this same historical situation, its theme of thanksgiving to God is certainly relevant to the events of 701 BC.

1 In Ps. 75 what characteristics of God's judgment are mentioned? What is the psalmist's response?

2 Ps. 76 falls into four sections of three verses each. How would you summarize the contents of each section? What was God's purpose in acting in judgment?

3 How does the teaching of Christ illustrate Ps. 75: 4–7? *Cf.* Lk. 14: 7–11; Mt. 20: 20–28. Does your belief in such teaching control your ambition and your ideas about promotion?

Notes

1 75: 8. A picture of divine retribution; *cf.* Is. 51: 17; Rev. 14: 10.

2 76: 5, 6. A vivid picture of the enemy, silent and inactive in death.

3 76: 10. Even the violent acts of the wicked will be turned to God's praise.

☐ STUDY 60 Psalm 77

1 Observe in detail the depth of the psalmist's depression. What was the chief question underlying his distress? How did he find an answer to it?

2 What particular aspects of the character of God are mentioned in verses 11–20? How do these begin to resolve the psalmist's problem? Do we in times of depression similarly 'call to mind the deeds of the Lord' (*e.g.*, Rom. 5: 8)?

☐ STUDY 61 Psalm 78: 1–39

1 A nation's history may teach many different lessons. From verses 1–8 what do you consider this psalm's main purpose is? What light do these verses throw upon the necessity and importance of family religion? *Cf.* Dt. 6: 6–9, 20–25.

2 From verses 1–39 make a list of (a) God's saving acts for His people; (b) the nation's sins; (c) God's judgments. In particular, from verses 34–37, consider the difference between true and false repentance. *Cf.* Je. 29: 13. Is your life free from a similar monotonous cycle of relapses? How, according to verses 1–8, may we avoid such failure?

☐ STUDY 62 Psalm 78: 40–72

1 The detail of verses 43–51 sets the people's disobedience (verses 40–42) in bold relief. What other purpose do you think the verses had? *Cf.* Ps. 103: 2; 2 Pet. 1: 9, 12, 13.

2 What disasters did idolatry bring upon Israel? How did God in His grace come to their aid? Of what is such action a foreshadowing?

Notes

1 Verse 61. A reference to the capture of the ark; see 1 Sa. 4: 21.

2 Verses 67–69. The tent at Shiloh, in the territory of Ephraim, was not rebuilt (for the reason given in verses 58–60), but Zion was chosen instead, in the territory of Judah, as the place for God's sanctuary.

☐ STUDY 63 Psalms 79 and 80

These two psalms are national prayers in times of national disaster. In Jewish synagogue worship Ps. 79 was prescribed for use in commemoration of the destruction of the Temple in 586 BC and in AD 70. Try to recapture the sense of desolation which pervaded the nation (79: 1–4, 7, 11; 80: 12, 13), together with the feeling that exile brought dishonour to the Lord's name (79: 10; *cf.* Ezk. 36: 20).

1 Ps. 79. Note here the plea for vengeance, coupled with prayer for forgiveness and deliverance. *Cf.* Is. 35: 4; 59: 16–19; 63: 3, 4. The New Testament is no less concerned for God's glory, but its spirit is different. *Cf.*, *e.g.*, Mk. 11: 25; Rom. 12: 19–21. How do you account for this difference?

2 Ps. 80. What do the Israelites here confess concerning God's attitude towards them and His treatment of them? Where does their only hope of salvation lie? What ought we to learn from this?

Notes

1 79: 3. 'There was none to bury them': a disgrace threatened in Dt. 28: 26; and repeatedly predicted by Jeremiah (7: 33; 8: 2; 9: 22).

2 80: 1, 2. The three tribes here mentioned camped west of the tabernacle in the wilderness, and immediately followed the ark when the people were on the march. See Nu. 2: 17–24.

3 80: 17. This verse points forward to the Messiah.

□ STUDY 64 Psalms 81–83

1 Ps. 81. What does God here demand of His people (verses 1–4)? Of what does He remind them (verses 5–7, 10–12), and with what promises and practical challenge does He confront them (verses 8, 9, 13–16)?

2 Ps. 82 is a dramatic picture of the judgment and condemnation of divinely appointed judges who have failed to fulfil their office. What does God demand of such men (verses 2–4), and what is the effect upon society of their failure (verse 5)? In such circumstances, what hope is there of justice being done?

3 Ps. 83. A strong coalition of enemy nations is plotting against Israel to destroy it. On what grounds does the psalmist plead for God to act? What in particular does he ask of God, and to what end? Contrast this with the prayer of Acts 4: 29, 30. Is a prayer like the psalmist's still legitimate?

Notes

1 81: 7. 'The secret place of thunder': *i.e.*, from the midst of the thunder-cloud. *Cf.* Ex. 14: 10, 24.

2 82: 1, 6. From Jn. 10: 34, 35 it is clear that earthly judges are here referred to. They were called 'gods' and 'sons of the Most High' in virtue of their high office as dispersing the divine justice. *Cf.* Rom. 13: 3, 4.

STUDY 65 Psalm 84

1 Verses 1-4. 'Blessed are those who dwell in thy house.' Consider the significance of the language which the psalmist uses. Note particularly the names he gives to God. What was the object of his deepest delight?

2 What characteristics of the pilgrim to Zion are mentioned in verses 5–9? Whence does he derive strength to continue his journey? What is the basis of his security? What self-discipline must he practise? What are his crowning rewards (verses 10–12)?

Notes

1 Verse 5b. The meaning seems to be 'those whose hearts are set on pilgrimage' (*i.e.*, to Zion).

2 Verse 6. 'The valley of Baca': some dry and barren valley where balsam trees (baca) grow, which the travellers approach with dread only to find that the God-given rain has transformed it.

3 Verse 7. Far from being wearied by their journey the pilgrims are also strengthened by the prospect of the vision of God in Zion.

4 Verse 9. A reference to the king, the Lord's anointed, *i.e.*, the Messiah.

STUDY 66 Psalm 85

1 Verses 1–7. To what does the psalmist make appeal in his prayer, and for what does he pray? Note that his prayers are not for himself, but for God's people. Do you have any comparable conviction and concern?

2 Verses 8–13. In His answer, what blessings does God promise, and to whom? What is the guarantee of fulfilment?

Notes

1 Verse 8b. The mg. suggests that there is here an abrupt warning to God's pious ones not to 'turn back to folly'. For what is meant by 'folly', see Ps. 14: 1; Rom. 1: 21, 22.

2 Verse 9b. The 'glory' is that of the revealed presence of God. *Cf.* Ex. 40: 34; Zc. 2: 5.

STUDY 67 Psalms 86 and 87

1 Ps. 86. List (a) the psalmist's petitions, and (b) the reasons for his confidence that his prayer will be heard. Note especially in verses 8–13 the concentration of his thought on God in worship and thanksgiving. Can you pray verse 11, and mean it?

2 Ps. 87 is a kind of prophetic expansion of Ps. 86: 9. Zion is seen as the city of God's special choice and sovereign purpose. Individuals from the nations that were Israel's enemies are to become citizens of Zion. Are you one? What is the significance of the birth register,

and of being 'born there'? *Cf.* Jn. 3: 3, 5; Heb. 12: 22–24; Rev. 21: 27.

Notes

1 86: 2. 'I am godly': the adjective speaks of devotion to God, and loyalty to His covenant.

2 86: 11. 'Unite my heart to fear thy name': *cf.* Dt. 6: 4, 5; Je. 32: 39. The psalmist desires in singleness of heart and harmony of purpose to be wholly and exclusively devoted to God's worship and service.

3 87: 7. The city resounds with joy, each worshipper declaring that the one source of all his blessings is Zion and Zion's Lord.

☐ STUDY 68 Psalm 88

In some respects this psalm depicts the sufferings of the Jewish nation in exile. The Christian may find in it a picture of the sufferings of Christ. But the language of the psalm is universal, and no one specific application exhausts it; hence its continuing relevance.

1 Summarize the main features of the sufferer's distress. The sufferer cleaves to God most passionately when God seems to have removed Himself most completely. How do you account for the persistence of his faith? *Cf.* Is. 50: 10; Hab. 3: 17, 18.

2 Verses 4–6, 10–12. With the psalmist's view of death and its sequel, *cf.* Ps. 6: 5; 30: 9; Is. 38: 18. Contrast it with that of the Christian and note whence light and hope come. See 2 Tim. 1: 10; Heb. 2: 14, 15; 1 Cor. 15: 17, 18, 51–57.

☐ STUDY 69 Psalm 89: 1–37

This psalm vividly depicts the conflict of faith. In the first part (verses 1–37) the psalmist praises the Lord, who is reverenced in heaven and on earth, as the Victor over chaos, and the covenant God and Father of Israel's king and people. In the second part (verses 38–52), however, it is clear that the king has suffered a serious military reverse.

1 Verses 5–18 expand verses 1 and 2. What attributes of God are extolled? How is the blessedness of God's people described?

2 Verses 19–37 expand verses 3 and 4 concerning God's covenant. Ponder the scope, the conditions and the generosity of God's promises.

Notes

1 Verse 3. The original occasion is described in 2 Sa. 7, recalled in 2 Sa. 23: 5, and celebrated in Ps. 132: 11ff.

2 In verses 9–14 the pronouns 'thou' and 'thine' are emphatic.

3 Verse 10. Rahab was originally used to refer to the forces of chaos subdued at creation (*cf.* Jb. 26: 12). But here and in Is. 51 : 9 (*cf.* Ps. 74 : 12ff.) the imagery is used to refer to the exodus from Egypt, when God's mighty power was shown in redemption.

☐ STUDY 70 Psalm 89: 38–52

1 Notice the repeated 'thou' in verses 38–46. It is the same God of steadfast love, faithfulness and power, extolled in the earlier part of the psalm, who has brought about the downfall of the king and the desolation of the land. This constitutes the psalmist's dilemma. What bold requests for God's speedy action does he make (verses 46–51), and on what does he base them?

2 What may we learn from the psalmist's example when circumstances seem to call God's character and promises into question? How does faith survive in such situations? *Cf.* Gn. 18: 25; Rom. 11: 29, 33; Phil. 1: 6.

Note. Verse 52 is a doxology to close Book III of the Psalms.

For Studies 71–84 on the Psalms see p. 409.

EZEKIEL 33 - 48

Introductory Note to Chapters 33–39

These chapters all belong to the second period of the prophet's ministry after the fall of Jerusalem (see Introduction and Analysis). The only mention of a date is 33: 21, but the prophecies all presuppose that God's judgment upon the guilty city and nation, long predicted, has come to pass.

☐ STUDY 22 Ezekiel 33

The prophet had known from the first that part of his commission was to be a watchman (*cf.* 3: 16–21), but now the time had come to put it into practice: for in the new era that was dawning, only those who individually repented and returned to God would live.

1 In what terms does Ezekiel express the need for repentance? What kind of behaviour is expected of the wicked man when he repents? *Cf.* Acts 26: 20; Rev. 2: 5.

2 Compare the two current sayings quoted in verses 10 and 24. Observe *where* they were current, and how the one is despairing, the other confident. What is God's answer in each case?

3 Why did the prophet suddenly become more bold to speak, and the people more curious to hear his words? See verses 30–33. What, however, was lacking in their new interest? *Cf.* Mt. 7: 26, 27.

☐ STUDY 23 Ezekiel 34

The new era will be different from what has gone before, because of a change of shepherd, *i.e.*, ruler.

1 What, according to verses 1–10, was the inherent vice of the rulers of the past, which brought disaster upon the nation? Contrast their methods (verses 4–6) with those of God (verses 11–16). *Cf.* 1 Pet. 5: 1–4.

2 What blessings are declared in verses 23–31 as following the coming of the Messiah? Interpreting them spiritually, what may we learn from these verses concerning God's gifts to us in Christ? *Cf.* Ps. 23; Heb. 13: 20, 21.

☐ STUDY 24 Ezekiel 35: 1 – 36: 15

In this section the prophet declares that the new era will be better than the past, because of the greater fertility of the land. When he uttered this prophecy, the land of Israel seemed ruined. Edom (Mount Seir) was seeking to obtain possession (35: 10; 36: 5), and the mountains of Israel lay desolate (36: 4). The prophet declares, first a judgment upon Edom (chapter 35), and then a return of Israel to enjoy times of unprecedented prosperity (36: 1–15).

1 Chapter 35. What are the three sins of Edom, mentioned in verses 5 and 10, for which they will be judged? Notice how frequently the punishment foretold exactly matches the Edomites' sin, *e.g.*, verses 5 and 9; verse 6; verses 14, 15. How does Ezekiel show that even in their hour of judgment God still identifies Himself with His people, Israel?

2 Summarize the blessings promised to Israel in 36: 8–15. If you interpret the restored land as a picture of our inheritance in Christ, what spiritual blessings are typified in these verses?

☐ STUDY 25 Ezekiel 36: 16–38

1 Consider carefully in this remarkable passage the following points: (a) why the Lord cast the people into exile (verses 16–19); (b) why He brought them back (verses 20–24); (c) the change wrought in their moral and spiritual condition (verses 25–31). Reflect how closely the prophet's teaching here anticipates the New Testament revelation of the steps by which God transforms a sinner into a saint. See particularly Rom. 3, 5, 6 and 8.

2 How will the change in the people and their restored prosperity affect the surrounding nations? See verses 35, 36 and *cf.* Jn. 17: 21, 23.

Notes

1 Verse 20. 'They profaned my holy name': because the nations, seeing them cast out, concluded their God could not protect them. *Cf.* Ps. 42: 10.

2 Verse 26. 'Heart of stone': *cf.* 2: 4; 3: 7; Zc. 7: 12. 'A heart of flesh': *i.e.*, sensitive to the divine Word.

☐ STUDY 26 Ezekiel 37

1 Why were the people unable to believe Ezekiel's prophecies of restoration and blessing? See verse 11. Did the vision of verses 1–10 show that things were not so bad as or worse than they seemed? Yet what happened, and why?

2 Notice that the regeneration of Israel came in two stages (verses 7–10). What would this have signified to Ezekiel? What part did he have to play in the change that took place? Are the spiritually dead coming to life as a result of your witness and praying?

3 Verses 15–28 are a glorious picture of the purified, restored and reunited Israel. Note the five great features of the Messianic kingdom described in verses 24–27. What light does this passage throw upon the conditions and blessings of Christian unity?

☐ STUDY 27 Ezekiel 38

In this chapter and the next the prophet foresees in the far distant future an invasion of Israel by nations lying beyond the circle of those with which Israel hitherto has had to do. They, too, must learn that the God of Israel alone is God, and they will learn it through meeting His power as they seek to plunder His land, and through being brought by Him to total defeat. Read Rev. 20: 7–10 in conjunction with this chapter.

1 In what two different ways are the causes of Gog's invasion described? Contrast verses 4 and 16 with verses 10–12. And yet may not all these verses describe one and the same cause? *Cf.* Rom. 9: 17, 18.

2 *Cf.* verses 18–23 with 37: 25–28. In what two ways will God bring the nations to know that He is God alone? *Cf.* Rom. 1: 16–18; 9: 22, 23; 11: 17–22.

Notes

1 Verse 2. The name 'Gog' is probably Ezekiel's own invention, formed by removing the first letter from the place-name Magog. It is pointless to try to identify these nations with modern states: they were simply tribes on the fringe of the known world in Ezekiel's day which he uses for these apocalyptic pronouncements.

2 Verse 13. These are merchant nations, stirred to excitement by Gog's invasion.

☐ STUDY 28 Ezekiel 39

1 A further prophecy against Gog emphasizes the completeness of his overthrow. In what three ways is this brought out in verses 9–20, and what attributes of God's character are thereby revealed (verses 21–29)?

2 What is meant by the expression 'I hid my face from them' (verse 23)? *Cf.* Dt. 31: 17; Pss. 30: 7; 104: 29; Is. 8: 17; 64: 7. Consider the great blessing that is contained in the promise of verse 29.

Introductory Note to Chapters 40–48

These chapters describe a vision given to Ezekiel some twelve years after the prophecies of chapters 33–37 (*cf.* 40: 1 with 33: 21). In these earlier prophecies he had declared to the exiles in Babylon God's purpose to restore Israel to the holy land as a nation purified, redeemed and re-united. The question must have been much in the prophet's mind how this restored community would be fashioned in its religious and political life; and in these chapters God gives to the prophet the answer to his questionings. There is first a description of the sanctuary, to which Jehovah will come in glory, and in which He will take up His dwelling (40–43); second, regulations with regard to the ministers of the sanctuary, and to the 'prince' who shall rule over the people; and third, the boundaries of the land are defined, and the territories of the tribes.

The question is sometimes asked whether the vision will be literally fulfilled. Why, however, should we suppose this, any more than that the vision of chapter 1 is a literal portrait of the divine Being? It is true that the prophets generally associate great changes in nature with the advent of 'the day of the Lord', and this is affirmed also in the New Testament (see, *e.g.*, Rom. 8: 21), but this is not to say that the vision which Ezekiel saw will find literal

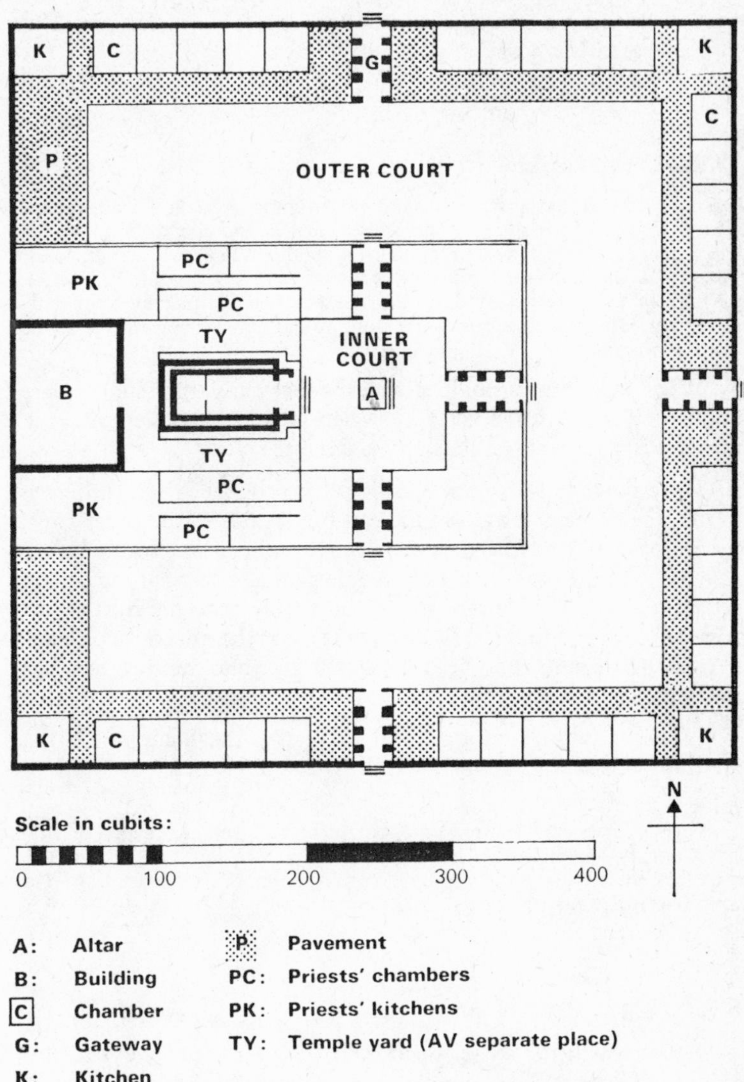

A: Altar
B: Building
C Chamber
G: Gateway
K: Kitchen
P Pavement
PC: Priests' chambers
PK: Priests' kitchens
TY: Temple yard (AV separate place)

DIAGRAM 1 Sketch Plan of the Temple Area

fulfilment. It is rather a setting forth, within the limits of Old Testament symbolism, of fundamental principles concerning God's relation to His redeemed and sanctified people when He dwells in their midst in His glory.

☐ STUDY 29 Ezekiel 40: 1–47

Having been cast into a trance and brought in spirit to the holy land, Ezekiel saw on the top of a high mountain what at first he thought to be a city but was in fact the Temple, with its courts and buildings. It was, however, a new Temple. While the sanctuary itself was similar to that of Solomon's Temple, the surroundings were very different. The prophet was met by a heavenly messenger, who had a measuring-tape of flax and a measuring-rod, and who acted as his guide.

1 What two responsibilities did the heavenly messenger place upon the prophet? See verse 4. When judged by these standards, how far is your own Bible study a success?

2 With the aid of diagram 1, follow the prophet's route as he was shown the outer gateway on the east (verses 6–16), the outer court (verses 17–19), and the gateways on the north and south (verses 20–27); then the inner court on a higher level, also with three gateways (verses 28–37). In the inner court, alongside the north gate, were a chamber and tables (verses 38–43), and there were two chambers for the priests, one near the north gate and another near the south gate (verses 44–47).

3 Note the symmetry of the ground plan of the Temple. Has this anything to teach us about God?

Notes

1 Verse 5. Two cubits were in use, one being eighteen inches long and the other twenty-one inches—a 'handbreadth' extra. The longer cubit was that used by Ezekiel. The measuring-reed would therefore have been 10 ft. 6 in.

2 Verse 12. 'A barrier': *i.e.*, a projecting wall.

☐ STUDY 30 Ezekiel 40: 48 – 41: 26

1 Follow with the aid of diagrams 1 and 2 the prophet's further examination of the Temple, as he comes first to the sanctuary itself, with its vestibule and two pillars (40: 48, 49), holy place ('nave', 41: 1), most holy place ('inner room', 41: 3, 4), and side chambers or cells built in three storeys (41: 5–11). The *interior* of the sanctuary is described in 41: 15b–26.

2 Note that Ezekiel, as a priest (1: 3; *cf.* 44: 16), entered into the

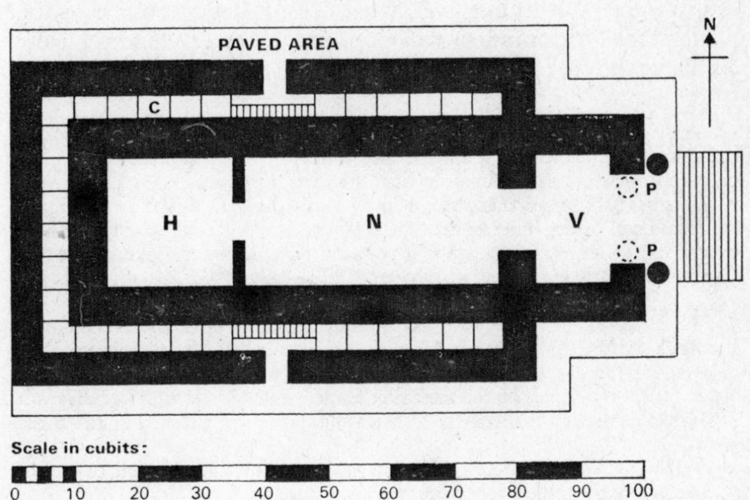

C: Side-chambers (41:5-7)

P: Pillars (40:49): position not certain

V: Vestibule (40:48, 49)

N: Nave, or holy place (41:1, 2)

H: Inner room, or holy of holies (41:3, 4)

For the paved area, or platform, see 41:8-11.

DIAGRAM 2 Sketch Plan of the Sanctuary

vestibule and the holy place, but not into the most holy place (41: 3, 4). Why did he not enter the most holy place? Contrast our privileges in Christ. See Heb. 9: 6–9, 24; 10: 19–22.

3 There were palm-trees both in the inner sanctuary (41: 18–20), and also on the gate-posts of the outer and inner courts (40: 16, 22, 31). So also in Solomon's Temple (see 1 Ki. 6: 29; 7: 36). Applying this to the temple of our lives, what does it suggest both as to the hidden life of communion with God, and the outer life seen by all? *Cf.* Ps. 92: 12–14; Je. 17: 7, 8.

Notes

1 Verse 7. The meaning is that at each storey the walls facing the cells were made less thick, to leave a ledge for the beams to rest on, and thus the rooms on each floor were a little broader than the rooms below.

2 Verse 11b. The sanctuary stood upon a raised platform six cubits higher than the level of the inner court (verse 8), and occupied the whole platform except for a marginal strip running round three sides on the outer edge (see diagram 2). This narrow strip is what is here called 'the part that was left free'.

3 Verses 12–14. Another strip of ground, at the level of the inner court, encompassed the sanctuary platform, and is here called 'the temple yard'. It marked off the sanctuary from other buildings nearby (see diagram 1, TY). One of these buildings, on the west side, is mentioned in verse 12 (see diagram 1, B), but its use is not specified. Other buildings are mentioned in 42: 1–14; 46: 19, 20.

4 Verse 22. The table here spoken of, which looked like an altar of wood, was probably the table of shewbread.

☐ STUDY 31 Ezekiel 42: 1 – 43: 12

This section opens with a description of other buildings in the inner court (42: 1–12), together with the purposes they are intended to serve (42: 13, 14). See diagram 1. The measurements of the outer wall, and of the whole Temple area are then stated (42: 15–20). In 43: 1–9 the prophet sees in a vision the glory of the Lord returning by the east gate, the gate by which, years before, he had seen Him depart (11: 1, 22, 23).

1 Observe the emphasis on the *holiness* of God. See especially 42: 13, 14; 43: 7–9, 11, 12. How was the holiness of the Temple to be safeguarded, in order to bear witness to this truth about the Lord?

2 How, for us, have the barriers been removed that separate us from the Holy One? And on what conditions may we draw nigh to God and render His acceptable service? *Cf.* 2 Cor. 7: 1; Heb. 7: 24; 10: 14, 19; 1 Pet. 2: 5.

Note. 43: 7–9. In Solomon's Temple there was no walled-off outer court separating the Temple from the unconsecrated ground without (*cf.* 42: 20). The Temple, royal palace and other buildings all stood together in one great enclosure, and the burial-ground of the kings was not far distant.

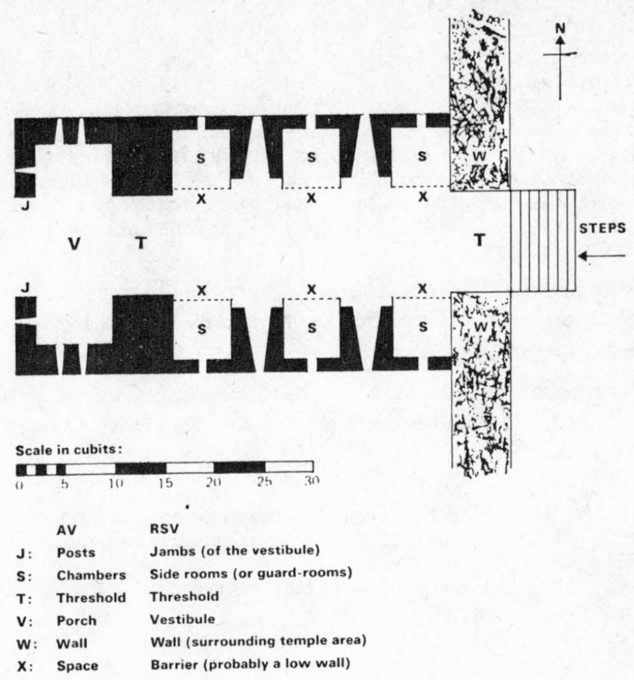

DIAGRAM 3 Sketch Plan of a Typical Gatehouse

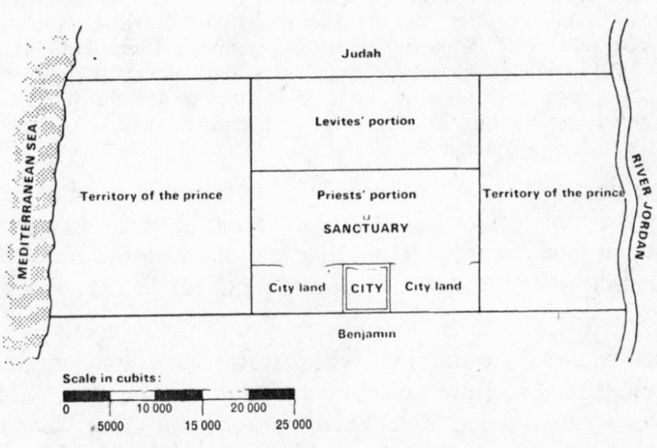

DIAGRAM 4 Apportionment of the Land

☐ STUDY 32 Ezekiel 43: 13 – 44: 31

This section opens with a description of the great altar in the centre of the inner court, together with the sacrifices by which it is to be cleansed and purified (43: 13–27). The altar rested upon a square base and was built of three square blocks of stone, each smaller than the one below, so as to leave at each level a projecting ledge. The uppermost block had four horns and was twelve cubits square. It was reached by steps on the east side. Chapter 44 lays down three ordinances, the first concerning the use of the east gate (verses 1–3), the second concerning the Levites (verses 4–14), and the third concerning the priests (verses 15–31).

1 Why had the altar to be cleansed before the offerings made upon it were acceptable to God? See 43: 27 and *cf.* Lv. 16: 18, 19; Col. 1: 19–22; Heb. 9: 23.

2 What lessons are taught in 44: 10–16 regarding God's judgments upon faithful and unfaithful service? *Cf.* Lk. 19: 17; 2 Cor. 5: 9, 10; 1 Tim. 1:12.

Notes

1 44: 7, 8. It had evidently been the custom before the exile to allow foreigners to officiate in the sanctuary and in its ministry, even though it may have been only in menial duties.

2 44: 19. They shall not bring their holy garments into contact with the people. *Cf.* Ex. 30: 29.

☐ STUDY 33 Ezekiel 45 and 46

Not only was the Temple different in many respects from that of Solomon, but the whole land was to be divided up in a new way. A broad strip of land, extending right across the country from the Mediterranean to the Jordan and including the Temple, was to be set apart for the Lord (45: 1–8). How it was to be used is shown in diagram 4. Verses 9–17 lay down regulations as regards weights and measures, and the dues to be paid by the people to the prince. The remainder is chiefly concerned with the feasts and offerings (45: 18 – 46: 15), but at the end are two notes, one about the right of the prince to bestow part of his territory upon his sons or servants (46: 16–18), and the other about rooms in the Temple courts to be used as kitchens for boiling the flesh of the sacrifices (46: 19–24).

1 How does 45: 8–12 show that the holiness which Jehovah requires is not only religious but moral? What light do these verses throw upon God's attitude to injustice and oppression, and to commercial dishonesty? *Cf.* 46: 18; Lv. 19: 35, 36; Pr. 11: 1; 1 Pet. 1: 14–16.

2 What is said three times in 45: 15–20 to be the purpose of the sacrifices? If they had not been offered, could the people have had any assurance in drawing nigh to God? What in the New Testament is revealed as the true ground of atonement? *Cf.* Heb. 10: 4–10; 1 Jn. 2: 1, 2.

Notes

1 45: 1. The holy district consisted of the area marked on diagram 4. 25,000 cubits was about eight miles.

2 45: 10–12. There was a vast amount of local variation in ancient Israel regarding weights and measures, and this was the cause of much commercial malpractice. Ezekiel is here demanding in God's name strict standardization.

3 46: 19 defines the positions of the priests' kitchens, as verses 21–24 do the position of the people's kitchens. See diagram 1.

☐ STUDY 34 Ezekiel 47: 1–12

The prophet is shown another aspect of what it means when God dwells in the midst of His redeemed and reconciled people.

1 Notice particularly where the river comes from. What may those who seek reform, whether it be social, political, or moral, learn from the revelation here given to Ezekiel? *Cf.* Ps. 46: 4; Is. 33: 21; Rev. 22: 1, 2.

2 What is symbolized by the increasing depth and extent of the waters? How long is it since you first came to Christ, and became a temple for His indwelling? Are the living waters flowing from your life in increasing measure? If not, what is wrong? *Cf.* Jn. 7: 37–39.

3 The river of life sought out the most desolate and seemingly irrecoverable region in all the land, and brought life and healing. Recall how this was also Christ's method. *Cf.* Mk. 2: 16, 17; Lk. 15: 1, 2; 19: 10; 23: 42, 43. What have these things to say to us?

Notes

1 Verse 1. The waters flowed from the sanctuary across the inner court, south of the altar, and appeared on the right-hand side of the outer east gate.

2 Verse 8. 'The sea': *i.e.*, the Dead Sea, in which nothing can live.

3 Verse 12. *Cf.* Ps. 1: 3; Je. 17: 8; Rev. 22: 2.

☐ STUDY 35 Ezekiel 47: 13 – 48: 35

Finally the prophet is shown in vision the boundaries of the land (47: 13–21) and the portions of the tribes (48: 1–29). The land was to be divided into parallel zones, running from the west coast to the Jordan.

1 What gospel principle is foreshadowed in 47: 22, 23? *Cf.* Eph. 2: 11–13, 19; Col. 3: 11.

2 How many tribes had their portion north of the broad zone assigned to the Lord in 45: 1 (see diagram 4, p. 393), and how many south of it? Which tribes had portions immediately adjacent to the central zone containing the sanctuary? What do you think was the reason for this privilege?

3 What does the new name of the city reveal about God's purpose in relation to His people? Looking back upon the vision as a whole, write down the main lessons which it teaches, and consider how these stand out still more clearly in the light of the revelation given us in Christ.

COLOSSIANS

Introduction

Colossae was one of a group of three cities (of which the other two were Laodicea and Hierapolis; *cf.* Col. 4: 13), situated in the Lycus valley about a hundred miles inland from Ephesus. Paul had not visited these cities himself (2: 1), but was given a full account of the situation at Colossae by Epaphras, who had founded these churches (1: 7; 2: 5; 4: 12, 13).

While there was cause for thanksgiving (1: 3–5; 2: 5), yet there was ground also for deep concern because of the dissemination of a plausible false teaching, which, dressed in the garb of an enlightened philosophy (2: 8), claimed to be a higher form of Christianity. Would they have full emancipation from evil? Then they must observe circumcision and practise a strict discipline. Would they have access to the divine presence? Then they must worship angelic beings, by whose mediation they might draw nearer to the throne of God. No doubt these teachers gave Jesus a high place, but it was not the supreme place.

Paul's answer is to set forth Christ Jesus as pre-eminent in every sphere, and as all-sufficient for the believer's need. This is the main theme of the letter, which stands out among all Paul's Epistles for the fullness of its revelation about the Person and work of Christ. It contains also in brief compass a wealth of practical instruction for Christian living.

Analysis

1: 1–8	Greeting and thanksgiving.
1: 9–14	Petition.
1: 15–20	The pre-eminence of the Son of God.
1: 21–23	The Colossians share in the blessings of the gospel.
1: 24 – 2: 7	Paul's part in God's plan.
2: 8–23	Answer to the Colossian heresy: the all-sufficiency of Christ as Saviour.
3: 1 – 4: 6	A new pattern of life.
	3: 1–17 Practical implications of participation in Christ.
	3: 18 – 4: 1 Acting rightly in household relationships.
	4: 2–6 Prayer and witness.
4: 7–18	Personal references, greetings, *etc.*

☐ **STUDY 1 Colossians 1: 1–14**

1 Of what blessings which God has made ours in Christ does the gospel speak? What results did this gospel produce in the experience of the Colossians who heard it? Have I made as much progress as they had?

2 In his prayer for the Colossians, for what further progress in the things of Christ does the apostle ask? Carefully note the items in Paul's prayer. In which of these directions do I most desire or need myself to make progress?

☐ **STUDY 2 Colossians 1: 15–23**

1 What is revealed in verses 15–20 concerning our Lord's relation to God, to creation, and to the church? What practical effects should this revelation have on our Christian faith and life?

2 Verses 21–23. From what condition, at what cost, and with what goal in view has Christ rescued us? What is required of those who desire fully to enjoy these benefits?

☐ **STUDY 3 Colossians 1: 24 – 2: 7**

1 In 1: 24–29 what does Paul say about (a) his sufferings (*cf.* Acts 9: 15, 16); (b) his commission; (c) his theme; and (d) the method, aim and inspiration of his ministry?

2 2: 1–7. What is essential if Christians are to stand firm in the faith and not be misled? How may they gain encouragement to continue and become more fully established? Do you (a) covet such progress for yourself; (b) pray like this for others?

Notes

1 1: 28. The false teaching suggested that full participation in knowledge and consequent maturity was restricted to a select few. The gospel makes it possible 'in Christ' for all alike—for 'every man'.

2 1: 29; 2: 1. 'Striving': a metaphor from the Greek games, a word used again in 4: 12. It describes here earnest conflict, straining every nerve, in prayer.

□ STUDY 4 Colossians 2: 8–23

1 What four defects does Paul find in the false teaching (verse 8)? In what ways does he then set forth Christ as the one absolutely sufficient Saviour (verses 9–15)? List the treasures and the benefits which are ours in Him.

2 Verses 16–23. It is quite clear that the false teachers stressed (a) the observance of holy days, (b) the worship of angels, and (c) ascetic practices. On what grounds does the apostle show all these to be mistaken, useless and hurtful as a means of salvation?

3 Verses 11–15. How is the way in which Christians have been 'circumcised' distinguished from the rite practised by the Jews? By what ceremony has Jewish circumcision been replaced for Christians? How is its symbolism related to the death and resurrection of Christ? *Cf.* Rom. 6: 1–14.

Note. Verses 11, 12. 'By putting off the body of flesh': the false teachers advocated the rite of circumcision as a means of purification. Paul's answer is that in the believer's identification with Christ in His death and resurrection the whole body which has been governed by fleshly desires is put off, and a new man emerges. This far more than fulfils all that the rite of circumcision signified.

□ STUDY 5 Colossians 3: 1–17

1 Verses 1–11. What results, (a) positive and (b) negative, should follow from being 'raised with Christ'; in other words, what should the experience make us (a) do, and (b) stop doing?

2 Verses 12–17. Make a list from these verses of the divinely-intended characteristics of active Christian living; and prayerfully examine your own living in the light of these standards.

☐ **STUDY 6 Colossians 3: 18 – 4: 18**

1 3: 18 – 4: 1. Observe how, in giving directions about the life of a Christian household, Paul urges 'upon each party its own duties and the other's rights'. What overriding concerns should influence all alike, and why?

2 4: 2–6. List the activities here demanded as essential (a) to prayer, and (b) to our relations with non-Christians. In my own practice of Christian self-discipline, to which of these points do I need to give more attention? Can I learn from verses 3, 4, 12 how to pray for others?

Note. 3: 21. 'Provoke': by excessive fault-finding and little or no praise.

PHILEMON

Introduction

The Epistle to Philemon contains no systematic presentation of doctrine. It has one avowed purpose—to ask Philemon to receive back a runaway slave who had been in his service and had absconded with his money. The man had come into contact with Paul in Rome and had been converted and transformed into a new man. It was not easy for Paul to let him go; it was harder still for Onesimus to face his former master. But it was hardest of all for Philemon to take him back. These men were Christians, however, and that made all the difference. The letter is one of great charm, tact, graciousness and love, and provides an unforgettable picture of Christianity in action. Though no place-names are mentioned, it is clear that the letter was written at the same time as that to the Colossians.

☐ **STUDY Philemon**

1 What light does this letter throw upon Paul himself? Is he putting into practice Col. 3: 12–14? Consider closely the appeal he makes and the arguments by which he reinforces it.

2 What had happened to Onesimus (whose name means 'useful' or 'profitable') to make him start living up to his name? Has acceptance of the Christian faith made us useful (a) to the person who led us to Christ; (b) to those who are our employers, or in a comparable position?

EZRA & NEHEMIAH

Introduction

The books of Ezra and Nehemiah continue the history of the Israelites from the point reached at the end of 2 Chronicles. The two books are closely linked together and cover between them a space of about one hundred years, from the first year of the reign of Cyrus, king of Persia (538 BC), to soon after the thirty-second year of Artaxerxes (432 BC). Other books of Scripture belonging to this period are Haggai, Zechariah, Malachi and Esther.

The events recorded in the books of Ezra and Nehemiah gather round three periods, as follows:

First Period (Ezr. 1–6), from the first return of exiles under Zerubbabel (or Sheshbazzar) and Jeshua the high priest (536 BC) to the completion of the Temple (515 BC). It is to be noted that, though these events are recorded in the book of Ezra, they occurred more than sixty years before Ezra himself appeared on the scene.

Second Period (Ezr. 7–10), describing the return of a second large company of exiles under Ezra, with some account of Ezra's ministry in Jerusalem (458 BC).

Third Period (Ne. 1–13), describing the arrival of Nehemiah as governor (444 BC), and his building of the city walls, together with his joint activity with Ezra.

Ezra and Nehemiah were men raised up of God to render invaluable service at a critical time in Israel's history. Ezra was a priest of the house of Aaron, a man of outstanding piety, a diligent student and capable teacher of the law of God, and a zealous reformer. Nehemiah was a public servant and a true patriot, who devoted himself to the improvement of the moral and material condition of his country. He combined watchfulness with prayerfulness, and energetic activity with conscious dependence upon God. While both men rendered notable service, the work of Ezra was the more enduring, for he gave to the law of God a place of supreme authority in the life of the people.

Analysis Ezra

1:1 – 2:70	The return of exiles to Jerusalem to rebuild the Temple.
3:1–13	The altar erected, and the Temple foundations laid.
4:1–24	The work opposed, and made to cease.
5:1–17	The resumption of the work, promoted by the prophets Haggai and Zechariah.
6:1–22	The completion of the Temple.
7:1 – 8:36	After an interval of nearly sixty years, Ezra's journey to Jerusalem in 458 BC.
9:1 – 10:44	Reformation, including expulsion of foreign wives, promoted by Ezra.

☐ STUDY 1 Ezra 1 and 2

1 First, what definite acts of God can be seen in bringing about this return to Jerusalem? With 1:1, *cf.* Je. 29:10. Then fill in the outline given here, by trying to imagine the feelings and actions of the people concerned. Note, *e.g.*, 1:5, 6; 1:7–11; the links with specific 'home towns' and positions; the claims in 2:59–63; the scene in 2:64–67; the generosity and contentment of 2:68–70.

2 In the light of these two chapters meditate on Jos. 23:14.

☐ STUDY 2 Ezra 3

1 As background to verses 1–6, see Lv. 23:23–43. What were the motives and purposes in the hearts of the returned exiles at this time?

2 In what further ways was the Lord put central in this settling-down period? Consider what challenge this study presents to you personally.

☐ STUDY 3 Ezra 4

1 Is not co-operation with others in work for God most desirable? Why then did the Jews refuse to co-operate with those who claimed to share their faith and who offered to help them to achieve their great spiritual objective? *Cf.* 2 Ki. 17: 24, 32, 33. See also Mt. 7: 15; and contrast 3 Jn. 8 with 2 Jn. 11.

2 What was the reaction of the frustrated adversaries? *Cf.* Am. 7: 10; Lk. 23: 2; Acts 17: 7 for similar incidents. What price did Zerubbabel and his fellow-Jews have to pay for their faithfulness? Do you know of any modern parallels? Note Eph. 6: 18–20.

Notes

1 Verses 1–3. 'The proposal to unite in building the temple was a political move; for in old-world ideas, co-operation in temple-building was incorporation in national unity. The calculation, no doubt, was that if the returning exiles could be united with the much more numerous Samaritans, they would soon be absorbed in them' (Maclaren).

2 Verse 5. 'Until the reign of Darius': *cf.* verse 24. It was a period of about sixteen years.

3 Verses 6–24. Ahasuerus and Artaxerxes are kings who succeeded Darius (*cf.* 7: 1). This indicates that these verses refer to a later period than do verses 1–5, and this is confirmed by the fact that the letters of verses 11–16 and 17–22 concern the rebuilding of the *city* of Jerusalem, not of the Temple. Some think the passage belongs chronologically to the time between Ezr. 10 and Ne. 1.

☐ STUDY 4 Ezra 5 and 6

1 When the work of rebuilding the Temple had ceased for many years (4: 24), by what various means did God cause it to begin again and bring about the fulfilment of His purpose? How does dedication strengthen faith and give guidance for prayer? *Cf.* Gn. 50: 20; Pr. 21: 1; Hg. 1: 14; 1 Tim. 2: 2.

2 Note the joy, dedication and worship when the task was completed (6: 16–22). *Cf.* Jn. 17: 4; Acts 14: 26; 20: 24; Col. 4: 17; 2 Tim. 4: 7; Rev. 3: 2.

☐ STUDY 5 Ezra 7

This chapter begins the second period covered by this book (see Introduction). Some sixty years have elapsed since the end of chapter 6.

1 What do we learn about Ezra from this chapter? Note particularly the order of the aims in verse 10, and consider the evidence which shows that he accomplished these aims. Have you any similar aims?

2 What called forth the doxology in verses 27 and 28? *Cf.* 2 Cor. 3: 5.

☐ STUDY 6 Ezra 8

1 How many males, all told, were with Ezra? These, with women and children (verse 21), would make a large company. They had also their goods and provision for the way, many precious vessels and much silver and gold. The journey was long (7: 9) and dangerous (8: 31). Would it have been wrong for Ezra to ask the king for an escort? *Cf.* Ne. 2: 9. Why did he not do so? Are we as careful as he to live out what we profess?

2 From Ezra's actions before setting out, what may we learn regarding undertaking work for God? See especially verses 15–20, 21–23, 24–30, 33–35, 36; and contrast Jos. 9: 14; Is. 31 : 1 ; Je. 48: 10a; Mt. 25: 3.

☐ STUDY 7 Ezra 9 and 10

1 For the background to this incident see Dt. 7: 1–4. In what ways had the people of God sinned? In what ways is it possible for Christians to commit similar sin today?

2 What can we learn from this chapter about (a) the responsibilities of leadership; (b) prayer and confession; (c) God's faithfulness; (d) the cost of repenting?

Analysis Nehemiah

1: 1–11	The distress of the Jews in Jerusalem. Nehemiah's prayer.
2: 1–10	Artaxerxes sends Nehemiah to Jerusalem.
2: 11–20	Nehemiah stirs up the people to rebuild the walls of Jerusalem.
3: 1–32	The apportionment of the work. List of helpers.
4: 1 – 6: 14	The work continued in spite of opposition and difficulties. Nehemiah's vigorous and exemplary leadership.

6:15 – 7:4	The completion of the walls. Provision for the protection of the city.
7:5–73	Register of those who returned with Zerubbabel.
8:1–18	Public reading and exposition of the law. Celebration of the Feast of Tabernacles.
9:1–38	Corporate repentance and confession.
10:1–39	A covenant to walk in God's law, publicly signed and sealed.
11:1 – 12:26	Lists of those who dwelt in Jerusalem.
12:27–47	Dedication of the city walls. Provision for the regular Temple services.
13:1–31	Separation from other nations. Reforms carried out by Nehemiah on the occasion of his second visit to Jerusalem.

☐ STUDY 1 Nehemiah 1

1 How long did Nehemiah brood over the news about Jerusalem before he took action (see Note 1 below)? Note the sequence of events—one which is often seen when God calls His servants to a particular task.

2 What can we learn from the example of Nehemiah's prayer? Note his attitude, his knowledge of the Scriptures, his grounds for expecting prayer to be answered. Dt. 7; 9–12; 29; 30 provide a background to the prayer.

Notes

1 Verse 1. The month Chislev corresponds to our November–December, and Nisan (2:1) to our March–April.

2 Verse 11. 'Cupbearer': a high official, who had the duty of tasting wine before it was handed to the king, lest it should have been poisoned.

☐ STUDY 2 Nehemiah 2

1 What is the order of events following Nehemiah's prayer? What difficulty did he have to face at each stage?

2 What light does the chapter throw on Nehemiah's secret communion with God? On what grounds was he confident that God would prosper him in his work? Are such communion and confidence lacking in your life?

Notes

1 Verse 3. Nehemiah had probably broken court etiquette in letting his grief be seen in the king's presence.

2 Verse 10. 'Sanballat': an important official, probably governor of Samaria. Tobiah may have been his secretary.

☐ STUDY 3 Nehemiah 3

1 Contrast the busy scenes of this chapter with the picture of the walls and gates lying desolate, broken and burned, in 2: 13, 14. What brought about the change? (Examine, if possible, a plan of the city at this time.)

2 Note how all classes in the city took part in the work, each being assigned his special place and task. What may we learn from this chapter of the value of (a) thorough organization, and (b) willing co-operation on the part of all?

Notes

1 Verse 5. The word 'Lord' should probably be 'lord', the reference being to Nehemiah. For the metaphor see Je. 27: 12.

2 The *Century Bible* divides the chapter as follows: verses 1–5, the north and north-west wall; verses 6–12, the west wall; verses 13, 14, the south wall and gates; verses 15–27, the south-east wall and gates; verses 28–32, the north-east wall.

☐ STUDY 4 Nehemiah 4

1 The successful progress of the work brought increasing opposition. Picture the characters concerned in the various scenes. What kinds of discouragement did Nehemiah meet, and how did he deal with each?

2 In verses 19–23 notice how Nehemiah shared in the hard work. Where did he plan to be if fighting broke out? What does this teach us about leadership?

☐ STUDY 5 Nehemiah 5

1 What social evil did Nehemiah put right (see verses 1–13)? And how did he do it?

2 What features of his conduct made Nehemiah an excellent governor? Are we developing similar characteristics?

3 What considerations ought to keep God's people from doing some things which others do as a matter of course? *Cf.* verse 15 and 1 Cor. 8: 13.

Note. Verses 1–5. The wealthier Jews were evidently demanding repayment at high interest of money lent by them to their poorer brethren, and were seizing the lands and property, and even the persons of the debtors whenever their demands were not met.

□ STUDY 6 Nehemiah 6

1 Nehemiah's enemies now tried intrigue. The proposal to confer together is often an attractive one. What made Nehemiah persistently refuse it? Contrast Eve's folly in discussing the question raised by the serpent (Gn. 3: 1–5). Do you ever parley with questions that should never be allowed consideration?

2 What were the special subtleties of the attempts to ensnare Nehemiah? Notice how Nehemiah's singleness of purpose and loyalty to God were as a shield about him. What may we learn from this?

Note. Verse 5. 'An open letter': so that others besides Nehemiah might see its contents.

□ STUDY 7 Nehemiah 7

1 What further steps did Nehemiah take in ensuring an orderly life in Jerusalem? Why was Hananiah put in charge of Jerusalem? Remembering that you may be called to responsibility in your work for God, what are you doing to develop these same qualities?

2 What makes a register of names so important? See verses 64, 65; and *cf.* Rev. 20: 15; 21: 27; Lk. 10: 20.

Notes

1 Verse 2. The 'he' refers to Hananiah. Possibly the appointment of two men in charge of the city means, as in 3: 9, 12, that each was ruler of half the district of Jerusalem.

2 Verses 64, 65; *cf.* Ezr. 2: 62, 63. The need was for a priest able to obtain guidance to decide whether these men were entitled to enjoy privileges as priests or not. For an example of the way in which Urim and Thummim were used, see 1 Sa. 14: 41.

□ STUDY 8 Nehemiah 8

1 Chapters 8, 9 and 10 describe a remarkable revival. What was its first manifestation, and what further characteristics developed from this?

2 Consider how great a change of heart had taken place since before the exile. *Cf.* Je. 11: 6–8; 32: 36–40; Ne. 1: 5–11. How are these verses an illustration of Ps. 119: 71 and Heb. 12: 11?

Notes

1 Verse 10. 'Send portions . . .': *cf.* Dt. 16: 11, 14; Est. 9: 19–22.

2 Verse 17. The Feast of Tabernacles had been observed (see, *e.g.*, 2 Ch. 8: 13), but not, it seems, the making of booths.

☐ STUDY 9 Nehemiah 9: 1–21

1 What marks do you find here of a genuine repentance? *Cf.* 2 Cor. 7:10, 11.

2 Meditate upon God's great kindness and many mercies, in spite of great provocation, as seen in this passage. How much cause have you for similar recollection, repentance and gratitude to God?

☐ STUDY 10 Nehemiah 9: 22–37

1 Analyse this summary (verses 6–37) of the history of God's people. What may we learn here about the heart of God, and the heart of man?

2 The Jews had learnt by bitter experience that disobedience brings penalty. Yet had God acted only in punishment? *Cf.* Ps. 130: 3, 4. What may we learn from this chapter about the principles of God's action towards His people when they sin? *Cf.* also Phil. 1: 6; 2 Jn. 8.

☐ STUDY 11 Nehemiah 9: 38 – 10: 39

1 Make a list of the seven specific ordinances included in the general covenant to walk in God's law (10: 29) and not neglect the house of God (10: 39).

2 What did the people agree (a) to give up, and (b) to give, that they might 'observe and do all the commandments of the Lord'? What does this teach us about the meaning of whole-hearted consecration? *Cf.* 2 Cor. 6: 14 – 7: 1; Pr. 3: 9, 10; Mal. 3: 10; 1 Cor. 16: 1, 2.

Notes

1 10: 29. 'Enter into a curse and an oath': *i.e.*, pledged themselves by an oath, invoking divine vengeance upon themselves, if they failed to observe it.
2 Verse 31b. *Cf.* Ex. 23: 10, 11; Dt. 15: 1–3.
3 Verses 35–39 give a general summary of such laws as Ex. 23: 19 and Nu. 18: 8–32.

☐ STUDY 12 Nehemiah 11

1 Though the Temple had been rebuilt and the city walls repaired, Jerusalem remained unattractive to dwell in (*cf.* 2: 3, 17), and the bulk of the people preferred to live in the country. By what two methods (verses 1, 2) were more inhabitants for the city secured? Are you willing to volunteer to serve in the place of greatest need? *Cf.* Is. 6: 8.

2 In verses 3–24 is given a list of those who dwelt in Jerusalem, in the following categories: (a) heads of families of the tribe of Judah (4–6); (b) of the tribe of Benjamin (7–9); (c) officials of the Temple—priests (10–14), Levites (15–19), other attendants, including singers (20–24). Try to picture the life of the city. Observe the prominence given to the house of God and its worship. Others helped in other ways, and some of them are described as 'valiant' or 'mighty men of valour' (literally 'men of strength and force'). Are you playing your part in the community to which you belong, helping it to become strong? *Cf.* Ec. 9:10a; 1 Cor. 15:58.

☐ STUDY 13 Nehemiah 12

1 How did the people celebrate the completion of the wall? See the further reminder in Lk. 17:15–18. As you read this passage, following in imagination the two companies as they marched in procession, remember Nehemiah's solitary journey as described in 2:12–15. Consider also how much you owe to God. *Cf.* 1 Cor. 15:10; Rom. 12:1.

2 'Nehemiah the governor' and 'Ezra the priest the scribe' (verse 26). Consider and contrast the office and character of these two great men, and how both alike were needed in this critical period of Jewish history. Have you discovered your gift and call of God or your variety of service for the common good? *Cf.* Rom. 11:29; 1 Cor. 12:4–7.

Note. Verse 30. 'Purified': by sprinkling the blood of sacrifices. *Cf.* Ezk. 43:19, 20.

☐ STUDY 14 Nehemiah 13

Nehemiah at some point in his governorship returned to King Artaxerxes, and later came again to Jerusalem (see verses 6 and 7), only to find that during his absence various abuses and backslidings had taken place.

1 Note in this chapter (a) five references to definite actions taken to deal with unsatisfactory features in the conduct and condition of the people; (b) the way in which Sanballat and Tobiah succeeded at last in gaining a footing in Jerusalem. What may we learn from these?

2 Have you the main sequence of events after the exile sorted out in your mind? In the light of 1 Cor. 10:11, what seem to you the main lessons to be learnt from this period in the history of God's chosen people?

PSALMS 90 – 106

☐ STUDY 71 Psalm 90

1 In verses 2–11 what is said about (a) man and (b) God? In view of these facts, what should be man's attitude (verses 11, 12)? What is meant by 'a heart of wisdom'? *Cf.* Pr. 9: 10; Je. 9: 23, 24; Jas. 4: 12–16.

2 Set down in your own words the petitions of verses 13–17. What convictions do they reveal concerning God's character and action? Can the petitions be transposed into a Christian key?

Note. Verse 11. It is only those who truly reverence the Lord who consider the reality of God's wrath against sin in all its intensity.

☐ STUDY 72 Psalm 91

The theme of this psalm is the security and blessedness of a life lived under God's protection. The change of pronouns has been variously explained. In verses 2 and 9a (see mg.) a solo voice declares its trust (in the first person singular), after which the choir respond with renewed assurances. Finally, in verses 14–16, God Himself speaks in words of gracious promise.

1 Life and health were insecure in ancient times. The world was haunted by unseen, malevolent powers. How does the psalmist's faith in God transform the situation? What comfort does the psalm bring to (a) the sufferer, and (b) one who anticipates suffering? *Cf.* the fuller statement in Rom. 8: 16–18, 28, 31, 35–37.

2 Verses 14–16. Note here seven gracious promises of God. Can you bear witness to their truth from your own experience and from the experience of other believers? *Cf.* 2 Pet. 1: 2–4.

Notes

1 The evils mentioned in verses 3, 5, 10, 13 refer to all kinds of adversity, insidious and hidden, or open and visible, explicable or inexplicable. Verse 13 refers not to Tarzan-like exploits, but to deliverance from dangers, natural and supernatural, not by magic (as in Egypt), but by faith.

2 Verse 14. 'I will protect': literally, 'I will set him inaccessibly high.'

☐ STUDY 73 Psalms 92 and 93

1 Ps. 92. The psalmist's eyes have been opened to discern the principles of God's working, which are hidden from those who have no spiritual understanding. What are these principles? How are both the emotions and the mind stirred?

2 Consider the picture of the life of the godly, as described in 92: 12–14. What is the secret of their vigour and beauty? *Cf.* Ps. 1: 3; Je. 17: 7, 8; Is. 40: 29–31.

3 Ps. 93. Might alone did not distinguish Israel's God from those of surrounding nations. What two unique features does this psalm mention? *Cf.* Ps. 90: 2c; Dt. 33: 27 and Ex. 15: 11b; Ps. 47: 8.

Notes

1 92: 1. 'To give thanks' means much more than 'to say "thank you" '. It involves public acknowledgment of God's grace by word, and probably with thank-offering.

2 92: 6. 'This' refers, as the colon shows, to the contents of verses 7 and 8.

3 92: 10. Horns symbolized power. *Cf.* Zc. 1: 18ff.; Ps. 75: 10. The figure is one of reinvigoration and reconsecration.

4 92: 12. 'Flourish': the same word as 'sprout' in verse 7.

☐ STUDY 74 Psalm 94

1 How does the psalmist find hope and comfort when oppressed by evil men? List carefully both the grounds and the content of his confidence.

2 What rebuke does the psalmist give to those in Israel who may have thought that evil men were right when they said (see verse 7) that God was indifferent to His people's need? What purpose does he see in the nation's present sufferings? See verses 8–15; *cf.* Pr. 3: 11, 12; Is. 49: 14–16.

Notes

1 Verses 1, 2. The fact that 'God of vengeance' is parallel to 'judge of the earth' shows that the former is not such an unpleasantly vindictive expression as the English might suggest. Both phrases indicate that God is concerned with the upholding of the moral order.

2 Verse 16. A court scene. 'Who is my counsel for the defence?' asks the psalmist. *Cf.* Rom. 8: 31, 33.

☐ STUDY 75 Psalms 95 and 96

These two psalms seem to have been associated with the new year festival. The renewal of the covenant was a special feature of this festival, and God was celebrated as Creator, King and Judge. Ps. 95 summons God's people to worship Him, a summons enforced by a grave warning against disobedience. Ps. 96 bids the whole creation join in worship of the Lord.

1 What is said in these two psalms to show that worship from all creation is the Lord's due? List the reasons why He ought to be worshipped. How should such worship find expression?

2 What special reasons are given in Ps. 95 why 'we' should worship God? Who constitute the 'we'? Of what danger are we warned to beware, and when, and why? *Cf.* Heb. 3: 7–15.

Notes

1 95: 3; 96: 4 (*cf.* 97: 9). The monotheism of the Old Testament is on the whole practical (*e.g.*, Ex. 20: 3) rather than theoretical. But 96: 5 expresses the logical conclusion of Old Testament as well as New Testament belief—that 'all the gods of the peoples are (literally) nothings'. *Cf.* 1 Cor. 8: 4–6.

2 95: 6. 'Our Maker': *i.e.*, the Maker of Israel as a nation—to be His people.

□ STUDY 76 Psalms 97 and 98

1 Ps. 97. What aspects of the Lord's character are revealed here, and what are the several effects of this revelation? Do they characterize your reaction in the presence of God? *E.g.*, note verse 10a, mg.; *cf.* Rom. 12: 9.

2 Ps. 98. What acts of the Lord, past and future, cause the psalmist to praise Him? Does your worship begin and end with thoughts of God, and does it find similar vocal and audible expression? *Cf.* Eph. 5: 19, 20.

□ STUDY 77 Psalms 99 and 100

1 Ps. 99. In what ways is the holiness or distinctive character of God here said to be demonstrated? What comfort and what warning can we take from the fact that God's holiness is not abstract but active? Do you share the psalmist's passion to see God publicly exalted in holiness? *Cf.* Rev. 15: 3, 4. Do you know what it means to call on His Name and to find that He answers (verses 6–8)?

2 Ps. 100. What does this psalm declare that we know about the Lord? And what should this knowledge make us do? In what spirit do you 'serve the Lord' (verse 2)?

Note. 99: 3. 'Terrible': *i.e.*, awe-inspiring. The same word is used in Dt. 10: 17; Ps. 76: 7, 12.

☐ STUDY 78 Psalm 101

Luther called this psalm 'David's mirror of a monarch'. Though the themes of the psalm are general, 2 Sa. 6: 9 may provide the clue to the historical situation—at the beginning of David's reign.

1 Verses 1–4. David could not sing to God without being aware that worship must have some effects upon his character and actions. Ponder the verbs of these verses. Is your Christian life as definite and decisive as this?

2 Verses 5–8. What company did David seek and shun? To what strenuous and sometimes violent action is the Christian similarly called? *Cf.* 2 Tim. 2: 14, 16, 19, 21–23.

☐ STUDY 79 Psalm 102

This psalm was probably written towards the close of the exile (see verse 13 and *cf.* Je. 29: 10; Dn. 9: 2). A description of the present distress (verses 1–11) is followed by a vision of a restored Zion (verses 12–22). The closing verses record the psalmist's assurance of the changeless character of God (verses 23–28).

1 What does this psalm teach us to do in time of trouble? See the title, and *cf.* Ps. 62: 8.

2 'For I . . . but thou' (verses 9, 12). Contrast with the extreme misery of verses 1–11 the vision of faith in verses 12–28. What has happened? Where is your gaze fixed—upon earth's sorrows, or upon God? *Cf.* 2 Cor. 4: 8, 9, 18.

Note. Verses 19, 20. *Cf.* Ex. 3: 7, 8. As then, so now.

☐ STUDY 80 Psalm 103

1 List the spiritual blessings mentioned in this psalm. Are you enjoying them yourself? Are you as mindful of their source, and as grateful to God, as the psalmist was?

2 What is emphasized by the mention of God's 'steadfast love' (verses 4, 8, 11, 17)? How is it demonstrated? What corresponding activity is demanded of those who would enjoy it? See verses 11, 13, 17, 18.

Notes

1 Verse 5. 'Like the eagle's': better, as in RV, 'like the eagle'. The meaning is 'made strong as an eagle'. *Cf.* Is. 40: 31.

2 Verses 11, 13, 17. The 'fear of the Lord' in the Bible does not refer to an abject, servile terror of the unknown or the terrifying. It is basically and consistently moral (see Ex. 20: 18–20), based on knowledge (see Pr. 9: 10), and means 'due reverence and awe'.

☐ STUDY 81 Psalm 104

This psalm has been described as a poetical version of Gn. 1. The two chapters may be compared with profit. Note the measure of agreement.

1 How is the dependence of the creature on the Creator brought out in verses 27–30? *Cf.* Ps. 145: 15, 16; Gn. 1 : 29, 30. Ponder the beautiful picture of God which this affords. What ought it to make us do? *Cf.* Mt. 6: 25–33.

2 Do we share the desires and resolves of the psalmist's heart, as expressed in verses 31–35?

Note. Verse 26. 'Leviathan' here refers to the sea monster. *Cf.* Gn. 1: 21; Am. 9: 3 for similar references.

☐ STUDY 82 Psalm 105

This psalm opens with a call to remember and recite the mighty deeds of the Lord. It is itself a historical retrospect, made, we may surmise from verse 45, with a view to encouraging obedience to the redeeming Lord. 'Remembering' was never a merely intellectual process in Israel's worship; it had a moral purpose.

1 Verses 1–5. List the imperatives used here. Think of appropriate times when you should obey them. *Cf.* Ps. 119: 164. Might it be particularly helpful to turn to these verses and this psalm when depressed?

2 What reason is given in verses 7–10 and 42 for God's intervention on behalf of the Israelites? *Cf.* Lk. 1 : 72–74. For what similar reason do we know that He will not fail or forsake us? *Cf.* Heb. 13: 5b, 6, 20, 21.

3 What may we learn from this psalm about the ways in which God protected, delivered, trained and provided for His chosen people? Will He do less for us? *Cf.* 1 Sa. 12: 22.

Notes

1 Verse 2. 'Tell of': the meaning is 'meditate on'; but the Israelites seldom meditated silently.

2 Verse 28b. A difficult clause. The LXX omits 'not'; and this may be the original reading. Or the Hebrew (see mg.) may be a rhetorical question, 'Did they not rebel?'

☐ STUDY 83 Psalm 106: 1–33

This section consists of a summons to praise the Lord, a prayer, and then (verses 7–33) a confession of seven instances of Israel's sin from the exodus to the entrance into Canaan.

1 What feature of Israel's failure is mentioned three times in these verses, and what were some of its consequences? *Cf.* Dt. 8:11–20.

2 Why did God, after delivering the Israelites, later overthrow them in the wilderness? Note the four things mentioned in verses 24, 25 which caused Him to change His attitude. With what awe and seriousness should the Christian take warning from this incident? *Cf.* Heb. 3:12, 17–19; 4:1.

3 The reference in verses 14, 15 is to Nu. 11 (see verses 4, 34). What inspired the Israelites' request, and what serious consequence followed? The New Testament indicates that we are involved in a war with fleshly lusts. How are we to fight them? *Cf.* 1 Cor. 10:6; 1 Pet. 2:11; Gal. 5:16.

□ STUDY 84 Psalm 106: 34–48

The ending of this psalm, particularly verses 45–47, suggests that, whereas the function of Ps. 105 was to stimulate obedience, the purpose of the historical retrospect here, which, dismal though it is, is crowned by a reassertion of God's steadfast love, is to strengthen faith among an exiled people, tempted to despair.

1 A new generation entered Canaan (see Nu. 14:29–32; 26:64, 65), but the sinning continued. What was their first failure, and to what sins of ever deeper degradation did it lead (verses 34–39)? How are Christians to avoid similar entanglement? *Cf.* 2 Cor. 6:14 – 7:1; 1 Jn. 2:15–17.

2 What wonderful comfort can we take from the fact, which this psalm demonstrates, that man's rebellion did not exhaust the compassion of God? See verses 1–5, 45–47. What challenge do these verses bring?

Note. Verse 48. Probably a doxology to mark the end of Book IV of the Psalms.

For Studies 85–111 on the Psalms see p. 436.

HAGGAI

Introduction

The prophets Haggai and Zechariah are mentioned together in Ezra 5:1 as prophesying at that time in Jerusalem. Ezra 5 and 6 should be read in order to fit the ministry and God-given messages of these prophets into their historical setting.

The exact date of Haggai's prophesying is given in Hg. 1:1 as being the second year of Darius, king of Persia, *i.e.*, 520 BC (*cf.* Zc. 1:1). In 538 BC, the first company of exiles, under Zerubbabel, had returned from Babylon to Jerusalem, and had set about the work of rebuilding the Temple. But Samaritan opposition and intrigue proved too strong, and the work ceased (see Ezr. 4:1–5, 24). The people became occupied with their own concerns, and said with regard to the Temple, 'The time has not yet come to rebuild the house of the Lord' (Hg. 1:2).

The prophecies of Haggai consist of four utterances (see Analysis), which contain repeated promises of God's presence and blessing, if only the people will give themselves to the work of building the Lord's house. Haggai's words express for our instruction the abiding truth that God gives Himself and His best to those who fully honour Him and seek first His kingdom. There is no other hope of survival in the day of trouble and judgment, when God Himself will shake all things and reveal the worthlessness of every other boasted confidence (see Hg. 2:21–23; and *cf.* Heb. 12:25–27). Thus did Haggai, by the light of the Spirit of God, discern the truth about life's immediate circumstances, and foresee the similar, if greater, certainties of the final consummation in the day of the Lord.

Analysis

1:1–15 First utterance. A call to the people to recommence the building of the Temple. The work resumed.

2: 1–9 Second utterance. The builders encouraged. God is with them to prosper the work.
2: 10–19 Third utterance. The people and their offerings have been unclean in God's eyes. But now He will bless them.
2: 20–23 Fourth utterance. The kingdoms of this world shall be overthrown, and the Lord's elect servant exalted.

☐ STUDY 1 Haggai 1

1 How did the Jews of Haggai's day reckon their priorities? What was the consequence? And what was the Lord's command? What lesson did God wish them to learn? Is there a present-day application? *Cf.* Mt. 6: 33.

2 How had the people failed to live up to the purpose for which they had been allowed to return? *Cf.* Ezr. 1: 2–4. Contrast their first beginnings with the conditions described by Haggai. Is this at all your experience? *Cf.* Rev. 2: 4. What happened once they obeyed God's voice?

Note. Verse 1. 'The sixth month': corresponding to our August–September.

☐ STUDY 2 Haggai 2

1 Picture the desolate scene and the despondency of the people (verse 3). But how did the prospect appear to Haggai's eye of faith (verses 4–9)? On what grounds did he reassure them, and to what vision did he direct their eyes?

2 Verses 10–19. How does Haggai show that (a) in the sanctified life contact with unholy things must be avoided, and that (b) mere contact with holy things is not sufficient? Is it possible to deceive ourselves today, as the Jews of Haggai's day did? *Cf.* 2 Tim. 2: 19–22.

3 What will be the fate of all human activity and organization carried on without God, and what is the work that will stand, whose doers are blessed from the day they set their hand to it? *Cf.* 1 Jn. 2: 17. Why would Zerubbabel be safe when the Lord would shake the heavens and the earth?

Note. Verse 23. 'Like a signet': a symbol of honour and authority. *Cf.* Je. 22: 24.

ZECHARIAH

Introduction

Zechariah began his prophetic ministry two months after Haggai (see Zc. 1: 1; Hg. 1: 1). His book falls into two parts (chapters 1–8 and 9–14), and these are so different in character that many have thought that the second part must have been written by someone other than Zechariah. Such a supposition, however, is by no means necessary. The differences may be explained by the change of theme, and by the fact that the second part was written many years later than the first. A close study also reveals remarkable resemblances between the two parts.

The first part of the book has to do mainly with the rebuilding of the Temple, and contains Zechariah's words of encouragement and warning to the people and their rulers. After an opening call to repentance (1: 1–6) there follows a series of eight visions, which supply an answer to doubts and questionings in the people's minds. The first part closes with the prophet's reply to an enquiry from the people of Bethel (7: 1–3) about the continuance of the fasts which the Jews had been observing in mourning for the calamities that had overtaken them.

The second part of the book consists of two oracles (9–11 and 12–14). Both sections, as David Baron says in his valuable commentary, treat of war between the heathen world and Israel, but 'in the first the judgment through which *Gentile world power over Israel is finally destroyed*, and Israel is endowed with strength to *overcome all these enemies*', is the main theme; and, in the second, the judgment through which '*Israel itself is sifted and purged* in the final great conflict between the nations, and transformed into the holy nation of the Lord, forms the leading topic'.

Zechariah's writings foreshadow the appearance of Zion's King both in meekness and in majesty, and declare both His rejection and His dominion over the whole earth. They are therefore frequently quoted in the New Testament with reference either to Christ's first or to His second coming to the earth.

Analysis

1: 1–6	A call to pay heed to the Word of God.	
1:7 – 6: 8	Eight visions.	
	1: 7–17	The Angel of the Lord among the myrtle trees.
	1: 18–21	The horns and the four smiths.
	2: 1–13	The man with the measuring line.
	3: 1–10	Joshua the High Priest.
	4: 1–14	The golden lampstand.
	5: 1–4	The flying scroll.
	5: 5–11	The ephah and the woman.
	6: 1–8	The four chariots.
6: 9–15	The crowning of Joshua.	
7: 1 – 8: 23	Reply to the deputation from Bethel.	
9: 1–17	A Gentile conqueror and Zion's King.	
10: 1–12	What the shepherd king will bring to His people.	
11: 1–17	The rejection of the true shepherd and its tragic consequences.	
12: 1–9	The deliverance of Jerusalem.	
12: 10 – 13: 6	The penitence and purifying of the people.	
13: 7–9	The smiting of the shepherd and scattering of the flock.	
14: 1–21	Messiah's appearing, and the establishment of His kingdom on earth.	

☐ STUDY 1 Zechariah 1 and 2

1 What do we learn from Zc. 1: 1–6 about the Word of the Lord and the different consequences of obeying and rejecting it? What is and always will be true of it, whatever men do? With verse 6, *cf.* Mt. 5: 18.

2 In these chapters are three visions (1: 7–17; 1: 18–21; 2: 1–13). How do these answer the following questions? (a) What is God's real attitude towards Jerusalem? (b) How can the nations which oppress them be subdued? (c) Can the city, now desolate, have any future?

3 Consider how much that is said here of Jerusalem is true spiritually for us in Christ. See, *e.g.*, 2: 5, 8b, 10–12. Is there not the same call to us to believe, as there was to the people of Zechariah's day? *Cf.* 2 Cor. 1: 20.

Notes

1 1: 11. There was no sign of any stirring among the nations to fulfil God's purposes towards Israel.

2 1: 20, 21. 'Four smiths': agents appointed by God to destroy the 'horns' (*i.e.*, strength) of the nations.
3 2: 4, 5. The proposed measurement of Jerusalem is cancelled, for the reasons given here.
4 2: 6. 'The land of the north': Babylon (or Persia), where they had been exiled. See verse 7.

☐ STUDY 2 Zechariah 3 and 4

1 Joshua, as high priest, acts as the representative of the people. How is the people's guilt to be removed? By whose intervention is Satan rebuked and Joshua cleansed? *Cf.* Rom. 8: 31–34; Heb. 7: 25; 9: 26.

2 What is the meaning of the vision of chapter 4? What is its relevance today? *Cf.* Ho. 1: 7; 2 Cor. 10: 4, 5.

Note. 3: 8, 9. 'My servant', 'the Branch', 'the stone' are all titles of the Messiah. *Cf.*, *e.g.*, Is. 28: 16; 42: 1; Je. 23: 5. The 'seven facets' may represent the omniscience of the Messiah. *Cf.* Rev. 5: 6.

☐ STUDY 3 Zechariah 5 and 6

1 Chapter 5 contains a vivid vision concerning those who practise wickedness, and of wickedness itself. What is to be the eventual fate of such? *Cf.* 2 Tim. 2: 19; 2 Thes. 1: 7–10; Rev. 21: 1–4, 8, 27.

2 What is foreshadowed in 6: 9–15 by the crowning of the high priest, and by the prophetic declaration that 'the man' (verse 12) thus signified shall be a priest *upon his throne*, and shall build the temple of the Lord? *Cf.* Jn. 2: 19–22; Eph. 2: 13, 19–22; Heb. 8: 1; 10: 11–13; 1 Pet. 2: 5.

Notes
1 5: 1–4. A vision of God's judgment pursuing the transgressor.
2 5: 6. 'The ephah': a barrel-shaped measure, having here a circular lid of lead.
3 5: 11. 'The land of Shinar': Babylonia.
4 6: 1–8. The vision in its details is difficult to interpret, but in general reveals the Lord ruling over the earth (verse 5), and exercising His judgment by unseen agents. *Cf.* 2 Ki. 6: 15–17.
5 6: 10, 11. A deputation from the Jews in Babylon had come to Jerusalem. Zechariah is commanded to make 'a crown' from some of the silver and gold which they had brought, and to set it on the head of the high priest.

☐ STUDY 4 Zechariah 7

See Introduction. Zechariah's answer to the delegation from Bethel consists of four parts, each beginning 'And the word of the Lord came to me'. The first two parts of his reply are contained in this chapter and the last two in chapter 8.

1 With what did God find fault in these fasts? See verses 5, 6 and contrast 1 Cor. 10: 31. In the light of this part of the prophet's reply, is there not much in men's worship today that is not acceptable to God?

2 With verses 9 and 10, *cf.* Is. 58: 6, 7. Where does a man's enmity towards his brother take its rise? *Cf.* Mk. 7: 21, 22. What attitude of heart towards God had the Jews shown?

□ STUDY 5 Zechariah 8

1 Enumerate the blessings which God here promises concerning Jerusalem, noticing also the emphasis placed upon them by the number of times the phrase 'says the Lord' occurs. Is God less willing to fulfil to us the 'precious and very great promises' (2 Pet. 1: 4), which He has given us in Christ? *Cf.* Heb. 6: 11–18.

2 What, however, are the conditions for obtaining the promises of God? In the light of the evidence we have of God's willingness to give, where does the hindrance lie, if we are not enjoying in personal experience the things promised?

3 What will ultimately happen to the fasts about which the deputation from Bethel had enquired in 7: 2, 3?

Notes

1 Verses 4, 5. 'Old men . . . boys and girls playing . . .': these indicate and illustrate the security and peace which is promised.

2 Verse 10. Three evils are here spoken of from which the people suffered when God's house was neglected, namely, scarcity, absence of security and disunion.

□ STUDY 6 Zechariah 9 and 10

1 The opening verses (9: 1–8) are a prophecy of an invasion of Syria, Phoenicia and the country of the Philistines. The prophecy was historically fulfilled in the conquests of Alexander the Great. But to whom is the prophet's eye directed? How does this account, on the one hand, for the fall of Tyre, notwithstanding its wisdom, strong defences and wealth, and, on the other, for the preservation of Jerusalem? *Cf.* 9: 15a and 2: 5.

2 In 9: 9–12 a picture is presented of Zion's King, in which, as often in the Old Testament, His first and second advents are merged into one. What is said (a) of His character; (b) of the manner of His coming; (c) of the final extent of His rule; and (d) of the benefits He brings? *Cf.* Ps. 40: 2, 3; Joel 3: 16b; Is. 61: 7.

3 The remaining portion (9: 13 – 10: 12) has for its theme what God will yet do for His people Israel. Make a list of the things here promised, and reflect how they are symbols of spiritual blessings which are ours in Christ.

Notes

1 9: 1–6. Hadrach and Aram are probably Syrian towns; Hamath, Tyre and Sidon are Syrian neighbours; Ashkelon, Gaza, Ekron and Ashdod (verses 5, 6) are Philistine towns.

2 9: 7. A prophecy of the abolition of idolatrous sacrifices, and the incorporation of the remnant of the Philistines among God's people. The Jebusites were the original inhabitants of Jerusalem.

3 9: 8. When Alexander invaded these parts and swept through the coastal nations, nothing could stop his armies, but he was restrained from attacking Jerusalem.

4 9: 13–17. A prophecy of victory for Israel, when the enemy shall be trodden down like sling-stones and Israel lifted up like the jewels of a crown. In verse 15b is another figure, representing the Israelites as drinking the blood of their enemies, with which they will be as full as the bowls used in sacrifice, or like the corners of the altar that were drenched in blood.

☐ STUDY 7 Zechariah 11

While plain in its main teaching, this chapter is obscure in many of its details. Its theme is grace and judgment. It opens with a vision of judgment sweeping over the land and making it desolate (verses 1–3). God shows to the prophet that the promises of the preceding chapter will not be realized without further uprisings of evil (*cf.* 10: 2, 3a). In verses 4–17 the prophet is bidden to impersonate first a good shepherd, and when he was rejected and despised, a worthless shepherd, under whom the flock will suffer many sorrows. The section is a vivid foreshadowing of the coming of Christ (verses 12, 13; *cf.* Mt. 26: 14, 15; 27: 9, 10).

1 Verse 7. The good shepherd's 'two staffs' (*cf.* 'rod' and 'staff' in Ps. 23: 4) were named 'Grace' and 'Union', indicating that He came in grace to bind the flock into one. How far is this a picture of Christ? *Cf.* Jn. 1: 14; 17: 20–22.

2 How is the lot of those who deliberately refuse the good described? *Cf.* Mt. 23: 37, 38; 2 Thes. 2: 8.

Notes

1 Verses 7, 11. 'Traffickers in the sheep': 'poor of the flock' (AV) fits the context better.

2 Verse 12. 'Thirty shekels of silver': the price of an injured slave (Ex. 21: 32). *Cf.* Mt. 26: 15; 27: 9.

☐ STUDY 8 Zechariah 12 and 13

These chapters contain a prophecy of a combined attack of many peoples upon Jerusalem and of the deliverance God will give (12: 1–9), together with the repentance and cleansing which will be wrought within the nation by their vision and recognition of Him whom they pierced (12: 10 – 13: 9). The ultimate fulfilment of this prophecy will take place at the end of the present age (*cf.* Rom. 11: 25–27), but it has a present application spiritually to all who belong to Him.

1 What is to be the secret of Jerusalem's survival when threatened by so many enemies gathered together against it (12: 1–9; *cf.* 14: 3)? Has the Christian similar hope of overcoming the world, the flesh and the devil? *Cf.* Ps. 27: 1–5; 1 Jn. 4: 4; 5: 4.

2 What four experiences of God's people are set forth in 12: 10 – 13: 9? Do you know them in your experience? (a) With 12: 10–14, *cf.* Jn. 16: 8, 9; Acts 2: 37–40. (b) With 13: 1, *cf.* Heb. 9: 13, 14. (c) With 13: 2–5, *cf.* 2 Cor. 7: 1. (d) With 13: 7–9, *cf.* 1 Pet. 1: 5–7.

Notes

1 12: 11. Hadadrimmon is thought to be a city in the plain of Megiddo (or Jezreel), where King Josiah was killed, the darkest and saddest event in Jewish history (*cf.* 2 Ch. 35: 22–25).

2 12: 12–14. Both the intensity and the universality of Israel's repentance are here emphasized.

3 13: 2–6. The prophets, having been proved false, shall be ashamed, and will seek to disguise the fact that they prophesied. The wounds (verse 6) are either wounds self-inflicted in their prophetic frenzy (*cf.* 1 Ki. 18: 28), or more probably wounds received by them through the attacks of people upon them (*cf.* verse 3c).

☐ STUDY 9 Zechariah 14

Verses 1–5 appear to be a prediction of the fall of Jerusalem in AD 70, together with a prediction of the Lord's return. In the Gospels (*e.g.*, Lk. 21: 20–28) these two events are also described as if they were one. Then follows an account of the blessings that will ensue.

1 Verses 1–5 describe the breaking in of the day of the Lord. Who will at that time be gathered against Jerusalem? What will happen to the city and its inhabitants? When and in what manner will the Lord appear?

2 In the day of the Lord what further results will come to pass as regards (a) Jerusalem (verses 6–11; *cf.* Rev. 22: 1–5; Jn. 4: 13, 14); (b) those who attacked Jerusalem (verses 12–15); and (c) the remnant of the nations that have escaped (verses 16–19)?

3 Picture the city as described in verses 20, 21. Are you aiming to see that your life is holy in every part? *Cf.* 2 Cor. 7: 1; 1 Thes. 3: 13; 1 Pet. 1: 15, 16.

Note. Verses 20, 21. Every aspect of the city's life will bear the mark of holiness —business life, religious life and domestic life. Verse 20b. The pots which were used for mundane purposes shall be as holy as the bowls which held the blood of sacrifice.

MALACHI

Introduction

Malachi (the name means 'my messenger'—see 3: 1) was doubtless a contemporary of Ezra and Nehemiah. He attacked the evils which arose at Jerusalem after the Temple was rebuilt and its services re-established, evils of which we have historical record in the book of Nehemiah. 'The religious spirit of Malachi is that of the prayers of Ezra and Nehemiah.' There is an ancient tradition which regarded 'Malachi' as a pen name, and assigned the authorship to Ezra himself.

This book is the more significant because it closes the Old Testament revelation. As a link between the law and the gospel, it combines severe insistence on the necessity of purity and sincerity of heart with the sure promise of the coming of a Deliverer to those who fear the Lord. Finally (4: 4–6), it appeals back to the law and the prophets (of whom Elijah is the chosen representative). The fuller revelation will not contradict its preparatory stages. The people are to find in the spiritual authorities they already know (*i.e.*, in the Old Testament) their assurance for accepting Him who should come. So, on the Mount of Transfiguration, when the Father called men to hear the Son, Moses and Elijah stood by to give their assent and to provide evidence that He was the fulfilment of all their anticipation. See Mt. 17: 3–5; Jn. 5: 46.

Analysis

1: 1–5	God's love for Israel.
1: 6 – 2: 9	The sins of the priests.
2: 10–17	The sins of the people.
3: 1–6	Warning that the Lord will come to judge and to purify.
3: 7–12	How to give practical expression to their repentance.
3: 13 – 4: 6	The future day of judgment.

☐ STUDY 1 Malachi 1: 1 - 2: 9

1 1: 1–5. The people of Judah, looking upon their condition and circumstances, were depressed and murmuring against God. What proof did the prophet adduce to show that God did love them as a nation? *Cf.* Pss. 34: 15, 16; 73: 26–28.

2 Of what particular sins were the priests guilty? With what will God punish them if they remain impenitent? What was the root of their failure?

3 What, by contrast, do we learn should be the quality and objectives of our service as messengers of the Lord of hosts? *Cf.* 2: 5–7, and *cf.* 2 Cor. 6: 3; 2 Tim. 2: 15; 1 Pet. 4: 10, 11.

Notes

1 1: 2–4. The Edomites were the descendants of Esau.

2 1: 5. 'Great is the Lord beyond the border of Israel': the people had too small a conception of their God, and this the prophet seeks to correct. *Cf.* verses 11, 14b.

3 1: 8. Perfect, unblemished sacrifices were demanded (Lv. 1: 3), and not the 'rejects' from the flock.

☐ STUDY 2 Malachi 2: 10 – 3: 6

1 2: 10–16. Although the people wept before the Lord, they found He would not regard their offerings. Why not? What particular sin was coming between them and God, and what 'heart condition' underlay it? *Cf.* Heb. 3: 12, 13.

2 How is 3: 1–6 an answer to the people's complaint in 2: 17? What similes are used to describe the day of the Lord's coming? What must be put away? And on what must my heart be set, if I am to be ready to welcome Him at His appearing? *Cf.* 1 Thes. 3: 12, 13; 1 Jn. 3: 2, 3.

Note. 2: 10, 11. 'Profaning the covenant of our fathers': *i.e.*, by marrying wives of other nations. *Cf.* Ex. 34: 10–12, 15, 16. 'The daughter of a foreign god' means a foreign woman of another religion.

☐ STUDY 3 Malachi 3: 7 – 4: 6

1 Of what are the people accused in 3: 7–15? What must we make our chief concern if we wish to obtain God's promised blessings? *Cf.* Pr. 3: 9, 10; Mt. 6: 30–33; 16: 25; Lk. 6: 38. In what practical ways ought I to respond to this call?

2 Two different classes of people are described in 3: 13–16. To which do you belong? The wicked may seem to have the best of it, but God says here that, in contrast to present circumstances, He is

going to make a day (3: 17 and 4: 3) in which the righteous and the wicked shall be openly distinguished and justly recompensed. How will this be effected? *Cf.* 4: 1, 2 with 2 Thes. 1: 7–10; 1 Jn. 2: 28; 3: 2; Rev. 6: 15–17.

Note. 3: 11. 'The devourer': *i.e.*, the locust.

JAMES

Introduction

It is generally believed that this letter was written by James, the brother of our Lord. During Christ's life on earth he was an unbeliever (Jn. 7: 5), but was converted when Jesus appeared to him after His resurrection (1 Cor. 15: 7). He was austere in disposition and practical in character. In the book of Acts (see 12: 17; 15: 13–21; 21: 18 and also Gal. 2: 9) he appears as leader of the church at Jerusalem. He was killed by the Jews about AD 61.

The letter is addressed 'to the twelve tribes in the dispersion' (1: 1), that is, to fellow-Jews living outside Palestine. It is terse and forceful, yet vivid and dramatic in style. It begins and ends abruptly, without any opening thanksgiving or final benediction. James seeks to encourage those who were passing through a period of trial and suffering; but at the same time rebukes such failings as profession of faith without the practice of it, sins of speech, strife and envying, eagerness to take the position of teachers, and a lack of steadfast endurance. He urges his readers to be 'doers of the word, and not hearers only', to express their Christian faith not in outward formality and barren profession, but by seeking to obey from the heart God's perfect law of liberty in the manifold relationships of life.

The central thought is that 'faith apart from works is barren' (2: 20). Justification is by faith, but the faith that justifies is a living faith which, by an inherent irrepressible necessity, must produce good works, or express itself in active self-committal and obedience.

Analysis

The letter is a homily rather than a treatise, and deals with practical religion; there is thus no continuous thread of argument through the book; rather, with sure touch, the author comments, encourages or chides on matters of doctrine and conduct as they arise, in vivid and energetic style.

1: 1–18	Dealing with temptation.
1: 19–27	Receiving God's word and doing God's will.
2: 1–13	Snobbishness and the royal law of love.
2: 14–26	Against an inactive faith.
3: 1–12	Control of the tongue.
3: 13–18	Earthbound and heavenly wisdom.
4: 1–12	Dealing with dissension and worldliness among Christians.
4: 13 – 5: 11	Warnings to the rashly confident and the callous rich; counsel and encouragement to the oppressed.
5: 12–20	Miscellaneous pastoral remarks; with emphasis on the place and power of prayer.

☐ STUDY 1 James 1: 1–18

A distinction is drawn in this passage between 'trials' (verse 2, 12), which may have positive effects (*cf.* 1 Pet. 1: 7), and 'temptation' (verses 13f.), which is the enticement to evil conceived within the human heart.

1 Verses 2–7, 12. What is our mental attitude to trials to be? What is their purpose and goal? In trying situations wisdom (*cf.* 3: 17) is necessary. How in particular is this wisdom to be obtained?

2 Verses 13–15. What is the origin of temptation, and what are the inevitable products of yielding to it? How can we avoid being deceived, and gain strength to overcome?

3 Verses 9–11, 16–18. Contrast the impermanence of men, poor and rich alike, with the changeless consistency of God our Father. What also is God's will for us, and what means does He use to fulfil it? How should these truths influence our attitude to life?

Notes

1 Verse 17b. The eternal Source of light is not, like the heavenly bodies, subject to variation or eclipse.

2 Verse 18. 'A kind of first fruits': the first fruits were evidence that the harvest had begun, and promise of more to follow.

☐ STUDY 2 James 1: 19–27

It is characteristic of James to pass from one paragraph to another by repetition of a key-word. Here, having spoken of God's word in regeneration (verse 18), he goes on to speak of the place God's word—as expressing His will—should have in the believer's life.

1 What are the possible hindrances and dangers which may prevent God's word from taking root and bearing fruit in our lives?

2 'Meekness' (verse 21) is not to be confused with inactivity. What lessons does James' illustration enforce concerning our reaction to God's word and His law? With verse 25, *cf.* Lk. 8: 15. How does your religion stand up to James' practical tests (verses 26f.)?

Notes

1 Verse 25. 'Looks into': literally 'peers closely at'; *cf.* Jn. 20: 5, 11; 1 Pet. 1: 12. 'The law of liberty': *cf.* Rom. 8: 2. The Christian gospel is a 'law of liberty' because God's Spirit creates within the hearts of those who receive it the will and power to obey God. So God's law becomes an inner constraint and is no longer chiefly an external restraint.

2 Verse 27. 'Religion': the word means the outward expression of faith. 'This is the ritualism which God loves,' says James, 'to visit orphans . . .'

☐ STUDY 3 James 2: 1–13

1 Verses 1–7. On what five grounds (three general and two particular) does James condemn the snobbish conduct described in verses 2, 3? With verse 4, *cf.* 4: 11. We, too, believe in the 'Lord of glory'. Are we free from the preoccupation with what people have rather than what they are? Do we love and learn from 'the rich in *faith*'?

2 Verses 8–13. 'This partiality business is just a minor matter.' How does James deal with this sterile objection? Why, in a life which may otherwise appear to be law-abiding, is one form of sin, like partiality, so serious?

Notes

1 Verse 12. Our freedom is not freedom *from* the obligations of moral law; it is freedom to *fulfil* (verse 18) the just requirements of the law.

2 Verse 13b. Mercy triumphs over (not justice but) judgment. The same word is translated 'condemnation' in 5: 12. Mercy will finally triumph because when the merciless are condemned, the merciful will be forgiven.

☐ STUDY 4 James 2: 14–26

James has already warned against an empty religion which is impure (1: 26, 27); here he warns against an inactive faith which is impotent.

1 Verses 14–20. Empty faith is words without action, profession without performance. *Cf.* 1 Jn. 3: 18 (NEB). How profitable is my faith by the test of James' illustration? How does my faith differ from that of the demons?

2 Verses 21–26. James illustrates his argument by reference to two very different people. How was the principle of verse 22 demonstrated in their lives? Is the principle at work in my own life?

Notes

1 Verse 14. The sense is: 'Can (that sort of) faith save him?' *i.e.*, from condemnation.

2 Verse 18. The objection that some have faith and some have works is specious, because without corresponding moral action faith is empty and barren, like that of the devils (verse 19).

3 Verse 25. 'Justified by works': *cf.* Rom. 3: 20, 28; Gal. 2: 16. Paul and James seem to contradict one another. But, in fact, Paul says, 'Faith can save apart from works of the law', and James says, 'Faith cannot save without the works of faith.' The two are therefore complementary.

☐ STUDY 5 James 3

In this chapter James returns to two subjects which he has already mentioned: the tongue (*cf.* 1: 19, 26) and wisdom (*cf.* 1: 5).

1 Verses 1–12. Why does James discourage undue eagerness to take up teaching? Ponder his vivid illustrations of the power, for good or evil, of the tongue. How is the malignity of the tongue most clearly shown, and why is it so serious? How does James also show that the tongue's inconsistency is monstrously unnatural?

2 Verses 13–18. What are the marks and results of the two kinds of wisdom described in these verses? Consider how the qualities of heavenly wisdom, described in verses 17, 18, were seen in the Lord Jesus. Are they evident in my life?

Notes

1 Verse 6. NEB translates: 'And the tongue is in effect a fire. It represents among our members the world with all its wickedness; it pollutes our whole being; it keeps the wheel of our existence red-hot, and its flames are fed by hell.'

2 Verse 13. 'Meekness': a word which today has lost much of its original nobility. For the Greeks it denoted a strong man's self-discipline and a wise man's humility. *Cf.* 1: 21.

3 Verse 14. 'Do not boast and be false to the truth': to boast of wisdom when the heart is full of envy and selfish ambition is mere sham. *Cf.* 1: 26.

4 Verse 18 is to be contrasted with verse 16. Disorder and vileness accompany envy and rivalry; but righteousness (or justice) is the seed and crop of the peacemakers.

☐ STUDY 6 James 4

1 Verses 1–10. How does James diagnose the condition of those to whom he is writing? Can you find in verses 4–10 seven steps to spiritual recovery? What cause is there for encouragement and gratitude in this often painful business?

2 Verses 11–17. The Christian community to which James was writing was further disfigured by evil speaking and rash confidence. What guidance does James give concerning our attitude (a) to our fellow-Christians, and (b) to tomorrow? What difference would it make to your life if you took seriously the definition of sin in verse 17?

Notes

1 Verse 4. 'Unfaithful creatures': literally 'adulteresses'. *Cf.* Ho. 3: 1. But the reference here is to apostasy, not immorality.

2 Verse 6. The quotation of Pr. 3: 34 is introduced to demonstrate the wonder of God's grace, which is able to overcome even the worldly spirit of James' readers, if they will humble themselves and respond to His Spirit's yearnings.

☐ STUDY 7 James 5

James denounces the callous rich in language which recalls that of the Old Testament prophets. *Cf.* 1: 9–11; 2: 1–7.

1 Verses 1–12. What is the outstanding fact underlying James' warnings to the rich, and his counsel to the oppressed? Do we, rich or poor, share this eternal perspective? What particular warnings should we take from verses 1–6? What reasons (verses 7–10) are there for self-control and what grounds for joyful peace of mind?

2 Verses 13–20. In what ways are we called upon to help others? In particular, what illustrations are here given of the power of prayer, and what conditions of effective prayer are laid down?

Notes

1 Verse 3b. NEB translates, 'You have piled up wealth in an age that is near its close.'

2 Verse 6. The reference is probably not to Christ, as some suppose (*cf.* Acts 7: 52), so much as to prevailing social conditions.

3 Verse 9. 'Do not grumble': the verse recalls 4: 11, 12, where open criticism is discouraged; notice the similar legal language.

4 Verse 11. 'The purpose of the Lord': literally 'The end of the Lord' (AV, RV), *i.e.*, what the Lord finally purposed for Job. See Jb. 42: 12.

5 Verse 12. It seems that James' readers were notoriously unable to control their tongues: *cf.* 1: 19, 26; 2: 12; 3: 5ff.; 4: 11; 5: 9.

6 Verse 16. 'Confess your sins': there must be no hushing up of sin if prayer is to prevail. *Cf.* Ps. 66: 18; Mt. 5: 23, 24.

1 CHRONICLES

Introduction

The two books of Chronicles, which are really one whole, were composed at a much later date than the other historical books, and frequent reference is made to former writings not now possessed by us. The date is after the carrying away to Babylon (1 Ch. 6: 15) and after the decree of Cyrus ordering the return (2 Ch. 36: 22, 23), which decree is found also in the first chapter of Ezra. The literary style is similar to the books of Ezra–Nehemiah, which suggests that all belong to the same period.

The books of Chronicles are placed last in the Hebrew Bible. They are separated from the other historical books, and form part of the section of the Hebrew Canon known as 'Hagiographa' or 'Writings'. The Hebrew title for the books of Chronicles is 'The Words of the Days', and the Greek title is 'Omissions'. The name 'Chronicles' comes from Jerome. The theme of the books is the need for God to be central in the life of the nation, and the frequent times in the history of the monarchy when the nation turned away from Him, with occasional times of reformation under such kings as Jehoshaphat, Hezekiah and Josiah. After the death of Solomon (2 Ch. 9) the story of the southern kingdom alone is told, with only occasional references to the northern kingdom. The work of the prophets as witnesses to the truth of God, when kings and even priests corrupted it, is shown again and again, as is the faithfulness of God to the people of His choice. The interest of the writer centres very largely in the Temple, its priesthood and its worship.

Analysis

1 – 9 Chiefly genealogies.
10 – 29 Events leading up to the building of the Temple. Reign of David.

10 – 12 Death of Saul and accession of David. The exploits of his mighty men.
13 – 16 The ark brought to Jerusalem—services arranged.
17 David's desire to build a Temple and the Lord's answer.
18 – 20 David conquers and subdues neighbouring peoples.
21 The numbering of the people.
22 David's preparation for Solomon's accession.
23 – 26 The ministry of the tribe of Levi.
27 Civil leaders of the nation under David.
28 David's address to the leaders of the people and to Solomon.
29 The people's response. David's death.

☐ STUDY 1 1 Chronicles 1–9

These chapters, which at first sight appear to be a mere wilderness of names, are seen on closer inspection to contain an orderly arrangement, like a garden divided into separate beds. The writer begins with the line of descent from Adam to Noah, and then gives the descendants of each of Noah's three sons (1: 1–27). Arriving thus at Abraham, he lists the sons of Ishmael, and of Keturah, and Isaac's two sons, Israel and Esau, with a list of the descendants of Esau (1: 28–54). With chapter 2 begins the list of Israel's sons, with their descendants. Judah comes first and is given the largest space (2: 3 – 4: 23); then Simeon (4: 24–43), Reuben, Gad and the half tribe of Manasseh (chapter 5), Levi (chapter 6), Issachar (7: 1–5), Benjamin (7: 6–12), Naphtali (7: 13), Manasseh (7: 14–19), Ephraim (7: 20–29), Asher (7: 30–40). It will be noticed that two tribes are omitted. In chapter 8 the descendants of Benjamin are given more fully, leading up to the family of Saul and his descendants; chapter 9 gives a list of inhabitants of Jerusalem, and repeats the genealogy of Saul as an introduction to the story of his death in chapter 10. Amidst these lists of names are a number of passages which may be spiritually applied with profit to ourselves.

1 Read 4: 9, 10 and 5: 18–22. What do you learn for your own life from the examples of (a) Jabez, and (b) Reuben, Gad and the half tribe of Manasseh about success and victory? *Cf.* Ps. 81: 10; Col. 4: 2; 1 Jn. 5: 4.

2 Build for yourself a mental picture of the lives and service of the Levites, as described in chapter 6. Are there lessons to be learned from this passage about the nature of true worship?

☐ STUDY 2 1 Chronicles 10 and 11

1 Chapter 10 is a sad story of failure. To what is Saul's failure ascribed? Are our own lives free from the sins which brought about Saul's downfall? *Cf.* Is. 8: 19, 20.

2 What instances are given in chapter 11 of the valour and loyalty of the men who followed David? What may we learn from the story concerning the nature of true fellowship, love and Christian service? *Cf.* Acts 20: 22–24.

Note. 11: 8. 'The Millo': probably the name of an ancient citadel in the city.

☐ STUDY 3 1 Chronicles 12

1 Observe the unity prevailing at this time among the followers of David—though drawn from so many different tribes—and also the diversity of gifts which were found among them. Make a list of these gifts and compare them with the gifts of the Spirit as set forth in 1 Cor. 12: 4–11. What was the secret of the unity that prevailed?

2 What qualities of character do you find commended in this chapter? Are they characteristic of the Christian church today? Are they true of you?

Note. Verse 18. 'Amasai': probably the same as Amasa of 2: 17; 2 Sa. 17: 25; 20: 10.

☐ STUDY 4 1 Chronicles 13 and 14

1 The story in chapter 13 will repay reflection. Was Uzzah alone guilty, or was the spirit of deep reverence lacking also in king and people? Was it too much like a heathen idol procession? What lesson would the judgment upon Uzzah impress upon the people? *Cf.* Heb. 12: 28, 29.

2 The Philistines were not willing to submit to the ascendancy of David, and three times made an all-out effort to regain the upper hand. What may we learn from the way David met the challenge?

Note. 13: 6. The power and majesty of God are emphasized, as also His presence. Note also the words 'before God' twice repeated in verses 8 and 10.

☐ STUDY 5 1 Chronicles 15: 1 – 16: 6

1 What reason does David assign for the failure of the first attempt to bring the ark to Jerusalem? Comparing chapter 15 with chapter 13, what was there common to both processions, and what peculiar to the second? What is the obvious lesson for us to learn?

2 'Sounds of joy' (15: 16; see also verses 25, 28, 29). What made David rejoice so greatly? What did the ark stand for in his eyes? What kind of activity should cause us similar joy?

☐ STUDY 6 1 Chronicles 16: 7–43

1 Verses 8–22, 34–36. What should be the response of God's people in return for all His goodness? Make a list of all the things the psalm calls upon them to do. Note for what purpose Heman and Jeduthun were 'chosen and expressly named' (verses 41, 42).

2 Verses 23–33. Here the psalmist looks beyond Israel, and summons all nations to worship the Lord. What reasons does he give why they ought to do so? Can you use this hymn of praise as a thankful acknowledgment of all that the Lord means to you?

☐ STUDY 7 1 Chronicles 17

1 From this chapter and other passages where Nathan is mentioned (2 Sa. 12: 1–15, 25; 1 Ki. 1 *passim*; 4: 5), work out what an important place he had in the lives of David and of Solomon. The revelation here made to him and through him to David is one of the chief Messianic prophecies in the Old Testament, and had a profound influence upon the development of the Messianic hope. *Cf.*, *e.g.*, Ps. 89: 26, 27; Lk. 1: 33; Heb. 1: 5.

2 In what sense did God deny David's desire, in what way modify it, and in what way answer it above all that David asked or thought? Note especially verses 4, 10b, 12a. Have you had any comparable experience of the Lord's dealing in your own life?

☐ STUDY 8 1 Chronicles 18–20

1 What indications do you find in chapter 18 concerning (a) David's heart attitude towards God, and (b) the way in which he exercised authority as king? What in turn did God do for him? How may we enjoy similar God-given blessing?

2 How do chapters 19 and 20 show what grave consequences may arise out of a misunderstanding, and what retribution may result from an act of folly?

3 What good qualities are seen in Joab in these chapters? How? then, did he come to the sad end described in 1 Ki. 2: 31, 32, 34,

☐ STUDY 9 1 Chronicles 21: 1 – 22: 1

1 What circumstances, do you imagine, may have left David particularly prone to temptation at this time? Why was the numbering

of the people displeasing to God? *Cf.* Je. 17: 5. What evidence do you find of the genuineness of David's repentance? *Cf.* 2 Cor. 7: 11.

2 What two proofs are there in this passage of God's forgiving mercy? Observe how God turned the incident into blessing by using it to show David the site of the Temple. *Cf.* 21: 18; 22: 1; 2 Ch. 3: 1.

□ STUDY 10 1 Chronicles 22: 2–19

The thought of building a house for the Lord had been in David's mind, but now the way for action was open. This passage tells of (a) the abundance of what David prepared; (b) his charge to Solomon; and (c) his charge to the leaders of the tribes.

1 What may we learn from David's high conception of the kind of building that alone would be worthy (verse 5), and from the abundance of his preparations? Contrast the spirit of the people in Malachi's day (Mal. 1: 6–8). What may we learn also from David's willing acceptance of God's decision that not he, but Solomon, should build the Temple?

2 Study David's charge to Solomon and the people. What did he lay down as the all-important secrets of success? What were the people to do before undertaking the task of building (verse 19)? *Cf.* 2 Cor. 8: 5.

Introductory Note to Chapters 23–27

These five chapters describe how David and the leaders of the tribes organized before David's death the administration of the kingdom. The first matter taken in hand was the ministry of the priests and Levites, who had charge of the Temple and its worship and also administered judgment. This is set forth in chapters 23–26. Chapter 23 speaks of the Levites as a whole, chapter 24 of the priests (verses 1–19), and their attendants (verses 20–31); chapter 25 of the choirs; chapter 26 of the porters (verses 1–19), and of the officers and judges (verses 20–32). Then in chapter 27 are given in lesser detail the civil and military leaders of the nation other than Levites.

□ STUDY 11 1 Chronicles 23 and 24

Chapter 23, after telling of the assembly at which these matters were decided (verse 2), first gives the division of the Levites according to their work (verses 3, 4), and then their divisions according to families or houses, as descended respectively from the three sons of Levi—from Gershom (verses 7–11), from Kohath (verses 12–20), and from Merari (verses 21–23). The remainder of the chapter defines their duties. Chapter 24 speaks of those who served within the Temple, distinguishing between the sons of Aaron, who were priests (verses

1–19), and the rest, who were attendants of the priests (verses 20–31). Together these made up the 24,000 of 23: 4a.

1 Compare the special duties of the priests (23: 13—see Note below) with those of the other Levites who were not sons of Aaron. What part of the Levites' former duties were now no longer necessary, and why (23: 25–32)?

2 Why has all this elaborate organization passed away? *Cf.* Heb. 7: 11–25. What has taken its place? *Cf.* Heb. 8: 1, 2; 1 Pet. 2: 4, 5, 9; Rev. 1: 6.

Note. 23: 13. 'To consecrate . . .': better, 'to sanctify as most holy him and his sons for ever', as in RV mg. The burning of incense implies also the sprinkling of the blood of the atonement. *Cf.* Ex. 30: 10; Lv. 16: 12–14.

☐ STUDY 12 1 Chronicles 25–27

These chapters record the family divisions and the work of (a) the 4,000 choristers mentioned in 23: 5 (see chapter 25), (b) the 4,000 doorkeepers (26: 1–19), and (c) the 6,000 officers and judges (26: 20–32). All these were Levites. Chapter 27 records the leaders of the tribes, the commanders of the monthly divisions, and the chief officers of state.

1 Who were the three chief leaders of praise? See 25: 1; also 6: 33, 39. 44; 15: 16, 17. Why is their ministry of praise called 'prophesying'? *Cf.* Eph. 5: 18, 19.

2 Amidst the many differences of function and service described in these chapters, notice the way in which all contribute to the worship and honour of the Lord. What developments of this lesson do you find in the teaching about Christian service in Eph. 4: 1–7, 11, 12; 1 Cor. 12: 18–21?

Notes

1 25: 1. 'The chiefs of the service': the phrase seems to refer here to those in charge of the Temple staff, 'the authorities of the temple' (Moffatt).
2 25: 3. 'Jeduthun': elsewhere called 'Ethan'. See 6: 44; 15: 17, 19.
3 26: 29. 'Officers and judges': the officers collected the tithes and other revenue and the judges gave judgment in matters of law.

☐ STUDY 13 1 Chronicles 28

When David had done all he could in his private and personal capacity in preparation for the building of the Temple, he summoned an assembly of the leaders in all departments of the nation's life to commend the scheme to them, and, as the next chapter shows, was greatly gratified by their response.

1 'I had it in my heart to . . . But God said to me, "You may not"' (verses 2 and 3). Have we known some such experience in our service of God? How does David bring out that God's plan was far better?

2 There are two charges to Solomon in this passage, in verses 9, 10 and 20, 21. Considering them together, (a) what was to be Solomon's first duty, (b) what the character of the God with whom he had to do, (c) what the two grounds of his confidence, and (d) what consequently the manner and spirit of his service? What lessons do you find in this for your life?

Note. Verse 19. Notice the distinct claim here made that the pattern of the Temple and of its service was given to David by revelation.

☐ STUDY 14 1 Chronicles 29

1 Study verses 1–9 as a lesson in giving to the Lord. What did David ask of the people, and on what grounds? What characteristics of their giving are specially emphasized? *Cf.* 2 Cor. 8: 3–5; 9: 7. Is our giving of similar quality?

2 Consider in David's prayer (verses 10–19) (a) what he says of God, (b) what he says of man and of his own attitude of heart, and (c) what he prayed for. Seek to learn how to enrich and enlarge your own praying.

PSALMS 107 - 138

☐ STUDY 85 Psalm 107: 1–32

This psalm has a general introduction (verses 1–3), then four examples showing God's steadfast love (verses 4–32), and a conclusion summarizing what is learnt about God from these experiences (verses 33–43).

1 What are the situations of difficulty from which God rescued His people? Study (a) the reasons for these difficulties, (b) the feelings of the people in them, and (c) the way in which they obtained relief.

2 What reactions are called for from those who have been delivered in these ways?

3 How do some of the acts of Jesus show the same pattern as God's acts here? *Cf., e.g.*, verses 23–32 with Mk. 4: 35–41; Mt. 14: 22–33. What does this show us about Jesus?

☐ STUDY 86 Psalm 107: 33–43

1 What is shown about God Himself and His love by these great acts of deliverance? What was required of men to enter into these experiences?

2 Study the evidences given here of God's control of human experiences and circumstances. *Cf.* verse 34 with Joel 1: 19, 20; 2: 3; Dt. 29: 22–26; and verse 35 with Is. 43: 19, 20; 44: 3.

☐ STUDY 87 Psalm 108

The first five verses of this psalm are taken from Ps. 57: 7–11 and the remainder from Ps. 60: 5–12.

1 Verses 1–5. What moves the psalmist to such determined praise? How do these verses show us the way to appreciate and worship God, and to include praise as a vital part of our prayer?

2 Verses 6–13. In the agony of wondering whether God is helping them any longer, how does the psalmist anchor his faith? *Cf.* Heb. 6: 17; 10: 23; 13: 5, 6.

Note. Verses 7–9. The promise God gave in the Temple enforces His sovereign claim over these territories. The mention of Shechem and Succoth emphasizes God's claim over both sides of Jordan (*cf.* Gn. 33: 17, 18). Ephraim and Judah, paired, bind north and south. (For the sceptre see the promise of Gn. 49: 10.) Moab, Edom and Philistia are traditional enemies and hostile neighbours of Israel. A campaign against Edom seems to be in mind (verse 10).

☐ STUDY 88 Psalm 109

This psalm falls into three parts. Verses 1–5 are a prayer to God for deliverance from persecuting opponents. Retribution is then invoked by the psalmist (verses 6–20) upon the leader of his enemies and all that belongs to him. In the third section (verses 21–31) there is a return to prayer, culminating in thanksgiving and faith.

1 Verses 1–5. How does the writer show that he has a good conscience, and is not being opposed because of his own offensiveness or evil deeds? Compare Jesus' attitude in parallel circumstances (Lk. 23: 32–43; *cf.* also 1 Pet. 4: 12–19).

2 Verses 21–31. Instead of himself taking revenge, the psalmist takes refuge in prayer. Study the attitude of prayer in these circumstances.

Note. Verses 6–20. The retribution invoked includes the man himself, his person and office, his wife and children, his property, and also his prosperity. The place and significance of the imprecatory psalms (of which this is one), as part of the fullness of revealed truth, belong to the general subject of the progress of revelation. It is to be remembered that in pre-Christian days New Testament standards were not yet revealed. Old Testament believers lived in a dispensation in which retribution was a fundamental principle. Their very faith in a God of righteousness, who would reward the righteous and condemn the wicked, encouraged them to pray for His blessing upon themselves and for His vengeance upon their persecutors; and in this they had scriptural support (*e.g.*, Lv. 24: 19; Pr. 17: 13). Retribution was therefore prayed for as part of the practical vindication of God's actual and righteous sovereignty. Note here that the psalmist does not take vengeance himself, but leaves it to God. The New Testament teaches us also to love and pray for them that despitefully use us (Mt. 5: 43–45; Rom. 12: 19–21).

☐ STUDY 89 Psalm 110

This psalm speaks of the enthronement of a king (*cf.* Ps. 2), and of God's proclamation to that king. At morning time (verse 3b)—symbolizing the newness of the era about to begin—a solemn procession (verses 3, 7) moves by way of the spring (verse 7; *cf.* 1 Ki. 1: 33, 34, 45; 2 Ch. 32: 30) to the coronation in the holy city. There the king, as God's representative, begins his reign.

1 In detail, what hopes are expressed for this new epoch, with reference to (a) the rule of the king, and (b) the response from the people? Jesus applies this psalm to Himself in Mk. 12: 35–37. How then is all this realized in His Messianic kingship over us and the world?

2 Study the use of this psalm in the New Testament. No Old Testament verse is cited more often in the New Testament than Ps. 110: 1. *Cf.* Mk. 14: 62; 1 Cor. 15: 25ff.; Eph. 1: 20; Col. 3: 1; Heb. 1: 13; 10: 12, 13. Of what are we thereby assured?

3 The promised king is also to be a priest but not an Aaronic one. How does the writer to the Hebrews expound verse 4? *Cf.* Gn. 14: 17–24; Heb. 5: 7–11; 6: 20 – 7: 28.

☐ STUDY 90 Psalms 111 and 112

1 Ps. 111. What does the study of God's works reveal about Him to those who make it their delight to examine them? What response to God should follow?

2 Ps. 112. What social and ethical obligations are laid on the man who wants to please God? *Cf.* Mi. 3: 1–4; Je. 22: 1–4, 16; Mk. 10: 21. What blessings can such a man look for from God, in his own life and in his family's?

☐ STUDY 91 Psalms 113 and 114

Pss. 113–118 are psalms of redemption, the Hallel or hymn of praise that was sung at Jewish festivals in the time of Jesus. Looking back on God's past acts of redemption, particularly in the exodus, the people were encouraged to believe God would so act again. Jesus and His disciples may have sung these psalms at Passover as He Himself prepared for His act of redeeming us. (*Cf.* Mk. 14:26.)

1 Ps. 113. What activities are here said to be characteristic of God? *Cf.* Lk. 1:46–55. What kind of response, in terms of both time and place, should their acknowledgment secure from men?

2 Ps. 114. What features of the Israelites' journey from Egypt to Canaan are referred to? *Cf.* Ex. 14:21, 22; 17:5, 6; 19:18; 33:14; Nu. 20:11; Jos. 3:14–17. To what truths were these events a permanent witness?

☐ STUDY 92 Psalm 115

1 What answer is here given to idolaters who suppose that their gods are real, and that our God does not exist? Of what may we be sure concerning 'our God'?

2 What ought this psalm to stir us to do? What concern and what resolve ought it to prompt in us?

☐ STUDY 93 Psalm 116

While this psalm is written in the first person, there are indications that, like the other psalms of this group, it has a national character, and sets forth the reaction of the nation to the deliverance from exile. At the same time it echoes the personal experience of any believer.

1 How did trouble test the faith of the writer, and what new realization did his experience bring?

2 What is shown about his prayer during the trouble and afterwards? What resolves and dedication sprang from his experience?

Note. Verse 15. God sets a high value on the life of His people and does not regard their death lightly.

☐ STUDY 94 Psalms 117 and 118

Ps. 118 was used on a great Feast Day (verse 24). It opens with solemn liturgical exhortations and repeated responses. Then a kingly procession moves from outside the Temple (verse 19) to the interior (verse 26), culminating in a ceremony at the altar (verse 27). The king himself, entering into his victory celebration, has come through great struggles and opposition (verses 10–14, 18) to the gladness of victory and salvation (verse 21). This psalm, therefore, takes us to the centre of Israel's faith as a nation, and particularly to the triumph of her king.

1 In both psalms what truths about God particularly move the people, and how do they express their worship? What can we learn from their example?

2 Ps. 118: 5–21. Examine in detail the more personal testimony o the king. What has he been up against? What has the Lord done for him? Have you any comparable testimony?

3 Study the use of Ps. 118: 22–26 in its application to Jesus. *Cf.* Mt. 21: 9; Mk. 12: 6–11; Acts 4: 10–12; 1 Pet. 2: 7.

□ STUDY 95 Psalm 119: 1–24

The psalm consists of twenty-two stanzas of eight verses each, and goes through the Hebrew alphabet letter by letter. Each stanza begins with a new letter, and each verse in that stanza begins with that letter.

1 How must God's Word be used so that a man may live a pure and sinless life? Conversely, what temptations have to be overcome so that our motives are right, both in coming to God and in living for Him? *Cf.* Jas. 1: 21–25.

2 What compelling reasons urge the writer to study God's law? In putting what we here read into practice, where is the responsibility for action ours, and in what matters must we look only to God?

□ STUDY 96 Psalm 119: 25–48

1 In daily life the psalmist is confronted with many choices and subtle temptations. What are these, and how does the Word of God lead him (a) into the right choices, and (b) to victory in temptation?

2 For what motives and longings, described in this passage, do we particularly need to pray?

□ STUDY 97 Psalm 119: 49–80

1 How have sufferings been used for good in the life of the psalmist? How does this lead us forward in understanding why suffering sometimes comes? *Cf.* Je. 2: 30; Heb. 12: 6–11; Am. 4: 6–11.

2 Each section begins with a statement about the Lord. How then is past experience of Him to be used in prayer, commitment and obedience?

3 What bearing have the commandments upon the relationships between God's servant and others who fear Him? See verses 63, 74, 79.

☐ STUDY 98 Psalm 119: 81–104

1 Study the various aspects of the psalmist's problems as described in verses 81–88. How is God's Word relevant in these troubles?

2 Verses 89–96. How is it helpful to know that the author of these commandments and promises is the God of creation?

3 How do verses 97–104 illustrate from the psalmist's experience that whole-hearted obedience is the practical condition for progress in knowing and understanding the truth? *Cf.* Jesus' words in Jn. 8: 31, 32.

☐ STUDY 99 Psalm 119: 105–128

1 The psalmist has pledged himself to be God's servant (verse 106), but is tempted from several directions to go back on it. Which tests does he find hardest, and what is the way through them?

2 Verses 113–120. What does the psalmist say God is to him, and does for him? Can you make each of his statements your own?

3 Verses 121–128. In what matters is the psalmist conscious (a) of his dependence upon God only, and (b) of the importance of his own obedience?

☐ STUDY 100 Psalm 119: 129–152

1 List the terms in which the psalmist expresses his appreciation of God's Word. What tests and demands does he find that it can stand up to? What does this awareness mean (a) to him, and (b) to you?

2 When did the writer set himself to pray and study, and what may we learn from the way he prayed? Are your requests as personal, definite and comprehensive?

☐ STUDY 101 Psalm 119: 153–176

1 The writer continually prays for help and understanding (see verse 169), even though he has clearly been taught deep things already. What may we learn from this? See, *e.g.*, verse 176; *cf.* Rev. 3: 17–19.

2 Why does the psalmist need God's help? On what grounds does he expect his prayers to be answered? What is his reason for continual praise?

3 In verses 161–168, find at least three characteristics of the psalmist's attitude to the Word of God, and three blessings which devotion to it brings into a man's life. *Cf.* Pr. 3: 1–4; 6: 20–24.

☐ STUDY 102 Psalms 120 and 121

In Pss. 120–134 we have a book of pilgrim songs, probably used on the way up to Jerusalem for the great national festivals. Gradually the pilgrim approaches Zion where God is, and where the people enter afresh into the blessings of His love and redemption.

1 What does Ps. 120 teach about the menace of the tongue and the way of control? *Cf.* Ps. 141: 3, and the very similar teaching in Jas. 3: 1–12; 4: 1–3.

2 In Ps. 121 the infinite concern and care of God is shown. How, when and where can a man look to this God? And what will He constantly do for us?

Note. 120: 5. Meshech is somewhere between the Black Sea and the Caspian Sea (Gn. 10: 2; Ezk. 27: 13; 32: 26); Kedar is a tribe of Bedouins in the Syrian-Arabian desert (Gn. 25: 13; Is. 42: 11). They are so far from one another that their significance here is probably as symbols of quarrelsome adversaries without any special reference to their geographical position.

☐ STUDY 103 Psalms 122 and 123

1 Ps. 122. What is this pilgrim's attitude to Jerusalem, and why does he obey the summons to come and to pray? *Cf.* Dt. 12: 5–7; Ps. 87.

2 According to Ps. 123, what is the best antidote to despondency? *Cf.* also Heb. 4: 16.

☐ STUDY 104 Psalms 124–126

1 Ps. 124. What salutary reflections does the psalmist draw from the narrow escape that is past? How do past experiences buoy up present faith? What ought we to learn from them?

2 Of what two things did the mountain beneath, and the mountains around, Jerusalem speak to God's people? With Ps. 125, *cf.* Dt. 33: 27–29a.

3 In Ps. 126, what are the effects of God's intervention? Note the significance of the illustrations used. What kind of hope does such recollection inspire?

☐ STUDY 105 Psalms 127–129

1 Ps. 127 and 128. What is the secret of true prosperity? *Cf.* Ps. 37: 5–7; Pr. 3: 5–8.

2 Ps. 129. What two permanent truths concerning the life of the servants of God in the world are here set forth? Compare the experience of the Servant in Is. 50: 4–10, and the example of Jesus as the Servant of God in 1 Pet. 2: 19–23.

☐ STUDY 106 Psalms 130 and 131

1 Study the psalmist's attitude in prayer. On what things does he particularly concentrate (a) about himself, and (b) about God? How does his renewed contact with the Lord enable him to encourage others?

2 What four things does the psalmist say about himself in Ps. 131? *Cf.* Mt. 11: 29; Phil. 4: 11–13, 17, 18.

☐ STUDY 107 Psalm 132

This is another psalm describing the procession into the Temple as the king enters for his coronation. With him he brings the ark, the symbol of God's presence, as David did on the first occasion of this sort.

1 What lessons do we learn about the presence of God among His people? What did it mean to the king as he looked at his responsibilities for his own life and for the life of the nation? *Cf.* 2 Sa. 7: 1–17.

2 How do failures to enjoy blessings and promises of this sort arise? See how some of the kings went astray (1 Ki. 11: 1–6; 15: 1–5; 2 Ki. 13: 1–6).

Note. Verse 6. 'Ephrathah' is the ancient name of Bethlehem, the home of David (see *NBD*, p. 383), and 'the fields of Jaar' mean Kiriath-jearim (1 Sa. 7: 1ff.; 1 Ch. 13: 5ff.), where the ark rested before David brought it to Jerusalem.

☐ STUDY 108 Psalms 133 and 134

1 Ps. 133. By what two similes does the psalmist depict the blessings of love and unity? What is the force of these similes? *Cf.* Jn. 13: 34, 35; 1 Jn. 2: 7–11.

2 Ps. 134. Note the 'two-way traffic' sustained in the house and from the city of the Lord. Where ought we to go to share in it? *Cf.* Heb. 10: 24, 25; 12: 22–24.

Notes

1 133: 2, 3. These similes both indicate copiousness. The oil was poured upon Aaron's head so plentifully that it reached even the collar of the robe. The dew of Hermon was also noted for its abundance.

2 Ps. 134 is a Temple song, consisting of the call of the worshippers as they left the Temple in the evening to priests who were to serve during the night, together with the priestly blessing in response. It forms an appropriate ending to the book of pilgrim songs.

☐ STUDY 109 Psalm 135

1 Who are summoned to praise the Lord? Why is it so reasonable to do so? See verses 1–5.

2 As is so often the case, the thought goes back to God both as the Creator and the Redeemer. Why are these two activities so significant? What does each reveal about God in contrast to idols, and what should contemplation of them move us to do?

☐ STUDY 110 Psalm 136

The psalm divides into a call to give thanks (verses 1–3), a description of God in His creative acts (verses 4–9), and then in His acts of salvation (verses 10–22), ending with a deduction and summary (verses 23–26).

1 By what titles is God described? See verses 1–3 and 26, and *cf.* Dt. 10: 17; Ne. 1: 4, 5. What acts demonstrate the appropriateness of these titles? And how do these acts show God's 'steadfast love'?

2 What permanent lessons does the psalmist draw out? Compare the same themes in Ps. 107.

☐ STUDY 111 Psalms 137 and 138

Ps. 137. The psalmist expresses the deep feeling of the exiles in Babylon, as the stinging experience of hostile surroundings and treatment, and the memory of the cherished city of Jerusalem, now a mass of rubble and ruin, overwhelm them.

1 Ps. 137. What interest and concern made the captives in Babylon weep rather than sing? Do you ever feel any similar constraint?

2 Whence does the writer of Ps. 138 gain the conviction that God is at work in his life? Examine the details of his confidence. How much of his confession can you make your own?

3 137: 6, 7. What place ought we to give in our thought, prayer and preaching to divine vengeance and just recompense? *Cf.* Ezk. 25: 12–14; Rom. 12: 19–21.

For Studies 112–119 on the final section of the Psalms see p. 478.

---

2 CHRONICLES

For Introduction, see p. 430.

Analysis

1: 1 – 9: 30	The building of the Temple. The reign of Solomon.	
9: 31 – 35: 27	The decline of the Temple.	
	9: 31 – 13: 22	First declension under Rehoboam. The kingdom divided and a rival worship established in the north.
	14: 1 – 20: 37	First reformation under Asa and Jehoshaphat.
	21: 1 – 22: 12	Second declension under Jehoram.
	23: 1 – 24: 16	Second reformation under Joash.
	24: 17–27	Third declension under Joash, after the death of Jehoiada the priest.
	25: 1 – 27: 9	Period of partial recovery under Amaziah, Uzziah and Jotham.
	28: 1–27	Fourth declension under Ahaz.
	29: 1– 32: 32	Third reformation under Hezekiah.
	32: 33 – 33: 25	Fifth declension under Manasseh and Amon.
	34: 1 – 35: 27	Fourth reformation under Josiah.
36: 1–21	The destruction of the Temple.	
36: 22, 23	The command of Cyrus concerning the rebuilding of the Temple.	

☐ STUDY 1 2 Chronicles 1 and 2

1 How did Solomon inaugurate his reign?

2 How do Solomon's request (1: 10) and God's response illustrate Mt. 6: 33? In my praying what do I 'seek first'?

3 What characterized the way in which Solomon went about the preparations for building the Temple? Is my service of God comparable?

Note. 1: 3. 'The tent of meeting': this was the Tabernacle used in the wilderness. After the Israelites entered Canaan, it was first pitched in Shiloh (Jos. 18: 1; 1 Sa. 2: 14b; 3: 21), then moved to Nob (1 Sa. 21: 1, 6), and then to Gibeon. Later Solomon brought it to Jerusalem (2 Ch. 5: 5), where it was probably stored and finally perished.

☐ STUDY 2 2 Chronicles 3: 1 – 5: 1

1 All that human skill and wealth could do (note how many times the word 'gold' occurs in these chapters) was done. Yet it was still inadequate. Why? See Heb. 9: 1–10, which, though spoken of the Tabernacle, is equally applicable to the Temple.

2 Solomon's Temple has long since passed away (see 36: 19), and the Temples that succeeded it also. Is there, then, today a place where men may draw near to God? See Heb. 10: 19–22, 'Let us draw near. . . .'

Note. 3: 3. 'The old standard': a reference to the cubit in use before the exile, which was a handbreadth larger than that used later.

☐ STUDY 3 2 Chronicles 5: 2 – 6: 11

1 This was one of the great days in Israel's history. How does Solomon interpret its significance in 6: 1–11?

2 We, who belong to the new covenant, are ourselves the temple of God (1 Cor. 3: 16; 6: 19). Is there any parallel between the place given here to the ark and the place we should give to Christ in our hearts? What is the ground of Christian praise, and what corresponds to the glory which 'filled the house'?

Note. 5: 5. See Note on 1: 3.

☐ STUDY 4 2 Chronicles 6: 12–42

1 On what grounds does Solomon base his prayer? See verses 14, 15 and 42. What three main petitions does he present in verses 16–21, and into what seven specific requests does he expand the third of these?

2 What conditions does Solomon's prayer suggest as being essential to effective prayer?

☐ STUDY 5 2 Chronicles 7 and 8

1 God's immediate answer to Solomon's prayer is given in 7: 1–3. What effect had it upon the people? *Cf.* Lv. 9: 24. How far should God's mercies affect us?

2 God gave a further answer to Solomon privately in the form of a promise and a warning (7: 12–22). What were the conditions upon which Solomon's petitions were to be granted? Do I fear the fulfilment of God's warnings as I desire the fulfilment of His promises?

☐ STUDY 6 2 Chronicles 9 and 10

1 What was the Queen of Sheba's testimony concerning Solomon? Has something similar been your experience of Christ? *Cf.* Phil. 3: 8.

2 What led Rehoboam to make such a disastrous mistake? What did he lack that Solomon possessed? *Cf.* 1 Ki. 3: 28.

Notes

1 Chapter 9. Another side to the portrait of Solomon is found in 1 Ki. 11: 1–13, and provides a background to the disruption. Note also 2 Ch. 10: 4.

2 From chapter 10 onwards students are advised to make a list of the kings of Judah as they work through the rest of the book, and to note the biblical assessment of each (*e.g.*, good or evil), with a brief mention of his contribution to the nation's religious life.

☐ STUDY 7 2 Chronicles 11 and 12

1 Was Rehoboam good or evil? Was there a fundamental fault in his character? *Cf.* Jas. 1: 8.

2 What did Shemaiah achieve on the two occasions when he intervened in national life, and how was he able to do this? Is there a parallel between his work and that of a Christian today?

3 What lesson did God mean to teach through Shishak's invasion?

☐ STUDY 8 2 Chronicles 13 and 14

1 Chapter 13. Jeroboam had the advantages of numbers (verse 3) and of military skill (verse 13), and he, too, had received promises from God (*cf.* 1 Ki. 11: 29–39). What, then, gave Judah the victory? *Cf.* verse 18 with 1 Ki. 12: 28–33.

2 Chapter 14. What did Asa do to mark him out as 'good and right' in peace and war?

3 What is the connection between 14: 2–4 and 14: 11, 12? *Cf.* 1 Jn. 3: 21, 22; 5: 3, 4. If Asa had not set God and His commandments in the forefront of his endeavours, could he have prayed with such confidence or won so great a victory? What did Asa's faith provide him with besides the victory?

Note. 13: 5. 'By a covenant of salt': *i.e.*, a binding covenant, not to be broken. *Cf.* Nu. 18: 19.

□ STUDY 9 2 Chronicles 15 and 16

1 Can you find in Azariah's message (15: 2–7) (a) a fundamental principle of divine government, (b) an illustration from Israel's past history, (c) an exhortation, and (d) a promise?

2 Chapter 15. How thoroughly and with what success were these lessons heeded by Asa (see especially verse 15)? *Cf.* Je. 29: 13; Mt. 11: 29.

3 In what ways did Asa backslide in his later years, and what were the consequences?

□ STUDY 10 2 Chronicles 17 and 18

1 The chronicler gives four chapters to the reign of Jehoshaphat, who was one of the best of the kings of Judah. What, according to chapter 17, were the reasons for his prosperity? Note the word 'therefore' in verse 5. What method did Jehoshaphat introduce to give religious instruction to the people?

2 Chapter 18. How did Micaiah seek to proclaim the word of God, and what difficulties did he encounter? What may we learn from him concerning faithfulness in such ministry?

3 In what ways do the characters of Jehoshaphat and Ahab differ?

□ STUDY 11 2 Chronicles 19 and 20

1 In the beginning of Jehoshaphat's reign he continued the policy of maintaining fortified cities for defence against Israel. But later he made peace with Israel through a marriage alliance (18: 1; 21: 6). How was this alliance with Ahab rebuked, and on what grounds? *Cf.* 2 Cor. 6: 14; see also 2 Ch. 20: 35–37.

2 After this rebuke, what further steps did Jehoshaphat take to establish true religion in the land?

3 When peril came, what did Jehoshaphat do first? What impresses you most in this story?

Note. 20: 2. 'Engedi': on the western shore of the Dead Sea, and therefore not far from Jerusalem.

☐ STUDY 12 2 Chronicles 21: 1 - 22: 9

1 Identify the sins here recorded of Jehoram. How did God deal with him, and why? To what did he owe his survival?

2 How far was the low state under Jehoram and Ahaziah directly traceable to the mistaken step of Jehoshaphat as recorded in 18: 1? What does this illustrate concerning the character and consequences of some sins?

☐ STUDY 13 2 Chronicles 22: 10 – 23: 21

1 *Planning*. Why had Jehoiada to wait seven years? What lessons may we learn from this for ourselves? *Cf.* Hab. 2: 3. Why did he have confidence that the plan would succeed?

2 *Action*. What lessons in careful planning and organization can we learn from Jehoiada in our service of Christ?

3 *Success*. Jehoiada was not content with half measures. How did he follow up his victory? See 23: 16–20.

Notes

1 23: 2, 3. This was the preliminary gathering, secretly convened in the Temple, in which all present pledged their loyalty to the boy king.

2 23: 11. 'The testimony': *i.e.*, the book of the law. *Cf.* Dt. 17: 18–20.

☐ STUDY 14 2 Chronicles 24

1 Joash was a weak character, who leant on others. To whom did he listen? What were the consequences? What lessons may we learn? *Cf.* 2 Tim. 2: 1.

2 Why was the stoning of Zechariah a peculiarly flagrant crime?

Note. Verse 16. This was a signal and unique honour. Contrast verse 25.

☐ STUDY 15 2 Chronicles 25

1 What would you say was the chief fault in Amaziah's character? How does the chapter illustrate the description of him in verse 2? See, on the one hand, verses 3, 4, 7–10; also 26: 4; and, on the other hand, 25: 14–16, 27. *Cf.* Je. 17: 9.

2 How does Amaziah's career, with its gradual drift away from God, show the peril of a half-hearted loyalty to Christ?

Note. Verse 10. The hired soldiers had been hoping for loot and plunder' hence their anger. See also verse 13.

☐ STUDY 16 2 Chronicles 26–28

1 How was it revealed that in Uzziah's heart, notwithstanding his piety (26: 5), there lurked the same evil tendency that had marred the life and reign of his father Amaziah before him? With 26: 16, *cf* 25: 19; Dt. 17: 18–20. What forms might his sin take today?

2 How did the sin of Ahaz affect (a) God, (b) His people, and (c) himself?

3 In the midst of a godless age how did Oded, the prophet, and the men mentioned in 28: 12 stand out? What may we learn from their example? *Cf.* 1 Tim. 5: 20.

Notes

1 26: 5. 'Zechariah': not otherwise known, and not the prophet of the biblical book who lived at a later period.

2 26: 18. See Nu. 16: 40; 18: 7.

☐ STUDY 17 2 Chronicles 29: 1 – 31: 1

1 Hezekiah as king desired to reform the religious life of the nation, and worked urgently to a definite plan. What steps did he follow? Note his speed (29: 3; 30: 2) and his priorities (29: 16–21).

2 What evidence do you find that the Passover (chapter 30) was not merely an outward form, but betokened a genuine turning back to God? What signs were there of true spiritual revival?

Note. 30: 2, 3, 13, 15. The king availed himself of the provision in the law which allowed the Passover to be kept in the second month, instead of the first (see Nu. 9: 10, 11), and thus avoided having to wait almost a year.

☐ STUDY 18 2 Chronicles 31: 2 – 32: 33

1 How far was Hezekiah's thoroughness in all matters connected with religion the secret of his success? See especially 31: 20, 21. *Cf.* Rom. 12: 11; Col. 3: 23.

2 What lessons can we learn from the way in which Hezekiah met opposition?

3 How far did this spiritually-minded king fall short of perfection? How may we learn from him?

Notes

1 32: 1. This reference to Hezekiah's faithfulness (31: 20) is introduced to show that the coming of Sennacherib was not because he had sinned.

2 32: 5. Archaeologists think 'the Millo' at Jerusalem was probably part of the fortifications or the foundations for them.

☐ STUDY 19 2 Chronicles 33

1 Make a list of Manasseh's idolatrous deeds, as described in verses 3–9. It has been termed 'a very delirium of idolatry' and was done in the face of protest and rebuke (verses 10, 18).

2 What means did God use to bring Manasseh to his senses? And what may we learn from this as to one of the purposes of human suffering?

3 What marks of true repentance are seen in Manasseh after his restoration? In what ways could it have gone further?

Notes

1 Verse 6. A reference to human sacrifice in honour of the god Molech. *Cf.* 2 Ki. 23: 10; Je. 7: 31.

2 Verse 14. 'Ophel': a mound south of the Temple. *Cf.* 27: 3.

☐ STUDY 20 2 Chronicles 34 and 35

1 At what age did Josiah begin to seek the Lord? What effects did this have on his subsequent life both publicly and privately?

2 What was the effect of the finding of the book of the law (a) upon Josiah, and (b) through him upon the nation? *Cf.* Ps. 119: 59, 60. Is the Word of God having the same effect upon you, and through your life?

3 What does 34: 23–28 teach concerning (a) the inevitable consequences of sin (*cf.* Dt. 11: 26–28), and (b) God's attitude to the sincere penitent?

Notes

1 34: 14. 'The book of the law' was quite likely Deuteronomy (*cf.* Dt. 31: 26).

2 35: 3. It is usually assumed that the ark had been taken out of the holy of holies during the repairs, and that the Levites were now bidden to restore it, with the assurance that they would not again be asked to undertake this work. *Cf.* 1 Ch. 23: 26.

3 34: 28 and 35: 24. Josiah was spared from witnessing God's anger poured out upon Judah (34: 25) by his death, and thus may be said to have died 'in peace'.

☐ **STUDY 21 2 Chronicles 36**

1 Alongside the cataclysmic political happenings, what is the one outstanding event in this chapter which overshadows all else?

2 In the indictment of this chapter, on what sin does the emphasis lie (verses 12–16)? How would you describe the cause of Judah's downfall? *Cf.* 7: 19–22.

3 In what particular matters did Zedekiah fail?

4 What does this chapter reveal about the character of God?

Note. A summary of the kings and events of this chapter. (a) Jehoahaz was king for three months (verses 1–3). (b) Jehoiakim (Eliakim) reigned for eleven years (verses 4, 5). He was an Egyptian vassal until the Babylonians (or Chaldeans, verse 17) defeated them at the Battle of Carchemish (605 BC) and became the dominant power. The first Babylonian invasion occurred during this reign (verses 6, 7). (c) Jehoiachin was king for three months, until the second invasion (verse 10) terminated his reign; 10,000 leading citizens were taken into exile. (d) Zedekiah reigned for eleven years (verse 10, 11). He was a Babylonian vassal and his rebellion precipitated the third invasion, devastation and exile (verses 17, 18) in 586 BC.

ESTHER

Introduction

The book of Esther is a swiftly-moving story which repays reading at one sitting. Its author and date of composition cannot be identified with certainty. The wealth of detail and local colour, however, suggests that it was written in Persia not long after the events recorded in the book had taken place. Perhaps its Persian origin may account for the long time that elapsed before it was accepted as canonical by the Palestinian Jews.

Ahasuerus is usually identified with Xerxes (485–465 BC), and the action takes place in Susa, one of the three capitals of the Persian Empire. Chronologically this places the events some years before those recounted in Ezra and Nehemiah, which relate to the following reign—that of Artaxerxes (465–424 BC).

One of the most unusual features of the book is the absence of any mention of the name of God. There is, however, a strong undercurrent throughout of patriotism and a sense of overriding Providence, as the Jews in exile are saved from destruction. Their deliverance provides the origin of the Feast of Purim.

Analysis

1: 1–22	Queen Vashti disobeys King Ahasuerus and is deposed.
2: 1–20	Esther, a Jewess, is chosen by the king to replace Vashti.
2: 21–23	Mordecai exposes a plot against the king's life.
3: 1–15	Mordecai refuses to bow to Haman, the king's favourite, who thereupon plans to massacre the Jews.
4: 1–17	Esther is persuaded by Mordecai to intercede with the king.
5: 1–8	The king receives Esther.
5: 9–14	Haman schemes to secure Mordecai's death.
6: 1–14	The king makes Haman honour Mordecai publicly as a reward for revealing the plot against him.
7: 1–10	Esther's plea is granted and in consequence Haman is executed.
8: 1–17	Mordecai is honoured further and an edict is published allowing the Jews to defend themselves.
9: 1–19	The Jews slay their enemies.
9: 20–32	Their deliverance is commemorated in the Feast of Purim.
10: 1–3	Mordecai is given a position of great authority.

☐ STUDY 1 Esther 1

1 Read this chapter in the light of 2 Cor. 4: 18 and 1 Jn. 2: 16, 17. What choice do such considerations force upon us?

2 What may we learn of the characters of Ahasuerus, Vashti and Memucan as seen in this chapter? *Cf.* Pr. 20: 2; Jas. 1: 19, 20; Eph. 4: 26, 27.

Notes

1 Verse 11. Persian women were usually present at feasts, so this would not be taken as a personal affront to Vashti.

2 Verse 14. 'Who saw the king's face . . .': *i.e.*, belonging to the inner circle of the king's counsellors.

☐ STUDY 2 Esther 2: 1–18

1 By what steps did Esther become queen? Consider the events and the timing in terms of God's overruling care for His people. See Note on verse 16; *cf.* Rom. 8: 28; Is. 65: 24.

2 How far should a Christian conform to the laws and customs of his country? *Cf.* Dn. 1: 8; 1 Pet. 2: 13, 14.

Notes

1 Verses 5, 6. 'Who had been carried away . . .': this refers not to Mordecai, but to Kish his grandfather.

2 Verse 16. *Cf.* 1: 3. Four years had elapsed since Vashti was deposed.

☐ STUDY 3 Esther 2: 19 – 3: 15

1 Mordecai made no secret of his Jewish faith, yet advised Esther to remain silent. What does this teach us for our own witness? Why did Mordecai not obey the king's command? *Cf.* Ec. 3: 1, 7b; Dn. 3: 8–12, 16–18; Acts 5: 28, 29.

2 What do we learn of Haman's character in chapter 3? See particularly verses 5–9 and 15. To what was he blind in the schemes that he made?

Notes

1 2: 19. 'Sitting at the king's gate': the phrase may imply that he was in the king's service in some way.

2 2: 21. 'Who guarded the threshold . . .': *i.e.*, of the king's sleeping apartments.

☐ STUDY 4 Esther 4

1 The Jews mourn Haman's decree, but for Esther the situation requires personal action. Consider (a) what factors influenced the decision she reached (see particularly verses 4, 8, 13, 14, 16), and (b) whether verse 14 is relevant to your own immediate situation.

2 Esther made careful preparations to enter the king's presence. In our own approach to the King of kings, what parallels and contrasts can you find? See also 5: 1, 2; *cf.* Ps. 33: 8; Heb. 10: 19–22.

☐ STUDY 5 Esther 5 and 6

1 Mordecai could reasonably have expected a substantial reward for saving the king's life (2: 21–23). However, his service was acknowledged only after a long delay and by an apparent coincidence. In what ways does this help us to understand delays and disappointments in our own life? *Cf.* Ps. 37: 7; Is. 55: 8, 9.

2 Consider the developments in the story of Haman as illustrations of such verses as Ps. 34: 15, 16; Pr. 16: 18. What ought we to learn from such a record?

☐ STUDY 6 Esther 7 and 8

1 How does chapter 7 illustrate the theme of certain psalms? See, *e.g.*, Pss. 73: 17–19; 94: 1–7, 21–23. How should this influence our faith?

2 After the fall of Haman what did (a) Esther and (b) the Jews still have to do to obtain the deliverance promised by the king? See especially 8: 3–8, 11, 12. What parallel is there in Christian experience? *Cf.* Phil. 2: 12, 13.

Notes

1 7: 3. 'My life . . . and my people . . .': for the first time Esther acknowledges her nationality.

2 7: 9. Notice how often the king's decisions are influenced by those around him.

☐ STUDY 7 Esther 9 and 10

1 Select from these and earlier chapters the outstanding features o Mordecai's character. What was the source of his moral strength?

2 Notice here the severity of the judgment on the wicked. Are we in danger of underestimating this part of 'the whole counsel of God' (Acts 20: 27)? *Cf.* Heb. 10: 30, 31; 1 Pet. 4: 17, 18; Rev. 20: 12–15.

3 Why was the Feast of Purim instituted? See 9: 22; *cf.* Ex. 12: 14–17. Do we ever encourage and challenge ourselves by the remembrance of God's mercies to us? *Cf.* Dt. 8: 2; 1 Cor. 11: 24–26.

Note. 9: 26. 'Purim . . . Pur': these words are derived from the Assyrian *puru*, meaning a small stone, which was used to cast lots. See 3: 7; 9: 24.

ECCLESIASTES

Introduction

This book speaks through the mouth of Solomon, but does not in any way build on his authority. In the earlier part the writer describes human life as seen by a shrewd observer, who disputes the arguments of those who find a satisfactory aim in life either in intellectual labour, or in the gathering of riches, or in pleasure, or even in the attainment of an ethical ideal, seeing that death terminates all, and comes to all alike.

Man cannot by searching find out the deep things of God (3: 11) but must bow before His sovereignty (3: 14). Whatever appearances may indicate, God judges righteously, though judgment may be long delayed (8: 12, 13).

The recurring phrase 'under the sun' may be regarded as indicating the purely human standpoint adopted by the writer in the earlier chapters, and as roughly equivalent to 'in the world as man sees it'. It is salutary for the Christian to contrast the vanity and meaninglessness of this world, its business and pleasures, as set forth in Ecclesiastes, with our glorious heritage in Christ as set forth in the New Testament.

The book is the record of a spiritual pilgrimage, reaching its culmination in chapter 12 (*cf.* 12: 13, 14 with Rom. 2: 16). In Ecclesiastes, perhaps more than in any other book of the Old Testament, the standpoint of the writer should be borne in mind, and particularly the fact that he saw nothing for man beyond death save judgment. His attention is concentrated upon this life, for 'our Saviour Christ Jesus, who abolished death and brought life and immortality to light through the gospel' (2 Tim. 1: 10) had not yet appeared.

Analysis

1: 1	The title.
1: 2–11	The endless monotony of human life on earth.
1: 12 – 2: 26	The Preacher's experiences—wisdom, pleasure, labour alike fail to satisfy. 'There is nothing better for a man than to eat and drink and enjoy himself, as he does his work' (2: 24, Moffatt).
3 – 6	Further illustration of the vanity of man's striving. His life is hemmed in by divine control, and ends in death. Various counsels. Riches do not satisfy.
7: 1 – 11: 8	The kind of life men should lead. Wisdom is better than folly. The fear of God brings a sure reward. God's works are unsearchable. Various counsels.
11: 9 – 12: 14	Childhood and youth pass; old age and death draw near. The ultimate conclusion: fear God and keep His commandments.

☐ **STUDY 1 Ecclesiastes 1 and 2**

1 In what ways does 1: 1–11 show the monotony of life? Why is such pessimism unchristian?

2 How did the writer discover that neither the pursuit of wisdom (1: 12–18) nor the enjoyment of pleasure (2: 1–11) can satisfy man's heart?

3 Though wisdom is better than folly (2: 13, 14a), what three facts rob even wisdom of its power to satisfy (2: 14b, 17, 18 and 23, 24–26)?

☐ **STUDY 2 Ecclesiastes 3: 1 – 4: 8**

1 What, according to 3: 1–15, is the best attitude to life? How does the Preacher illustrate his conviction? *Cf.* Mt. 10: 29, 30. To what practical conclusion does he come?

2 In 3: 16 – 4: 8, what four instances are given of the futility of life, and what reflections do they arouse in the writer's mind?

Note. 3: 1. 'Season . . . time': the two words express two thoughts, (a) tha everything happens at an appointed time; and (b) that the time is appropriate in relation to the working out of God's purpose.

☐ **STUDY 3 Ecclesiastes 4: 9 – 6: 12**

1 What are the blessings of friendship described in 4: 9–12? How does this apply in the spiritual life? See, *e.g.*, Mt. 18: 19, 20; Lk. 10: 1.

2 What does 5: 1–7 teach concerning worship, in respect to (a) the right attitude of spirit, (b) words spoken in God's presence, and (c) the importance of fulfilling vows?

3 What is the teaching of 5: 8 – 6: 12 regarding money and the evils it brings?

Notes
1 5: 1. 'Guard your steps': *i.e.*, 'Never enter God's house carelessly' (Moffatt).
2 5: 3. As cares and labours cause a man to dream, so do many words in worship give rise to folly.
3 5: 20. 'Then he will never brood over the fewness of his days' (Moffatt).
4 6: 10, 11. 'Whatever happens has been determined long ago, and what man is has been ordained of old; he cannot argue with One mightier than himself' Moffatt). The meaning is that much talking against God's dealings is profitless.

☐ STUDY 4 Ecclesiastes 7 and 8

The Preacher has declared several times that man's best course in this present world is to enjoy the portion in life which God has given him, and the fruit of his labour. In these later chapters, while still holding to this view, he inquires more closely into the kind and quality of life which men should lead.

1 In the practical wisdom of chapter 7, what emerges as the guide-principle for life?

2 Though the future is hidden from man, what course of action is advocated in 8: 1–7? How is the problem of death approached in 8: 8–17?

☐ STUDY 5 Ecclesiastes 9: 1 – 10: 7

1 Why, from a Christian standpoint, is the view of life containec in 9: 1–10 untenable? *Cf.* Lk. 23: 39–43; and note how and why one of the criminals rebuked the other and found hope for himself.

2 What do 9: 11, 12 teach regarding a man's attitude to natura talents? In what way is the value of wisdom shown in 9: 13 – 10: 4?

☐ STUDY 6 Ecclesiastes 10: 8 – 11: 8

1 List the spheres in which the practical wisdom of 10: 8–20 apply, and deduce any general principles for your practical guidance.

2 11: 1–8. Since the future cannot be known, what advice does the writer give regarding an appropriate attitude in life? *Cf.* 9: 10.

Note. 11: 1, 2. 'Trust your goods far and wide at sea, till you get good returns after a while. Take shares in several ventures; you never know what will go wrong in this world' (Moffatt).

□ STUDY 7 Ecclesiastes 11: 9 – 12: 14

1 In the Preacher's counsel to youth, (a) in what is youth to rejoice, (b) to what all-important fact must heed be given, and (c) who is to be remembered? What is the reason for this counsel?

2 Contrast the joyful hope of the Christian with the picture of death and old age given here. *Cf.* 2 Cor. 4: 16–18; 2 Tim. 4: 6–8; 1 Pet. 1: 3–5.

3 In summing up man's duty, what place is given to God? How, in consequence, ought we to live?

Notes

1 11: 10. 'Vanity' has here the meaning of 'transitory' or 'passing'.

2 12: 2. Old age is here compared to winter weather, when storm succeeds storm.

3 12: 3–6. A series of pictures of the failure of man's various bodily faculties in old age, such as strength of limb, number of teeth, keenness of sight, *etc.* 'When old age fears a height, and even a walk has its terrors, when his hair is almond white, and he drags his limbs along, as the spirit flags and fades' (verse 5, Moffatt).

SONG OF SOLOMON

Introduction

The Song of Solomon is unique not only for its exquisite literary charm, but also for its rich appreciation of human love and the beauty of nature, and its deep insight into the human heart. It has also appealed to Christians as a picture of the love of Christ for His church, and gives to them words in which to utter their hearts' devotion to Him.

It is uncertain who wrote it. The phrase 'which is Solomon's' in 1: 1 may equally mean 'which is for Solomon' (as in the title of Ps. 72) or 'which is about Solomon'; and there is no other clue to its authorship.

According to the earlier and more traditional interpretation, there are only two main characters—Solomon and his bride. Many commentaries of great devotional beauty and insight have made this interpretation familiar, in which the bride is regarded as a 'type' of the church, and Solomon of Christ.

Others, however, discern in the background of the story another figure, that of a shepherd, who is the girl's true lover. It is he whom she calls 'my beloved'. A girl from the village of Shulem, she had gone one day to visit her garden, when she fell in unexpectedly with some of Solomon's retinue, who took her captive to the palace (6: 11–13). There the king visits her, and struck by her great beauty seeks to win her for himself. But she has a shepherd lover to whom her heart is pledged, and to whom she remains faithful. Three times the king visits her, wooing her with growing ardour, until at last, finding all his efforts of no avail, he sets her free. At the close of the book she is seen leaning on the arm of her beloved, returning to her village home, where she is received by her family and friends as the shepherd lover's acknowledged bride. In this view, much of the book consists of reveries in which the girl communes in thought with her beloved; and of incidents and dreams connected with him, which with artless simplicity she tells to the ladies of the court.

With these different interpretations to choose from, we must obviously form our own view from a study of the book itself. If we take the Song as it stands it is clear that we must look at it first of all as a poem, or collection of poems, about human love between man and woman. The study questions are therefore designed primarily to discover the meaning of the Song of Solomon at this level.

Analysis

It is exceedingly difficult to analyse the Song. The following scheme is based on the three-character interpretation outlined above:

Section I

1: 2 – 2: 7 Scene in the private apartments of Solomon's palace.

1: 2–8 The girl, soliloquizing, expresses her longing for her absent lover (verses 2–4). Then, seeing the ladies of the court eyeing her, she explains to them the darkness of her complexion (verses 5, 6), and breaks out into a cry that she might know exactly where her lover is, to which the ladies of the court reply that she should go to seek him (verses 7, 8).

1: 9–11 The king enters, praises her beauty, and promises to adorn her with jewels.

1: 12 – 2: 6	The king having gone to his repast, the girl falls into a reverie, in which, in imagination, she communes with her beloved in some forest glade.
2: 7	She bids the ladies of the court not to seek to arouse love by artificial means.

Section II

2: 8 – 3: 5	The girl relates an incident of the past.
2: 8–15	Her beloved came one morning to call her to go with him, and to warn her of danger to love's fulfilment.
2: 16, 17	She bids her beloved return at the end of the day.
3: 1–4	When he did not return, she could not rest, but went out into the night to seek him.
3: 5	The same charge as in 2: 7.

Section III

3: 6 – 8: 4	The struggle is intensified, but ends in victory.
3: 6 – 4: 7	Solomon, appearing in royal splendour, makes a determined attempt to capture the girl's affections.
4: 8 – 5: 1	Alarmed, she flees in thought to her beloved, whose voice she hears, bidding her escape with him from the dangers of the palace (4: 8). He pours out his love for her (4: 9–15) in words far excelling the conventional tributes just paid to her by the king. Her heart opens to her lover, and she sees their marriage day as if already come (4: 16 – 5: 1).
5: 2–16	The girl relates a disturbing dream which she has had; and in answer to a question from the ladies of the court gives an impassioned description of her beloved.
6: 1–3	The ladies of the court ask where he is, that they too may seek him, a suggestion that leads the girl to declare that no other can share her privilege of possession.
6: 4–10	The king enters, and tells her in words of admiring praise that there is no-one who can compare with her, and that even his queens have sung her praises.
6: 11–13	The girl interrupts to explain how she came to be in the king's palace.
7: 1–9	The king continues to urge his desire.
7: 10 – 8: 3	The girl, refusing, turns in heart to her beloved to commune in spirit with him.
8: 4	The same charge as in 2: 7 and 3: 5.

Section IV

8: 5–14	The scene is the girl's village home.
8: 5	The girl, released, returns with her beloved to her home.
8: 6, 7	The girl's panegyric on true love.
8: 8–12	She recalls her brothers' words, and declares her faithfulness.
8: 13, 14	Her lover bids her speak and in the presence of his friends she calls him her beloved.

☐ STUDY 1 Song of Solomon 1: 1 – 2: 7

1 Much of this passage consists of conversation. The Analysis provides one answer to the problems of how many characters are speaking and where the break occurs. What do you think is the basic situation?

2 Can we learn anything from the different imagery used by the man (1: 15–17; 2: 2) and the woman to express their love and longing for one another? Does this suggest anything of the different qualities, or needs, of each?

Notes

1 1: 12–14. Women wore small bags of myrrh suspended from the neck under their dress. To the girl, her beloved was as the costliest perfume.

2 2: 1. The girl describes herself as an ordinary wild flower of the meadow.

3 2: 3. The apple tree affords both shade and fruit.

4 2: 4. 'The banqueting house': literally 'house of wine', signifying 'a place of delight'.

5 2: 7. A difficult verse. It seems to mean that love should awake or come to life of itself or in its own time, not by artificial stimulation and not before the beloved one is pleased to respond. Gazelles or hinds are noted for their timidity.

☐ STUDY 2 Song of Solomon 2: 8 – 3: 5

1 What purpose do the various pictures from nature serve in revealing the quality of love?

2 What characteristics of true love emerge in 2: 16, 17 and 3: 1–5?

Notes

1 2: 10–12. An appeal to respond to the approach of love, like nature to the return of summer.

2 2: 15. The enemies may be small—'little foxes'—but the mischief done great. If the blossom is spoiled, there will be no fruit.

3 2: 17. A picture of evening, not of early morning. The shadows flee away when the sun that causes them sets. The bride asked her beloved to wait until the evening. When it came, she 'sought him but found him not' (3: 1).

☐ STUDY 3 Song of Solomon 3: 6 – 5: 1

1 What do you make of Solomon's entrance here, and of his part in the whole of the Song? See also, *e.g.*, 1: 1, 12; 6: 8, 9, 12; 7: 1, 5; 8: 11, 12.

2 What do these frank expressions of a man's physical delight in his bride teach us about the place of sexual attraction in love and marriage? What is the significance of the private garden image?

3 Scripture uses marriage as a picture of God's relationship to His people and Christ's relationship to His church. See, *e.g.*, Is. 62: 4, 5; Eph. 5: 21–33. Is there, therefore, a sense in which 4: 8–15 illustrates this relationship? *Cf.* Pss. 147: 10, 11; 149: 4. Is our heart reserved for Christ alone?

Notes

1 3: 7. 'Litter'; in verse 9, 'palanquin': a couch covered by a canopy borne by four or more men.

2 4: 4. The neck, decked with ornaments, is compared to a battlemented tower, hung with shields.

3 4: 8. On the three-character analysis the bride hears the voice of her beloved, calling her to himself, and the verse may be taken as a poetic description of the dangers to which she is exposed in the palace.

☐ STUDY 4 Song of Solomon 5: 2 – 6: 3

1 Is there any underlying reality in the disturbing dream of 5: 2–7? Would we be right to see in this passage teaching about, *e.g.*, the importance of response in love, or the likelihood of suffering if response is lacking?

2 How far is the bride's delight in, and praise of, her lover a feature also of our relationship to Christ? Do we meditate on Him as our 'beloved' and our 'friend' (5: 16)?

Notes

1 5: 2. 'I slept': these words indicate that the bride is relating a dream.

2 5: 4. The door was bolted—on the inside (see verse 5).

3 5: 10. 'Distinguished among ten thousand'; literally, 'marked out by a banner', *i.e.*, as outstanding among the rest as a standard bearer.

☐ STUDY 5 Song of Solomon 6: 4 – 8: 4

1 In 2: 16 the girl's first thought was of her claim upon her lover. Now (6: 3) she thinks first of his claim on her. In 7: 10 her claim is no longer mentioned. Her concern is to satisfy him by giving herself. The importance of this for human marriage relations is clear. But can these stages in love apply to our relation to Christ? If so, how?

2 8: 4. The warning is repeated here for the third time (see also 2: 7; 3: 5). Why do you think it was given, and with such emphasis?

Notes

1 6: 4. 'Tirzah': the name (meaning 'delight') of a beautiful town, which later became the royal residence of the kings of northern Israel.

2 6: 12, 13. A possible translation, in line with the three-character analysis, is 'My soul has unwittingly brought me to the chariots of the companions of my prince'; *i.e.*, she fell in with some of Solomon's retinue. She fled, but they called her back, and gazed upon her, as she put it, as if she were a company of dancers.

3 7: 1–6. These verses may be part of the song composed by the women (6: 9b, 10), or may be spoken by Solomon. In verses 7, 8 he is certainly the speaker.

☐ STUDY 6 Song of Solomon 8: 5–14

1 What does this passage add to all we have already learnt of the nature of love? What attacks may true love have to face?

2 What qualities are here shown to be characteristic of true love?

Notes

1 8: 6. 'Set me as a seal . . .': in ancient times men carried their seal fastened to breast or wrist for safe preservation. The girl desires to be thus held fast on the heart and arm of her beloved. 'Jealousy is cruel as the grave': better, 'Ardent love is unyielding as Sheol'.

2 8: 8–10. The girl recalls her brothers' earlier words. They had waited to see if she would be as a wall against temptation, or as an open door to give it entrance. Here she claims that she has shown herself as a wall.

3 8: 11, 12. Solomon appears to have offered her a vineyard of great wealth; but she put it aside in favour of the vineyard which was hers in her beloved.

☐ STUDY 7 The whole Song of Solomon: Revision

Most of the study questions have been concerned with the Song's meaning at the level of human love between the sexes. Re-reading the Song, draw out some of the lessons it can teach us about Christ's love for us, and our love for Him. How does our personal devotion to Christ measure up to these very high standards?

2 PETER

Introduction

The second Epistle of Peter was written just before his death (1: 14, 15). We may regard it as his last word, and this fact lends added significance to the final message, 'Grow in the grace and knowledge of our Lord and Saviour Jesus Christ' (3: 18).

Peter is obviously concerned about the heresies and moral evil which have crept into the church, and is writing to warn, to exhort and to comfort. In contrast with the gloomy picture which he draws is the prominence he gives to the hope of our Lord's return. He explains that this is delayed, not through any slackness on God's part, but through His forbearance (3: 9). He is afraid that the Christians, under the stress of persecution and temptation, will forget the commandments which have been delivered to them through the prophets and the apostles. He writes to remind them of their calling and to stir them up (1: 9, 12, 13, 15; 3: 1, 2).

Chapter 2 is strikingly similar in content to the Epistle of Jude. As Peter dwells on the evil which is rampant, he stresses more than ever the call to holiness which he had given in his first letter. 'You therefore, beloved, knowing this beforehand, beware lest you be carried away with the error of lawless men and lose your own stability' (3: 17). The essential antidote to error is the true knowledge of God and of the Lord Jesus Christ. This is the key to this Epistle. See 1: 2, 3, 8; 2: 20; 3: 18.

Analysis

1: 1, 2	Introduction.
1: 3–15	The call to progress in Christian character and fruitfulness.
1: 16–21	The veracity of the Christian message.
2: 1–22	Description and condemnation of evildoers and false prophets.
3: 1–7	Warnings for the last days.
3: 8–18	The longsuffering of the Lord, and the certainty of His coming.

☐ STUDY 1 2 Peter 1: 1–11

1 How do verses 1 and 10 describe the Christian's relation to God? What is meant by 'knowledge' in verses 2, 3, 8? What provision has God made for our present life, and what will be our final position (verses 3, 4, 11)?

2 If our salvation is the product of God's call and power (verses 10, 3), why are we urged to zealous effort (verses 5, 10)?

3 Analyse the picture of the fully developed Christian, given in verses 5–7, in relation to (a) his personal character; (b) his attitude to God; and (c) his dealings with others. Observe that all rests upon a basis of faith, but faith without these added qualities is not enough.

☐ STUDY 2 2 Peter 1: 12–21

1 Of what does Peter take such care to remind his readers? Does any Christian not need this kind of reminder? *Cf.* 3: 1, 2; Dt. 32: 18; Heb. 2: 1.

2 How do verses 16–21 provide an answer to theologians who claim that truth does not require a basis of historic fact?

3 Explain from verses 20, 21 the nature of the inspiration of Scripture. What gives it its authority, and what should govern its interpretation.

Note. Verse 19. 'The written word of prophecy has been confirmed by the vision of the Lord's glory . . . on the mount of Transfiguration, and Christians may well trust themselves to its guidance in this dark world, till light has dawned, which will render the lamp of an external revelation unnecessary' (Swete). This lamp of prophecy is referred to again in 3: 2.

☐ STUDY 3 2 Peter 2

1 Although we have the lamp of prophecy it is necessary to beware of *false* teachers. Note from today's passage the forms of evil in which the false teachers, of whom the apostle speaks, indulged. By which are you most liable to be snared? How far is this kind of behaviour seen in modern society? How would you meet the claim of those who profess to be free from the restraints of convention (verse 19, *cf.* Jn. 8: 34–36)? *Cf.* verse 20 with Mt. 12: 43–45; Heb. 6: 4–8.

Note. Verses 4–10 are parenthetical, interrupting the description of the false teachers, which is resumed in 10b.

☐ STUDY 4 2 Peter 3: 1–10

1 What arguments do the scoffers of verse 3 use? What is the best defence against them (verse 2)?

2 In verses 5–7 Peter refutes the scoffers by reference to the unfailing fulfilment of God's word. Explain from these three verses how the words and actions of God in the past assure us that in the future He will again do what He has said. Is there a similarity between the people of Noah's day and our own (*cf.* Mt. 24: 37–39)?

3 Why is 'the day' so slow in coming (verse 9)? *Cf.* Ezk. 18: 23, 32.

Note. Verse 10. 'Elements' : the material elements of the universe; but, as many think, with specific reference to the heavenly bodies.

☐ STUDY 5 2 Peter 3: 11–18

1 Make a list of the practical conclusions which Peter draws from the certainty that the day of the Lord will come. How do these work out in the way you yourself live?

2 Verses 17, 18 sum up the theme of the whole Epistle. How are we to maintain stability in the Christian life? Show that to be stable is not to be static.

Note. Verse 12. 'Hastening' (RSV) is better than 'hasting unto' (AV). The day is being hastened as by our repentance and zeal we remove the need for God's forbearance (verses 9, 15). *Cf.* Rom. 2: 4.

JUDE

Introduction

The writer of this Epistle has been generally identified with Judas, one of the brothers of the Lord (Mt. 13: 55). The letter was probably written after the fall of Jerusalem, possibly between AD 75 and 80.

The message of the Epistle is very similar to that of 2 Peter. Both authors write out of a sense of deep urgency (*cf.* Jude 3, 'I found it necessary'). Evil men and evil ways had crept into the church, and were endangering its life. This evil must be fought; and the object of both Epistles is to stir up the Christians. Jude, like Peter, looks to the past for illustrations of divine judgment upon sin, and declares that judgment will fall as certainly as in the past upon those who are now turning their backs upon truth and righteousness. Finally, he exhorts his readers to keep themselves in the love of God, who will hold them fast, through Jesus Christ our Lord. Peter foretold the coming of false teachers, but they were already active when Jude wrote.

Analysis

1–4 Introduction, and purpose of the letter.
5–7 God's judgments in the past.
8–16 Description and condemnation of the evil which has crept in.
17–25 Exhortation and benediction.

□ STUDY 1 Jude 1–16

1 Contrast, clause by clause, the threefold description in verse 1 of the faithful believers, to whom Jude is writing, with the description in verse 4 of the false intruders into the church, whom he condemns.

2 Compare Jude 4–16 with 2 Pet. 2: 1–18. What resemblances and differences do you find?

3 Verse 3. Are you contending for the faith? If it was once for al delivered to the saints, is there any scope for modification as the church develops?

Note. Refer to the *NBC* for explanation of verses 9, 14, 15.

□ STUDY 2 Jude 17–25

1 Verses 17–21. When confronted by the adverse influences of the world, what are we to do, and what will God do, to maintain our spiritual development?

2 What should be our attitude as Christians to those around us who may be going astray, and what to the sin that has defiled them?

3 What may we learn from verses 24, 25 concerning the ground of our confidence, the source of our joy, and the object of our aspirations? What should such awareness move us to do?

DANIEL

Introduction

The book of Daniel is rich in spiritual instruction, and will reward prayerful study. It shows, first of all, how those who believe in God can take their place in the society where they find themselves, play their part in current affairs, and yet remain true to God, thereby bringing glory to Him and blessing to men. Such men and women are needed among the nations today.

The book of Daniel is also a tonic to faith. The overthrow and exile of the Jews raised the question 'Where is their God?' (Ps. 115: 2). The book of Daniel reveals God as sovereign over the nations, watchful over those who trust in Him, and working all things 'according to the counsel of his will'. The earlier chapters helped to bring home to the Jews the great truth of the sole Deity of the Lord. This weaned them from idol-worship (*cf.* Ps. 115: 3–11). The later chapters of the book, with their exact prediction of the course of events, were the means by which the faith of the remnant was sustained amid the troubles and persecutions that they endured. This book should help also to sustain our own faith in days of darkness.

The book of Daniel is also an integral part of Scripture in its revelation of things to come. This assumes that the book is a true record and prophecy belonging to the time of the exile. There has been a strong trend in recent times to dispute this, and to assign the composition of the book to a period 400 years later, when many of its predictions had already become facts of history. The older view is not without its difficulties, but the progress of archaeology has already removed some of these, and in holding to the authenticity of the book, we are in line with the New Testament, which bears witness to its miracles and predictions (see, *e.g.*, Heb. 11: 33, 34; Mt. 24: 15), and quotes from or alludes to it frequently, especially in the synoptic Gospels and the book of Revelation.

Analysis

History (chapters 1–6)

1 Daniel and three other youths selected, proved, educated.
2 Nebuchadnezzar's dream and its interpretation.
3 Nebuchadnezzar's golden image, and the fiery furnace.
4 Nebuchadnezzar's second dream, with its fulfilment, and his testimony.
5 Belshazzar's feast, the writing on the wall, the fall of Babylon.
6 Darius' edict. Daniel in the den of lions.

Prophecy (chapters 7–12)

7 Vision of the four great beasts, in the first year of Belshazzar.
8 Vision of the ram and he-goat, and of four kingdoms, and of the little horn, in the third year of Belshazzar.
9 The prayer of Daniel; the revelation concerning Messiah.
10–12 Vision of the future, and of 'the time of the end', in the third year of Cyrus.

☐ STUDY 1 Daniel 1

1 What were the motives which lay behind the resolve of Daniel and his three friends to avoid defilement? *Cf.* Lv. 3: 17; 20: 24–26. How did they set about achieving their aim? What Christian qualities did they display in their approach to authority? With what gifts did God reward them?

2 What light does the story throw upon what it means to be 'in the world' (Jn. 17: 11), but 'not of the world' (Jn. 17: 16)? Notice how firmness of conviction in youth laid the foundation for later steadfastness.

Notes

1 Verse 1. The year is probably 605 BC, and the reference is to a Babylonian foray immediately after their victory at Carchemish.

2 Verse 2. 'Shinar': an ancient name for Babylon.

☐ STUDY 2 Daniel 2: 1–30

1 Daniel and his companions were brought suddenly into great peril through no fault of their own. Note carefully what steps Daniel took. What may we learn from his example as to how to act in any such time of sudden danger? *Cf.* Acts 4: 23, 24; 12: 5.

2 Watch the four at prayer. They might have asked God to change the king's mind, for he was acting very unreasonably; but what did they ask? Consider the faith behind their petition, and how God answered them above what they had asked. See 2: 47–49; and *cf.* Eph. 3: 20, 21.

☐ STUDY 3 Daniel 2: 31–49

1 Observe that the four kingdoms, though historically appearing one after the other, are yet all parts of the one image. Also, it is not only the last kingdom of the four, but the whole image that is broken to pieces by the stone that smites it. What does the dream reveal as to God's final purpose? And what differences do you find between the kingdoms of the world that compose the image and the kingdom prefigured by the stone? *Cf.* Rev. 11: 15.

2 What divine purposes did the dream serve in relation to (a) Nebuchadnezzar, (b) Daniel and his friends, and (c) all who knew, or know of it?

Note. Verses 39, 40. Those who assign the book of Daniel to the Maccabean period take the four kingdoms to be those of Babylon, the Medes, the Persians and the Greeks. This, however, apart from other objections, seems to go contrary to the book itself, which regards Medo-Persia as one kingdom (see 5: 28; 6: 8; 8: 20, 21). The older interpretation, therefore, which takes the four kingdoms to be Babylon, Medo-Persia, Greece and Rome, is to be preferred.

☐ STUDY 4 Daniel 3

In the opening part of this chapter the king manifests a very different attitude towards the Lord from that of 2: 47. The probable reason is that between chapters 2 and 3 there is an interval of several years, during which Nebuchadnezzar had evidence that his own god was greater than the God of the Jews (*cf.* verse 15b). It accounts also for the enmity of the Chaldean officials against Shadrach, Meshach and Abednego. They would resent Jews continuing to hold rule over the province of Babylon.

1 What threefold accusation was brought against the three Hebrews? Consider how subtly it was worded to stir the king's anger.

2 How does this trial of faith differ from anything these men had had to meet hitherto? For similar instances of courage see Acts 4: 8–12; 5: 29–32; 2 Tim. 4: 16, 17. What purposes were served by the miracle of deliverance which God wrought?

☐ STUDY 5 Daniel 4

The theme of this chapter is pride. It takes the form of a decree by Nebuchadnezzar announcing the strange psychical affliction he has undergone, through which he has learnt the all-important lesson that 'the Most High rules the kingdom of men, and gives it to whom he will' (verse 25). It can be compared with Is. 14: 8–17 and Ezk. 28: 1–10, passages which in their turn look back to the basic sin of humanity (Gn. 3).

1 How effective was the king's experience in bringing him to humility? Contrast his attitude to God and confession of Him in this chapter with his previous utterances in 2: 47; 3: 29. How would you define the change?

2 What are the main themes of Daniel's teaching in this situation? With verse 27, *cf.* Mi. 6: 8.

Notes

1 Verse 13. 'A watcher, a holy one': *i.e.*, an angelic figure who acted with the authority of God.

2 Verse 33. The mental derangement, known as zoanthropy, lasted for a set period described as 'seven times' (verse 16). This could mean 'seven years' or simply 'a substantial period of time'. In the apocryphal 'Prayer of Nabonidus', found at Qumran, it is recorded that King Nabonidus, a successor of Nebuchadnezzar, spent seven years of his reign in isolation at Teima because of some strange illness. So this chapter is not without parallel in ancient traditions

☐ STUDY 6 Daniel 5

Babylon fell in 539 BC, twenty-three years after the death of Nebuchadnezzar. A quarter of a century, therefore, has elapsed since the events of chapter 4.

1 What four accusations did Daniel bring against Belshazzar? In what two ways was Belshazzar's sin aggravated and made more heinous?

2 Consider the judgment pronounced upon Belshazzar as symbolizing the divine judgment upon all ungodliness, whether in national or individual life. See verses 26–28, and *cf.* Pr. 15: 3, 9; Ec. 8: 11–13.

Notes

1 The identity of Belshazzar was for long unknown, but he is now known to have been the eldest son of King Nabonidus (556–539), and to have shared the duties of the throne with his father. While Nabonidus was away from Babylon, his son had supreme authority there.

2 Verse 10. 'The queen': probably the queen-mother, widow of Nebuchadnezzar.

3 Verses 25–28. The words represent three weights or coins, *viz.* mina, shekel, and peres or half-mina. But the interpretation conceals numerous plays on words, for the verbal roots mean 'to number, to weigh and to divide'. In the case of 'peres', 'to divide', a further similarity to the word for Persian has been used.

☐ STUDY 7 Daniel 6

The identity of Darius the Mede is still a matter for debate, but the most likely candidates are Gobryas (Gubaru), the governor of Babylon, or Cyrus the king. This is one of many instances of biblical interpretation over which the reader has to admit that he simply does not know the answer until fresh evidence comes to light to help to solve the mystery.

1 Neither pressure of business nor the threat of death kept Daniel from prayer. How is it with you? Do you think that other qualities in Daniel's character revealed in this chapter were the outcome of his prayer life? What were those qualities? *Cf.* Is. 40: 29–31; Phil. 4: 5, 6.

2 Is your faith of such a kind that you can stand alone in obedience to God without external support? Are we so living that even our keenest critics take it for granted that the will of God comes first in our lives, come what may?

☐ STUDY 8 Daniel 7

The chapter records, first, the vision (verses 2–14); then the general interpretation (verses 15–18); then Daniel's enquiry concerning three features of the vision (verses 19, 20); and lastly, the answer given to these enquiries.

1 Assuming the four kingdoms to be the same as those which Nebuchadnezzar saw in his dream (chapter 2), what is there new in this vision which caused Daniel such distress and agitation of spirit (verses 15, 28)?

2 To Nebuchadnezzar the kingdoms of this world appeared in the glittering splendour of material wealth and power, whereas by Daniel they are seen as beasts of prey. What is the difference between these points of view, and which is the deeper and truer view? *Cf.* 1 Sa. 16: 7; Mt. 4: 8; 1 Jn. 2: 16, 17.

3 What is to be the final goal of history to which this vision looks forward? Who are meant by 'the saints of the Most High' (verse 18)? What privileges will they have in the days to come?

Notes

1 Verse 5. The bear represented the Medo-Persian Empire, noted for its greed for further conquest.

2 Verse 6. The wings on the leopard's back indicate the swiftness of Alexander's campaigns. After his death his empire was divided into four parts.

3 Verse 7. The fourth beast is either the Seleucid Empire, with its many kings (horns), of whom Antiochus Epiphanes was the most deadly, or Rome with its many emperors, under one of whom arose the Son of man.

☐ STUDY 9 Daniel 8

The vision of this chapter received historical fulfilment in the overthrow of Persia by Alexander the Great (330 BC), the division of Alexander's kingdom into four ('but not with his power', verse 22), and the rise of Antiochus Epiphanes, who did what is here foretold of him in verses 9–12 and 23–25 (170–164 BC). Gabriel's emphasis, however, upon the vision having to do with 'the time of the end' (see verses 17 and 19) suggests that its meaning is not exhausted in Antiochus, but that he is only a type of one greater than he, and yet to come, who will act in a similar way. *Cf.* 7: 24–26 and Mt. 24: 15; 2 Thes. 2: 8–10.

1 What expression is used both of the ram and of the he-goat in the time of their prosperity, and also of the king of verse 23? Yet what was the end of these kingdoms? Notice the repetition of the verb 'to break'.

2 Why was Daniel so deeply affected by this vision? Consider how the prophecies of Jeremiah and Ezekiel seemed to indicate that the return from exile would coincide with the advent of the kingdom of God (see, *e.g.*, Je. 32: 37–44; Ezk. 37: 21–28); but this vision shows long vistas of history stretching into the future, and *further suffering for the Jews.*

Notes

1 Verse 9. 'The glorious land': *i.e.*, Palestine.

2 Verse 10. 'The host of heaven . . . stars': used figuratively of Israel and her leaders.

3 Verse 11. 'The prince of the host': *i.e.*, God Himself. *Cf.* verse 25.

4 Verse 12. Israel was to be given over into the power of the 'horn' because of transgressions, and true religion was to be suppressed.

5 Verse 14. If the burnt offering ceased for 2,300 times, that would be 1,150 days, which is a little more than three years. It is known that Antiochus did suspend the burnt offering for three years and possibly a little longer.

□ STUDY 10 Daniel 9: 1–19

1 Consider the effect of the fall of Babylon upon one who, like Daniel, saw in it a fulfilment of prophecy (verse 2; *cf.* Je. 25: 11; 29: 10–14; 50: 1–5). What did it lead him to do (*cf.* Ezk. 36: 37), and what light do verses 2 and 3 throw upon the use of Scripture in our praying?

2 As you read through Daniel's prayer, how would you describe his praying? See especially verses 3 and 19. In his confession, how does he speak of God? How of himself and his people? In his petition, on what does he base his plea for mercy, and for what does he ask?

□ STUDY 11 Daniel 9: 20–27

Daniel had assumed that a period of seventy years would finish 'the desolations of Jerusalem' (verse 2), and in his prayer had pleaded with God for this (verse 18). God sends Gabriel to give him fuller understanding (verses 20–23), by conveying to him 'a word', which speaks not of seventy years, but of seventy weeks of years. The message is very condensed, and every clause is significant.

1 Verse 24. What are the six things here mentioned? Notice that they all concern the Jews and the holy city, and are to come to pass at the end of the full seventy weeks of years.

2 The seventy weeks of years are divided into three periods of seven weeks, sixty-two weeks and one week respectively. What the first period signifies is not certainly known, unless it is the time taken to build the city. What event, however, is stated as happening at the end of the second period?

3 The remainder of the passage has been variously interpreted, even by those who regard it as inspired prophecy. If verse 26a is a reference to the cross of Christ, then verse 26b seems to point to the destruction of Jerusalem and the Temple by the Romans in AD 70. But such questions as these arise: (a) Does the fall of Jerusalem in AD 70 exhaust the prophecy? (b) Who is the 'prince that shall come', and is he to be identified with the little horn of 7: 8, 24, 25? See Note 3 below.

Notes

1 Verse 24. 'To finish the transgression' and 'to put an end to sin' are parallel expressions meaning to bring Israel's sinning to an end. *Cf.* Rom. 11: 26, 27. 'To seal both vision and prophet': *i.e.*, to ratify them as being fulfilled. 'To anoint a most holy place': *i.e.*, the consecration of the Messianic Temple, fulfilled in the establishment of the church, the body of Christ.

2 From the decree of Artaxerxes I, referred to in Ezr. 7: 11ff. (458 BC), sixty-nine weeks of years bring us to the period of Christ's ministry. This prophecy of Daniel may account for the widespread expectation of a Messiah at the time Jesus appeared (*cf.* Mt. 2: 1, 2; Lk. 2: 25, 26; 3: 15), and may lie behind our Lord's own words in Mk. 1: 15a.

3 Verses 26, 27. Many hold that in this prophecy, as in other Old Testament passages, the beginning and end of the Christian era are telescoped together, and that the prophecy here leaps forward to the end of the age. If so, the last 'week' is separated from the first sixty-nine by the whole interval between Christ's first and second comings. With verse 27, *cf.* 2 Thes. 2: 8.

□ STUDY 12 Daniel 10: 1 – 11: 1

1 This chapter is introductory to Daniel's last vision. Consider the date (10: 1) and trace out from Ezr. 1; 3; 4: 4, 5 what was happening at that time to the first contingent of those who returned from exile. What light does this throw upon the mourning of Daniel (verse 2) and upon the purpose of the vision?

2 What does this passage teach of the costliness of communion with God, and of true prayer?

3 Read Eph. 6: 10–13 in the light of this chapter; also 2 Ki. 6: 16–18; Ps. 34: 7. In the presence of the mysterious spirit-world, what comfort may we draw from the New Testament revelation that our Lord is supreme there also? *Cf.* Eph. 1: 20–23; Col. 1: 16; 2: 15.

Notes

1 Verses 5, 6. It is not said who this august being was. Some features of his appearance and person remind us of the visions of Ezekiel and John (Ezk. 1: 13–16; Rev. 1: 13–15).

2 Verse 8. 'No strength': 'Before God gives strength and power unto His people He makes them sensible of their own weakness.'

3 Verse 13. 'Prince': used here of guardian angels of the kingdoms.

4 Verses 16, 18. The angelic figure described in these verses is probably the same as the original being of verse 5, but the text is not very clear.

☐ STUDY 13 Daniel 11: 2–20

This passage is a forecast of history, not continuous, but selective. The period is one of nearly 400 years, from the time of Daniel's vision to the reign o Antiochus Epiphanes. Verses 2–4 are introductory, having reference (a) to the rulers of Persia, up to Xerxes (verse 2), and (b) to the rise of Alexander the Great nearly 150 years later, and to the division of his kingdom into four (verses 3, 4). From this point the prophecy confines itself to two of these four kingdoms: Egypt, whose ruler is called 'king of the south', and Syria, whose ruler is called 'king of the north'. The successive rulers of these kingdoms in historical succession were (a) *Egypt*: Ptolemy I (304–285 BC); Ptolemy II (285–246 BC); Ptolemy III (246–221 BC); Ptolemy IV (221–205 BC); Ptolemy V (205–180 BC); Ptolemy VI (180–145 BC); (b) *Syria*: Seleucus I (312–280 BC); Antiochus I (280–261 BC); Antiochus II (261–246 BC); Seleucus II (246–226 BC); Seleucus III (226–223 BC); Antiochus III, called the Great (223–187 BC); Seleucus IV (187–175 BC); Antiochus IV, called Epiphanes (175–163 BC).

Verse 5a of our chapter refers to Ptolemy I, and verse 5b to Seleucus I, who for a time was one of Ptolemy's generals, but became ruler of a wider empire then Ptolemy's. Verse 6 refers to Ptolemy II, who gave his daughter Berenice to Antiochus II in marriage upon certain conditions. The conditions were, however, broken and Berenice lost her life. Verses 7 and 8 refer to Ptolemy III, brother of Berenice, who successfully attacked the kingdom of Syria under Seleucus II and returned with great spoil. Seleucus II later invaded Egypt, but without success (verse 9). Verses 10–19 predict continued wars between the kings of Syria and Egypt in the reigns of Antiochus III, Ptolemy IV and Ptolemy V. The victory turned now to the north (verse 10), and now to the south (verses 11, 12). Then Antiochus brought Egypt low (verses 13–17), but, wishing to press westwards (verse 18), made an alliance with Egypt by giving Ptolemy V his daughter Cleopatra in marriage (verse 17). The plans for a conquest westward were, however, defeated by a Roman commander (verse 18), and Antiochus had to retire to his own kingdom, where he died (verse 19). Verse 20 refers to Seleucus IV, who imposed heavy taxes upon Palestine to build up his kingdom's finances. In all this time Palestine, named 'the glorious land' (verse 16) and 'the glory of the kingdom' (verse 20), was the pathway of marching armies, and a bone of contention between the warring nations. But it had not yet suffered what it was soon to suffer under Antiochus IV.

1 What was the purpose of this detailed prediction? In what way would it help the remnant during the persecution which was to come?

2 Ponder the words in verses 3 and 16 'shall do according to his own will'. See also verse 36, and contrast Jn. 4: 34; Rom. 12: 1, 2; 1 Jn. 2: 17. Are you learning to say with Christ Mt. 26: 42 and Heb. 10: 7?

Note. Verse 14. A party among the Jews will rise up, thinking by violence to bring to pass the fulfilment of prophecy.

☐ STUDY 14 Daniel 11: 21 – 12: 13

At chapter 11: 21 the predicted course of events as told in the vision reaches the reign of Antiochus Epiphanes, and the historical fulfilment can be traced with accuracy up to verse 35. The career of Antiochus is revealed in four main features: (a) the craft by which he obtained the throne and won his way to power (verses 21–23); (b) his love of munificent and lavish giving (verse 24a); (c) his plans for war (verse 24b), and especially his wars against Egypt (verses 25–30); and (d) his acts of sacrilege against the Temple in Jerusalem and persecution of the Jews (verses 31–35).

The remainder of the passage (11: 36 – 12: 4) seems at first sight to be a continuation of the career of Antiochus, but on closer examination is seen to go beyond it, alike in its description of the king (verse 36; *cf.* 2 Thes. 2: 4), in the events which it records (*e.g.*, 12: 1, 2), and in the emphasis laid upon its being 'the time of the end' (11: 35, 40; 12: 4). The figure of Antiochus seems here to merge into the more sinister figure of the Antichrist. With 12: 2, 7, *cf.* 7: 25; 9: 27.

1 Gather out the evidence given here on the one hand of man's sinfulness and lust for power, and on the other of God's overruling control and purpose. *Cf.* Je. 17: 5–14.

2 What are the characteristics of those who will be glorified and of those who will be put to shame at the last?

Notes

1 11: 21. *I.e.*, he was not the recognized heir to the throne.

2 11: 22–24. 'The prince of the covenant' is probably Antiochus, the infant son and heir of Seleucus IV. 'The strongholds' are those of Egypt.

3 11: 27. Antiochus actually captured the king of Egypt, but they pretended to be friendly.

4 11: 30. 'Ships of Kittim': *i.e.*, Roman ships, which refused Antiochus liberty to proceed. He vented his anger, therefore, upon Palestine.

5 11: 31. 'The abomination that makes desolate': a small altar was placed upon the altar of burnt offering and sacrifices were offered to idols.

6 11: 37. 'The one beloved by women' refers to the god Tammuz. See Ezk. 8: 14.

PSALMS 139 - 150

☐ STUDY 112 Psalm 139

1 Verses 1–18 describe in three sections the psalmist's consciousness of God's scrutiny of his life. What departments of life are singled out as known by God in verses 1–6? What truths about God are emphasized in verses 7–12, and in verses 13–18?

2 Why is it that the psalmist can pray as he does in verses 23, 24, especially in the light of what he confesses in verses 1–4? Do you regularly pray this kind of prayer?

☐ STUDY 113 Psalms 140 and 141

1 In Ps. 140 note carefully the psalmist's description of his enemies: their character, their methods, their purpose. In these circumstances of intense danger, what does the psalmist do, what does he pray for, and how is his faith sustained?

2 Ps. 141 deals with some of the more insidious temptations which threaten to involve God's servant in evil. Note in detail what they are. Note also the kinds of help for which he prays. How does the influence of other people work here?

3 Both psalms mention the far-reaching significance of speech. Study how the things men say can do evil. How can greater control be gained over the tongue?

☐ STUDY 114 Psalms 142 and 143

1 Ps. 142 shows how God's servant is not immune from the depths of distress and despair. How does he describe how he feels? And then, what does he do? What does he believe? And what does he expect? *Cf.* Ps. 138: 7, 8; Jb. 23: 10; 2 Cor. 1: 8–11.

2 Ps. 143 consists of an invocation (verses 1, 2), a lament (verses

3, 4), a retrospect (verses 5, 6) and a petition (verses 7–12). Study how one important fact comes to mind in each of these first three sections. Note what reaction is caused each time in him. The petition itself falls into a pattern like this too. What solution does he now pray for in each aspect of his need? Note particularly his morning prayer in verse 8. Learn from such an example how to be more pointed in your praying.

☐ STUDY 115 Psalm 144

1 What does David confess (a) that he is in God's sight; and (b) that God can be to him and do for him? Have you similar cause to 'sing a new song' (verse 9)?

2 What special lessons for spiritual leaders of others can be learnt from this psalm? In particular, how do David's prayers express the special needs of a person with responsibility?

Note. Verses 8, 11. The meaning is that when they raised their right hand in solemn oath, they lied.

☐ STUDY 116 Psalm 145

1 How many different aspects of the character of God are mentioned in this psalm, and what kinds of appreciation and response should such contemplation of His character call forth?

2 How is the kindness of God shown to all, and how more specifically to those who fulfil certain conditions? *Cf.* and contrast Mt. 5: 4, 5; Rom 3: 22; 8: 28.

☐ STUDY 117 Psalm 146

1 In verses 3 and 4 the psalmist is warning Israel against trust in alliances which are a substitute for trusting God. *Cf.* Is. 30: 1–5; 31: 1. Why is trusting in man such a mistake? *Cf.* Is. 2: 20–22; Je. 17: 5.

2 It was always important to Israel to be a remembering people. See how God's acts in their experience long before illustrate the statements about God in verses 6c, 7a, 7b, 7c. Look up Jos. 23: 14–16; Ex. 3: 7, 8; 16: 2–4; Ps. 126: 1, 2.

3 Jesus takes up these themes making them the programme of His whole ministry (see Lk. 4: 16–21), and explaining His miracles in these terms (see Mt. 11: 2–5, echoing Is. 29: 18, 19; 35: 5, 6). What does He mean to teach about Himself in this way?

☐ STUDY 118 Psalm 147

1 In each of the three sections of this psalm (verses 1–6, 7–11, 12–20) one attitude or attribute of God is being highlighted. Discover each of these. What are, then, the point and logic of the references in each section to God's control of the natural universe and of created things?

2 Faith and praise are here supported by concrete reasons. What do we thus learn to be the greatest reasons for trusting and praising God?

☐ STUDY 119 Psalms 148–150

These psalms again find their best setting in the gathering of Israel in the Temple, celebrating God's greatness particularly in terms of His works in creation and history.

1 Summarize as expressed here the psalmist's view of God in His cosmic magnificence and creative omnipotence. To what one end should everything be used, and all creation united?

2 How is God's special relation with His people shown, and of what things do they feel they can be assured as they dwell on what He is known to be?

REVELATION

Introduction

Many have been put off the study of the book of Revelation by fears of its difficulty, or the intricate nature of some interpretations. But no book of the Bible will more surely reward the student who approaches it for its present relevance rather than as an eschatological enigma. It is important to remember that the visions which occupy so large a part of it are not to be regarded as literal pictures: the book is written in the literary form known as 'apocalyptic', which expresses heavenly and spiritual realities by means of a conventional and elaborate symbolism.

It is generally agreed that it was written by John the apostle, and in days of persecution, as his exile proves (1:9). Some think that his exile was suffered under Nero, who died in AD 68; some under Domitian (81–96). The later date seems more probable. The struggle between the people of Christ and the power of Rome had now reached a state more advanced than that which is reflected in the Acts of the Apostles. Emperor worship became common from Nero's reign onward, and the outlook was dark and threatening.

The reference to Rome in chapter 17 is but thinly veiled. Some interpreters ('Preterist') regard all the references as being to contemporary events, so that for us the book speaks of things already past; some ('Historicist') have seen in chapters 2–19 references to Christian history before and after the fall of Rome, and to the conflict of evangelical religion with the Roman church, so leading on to the times of the end; others ('Futurist') regard chapters 2 and 3 as an epitome of Christian history, and the rest of the book as a prophecy looking forward to events at the time of the Lord's return.

A true interpretation may well find something of value in all these points of view. It is best to study the book with the assurance (1) that it had a real message for its own time; (2) that its lessons have been illustrated by the history of the church; and (3) that it contains prophetical references to the future. The reader should not be so troubled by the obscurities that he cannot rejoice in the message of what is clear. We can learn lessons of tremendous value about the place of Christ's people in the purposes of God and the glorious future awaiting them, the heavenly nature of our earthly conflict, which can be carried on only with divine aid, the need to overcome in the struggle, the eternal judgment of God upon Satan and sin, and the certainty of the complete victory, the lordship over history and second coming of Jesus Christ our Lord.

Analysis

1:1–8	Prologue.
1:9 – 3:22	Vision of Christ, alive for evermore, in the midst of the churches.
4:1 – 5:14	Vision of the throne of God, and of the Lamb in the midst of the throne, to whom is committed the sealed book of the judgments of God.
6:1 – 8:5	Vision of the 'seal' judgments, with two visions interposed for the comfort of Christ's people (7:1–8, 9–17).

8: 6 – 11: 19	Vision of the 'trumpet' judgments, with three visions for the comfort of Christ's people (10: 1–11; 11: 1, 2, 3–13).
12: 1 – 14: 20	Vision of the man-child, and of the dragon and the two beasts, with three visions for the comfort of Christ's people (14: 1–5, 6–13, 14–20).
15: 1 – 16: 21	Vision of the 'bowl' judgments.
17: 1 – 19: 10	Visions of Babylon, the harlot city, and her destruction.
19: 11 – 20: 15	Vision of Christ's return, of His triumph over all His enemies, and of the last judgment.
21: 1 – 22: 5	Vision of a new heaven and earth, and of the new Jerusalem.
22: 6–21	Epilogue.

□ STUDY 1 Revelation 1: 1–8

1 Trace in verses 1 and 2 the course of the 'revelation' from its source in the mind of God by four successive steps to us who read and receive it. How is it described in its content, character and value, and what is required in those who read or hear? *Cf.* Lk. 11: 28.

2 Observe the place given to Jesus Christ in relation to God, and consider each title given to Him in verse 5a. *Cf.* Jn. 3: 11, 32, 33; 18: 37; Col. 1: 18; Rev. 19: 11–16. How does John describe His attitude to us, and what He has done for us? *Cf.* Jn. 13: 1; Eph. 1: 7; 1 Pet. 2: 9.

3 With 1: 7, *cf.* Dn. 7: 13 and Acts 1: 9–11. Is the thought of His coming a joy to you? *Cf.* 6: 15–17; 1 Thes. 4: 15–18; 5: 1–4; 2 Thes. 1: 7–10.

Notes

1 Verse 1. 'The revelation of Jesus Christ': *i.e.*, communicated by Him; and intended not to mystify but to disclose.

2 Verse 3. 'He who reads': *i.e.*, the one who reads this book aloud to his fellow-believers. 'The prophecy': a significant claim. *Cf.* 22: 7, 10, 18, 19.

3 Verse 4. 'The seven spirits': *i.e.*, the Spirit in His sevenfold fullness.

4 Verse 5. 'The faithful witness': this includes the thought of martyrdom. *Cf.* 1 Tim. 6: 13. Note the sequence—death, resurrection, enthronement.

□ STUDY 2 Revelation 1: 9–20

1 What, according to verse 9, is the twofold experience in which all believers share, and what should characterize their lives? *Cf.* Jn. 16: 33; Acts 14: 22; 2 Tim. 2: 12a.

2 We are not for a moment to suppose that Christ is literally like this. What John sees is a vision, each feature of which is symbolic of some aspect of our glorified Lord. Write down against each feature here portrayed what trait in our Lord's character it suggests. What is the total impression left upon your mind?

3 What does Christ say of Himself and of His relation to the churches in verses 17–20? With verse 17, *cf.* Dn. 10: 8–11, 15–19, and with the figure of the 'lampstands', *cf.* Mt. 5: 14–16.

Notes

1 Verse 17: see also 22: 13. Note that Christ applies to Himself words spoken by God of Himself in verse 8.

2 Verse 18. 'The keys of Death and Hades': according to the teaching of the Rabbis these keys are in the hands of God alone.

3 Verse 20. 'Mystery': *i.e.*, something with a hidden meaning here explained. *Cf.* 17: 7; Mt. 13: 11. 'The angels of the seven churches': sometimes taken to mean the pastors or bishops of each church, but more probably denoting a guardian angel (*cf.* Dn. 10: 21; Mt. 18: 10).

☐ STUDY 3 Revelation 2: 1–7

The seven letters of chapters 2 and 3 are all similar in structure, beginning with titles descriptive of Christ, which have already occurred in the vision in 1: 9–20; then giving Christ's message to the church, and closing with a summons to hear and a promise to 'him who conquers'. In the last four letters the promise precedes the summons.

1 State in your own words what Christ found to commend in the church at Ephesus (verses 2, 3, 6).

2 What was the proof that their love had declined? How could this condition be remedied? What further danger otherwise beset them? How should we take such a warning to heart?

3 Verse 7a. Note the present tense 'says', and the combination of individual appeal and universal application. How does Christ still speak through these scriptures, and to whom? *Cf.* Mk. 4: 9, 23; 8: 18. How may the hearing ear be obtained?

Notes

1 Verse 6. 'Nicolaitans': see also verses 14, 15. '*Nicholaos*' may be meant as a Greek equivalent of 'Balaam', intended to describe a person who lays waste the people of God, as Balaam did through the introduction of idolatrous and immoral practices. *Cf.* 2 Pet. 2: 15, 16.

2 Verse 7. 'The tree of life': in contrast to the corrupt fruits of idolatrous and sensual self-indulgence. *Cf.* 22: 2.

☐ STUDY 4 Revelation 2: 8–17

1 Reconstruct from verses 8–11 the situation with which the believers in Smyrna were confronted. What does Christ declare

concerning (a) their immediate, and (b) their final future? In what ways were they already rich? How were they to conquer? To what result would such conquest lead?

2 Satan could not break the rocklike steadfastness of the church in Pergamum by frontal attack (verse 13), so he employed another method, tempting believers to ask, 'Is it necessary to be so uncompromising in our attitude towards idolatrous practices and pagan morals?' What is Christ's answer to this sort of question?

Notes

1 Verse 10. 'Ten days': *i.e.*, for a short period.

2 Verse 11. 'The second death': *cf.* 20: 14, 15; 21: 8.

3 Verse 13. 'Where Satan's throne is': Pergamum was the official residence of the Roman proconsul of the province, and the chief centre of the worship of the emperor.

4 Verse 17. 'The hidden manna': the Rabbis taught that the Messiah when He came would give the people manna to eat, now hidden in heaven. What is said here is that Christ is the true manna, the bread of life. *Cf.* Jn. 6: 48–51. 'A white stone': stones engraved with names supposed to possess magical qualities were highly valued in heathen circles. Christ gives privileges, personal to each recipient, which exceed all that can be found outside of Him.

□ STUDY 5 Revelation 2: 18–29

1 In what ways is the description of Christ in verse 18 relevant to what follows? In what character is He here revealed? How should awareness of these truths affect our own behaviour?

2 The religious compromise and moral laxity that were creeping into the churches seem to have proceeded further in the case of Thyatira, and to have become a doctrine and almost a sect. What responsibility had the church as a whole towards the presence of such evil in its midst? What advice is given to the individual members who do not hold this teaching?

Note. Verse 20. 'The woman Jezebel': so called because of her moral likeness to Jezebel of old. *Cf.* 1 Ki. 21: 25, 26; 2 Ki. 9: 22, 30.

□ STUDY 6 Revelation 3: 1–13

1 Verses 1–6. What was wrong with the Christians in Sardis, and what was needed to remedy the situation? Upon whose action did change and better living depend? Is our condition at all similar?

2 In verses 7–13 what Christian quality is shown to be essential? For how long ought it to be exhibited? To what rewards will its practice lead?

Note. Verse 8. 'An open door': *i.e.*, a missionary opportunity. *Cf.* 1 Cor. 16: 9; 2 Cor. 2: 12.

☐ STUDY 7 Revelation 3: 14–22

1 How do you think the church in Laodicea had become so blind to its true spiritual condition? *Cf.* Mt. 23: 25, 26; 2 Cor. 4: 18. Who undertakes to deal with them, and how?

2 What three qualities of Christian character are symbolized by 'gold refined by fire', 'white garments' and eye salve respectively? See for the first, 1 Pet. 1: 7; for the second, verses 4 and 19: 8; Ps. 51: 7; and for the third, Ps. 119: 18; 2 Pet. 1: 9; Eph. 1: 18, 19. How may these things be obtained?

3 How in its context is verse 20 to be understood? If a church as a whole is 'lukewarm', may individuals within it enjoy a close relationship with the Lord? What does the Lord promise to such? What are the conditions to be fulfilled in order to obtain what is promised? *Cf.* Jn. 14: 22, 23.

Note. Verse 17. Laodicea was prosperous and wealthy. After its overthrow by an earthquake in AD 61 it was rebuilt by its own citizens without imperial subsidy. 'We need nothing' was virtually what its inhabitants said.

Introductory Note to Chapters 4–11

We are now entering upon the main revelation of the book (see 1: 1 and 4: 1). We have seen the condition of the churches. Persecution had begun, and times of greater trial loomed ahead (see 2: 10, 13; 3: 10). The question, 'What of the future?' must have troubled every thoughtful Christian, and is now about to be answered. But first in chapters 4 and 5 God shows John a vision of the heavenly realities which abide unshaken behind and above the changes and uncertainties of earth.

☐ STUDY 8 Revelation 4

1 When John looked into heaven, what is the chief and outstanding sight which met his eyes? What may we also learn from this vision about the origin, the control and the purpose of the created universe? What kind of response ought this awareness to call forth from us?

2 What is here indicated or symbolized concerning the nature and character of God, and concerning the way in which He ought to be worshipped?

Notes

1 Verse 3. 'Like jasper': *i.e.*, radiant; *cf.* 21: 11. 'Like . . . carnelian': ***i.e.***, red like fire or blood. The 'rainbow' suggests God's faithfulness. *Cf.* Gn. 9: 12–17.

2 Verse 4. These elders are normally taken to represent the church of Old and New Testaments.
3 Verses 6–8. 'Four living creatures': similar to those of Ezekiel's vision. See Ezk. 1: 5ff.; 10: 12. Their appearance suggests the characteristics of strength, service, intelligence and swiftness. For their song, *cf.* Is. 6: 3.

□ STUDY 9 Revelation 5

1 Of what does this vision assure us concerning the purpose and the results of Christ's earthly sacrifice—as 'the Lamb who was slain'?

2 What is it that here prompts 'a new song' (verse 9)? How many ultimately join in the singing? What difference is there in qualification to sing on the part of those who do sing? See 14: 3. Have you discovered why you should sing?

Notes
1 Verse 1. 'A scroll': this is the book of destiny. It declares God's purposes of judgment and blessing for this world. Some regard it as the title-deed to the inheritance which Christ has procured for Himself and for His fellow-men by His redeeming work.
2 Verses 5, 6. Note the tense, 'has conquered'. The victory is already won. *Cf.* 3: 21. See also Jn. 12: 31, 32. The occasion here seen in vision is that of Christ's return from the cross to the throne of God as the Lamb that 'had been slain'. He is at once invested into His universal dominion. *Cf.* Mt. 28: 18; Heb. 2: 9; 10: 12, 13.

□ STUDY 10 Revelation 6

1 As the book of future events is opened seal by seal, what points of correspondence do you find with Mt. 24: 4–14? *Cf.*, *e.g*, verses 4, 6 and 9 with Mt. 24: 6, 7 and 9. (For the meaning of the white horse, see Note 1 below.) What does this teach about the present course of world history?

2 To what climax of judgment do all these things mount up? See verses 12–17 and Note 3 below. *Cf.* Mt. 24: 29, 30. What is more to be dreaded than death? *Cf.* Is. 2: 19–21.

3 For what were the martyrs willing to lay down their lives? Are those right who think that God takes no action either for their reward or their vindication? May similar sacrifice still be called for?

Notes
1 Verse 2. Two principal interpretations have been given of the white horse and his rider. Many take it to be a picture of Christ going forth in the conquests of the gospel. *Cf.* Mt. 24: 14; Ps. 45: 3–5. Others regard it as a picture of invasion and lust of conquest, leading to the miseries of war, famine, pestilence and death. The latter seems more likely. The four horses, as in Zc. 6, form a series whose mission is to execute judgment.

2 Verse 6. Such was the scarcity that a day's wage (Mt. 20: 2) would suffice to buy only a small measure of wheat.
3 Verses 12–14. The imagery of these verses is such as is frequently used in the Old Testament to symbolize great upheavals among the nations. See, *e.g.*, Is. 13: 9–11, 13; Ezk. 32: 7–9; Na. 1: 5.

☐ STUDY 11 Revelation 7

Before the revelation of further judgments, two visions are interposed for the comfort of believers. In all that has been shown so far, nothing has been said of the church, exceup with regard to those who have been martyred. This passage shows the church first in this life, on earth, and so always limited in number (verses 1–8), and then, numberless in heaven, having life for evermore.

1 What assurance is given in verses 1–8 concerning God's watchful *care* over His people? *Cf.* Ezk. 9: 3–6; Jn. 6: 27; 10: 27–29; Rev. 9: 4.

2 In verses 9–17, who compose the great multitude, and where are they standing? How came they to be there, and what is now their occupation? Make a list of the blessings that they enjoy, translating the symbols into the realities which they represent.

Notes
1 Verse 1. It is a task given to angels to control forces of nature. *Cf.* 14: 18; 16: 5; Heb. 1: 7.
2 Verses 4–8. Some have thought that those who are 'sealed' represent believers from among the Jews, but in the light of 14: 1–4 it is better to regard the vision as including the whole 'Israel of God' (Gal. 6: 16).
3 Verse 14. 'The great tribulation': *cf.* 3: 10. Here both visions show that all who are the Lord's will be brought safely through this earthly trial.

☐ STUDY 12 Revelation 8 and 9

We are brought back, after the interlude of chapter 7, to the opening of the seventh seal. Will it usher in the final end? All heaven is silent, as if in suspense and expectancy (*cf.* Mk. 13: 32), but there follows a new series of judgments (*cf.* Mk. 13: 7, 8).

1 In 8: 3–5 we see, in the heavenly sanctuary, what happens to the prayers of Christ's people. What are we taught as to the efficacy of prayer when mingled with the incense of Christ's intercession and fire from the altar of His sacrifice? In this case what kind of answer is granted? *Cf.* 6: 9, 10; Rom. 8: 26; and see Note 5 below.

2 Contrast the first four trumpet judgments with the fifth and sixth, (a) in the objects affected, and (b) in the severity of their character and result. What was the purpose of these trumpet judgments? See 8: 13; 9: 20, 21. *Cf.* Lk. 13: 1–5.

3 What do we learn from these chapters concerning God's control over all that happens? See especially 8: 2; 9: 1, 4, 13–15.

Notes

1 8: 3, 5. Two altars are to be distinguished, the 'golden altar' of incense, and the altar of sacrifice. See Ex. 37: 25 – 38: 7.

2 8: 6. 'Trumpets': indicating that these judgments were sent in warning. *Cf.* Am. 3: 6; Ezk. 33: 1–5. The destruction wrought is therefore only partial—'a third'.

3 9: 1. 'The bottomless pit': better, 'the abyss' (RV), the abode of the powers of evil. *Cf.* 11: 7; 17: 8.

4 9: 11. 'Abaddon' and 'Apollyon': both mean 'destruction'.

5 9: 13. 'The golden altar': indicating that the prayers of the saints were being answered.

☐ STUDY 13 Revelation 10

Rev. 10: 1 – 11: 13 is an interlude between the sixth and seventh trumpets, corresponding to chapter 7 (see Analysis). The seer first tells of his new commission (10: 1–11), and then describes the church as God's sanctuary (11: 1, 2), and as bearing witness in the world (11: 3–13).

1 In what two ways does chapter 10 show that the revelation thus far given to John, though it extends to the end of the age (verses 6, 7), is by no means a complete disclosure of the hidden counsel of God? *Cf.* Dt. 29: 29; Jb. 26: 14. Of what was John now solemnly assured concerning truths which had been revealed?

2 What made God's Word sweet to taste, but bitter to digest? What responsibility did the reception of such revelation place upon John? *Cf.* Ezk. 2: 8 – 3: 4; 1 Sa. 3: 15–18; 1 Cor. 9: 16, 17. Have you any comparable privilege and responsibility?

Note. Verses 6, 7. The mysterious purpose of God, as revealed through the prophets and worked out in earthly history, is thus to be completed or finished.

☐ STUDY 14 Revelation 11

1 The question, 'Who are the two witnesses?' in 11: 3–12 has received many answers. Assuming that they represent the witness of the church throughout the present age, what lessons may we learn from this passage concerning true witness for Christ, the authority of His witnesses, their preservation, their suffering to death, and their final triumph? *Cf.* Lk. 10: 19; Jn. 16: 2; Acts 7: 54–60.

2 When God's purposes are completely fulfilled by the sounding of the seventh trumpet (see 10: 7), who is seen to be triumphant at the last? What attributes and activities of God make certain His triumph over all opposition? What ought this prospect to make us do?

Notes

1 Verses 1, 2. The purpose of the measuring is to mark out what is to be preserved. If the Temple represents Christ's people (1 Cor. 3: 16), the outer court may represent the Jews in their unbelief (Lk. 21: 24).

2 Verses 2, 3. 'Forty-two months' is the same length of time as 'one thousand two hundred and sixty days' and as 'a time, and times, and half a time' (3½ years) of 12: 14. *Cf.* 12: 6. It appears here to be a conventional description of the duration of the present age. Note the contrast in verse 11—only 'three and a half days'.

Introductory Note to 12: 1 – 19: 10

At this point a new division of the book begins, and a new series of prophecies (*cf.* 10: 11). The earlier part of the book has been occupied mainly with outward events and acts of divine judgment, together with visions of the church and her sufferings; and it has been shown that behind all is God's throne, and that all that is happening is under His control, and in the hand of Christ. The present section of the book reveals another and graver aspect in the situation, namely, the enmity of powerful spiritual foes, of Satan and the world. This has so far only been hinted at (2: 9, 13, 24; 3: 9; 9: 11; 11: 7), but is now brought into full view, and it is shown that the sufferings of the church have their origin in the conflict between Satan and Christ.

☐ STUDY 15 Revelation 12

The chapter gives a symbolic picture of the birth of Christ, and of His return to the throne of God, but its main purpose is to show the power and malignity of Satan as the enemy of Christ and His people.

1 Gather out what is said about Christ. *Cf.* Ps. 2: 6–9; Lk. 10: 18; Jn. 12: 31; Eph. 1: 19–21. What is the significance of verse 10? *Cf.* Rom. 8: 33, 34.

2 Why, according to this chapter, is the lot of the church on earth one of constant conflict? *Cf.* Eph. 6: 10–13; 1 Pet. 5: 8. How is the fearful power of Satan depicted? How do or may we share in Christ's victory over him?

Notes

1 Verses 1, 2, 4–6, 13–17. The woman represents the true Israel, which, after Christ's ascension, forms the Christian church. For the imagery, see Gn. 37: 9; Ct. 6: 4, 10; Is. 66: 7–10.

2 Verses 3, 4a. 'Red': the colour of blood. *Cf.* Jn. 8: 44. The seven heads and diadems indicate far-reaching dominion, the ten horns, great power, and the tail, his vast size and strength. Note verse 9; and *cf.* Gn. 3: 15.

3 Verses 6, 14–16. The exact meaning of the symbolism is obscure, but the general sense is clear, that the church is under God's protection, and although Satan will seek to destroy her, his plans will be thwarted.

☐ STUDY 16 Revelation 13

Satan in his war against the saints uses two chief instruments: (a) totalitarian world power, hostile to the true God, subservient to Satan, and claiming worship for itself (verses 1–10); and (b) established religion, supporting the claims of the world power, by false miracles and signs (verses 11–18). Such 'beasts' were found in John's day in the Roman Empire and the cult of emperor worship. They have appeared also in later history, and may appear again.

1 Note how true Christians are here distinguished from others (verse 8; *cf.* 17: 8). What experience is inevitable for them in such a world situation as verses 1–10 depict? How is it appointed that they should show their faithfulness? *Cf.* Mk. 13: 13.

2 In what respects does the second beast differ in outward appearance from the first? *Cf.* 1 Pet. 5: 8 with 2 Cor. 11: 14. How does its aims and methods bring Christians into direct conflict with it? *Cf.* Dn. 3: 4–6; Jn. 15: 18–21.

Notes

1 Verse 2. Note a combination of the characteristics of the first three beasts in Daniel's vision. *Cf.* Dn. 7: 4–6.

2 Verse 3. This suggests a counterfeit to Christ's death and resurrection, intended to lead men to faith and worship.

3 Verse 4. The reason for worship is not moral greatness but brute force.

4 Verse 10 echoes words in Je. 15: 2. In the face of such treatment Christians are not to try to resist or retaliate.

5 Verse 12. This second beast completes the satanic trinity. It is called 'the false prophet' in 16: 13; 19: 20; 20: 10. He is the Lie dressed up like the Truth. *Cf.* Mt. 7: 15; Mk. 13: 22; 2 Thes. 2: 9–12.

6 Verse 18. Many take the number 666 to refer to 'Nero Caesar'. Others, because every digit falls short of the perfect number 7, regard 666 as a symbol of Antichrist.

☐ STUDY 17 Revelation 14

This chapter, like chapters 7 and 10: 1 – 11: 13, is an interlude introduced for the comfort of believers.

1 Verses 1–5 present a picture of the true followers of Christ. Although outwardly scattered, suffering and in danger of death, spiritually they are with the Lamb on the impregnable rock of Mount Zion, owned of God, not one missing (verse 1), and sharing in the worship of heaven (verses 2, 3). To what do they owe their position and what four characteristics mark their life? See verses 4 and 5, and *cf.* Mt. 5: 3; Lk. 14: 27; Eph. 4: 25; Phil. 2: 15. How does your own life appear in the light of these standards?

2 In verses 6–11 are shown three angels, each with a message for all who dwell upon the earth. Examine the contents of their threefold message Verses 12 and 13 are addressed to believers. What

encouragement do they give to those who may have to die for Christ's sake?

3 In the twofold vision of verses 14–20 what are the differences between the two parts of it (verses 14–16 and 17–20)? *Cf.* Ps. 1; Mal. 3: 16 – 4: 3; Mt. 13: 39b–43.

Notes

1 Verse 3b. The song is 'from heaven' (verse 2); the saints on Mt. Zion are learning to sing it.
2 Verse 4. A symbol of purity of heart. *Cf.* 2 Cor. 11: 2.
3 Verse 6. 'An eternal gospel': *cf.* Ec. 12: 13, 14; Acts 14: 14–18; 17: 24–31.
4 Verses 9–11. The very marks, which once ensured benefits (see 13: 15–17), now single out individuals for judgment.
5 Verse 13b. The weariness of labour will be over, the reward of their deeds awaits them. *Cf.* Mt. 25: 34–40. Contrast verse 11: 'they have no rest'.

□ STUDY 18 Revelation 15 and 16

The series of judgments here described, though similar to those of the seals and trumpets, is seen as a separate 'portent' in heaven. What follow are no longer warnings but a final outpouring of the wrath of God.

1 John is looking at the seven angels, when his eye is caught by another vision, which he describes in 15: 2–4, no doubt for the comfort of believers, in face of the terrible judgments which are about to fall. What great truths are they thereby assured of, and encouraged to rejoice in? What should such awareness make them—and us—do? *Cf.* 16: 5–7.

2 In what respects are the 'bowl' judgments more severe than those of the seals and the trumpets? What was the reaction to them (a) of men, and (b) of the dragon and his allies? Before such a prospect, what ground have we for hope, and what reason for watchful concern? With 16: 15, *cf.* Mt. 24: 42–44.

Notes

1 15: 3, 4. 'The song of Moses': *cf.* and contrast Ex. 14: 30 – 15: 19.
2 16: 16. 'Armageddon': meaning 'the hill of Megiddo'; *i.e.*, the plain of Megiddo, where more than one famous battle was fought (Jdg. 5: 19; 2 Ch. 35: 22), and the hills around.

□ STUDY 19 Revelation 17

The people of Christ have another enemy—Babylon. Babylon is the name of a city, and John uses it to denote the Rome of his day, seated upon her seven hills (verse 9), and also upon many waters, *i.e.*, upon nations and kingdoms making up the Empire (verses 1, 15, 18). But Babylon, like the two beasts of chapter 13, is a symbol; not, like the first beast, a symbol of material power; nor, like the second beast, of false religion; but rather a symbol of the world's lust, love of gain, pride and corruption. Wherever these aspects of the worldly spirit find embodiment there is Babylon, and there God's judgment will fall, unless men repent.

1 John's wonder at the woman (verse 6) should lead us to examine her closely. What does each feature of the picture symbolize? Contrast the woman and her brood with the woman of chapter 12 and her seed (with 17: 14, *cf.* 12: 17). What, in the face of such a foe, is the prospect before those 'who follow the Lamb' (14: 4)?

2 Verses 7–13, as the interpreting angel himself admits, require for their understanding a mind that has wisdom (verse 9). Observe that two different meanings are assigned to the heads of the beast. Note carefully also the difference between the heads and the horns. The main lesson of the chapter is the certain 'doom' of Babylon. How is this brought about? What does this illustrate concerning God's judgments?

Notes

1 Verse 2. 'Committed fornication': a reference to the immoral practices which kings and rulers committed in response to the seductions of Rome.

2 Verse 8. It 'was, and is not, and is to ascend': the beast is a satanic counterpart of God Himself. See 1: 4.

3 Verses 10, 11. The Emperor Nero committed suicide, and the historian Tacitus says that a rumour spread abroad that he was not dead and would return. It is commonly thought that there is an allusion to this belief in verses 8a and 11. This is a satanic counterpart to the death and resurrection of Christ. Assuming that the seven kings of verse 10 were Roman emperors, the most probable theory sees in the five who 'have fallen', Augustus, Tiberius, Caligula, Claudius and Nero; in the one who 'is', Vespasian (AD 69–79), and in the one who 'has not yet come', Titus. After Titus came Domitian, who would be the 'eighth' (verse 11), and who resembled Nero so closely, especially in his persecution of the Christians, that he might well seem to be Nero come to life again.

4 Verses 15–17. The harlot city will eventually be brought down by a united revolt on the part of the provinces and their local rulers.

□ STUDY 20 Revelation 18: 1–20

1 Consider first the messages of the angel and of the voice from heaven. What aspects of God's judgments do these emphasize? What urgent imperative does the Lord here speak to His own people? *Cf.* 2 Cor. 6: 14–18.

2 In contrast, listen to the voices of earth on Babylon's fall. Who are the speakers? To what fact about Babylon's fall do they refer, and for what reason did they thus mourn for Babylon? Observe the difference between the points of view of heaven and of the world. In such circumstances, in which would you join—mourning or joy?

3 When time permits, read Is. 13 and 47; Je. 50 and 51 and Ezk. 27 to see how deeply steeped is the mind of John in the visions and prophecies of the Old Testament.

☐ STUDY 21 Revelation 18: 21 – 19: 10

1 What thoughts does the action of the angel in 18: 21 suggest as to the purpose of God towards 'Babylon'? Notice especially how many times the words 'no more' occur in 18: 21–24. *Cf.* 19: 3. What truth is thus enforced concerning the whole system of godless luxury and lust which the name 'Babylon' represents? *Cf.* 1 Cor. 7: 31b; 1 Pet. 1: 24, 25; 1 Jn. 2: 17.

2 What calls forth the praises of 19: 1–3, 4, 5–8, and by whom respectively were they spoken? What truths about God's character and ways are here acknowledged? *Cf.* 19: 10; Is. 45: 21–25.

Notes

1 19: 3b. Symbolic of final destruction. *Cf.* Is. 34: 10.

2 19: 7. 'The marriage of the Lamb': the fulfilment of God's purpose as described in Eph. 5: 25b, 26. A final decisive contrast to the harlot and her impurities.

☐ STUDY 22 Revelation 19: 11–21

Following upon the destruction of 'Babylon', the beast, and the kings in alliance with him (*cf.* 17: 12–14), make war upon Christ, who comes forth from heaven in judgment to overthrow them. The end of the present age, prophesied throughout the book, has now come, and we have in today's portion Christ's second coming described, in its aspect of judgment upon His enemies, as in 2 Thes. 1: 6–10 and Ps. 2: 9.

1 Verses 11–16. In this symbolic picture of Christ seek to appreciate the suggestive significance of each descriptive phrase. Contrast some of the phrases of Zc. 9: 9, 10. In what ways will Christ's second coming be different from His first coming? Should this prospect fill us with fear or joy?

2 Verses 17–21. This is the battle of Armageddon, spoken of in 16: 14–16. Note the contrast between 'the great supper' of judgment and 'the marriage supper of the Lamb' (verse 9). *Cf.* the contrast in 14: 14–20 between the two harvests. See also Mt. 13: 30, 40–43. What truths are thus repeatedly emphasized concerning the final settlement and issue of world history?

Notes

1 Verses 13a, 15b. *Cf.* Is. 63: 2, 3.

2 Verse 14. These are armies of angels. *Cf.* Mt. 16: 27; 2 Thes. 1: 7–9.

3 Verse 20. 'The lake of fire'; so also in 20: 10, 14, 15; 21: 8; elsewhere called 'the eternal fire' or 'the Gehenna of fire' (Mt. 18: 8, 9; 25: 41); also 'the furnace of fire' (Mt. 13: 42, 50). It is the place of final destruction.

☐ STUDY 23 Revelation 20: 1–10

Great differences exist among Christians concerning the interpretation of 'the thousand years' and 'the first resurrection'. Either the thousand years follow Christ's second coming, or this section is a fresh symbolic description of the period between Christ's first coming and His second coming. There does seem to be a parallel sequence in the main events of Rev. 11–14 and 20. It was through Christ's first coming that Satan was bound. *Cf.* Mk. 3: 23–27; Lk. 10: 17–19; Jn. 12: 31. Rev. 20: 7–9 can be understood as yet another reference to Armageddon. *Cf.* 16: 14–16; 19: 19. 'The first resurrection', however understood, is a privilege shared in only by faithful followers of the Lamb. Some think the phraseology symbolically predicts that the age of the martyrs would be followed by a far longer period of Christian supremacy during which the faith of Christ for which the martyrs died would live and reign. (See *NBC* and *More than Conquerors* by W. Hendriksen, Tyndale Press, 1962.)

1 What activity is particularly attributed to Satan? In what different ways is he dealt with? How is his activity made to serve God's purposes? *Cf.* 2 Thes. 2: 9–12. What will be his end? Who will share the same fate? *Cf.* Mt. 25: 41.

2 What are the rewards of the martyrs who are faithful to death? *Cf.* Lk. 22: 28–30; 2 Tim. 2: 12; Rev. 2: 10, 11; 5: 10. What grace should such awareness make us covet?

Notes

1 Verses 1–3. 'The bottomless pit': as the abode of evil spirits (*cf.* 9: 11) this is to be carefully distinguished from 'the lake of fire' (verse 10).
2 Verse 3. 'Must': for reasons hidden in the divine will.
3 Verse 8. 'Gog and Magog': the reference here is to Ezk. 38; 39, where the prophet conceived of a great invasion of the land of Israel.

☐ STUDY 24 Revelation 20: 11 – 21: 8

1 20: 11–15. We have here depicted the final settlement of the destiny of the present world order and of all who belong to it. Who is to be the Judge? How is each man's destiny to be determined? What are the only alternatives? *Cf.* Mt. 16: 27; Jn. 5: 28, 29; Rom. 2: 6, 16; Rev. 21: 8; 22: 12.

2 21: 1–7. A revelation of the new world order is now given. *Cf.* Is. 65: 17; 2 Pet. 3: 13. What is its metropolis? Contrast Rev. 18: 10. Who are its citizens? What are their privileges? Of what blessings are they assured, and by whose word and deed?

□ STUDY 25 Revelation 21: 9–21

This vision of the city of God is no more to be taken literally than was the vision of Christ in 1: 12–20. It is a symbolic picture, and we have to see in and through the symbols the spiritual realities which they represent.

1 For example, the size of the city (verse 16; see Note 2 below) expresses the same thought as the phrase 'which no man could number' in 7: 9; the shape of the city as a cube (21: 16) suggests its perfection of design and its permanence; the gold and precious stones its brilliance and perfection of quality, and so forth. What other spiritual realities does this passage suggest to you?

2 How is the contrast between this city and the harlot city Babylon brought to the mind of the reader? *Cf.* verse 9 with 17: 1. Work out this contrast in some of its features. What are the outstanding differences between Babylon and the New Jerusalem? *Cf.* Zc. 14: 20, 21; Lk. 16: 15; 1 Jn. 2: 16, 17.

Notes

1 Verses 12–14. The city, while offering entrance from all directions, is determined in character by the revelation given to Israel and through the apostles.

2 Verse 16. 'Twelve thousand stadia': about 1,500 miles.

3 Verse 18. 'Pure gold, clear as glass': see also verse 21. There is nothing not genuine, nothing not transparent.

□ STUDY 26 Revelation 21: 22 – 22: 5

1 Make a list of all that is said not to be found in the perfected kingdom of God, *i.e.*, of all in 21: 1 – 22: 5 of which the words 'no' or 'no more' or 'nothing . . . nor any one who' are used. Over against these, set the positive blessings here spoken of. Comparing these blessings with those of the Garden of Eden (Gn. 1: 28, 29; 2: 8–25), how do they transcend them, and what is their chief glory? *Cf.* 1 Cor. 15: 46; Eph. 1: 3.

2 Would a non-Christian be able to enter the city (see 21: 27), and if he did enter would he find satisfaction in its blessings (*cf.* Eph. 2: 3; 1 Cor. 2: 14)? In the light of this, consider the absolute necessity of 'the blood of the Lamb' and of regeneration for every man. *Cf.* Jn. 3: 5; Lk. 10: 20.

Note. 22: 1, 2. Some interpret this to mean that there is one broad street which intersects the city, beside which the river flows, with trees on either bank. Others take 'street', 'river', and 'tree of life' as being collective nouns, and picture many streets and streams of the river flowing by them and many trees bearing fruit every month, all being symbolic of 'the superabundant character of God's provision'.

☐ STUDY 27 Revelation 22: 6–21

1 What word of Christ is repeated three times in these verses? See also 3: 11, and *cf.* 1: 7; 16: 15. How are we to reconcile this word with the fact that even now He has not come? What should be our attitude and response to this word of our Master? *Cf.* 2 Pet. 3; Mt. 24: 43–51; Heb. 10: 36–39. Can you join in the prayer of verses 17 and 20 as the spontaneous yearning of your heart?

2 How are the truth and the importance of the contents of this book confirmed to us in this passage? By what name is it four times described? What is its origin? Whence does it derive its authority? How ought we to express our regard for it and our response to it?

Notes

1 Verse 6. This book springs from the same divine source from which all the prophets have derived their inspiration.

2 Verses 8, 9. *Cf.* 19: 10; Col. 2: 18. John emphasizes both the attraction and the error of angel worship. The same might be said of the worship of the saints.

3 Verse 11. An emphatic warning that the time of the end is near, and the opportunity of a change of character is passing. *Cf.* Dn. 12: 10; 2 Tim. 3: 13. Yet see verse 17b below, and 21: 6.

4 Verse 16. 'The root and the offspring of David': *cf.* Mk. 12: 35–37.

☐ STUDY 28 Revelation 1–22: Revision

1 How would you sum up the chief message of this whole book? What abiding truths are we meant to learn from it for our instruction and encouragement? *Cf.* Jn. 16: 33; Acts 14: 22; Rev. 1: 9; 12: 10, 11. What are the things in which we are called to share 'in Jesus'?

2 Consider the seven beatitudes in this book. See 1: 3; 14: 13; 16: 15; 19: 9; 20: 6; 22: 7 and 14. Are you observing the conditions, and, in so far as is yet possible, are you beginning to know the wealth of the blessedness?